P9-AEU-064

RETHINKING FRANCE

RETHINKING FRANCE

LES LIEUX DE MÉMOIRE

VOLUME 2

SPACE

☙

Under the direction of

PIERRE NORA

☙

Translation directed by

DAVID P. JORDAN

THE UNIVERSITY OF CHICAGO PRESS
CHICAGO AND LONDON

Pierre Nora is editorial director at Éditions Gallimard. Since 1977, he has been directeur d'études at the École des Hautes Études en Science Sociales. He is the founding editor of *Le Débat* and has directed the editorial work on *Les Lieux de mémoire* since 1984. In 2001 he was elected to the Académie Française. **David P. Jordan** is the LAS Distinguished Professor of French History at the University of Illinois at Chicago and the author of *Transforming Paris* and *The Revolutionary Career of Maximilien Robespierre,* both published by the University of Chicago Press.

The University of Chicago Press, Chicago 60637
The University of Chicago Press, Ltd., London
© 2006 by The University of Chicago
All rights reserved. Published 2006
Printed in the United States of America
15 14 13 12 11 10 09 08 07 06   5 4 3 2 1

ISBN (cloth): 0-226-59133-6

Originally published as *Les Lieux de mémoire,* © Éditions Gallimard, 1984, 1986, and 1992.

The University of Chicago Press gratefully acknowledges a subvention from the government of France, through the French Ministry of Culture, Centre National du Livre, in support of the costs of translating this volume.

Library of Congress Cataloging-in-Publication Data

Lieux de mémoire. English
   Rethinking France = Lieux de mémoire / under the direction of Pierre Nora ;
  translated by Mary Trouille ; translation directed by David P. Jordan
     p.   cm.
   Includes index.
   Contents: v. 1. The State.
   ISBN 0-226-59132-8 (cloth, v. 1: alk. paper)
    1. France—Civilization—Philosophy. 2. Memory. 3. Symbolism. 4. National
  characteristics, French. 5. Nationalism—France. I. Nora, Pierre. II. Title.
   DC33.L6513   2001
   944—dc22

                          2001000375

CONTENTS

INTRODUCTION   *vii*
   ❧   *Pierre Nora (translated by Richard C. Holbrook)*

1. NORTH–SOUTH   *1*
   ❧   *Emmanuel Le Roy Ladurie (translated by Jennifer Gage)*

2. FRANCE, THE COAST, AND THE SEA   *25*
   ❧   *Michel Mollat du Jourdin (translated by Richard C. Holbrook)*

3. THE FOREST   *83*
   ❧   *Andrée Corvol (translated by Richard C. Holbrook)*

4. THE REGION   *149*
   ❧   *Jacques Revel (translated by Janine Maltz Perron)*

5. THE DEPARTMENT   *183*
   ❧   *Marcel Roncayolo (translated by Christine Haynes)*

6. THE LOCAL: ONE AND DIVISIBLE   *231*
   ❧   *Thierry Gasnier (translated by Richard C. Holbrook)*

7. THE PAINTER'S LANDSCAPE   *295*
   ❧   *Françoise Cachin (translated by Mark Hutchinson)*

8. THE SCHOLAR'S LANDSCAPE   *343*
   ❧   *Marcel Roncayolo (translated by Richard C. Holbrook)*

9. THE VENDÉE, REGION OF MEMORY: THE BLUE
AND THE WHITE   *383*
   ❧   *Jean-Clément Martin (translated by Richard C. Holbrook)*

10. A FRONTIER MEMORY: ALSACE   *409*
   ❧   *Jean-Marie Mayeur (translated by Richard C. Holbrook)*

ILLUSTRATION CREDITS   *443*

PLAN OF THE VOLUMES   *451*

INDEX   *455*

PIERRE NORA

The word "space," in its philosophical, geometrical, and topographical neutrality, is torn, like the word "State"—the title of the preceding volume—between two poles of meaning. In one respect, it refers
to the notion of *territory*, by definition limited, therefore presupposing
borders inside which power is exercised and, in consequence, history
evolves. In another respect, it refers to the idea of *nature*, with its climate,
resources, landscapes—in short, everything an old peasant society calls
the "land." In this case, the word is subsumed under geography.

Territory and nature—or, if one prefers, history and geography. The
powerful originality of France is to see these two poles linked indissol-
ubly in the definition of its national identity. Hence the intensity of the
connection the French traditionally have felt with "space."

Many recent transformations since about the 1960s could have made
this connection disappear: the sudden growth of industry in the 1960s
and 1970s and the uniformity it imposed; the opening of borders to a European collectivity rightly named "Schengen space";[1] the speed of communication that puts Marseille three hours from Paris by high-speed
train; the push to decentralization; and, with the development of large
regional centers, the end of the Paris-versus-France dichotomy that
nourished so much of the literature of the nineteenth and twentieth
centuries.

This intimate connection to space has not been altered by such profound upheavals only because that connection is deeply anchored in the

consciousness as well as in the imagination and sensibilities of the French. This anchoring rests on two antithetical and complementary themes that form the leitmotif of a long, descriptive tradition of travelers, writers, and scholars: from Strabo, first-century B.C. Greek geographer and historian, to the leading figures now studying human geography, people have not stopped celebrating the overall balance of form and seeing in it both a providential blessing and a natural act of charity; nor have they stopped admiring the richness and infinite diversity of detail. Unity and fragmentation have been the two constant themes of any evocation of French space.

The idea of a preestablished harmony is fed by an imagined continuity with Gaul (the original and founding figure ever since the Renaissance), bordered, according to Julius Caesar, by the Atlantic Ocean, the Pyrenees, and the Rhine—a harmony that the theory of "natural frontiers" will consolidate, an ideal form that will later be represented in geometric terms. Thus, Gilles le Bouvier, the herald of Charles VII and author of *Livre de la description des pays* in the fifteenth century, describes the kingdom as a "lozenge, for it is neither long nor square." Over the centuries, the incremental building of national territory, beginning with the royal *pré carré*, or royal preserve, will metamorphose through the circle, the pentagon, and the octagon, to become fixed in the consecrated expression of the "hexagon" whose history the American historian Eugen Weber traces.[2] The hexagon is perfection won and the fruit of long obstinacy for this reason: the exceptional dynastic continuity, beginning with the accession of Hugh Capet in 987, merged with the steady extension of the royal domain and progressive unification of acquired land into a single kingdom. Here history comes to the aid of nature to work in what Gilles le Bouvier described still and again as "the most beautiful, the most pleasing, the most gracious, and the best proportioned of all the kingdoms."

This abundant ensemble has its counterpart in an extraordinary variety and in a capacity for fragmentation that is almost infinite. Here again, France derives its uniqueness from a natural wealth of climates, the variety of its terrain, and landscapes of a very particular density on which is layered the historic succession of divisions of every order—ecclesiastical, seigneurial, and administrative. This richness and diversity give pleasure to the traveler and tourist but discourage the geographer and scholar. How to make of the one, with its infinite multiple, a whole with the eternally fragmented? This is the constant theme in an immense literature, which reaches its culmination in 1903 in that classic masterpiece *Tableau de la géographie de la France* by Paul Vidal de La Blache, founder of the French school of human geography. This is one of those key books that one encounters at every turn on any question about space. Reality generally defies any precise and definitive response to this enigma. A student of Vidal de La Blache, René Musset, in his fine dissertation on the Bas Maine (1917) dealing with terrain in all aspects, detects, for example, that in western France "division goes well beyond the region and the country; it extends to infinity: as every parish is shut off from the rest of the world, so too every hamlet within a parish. Life is not provincial," he concludes, "not even down to the village level. It is familial."

Given these inalterable facts, two periods have played a crucial role in crystallizing the very special link that the French feel toward their national space: the Revolution of 1789 and the Third Republic.

The Revolution is the decisive moment when the complex that ties the national idea to the space of sovereignty is put in place (the State to the kingdom, if you will). All the revolutionary events combine to bring about this creation of national territory, beginning with the sanctification of the "national frontiers." The theme is ancient. One finds the sources of it in ancient France, but it is the Revolution that gives it explosive power: "Here begins the country of liberty." Externally, the theme dominates, in the self-exile of mainly aristocratic emigration, the physical development of the attachment to a land the Revolution took from them. Within France the theme is expressed in the sanctification of an invaded space and the peasant reflex found in the *levée en masse*—the response to a national call to arms. As the refrain in the *Marseillaise* says, "qu'un sang impur abreuve nos sillons" (let impure blood soak our fields).

In any unifying work on the Revolution, one has to deal with the creation of the departments, the eighty-three more or less equal administrative units into which the entire country was divided. The eighteenth century saw the development of the idea, following Montesquieu, that a more rational spatial allocation was the necessary condition for the proper functioning of the monarchy. But the Revolution, in the very first months, went even further, making the kingdom and then the republic "one and indivisible." From then on it was expected from the organization of the territory that it become the guarantor of that egalitarian representation of the nation that its ancient partitions, tangled over time, had made impossible. The new divisions, which for a while were pictured, in a spark of utopian realism, as a purely geometric overlay, became the very image of an egalitarian participation of each of the territorial parts in the unity of the nation. Rationalize, equalize, standardize—these all gave to each territorial unit the same chances, the same rights, the same means of being associated with the collective destiny of the nation in the process of creation. Such was the inspired thought of Abbé de Sièyes, the true father of departmentalization as well as the author of *Qu'est-ce que le Tiers État?* (What Is the Third Estate?). There is no need to dwell on this history, since it is analyzed in this volume at length,[3] but let us recall its importance: no act has done more in an instant to give an undifferentiated space its dynamic.

To this political union of space and nation the Third Republic gave democratic, civic, and popular sanction, marked by the marriage of history and geography. It was henceforth the fundamental association in the definition of national identity, at least until recently, and which in all respects was incarnated by Ernest Lavisse,[4] the author of little teacher manuals, which at that time had great influence on mass education, and the editor of an *Histoire de France* in twenty-seven volumes, which established a standard version of chronology. It is precisely to introduce this *Histoire de France* that Lavisse demanded from Vidal de La Blache a *Tableau de la géographie de la France* that was to put the accent on "that which is fixed and permanent." The work appeared the very year of the first staging of the Tour de France for cyclists.[5] The connection is somewhat symbolic: popular training in the plains and valleys, through muscle and sweat, on the democratic steed that the bicycle represented, is exactly contemporaneous with that scholarly knowledge of France that was destined to become classic.

The appropriation of space is not a new theme. Ever since the Renaissance and the formation of the monarchical state, space was invested by the forms of power: the voyages of the king, administrative statistics, the steady improvement in maps from Cassini (1744) to the one known as the *État-major,* so many instruments for the mastery of space by the State. Yet it was the marriage of geography to history, promoted to the first rank as the chief instrument in the formation of awareness and of national instruction, that was to set down roots that are much more fundamental. Primary education taken as a whole can be interpreted as an apprenticeship in distinguishing the *petite patrie,* that is, the neighborhood, from the *grande patrie,* that is, the nation, to which the future citizen will feel attached through a contractual and constraining bond, since the future soldier he is to be will also have to "learn how to die" for the *grande patrie.* Lavisse had a happy definition of geography: "It is history as surface." And on the cover of his celebrated manual one can read: "Child, you must love France because nature has made it beautiful and history has made it grand."

※

In their own configuration and logic, the volumes of *Les Lieux de mémoire,* in the French version, have covered almost all the angles of attack that allow for the influence of "space" to be understood and measured in the national memory. Five of the original French essays seemed too specific to be included in the American edition. They are, however, too important not to be brought to the attention of the American reader who may be interested. They concern the formation of the frontiers "from feudal limits to political frontiers" (D. Nordman, B. Guenée); they concern the idea of the "hexagon" that Eugen Weber took up in his collection of essays, *My France: Politics, Culture, Myth* (Harvard University Press, 1991); they concern "the general statistics of France" (H. le Bras), that vast enterprise launched in 1833 that developed, organized, and centralized demographic, economic, and social observations for 110 years until brought under the Institut National de la Statistique et des Études économiques (I.N.S.E.E.) in 1945. They deal, moreover, with the Joanne guides (D. Nordman), forerunners of the *guides bleus,* well known by tourists and competing today with the Michelin *guides verts,* which no longer exist except in simplified versions. They deal lastly with the "center and the periphery" (M. Agulhon) or, put another way, with the never-ending tension in France between forces that tend to unification through centralization and those that remain more sensitive to all forms of particularism, whether regional or linguistic.[6]

Four basic approaches can be consulted in *Realms of Memory* (3 vols., Columbia University Press, 1996–99): (1) the diagonal "Saint-Malo–Geneva line" that locates the major contrasts in language, culture, and civilization that make the two Frances that meet there so dissimilar (R. Chartier); (2) "Paris–Province" (A. Corbin), in which the contrasts and the comings and goings have played such a role in the social reality and imagination of the French; and those two key works, (3) "Vidal de La Blache's *Geography of France*" (J. Y. Guiomar) for the scholarly level, and (4) "*Le Tour de la France par deux enfants:* The Little Red Book of the Republic" (J. and M. Ozouf) for the pedagogical level.[7]

The ten essays gathered here have the advantage—and this connection is not by chance and seemingly extraneous—of covering, in an original way, the most typical required approaches to French space: the external and internal boundaries and divisions; the basic unit of local space; and the mental construction that gives a general idea of the concept of landscape. To be sure, these approaches are illustrated here only through strongly differentiated angles of attack, with many levels of meaning, and each aimed at shedding light on the idea of *lieu de mémoire.*

Then there are the boundaries. The analysis was focused not on the political and national boundaries in their long historical development, but on three aspects of the external and internal boundaries dictated by nature: the coastline, the forest, and the north and south. Again, the question is not at all intended to describe them, once situated, as a geographer would. Those are the divisions of space-time. To compose them as a *lieu de mémoire* is to measure what France's maritime façade, or rather façades—there are at least three—still show of a failed historical calling in the national dynamic. It is to measure what this forested surface, today the largest in Europe, still conceals of the profound depths of the imagination. It is to measure the core tension implied in all respects by the major dichotomy of the territory—the France of the north and the France of the south.

Then there are the internal limits and divisions represented here at their three key levels, above and below the unavoidable department, which imposed administrative division yet were quickly internalized by the national consciousness. What French child has not had to learn by heart the eighty canonical departments and their capitals? Above them is the region, a concept fundamental for grasping the diversity and the space—a hazy idea—between the province and the country, a "haunting and elusive reality." Below, and very much below, the basic unit for perceiving the territory is the "local." The authors here have sought to demonstrate and construct at the opposite pole of the national, as the elemental unit with its deep roots, the framework and mirror of the particular in opposition to all forms of the general, the laboratory of the basic elements or mother cell of the national, isolated as a whole and which the reader will here for the first time see placed under the microscope of the historian: the *lieu de mémoire* par excellence of French space, dense to the extreme in its interwoven networks.

The reader will find here two exemplary pieces of Harlequin's costume, with its two separate sides, that is the national territory. Regions, if you will; provinces or country. The designation is unimportant. Here they are the Vendée and Alsace. Why these two? Because at the very core of the identity that forms them is memory. The authors show it well: It is civil war and the traumatic memory of the revolutionary uprising and its repression that forms the Vendée and individualizes it more than any administrative or geographical limit. It is Alsace's frontier position and its history, buffeted between France and Germany, that forged the awareness there of an identity radically different from that of interior France and entrusted Alsace, for all of France, with a symbolic power of exception, itself a type of memory region and thus frontier memory.

There remains the landscape, another typical form of the *lieu de mémoire,* an idea that stands out from the evidence and yet is not so simple, developed by the combined forces of nature, man, and time, a piece of space carved up and constructed. But carved up and constructed by whom and for whom? To whom does the landscape belong? To the geographer who turns to the historian? To the traveler? To the surveyor, the photographer, the writer? The landscape belongs to the senses, perhaps therefore to the person who looks at it and translates it: the painter, about whom we have not said much. In this variegated France is there a "national" landscape? The answer is neither simple nor unequivocal, but the question of this landscape of the painter is worth posing. The evidence for the most common forms of awareness, however, is at the other end of the spectrum, the unconscious fruit of all the knowledge that gives it shape: statistical, topographical, cartographical, geological, and historical knowledge. There is indeed a landscape of the scholar.

Natural diversity *against* unity, national unity *because of* diversity? The eternal question that inhabits all these *lieux de mémoire* of space has become, in itself, the true *lieu de mémoire* of French space. And like all the *lieux de mémoire,* it is inexhaustible, insoluble—and fertile.

NOTES

1. Schengen space, or sometimes Schengenland, refers to that area of free circulation within the European Union created by Belgium, the Netherlands, Luxembourg, France, Germany, Portugal, and Spain and ratified in the Schengen Agreement in 1985 in the village of that name in Luxembourg. Its purpose was to remove all controls at internal land, sea, and airport frontiers. Fifteen European countries, including two non–European Union members (Norway and Iceland), are current signatories.

2. Eugen Weber, "L'Hexagone," in *Les Lieux de mémoire,* under the direction of Pierre Nora, 3 vols. in 7 (Paris: Gallimard, 1984–92), vol. 2, book 2, 97–116.

3. Marcel Roncayolo, "The Department," below in this volume.

4. See also Pierre Nora, "Lavisse, instituteur national," in *Les Lieux de mémoire,* vol. 1, 247–90.

5. See also Georges Vigarello, "Le Tour de la France," in *Les Lieux de mémoire,* vol. 3, book 2, 884–925.

6. Daniel Nordman, "Des limites d'État aux frontières nationales," in *Les Lieux de mémoire,* vol. 2, book 2, 35–62; Bernard Guenée, "Des limites féodales aux frontières politiques," in *Les Lieux de mémoire,* vol. 2, book 2, 11–34; Weber, "L'Hexagone"; Hervé Le Bras, "The Government Bureau of Statistics," in *Rethinking France: Les Lieux de Mémoire,* under the direction of Pierre Nora, vol. 1: *The State* (Chicago: University of Chicago Press, 2001), 361–400; Daniel Nordman, "Les Guides-Joanne," in *Les Lieux de mémoire,* vol. 2, book 1, 529–68; and Maurice Agulhon, "The Center and the Periphery," in *Rethinking France,* 1:53–79.

7. Roger Chartier, "La Ligne Saint-Malo−Genève," in *Les Lieux de mémoire,* vol. 3, book 1, 738−75; Alain Corbin, "Paris-province," in *Les Lieux de mémoire,* vol. 3, book 1, 776−823; Jean-Yves Guiomar, "Le *Tableau de la géographie de la France* de Vidal de La Blache," in *Les Lieux de mémoire,* vol. 2, book 1, 569−98; and Jacques and Mona Ozouf, "Le *Tour de la France par deux enfants,*" in *Les Lieux de mémoire,* vol. 1, 291−322.

CHAPTER I

NORTH-SOUTH

EMMANUEL LE ROY LADURIE

The perspectives of memory and of historical scholarship readily intersect, without merging, when it comes to the binary partition between north and south, a geographic or rather geohistorical division that affects French territory. The average French citizen, made aware through seaside vacations and televised weather maps, knows quite accurately that the Hexagon contains different climatic zones, ranging from warm to cool as one moves from the Midi to the north of France. Some, perhaps even most, minds, with a historical awareness acquired through school or other means, have even heard accounts of a certain oppression—real or supposed—suffered by the *pays d'oc* at the hands of the *pays d'oïl,* and considered by some (who are legion) to go back as far as the Albigensian Crusade. This crusade is blamed for having made the inhabitants of the Midi bow down under the harsh fist of the baron-knights who descended on them from the Parisian Basin. As for the web of French railways woven around Paris, as early as the nineteenth century it was regarded as demarcating the fallow spaces of the French desert beyond the Loire.

Such bracing views reveal the contents—not necessarily ridiculous—of the common memory as much as they bear witness to its deficiencies. This memory is indeed nourished by a vague yet nonetheless pertinent knowledge that gradually, and not always explicitly, assimilated certain facts from the research of statisticians of the past and present. Baron Dupin, d'Angeville, and then Maggiolo, followed by Furet, Ozouf, Chartier, and others, have successively underlined the importance of the Saint-Malo–Geneva line. Running along an imaginary border, a more or less straight line from Mont-Saint-Michel to the westernmost point of Lake Leman, it separates the most developed regions of the *pays d'oïl*—Normandy, the Parisian region, or Picardy—from all the provinces of the *pays d'oc,* and also from certain backward *oïl* areas located "as if by chance" to the south of the strategic border in question; these may include, for example, the Vendée and the Berry region, among others. The criterion used to define this cartographic dotted line is the ability to read, write, and sign one's name on a marriage contract. The Saint-Malo–Geneva line, if we are to believe the surveys of these historians, was already in place in the 1680s; that is to say, it was "constructed" early in the seventeenth century or even before, a construction most probably stimulated by the Renaissance and the accompanying boom in printing, along with an initial wave of schooling. Be that as it may, toward 1680–85, when official France was pursuing a reactionary policy of anti-Huguenot measures that was to culminate in the revocation of the Edict of Nantes, the advances of the Enlightenment, even in attenuated form, were an effective presence in northeastern France. These advances expressed the threefold wish to promote literacy, simultaneously supported by municipalities, the church, and wealthy peasant and bourgeois families. . . For subsequent periods, in particular the 1780s, 1820s, and 1860s, Maggiolo's survey confirms the significance of the Saint-Malo–Geneva line. It was to disappear only gradually, with the spread of mandatory schooling in the course of the last quarter of the nineteenth century instituted by Jules Ferry. This old border, so durable, delineated in its time (1680–1870) a north–south division that can also be found in many other sectors. Thus, in the 1830s, d'Angeville observed that tall individuals were to be found in greater proportion in the northeastern zones, which in addition were far more advanced in literacy and schooling. Naturally, the relatively greater heights are not to be explained by some racial factor; they must be correlated, regionally, with superior nutrition, itself the result of more substantial per capita income in the region. Incidentally, this higher income also financed and spurred the region's progress in literacy relative to poorer areas; whence the multiple correlations among phenomena that at first appear heterogeneous.

Starting from the same viewpoint, we can also quantify the progress of national integration. According to d'Angeville, the "enlightened" populations of the great northeast, as just defined, were characterized by loyalty to the State, faithful payment of fiscal taxes and performance of military service, and the more frequent presence of young people among the elite. In contrast, we find a vast zone of military insubordination and resistance to taxes in the "Occitanian" south, particularly in the

mountains and still more in the Massif Central. These mentalities—
loyalist tendencies in the Ardennes and rebelliousness in the Corrèze—
are not recent phenomena. They belong to elements of the collective
memory, which moreover includes (both before and after the revolutionary decade) the geography of crime: hoodlums committing violence
to property were more preponderant in the developed regions, such as
Normandy and Île-de-France. . . On the other hand, murder, reflecting
the Iberian and Mediterranean models, expressed a certain archaic tendency of the south. These remarks, which apply to murder, no longer
pertain as soon as one looks at suicide rates: as the sin of civilization, of
individualism, suicide was most prevalent among the men of the developed north, in contrast to the southern (as well as the westernmost)
zones, which were happily more conservative and resistant to personal
self-destruction for a long time to come.

Let us go farther: an exhaustive survey by Michel Demonet (1985)
located and defined similar divisions in the hexagonal landscape during
the 1850s. These partitions are contemporary with a collection of rural
statistics that, though already highly detailed, were fortunately representative of a still traditional society. The north—south opposition still obtained, according to Demonet. But it no longer strictly followed the
Saint-Malo—Geneva line. It simply implied the coexistence of two powerful areas defined according to latitude, and whose extended surface was
in little doubt at many of these latitudes. The respective outlines of these
areas may have blurred or shifted according to the variable under examination; their common border was not necessarily fixed once and for all.
Let us briefly sketch some of the significant details of this picture: the
north contained the most widely cultivated regions, with the highest net
yield of flour per hectare of wheat. It also possessed most of the flax, a
plant of the coastal perimeters from Finistère to Flanders, and nearly all
the nongrain cultivated crops (sugar beets, for example). In southern
France, on the contrary, there were vast, unproductive fallow lands. The
north also had precious vines, mixed wheat and rye fields, and oats
(grown exclusively for the "noble beasts" of the military and agricultural
cavalry). These equine populations, so numerous to the north of the
Quimper—Colmar line, corresponded, in their own kind, to the old
zones of medieval chivalry. Herein lay something of nostalgic memory,
unexpectedly preserved through animal husbandry practices. These four-
legged beasts, often gelded in the northeast and near cities, drew the map
of a certain pattern of equine domestication by this simple fact of what
they lacked. Moreover, in various sectors of livestock breeding, castra-
tion was an unexpected sign of another development. To the north of the
Nantes—Mulhouse line, there were more oxen and fewer bulls than was

the case in the highly bullish breeding spaces for horned beasts in the center and, incidentally, in the Midi. Raised for meat, butter, and cheese, the idle cows of the north, with their greater weight and more abundant milk production, presented a stark contrast to the hardscrabble cows of Occitania, virtually skin and bones, constantly hitched to the swing plow—so different from the large horse-drawn plow of the north. A homologous contrast is found in sheep and pig husbandry: the merinos descended from the perfect breeds of Rambouillet's model sheepfold improved the northern flocks. In contrast, less distinguished types of sheep inhabited the natural meadows of the Massif Central, as well as the scrublands, moors, and pastures of the Midi and the extreme south. In the north, swine raised for quick slaughter for nervous speculative markets were killed earlier than the old, fat, oafish pigs of the Midi.

More generally, the models of wealth differed from one zone to the other. The indisputable prosperity of the north was linked to a diversified, balanced, and fairly stable system of mixed farming (varied crops plus livestock). This was the case in Normandy, in the department of the Nord, and in Alsace. The wealth of the south, when it existed, was narrowly correlated with the capricious and fragile fortunes of the vineyards and indexed according to the wildly fluctuating prices of wine, in zones including the Mediterranean, the Rhône Valley, the Gironde, and the Loire Valley. The geography of farming equipment was also telling with respect to the superiorities or in any case the differences of the north, where, as mentioned above, there was a strong equine presence, along with the horse-drawn plow, the four-wheeled barrow, and the flail; these contrasted with the ox and draft mule, the swing plow, and traditional threshing methods, whose prevalence began, along various borders, south of the Loire.

Finally, in the realm of social structures, the proportion of nonresident landowners was higher and the size of their holdings greater in the more developed France of the north. As for the widespread phenomenon of tenant farming, the corollary to the prevalence of nonresident landowners in the north, this was a cause not of backwardness but of progress. Consider England, where those working the land were by definition *farmers*—in other words, tenants renting the land, precisely like the farmers of the Parisian basin. Cartographically, the farmers of this extensive region and its surroundings formed a sort of "Anglicized France" dominated by tenant farming from the Charentes to the Meuse, and all the way to the channel and the North Sea. The long leases, of nine years and more, afforded these farmers, alias tenants, stability, a degree of employment security, and thus positive incentive to invest. It so happens that these farmers were found to the north of a line from La Rochelle to Geneva. The regions included, among others, all those characterized by large-scale, efficient croplands that were so dear to the physiocrats, from the Somme to the Loiret, and from the Aisne to the Basse-Seine.

In contrast to these northern blocks, the south and the extreme west of France, also considered from an agricultural viewpoint, will be presented here in a schematic manner at first (an attempt will be made to fill in details later). The various characteristic features of the south to be noted include:

1. lands left continually fallow, with triennial or, much more often, biennial, rotation;
2. second-zone grains (Breton buckwheat, Massif Central rye, Aquitanian maize), which, of course, do not exclude the presence of wheat in most fertile zones of the Midi;
3. democratic vineyards, spread over a vast area in the manner of Languedoc; their products were often mediocre and low cost in comparison to the small, elitist, highly refined vineyards of Champagne or Bourgogne; and, finally,
4. meager arboriculture, exemplified by the vast chestnut groves of primary land formations, elsewhere flanked by rows of cash orchards, at the mercy of sunshine and geology (Dauphinois walnut trees, mulberry trees, and olive groves in the southwest).

As far as raising livestock is concerned, I have already mentioned the mules raised, for lack of good horses, in Poitou, Languedoc, and Provence. To these should be added the scrawny cows of the Midi, used to scratch the soil with the swing plow. While sorely lacking in horses, the Midi was, on the other hand, determinedly well-stocked with goats, to such a point that eighteenth-century *intendants* from time to time waged a war against goats, "southern beasts of the poor soils" that laid waste forests, or what was left of them. The uninterrupted chain of goat country thus ran from Poitou-Limousin to Provence and the Dauphinée, not to mention Corsica.

The rural geography of bipeds converged by other paths with that of the quadrupeds. The south, less developed, was home to a higher percentage of farmers, to the detriment of other professions—a typically archaic feature. This was true particularly below the La Rochelle—Geneva line. Alongside the micro-landowners, who were particularly numerous in this zone, there were also tenant farmers in the center and in the Midi; but their lives were less rosy than those of their comfortable counterparts in Great Britain or in the north of France, and they could even be said to have been oppressed by the landowning class, which exploited the native labor. These tenants paid the landowners a particularly high rent.

Thus, land capital was (relatively) profitable to the south of the line between Bordeaux and Pontarlier, but clearly this was in no sense a sign of good economic health—far from it: southern salaries were often low. It will come as no surprise that patterns of consumption, once again, find the south disadvantaged: the northwest showed itself to be more modern in spending more for heating and housing. The poorly sheltered south tightened its belt in order to pay taxes and to dress somewhat ostentatiously—one way of masking certain deficiencies in other aspects of the standard of living.

A notorious triangle of poverty inscribed in the southwest area (and even beyond, since it included a fair portion of the Breton peninsula) stood out within and at the margins of France's prevailing underdevelopment. This infertile crescent of the nation, a horseshoe of marginal lands, formed a more or less discontinuous zone extending from Brittany to the Massif Central and the Landes. This was in a sense the realm of the excluded third, of dead angles, a place where the standard of living was poor and the agricultural salaries low: women employed in field or other farm labor were particularly badly paid; live-in help, for the most part female, living under the yoke of semiservitude, was widespread; the proportion of salaries that was nonmonetary, or paid in kind, remained substantial; and these paltry wages, in any case, were used to obtain food and above all bread for the families of these proletarians.

This clearly delineated triangle, with its bitter misery, reminds us, by its very emergence, that it would be unreasonable to present the south of France as uniformly underdeveloped *as a whole*. Far from it! The contrast between expanses of development (in the northeast) and of less development (in the far west, the center, and even the Midi) nevertheless remains relevant. It parallels, moreover, on a larger scale, the recognized contrast between northern Europe, which was in the throes of rushing modernization, and Mediterranean Europe, which was gradually sinking into archaism. But even admitting this point, the lot of southern France was not one of unmitigated deprivation. Indeed, it contained, if not expanses, at least strips and even swaths of development, which show up clearly on our map. The largest of these strips bordered and followed the Garonne Valley, broadly sketched, from Bordeaux to Toulouse; then it bifurcated above the threshold of Naurouze, toward Languedoc and Provence. It extended up in the form of a Y toward the Rhône Valley and all the way to the hubs of Lyon and Saint-Étienne. Rich and productive agriculture, large farms, a plentiful supply of agricultural laborers who were relatively well paid (if only in comparison with those in the truly impoverished zones), and high income from the land are what might characterize this long strip of "privileged Occitania," where the baroque and ornamental forms of southern sociability energetically thrived. There was a clear contrast with the mountainous Occitania of the Massif Central (and tangentially of the Alps and the Pyrenees), which often, to varying degrees, bore the marks of a certain poverty.

The geography of development in traditional France was thus finely drawn in its expanses and swaths, broad spaces and narrow strips. Nevertheless, the basic division, which is of the highest relevance, did oppose a "north" and a "south" in large blocks, a division that now calls for nuance or refinement.

The cartographic contrast thus established between northern France and the Midi is quite dated, since in our time as well the theme of "wealth and poverty" would be played out more from east to west, and thus to a lesser degree from north to south. The spatial memory dealt with in the present text is therefore all the more deeply rooted in the historical memory because it tends toward fossilization in the face of contemporary realities.

✿

For centuries and even millennia, the north—south split was to varying degrees alive. Going back as far as the Flood, the earliest agriculture, termed "Neolithic," arrived in the Midi via the Mediterranean (from Palestine, the Middle East, and Asia Minor) starting in the sixth millennium before our era. In contrast, agriculture (here too including livestock breeding) did not arise in the "French" north until around 4500 B.C. It was imported *chez nous* along a land route, through the civilizations of the Danube region: there was, roughly speaking, a fifteen-century gap.

The final millennium, "before 1 A.D.," was likewise rich in specific developments that correlated with latitudes. The south was first to acquire the advantages of Hellenism, thanks to the foundation of a Rhodian colony in Marseilles, and the advantages of Roman civilization, as a result of the early establishment of a grape- and olive-growing "Narbonnaise" province annexed to the Italian metropolis. This Gallia Narbonensis even claimed the sad privilege of being exploited by greedy bureaucrats from the *urbs,* whose memory is perpetuated by Cicero in his celebrated *Pro Fonteio.* Even today, the Maison Carrée in Nîmes, the "Antiques" of Saint-Rémy-de-Provence, and the Pont du Gard bear witness to the "imperialism" that hailed from the south and was particularly penetrating. The hub of the Roman road system was in Lyon, in the southern half of Gaul. The geochronological gaps continued to make themselves felt, even if counted in centuries and no longer in thousands of years. Vineyards, for example, were confined to the south of the Libourne—Geneva line, a border that was not crossed until viticulture triumphantly made its way toward the north starting in the third century A.D. At the end of that same century, there were two administrative Gauls: that of Trèves and that of Arles, already probably separated by linguistic differences. Then came the barbarian invasions. Penetration by the Franks, so marked in the north, was infinitely less so in the Midi, where various kingdoms flourished—Visigoth or Ostrogoth, depending on the era. Their cultural fecundity was not negligible. The perambulations of the Gascons (or Vascons), who came from Spain and fanned out around Toulouse as early as the sixth century, added an extra touch of originality to what would one day become Occitania. Clovis's southern conquests or reconquests did not prevent the reemergence around 670 of an autonomous Aquitania. In the face of the full-blown Muslim threat at the beginning of the eighth century, the Occitan ideal of self-determination even seems to have been momentarily realized—though in the worst of conditions, it is true—with the coexistence of Aquitania, Provence, and Languedoc, each of which, for the time being, functioned independently! The northward push of the Muslims, who were first defeated in Poitiers in 732, set off repercussions in the form of renewed Frankish inroads. These paved the way for the integration of what is now southern France and of Catalonia into Carolingian structures, which were lasting in cultural terms but fragile in the everyday sphere of administration.

Changing political fortunes are one thing; the pre-Christian and then the Christian Midi, as we have seen, was at times incorporated with the north[1] and at other times separated from it.[2] Cultural originality, on the other hand, persisted and was affirmed during the barbarian and Merovingian period: a sizable intelligentsia, renowned for such writers as Ausonius, Sidonius Apollinaris, Fortunatus, and the Auvergnat Grégoire "of Tours," embodied the intellectual preeminence of southern Gaul between Clermont and Bordeaux. Provence was at that time a reservoir of monks and bishops. The Midi, seduced by Arianism and Adoptianism, also entered into a long career of heretical leanings.

The future of the difference, however, belonged to the linguistic facts; our *français d'oïl* was the bastard child of Latin dialects, themselves overdetermined in this case by a Celtic substratum (earlier) and a powerful Germanic "superstratum" (subsequently). In contrast, in the south, another scenario was played out beyond the human desert that was temporarily inserted between the Loire and the Garonne after the invasions: from the Gironde to Camargue, starting in the ninth and tenth centuries, the pre-Occitanian cluster of "southern Gallo-Roman" took on a distinct identity. In these regions, the vernacular speech of the Romans, pagan legionnaires, and Catholic preachers was more effectively preserved under the auspices of a richer, more authentic Latin purity; the presence of Celtic and, later, German idioms was less marked. Analogous phenomena of remarkable language conservation also occurred in Spain and in Italy, but it goes without saying that the dialectical modalities in those regions were not identical to those in the *pays d'oc*.

The temptation of longitudinal divisions, from east to west, could never be completely exorcised. In the ninth century these were incompletely exemplified in Lotharingia. However, as the end of the first millennium approached, north–south divergences continued to dominate in various ways. With respect to agriculture and the landed aristocracy, feudalism and serfdom were less developed in the southern half between the Loire and the Meuse. Seigneurial domains, the precursors of our large agricultural holdings, were smaller in "Occitania" than elsewhere, and this feature was to persist in other forms until the nineteenth century, even into the present day.

The *pays d'oc* was not lacking in initiative, nor was it incapable of creating institutions: it was in this region that the idea of the truce of God originated in the tenth and eleventh centuries, quickly spreading throughout Europe. But the drive to centralize was lacking: the tendency to infraregional dispersions triumphed, despite the inchoate unifying impulses that emerged around Toulouse and remained in a state of stammering infancy. Between Auvergne and the Pyrenees, there was nothing comparable to the patient attempts at Capetian conglomeration that held sway farther north starting in A.D. 987—a symbolic date. The aristocracy of the Midi, not highly militarized, was weakened by the very behavior that made it appealing: the moderate but indisputable "feminism" to which it was home. Its wealth was indeed undermined by the constant division of inheritances, which were conferred upon daughters as well as sons. This southern aristocracy therefore lacked the necessary courage at the critical moment of confrontation with its powerful northern sister, clad in steel armor and brandishing tough ideas.

At the threshold of the Middle Ages, literary creation—oral, written, poetic—once again (as had been the case six or seven centuries earlier, at the time of Ausonius, Sidonius, and Gregory) gave free rein to the special talents of the Midi. The troubadours exalted the *langue d'oc* at the expense of Latin; they celebrated aristocratic values and disparaged the clerical model. The woman of noble extraction was exalted and subjected to the desires, crude or courtly, of poet-lovers. The resurgence of Roman law, brought back from Italy to southern France via Provence, spurred the first rash of notaries, those troubadours of the daily grind. The *consulats,* the first municipal organisms, were livelier and more active than in the *pays d'oïl,* endowing cities, and later peasant villages, with the status of legal communities. They conferred powers first to the nobility, then to the bourgeoisie, and even to artisans and peasants. Cellular municipalism, coupled with the absence of multiregional unity, became an essential aspect of political life in our Midi: at least three powers—the Plantagenets, renowned for Eleanor of Aquitaine; the counts of Toulouse; and the sovereigns of Catalonia or of Aragon—vied for the biggest piece of the pie, attempting to impose order in the larger south, which, bounded by the Pyrenees, was still no more than a geographical expression. *Trois larrons en foire, soit deux de trop.*★ A major cycle of Romanesque art, however, gave concrete local expression to southern originality, which was radically opposed to a later Gothicism that was to take its inspiration rather from Île-de-France and Normandy. At the heart of the *langue d'oc* zone, and setting aside short-lived administrative boundaries, a well-defined geographic area spawned the language shared by the poets of the *trobar* and the *chancelleries.* This area included, and exceeded by a generous margin, the south of the Massif Central; it corresponded roughly to what were formerly the provinces or subprovinces of Quercy, Toulousain, Albigeois, Rouergue, Gévaudan, Narbonnais, and Nîmois. The terms "Provençal" and "Limousin" for language and poetry (sometimes used by historians) are therefore inexact under the circumstances. Military-religious orders such as the Hospitalers of Saint John or the Knights Templar played a key role in crystallizing a way of writing and speaking in the *langue d'oc.* The tiny community of Saint-Eulalie, in Rouergue, well supplied with religious knights, weighed more heavily in this process than did the vast groups of Romanic speakers in Limoges or Marseilles.

The "French" incorporation of the southern nebula, definitively captured by a Capetian galaxy, took place in the thirteenth century, through the Albigensian Crusade and the subsequent annexation. I will not dwell on this: the overall problem of "Montségur," as an event symbolizing and summarizing this entire "Cathar" period, will come up in the following volume of *Les Lieux de mémoire.* I will simply note here that the annexation, which was not lacking in bloody acts, marked the Midi's definitive swing toward the north, and in a sense wrested the south away from its old Mediterranean tropisms. "France" took advantage of the situation to push the Catalan-Aragonian State back beyond the Pyrenees (for the disputed possession of Roussillon, this repulsion was not to take full and irreversible effect until 1659). Some time before this still distant

★ Three thieves together are two too many. TRANS.

date, it became apparent that the French kingdom, as early as the thirteenth century, had a hold on Occitania's heart and belly, Auvergne and Languedoc, respectively. The incorporation of the two wings was under way. The Provençal wing was peacefully digested starting in the 1480s; the Girondin and Gascon wing lost its autonomy in 1453, when the English were evicted from Bordeaux.

Let us attempt, in this connection, to avoid anachronistic expressions such as "colonialism" or "genocide." Occitania, at least in its Languedocian parts, was at first indisputably violated by French power. But subsequently, as often happens with old couples in forced marriages, Occitania gave herself fairly freely to the northern State. The Capetian royalty did not arrive empty-handed; it brought something for everyone. The clerics, in Toulouse or Carcassonne, were grateful that it consolidated the (quite oppressive) monopoly of papist beliefs. It also legitimized the municipal structures upon which the bourgeoisie *d'oc* prided itself. Finally, the Capetian State offered both a modicum of justice and an opportunity for military careers, fulfilling the respective wishes of the peasants and the nobility. It is impossible, of course, to paint a rosy picture of a union that had its share of conflicts and marital quarrels, some of them quite violent. But never did the parties go so far as officially to threaten divorce proceedings.

The fourteenth and fifteenth centuries, severely marked by grave crises—plagues, the Hundred Years' War—saw the birth and local development of large regional entities. These were moreover desired by the monarchy, which, in the state of institutional infancy to which it was still confined, had neither the means nor the desire to practice a massive policy of direct administration; under the circumstances, such a policy would have proven absurd. Among the strong local organizations that formed the uniqueness and the pride of the south, let us point first of all to the Estates (legislative body) of Languedoc and the Parlement de Toulouse (law court of Toulouse).

In any case, at the end of the fifteenth century, after the definitive annexation of Provence and Marseille (1481), "Occitania," or at least the geographical expression that was sometimes to be designated by this name, assumed something close to its present-day configuration. The only entities left out of this system were the regions of Nice (until 1860), the Comtat (which remained under papal control throughout the ancien régime), and the Béarn, which for more than another century was to remain subject to the Pyrenean Albret-Navarre dynasty (which was to produce Henri IV). It becomes possible, in this context, to define, if only negatively, the said "Occitania," which was already almost fully constituted: in actual fact it corresponded to the vast zone of Romanic (i.e., not *d'oïl*) languages that the French had assembled between the Alps and the Pyrenees and that, as a result, escaped once and for all the Italian, Catalan, and Iberian spheres of influence. After all, with respect to this zone, all three powers would have been completely at the ready, but history failed them. The "southern accent," which in fact varies widely but which strikes the Parisian ear as a unique or unified phenomenon, continues today to mark the majority of the region's inhabitants, the "natives" of this strange Occitanian country that is not one.

At the dawn of the Renaissance, a diversity of cultures developed: the French *langue d'oïl* first penetrated this extensive area, thanks to Gutenberg's printing technology, starting in 1480–90. Acts of patronage, happily initiated by the good King René in Aix-en-Provence, the Pope's agents in Avignon, and the Gai Savoir and Jeu Floraux in Toulouse, sponsored or locally underpinned literary and artistic creativity that was not entirely derived from Parisian, Ligerian, or Lyonnais models—far from it. The creative void left by the troubadours, who had disappeared from the scene, was filled in a provincialist mode by theater dramatizing religious subject matter in dialect. More concretely, land tenure was characterized by a relatively liberal, even modern, system. Freeholds (property wholly owned by commoners, without seignieurial interference) were much more numerous in the south than in the north: this time, the archaic tendency was not where one would expect to find it! Moreover, the peasants in the *pays d'oc* were quite enamored of the generous maxim "No lord without a title," whereas those in the *pays d'oïl* had to make do with the rigid motto "No land without a lord." In Languedoc and Provence, taxes were "real," more or less equitably established according to the area and quality of the farmlands; in the Parisian basin, they were "personalized," arbitrarily imposed on individuals at the pleasure of the collector. The southern populations were in theory (and therefore in fact) subject to the king of France. But in the sixteenth century nearly everywhere they were still governed by assemblies representing the three orders or estates (clergy, aristocracy, and commoners). Thus the municipal or communal semi-democracies that characterized local power in this region were accompanied by a regional semirepresentative system, a sort of constitutional regime *avant la lettre*—one with highly oligarchical tendencies, to be sure. There were other objectively "democratic" factors, at least in the long run: the great princely families of the Midi (Albret, Foix, Armagnac, and others) were headed for extinction, albeit a glorious one (Henri IV was an Albret on his mother's side); at best, their leadership role was temporarily taken over by their more powerful counterparts, who "parachuted" into the south from their northern origins. In this connection, consider the Rohan and Montmorency families, from Brittany and Paris respectively, who spearheaded the Midi's powerful revolts against royal power in the seventeenth century. The failure of these leaders, in turn, facilitated the rise to power of the Occitanian bourgeoisie.

The particularity of the south was also solidified through the preferential adoption of Protestantism, *hic et nunc*. This process, of course, must not be idealized. Early on, Huguenots gained a following throughout urban France, in Meaux and Grenoble alike, from Caen to Montpellier. The tipping of the scales toward the south was, at first, the opposite of an indirect effect: Huguenots were progressively driven outside the northern territory by harsh repressive measures issuing from the monarchic State, by military force, and by the Parlement de Paris. Now this Catholic "iron hand" lost its vigor and waned as a function of distance from the geographic sites or effective summits of centralized Parisian decision-making. By a simple effect of residual survival, the Protestant sphere of influence thus settled, crystallized, and solidified in a curve at a respectful distance from the capital, in the Huguenot fertile crescent arcing from La Rochelle to Nîmes and to Geneva, traversing Agen, Montauban, and Sommières. Nevertheless, in the Midi and particularly in the southern Massif Central (Rouergue, Gévaudan), powerful blocks of Catholic loyalty remained in existence.

Religious originality is not everything. A corroborating cartography was also delineated by resistance to taxes. The allergy to fiscal taxes was more severe among populations of the Midi, and principally of the southwest, than elsewhere, and indeed caused a disproportionate multiplication of acts of rebellion, minor or major, against revenue agents, customs officers, and other tax collectors (to use more modern terminology). These peculiar and often bloody agitations marked a long period that was rife with uprisings, extending from the precocious revolt of the Pitauts in the Bordelais and Angoumois (1548) to the final action of the "Croquants tardifs" (1707). In the limited scope of the present text, I can only point to this particularly antiestablishment bent of the Aquitanians, without attempting to explain it.

This tendency did, it is true, go some way toward defining a multiregional autonomy: the close alliance of Protestants and moderate Catholics, in proximity to each other and far from Paris, led to the formation of the very short-lived Republic of the United Provinces of the Midi, a perhaps exaggerated expression. This scattered archipelagic entity, resembling a leopard's skin, covered in part the often Calvinist irredentist lands of Languedoc and Gascogne; it experienced a brief apogee during the crucial decade of the 1580s but would not survive the definitive return of royal and national unity implemented by Henri IV. More durable, in contrast, was the new wave of cultural, or strictly

Figure 1.1
Protestantism in France in the 17th century.

literary, production. In the vast south, where elites were learning French, great Francophone writers appeared for the first time on the local scene: between 1550 and 1600, Montaigne, La Boétie, Monluc, Brantôme, even d'Aubigné. But the invading forest (*d'oïl*) must not be allowed to obscure some fine trees (*d'oc*). At the end of the sixteenth century, and during the first two-thirds of the seventeenth century, a strictly dialectal literature (which was innovative in its picaresque, theatrical, and baroque aspects) flourished in Aix, Avignon, Béziers, and Agen. Under the aegis of Brueys, Zerbin, Cortète, Michalhe, and a few others, it lacked neither zest nor appeal. The Provençal prophet Nostradamus, for his part, remains to this day—and this is no small achievement—one of the most popular, if not the most widely read, writers of French literature, as soon as we cease to confine our analysis exclusively to the most "distinguished" readership. More generally, the economic underdevelopment mentioned at the beginning of this essay did not prevent some remarkable achievements during the classical and postclassical age (the seventeenth and eighteenth centuries). Some of these emanated "from above," in other words from authorities in Versailles or Montpellier (via the Canal du Midi or the network of roads created by the States of Languedoc). Others arose "from below," so to speak, such as from the small or middle-sized backers of manufacturing concerns (Languedocian or Carcassonian cloth manufacturers exporting toward the Levant). Such achievements in the Midi implied a type of growth that was no longer strictly agricultural. Under the circumstances, is it possible to speak, as scholars of Occitania often do, of a Midi that was already marginalized at the beginning of the ancien régime's final century? The urban evidence, in fact, contradicts this overly assertive claim. From Louis XIV to Louis XVI, the Hexagon's dynamic cities par excellence were Lyons, Bordeaux, Nîmes, and even Marseilles (despite the 1720 plague). The persistent lag, which in any case decreased, must not be allowed to mask the region's constant and often successful attempts to catch up.

   The classical era and the Enlightenment were marked, in any event, by a double movement: on the one hand, there was the (widely known) increase in monarchic centralization, embodied in the regional *chefs-lieux* (Aix, Bordeaux . . .) by the *intendants de généralités* (provincial administrators), who came from the Parisian technocracy and were backed by the Catholic hierarchy. Basville, the *intendant* of Montpellier, a heavy-handed administrator known as a persecutor of Protestants, was the uncrowned king of Languedoc during the second part of Louis XIV's reign. The revocation of the Edict of Nantes (1685) made Basville (rightly or wrongly), along with Simon de Montfort, one of the chief villains of Languedoc's historical dramaturgy. The 1685 act clearly signaled the will of Versailles to eclipse the Huguenot crescent once and for all, in the name of a heartless centralism locally purveyed by the bishops.

Simultaneously—and this is quite a paradox—regional institutions conserved their power and, during the Enlightenment, even increased it, at least in the vast provinces where these institutions were lucky enough to be preserved. The contradiction with respect to the centralizing process described above is more apparent than real. After all, the States of Languedoc, so proud of their regionalist autonomy, allowed themselves to be guided by the local bishops, who were the best agents of national power in the matter of anti-Calvinist repression. A dialectical and Jesuitical synthesis of pro (royal) and con (local) . . . It is therefore not surprising that, in this (ambiguous) Languedoc, the Assemblée des États retained the upper hand in the collection of taxes and dealt with Louis XV (who was, to be sure, less domineering than was his great-grandfather Louis XIV) as one power with another. At the end of the eighteenth century, the synthesis (naturally an uneasy one) and the *connubium* between the two entities—centralism and regionalism—intensified, at least in certain zones, producing some strange bedfellows. Certain *intendants,* for example in Provence, turned into outright renegades, becoming strictly advocates for their constituents before the King's Council.

The French Revolution, in the end, was to catch Occitania off balance. The Occitanians had difficulty accepting first the abolition of large regional institutions, then de-Christianization, and finally the economic crisis resulting from the wars and the interruption of various commercial circuits. With the disappearance in 1815 of Napoleon and his followers, who were the remnants of the revolutionary decade, suddenly the Midi emerged with its true colors starkly exposed: overwhelmingly "ancien-régimist," Bourbonophilic, furious, bent on revenge, and responsible for a White Terror. The Restoration therefore brought nobles or notables of the Midi to power (albeit a centralist, Parisian, and supreme form of power) in the persons of Decazes and Villèle, whose right-mindedness, imbued nonetheless with a muted liberalism, seduced the good Louis XVIII.

A new mutation, devoid of unanimism, surfaced in the Midi (after 1830) in the shadow of Louis-Philippe's umbrella and continued after the fall of that sovereign. In privileged Occitania (see above), it was due primarily to the influence exerted on the lower class by bourgeois and petit-bourgeois who had become republicans; the propaganda of the first socialists also played a certain role in this development. In 1849–51 there emerged a "Red Midi" along the Languedocian border as far as Limousin. Through many twists and turns, this peculiar leftist phenomenon was destined to take century-long root throughout a broad area. In the course of time, it was to furnish the final push needed to consolidate the Third Republic and the leftist victories during the period of Mitterand's socialism, including those of 1981. Occitania, however, is nothing if not diverse. It preserved enough white (the Old Bourbon color) among the red for the Vichy regime and then the Resistance to find rich diggings there, each concentrated in a certain area: the former in the northern and southern Massif Central, the latter in Limousin or Gard.

Whether in the Midi or elsewhere, the Socialist (Aude) and then Communist (Bouches-du-Rhône) choices are, in any case, indicative of a universal signifier that is not a priori geographically motivated. It was therefore logical that, in more well-defined areas, a "Provençal" and then "Occitan" choice made itself known, at once modest and enduring, atomistic and pervasive. On the east bank of the Rhône, the Mistralian Félibrige was monarchist and rightist from 1850 to World War II.* On the western side of the great river, Occitanism was symbolically leftist, especially after 1945: René Nelli, Robert Lafont, Yves Rouquette, grandfather, father and son, were spurred on by Oedipal rivalries. The *félibres* and the Occitans wrote the *langue d'oc* using two different orthographic systems: the battle of the final *a* versus *o* has drawn more ink than blood.

With the Socialist victory of 1981, once again the militants of the nationalist Left, in Montpellier and Toulouse alike, were left without a convenient scapegoat in the form of the northern Giscardian Right, which was henceforth excluded from power for at least one legislative term. But the future remains open to Occitanian regionalist demands, thwarted though they may be by the escalating pro-French nationalism provoked among Languedocian and Provençal voters by a double influx of Algerian immigrants. Both *pieds-noirs* and Muslims are present in great numbers along the Mediterranean coast, and there is little love between them. Their mutual resentments contribute to the local successes of the National Front, which is so dear to the former French of Algeria and which clearly finds Occitanism the least of its worries.

I should not like to close the second part of this essay, however, on such an anecdotal, short-term vision of questions concerning the Midi. Let us say that delving deep into the past has enabled us to diagnose the effects of a fourfold hysteresis, four lingering influences of previous magnetic forces: (1) *Huguenot survivals in the south,* Protestantism having been

---

* The Félibrige was a society of writers formed in 1854 with the object of preserving the Provençal language. Mistral (1830–1914) was a Provençal poet. TRANS.

progressively driven out of northern France; (2) *the vestiges of a decentralized system,* which arose once again in the form of urban and peasant revolts in the southwest, in opposition to the increasing centralization implemented in the seventeenth century by the Bourbon monarchy; (3) *the persistence of a defunct ancien régime,* re-emerging after the French Revolution and the Empire (embodied in the period of the White Terror); and finally, (4) *the residue of the Revolution itself,* that great event formerly concentrated within a decade at the end of the eighteenth century and completely exported toward the Midi beginning only in the years 1840–50. Thus the Red Midi was born and survives to our day. The effects of the southern "crescent" that I have discussed in connection with the Huguenots can also be applied to these various phenomena, spaced out over successive and widely differing periods of time from the sixteenth to the twentieth centuries.

Having considered retrospective and comparative history, I should like to conclude with a third aspect of the "north–south division": the opposition between north and south over the classic contrast between customs and Roman law (the latter also known as written law): in short, legal and geographical ethnography, which once again reveals the juxtaposition of two blocks, just as slate gives way to tile.

The more thorough implantation of Roman law in the Midi corresponds fundamentally to facts of culture. In this region, the late Middle Ages had to some extent forgotten the ancient imperial legal system in favor of a variety of laws, stemming in part from barbarians or simply arising out of local habits. Starting in the twelfth century, Justinian's compilations "landed" on the territory that was to become present-day France. They were received with particular favor in the south, where the dark centuries of the intervening phase, notwithstanding what has just been asserted, had never entirely eclipsed what remained of the Latin legal system. Between 1124 and 1190, the two banks of the Rhône, to the south of Valence, were won over by this second incarnation of Roman law. A professional infrastructure made up of *notarii* (notaries) was established simultaneously, as early as 1125, in Bas-Languedoc and Camargue. In the thirteenth and fourteenth centuries, these legal experts, who in any case were to remain far more numerous in the south than in the north, were among those practitioners who were most active in adopting Roman practices. Paradoxically, beginning with the reign of Philippe Auguste, the royal authorities encouraged the diffusion of Roman law in the Midi, which they considered a useful instrument of power. In contrast, in the north the same authorities were content with custom, which seemed more likely to thwart the ambitions of the Empire, whose advocates had readily adopted Romanist arguments. In 1251 and 1278, the official texts issued by the Parisian monarchy already distinguished between the France of written law (the regions of Toulouse, Carcassonne, Beaucaire, Périgord, Rouergue, Quercy . . .) and the rest of the kingdom, which obeyed only custom (*consuetudo*). The border thus delineated was not dissimilar to the linguistic border between the *langue d'oc* and *langue d'oïl*. The barrier was far from impenetrable: the northern customs themselves, particularly in the Orléanais, were permeated, or "infiltrated," by certain influences of learned law; nevertheless, despite these admixtures, they retained their irreducible originality, their local flavor.

In the Midi, then, Roman law was early on superimposed upon local customs, which perished in its formidable clutches. Traces of some of these customs, however, survived, still vigorous and poorly effaced, particularly in the Pyrenees. Then again, Roman law itself, seen from this angle, was not without ambiguity. It always promoted the will of the paterfamilias in his desire to favor the one child who alone, or almost alone, was to succeed him in matters of inheritance. While doing so, it revived or simply perpetuated, under another name, much older habits that had existed long before it. Particularly in its mountainous regions, the Midi was by no means unfamiliar with the communitarian family, rooted in its traditional bedrock and endeavoring in its own way to favor one son in inheritance, in order that he might, with and after his parents, ensure the posterity of their land and "house." Roman law was limited in this setting to supplying a posteriori justification for preferential inheritance arrangements, which did not need it to begin their career; the effect was more or less the same.

During the first half of the fifteenth century, the creation of the Parlement de Toulouse, boasting a vast geographical jurisdiction, marked another stage in the continuous progress of the new law in the south. Between 1451 and 1477, this stage was reinforced by the establishment of other pro-south *parlements* in Grenoble, Bordeaux, and Aix-en-Provence, which preferred Roman law.

At the heart of the "Romanizing" process—further stimulated starting in the fourteenth century by the ad hoc influence of the universities of Toulouse and Montpellier—lay the notion of property without legal hindrance, and of the all-powerful Will. It conferred upon the paterfamilias, as we have said, the ability to designate a sole heir and to deprive his other children of inheritance. Such provisions created the fortune of the great seigneurial house of Albret, whose members were indeed early practitioners of strict Roman primogeniture; and many nonnobles hastened to imitate them.

We thus find ourselves contemplating an ambivalent situation: on the one hand, the omnipotence of Roman habits in the Midi provided de facto encouragement for certain antiegalitarian tendencies—they might as well be termed reactionary—such as primogeniture among commoners, a practice that had a far more extensive social impact there than it did in the northern lands, where it was almost exclusively limited to the nobility. In contrast to the south, on the other hand, the north left a lot of leeway for equality among nonnoble heirs beginning in the sixteenth century, and even earlier. Thus the overwhelming majority of northern families—all but the bluebloods—were shaped by egalitarianism.

Roman law in the Midi, in addition, exalted the individual's freedom and sense of responsibility. It affirmed the ascendancy of quiritarian property, without limitations, and it did so in opposition to the various inheritance claims for divided usufruct and multiple ownership imposed on a single property by various individuals, as sanctioned by the customs of the north. Finally, let us add that Roman law was entirely on the side of contractual logic, which was itself hostile to family ties and to outmoded statutes; it favored commercial and monetary practices.

The complexity of the picture, however, is all the greater because of the ambivalence that also existed in the northern region. The movement to record customs to the north of the Loire culminated for the first time under the reign of Louis XII and a second time, a little later, during the period of Henri II. This movement (under both of these monarchs; the time that elapsed between them changed nothing) was, it might be said, doubly triggered. On the one hand, it consolidated certain antiquated archaisms of custom, by the very fact that they were from that day forward set down in a register in black and white. But, in addition, the great Parisian jurists, with their smattering of renascent culture, were unable to resist quietly Romanizing certain articles of one or another regional custom, with the voluntary or forced consent of the local elites, on the occasion of the scriveners' cavalcades or tournaments in which they participated outside the capital.

Whatever the case, the "quiritarian" advantages of the Midi persisted (despite contradictory variations, here and there). The south has long since boasted many more *alleux* (freeholds, or lands owned outright) than the north. Is it for this reason, along with others, that the maxim prevailing in these sunny lands was the liberal—indeed virtually "progressive"— adage "To every landlord a title," in contrast to the universal "feudalism" of the northern zones, with their revealing motto "To every land a lord"? The same sense of equity obtained—and this is no coincidence—in the matter of direct taxes, or the *taille*. As we have seen, in Languedoc property taxes were fairly calculated on the basis of the owner's wealth. In the northern provinces, the *taille* was a tax on income, imposed solely upon heads of household, who were all too often assessed capriciously. Still, in connection with the claims of the State, of which taxes were after all only one aspect, the Midi took great advantage of the fact that Roman law, which emphasized quiritarian property, readily thwarted seigneurialism, which on the contrary would have broken down proprietary rights to its own advantage. Therefore, the south had no problem (here is another "progressive" tendency, in the best sense of the word) effectively keeping in check the *directe universelle* of the king of France: His Majesty's ambitions, his desire to extend his seigneurial and nationalizing claims abusively over all the lands of the kingdom, wherever or whatever they might be. In the Midi—in another offensive of the "quiritarian" mentalities that were encouraged by the local *parlements*—easements (for right of way and use of grazing land), in other words the joint ownership or common use of the boundary areas between adjoining properties, were kept under strict surveillance by jurisprudence, which allowed them only in cases of immemorial presumption. Such severity shocked the apostles of customary law, for whom any passerby (northern. . .) could gather the fruits growing on bushes—for whom, indeed, any wall was automatically common property. As for complaints concerning real estate acquisitions considered to be unwarranted by the plaintiff, the statute of limitations was for one or five years according to northern customs, but for thirty years in the jurisdiction of Toulouse! For in its jurisprudence, the pink city showed a fastidious (Romanist. . .) respect for property law: landlord absenteeism that to their great dismay led to the forfeiture of their rights was proclaimed at a distance of merely ten leagues from the land or the house under contention, or simply outside the bailiwick, in the customs of the north. But the Parlement de Toulouse, ever attentive to the quiritarian spirit, affirmed absenteeism only if the landlord in question had left the kingdom. The free alienation of real property was normally permitted in Provençal and Languedocian lands, which, on this point, once again proved to be in the vanguard in bourgeois matters (how far we are in these cases from the indexes, nevertheless so real, of underdevelopment in the south, which were discussed in the first part of the present text in an altogether different connection, that of economics). In contrast, north of the Loire there remained quite numerous traces of lineal reclamation, in the name of which families could oppose one member's dissipation of inherited real estate, even if in principle that member held official title to the land. This "heinous practice" in the eyes of written law—"this northern shameful vestige of feudalism" that was the ridiculous formality of lineal power—was not to be completely abolished until 1790, with the French Revolution.

In matters of inheritance, Roman law—in itself, as well as in the Midi of old—was far from feminist (see in this connection the disillusioned remarks by Alphonse Daudet, whose *Numa Roumestan* laments the male chauvinism of his Provençal compatriots). This law always gave preference to relatives on the paternal side, or agnations, at the expense of maternal relations. On the other hand, *customs,* particularly in the west, in Île-de-France and in Picardy-Wallonia, favored women's interests in succession. The southern Romanist paterfamilias chose his heir and successor "at his pleasure and will," whereas (renewed) northern customs often encouraged equal treatment of heirs, or again the representation ad infinitum of various lineal descendants; or yet again they linked inheritance rights to cohabitation.

Where adoption was concerned, in the Midi and particularly in Provence, there was persistent loyalty to the positive provisions (the father's will, always!) that had originated in classical Roman law. This, of course, contrasted with customary law, which did not allow the intrusion of a stranger to infringe upon the prerogatives of blood relations. In the matter of a father's emancipation of his children, beginning in the sixteenth century customs graciously accorded some opportunities, whereas in the Romanist Midi, the formidable fathers retained usufruct of the goods of their offspring. They could refuse to emancipate them, even in the event of marriage. They continued to hold sway, if possible, even over their grandsons.

As for the dowry system, the *parlements* of the Midi jealously clung to Roman rules governing the inalienability of women's dowries, rules intended both to guarantee wives a means of subsistence and to protect families, for whom dowries provided an assurance of emergency resources in case of need. In the north, the dowry was often pooled with or considered as part of the combined marital assets, of which the husband was lord and master. Can this be seen as a brand of southern feminism evening the score, making up for what was lost in inheritances by claiming its due on the question of dowries? In any event, what was essential, in both cases, was the ultraproprietary (and therefore modernist and bourgeois) spirit of Roman law. It preserved the quiritarian rights of fathers in their role as testators; but the same logic motivated its vigilance in guarding wives' dowries, which were, after all, originally bestowed by none other than the fathers (or fathers' widows) of these wives.

In the Midi, the last will and testament rejected the equal division of goods; it excluded daughters, who, in any case, had previously been either dowered or else placed in a convent. It favored the oldest son the better to preserve rank (among the nobility) or the integrity of farmlands (among commoners). In contrast, as early as the sixteenth century, egalitarian tendencies began to appear in the vicinity of Paris. In the west, their existence was attested even earlier, starting in the Middle Ages. For the benefit of family members who were disadvantaged by the inheritance of one of their deceased parents, the north provided consolation in the form of a "lineal reserve," to which any lineal relative, even a distant one, could lay claim if need be. With its very Roman distrust of extended lineage, the Midi implemented not a *reserve* but a *légitime,* a child's entitlement to a portion of his parent's estate; this applied only to children, and in exceptional to the brothers and sisters of *de cujus.* Substitutions, moreover, were a perfect expression of the testamentary freedom favored by the Romanist southerners, and of the tendency that was dear to them in the system of succession. From this standpoint, substitutions favored redundancy, allowing the father to designate a second heir, should the first one not claim the inheritance. In more scholarly terms, they corresponded "to the subrogation of another person to collect the benefits conferred by the provisions of a will." It is hardly surprising that such substitutions were widely favored in the Midi as an extension of the system espoused by Bartole, the celebrated Romanist of the 1340s, whose tree of substitutions was made up of five main branches, themselves subdivided into fifty-one smaller branches. On the other hand, substitutions were often viewed askance or prohibited outright by various northern customs. . .

On these various points, the contrast between the north and the south was dramatically asserted on the occasion of the first revolutionary assemblies. Robespierre, a child of France's extreme north, defended the notion of absolute equality among heirs, whereas Cazalès, taking the opposite position, "spoke for the south," ever in favor of the testator's freedom to dispose at will. In fact, in the nineteenth century, unequal division, giving one child priority over the others, was still being practiced unofficially in many regions of the Midi, in the earlier lands of written law. In contrast, northern France, despite major exceptions, was to prove more egalitarian, showing greater support for dividing up inheritances as advocated henceforth by the Revolution.

This having been said, it would be wrong to portray a south of written law and a north of customary law as two homogenous blocks in opposition to each other. For the north with its customs must in turn be broken down into at least two groups: the customs in the west, in matters of inheritance as in many other areas, privileged lineage; the customs of the Parisian region and of Picardy-Wallonia (among others) are more interested in the conjugal household. The Normans' lineage tree stands in contrast to the kitchen table, kettle, and hearth fire of the Walloons, the Picards, and others in the Île-de-France area with—the image is irresistible—their *pot-au-feu,* contents included. Even keeping in mind these nuances, the details of which are beyond the scope of this essay, the north–south division, limned by latitudes, linguistic borders, and juridical habits, remains a fact. The French Revolution, that great steamroller or scythe (just two of the plethora of metaphors that suggest themselves) that promised equality, was to triumph only belatedly, and then incompletely.

✲

This foray into the south has thus taken us on a rather rambling itinerary along the paths of retrospective economics, long-term history, and comparative law. The underdevelopment of the traditional society of the south is indisputable. But this underdevelopment cannot eclipse the authentic and original richness of growth in the Midi over the course of several millennia, nor the surprisingly positive (to the point of being ferocious in its inegalitarian, patriarchal, and willfully antifeminist thrust) progress—albeit relative—in these areas, in comparison with the north, owing to early adoption of Roman law, with its zealous protection of quiritarian property (soon to be bourgeois). However imprecise or variable its geographic boundaries, the south is other, and France is dual.

NOTES

1. Celtic Gaul, the Roman and post-Roman Empire; Carolingian Gaul.
2. Pre-imperial Roman Narbonnaise; and various periods of Aquitanian or Provençal autonomy, during the second half of the first millennium.

BIBLIOGRAPHICAL NOTE

For the arguments and literature on the Saint-Malo–Geneva line see especially Emmanuel Le Roy Ladurie, "Un théoricien du développement: Adolphe d'Angville," in *La Territoire de l'historien* (Paris: Gallimard, 1973); François Furet and Jacques Ozouf, *Lire et écrire: L'Alphabétisation des Français de Calvin à Jules Ferry* (Paris: Ed. de Minuit, 1977), vol. 1; and Roger Chartier, "Les Deux France: Histoire d'une géographie," *Cahiers d'histoire* (1979): 393–415.

The opposition of north versus south forms the central or marginal subject of innumerable works, including my own. Here I cite only three important books. The thesis (still unpublished) of Michel Demonet, *La Statistique agricole de la France vers 1850* (Paris I, 1985); Robert Lafont and André Armegaud, directors, *Histoire de l'Occitanie* (Paris: Hachette, 1979); and, lastly, Paul Ourliac and Jean-Louis Gazzaniga, *Histoire du droit privé français* (Paris: Albin Michel, 1985).

CHAPTER 2

'FRANCE, THE COAST, AND THE SEA

❧

MICHEL MOLLAT DU JOURDIN

Whether it is the training ship *Jeanne-d'Arc* under full sail paying a visit to one of the great ports of the world or the ocean liner *Normandie* raising the blue pennant on its triumphal entry into New York harbor in 1936 or French sailors competing for France in a transoceanic race, people respond each time as though France itself were paying a visit. Any ship flying the French flag is, legally speaking, national territory. The law of *jus soli** is not just symbolic. The national personality is made manifest and is projected with all the weight of its past and its being. Is this to say that the entire French nation is unaware of its ties to the sea except for isolated incidents colored by superficial sentimentality?

The sea, let us admit, seems hostile to many forms of memory. When it attacks the coast, covering it with sediment, it alters the features of the land. In its fury, the "great devourer" consumes what it rips out and buries what it destroys. A monster of prey that terrifies men, it swallows up its prizes, and only recently have stubborn deep-sea divers, with great difficulty, wrested remains from it that up to then were consigned to oblivion. Even when the sea is calm, stretching out peacefully, it appears indefinite, infinite, immutable, and impervious to the flow of time.

---

* EDITOR'S NOTE: "Right of the soil": in common law, allegiance or citizenship is determined by the place of one's birth.

Figure 2.1
Naval map of Western Europe in G. de Brouscon du Conquet, *Pilot's Manual for Use by Breton Pilots* (1548).

The land, by contrast, displays the slow changes of a stable world. Its features do alter over the course of time, but at a rhythm set by man, who bestows on it the mark of his presence and the evidence of his labor. Through the land societies become rooted in their past. Fundamentally speaking, the land is memory. But the sea? To a degree sailors themselves subscribe to this vision. They set sail not to wander the seas driven by some dreamy impulse. They leave for a destination and return to touch the soil of their homeland. For the late Middle Ages in France, Jacques Bernard has provided a good description of the homesickness sailors felt even though they went back to the sea at the first opportunity. Unstable men, like the ocean that bore them? Furthermore, do not the shorelines reveal the memories of the maritime history the people have left, particularly in the way they have fashioned the coastline and constructed the ports? Thus it is the men who go down to the sea, more than the sea itself, who have built the places of memory out of their reciprocal interactions with the sea.

The intimacy of these interactions, especially for France, is close. Seen from a satellite, our country follows the outline of a tiny peninsula at the extreme end of the Eurasian landmass. Yet, France is so much a part of the continent that its inhabitants have never spontaneously paid any attention to the surrounding seas, whose influence has so profoundly affected their landscape. The ocean still seems to many to be accessible only to the adventurous. It is therefore not in the fields deep in the interior of France that we will find the reflection of its maritime image.

The lack of understanding of sailors and the sea by those on land is ancient and lasting. Once it was the boundary beyond which the Capetian domain did not extend. Philip Augustus found the coasts of Poitou too far to adventure to.[1] It took the Hundred Years' War and the so-called English insults for the chronicler Froissart in his writings to extend the "border" to the seacoast. Up to that time, the term only applied to the lands of the kingdom.[2] In fact, even in our time, the coastline of France, stretching over five thousand kilometers, rarely attracted the attention of historians of France's borders. Vidal de La Blache conceives his *Tableau géographique de la France* (Geographical Chart of France) "as man in relation to the land, not to the sea."[3] Roger Dion limits his small book to the land borders.[4] In their defense, note that the gaze of many generations was stubbornly set on the "blue line of the mountains of the Vosges."[5] Nevertheless, it took the historian Fernand Braudel five pages to pose the problem and to demand the sea had a right to figure in France's memory: "The sea exists; the coasts exist; the fleets exist. And the maritime borders themselves, incontestably natural, do exist."[6]

That memory functions selectively is a recognized fact, and even then selectivity varies from person to person. So, let us first look at the place of the sea in the minds of Frenchmen. Then let us locate the geographic and social sectors as well as the specific historical circumstances that have brought forth sufficiently distinct "memories" that could be integrated into the national consciousness. Can a maritime image in the French personality be found? Where? And what realities does it express?

WRITINGS AND IMAGES

Writers and Artists of the Sea

Investigation into the maritime memory of the French leads to the literary evidence of writers. That evidence is most authentic when it comes from authors who know the sea and are strangers to the cliché.

Their visions of the maritime world express those of their respective generations. The sinking of the *Saint-Gérand* is depicted by Bernadin de Saint-Pierre with emotion appropriate to the Age of the Enlightenment. The shipwreck Chateaubriand described on the Normandy coasts draws on the real-life experience of someone from Saint-Malo. The wreck of *La Sémillante* gives the Provençal narrator the opportunity to sublimate the truth. Alphonse Daudet knew the island of Lavezzi. Poetry is a more complex place of memory. Talent rarely compensates for lack of experience about the sea. Even in *L'Homme et la mer* Baudelaire's ability to evoke cannot hide an ignorance of maritime realities, as evidenced by such imprecise formulations as "the twinkling of the lighthouses," "the slender forms" of the ships, the "complicated" rigging, the "harmonious" oscillations of the waves. Rimbaud, it appears, had never seen the sea when he wrote *Le Bateau ivre;* yet a storm "blessed its maritime awakenings," and in *Les illuminations*, the sea depicted as a "plowed field" is not without interest. These works are in any case "exercises in style," according to Étiemble. By contrast there is no ambiguity in Victor Hugo, either in *Les Voix intérieures* or in *Les Rayons et les ombres*, and still less in *Oceano nox*, where the breath of the poet transmits the savage roar of the breaking waves and the sinking vessel in death's grip. Let us recall, for example:

Matelots! Matelots! Vous voguez joyeux parfois, mornes souvent.

. . . .

On s'entretient de vous, parfois, dans les veillées,
Tandis que vous dormez dans les goémons verts.

Le corps se perd dans l'eau, le nom dans la mémoire.

[Sailors! Sailors! At times cheerful, often gloomy you are when
    sailing.

.   .   .   .

They will think of you, from time to time, during the vigils,
While you sleep in the green wrack.
The body disappears into the water, the name into memory.]

Paul Valéry, in *Le Cimetière marin*, is another author who was able to
evoke authentic and poignant recollections of those lost at sea. The
cemeteries for sailors are realities in Brittany and Saintonge as in Languedoc, and so are the lanterns for the dead on our Atlantic coasts. The memorial walls of those who perished at sea at Gruissan (department of
Aude), and at Canale and Ploubazlanec (department of Côtes-d'Armor)
show the same family names over and over again for several generations.
There are also blank spaces for those who have disappeared leaving behind the unceasing hope that the sea will return their bodies. Anguish,
hope, nostalgia, memories—all constitute an endless litany of emotions
more often unspoken than expressed.

Poetry has the merit of giving verisimilitude to sentiment. Prose can
warp the image of reality while anxiously seeking to convey it, even for
the nineteenth-century historian Michelet. The sea furnished him with
the theme and title of a small book, which he turned into his *Tableau de
la France* (Picture of France).[7] To his credit he wrote, "One must develop
true knowledge of the sea and not yield to the false ideas that the adjacent land might convey." Like a prophet, and well before the oceanog-
raphers of the depths, he felt that "the sea is the creator of life." While
he contributed to awakening the interest of the French in their maritime
memories, he did not satisfy all curiosity, nor did he construct a memorial. He saw the coasts, the sea, and the sea's surroundings as a continental tourist would, without penetrating into their soul.

Exciting the interest of schoolchildren was the purpose of two books
written a hundred years later. In one, *Le Tour de la France par deux enfants*
(Two Children Tour France), the author Fouillée, writing under the
pseudonym of G. Bruno, made certain choices. Her two heroes see Marseille, but not Toulon. A journey by sea brought them to Nantes and
Brest. The historical allusions are brief, for the tour is above all a "study
of nature." The young reader is given the names of Jean Bart and La
Pérouse, but not those of Richelieu and Colbert, nor even the story of
the *Vengeur,* which is astonishing. The young reader will also remember
a terrible storm.

By contrast, the second book, *Le Tour de France par Camille et Paul, deux enfants d'aujourd'hui* by Pons (Camille and Paul Tour France: Two Children of Today) (1977), gives more attention to the sea, but the prose shows less spontaneity. The journey from Yvetot to Bayonne and then into the Gulf of Lion collects memories of maritime life long ago with recent facts (the landing at Omaha Beach in 1944) and the technology of today (the tidal power station on the Rance, modern naval ships at Brest). "France is in the process of changing its way of thinking," the author writes. To recall the beginnings while prospecting the future, to tie the future to the past, is to demonstrate the reality of places of memory.[8]

Clearly more competent than pedagogues and educators are the ones who know the sea firsthand: the sailors or men whose bodies and spirits have been infused with sea air from the time they were young. The combination of literary talent and the ability to draw on authentic evidence is not given to everyone. Following Chateaubriand,[9] we find other authors, such as Eugène Sue and, closer to our own time, Pierre Loti, Claude Farrère, La Varende, who bring us tales of sailing around Cape Horn, trading along the shores of the New World and Iceland, and exploring Antarctica.[10]

The navy today has several poets, but discretion does not permit us to name them. What they write about they know and feel.

The same observations pertain to the way certain artists view the sea. Flemish intimist painting brought to seascapes a sincerity that is absent from the mundane and mythological voyages crafted by the workshops of the eighteenth century. Nevertheless, during the same period, Joseph Vernet's faithful adherence to an official command left us with an image of the great ports of France that is remarkable in its exactitude. In other cases, the intense pathos animates many scenes of the sea because the painter lived them: Géricault created *Le Radeau de la* Méduse, but he sought precision at the same time. Recent investigations done with sophisticated scientific apparatus have confirmed the location of the drama but without coming across the wreck.[11]

Less dramatically, the image Épinal played in the nineteenth century corresponds to today's comics, fixing, for example, certain memories of the Crimean War, the opening of the Suez Canal, and the campaigns of Admiral Courbet in the Far East, not to mention fishing on the high seas. During World War I, the memories of children were filled with stories and drawings found in a series called the Little Pink Books, which recounted the heroism of the marines under Admiral Ronarc'h in Flanders, the sinking of the *Gneisenau* and *Scharnhorst* in the Atlantic, the feats of the raider von Luckner in the Indian Ocean, and the torpedoing of the

Lusitania. The same can be said of photography or the cinema in its capacity to deliver to posterity images of Charcot's polar expeditions and the memory of the *Casabianca*, the submarine that escaped while the rest of the fleet was scuttled at Toulon.

Without being poets, the seamen who fashioned plaques of thanksgiving imbued their works with a simple but emotional charge. The craftsmanship of the painting on these plaques was often naive, done with humble or rustic materials such as paper and cardboard. The creators were in some cases survivors of shipwrecks. But the talent of some made them professionals in the service of other seaman. They won a reputation: Bommelaer at Dunkirk, Grandin at Fécamp, Adam at Honfleur, Pajot at Sables-d'Olonne, and especially the Roux family at Marseille. The thanksgiving plaque on a nautical theme was displayed at the salon of 1831 with Jugelet of Dieppe. The scene of a shipwreck sometimes diminished the place of the divine intercessor but did not conceal the significant convergence of the divine offer of mercy with the entreating look of the supplicant. Other types of thanksgiving plaques (e.g., models and heads of fish, naval instruments, buoys, decorations, etc.) were not so expressive, but they were specific to their original background. The inventory of this patrimony locates them by the thousands in coastal sanctuaries, their natural place, where their donors offered them to the Virgin Mary or to a local patron saint of the shipwrecked. These places are scattered along the coast from Notre-Dame-des-Dunes at Dunkirk to Notre-Dame of Lavesina on Corsica. In between there are Notre-Dame-de-Grâce at Honfleur, Sainte-Anne of Auray, Notre-Dame-de-Consolation at Collioure, Notre-Dame-de-la-Garde in Marseille, and so many other places.[12]

The men of the sea often left the memory of their concerns in rough, sketched forms carved into the wood or stone of a church, a chateau, a house, or even a prison. Such graffiti depicted ships, anchors, and sails. The professional specificity that guided their makers' stilettos or knives gave these objects technical authenticity, but the sentiments that inspired the images are unknown to us. The pioneering work of Olivier de Prat and Henri Cahingt has opened the way to fruitful research in the Seine valley and in Brittany, as well as at La Rochelle and Tarascon.[13]

Navigation Journals: Maps and Plans

The adage "he tells good lies who comes from afar" does not really apply to commissioned and noncommissioned officers going on long voyages. During the ancien régime, tradition obliged them to keep a journal of the expedition, which they filled with profiles of the coasts, plans for ports, and navigational calculations—material hardly compatible with fantasy. The result is a prodigious abundance of reports in the maritime archives, the Museum of Natural History, various libraries, and private collections. Some of these reports have been published. Those by Bougainville, La Pérouse, Baudin, Dumont d'Urville,[14] and Pagès show an appreciation for the people, the shoreline and sites for ports, geographical surroundings, and the flora and fauna.

Eighteenth-century naturalists brought collections of animal, vegetable, and mineral specimens back from the South Seas. These marks of the past, as impersonal as they are, constitute the scientific capital of the Museum of Natural History in Paris as well as that of museums around the country. For lack of funds, the study of this material has still not been completed after two centuries. The legacy of the drawings, watercolors, plans, and maps with their accompanying narrative has been better exploited. The Lesueur collection at Le Havre, among others, contains the abundant documentation brought back by Baudin at the beginning of the nineteenth century.

Finally, contrary to widespread opinion, such evidence of memory does not come just from cultivated sailors and educated observers. The spontaneity in the writing and the rusticity of the spelling by the quartermaster Dumont d'Urville hold up well over the science of the "skipper."[15]

Drawing and painting, like journals, were also part of the tradition that was solidly maintained by an officially designated unit of painters within the navy. Limited to the chosen few by ministerial authority, they exercised their art on board naval ships and almost every year held an exposition of their works at the Marine Museum.

More important still is the received heritage of the Depository of Maps and Plans, founded in 1720. Although the navy's Hydrographic Service in 1947 did entrust the pre-1800 part of this heritage to the Department of Maps and Plans at the Bibliothèque nationale de France— nothing shocking in that—it was an absurd move in actuality. The maps became separated from the navigation journals. The old maps contain an important part of our memory. Although they did not invent it, French navigators, like the Italians and Portuguese, adopted the portulan chart— highly accurate coastal maps with lines representing the major winds of the area. From the sixteenth century on, the mapmakers of Dieppe and Le Conquet enjoyed international renown. They recorded, with a sprinkling of dotted lines around the New World and Iceland, the location of the fishing banks frequented by their compatriots. It is perhaps to them that we owe the first sketches of the Australian coast. In the seventeenth and eighteenth centuries, our marine maps rivaled what the Dutch and English produced.

The old *routiers*, transcriptions of oral navigation commands, have bequeathed a venerable legacy to our *Instructions nautiques*. The instructions found in the *Grand routtier*, drawn up in the sixteenth century, can still serve in our own day as the appropriate course to take for navigating between Noirmoutier and Penmarc'h. Such precedents, though drawn from evolved methods of noting the sea depths and coastal profiles, have not been forgotten by the present Oceanographic and Hydrographic Service of the Navy, headquartered at Brest.

Archives, the Naval Academy

The changes in the history of the maritime archives merit the same attention. In this matter, as in many others, we must go back to Louis XIV's finance minister, Colbert. He kept his correspondence relating to naval and colonial matters at Saint-Germain-en-Laye. His successor, Pontchartrain, transported the collection to Paris in 1699 and put it in a garden pavilion belonging to the Augustinian order of the Little Fathers (today the Place des Victoires). Custody was then entrusted to Clairambault, whose name on a major manuscript collection at the Bibliothèque nationale de France reminds every historian of importance of the maritime manuscripts there.

The maritime archives have suffered from numerous moves: from Paris to Versailles in 1763, from Versailles to Paris in 1837, to a location on the Rue Royale, where they remained as a completed collection until 1899, when they were divided into two collections—the old records given to the National Archives[16] and the modern ones kept by the navy. In 1919, the latter created the Service des archives et bibliothèques (Archive and Library Service), located today at the Château de Vincennes and responsible also for the annexes at Cherbourg, Brest, Lorient, Rochefort, and Toulon.[17] Then the naval archives were amputated from the colonial archives just when a ministry for the colonies was established. Likewise, the establishment of a ministry for the merchant marine in 1913 and, a little closer to our own day, another for affairs of the sea in general (with the exception of the navy) presented opportunities for further division of the documents.

Administrative distortions, though bothersome, do not distort the coherence of memory. The emigration to Aix-en-Provence of the Archives de l'Outre-Mer (overseas archives), the former colonial archives, causes transportation (and thus monetary) problems for researchers. It is the same for certain documents from the navy's central administration, the only copies of which are kept in Brest and Toulon. Much more detrimental have been those infringements of the principle, sacred to scholars and archivists, that the integrity of the collection be respected. The maritime archives did not escape this fate in the nineteenth century, and, to compensate for the ensuing drawbacks, detailed analytical inventories had to be drawn up with reference tables. Someday, perhaps, computerization of the documents may facilitate access. In any case, the cooperation of the maritime authorities and the administration of the archives of France provide for the proper conservation and consultation in Cherbourg, Brest, Rochefort, and Toulon, as well as in Paris, of the documents that are essential to our maritime memory. In addition to these centers, the maritime authorities have recently added a photographic and cinematographic service at Ivry-sur-Seine responsible for the visual and auditory memory of the documentation.

The merchant marine has benefited, in several exemplary cases, from analogous efforts. Suffice it to mention the importance of the collections found in the chambers of commerce, of which Marseille offers a remarkable case. Several large companies have taken pains to preserve their ship models and archives, like that of the Company of the Suez Canal. The current Compagnie générale maritime is the heir to the exceptional document collection of the Compagnie générale transatlantique and of the Messageries maritimes. A similar situation exists for the Chargeurs Réunis and various corporations such as Fabre, Paquet, Delmas-Vieljeux, Bordes, and many others. The information contained in the collections of the Bureau Veritas, a company modeled on Lloyd's of London, should not be overlooked. Founded in Antwerp in 1828, it moved its headquarters to Paris five years later. It classifies ships according to their technical characteristics, and its center for electronic calculations, created in 1967, has assembled a database that is totally flexible and reliable. The memory of the sea will not become fossilized.[18]

In 1752, a group of sailors set up the first marine academy to promote all disciplines useful to navigation: the natural sciences, mathematics, astronomy, physics, geography, and naval architecture. The group also drafted a dictionary of naval terms. Founded at Brest by Bigot de Morogues and Duhamel du Monceau, two men of bold spirit, the academy numbered at the outset thirty-two members from Rochefort, Toulon, Marseille, Dieppe, and Paris. It linked up with the Academy of Sciences. Over the next twenty-five years, until its suppression during the Revolution, it held eight hundred meetings. But affairs of the sea have a long memory.[19] In 1921, a new marine academy was established, this time in Paris, although the rich library of its predecessor (six thousand volumes as of 1793) remained in Brest. The academy aimed at nothing less than forming a living organ, comprising six sections: four technical and scientific (including the merchant marine) following the tradition of the eighteenth century, one legal, and one dedicated to the arts, letters, and history.[20]

SITES AND PORTS

Riverbanks and Ghost Harbors

Certain sites, as much as the works of men if not more so, call for meditation. Maritime life, to begin with, has benefited some sites and deserted others.

It is doubtful, and the question has been disputed, whether low-lying coasts bring about maritime activity. Breeders of salt-meadow sheep in the bay of Mont-Saint-Michel and of cattle in the Charentais basin cannot be likened to those who engage in maritime activities. By contrast, commerce during the Middle Ages and after prompted salt-marsh workers from Brittany, Poitou, and the Saintonge to construct, and cordon off from the ocean, a landscape of levies and seawater channels to the reinforced enclosures that produced salt for the northern European countries. The checkerboard landscape, today overgrown by halophytic plants, recalls a time gone by. Not far from there, in the shallow depths, other pieces of memory await the marine archaeologist: wrecks of ships and the heavy stones that the Hanseatic traders used for ballast on their ships.[21] On the Mediterranean coasts, with their summer weather, traditional enterprise has a better chance of survival in the markets of the chemical industry: it is not widely known that the Compagnie des Salins du Midi bases its property titles on charters given by Louis IX (also known as Saint Louis).[22]

This example leads us straight to the port of Aigues-Mortes, constructed at the wish of Saint Louis. This king wished to have his own base of operations for the Crusades. It is a place of memory, like the Venice that Maurice Barrès describes in Le Jardin de Bérénice, where he found a reflection of eternity. Now only memories haunt its ramparts and its twenty towers. The sea no longer reaches the walls, and for that reason it is understandable why, in the fifteenth century, a wealthy merchant such as Jacques Cœur would desert the port for Marseille. The memory of Aigues-Mortes rests in the archives.[23] A leap of four centuries to the Atlantic brings us to Brouage: same natural conditions, same hopes, same destiny. Men who up to the seventeenth century believed in the usefulness of the site gave as its justification the fame of the location. It was known as far away as the Baltic as the place where salt was produced from

the surrounding marshes. It was also known for its location on the Saintonge coast along maritime routes and especially for the role it played in
ending the insubordination of La Rochelle. Once that city was subju-
gated, in 1628, Cardinal Richelieu declared, "Brouage no longer
matched its initial reputation." An uncared-for exterior of an uncompli-
cated town, the wall had as its only purpose to limit the inexorable invasion of silt and to commemorate an illusion. But at least this place recalls,
as an overseas extension of its ambitions, the expedition to Canada in
1608, led by Samuel de Champlain.[24]

Islands, Keepers of Tradition

Islands deserve special attention. On all of them, but especially on the
coasts of Brittany, the inhabitants show a tenacious will to survive despite
the limitations of their resources, the hostility of nature, and above all the
distance from the mainland. These conditions underlie the problem that
arose in linking the islands to the mainland by the bridges at Oléron, Ré,
and Noirmoutier. There can be no doubt that these bridges will transform the character of the three islands.

As the etymology of the term reveals, islands [isolates] are predisposed
to a conservative role. Each case is unique, but a comparison should lead
to one or more works of synthesis. Whatever it is that is original in the
islands off the north and west coasts of Brittany, in the region between
the Loire and Gironde rivers, and in Provence, the place of islands in the
national memory comes down to two circumstances. First, depending on
their distance from the coast, islands throughout history have served to
protect or threaten the coastal areas, and at all times they have kept watch
over the coast or the open sea. History dating back to the beginnings of
France let the islands of Hyères off Provence and the islands off Brittany
serve as a bridgehead. Through the islands the monastic influence,
Middle Eastern in Provence and Celtic (meaning chiefly the Irish) on the
Breton coasts, entered in the wake of a multitude of monks and hermits.
Their migration is attested to in such place names as Saint-Honorat,
Saint-Malo, Locronan, and Saint-Cado.

The revival of monasticism at the end of the Middle Ages left its
marks, for example, at Bréhat. The reminders are sometimes harsh. The
islands of Hyères were exposed to Saracen raids, and for centuries, notably during the wars of Louis XIV, the Revolution, and the Napoleonic
Empire, they were fought over by the fleets of France, Spain, and England. On the Atlantic side, the Hundred Years' War saw the islands enter, by turn, into the hands of the French, English, and Spanish. Some of
the islands off Brittany were fortified at the end of the Wars of Religion;

others, specifically Ouessant, Sein, Grois, and Belle-Île, became the key points on which the security of Brest and Lorient depended between 1745 and 1815. The fate of the Anglo-Norman islands, made an issue by the confiscation of John Lackland's possessions in 1204, was resolved, as far as the Minquier Islands were concerned, only in 1953, in a hotly debated decision by the International Court of Justice in The Hague in favor of England. Debated, disputed, conquered, retaken, reconquered—these islands have retained the memory of their trials and tribulations. Perhaps it took the courageous escape of the inhabitants of Sein and Ouessant to England during the World War II for the nation to take notice and remember the role these islands play in their defense.

This long misreading results from a second series of circumstances: isolation, for which the distance from the "main land" and the special difficulties in communication are the essential elements. Uniqueness, more or less marked, for each island's ethnological, sociological, economic, cultural, and religious point of view has resulted. The historical memory on each island displays traits that are sometimes incomprehensible to mainlanders. The most typical examples, without doubt, are Sein and Ouessant.

Ouessant has been the subject of a major study.[25] This "island sentinel" is not so much separated from the mainland by distance, a mere twenty kilometers, as it is by the Iroise Sea reefs and the violent currents, called the Fromveur and the Fromrust, which run at nine knots of white water. They surround the island and create dangerous eddies where they meet. There were no regular connections before the end of the sixteenth century. The comment made long ago describing the island as "a very difficult and perilous place, and dangerous to get to" still holds true. The first postal steamer began operations in 1880; even today the island is cut off from the world several days each year. Confined to some 1,500 hectares of windswept rocky soil, the people of Ouessant form a microsociety where endogamy existed up to a short time ago, a universe all but closed off to the outsider. Without a doubt, electrification suppressed nighttime parties and trysts and introduced some comfort into daily life. The men sail on the nation's ships or seek work in Brest, while the women who stay behind watch over the traditions. The island's memory is tied not to ancient monuments (there are hardly any) but to tenacious legends and to customs marked by the domination of the sea. The background is a past made up of shipwrecks, poor fishing, resistance to taxes formerly feudal but now national, and the presence of soldiers from the mainland. Nor have the sacrifices, from the time of the Seven Years' War and the American War of Independence down to the Nazi occupation, been tallied. The memory of the missions by a Nobletz or a Maunoir in

Figure 2.4
Ouessant, the island sentinel, with its many lighthouses.

the seventeenth century is not totally obscured, any more than the musty smell of practices dating back centuries. The rite of *proëlla*, noted in documents dated 1734 and celebrated for the last time in 1962, called for a funeral celebration in which the population of the island gathered, first to visit the house of the person who had perished at sea and then to visit the cemetery for a simulated burial, represented by a cross. The custom is obsolete, but the nostalgia remains. Death cannot be effaced from the popular memory even if it is scrubbed clean of legends.

Ouessant is an extreme example. Analogous examples can be found for the other islands, such as Sein[26] and Groix, and even for the less isolated islands of the Morbihan. Farther south the isolation is more attenuated, for example, Noirmoutier and Yeu. Nevertheless, on all the islands the spirit of insularity remains, a guardian spirit forgetting nothing.[27]

Fishing and Coastal Traffic

If our ports could tell their story, the result would be cacophony. There are so many ports. History does not bring rigor to this diversity. On the contrary.

This richness results from the configuration of the shoreline, which has created a multiplicity of sites, and from the small volume of the tonnage, an adaptation to the shallow draft of the ships. The division of the seigneuries in the provinces made each region responsible for maintaining its fishing and trading ports. Memory for the French, in its entirety, may be something evanescent, as far as the sea is concerned, but not at the local level.

Although history does not show a standard type of harbor or estuary port or Atlantic or Mediterranean port, certain characteristic features have been retained. Some ports were fortunate in keeping, intact or restored, the appearance that geographic conditions or historic circumstances bestowed.

Undisturbed at one end of the "Coast of Grace," the old port of Honfleur is an enclosure formed on one side by its old church, with its wooden nave resembling an overturned hull, and its officers' quarters, its salt storehouse, and its merchant halls on the other sides. The names of its streets, lined with half-timbered houses, recall Admiral Jean de Vienne and Gonneville, called "The Brazilian."[28]

Seen from a distance, Saint-Malo still has its traditional silhouette: the ramparts, the high stone houses of the ship owners (Duguay-Trouin, Surcouf). The spire of the cathedral dominates the scene, and in that cathedral Jacques Cartier took communion before setting sail for Canada in 1524, ten years after Verrazano's American expedition.[29]

Figure 2.5 Honfleur.

Clio sometimes arranges unexpected encounters. The writer Chateaubriand is buried on le Grand Bé right beside the remains of Hitler's Atlantic Wall, while farther on the Solidor Tower, the high point in the ruins of Alet, loftily watches over the flowing Rance River. The Breton coasts are marked by similar towers and chateaus faithful in their guard duty: the La Latte Fort at Cape Fréhel, the Taureau castle at Morlaix, the Saint-Mathieu Abbey, Suscinio on the outskirts of Morbihan, the Pornic castle. They guard access to the coastal ports and rivers where the fleet found rest and shelter after a raiding expedition.[30] In fact, most of the harbors have kept their appearance, if not their function, from days gone by. History carries on at a slow pace in these spots, like a light turned low. It is impossible to name them all: a few chosen at random include Morlaix, Roscoff, Landerneau, Le Conquet, Quimper, Concarneau, Bannes, Redon, Le Croisic.

One of the perfect types of ports must be La Rochelle, whose spirit of independence matches that of Saint-Malo. Its central position, midway between Spain and Brittany, explains the presence of Italian merchants at the moment (1224) when the Capetian monarchy took this important communications hub between England and the province of Aquitaine away from the Plantagenets. The strategic importance of La Rochelle likewise did not escape Cardinal Richelieu. In 1628, he prevented the city from falling under Dutch and English control through their intermediaries, the Huguenots. The sunken vestiges of the famous dike, the walls, and the guard towers—all bear witness to fierce autonomy and the rebellious spirit of this city. The memory of the mayor, Guitton, is present, as well as that of the Four Sergeants whose names are affixed on the tower that was their prison. Another place, called the Lanterne, evokes not only the age-old trade in wine and salt to the countries of northern Europe, but also the beginnings of commerce across the ocean. Not by chance did Rabelais, always well informed, make this the base of operations for Pantagruel's adventures.[31]

Further south, the ports of the past were nestled into the indentations of the coast that assured their security: at the western end of the Pyrenees on the Basque coast, Bayonne and Saint-Jean-de-Luz; and at the eastern end of the Pyrenees on the Catalan coast, Port-Vendres and especially Collioure, once a medieval castle, which Vauban saw fit to transform into a powerful fortress.[32]

We need not reconsider Aigues-Mortes, which in archaeological terms is connected to Arles in the same way that Sète is to Narbonne. Marseille and Toulon will occupy our attention later on. There are other sites along the coast that the small yet deep rivers of Provence and the alpinelike cliffs have preserved. The walls of Saint-Tropez protect the pleasure boats as once they did the coastal raiders, the so-called corsairs. Up to the end of the era of sailing ships, the walls at Antibes. with their Roman foundations, at the base of the La Garoupe pinnacle formed a safe stopover on the route to the "Genoese Riviera." Nice,[33] Villefranche, Calvi, and especially Bonifacio, with its deep and narrow shelter, all have a similar past. Each preserves its specific character.

In other places where war ruined practically everything, memory of the past has been reasserted. The restorations, even if imperfect, reveal a concern that is praiseworthy, apart from the blunders and anachronisms that conceal particular memories. Besides, even the modernity of new construction, without even yet qualifying as historical, bears witness in its own manner to the suffering endured and the will to survive, right next to the remains from the past.

In Boulogne-sur-Mer, for example, if it is not a question of restoring the Tour d'Ordre at the entrance to the harbor, a tower dating back to Caligula (A.D. 44) that had fallen into ruin by the seventeenth century, people continue creating images on medals or in drawings of the Virgin Mary on a ship with no mast or sail. The urban vista still offers the contrast between the chateau, still intact, in the upper part of the city, and the new city, evoking the sad necessity of reconstruction.[34]

Figure 2.6
Fishermen bound for Newfoundland at the end of the 19th century. Title on picture reads: Fécamp: The basin at mid-tide.

The same can be said for Dieppe. Only one door survived the ravages of the Hundred Years' War, a bombardment by the English in 1694, and the abortive Canadian attack fought nearby in 1942. Fortunately, Saint-Remy and Saint-Jacques have been preserved in the parish of Jean Ango. Everything else has been reconstructed. The foundation of Ango's house on the quay still remains. It was from this house that Verrazano departed in 1524 to discover the roadstead known as New York. He called it Angoulême. Everything in Dieppe recalls a memory—for example, the first French expedition into the Indian Ocean, led by the Parmentier brothers in 1528, and the expeditions to Canada in the seventeenth century.[35]

The desire to restore the physical aspect of port cities on their ancestral site despite the encroachments of nature is also the result of other often-ancient activities: fishing, commerce, and exploration. The force of memory appears all the more restrictive when it comes into conflict with hostile circumstances. Economists deplore the excessive number of harbors and then find themselves in conflict with the once legitimate but now outmoded conservatism of the many chambers of commerce. History weighs heavy and will do so heavier still when the importance of each port is measured on a European scale. Already the coastal shipping in Brittany is scarcely more than a memory except for trade with English ports across the channel. The reason for the decline is not the increase in unit tonnage by ship, but market conditions. That is especially true for fishing, and especially during the last half of the twentieth century.

Traditional fishing is dying out. Seen no more along the Breton coast, the silhouette of the tuna fisherman's boat with its spinnaker unfurled on the seas has now joined the fishing boats, the *sinagots*, used in the Gulf of Morbihan as another archaeological image. The initiative taken at Douarnenez to assemble in one place different kinds of old ships is as happy an occasion as the founding of the ocean museum at Port-Louis. The cooperative structure of the herring industry in the English Channel from Dieppe to Flanders has medieval roots. What Lecat wrote in the *Marin-Pêcheur* (Sea Fisherman) has value as an ethnologic memory. Even industrial fishing is threatening to drift into the past in those places where the concentration of activity is limited. Quotas set by international authorities and competition between countries may turn it into a historical relic. Loti sketched a classic type in the fishermen of Iceland; the film *Le Crabe-tambour* (The Crab Drum) gave us an image of fishing in Newfoundland; the authors J. Recher in *Le Grand métier* (The Grand Profession) and L. Martin in *Les Forçats de l'océan* (Ocean Convicts) described the perils of the far north, with its excitement and danger, and the southern seas, in their oppressiveness. Each author sought to maintain the memory of a world in decline. In this regard, it is significant that a specialist, Olivier Guyot-Jeannin, saved the archives of Saint-Pierre-et-Miquelon, and that an archaeological expedition is searching the cold waters off their shores for some of the many wrecks.[36] Shipping and commerce have strewn their memories along the whole shoreline in rhythm to the expansion overseas.

Sanctuary for Large Commerce and Ocean Liners

In the realm of maritime commerce, the ravages endured between 1940 and 1945 did not obscure the awareness of a prestigious past, even in the ports most affected by the war. The opposite is perhaps true, for a break with one's roots often sparks the effort to find them again. Jean Bart, whose solitary statue stands over the ruins of Dunkirk, with his hand raised as if to inspire his fellow citizens to rebuild their city and restore the towers of the belfry and the Leughenaer, as well as reconstruct the *hôtel de ville*, the Saint-Éloi church, and the Marine Park gate (built by Vauban), not to mention rebuild the harbor. Even the present aspect, a consequence of misfortune, will perpetuate memory.[37] In Le Havre the new city expanded the center envisaged by Francis I, whose name the people of Le Havre, ever faithful to the memory of their founder, gave to the tower that once commanded the entrance to the harbor. They named a boulevard after him, and in 1970 they bestowed his name on the locks in the harbor, which at that time were the biggest in the world. Two monuments attest to the union of the past with the present: the Church of Saint-François, which became a cathedral in 1974, and the Gate to the Ocean, a work by the architect Auguste Perret, which opens to the sea and to the future.[38]

The other great ports are also faithful to their past. Although situated on rivers, Rouen, Nantes, and Bordeaux are gathering in the memories of their ties to the sea, starting with the quays: at Rouen it is the riverfront on the Seine where opinions differ about its reconstruction after 1945; at Nantes, the old hotels on the Quai de la Fosse and on Feydeau Island, which in the eighteenth century was the property of certain ship owners (Feydeau Island was known as "Little Holland" because of the Dutch who settled there); and at Bordeaux, the buildings on the Quai des Chartrons, with their well-kept-up appearance. Rouen has not forgotten its role as intermediary between the Baltic and the North Seas and the Atlantic Ocean and beyond. At Bordeaux, and especially at Nantes, the "islands" (Antilles and Mascareignes) have maintained, and still maintain, up to a certain point, a certain attraction.[39] The museum known as the Salorges (in the castle of the dukes) preserves these memories. It was about 1912 when the Martinière canal (which runs parallel to the Loire upstream from Nantes) turned into a kind of cemetery for rotting sailing ships built around the turn of the century. The absurd destruction of these ships has deprived us of what could have been a floating museum. The losses of these years have been made up, though only to a degree, by the purchase and restoration of the *Belem*, a three-masted ship built in 1896 at Nantes and since 1914 run first under an English and then an Italian flag. Thanks to a contribution from the Écureuil savings bank in 1985, the ship has been returned to its home.[40] An effort is thus taking shape in France to catch up with other countries.[41]

Commercial ships are indeed witnesses to the technological evolution in shipbuilding. They have acquired historical value through their condition of service. The history of French ocean liners in the North Atlantic has just been written. That is one example, for our maritime memory goes beyond limits of the sea—into Africa, the Far East, the coasts of Chile.[42] Cape Horn deserves more than just the attention of novelists, although one of them, Joseph Conrad, who was a sailor, was able to evoke the cape's "unchained fury" better than anyone else.[43]

For safeguarding its maritime patrimony, Marseille, specifically its chamber of commerce, is an exemplary case. No doubt the Arsenal of the Galleys is no more than a local memory, but at least for it the Old Port has been set aside as a protected area where once its two forts defended access.[44] Especially noteworthy is the national organization for the preservation of the nation's heritage directed toward underwater archaeological research (the Direction des recherches archéologiques sous-marines, or DRASM). It is headquartered in the Chateau of Saint John of the Hospitalers of Jerusalem. Indeed, the discovery of the ruins of the ancient port of Massilia, which date back well before the Christian era, confirms the city's title as the center of France's archaeological memory. Wise collaboration now brings together the city of Marseille, which provides the location; the CNRS, which provides the scientific personnel and a specially equipped ship, the *Archéonaute;* and the French navy, which has assigned a crew and turned over its laboratories in Toulon for use by the researchers. As a result, the exploration of our underwater patrimony is moving ahead through excavation of ancient shipwrecks. Starting a half century ago on the Mediterranean coast, researchers began exploring the wreck of the *Patriote*, sunk just outside Alexandria at the time of the Egyptian expedition. They are now doing work in the Atlantic and in the English Channel. Research has also extended to the Pacific. Investigations have resumed at the site where La Pérouse lost his ship at Vanikoro.[45]

Like Paris, with its Naval Museum, Marseille has a unique collection of models of commercial ships. Spectacular objects in the public's eyes, they demonstrate first-rate technical evidence. Along with drawings and photographs, they give life to written documentation, which can only list the characteristics of some remarkable ships. How can the lineage of the *paquebots* (packet boats) be forgotten? This was a lineage born in the eighteenth century, whose descendants included the *Impératrice-Eugénie* (108 meters) in 1850, the *Île-de-France* (242 meters) in 1927, the *Normandie* (313 meters) in 1935, and the *France* (316 meters) in 1960. The destiny of our grandest and most beautiful ships needs no commentary. Our first *France*,[46] built in Bordeaux in 1911, had five masts, twenty-nine square and twelve latine sails, and two auxiliary nine-hundred-horsepower motors for emergency use. With a speed of eighteen knots, it sailed the Nouméa line around Cape Horn for eleven years until it wrecked on coral reefs on the west coast of New Caledonia on July 5, 1922. This honorable end contrasts with the unfortunate fire on the *Normandie* in New York Harbor in 1942 and with the totally humiliating transfer of the second *France* in 1979, after five years of stagnating in the backwaters of

Le Havre, to the better administrators of Norway. "To sail on the sea was its vocation," its former captain sadly concluded, "and there are many of us who think that it is better to see a free *Norway* (its new name) than an enslaved *France*."[47] These great ships have been characterized as "romantic relics,"[48] and for them the blue pennant means nothing. In their turn the supertankers will join the superliners, another forgotten page in the history books. But this is just the point. Is it not these forgotten pages from the past, if history is to stand for anything, that history does not know and ought to know?

LA ROYALE

The navy preserves its historic patrimony, but not without difficulty. One episode is particularly revealing. In 1949, the British navy offered to return to France a troublesome trophy: the *Duguay-Trouin*, a ship of seventy-four guns that had seen battle at Trafalgar, only to be captured at Cape Ortegal two weeks later, on November 4, 1805; the British then took over the ship, first naming it the *Lion* and then the *Implacable*. The French government declined the offer, claiming that it lacked sufficient funds for the ship's restoration. With that refusal the ship, its masts and stern castle amputated, was destroyed and sunk by cannon fire off Portsmouth on November 2, 1949. Subsequent military honors did not compensate for the frustration our navy suffered, deprived of a location of memory equivalent to the *Victory*.

Nor is there compensation in the name "La Royale," the term currently used to designate the Marine nationale, military ships sailing under the French flag. Different reasons may be adduced to explain the origin of this term. The ancien régime recognized only *vaisseaux du Roi* (ships of the king). The Marine nationale does not use this designation. Many see the term "La Royale" as an invention of landlubbers ignorant of things of the sea and spread by journalists in search of a style that covers their historical ignorance. Vanity aside, the origin of this term might better be sought in the merchant marine of the nineteenth century. The "sailors of commerce" in all probability wanted to set themselves apart from the "sailors of the state" and to take advantage of the renewal in maritime commerce under the Second Empire to assert themselves. Mixed with this perhaps is a hint of admiration and envy of the fleet and a touch of irony directed against ways of thinking judged outmoded or excessive.

Perhaps, too, this term represents an unconscious homage to the permanence of the Marine nationale over the previous two centuries. During that period, "La Royale" appeared as a symbol. Such is the interpretation given by Admiral Joybert in his preface to the book *La Royale,* written by Commander Randier, a sailor in the merchant marine.

In any case, to close the gap between the ways the navy and those on land use the term is not a rash idea. The navy up to quite recently used the term "rue Royale" to designate the Ministry of the Navy. Its precise address is 2 rue Royale in Paris.[49]

Today it is the location of the navy's chief of staff.

The Hôtel de la Marine in Paris

Through this door we enter the "holy of holies," the Hôtel de la Marine. For nearly two centuries, the supreme body, in turn the secretary of state and ministry, and the headquarters of the navy, have occupied one of the private residences designed by Gabriel and built on the Place de la Concorde in the last years of Louis XV.

Without looking for too much significance, there are some curious coincidences. At Versailles, it was in the residence that Choiseul allocated to the navy that the treaty consecrating American independence was signed, a triumph to which the French fleet had greatly contributed. Also, the navy was located in one of the two residences constructed by Gabriel on either side of the rue Royale; American independence was recognized in 1778 in the other building, the Hôtel de Crillon, next door to the American Embassy. Perhaps such attention to the navy was deliberate, but then it could have passed for homage in revenge for the Seven Years' War. Never had the fleet known such brilliance. Then, too, the lover of coincidences could go on, for example, to imagine what those naval officers must have been thinking that day on the balcony overlooking the Place de la Concorde when they witnessed the execution of the only king who had ever paid serious attention to the fleet. That king—Louis XVI—had given them the means to achieve a presence on the oceans of the world.

The Maritime Legacy

If the brains of the navy are in Paris, then its heart beats on the coast, especially at Brest and Toulon. The rhythm is not so quick these days at Cherbourg, Lorient, or Rochefort. The maritime patrimony is concentrated in these five places. This legacy exists, even if it is often omitted in definitions of our national patrimony. It possesses the characteristics of "the common good" and "the collective heritage of what has traditionally been at stake as far as memory is concerned."[50] Its components, easily discernible, consist of geographical limits and topography as well as the type of naval installation and technical equipment, which includes first and foremost the naval ships themselves. But this patrimony is not just material. Just as important is the question of morale, where patrimony includes intellectual equipment, meaning traditions, spirit, and missions to carry out. In sum, whoever speaks of patrimony is thinking of both material and spiritual or even symbolic capital, accumulated and transmitted by inheritance and by tradition. The navy has entrusted part of this patrimony to each of its bases.

Cherbourg and Its Dike

Certain individual contributions to memory in France are of a technical nature. History presents several examples, starting with Cherbourg and Rochefort. For Cherbourg the contribution is a victory over the sea, something that eluded Rochefort. Rochefort, squeezed in alongside marshes, stands in contrast to Cherbourg, long exposed to ocean storm and enemy attack. But even with the two cities' different pasts, they are each witnesses to technological tenacity. Cherbourg has few ancient monuments. It owed its rise to the boldness of the engineers. The construction of a dike against the winds and tides was begun by Louis XVI in 1787 and completed sixty years later by Napoleon III. Another technical innovation, in our own time, was the transformation of the shipyard into France's first shipbuilding area for nuclear submarines. This is an initiative from the future that adds to an already well-stocked memory.

Rochefort: The Corderie and the Hospital

The innovations that marked the beginnings of Rochefort were no less remarkable, thanks to their creators in the seventeenth century. To compensate for the silting up of the port of Brouage, a new harbor had to be created from scratch, at great cost, and with enormous difficulty twenty-four kilometers from the sea upstream along the sinuous course of the Charente River. The seventeenth century loved to build sites on rivers. Starting with Colbert in 1666, the intendants (who included Colbert's nephew Colbert de Terron, then Arnoul, and Bégon) laid out quays, pits for logs, posts for anchoring and careening a vessel, equipment for masting a ship, workshops for food and equipment. Two installations of this new kind of shipyard were particularly notable. The first is in the old form of a graving dock (fifty-eight meters long, twenty-nine meters wide, and over five meters deep), constructed in stone between 1669 and 1671. It predates the one at Portsmouth, which was built in 1690. The installation is the Corderie royale, the royal rope works. It is a factory

Figures 2.7–2.9
The Corderie at
Rochefort at three suc-
cessive points in time
(*from top*): In the 18th
century, design by
Ozanne engraved by
Le Gouax. In 1979,
in ruins after the fire
of 1945. In 1991,
restored.

as well as an exceptional architectural landmark, built in harmony with its pavilions, which run a length of 374 meters. An enormous effort was required to save this edifice, which has importance from an artistic, industrial, military, and thus historical point of view. The fire set by the

Germans just prior to their retreat in 1944 so totally ravaged the structure that its restoration remained problematic until 1967. That restoration was such that the minute exactitude of Joseph Vernet's picture (1762) is easily recognized in the details, the construction, the ships, and the men working. This painting itself is a document and a place of memory.[51]

Just like the shipyard, the city of Rochefort is a privileged witness to maritime history through the architectural unity of its urban center. The geometric layout is faithful to the original plan. The command center of the navy, the archives and library of the port, and different services for the fleet still occupy some of the former residences and old buildings. The entire place contains echoes of the seventeenth and eighteenth centuries.

The naval hospital at Rochefort occupies a noteworthy place in the navy's patrimony. The present edifice, begun in 1788, was conceived by Pierre Toufaire, the engineer for the navy's administration, who also built the cannon foundry at Indret, further up the Loire from Nantes. The overall conception is imposing. The architect modified the arrangement of the courtyards at the Hôtel des Invalides in Paris. His idea broke new ground through functional considerations, assigning the 2,300 patients to different pavilions according to their medical complaint. The first hospital in Rochefort, which opened in 1683, needed to be replaced just about the same time as the hospital in Toulon. Its inadequacy and new developments in medical science demanded it. The intendant Bégon undertook two initiatives. First, he created a botanical garden, for research into new drugs. The garden was to be enriched by the huge numbers of plants that the explorers in the seventeenth century were bringing back from overseas. Second, he prevailed on Jean Cochon-Dupuy to come to Rochefort. In 1722, Cochon-Dupuy founded the first French school of surgery. Thanks to this scientist and to his son and nephew, who succeeded him, the school at Rochefort was renowned for over a century as the place where scientific experimentation cut through the lingering dogmatism of the medical establishment. The hospital treated a great variety of illnesses and from 1766 to 1855 maintained an amphitheater for dissection using cadavers from a prison. It also had departments of surgery and natural sciences, a museum, and a library of 2,500 volumes. The collections, typical for the eighteenth century, remain, and their preservation in their original setting seems essential. The city was vibrant and grew in importance thanks to all the medical activity there. The Viand family is one example: Gustave, a physician in the navy who had campaigned in the Far East, exercised great influence on his youngest brother Julien, in whom the writer Pierre Loti may be recognized. The latter's house, now a museum, adds a picturesque evocation to those memories that Rochefort already possesses.

Yet the nearby marshes made Rochefort an endemic spot for malaria and gave the city an enduring reputation in the eighteenth century as the tomb of the navy. Vernet was careful not to bring his family there, housing them in La Rochelle instead while he journeyed back and forth to Rochefort to paint its landmarks. The wretched nature of this location no doubt contributed to its being given the role as the place where the navy's medical corps was first developed. Rochefort became the example for Brest, where a college of surgery was established in 1731, and Toulon, where one was founded in 1740 and made official in 1755. The practices of Rochefort were adopted elsewhere, but Brest won the chief recognition in the eighteenth century because of wars and violent epidemics. Thus was launched the structured organization for training naval surgeons. That structure was undermined by the Revolution, which abolished diplomas, but was reorganized in fits and starts over the course of the nineteenth century. Through a kind of return to the sources or at least to a point near those sources, the École de santé de la marine et des colonies (School of Health for the Navy and the Colonies) was established in Bordeaux in 1890, with subsidiaries in Rochefort, Brest, and Toulon. Students of the school at Bordeaux, anxious like the rest of the navy about their traditions, did not forget what they owed to Rochefort.[52]

Lorient and the Heritage of the Compagnie des Indes

Lorient even more than Rochefort met the conditions of an ideal port in the seventeenth century. Three rivers flowing together—the Blavet, Scorff, and Ter—create a vast stretch of water, access to which, through a long inlet guarded at the entrance by the island of Groix, is easy to control. Up to the time of Richelieu, only two names are found in the annals and documents: Blavet, which like Morbihan refers to a series of harbors, and Loc Péran, the point of land that closes off the anchorage on the south side. There, during the Wars of Religion, the Spanish, under Philip II—called in by the duc de Mercœur, a Catholic Leaguer and governor of Brittany— constructed the fort of Aigle. After its recovery by Henri IV, it was renamed Port-Louis for the king's son and designated the headquarters of the Compagnie des Indes Orientales (East India Company). In 1664, Colbert reorganized the company and relocated it to the anchorage where the Scorff empties into the ocean. The site was ever afterward known as "l'Orient" and later, in 1793, simply as Lorient, following the misadventures of schemes hatched by Law in 1719 and Calonne in 1785.

An air raid on February 13, 1943, dropped sixty thousand incendiary bombs and leveled 95 percent of the city. Lorient sets next to this memory of martyrdom the enduring memory of the Compagnie des

Indes that its name evokes.[53] Many of its objects have disappeared there, but many others can be found in Nantes where until 1733 the Compagnie transacted sales of spices, calico, lacquerware, and porcelain. The archives contain a trace of this past. A good part of the archival material can be found in Nantes, Paris, and even Lorient. Philippe Haudrère based his thesis on such archival material as well as on the work of Jean Boudriot.

The Compagnie built considerably. Bernardin de Saint-Pierre, on leaving for Mascareignes, described the city in 1768, two years before Lorient became the naval harbor and shipyard of the king in 1770. Since that time the shipyard has been totally transformed. While it is still located on both sides of the Scorff River, new buildings occupy the places of the old. The maritime prefecture is one survivor of the construction undertaken by Louis de Saint-Pierre, the Compagnie's architect, and by Jacques Charles Gabriel, first architect of the king. The complex remains dominated by the Tour de la Découverte, erected in 1740. Not far from there, the Quai des Indes recalls the commercial purpose. The headquarters was moved elsewhere.

The coexistence of the navy and commercial shipping is a constant in the history of the harbor at Lorient. Between 1720 and 1770, the Compagnie des Indes possessed up to 750 ships of six hundred to seven hundred tons each, on average. Though these ships functioned as ships of commerce, they were constructed according to the design for warships. In addition, the Compagnie developed plans to fund a military force to protect its merchant ships. But in 1767, it was too late. Two years later, the Compagnie suspended operations. Lorient became, definitively, a military port, and in the harbor commercial and naval activities took place without overlapping. The German occupation would reinforce this duality. A powerful U-boat base was constructed close to the fishing port built at Keroman between the two world wars.

Two Great Points of Anchorage: Brest and Toulon

To every lord, all honor. No military ports can better represent the memory of the French navy than Brest and Toulon. We will not describe their physical aspects or present their histories. Rather we will attempt to decode their historical personalities and show what marks them for inclusion in actualizing the past.[54]

Their situation and their respective sites evoke dramatic roles that are constantly being renewed. Their differences are, however, notable. To be sure, Brest and Toulon were put at the disposition and the service of the navy, both at about the same time thanks to the unification of Provence and Brittany with the French kingdom. But the people of Brest never

Figure 2.10
The narrow inlet of the Brest harbor. E. Petit, *Carte topographique de Brest* (1640).

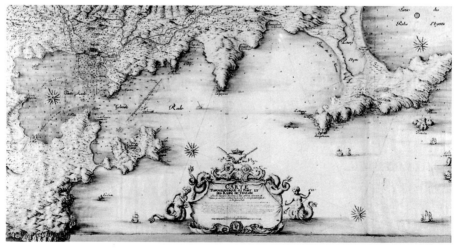

Figure 2.11
The large harbor of Toulon. *Carte topographique de la rade et du port de Toulon*, (1703).

forgot that it was for control of their city that the Valois and Plantagenets fought during the Hundred Years' War, well before Toulon came to serve as a naval base in the wars of Charles VIII in Italy, in particular at Naples in 1494. These campaigns led the sailors of the Ponant, the Atlantic, and the sailors of the Levant, the Mediterranean, to collaborate with each other, as Antoine de Conflans noted in his *Faiz de navigaige* (Deeds of Navigation).[55]

Brest was more vulnerable by sea than by land because the narrow entrance, difficult to force from the outside, could turn it into a trap and subject it to blockade by the enemy. During the Hundred Years' War, after the English took over the islands of Le Conquet, Saint-Mathieu, Sein, and Ouessant, they entrenched themselves at Brest, making it impossible for Du Guesclin to take possession. During the Seven Years' War and the Revolution, freedom of movement for the fleet at Brest became a problem several times. The same problem came up again between 1941 and 1944, this time for the Germans, with their U-boats blocked up in the pens at Lannion.

By contrast, at Toulon, where "nature did things in a grand manner," as the historian Fernand Braudel declared,[56] the entrance to the harbor between Cape Brun and Cape Cépet is completely open to the sea. Toulon can recall more than once that its fate was decided on land: in 1536, when Charles V sought to take possession; in 1707, when Eugene of Savoy laid siege; in 1793, when Napoleon invested the city from all sides except from the sea; and finally, let us not forget, it was by land that the Germans carried out their attack on Toulon on November 27, 1942.

Sites freighted with memories are therefore not lacking for either Brest or Toulon. The siege of 1795 showed the importance of the redoubts of Mont-Faron, which dominate Toulon, and likewise Fort L'Éguillette and the Balaguier Tower to the west and Fort Lamalgue, the old royal tower, to the east, which are on both sides of the Grande and Petite Rade, the two anchorages. In Brest topography has played a more complicated role. The different levels and contours offset the slight differences in altitude. The Penfeld river shields the harbor installations, which are dug into the crystalline rocks, while at Toulon the installations extend from the Petite Rade to La Seyne. Sedimentary soil on the southern side of the anchorage at Brest offers much space for the naval academy at Le Poulmic and an area that affords protection to the submarine base on Île Longue. By contrast, there is little space at the foot of the hills around Cape Cépet in Toulon.

History has thus spoken at both places. In Toulon recovery of the wrecks of two Roman ships enabled researchers to locate the piers of the ancient port. The royal tower at the Mourillon bears witness to Louis XII's wish to fortify the port. Vauban, Louis XIV's great military engineer, was responsible for the plans used in constructing the port, although most of it disappeared as the city expanded. The war did the rest. Of the urban center the only sections that remain, like witnesses, are the celebrated caryatids of Pierre Puget, which used to adorn the balcony of the town hall, and the just-as-popular statue of the *génie de la mer* on what was called the Kronstadt pier, which recalls the Franco-Russian alliance prior to World War I. Another memory: the gate of the naval yard and the rope-making factory, a totally separate entity from the one at Rochefort.

Brest has lost many of its memories. The distinction between the urban center and the Recouvrance quarter has become blurred. The rue de Siam, which evokes campaigns in the Far East, is unrecognizable. Now, to add to the near total ruin resulting from the war, there are regrettable acts of demolition, like that of the old prison, which was an imposing monument filled with memories. At least in the Recouvrance quarter the parish church, Saint-Sauveur, and the Tanguy Tower, next to the Penfeld remain, and on the opposite bank, the castle, with its imposing structure. The castle alone evokes the entire past for Brest, from the Roman assizes down to the maritime prefect's structure, built between 1951 and 1953 after the castle was turned over to the navy in 1945. Built on a rock lying perpendicular to the Penfeld and flanked by ramparts and towers, for which the presumed dates range from the sixth to the eighteenth centuries (notably Vauban's period in the seventeenth), the castle is intimately linked to Brest's maritime experience. If one more observation can be made about Brest and Toulon, it would be this: it seems natural that in each of these two ports the maritime prefects of the Atlantic and the Mediterranean would maintain, from their respective residences—the one at the castle in Brest and the other at Cape Brun—a global vision of the harbors to which the destiny of each has been entrusted.

TRADITION AND MODERNITY

The navy does not manage pantheons. The places for its memories are not the museums, but the places where it lives and functions. Its legacy grew and prospered before it was handed down. Tradition in these places is not dead.

The Borda, the Jeanne, and the Jacques-Cartier

What do the midshipman of today and a writer such as René de Chateaubriand or Augustin Jal have in common?[57] Both of the latter, the first a little before 1800 and the other a little after, "discovered" Brest through a kind of reverie. For Chateaubriand it was the image of himself "sitting on a mast lying on the Quai de Recouvrance." For Jal it was the image of himself leaning on the wall of the Ajot Promenade, unable to take his eyes from the grand view of the harbor. The first had breathed salt air since his youth; the other, from Lyon, had never until that moment seen the sea. Since that time, romanticism has not been part of the training of young officers. Yet, though of secondary importance, the differences do exclude the continuities.

Certain experiences in the eighteenth century, as well as initiatives undertaken at the beginning of the nineteenth century, proved the necessity of joining theory developed on land with practical applications, in stages, at sea. At one time the ships belonging to the Order of Malta had been the preferred location for such instruction. To replace it a system of training ships was created using the "Borda."[58] In 1840, renaming a ship after Borda and turning it into a school signified the intention to perpetuate in the navy the scientific legacy of the eighteenth century. Jean-Charles Borda, a naval engineer, had come to symbolize that legacy of his work, first as a navigator in the southern seas, then as director of the School of Naval Construction, and finally as a member of the Marine Academy and Office of Longitudes. For nearly a century, "Borda" was another term for the naval academy. The first *Borda* was in service for twenty-four years. Its name passed to the *Valing* (1864), then to the *Intrépide* (1890), and lastly to the *Duguay-Trouin* (1913), until *Jeanne-d'Arc*, a name that was assigned consecutively to two ships (1920, 1928), came to be a substitute for it. Borrowing the English word "midshipman" does not mask the traditional appellation *bordache* (naval cadet). The cadet's image took shape then, and it is worth mentioning that the service cap introduced in 1836 was reestablished by Georges Leygues. The fact is that the Naval Academy inherited all the traditions. Once at Saint-Pierre-Quiebignon, then shifted to the Poulmic on the other side of the harbor at Brest, the school has been training young ensigns at sea—first on the two schooners, *Belle Poule* and *Étoile*, and then on the *Jeanne* ever since the end of World War II. Nothing has been omitted to bring together tradition and modernity. The former includes initiation into the "Argot Baille,"* the familiar name of the school. The *sommets* are the celebration of the "Capital C" and the award of the saber to the *fistots*, the first-year naval cadets. As for modernity, it is summed up in few words: on the one hand, predominance of the scientific disciplines, although literature and history are not totally ignored; on the other hand, a degree in engineering from the Naval Academy conferred

* EDITOR'S NOTE: *Argot* means jargon, and *baille* means an old tub of a ship, or water.

Figure 2.12
The Borda, Naval School: The Arrival of the Professors, engraving after a drawing by P. Renouard that appeared in *Le Journal universel* (September 26, 1885).

Figure 2.13
The triumphal arrival of the *France* in New York after its maiden voyage across the Atlantic, 1962.

on the young officers. Admittedly our epoch has seen diversification in the schools for the navy, with centers of specialization located in the cities of Brest, Toulon, Rochefort, and Cherbourg that rely heavily on internal recruitment. For all that, the navy has not forgotten its lineage. Whoever closely examines, for example, the "bible"—the *Annuaire des officiers d'active de la Marine* (Directory of Active Naval Officers)—will be struck by the persistence of certain names alongside those with no hereditary tie to maritime life.

On a different but parallel plane, schools of hydrography are designed to train merchant marine officers, first at one of fifteen centers on land, and then on the training ship, the *Jacques-Cartier*. Their particular originality is rooted in the traditions of the merchant marine, from times gone by up through the changes in ships today.

From the System of Classes to Maritime Affairs

In their way, crewmen have not been impervious to the weight of history. The disappearance of the Maritime Inscription did not entirely do away with the system of classes established by Colbert. The constraints he instituted to maintain crews at full strength through rotating recruitment levies were no doubt unpopular, but they did offer compensation in the form of pensions to veterans and their families and a fund for the disabled, the latter being a kind of embryonic social security. All this explains the paucity of grievances on these matters in the *Cahiers* of 1789. In the maritime regions, it was not the suppression of the system but its strict application that was called for. The consequence was the survival, with few changes, of a special system for sailors. The 1938 law setting up the Établissement national des invalides de la Marine (National Institution for the Disabled of the Merchant Marine), a system quite different from the original, still maintained certain original principles. Officials in the Maritime Affairs offices succeed their predecessors in the inscription, but within the Merchant Marine international recruiting and the use of flags of convenience have totally changed conditions.[59]

The Memory on Board

Ships by their designation participate in the conservation of memories. How else, except by tradition, can the use of terms like "corvette" and "frigate" be explained without, on the one hand, direct reference to the old types of ships of the same name? On the other hand, the central government, alone qualified in the matter, selects the individual or abstraction that will serve as the eponymous name of a particular ship in the fleet. That choice offers in itself an ideal or example for the human community that sails on the ship.

The memory a ship bears is closely tied to the eponym. A chamber of memory and the captain's wardroom maintain like a sanctuary the legacy of the entire unit. The legacy of a ship, for example the *Tourville*, includes a portrait of a person after whom the ship is named, its coat of arms, and a chart showing its record in service. To that can be added a list of the ships that bore the same name, with the historical record appended. An engraved copper plaque contains a list of the officers who have succeeded to command of the ship. Among the memories there figure insignia, decorations, or plaques conferred on the ship by French or foreign authorities. The objective is to affirm, in the collective consciousness of the crew as well as in the outside world, the personality of the ship in its historical setting. It is the custom to offer visitors from the outside world an object—a medal, a cup, or a sash bearing the silhouette, the coat of arms, and the name of the person after whom the ship is named.

These practices may seem unsuitable to the technical modernity of the navy. That is not the case. Commissioned and noncommissioned officers are engineers and technicians, and ships resemble laboratories, if not factories. To appreciate this, one only has to visit the ship's command center, with its up-to-date equipment in computers, television monitors, acoustics, and ballistics. It is the equivalent, on water, of the complex of operations found in command centers on land. The rule of the machine and calculations does not make perspicacity and judgment any less necessary to the quick decisions on which the fate of the ship and its personnel, not to mention the operation, may depend. Responsibility no longer functions according to the conditions and methods of long ago, but it still requires lucidity and authority.

Ceremony in the Navy

Life on board is subordinated to a rigor that is well understood. The measures that regulate it, far from being outmoded practices, correspond to necessities. Let no one be mistaken about this. No doubt the author of *L'Argot Baille* justified his work by the need to maintain traditions disrupted by the last war. Following in the same path, another author believed a reminder of childish and honest civility was necessary for these men charged with representing French customs abroad.[60] But these works do not touch the essential. The recent *Instruction sur le cérémonial dans la Marine* (Directive for Ceremony in the Navy)—a volume of 562 pages[61] —brings together, on the basis of historical research, a certain number of rules, some of which date far back. One detail will illustrate this: the blue

Figure 2.14
The *Jeanne d'Arc* with all flags flying, New York, 1986.

uniform of the navy dates from 1665, when it was first used to contrast with the vermilion of the frock coat of the Knights of Malta. From that came the distinction between red officers and blue officers, which caused much ink to flow. The spirit of the *Instruction* corresponds to what is elsewhere called "the dynamism and fecundity of symbolic history."[62] The *Instruction* deals with the honors to be accorded to officers or eminent personages as well as persons crossing the gangway. It stipulates the number of times the whistle is blown for the officer and the cannon fired for the eminent person, as well as the way to salute a foreign land. It sets forth the honors given to the national flag, "the country's symbol and the mark of the ship's nationality." It establishes the ritual (music, gestures, words, etc.) in the ceremonies for the assumption of command and the first fitting out of the ship. Precedence is set. To avoid a gaffe of any sort, nothing is left to chance or to the capricious initiative of individuals. Each prescription rests on precedent, sometimes an ancient one. How well is it known, for example, that the halberdier on guard outside the quarters of an admiral on duty is the successor to the "guards of the admiral's flag" from the eighteenth century?

The merchant marine also enjoys some customs that are inherited from olden times. Here too discipline and hierarchy are necessities, at times vital, for all those on board.

Lastly, one ritual used by both the navy and the merchant marine for centuries has been in effect right up to recent technological changes: the launching of a ship. Ships of heavy tonnage are no longer launched, but lowered into the water inside a dry dock. Previously a ceremony, religious and profane, marked the event. The moves and gestures are old, if not ancient. They were Christianized in the Middle Ages in the West as well as in the East. A liturgy laid out the scriptural readings, the benediction, and the bestowal of a name in the presence of godparents. Rites and symbols tend to personify and sanctify a ship in order to attract celestial protection for the crew and passengers. These symbolic acts are bearers of a charge, the contents of which the past alone can express.[63]

Testimony

The events in the career of ships and sailors have not been shown to be less memorable than their beginnings. Their commemoration has brought about the erection of monuments, the stamping of plaques, the striking of medals and tokens, and, starting in the nineteenth century, the issuance of postage stamps. As an example, let us note the black marble obelisk that, until the destruction of Brest, stood in the apse of the Church of Saint Louis, inviting young people to imitate the courage of

Charles du Couédic, who was mortally wounded at Ouessant in 1779.[64] The plaques are too numerous to be counted. So too the medals and tokens. Under Louis XIV, medals of rare quality were struck. Some of them illustrate the role Brest played when Camaret led the resistance to an attack by the English in 1694. Its motto—"Custos Orae Armoricae" (Guardian of the Coast of Armorica)*—aptly describes the city. A medal from 1680 speaks of Toulon as "Tholonii Portus et Navale" (Toulon, Harbor and Shipyard). The confidence of the king was not shaken by the defeat at La Hougue; in 1693, the memory of Bévéziers inspired two encouraging legends: "Emergunt meliora" (Better things will come forth) and "Clarior emergit" (It will appear more clearly). In the course of the following years, France appears with the features of Thetis, queen of the sea, seated in Neptune's chariot, with the legend "Splendor rei navalis" (Brilliance in naval affairs). Naval motifs abound in the production of currency and deserve a systematic study.[65]

Philately contributes other more recent but no less significant examples. In 1988, an exposition in Paris provided evidence, drawn from the storerooms of the postal administration and private collections, of what the postage stamp had been revealing for a century and a half of the navy's influence in the world and French expansion overseas.[66]

Even the language of the sailors, apart from its unique technical style, expresses original forms of thought that often reflect a distant past. Changes, notably the disappearance of the sail and innovations of every kind, have enriched more than rendered obsolete the old ways of speaking. Note the genealogy of marine dictionaries since the eighteenth century. Of the many such dictionaries, a special place is due the *Glossaire nautique* by Augustin Jal.[67] The language of the sea is made up of successive contributions taken from the extreme diversity of the French language. Each variation in its own uniqueness deals with a particular aspect of maritime life, each forming a linguistic layer subsequently intermixed with all other layers.

In a related field the judicial sector shows that the law of the sea, even today, is dependent on the past. Three texts attest to the stages of this development: the *Rôles d'Oléron*, a collection of jurisprudence dating back to the twelfth century and compiled in the thirteenth and fourteenth centuries;[68] the *Guidon de la mer*, a kind of commercial code from the sixteenth century; and, lastly, Colbert's great *Ordonnance de la Marine*.

Finally, in all the texts, memorials, rituals, and customs, one common denominator of the maritime mentality comes through: solidarity

---

* EDITOR'S NOTE: Armorica was the Roman name for northwest Gaul, today Brittany and part of Normandy.

Figure 2.15
Joseph Vernet, *View of the Port of La Rochelle from the Petite Rive* (1762), detail.

in the face of shared risk. On land, the "quarter" [*quartier*] of the town, with its class system, was the privileged spot in the eighteenth century for maritime memory, and it provided the feeling of belonging to a community. In some ports—Dunkirk, Dieppe, Brest, and Les Sables-d'Olonne, to name a few—certain distinctive quarters preserved the memory of the group. The perils encountered at sea have enriched the collective memory of unforgettable facts. Among these memories, however glorious, humiliating, or merely tragic they may be, along with dangers shared and overcome, the most distressing one comes from the infamous floating hulks in which England detained thousands of prisoners captured between 1793 and 1815. These "floating sepulchers" imprinted a sinister memory in those who survived.[69]

NAVY AND SOCIETY

From Misunderstandings to Trends

The unhappy fate of the captives on the English hulks did cause a momentary stir. But only for a moment, for in matters of the sea the French have a short memory. The "enlightened" spirits of the eighteenth century left behind some examples. Voltaire stands out for his disdain of "Canada's snowy slopes," a remark that reveals his lack of understanding of naval operations overseas. Rousseau and Diderot also shared his disdain, not to mention scorn. Rousseau went so far as to wonder whether sailors were men or beasts—at a time when he was exalting the native virtue of the "noble savage."[70] Diderot considered maritime votive practices the height of obscurantism. Still, in the scientific milieu of the eighteenth century, there can be found certain minds who were quite interested in the sea and in the worlds to which the sea gives access, and who were personally quite open to participating in voyages of exploration. Indeed, they sought out such opportunities. We have met Borda and the Académie de Marine. We must remember the scientists who went along with Bougainville, La Pérouse, d'Entrecasteaux, and Baudin. One colloquy held at Brest in 1985 had as its subject the sea during the century of the encyclopedists.[71] It was during this period for the first time that a king, Louis XVI, manifested an active and informed interest in the navy.

Since the king set the example, it came to be in good taste, for a few years, to be interested in the sea. From Tahiti Bougainville brought back Aotourou, who became the idol of the Parisian salons. A new cause had arisen—the sea—and it coincided with the spirit of the Enlightenment, like the cause of liberty in America. With Franklin debarking at Auray, a port southwest of Lorient, naval victories had repercussions in high society, seen in such hairstyles as *à la Belle Poule* and *à la Frégate*. Later, people were touched by the fate of La Pérouse, though they forgot him the next moment. Propaganda celebrated the battling *Vengeur*, but the battle of Trafalgar had a greater impact than all the successes accumulated in the war for America's independence.

Short lived and somewhat masochistic: such has been the very selective memory of the French. What memories do people retain of the Hundred Years' War? The disaster of Béhuchet at Sluis in 1340, but only barely the name of Jean de Vienne. Of the Habsburg Wars in the fifteenth century, there is not a whisper of a memory of the fact that the navy kept the kingdom of Naples supplied. As for the discoveries in the New World, if the name of Jacques Cartier is recalled, it is (except at Saint-Malo) to note his failure. And one has to go to New York to learn that a Florentine—Verrazano, who became French—was the first to explore the east coast of North America. It is known that Colbert had ships built, but what is remembered is that these ships were destroyed at Barfleur. Forgotten is the fact that Tourville had just won a victory at Bévéziers (1691). The list of the gaps in memory would be long indeed.

How to explain it? Admittedly sailors themselves have a share in the responsibility for the landlubbers' lack of understanding. Up to recent times, they have wrapped their memories in the cowl of collective dignity that displays a sense of embarrassment, an impression of marginality, but also a feeling of superiority with respect to the *glaiseux* (people of clay, or peasants) and the *biffins* (foot soldiers). The land dwellers, for their part, experience similar mixed feelings. By wondering, "How can you be a sailor?" they evince astonishment, curiosity, a little admiration, and perhaps the beginnings of respect. All that must be taken into account if an appreciation for the place of matters of the sea in our national memory is to be attempted. The lack of appreciation stands in sharp contrast to English attitudes.

Awareness of the country's long coastline and maritime past has surely required the French to develop ways of communicating. The unlocking of the Breton coast is recent, but has it been achieved? Information and style have had a considerable impact.

The romantic generation was deeply touched by the wreck of the *Méduse* thanks to the painter Géricault, but the reality portrayed by Vernet was no less affecting. At least that generation discovered the pleasures of the beach and bathing in the sea, as did the duchesse de Berry on the coast at Dieppe around 1825. People expressed concern about the fate of convicts at Brest and Toulon, all the while considering the conditions for oceangoing fishermen normal because they had been so for centuries. Perhaps the chief merit of Jules Verne is that he aroused interest in

Figure 2.16
Sketch by Géricault, *The Raft of the* Méduse.

Figure 2.17
Géricault, *The Raft of the* Méduse (1819).

nautical adventure by drawing on the authentic traditions of his forefathers in Nantes.

Was it sufficient? There the vogue of "sailing" finds, without doubt, one of its original motifs. Inclined to imitate sailors, land dwellers have borrowed certain expressions from them. Thus they commonly say: to watch out for a squall, to remain in the harbor, to come to a standstill, to beat windward or tack, to slide down something like a ladder, to take on board someone or something, to fit out, to disembark. They make use of local expressions, often from Brittany, as, for example, "to be rigged like a schooner in good weather," meaning to be dressed in one's Sunday best. Someone in a bad mood is said to be facing a headwind. To attribute to sailors the expression *dessaler*, meaning "capsize," is incorrect. It belongs elsewhere. Windsurfing is a sport, but it is not sailing, and in any case the origin of the expression is too recent. Further, the only memories attributable to windsurfing come from games of skill and a few accidents.

To imitate sailors without sufficient experience, which means without memory, is to expose oneself ill-advisedly to the same dangers they face. How many inexcusable acts of carelessness have led us to expect and even demand help from true sailors? It is at such times that one appreciates the facilities available on the coasts for safety at sea and the mission the navy carries out freely and without credit.

Safety at Sea, the Ever-Alert Guardian Angels

Sounds and lights in the fog: lighthouses and buoys. Only if one has gone into a cove on the Brittany coast in overcast weather, even in midsummer, hearing the call of the sirens and foghorns and catching the veiled and intermittent flash from a lighthouse, can the tension of a navigator anxious to keep his course be understood. Radar and procedures using the transmission of sound and light do not, even in our own day, do away with watchful attentiveness. The coastline of France has about 1,300 lighthouses and 3,700 beacons, all managed by an agency in Paris that dates back to 1792. That agency has accumulated a legacy charged with history. If the lighthouses could tell their past, they would stand out like milestones over the course of time, marking the vicissitudes of war, the traffic in the harbors, and especially the progress in technology.

Natural conditions and the requirements for navigation fixed the sites of the first lighthouses in Roman times, such as the one at Fréjus, later asphyxiated by alluviation, and at Boulogne, the celebrated Tour d'Ordre. The Middle Ages saw the use of unreliable fires, such as candles on the balcony. Louis the Pious in the ninth century established a fire at the entrance to the Gironde River on the Cordouan Rock where, four centuries later, the Black Prince had the first French lighthouse constructed. At the top of the tower a wood fire, fueled by wax and coal tar, indicated the river's opening to the vineyards of Aquitaine. Maintaining the fire as a charitable service for sailors was assured by a religious order of hermits.[72] Incontestably useful, this lighthouse was duly noted in the portulans and cited in the charts. It required constant maintenance, and at the end of the sixteenth century reconstruction began under the direction of a renowned architect, Louis de Foix, who had worked on the Escurial, the royal palace in Spain. There were others. Fire by night and smoke by day were seen on the coasts at Oléron, La Rochelle, and Guérande in Brittany, as were the fires, dating from the fourteenth century, that were set at the entrance to the Seine. Fires were also set at Fécamp, Dieppe, Le Tréport, Calais, and the approaches to Marseille. The smoky illumination did not carry far, and so sailors rarely set to sea at night.[73]

Maritime memory uses the end of the seventeenth century as the point when the number of lighthouses began to increase along our Atlantic coasts, behind England but to some degree ahead of the Mediterranean. Vauban was there pushing for their construction for reasons of military and commercial necessity.[74] Memories are arranged, down to our own days, around the technology of architecture, light, and optics. To that may be added the essential human issues of provisioning and relief. Certain dates are significant: Chassiron at Oléron (1680), the Baleines at Ré (1682), Cape Fréhel (1695), and, in the last three decades of the eighteenth century, the Planier at Marseille (1771), La Hève (1774), the Ailly Point and Gatteville (1775) on the English Channel, Eckmühl at the tip of Brittany (1757). There were 24 lighthouses in 1800, 169 in 1853, 361 some thirty years later, and, in 1984, 1,300. This progression has known some memorable episodes, of which the most heroic are not so distant from us.

Cordouan, the king of the lighthouses, was visited by Michelet and by Fromentin in 1862.[75] The place was classified as a historic monument the same year as was Notre-Dame in Paris. In his excitement Michelet considered the lighthouse to be "a person." The tower was always the object of the attentive care of its builders. Its image presents a high silhouette, which was extended from thirty-seven to sixty-three meters in the nineteenth century to meet certain technical specifications (installation of mirrors) set by Teulère and Borda.[76] The stages in equipping the lighthouse with new technology are those of the history of "pharology." Thus it is that the source of energy went from charcoal, to vegetable and mineral oil in the eighteenth century, then to gas from petroleum in 1907, and finally, in 1948, to fueled power plants. The Fresnel lens was introduced in 1823. In 1847, the occultations were grouped in white,

TOUR DE   CORDOÜAN

Figure 2.18
Cordouan, the king of lighthouses, visited in 1826 by Michelet and Fromentin and classifed as a historical
monument at the same time as Notre-Dame Cathedral in Paris; watercolor (17th century).

green, and red beams. Putting the lighthouse back into service after
World War II was facilitated by the preservation of the optical apparatus,
hidden in the natural grottos of Meschers. Cordouan is now exposed to
the vandalism of tourists who go there on a kind of pilgrimage. Their curiosity is understandable, for the interior of the lighthouse is decorated
according to the tastes of the eighteenth century. That is what struck
Victor Hugo (*L'Homme qui rit*). At Cordouan the king's apartment on the
first floor and the chapel on the second, decorated in the baroque style,
cede nothing to the "fantasies" of the tower's English counterpart at Cas-
quets, near Portland. It forms "a plume at the edge of the sea."

Such is not the case with the imitators of Cordouan. The classic silhouette of the lighthouse, the watchtower, and the signal has hardly
changed even with added height. What changes have taken place lie in
the boldness of the structure and the functional improvements, aimed
principally at increasing the projection of the light. The lighthouse at
Antifer reached its height of 128 meters back in 1835. Even though barely
half that height at fifty-one meters, the one at Les Heaux de Bréhat
(1836–39) had, in Michelet's eyes, "the sublime simplicity of a marine
plant." The construction of the Isle of Sein lighthouse on the rock that
gave it its name, Ar Men, with a diameter of just over seven meters, took
fourteen years (1867–81). Enormous difficulties were experienced. So
hard was the rock and so violent the current in a distance across less than
one mile that of 404 attempts to land, 13 ended in failure. Rightly called
the "specter of the caretakers," it held one of them captive for ten days
during a storm in 1923. Worse befell the caretakers of La Vieille lighthouse on the coast of Léon when they were isolated without help from
mid-December 1925 to the end of the following February. Some caretakers in other cases went mad. But as a recent work put it, "True pathos,
widows and orphans, is required before the land dwellers become interested in the caretakers of lighthouses."[77] Let us hope that the automation
of the lighthouses will make such facts a thing of the past without effac-
ing their memory.

Although less ancient, the lighthouses that dot Ouessant have as
much right to be in the popular memory.[78] Vauban built two towers at
the Pointe du Stiff on the northeast side. Not until 1863 was the Creac'h
lighthouse built on the northwest side. The Jument lighthouse to the
southwest was completed in 1911, the one at Kéréon to the southeast in
1916, and the one at Nividic in 1936. The people of Ouessant remember, as do others, the race against the clock and the currents at eight
knots to build Jument. A giant conger eel attacked one diver, and the
lighthouse had hardly been completed when an autumn storm knocked
it down and kept five men prisoner for the storm's duration. The most

powerful lighthouse, Creac'h, with a height of forty-seven meters, shines
a beam that reaches thirty-four miles. Plans were drawn up to double its
size, turning it into a giant lighthouse 105 meters high, angled more to
the open sea, for directing and controlling the more than fifty thousand
ships that each year, sailing between the Atlantic Ocean and the English
Channel, travel along the maritime route called "R.A.I.L.," thereby en-
suring that they steer clear of the coasts of Brittany and prevent another
so-called black tide. The Marine nationale administers the Surveillance
maritime, commonly called the Sur Mar, by night and by day as an indispensable rescue force in these "places of memory" where sinister
events are not just anecdotes from the past. Rescuers are called upon to
intervene, any time of the year and in all kinds of weather.

Piloting and Rescue at Sea

A map that shows safety problems at sea should not just indicate lighthouses and beacons. Piloting and lifeboat stations must also be included.
Noting the location and dating certain famous shipwrecks would fix in
memory the most dangerous sites and usefully recall the debt of recognition due to the rescuers.[79]

The risks to navigation are greatest at the harbor approaches: when
coming into port, using a pilot is advisable. Piloting has a long tradition,
and in the mid-sixteenth century a distinction appears between oceangoing pilots and harbor pilots. Piloting, a delicate operation at all times,
sometimes has cost men their lives. History especially recalls the heroism
of those pilots on the northern coast of France during the evacuation in
1940, as well as the mine removal operations along the coast in 1945
where the navigational warning system had been disrupted.[80]

Before it was organized, in the late nineteenth century, help for those
wrecked at sea was uncertain, which contributed to the bad reputation
the coastal populations had and, as a result, the bad reputation of mariners
and the sea itself. Did a sailor in distress dare call for help when he knew
what the coastal residents would likely do? After attracting a ship to the
coast by false signals, they were known to reward themselves by sparing
the survivors' lives but robbing them of everything and plundering the
wrecked ships. The merchant Jacques Cœur, returning from the East in
1432, doubtless owed his life to the people of Calvi, but they did ransom
the travelers *usque ad camisas* (down to their shirts). In Brittany the
Seigneur du Léon boasted of possessing a reef that brought him much
profitable revenue. Such medieval customs brought both seaside residents
and lords of local estates into collusion. To lower the number of these
mishaps, the dukes of Brittany instituted the "sea convoy," assuring

sailors of an armed escort in autumn and spring.[81] Colbert's *Ordonnance* of 1681 and maritime law defined responsibilities and set forth punishment for offenses. Improvements in security at sea in dangerous areas, however, did not occur until permanent organizations providing immediate assistance, sustained by a moral effort, were established.

Those who were long stigmatized with the name of shipwrecker more often than not provided real help to the shipwrecked. At Ouessant, for example, even today the idea remains that whatever is washed up from the sea is a treasure to be taken. Yet the inhabitants of Ouessant earned the gratitude of Queen Victoria for having saved 250 passengers from the *Drummond Castle* in the strong current off Fromveur in June 1896. Seven years later at the Sorbonne, a woman from the same island received the grand medal from the Société centrale des naufragés (survivors).[82]

A noteworthy competition beginning in 1825 sparked first local then national initiatives.[83] The English example had encouraged a pioneer, M. de Bernières, to provide a rescue boat for Le Havre in 1775, and it was Le Havre again that set the example in 1825 for other cities along the coast up to Dunkirk when it established the Société humaine des naufragés. What drove this effort was the shock caused by several sensational shipwrecks, the *Méduse* and especially the *Sémillante*, when several hundred soldiers perished on February 15, 1855, on their way to the Crimea. The government took up the matter. An inquiry revealed that over a three-year period (1862–65) there had been 986 disasters at sea with 6,238 victims. This sad experience provided the urgency needed to create some seventy-five rescue stations equipped with specialized boats. Two organizations were charged to implement the program: the Société centrale des naufragés, the first president of which was Admiral Rigault de Genouilly, who had distinguished himself in the Crimean War; and the Société des hospitaliers sauveteurs bretons (Charitable Society of Breton Rescuers), founded by the grandnephew of the naturalist Buffon. For reasons of efficiency, the two organizations joined in 1967 to form the Société nationale de sauvetage en mer (National Society for Rescue at Sea). Their work is inscribed in maritime memory by the assistance they had rendered by that date to 61,000 ships and the rescue of 45,000 lives. In 1987, the number of stations on the French coast totaled 255. These stations are equipped with 461 inflatable dinghies, 36 unsinkable boats, and about 60 launches, all operated by 3,000 volunteers.

Just like the stations spread out along the coast, each of these rescue boats recalls many memories. The quality of these boats poses a constant problem, for they must be light hulled, unsinkable, and fast, capable of over twenty-five knots. Certain boats have acquired titles of nobility. So it was with a boat built in 1897 at the Augustin-Normand shipyard in Le Havre that served at the Roscoff station for fifty-six years before being turned over to the Société des régates de Paimpol and exercising its retirement rights. Restored and presented at a nautical exhibition in 1976, it found a place in the Musée de l'Atlantique in Port-Louis. Its name: *Commandant-de-Kerhallet*. This veteran has indeed earned its place among veterans.

The volunteer rescuers have an even greater right to the thankful memory of those indebted to them. Many paid with their lives in performing their lifesaving service. One example suffices: at Penmarc'h, on May 23, 1935, a single storm engulfed two rescue boats and two small fishing boats, drowned twenty-seven men, and left behind twenty-three widows and forty-five orphans.

There are the foolhardy who, not content to put their own existence at risk, engage, sometimes frivolously, the lives of the men of the Marine nationale and the rescue organizations (they are often the same) from whom they expect their salvation. Something here merits reflection. Memory ought to encourage caution, discretion, and gratitude.

There exists a maritime France. The past attests to it. The present confirms it. But is there only one maritime France? In one place no tide, in another tides that range between 30 and 130 centimeters. The northwesterly wind known as the *suroît* has nothing in common with the northerly wind in the south called the mistral. The sociability of seasonal fishing in the north used to contrast with artisan fishing in Brittany and Mediterranean individualism. There is variation in human reactions: northern violence, Breton anger, southern explosiveness. The language itself exhibits differences, and sailors of days long ago had to take that into account.

Diverse yet one, that is maritime France. It is felt through a common legacy. First of all, the sea, because it is the sea. The community on board ships is a shared solidarity. It would not take a moment in a brawl between land dwellers and sailors in a bad place for other sailors to join in whoever they are, setting aside all differences and rivalries. The interests of the craft are identical, including passions and personal sufferings. History has done the rest: the confraternity of combat, the maritime inscription. It has made of Brittany and Provence a pair: the telephone directory of the Var department contains many Breton names, and cars with license plate 83 (Var) are as numerous in Brest and Lorient as 29 (Finistère) and 56 (Morbihan) are in Toulon. Another detail: the recent attempt to reintroduce the terms

Figure 2.19
A cemetery for
sailors? At Ouessant a
small tomb surrounded
by flowers encloses
crosses from *proëllas*,
funeral ceremonies
performed for sailors
whose bodies disap-
peared at sea.

"Ponant" and "Levant" to designate the Atlantic and Mediterranean fleets, respectively, seems to have gone nowhere.

What did and still does weld our maritime regions together, with the community of a shared history, is the feeling of being misunderstood by land dwellers. Another shared conviction is they have paid the costs of the opportunities France missed when it failed to realize its maritime vocation. A stumble here and there, on which memory is too much focused, has left the bitter taste of a destiny that is behind us. This is serious because it concerns not only military reverses at sea, trotted out at the expense of happier episodes, but also the maritime economy's lack of success. In particular, commerce and fishing, together with the naval forces, support each other and constitute what the Anglo-Saxons call "sea power." And yet sea power is not divisible—something that has been understood only partially, belatedly, and fleetingly.

Those lost opportunities stand out over the last six centuries. The end of the Hundred Years' War made France and England confront choices in their destinies. England was willy-nilly driven back by the loss of its continental territories. It turned to the sea. France found itself confronting the everlasting difficulty of two well-balanced options: continental and maritime. During that period, certain individuals did perceive the extent of its maritime, military, and economic possibilities.

Thus the author of the *Débat des hérauts d'armes* put into the mouth of the herald of France: "I say that a prince who wants to be king of the sea must necessarily have three things: good harbors, deep and sufficiently strong, to hold ships; secondly, he must have a sufficient number of large and small ships; thirdly he must have goods that allow him to exploit his ships."[84] We know what came of the projects undertaken by Louis XI and Francis I, because, with the end the Italian dreams, the necessity to react against the powerful stranglehold of the Habsburg emperor, Charles V, and the cancer of the Wars of Religion diverted already insufficient efforts from the sea and concentrated them on the continent.

In the time of Cardinal Richelieu, the necessary coordination between the maritime economy and naval power was once again understood. For example, in 1629, at the end of an inspection of the coasts requested by Richelieu, Leroux d'Infreville defined the qualities of Le Havre: "the most convenient harbor in all France for finding there the things necessary for outfitting a ship because of the great commerce along the Seine."[85] Every renewed effort since Colbert, in the seventeenth and eighteenth centuries, starts from that point. Yet without fail it was thwarted by the ever-recurring land and continental demons. The growth in naval power after the American War of Independence very nearly attained success. The upheavals of the Revolution and twenty years of nearly uninterrupted warfare on the continent left disappointment inscribed in the memories of the French with the names of Trafalgar and the Continental Blockade.

New attempts, new disappointments have transpired since the middle of the nineteenth century. Naval construction bringing in state-of-the-art technology, a resurgence in commerce, and the opening of colonial markets produced hope for a durable maritime development despite the exhausting constraints of conflicts on the Continent. Disenchantment came. Is there nothing left, then?

So what purpose can memory serve? The future lies not totally in the past. The technical achievements of the navy are expensive, commerce lacks freight, fishing no longer sustains competition, and shipyards are closing one after another. Some are looking for relief in the vogue of sailing for pleasure—so be it! After all, surfboarding and, even more, yachting can be schools of lucidity and courage as well as opening eyes and minds to the sea. The French can play a great part in exploiting the oceans. Initiative will likewise be necessary in dealing with European integration. France can usefully appeal to its experiences and remember that a part of itself is maritime, that peace like war is won on the sea, and luck is an entrée on the menu that does not pass by twice.

NOTES

1. Henri-François Delaborde, *Recueil des actes de Philippe Auguste* (Paris, 1943), vol. 2, no. 926; Léopold Delisle, "Cartulaire normand," *Mémoires de la Société des antiquaires de Normandie* 16, no. 1082 (1852).

2. "Quant li rois de France eut ensi ordoneet et fet pourveoir, rapareiller et rafrescir toutes les frontieres de son royaume, tant sur mer comme par terre" [When the king of France had thus so ordered and had provided, repaired, and reconstituted all the borders of his kingdom, both on sea and on land]. Jean Froissart, *Chroniques*, ed. Siméon Luce (Paris, 1869–88), 406–7.

3. Observations of Jean-Yves Guiomar, "Le *Tableau de la géographie de la France* de Vidal de La Blache," in *Les Lieux de mémoire*, under the direction of Pierre Nora, 3 vols. in 7 (Paris: Gallimard, 1984–92), vol. 2, book 1, 571.

4. Roger Dion, *Les Frontières de la France* (Paris, 1947).

5. See Jean-Marie Mayeur, "A Frontier Memory: Alsace," below in this volume, 409.

6. Fernand Braudel, *L'Identité de la France*, vol. 1, *Espace et histoire* (Paris, 1986), 292–96. Seventeen study groups at the École nationale d'administration took up the challenge posed by Braudel in 1988. Their efforts focused on maritime problems from a French point of view within a world context. The collective reports were published as *La Mer: Hommes, richesses, enjeux* (IFREMER, 1989).

7. Jules Michelet, *La Mer* (Paris, 1861), and *Tableau de la France*, ed. L. Refort (Paris, 1949).

8. Tourist guides have used these linkages as a lens through which to view the maritime side of France. This approach deserves further study, particularly for the latter half of the nineteenth century.

9. René de Chateaubriand, *Mémoires d'outre-tombe*, ed. M. Levaillant (Paris, 1982). Bernard Chenot, "Chateaubriand et les bruits de la mer," speech given at the Académie des sciences morales et politiques, November 30, 1987.

10. Jean Recher, *Le Grand métier: Journal d'un capitaine de pêche de Fécamp* (Paris, 1977); Lionel Martin, *Les Forçats de l'océan: La grande pêche de Terre-Neuve aux Kerguelen* (Paris, 1977).

11. Painting has fixed memories by interpreting them; Françoise Cachin, "The Painter's Landscape," below in this volume. Three other references may be added: "Joseph Vernet (1714–1789)," exposition at the Musée de la Marine, Paris, 1976–77, presented by Luc-Marie Bayle and Philippe Conisbée, Paris, 1976; Jean Bourgoin, "La Localisation du naufrage de la *Méduse*," *Navigation* 29 (1981): 92–100; and Yves Le Pichon, *La Mer sous le regard des peintres de la marine* (Paris, 1988).

12. Monographs and expositions generating catalogs have multiplied over the last few years, particularly with the impetus given by the Association pour le sauvegarde et l'étude des ex-voto marins [Association for the Preservation and Study of Commemorative Sea Plaques], now merged with the Association des amis du musée de l'Atlantique [Association of the Friends of the Museum of the Atlantic]. Several expositions may be noted: "Ex-voto marins du Ponant" (1975), "Ex-voto marins de Méditerannée" (1978), and "Ex-voto marins dans le monde" (1981). Two publications may also be noted: François and Colette Boullet, *Ex-voto marins*

(Geneva, 1978), and Bernard Cousin, *Ex-voto de Provence: Images de la religion populaire et de vie d'autrefois* (Bourges, 1981).

13. M. Vincent, "Les Graffiti de Brouage," in *Recueil de la commission Arts et Monuments* 19 (Saintes, 1913–29), 1350; Henri Cahingt, "Les Graffiti dieppois," in *Colloque d'histoire maritime, 1957* (Paris, 1957), 53–71; Lucien Bucherie, "Les Graffiti de la Maison Henri II," *Publications de la Société d'archéologie et d'histoire d'Aunis* 2 (1977): 1–5; "Les Graffiti de la Tour de la Lanterne à La Rochelle," in *Publications de la Société d'archéologie et d'histoire d'Aunis* 3 (1978): 1–51. Research conducted by Anne-Sophie Auger has led to a series of articles in *Neptunia, Cols Bleus,* and *Le Chasse-marée,* following an exposition in 1985 at the Musée de la Marine. J. Peuziat, "1. Nefs de pierre dans les églises bretonnes," *Le Chasse-marée* 8 (1983): 9–21, and "2. Navires de pierre (sculptures des églises bretonnes)," *Le Chasse-marée* 15 (1985): pp. 34–47.

14. The collection *Voyages et découvertes,* published by Imprimerie Nationale, includes *Bougainville et ses compagnons autour du monde,* ed. Étienne Taillemite (Paris, 1977) and *Les Voyages de La Pérouse,* ed. Maurice de Brossard and John Dunmore, 2 vols. (Paris, 1985). Forthcoming editions in the series will include journals by Baudin and by Dumont d'Urville.

15. *Dumont d'Urville en Antarctique: Journal de bord de Joseph Seureau, quartier-maître de la Zélée (1837–1840),* ed. Catherine Mehaud and Hélène Richard (Paris: Publisud, [1995]).

16. Jean Favier et al., *Les Archives nationales: État général des fonds,* vol. 3, *Marine et outre-mer* (Paris, 1980); Étienne Taillemite, *Les Archives de la marine conservées aux Archives nationales* (Vincennes, 1980).

17. Most of the local document collections are the subject of catalogs or numeric indexes, the enumeration of which is impossible.

18. Pierre Blanc et al., *Bureau Veritas, 1828–1978: Cent cinquante ans d'histoire* (Paris, 1978); Pierre Blanc, "Le Bureau Veritas," *La Revue maritime* (1979): 482–88.

19. Philippe Henwood, "L'Académie de Marine à Brest au XVIIIe siècle," in *La Mer au siècle des encyclopédies,* colloquium, Brest, 1985, (Paris-Geneva, 1987), 125–35.

20. Étienne Taillemite, *L'Histoire ignorée de la marine française* (Paris, 1988), 256–78.

21. Marcel Delafosse, *Le Commerce du sel de Brouage aux XVIIe–XVIIIe siècles* (Paris, 1960); J. Poisbeau-Hémery, "Le Sel et les marais salants de la presqu'île guérandaise," in *Colloque sur le sel: Actes du 99e Congrès national des sociétés savantes, 1974* (Paris, 1976), 101–10; Pierre Tardy, *Sel et sauniers d'hier et d'aujourd'hui* (Sainte-Marie-de-Ré, 1987).

22. Michel Mollat et al., *Le Rôle du sel dans l'histoire* (Paris, 1968).

23. George Jehel, *Aigues-Mortes, un port pour un roi: Les Capétiens et la Méditerranée* (Roanne, 1985).

24. Charles de la Roncière, *Histoire de la marine française,* vol. 3 (Paris, 1923), 615–16.

25. Françoise Péron, *Ouessant: L'Île sentinelle* (Brest–Paris, 1985); Péron, *Essai de géographie humaine sur le milieu insulaire: L'exemple de l'île de Ouessant et les petites îles de l'Ouest français* (Paris, 1990).

26. Philippe Brémont, "Île de Sein: La médecine au péril de la mer" (thesis, Angers, 1979), cited in D. Goett, *Histoire de la médecine navale et d'outre-mer,* Séminaire

Niaussat, book 8 (1986–87), 1–14; Charles Floquet, *Belle-Île, Houat et Hoedic au cours des siècles* (Loudéac, 1997).

27. Jean-François Henry, *Des marins au siècle du Roi-Soleil: L'Île d'Yeu sous le règne de Louis XIV* (Janzé, 1982); D. Duviard, *Groix, île des thoniers: Chronique maritime d'une île bretonne, 1840–1940* (Grenoble, 1978).

28. Jean Mallon, "Un port normand au Moyen Âge: Honfleur du XIIIe siècle à la fin du XVe" (thesis, École des Chartes, Position des thèses de l'École des Chartes, 1926).

29. André Lespagnol et al., *Histoire de Saint-Malo* (Toulouse, 1984).

30. It can only be hoped that the ongoing study of castles will produce, in France, a study specific to castles on the coast analogous to what was done in England with the *Cliff Castles*. Interesting comments by Alain Guillerm may be found in his work *La Pierre et le vent: Fortifications et marine en occident* (Paris, 1985).

31. Marcel Delafosse et al., *Histoire de La Rochelle* (Toulouse, 1985).

32. Eugénie Cortade, *Le Château royal de Collioure* (Collioure, 1968).

33. Maurice Bordes, *Histoire de Nice et du pays niçois* (Toulouse, 1976).

34. Alain Lottin et al., *Histoire de Boulogne-sur-Mer* (Lille, 1983).

35. Henri Cahingt, *L'Église Saint-Jacques de Dieppe* (Dieppe, 1983).

36. Recher, *Le Grand métier*; Martin, *Les Forçats de l'océan*; see also Thierry du Pasquier, *Les Baleiniers français au XIXe siècle, 1814–1868* (Grenoble, 1982); Michel Mollat et al., *Histoire des pêches maritimes en France* (Toulouse, 1987); Olivier Guyot-Jeannin, *Histoire de Saint-Pierre-et-Miquelon* (Paris, 1986); Éric Rieth, Jean Chapelot, and Aliette Geistdorfer, *Recherches archéologiques, ethnologiques et historiques des îles Saint-Pierre-et-Miquelon* (Paris, 1987).

37. Alain Cabantous et al., *Histoire de Dunkerque* (Toulouse, 1983).

38. André Corvisier et al., *Histoire du Havre* (Toulouse, 1983).

39. Michel Mollat et al., *Histoire de Rouen* (Toulouse, 1978); Charles Higounet et al., *Histoire de Bordeaux* (Toulouse, 1980); Paul Bois et al., *Histoire de Nantes* (Toulouse, 1977).

40. Jean Randier, "Opération *Belem*," *La Nouvelle revue maritime* 365 (1981): 28–53.

41. The following organizations may be noted: Association des amis du musée de l'Atlantique, the francophone summer university [*université francophone d'été*] of Aunis-Saintonge (Rochefort and Château d'Oléron center), and the Douarnenez center where the journal *Le Chasse-marée* is published.

42. Pierre Derolin, *Les Premiers paquebots des isles françaises d'Amérique, 1762–1765*, memoir, E.P.H.E., 4 (1975); Pierre Derolin, *Les Paquebots du Havre à New York, 1814–1864*, 2 vols. (thesis, 1978, 1984), book 4, "Le Transport des émigrants aux États-Unis au temps des paquebots à voiles," published in *Recueil de l'Association des amis du Vieux Havre* (1985), 57–76.
Marthe Barbance has focused her research on the chambers of commerce, in particular the Compagnie Générale Transatlantique and the Compagnie Bordes. The Compagnie des Messageries Maritimes published articles based on its archives in the *Courrier*, its periodical organ. See Marthe Barbance, *La Vie commerciale de la route du cap Horn au XIXe siècle* (Paris, 1969).

43. Joseph Conrad, *Typhoon* [chap. 3, online ed. at www.online-literature.com. ED.].

44. Édouard Baratier et al., *Histoire de Marseille* (Toulouse, 1973). The journal *Marseille*, published by that city's chamber of commerce, contains good historical articles.

45. Marc Guérout, "Comment l'épave du *Patriote* fut retrouvée dans les passes d'Alexandrie," *Chronique d'histoire maritime* 15, no. 1 (1987):1−5. On the Atlantic coast searches were made of, among others, the *Juste* (Bay of Quiberon), the *Maidstone* (Noirmoutier flats), the *Goulimine* (narrows at Brest), and a medieval ship at Aber-Vrac'h; at Cherbourg explorations are under way on the *Alabama*. The site of the shipwreck of Paul and Virginie on Mauritius is being explored, and they are still finding objects from the ships lost by La Pérouse at Vanikoro.

46. Anonymous, "Le Défi de *France II*," *Le Chasse-marée* 16 (1985): 17.

47. Georges Croisile, "C'était *France* dont la France était fière," *La Revue maritime* 348 (1979): 629−36.

48. Jean Randier, "À la conquête du 'Ruban bleu,'" *La Nouvelle revue maritime* 361 (1981): 96−114.

49. The expression "la Royale" has caused much ink to flow, notably among sailors. See Jacques Thibault on the name of the Marine Nationale (*Cols bleus*, October 17, 1987) and Olivier de Veyrac, "'La Royale,' moi j'aime," *Bulletin A.E.M.* 218 (1987). The title *La Royale* was used in 1972 by Jean Randier for a history of the navy (Éditions de la Cité). La Varende, whose *L'École navale* (p. LXVI) could also be noted, interpreted the facts as reflecting something permanent: "The navy, it was said, is a royal matter thus indicating that its work must not be left subject to ministerial changes." Let us add the conclusion of vol. 2, book 3, of *Les Lieux de mémoire* (647), which mentions "the function of assuring preeminence, prestige, embodying the sacredness of the homeland and the nation in a permanent fashion." Note the absence of the expression "la Royale" in the index of Commander Roger Coindreau, *L'Argot Baille* (1957). Special note should be made of a work entitled *La Royale et le roi* by Admiral Jean Armand Marc Philippon (Paris, 1982) and *La Marine: Place de la Concorde, Exposition 1789−1989* (Paris, 1989).

50. André Chastel, "La Notion de patrimoine," in *Les Lieux de mémoire*, vol. 2, book 2, 405−50; Pierre Nora, conclusion, in *Les Lieux de mémoire*, vol. 2, book 3, 650.

51. There is a vast literature on Rochefort, in particular: René Mémain, *La Marine de guerre sous Louix XIV: Le matériel, Rochefort, arsenal modèle de Colbert* (Paris, 1937); Jean Bourdriot, "Le Port de Rochefort, par Joseph Vernet," *Archives de l'Université francophone d'été Saintonge-Québec, 1979* (Saint-Jean-d'Angély, 1981), 65−81; Bourdriot, *Rochefort et la mer: Techniques et politique maritimes aux XVIIe et XVIII siècles* (Jonzac, 1985); M. Acerra, "Rochefort: L'Arsenal, l'eau, les vaisseaux," in Martine Acerra, José Merino, and Jean Meyer, *Les Marines de guerre européennes, XVIIe et XVIIIe siècles*, colloquy held at the Sorbonne (Paris, 1985); Maurice Dupont and Marc Fardet, *L'Arsenal de Colbert: Rochefort* (Rochefort, 1986); J. Gay, *La Fabrication des cordages au XVIIe siècle*, publication of the Université francophone (Jonzac, 1987).

The maritime patrimony of Rochefort includes the only remaining transporter bridge in France. Constructed in 1900, it was classified as a historical monument in 1976.

52. On the School of Naval Medicine at Rochefort, see the paper by Pierre Huard with bibliography in *Histoire de la médecine navale*, seminaires Niaussat, book 1

(1981–82). Niaussat was chief naval physician. On the history of naval medicine, refer to the reports of the above-mentioned seminars, to the works of Pierre Niaussat, Adrien Carré, and Jean-Pierre Kernéis, to numerous memoirs and the dissertations directed by Kernéis, and to Jacques Léonard, *Les Officiers de santé de la marine française de 1814 à 1835* (Rennes, 1967). A collective work of a general nature was published by Pierre Pluchon under the title *Histoire des médecins et pharmaciens de marine et des colonies* (Toulouse, 1985).

53. *La Vie quotidienne à Nantes au temps de la Compagnie des Indes*, Exposition "1717–1967" (Nantes, 1967); *Lorient et la mer: Trois cents ans d'histoire, 1666–1966*, Catalogue de l'Exposition (Lorient, 1966); R. Picard, J.-P. Kernéis, and V. Bruneau, *Les Compagnies des Indes* (Grenoble,1966); Philippe Haudrère, *La Compagnie française des Indes au XVIIIe siècle* (Paris: Librairie de l'Inde, 1989), 4 vols. Jean Boudriot, *Compagnie des Indes: Vaisseaux, hommes, voyages, commerces* (Paris, 1983). Claude Nieres et al., *Histoire de Lorient* (Toulouse, 1988).

54. Yves Le Gallo et al., *Histoire de Brest* (Toulouse, 1976); Maurice Agulhon et al., *Histoire de Toulon* (Toulouse, 1980); Philippe Henwood, *Les Bagnards de Brest* (Rennes, 1986); André Zysberg, *Les Galériens, 1680–1748* (Paris, 1987); anon., *Le Château de Brest*, copy (Brest, 1976); A. Boulaire, *Brest et la marine royale de 1660 à 1790* (thesis, Université Paris IV, 1988).

55. Michel Mollat and Françoise Toutée, "Le *Livre des Faiz de la Marine et Navigaiges* d'Antoine de Conflans (ca. 1516–1520)," *Actes du 107e Congrès national des Sociétés savantes*, Colloquy on Maritime History (Brest, 1982; Paris, 1984), 9–44.

56. Braudel, *Identité de la France*, 1:317.

57. Étienne Taillemite, *Dictionnaire des marins français* (Paris, 1982), s.v. "Borda," "Jal." On Jal refer to his *Souvenirs d'un homme de lettres (1795–1873)* (Paris, 1877), 127–30.

58. Pierre Sizaire, "Croquis oubliés du Vieux Borda, " *La Revue maritime* (1975): 1128ff.; Coindreau, *L'Argot Baille*.

59. Jacques Captier, *Étude économique et sociale sur l'Inscription maritime* (thesis, Paris, 1907); Florian Cordon, *Les Invalides de la marine: Une institution sociale de Louis XIV; Son histoire de Colbert à nos jours* (Paris, 1950); Adrien Carré, *Origines et histoire des invalides de la marine* (Paris, 1975); Marc Perrichet, "L'Administration des classes de la marine et ses archives dans les ports bretons," *Revue d'histoire économique et sociale* 37 (1959): 89–112; Philippe Henwood, *La Bretagne maritime aux XVIIe et XVIIIe siècles, Administration et Archives*, in *Mémoires de la Société d'Histoire et d'archéologie de Bretagne* 66 (1987): 65–113 (with bibliography); Alain Cabantous, "Les Populations maritimes de la mer du Nord et de la Manche orientale, vers 1680–1793: Essai d'histoire sociale comparative" (thesis, University of Lille III, 1987), 1:259ff, 3:776–77. For the overall view, Jacques Godechot, "La France et les problèmes de l'Atlantique à la veille de la Révolution, " *Revue du nord* 36 (Mélanges Louis Jacob), (1954): 231–44.

60. Coindreau, *L'Argot Baille;* Admiral Roger Vercken, *Marine et bons usages* (Brest, 1986).

61. "Instruction sur le cérémonial," *Bulletin des Officiers de Marine (B.O.M.)*, no. 143, February 27, 1986. On the flags of the navy see Pierre Charrié, *Drapeaux et étendards du Roi* (Paris, 1990).

62. Nora, *Les Lieux de mémoire*, vol. 2, book 1, xx.

63. One example is discussed by F. Attoma, "Le Rite du lancement des navires," *Bulletin technique du Bureau Veritas* (September 1981): 417–25.

64. Le Gallo et al., *Histoire de Brest* 137–38.

65. Marie-Joseph Jacquiot, *Médailles et jetons de Louis XIV d'après le manuscrit de Londres (Add. Mss. 31 908)* (Paris, 1968), 3:606–11, 684–92; Alfred Guichon de Granpont, *Notice sur les jetons de la marine et des galères* (Paris, 1854); Le Gallo et al., *Histoire de Brest*, 122, 130; Agulhon et al., *Histoire de Toulon*, 64; Anne-Marie Lecoq, "The Symbolism of the State," trans. Mary Trouille, in *Rethinking France: Les Lieux de Mémoire*, under the direction of Pierre Nora, vol. 1: *The State* (Chicago: University of Chicago Press, 2001), 217–67.

66. "Latitudes Sud" exhibition, Musée de la Poste, February 19, 1988.

67. Augustin Jal, *Glossaire nautique* (Paris, 1848); revised edition in process to be published under the title *Nouveau glossaire nautique de Jal* (Paris, since 1970), 5 fascicles published (A–G).

68. The *Rôles d'Oléron* is the subject of an exhaustive study by John W. Shepherd as a thesis, in French, done at the University of Poitiers (forthcoming).

69. Philippe Masson, *Sépulcres flottants: Les prisonniers français en Angleterre sous l'Empire* (Rennes, 1987); A. Cabantous, "Les Populations maritimes," 1:269ff., 3:780–85; R. M. J. Guillemin, "Les Pontons de Cadix, " *La Revue maritime* (1978): 1523ff.

70. Taillemite, *Histoire ignorée*, 70.

71. *La Mer au siècle des Encyclopédies;* Michel Vergé Franceschi, *Les Officiers généraux de la marine royale, 1715–1774* (Paris: Librairie de l'Inde, 1990); Marine Acerra and Jean Meyer, *Marines et révolution* (Rennes, 1988).

72. Jacques Bernard, *Navires et gens de mer à Bordeaux, vers 1400–vers 1550* (Paris, 1968), 1:93, 94, 433, 434.

73. Kerhervé, 1:336; Bernard, *Navires et gens de mer;* Édouard Baratier and Félix Reynaud, *Histoire du commerce de Marseille*, vol. 2 (Paris, 1970), 33ff.

74. René Gast, J.-P. Dumontier, et al., *Des phares et des hommes* (Paris, 1985).

75. Michelet, *La Mer*, 87–97.

76. René Faille, "Les Phares et la signalisation au XVIIe siècle," *Dix-septième siècle (La mer et la marine en France au XVIIe siècle)* 86–87 (1970): 39–82; Faille, *Les Trois plus anciens phares de France: Cordouan, les Baleines, Chassiron* (La Rochelle, 1974); Philippe Lafon, *Guide historique des phares de Chassiron* (La Rochelle, 1987).

77. Gast, J.-P. Dumontier, et al., *Des phares et des hommes*, 116.

78. Péron, 359–69.

79. A map of this kind was drawn in 1865, similar to the English "Wreck Charts." It was part of the 1987 exposition at Brest featuring the objects found on the wreck of the *Columbian*, which was wrecked at Molène in 1865. See also P. Lizé, *Répertoire des naufrages*, preface by É. Taillemite (Dreux, 1977).

80. Jacques Messiaen, *Pilotes maritimes*, collected texts (Dunkirk, 1984). This work includes the entire coastline of France except for Collioure, Marseille, and Toulon.

81. Kerhervé, 2:682–86.

82. Péron, 132–48.

83. J. Pillet, *Le Sauvetage en mer au temps des avirons et de la voile* (Douarnenez, 1986).

84. Léon Pannier, ed., *Le Débat des hérauts d'armes de France et d'Angleterre* (Paris, 1877), para. 68ff.

85. Bibliothèque nationale, ms. fr. 8024.

CHAPTER 3

THE FOREST

ANDRÉE CORVOL

In every generation a great divergence emerges between the actual reality of the forest and its imagined reality. The forest constitutes cultivated space, subject to precise rules set by the proprietor or by the public authorities. Despite these constraints, a vision persists of turning our remaining wild areas into wooded space. Growing urbanization even accentuates this phenomenon. This is not to say that the peasants of old knew this milieu intimately. If some aspects of trees and woods were familiar to them, they were still ignorant of much of the rest. Their ignorance has endured right down to the present. Nonetheless, the true peasants, those raised in contact with trees, have a knowledge infinitely more vast in this matter than do city dwellers.

The attitude toward cutting trees reflects this difference. The person from the city, who sees trees only while strolling through the woods, points to the upheaval caused by bringing down a tree. The person from the fields, who represents permanence, knows that this is nothing more than the long cycle of the forest. Cutting a tree for him is a necessary stage of renewal. In the eyes of the passer-by it seems like inconceivable havoc. Points in time for the cities and for the countryside do not coincide. The sight of trees evokes memories that are thus not alike.

The rural exodus has thinned the ranks of those who hold views illuminated by the experience of generations. Such views predominate for the person who is conditioned by contemporary existence. In response to the attacks inflicted on a forest landscape postulated to be immutable,

Figure 3.1
"What Do You Think of the Universal Soul, My Lord the Oak?" Engraving by Théophile Schuler for Émile Erckmann and Alexandre, *La Maison forestière* (Paris: J. Hetzel and A. LaCroix, 1866). The tree has seen generations of men pass and seems to bear the weight of the world.

the new "consumers" of this space have raised their voices. The feeling is to keep the expanses intact, clear of human activity. The fear of such people is that they will see tree populations disappear that once filled ancestral needs and now help overcome the trauma of modern life. This is what motivates the waves of ecologists and, in a more general way, every friend of the forest.

Threatened nature, they insist, finds refuge only in the depth of the woods. Nature was once open to everyone. It is fitting now to protect it from everyone. Is there any need to recall that never has the forest been so threatened as today? True, forested areas do comprise in fact 13.7 million hectares—25 percent of France!—not to mention the one to two million hectares of man-made forest groves, clusters of trees, and trees arranged in rows: more than 40 percent of the forest in the European Union and 0.3 percent of the world's forests, 1.6 billion cubic meters in volume.

The good health of the forest will not keep it from the deadly fate that lies in wait for nature as a whole. Such a comparison reveals nothing surprising. It has been happening for a long time, though no one can date its origins, and no one has followed its development. He who maintains it will not harvest its fruits. He who attempts an experiment will not see the results. Because the forest is outside the norms of time, it seems to be the land of freedom. This fact alone allows it to assume certain symbolic functions that will haunt memory long after their disappearance.

THE WEIGHT OF MYTH

After playing around "in the beautiful woods close by the farm" of that name, Baby Bear finds Goldilocks "sleeping so peacefully as if she were asleep in a fine bed."[1] After believing he has seen Uglyane, Prince Hjalmar comes upon Maleine, terrified by "this forest darker than the night."[2] The one is a child, the other a young woman—both charming. Baby Bear and Hjalmar are dazzled by their charm, as if caught in a spell. Words sometimes retain an innocence denied to them by what people know. Here the thick forest where charms dominate protects youth and purity.

But the shade of the great trees also announces imminent dangers and horrible punishments. At the edge of the forest the Big Bad Wolf lies in wait for carefree Little Red Riding Hood. In the midst of the tall trees Tom Thumb and his brothers become lost, their precautions having made them too confident. In the forest mistakes are not forgiven. It is the place of punishment. The hunter brings poor Snow White there to please her rival. As for the ungrateful Blondine, she must remain "three months before leaving the forest" to expiate her mistake and give life back to her companions. These stories, which never cease to nourish dreams, bequeath to the forest an ambiguous image indeed, turning it into both a refuge for pure souls and a menace for those daring to venture into it.

The Path through the Woods

It matters little that these stories are lost in the mists of time, that they are altered as they are transmitted, and that they have furnished material to more than one writer, from Charles Perrault to Michel Tournier, not to mention the Countess Sophie de Ségur, Gustave Flaubert, and Maurice Maeterlinck. The primordial element—the forest—finds a central place in every tale; without its presence the narration could not begin.[3] The hero clears a path, jumps over a chasm, and reflects, sitting on a rock: the curtain pulled back, the plank crossed, the boundary marked—beyond these limits lies the sylvan glade. In crossing over into it he leaves behind the open fields and with that the land of the peasants, the common people of the ancient world.

Thus, through a physical displacement, rationality fades away before the marvelous set like an extravaganza in a vast theater. On this stage, however, no distinction is made between stage left and stage right. The actor turns his back to the public. He plays his role only if he forgets the footlights so that he may enter the dark zones behind the flies. It is a delicate exploration, for it is filled with pitfalls. Witches and wizards, enchanters and spirits, hermits and ogres all speak to him and help or reject him. They become the heroes. Each one, taken individually, is no more than a mask that nature likes to assume to hide its true face. Taken together, they point to what modern language has baptized "environment." Reflecting a fundamental change, the old notion, dressed up in new attitudes, has assumed an anthropomorphic turn that it did not formerly have. The man of the twentieth century wants to modify what surrounds him—restore a site, utilize resources—all for his happiness. As for the hero of the tale, he does not have this ability. He enters into contact with those powers that are over him only in spite of himself and always for someone else—his father or his beloved, it makes no difference in the circumstances. These natural forces are going to fashion him, educate him, and, in short, give him the ability to confront life. He is quite incapable of imposing his desires on them. He is the one who has to learn everything about this strange universe where triumph belongs to the plant kingdom.

The narrative follows the ways of the fantastic, and the changes in plot only reflect rituals buried in the collective unconscious, ready to be reborn as soon as the political situation is right. The history of France is rich in such resurgences. One need only recall the conspiracies of the

Counterrevolution, the anti-Bonapartist societies under Napoleon III, and the meetings of the woodcutters on the eve of the great strikes of 1891–92. It is always in the forest where conspirators seek a secluded and therefore discreet place where one can hear the enemy coming. No questioning or hostile look will bother them. What better terrain than the underbrush to guarantee the safety of everyone? The twig that snaps under the steps of the untimely guest betrays the intrusion. The branches that close in behind disorient him. Yes, the forest protects the mysteries that are celebrated there, be they political or religious. People have always preferred the verdant forest as the place for ceremonies at which an initiate accedes to precious knowledge. The participants are loath to reveal their identities: their hidden goals make them suspect to the authorities. Their projects, once unveiled, would cause much inconvenience. To work with no interruption, they have to know the art of camouflage, especially if the prince and society warn against secret meetings. To divulge the words and gestures—is that not to vulgarize them? The ceremony then loses its prestige and, worse yet, its power. The fairy tale bears the imprint of such concerns and fears. The heart of the narrative eludes those who are not in the know. Only the hero rushes into the forest. There the tragic thread is formed from which his destiny is woven.

The Mystery Forest

The path leads deep into the woods, a theater of verdure seen from afar as a haven of peace. Little Red Riding Hood skips gaily along, her mother suffering for having described the road for her only too well. As for Hansel and Gretel, they make a second mistake when "toward midday they see a beautiful bird, white as snow and singing so wonderfully that they stop to listen to it. . . . They follow it right to a little house where it is sitting on the roof," the cottage of the gingerbread lady. They run to it, tortured by hunger.[4] Donkey Skin for her part aspires to nothing more than rest after a very long walk:

> She went thus quite far, quite far, and still farther.
> Finally she arrived at a small cottage
> Where the farmer's wife needed
> A scullery maid whose skill
> Went to knowing how to wash an apron.[5]

Having reached the strategic point, the hero begins a long conversation with the forest. No one will drop in to trouble their talk, not that there is anyone who would dream of doing that even on a whim or out of necessity. The discussion, however, comes to naught. The prince in "Donkey Skin" several times comes close to the secret but has no inkling about the connection between the miserable servant girl and the radiant beauty glimpsed in the charcoal burner's cabin. The peasants want to slay the wolf, killer of children, but they do not think that his latest victim is still alive. The prince will find Beauty only in the father's castle where the ring is being assayed. The villagers will not flock to the abode of the Great Mother except under the influence of voices that, as various accounts have it, rise up from the chimney or come down from the trees. Only heroes take the initiative. That is the power they have that lets them escape the drama.

A jolt of courage, and all existence is changed. Others must not whisper guidance in the ears of the hero lest his decision to act not be meritorious. The character has to survive deprived of the warmth of his fellow man. Neither amusement nor consolation is provided for him. The woods extend as far as the eye can see. He plunges into them without the assurance of reaching the golden day. The sister in "The Six Swans" never wavers in her decision.[6] She "begins to walk straight into the forest. She continues thus the whole night and the whole day until fatigue prevents her from going any farther." Only after taking the measure of his forces does the hero reach his goal.

The mythic forest that he discovers defies description. The trees, their age, species, shape, or height—none of this gives the forest any material character. Truly, to make it concrete would remove its aura. It therefore appears as an incommensurable element: man must know his own limits, not those of nature. Somber, obscure, vast, infinite, immense—such are the fitting terms for a forest. They would also suit the earth, sea, and sky. One's immersion in the forest is total. Uniformity of trunks, thickness of the foliage—the guideposts have been eliminated, the sun no longer penetrates. On the magic road the initiate progresses, traversing spaces where time eludes man's clock. He forgets the reality of the hours that glide by. He travels leagues and covers places without encountering a living soul. He is not to be distracted. He is not to be pushed. The quest for self demands that the individual schedule his time and that he master the fleeting character of thought. The forest thus becomes a source of instruction: the knowledge of self, of others, and of the universe.

The Primacy of Instinct

The hero penetrates the forest—the forest of his thoughts—for the purpose of testing himself and therefore submitting to a series of ordeals that will in the end make him better. To reject the inessential and to develop the will, that is what he will have to learn in this strange, long, and complicated journey, which is above all a journey into the self. The doors of the school of life open before him. By crossing the threshold, he rids himself of the attachments that as a rule give rise to social position. The loss of his beloved, her abduction, and her sorrows—do they not show him that unhappiness strikes rich and poor alike, the wretched and the powerful? So it is in the tale of *Beauty and the Beast,* one of the many variations on the theme of Andromeda: for having offended the monster, the father has to hand over his daughter. He comes from every social category, although he is more often than not a merchant rather than a person of great renown or a man of humble origin. The heart beats under the old clothes of a day laborer the same way it does under the finery of a king. The universality of feelings turns all appearances into vanity. Neither possessions nor their absence spares suffering. Social status does not set right the human condition. One has to accept the world as it is and hope that, despite all, it will improve, a contradiction intentionally optimistic.

It is this ambivalence that turns the tale in the forest into a history of an aborted metamorphosis, aborted because the transformation does not deal with the physicality of the hero and only partially modifies his character. The caterpillar becomes a butterfly. It flies only long enough to appreciate the sensation of flight. Thus the hero's initial state has importance only until a fantastic whirlwind carries him off. The smallest detail furnished about his appearance acquires precise meaning as to moral behavior and social status. In fact, the pedagogical quality of the narrative depends on such minute detail, for, if the hero plunges into the delights of introspection, the narrative undeniably includes the audience of the narrator as well.[7] The message will be understood only as a function of scattered points of reference.

Once the edge of the forest is left behind, the hero sees that appearances are vain. In the depth of the woods he learns to his cost that they are deceptive. The forest, land of illusions, reveals for him the fragility of perceptions and forces him to assume the risks of disguise.

The sensual man. He is passionate about a maiden of whom he knows nothing or knows only that she is of humble birth. In the shade of the large trees only the sheep are her companions. To complicate the matter further, the noisome shrew and the vile hag fascinate just as much. It is up to the prince to repudiate, in either case, caste prejudices to keep the woman. The obstacle of convention is easy to overcome with the breath of love.

The important man. He is disguised as a poor wretch, in some cases deformed (humpbacked, pustules—it all depends), reduced to the level of brute or beast. These extreme disgraces severely diminish his abilities to seduce. In the forest he can fall in love with anyone, but he can make someone love him only with difficulty. It is quite nearly an impossible undertaking for him to obtain the sweetness of consent! And it is a lucky break if he does not have to claim the ultimate sacrifice from the beautiful damsel: that she assume his ugly skin, which presupposes a grand passion despite everything.

The virtues of the heart are the sole rewards. For him who has not shrunk from the hour of decision, recompense will come: The ill-favored woman is revealed as a princess; the atrocious gnome, a handsome god. Having reconciled himself to his downfall, the hero returns to his initial state. All's well that ends well? Yes, since harmony earlier in the cycle is reconstructed in the last sequence: The link between opposites is erased, and order, in one moment overturned, is reestablished. Grace and wealth walk in concert and will emerge anew. What has been gained is the equality of men battered by the hazards of life.

The Love of Others

The stay in the forest is thus akin to a bad dream. The terrors dissipate upon awakening. And still, in the course of his wanderings, the hero who believes the trees hostile meets behind each one of them other beings ready to help him if he shows himself worthy of their concern. He certainly needs that assistance, being someone whose only desire is to leave this labyrinth that seems to have been winding on for an eternity. He suffers bewilderment in the forest. It would not be a true forest if the visitor did not fear getting lost in it. When the author Évelyne Chaussin interrogated an old woman from Lézinnes (Yonne), the woman avowed that she never failed to leave her basket next to a big tree before venturing into the forest. Her dog would always find her tracks.[8] The reason is that "they will know the path someone has taken into the woods." In the forest distances, like hours, are not measured as in open country. Also, at the beginning of his adventure the hero does not know the right way. The roads are too numerous (he will exhaust himself trying to make headway) or too overgrown (he will tear himself to shreds in the entangling brambles). He needs someone to show him the way, and he makes inquiry to find someone who can assume that role. It is not easy, as the disappointments of Tom Thumb illustrate: "He saw a small light as if from a candle, but which was quite far away, beyond the forest; he came down from the tree and, when he was on the ground, he no longer saw anything. That caused him great sorrow."[9] There was good reason.

During his wanderings, he meets people who claim to be prisoners of the sylvan depths. Because they have chosen to consecrate themselves to praying in the forest or because their trade compels them to live off the forest, gold does not attract them. For the woodworkers, the wood-cutters, the stick carriers, and charcoal burners, gold exposes them to contempt and distrust. For religious hermits in the forest, gold signifies earthly temptations. All of them have their reasons for breaking with civilization. The forest represents for them a desert where they are free to assume the role of marginality. This does not imply the exercise of freedom but the comforting submission to an order that is not of man. They do not wish to explore other ways of living. So it is with the worker summoned while tying up bundles of sticks. He agrees to instruct the three brothers grieving for their sister, whom the Lord of the Shadows holds captive across the dark sea.[10] His reticence toward a problem elsewhere is strong: "There is in the forest [the dark sea] a road that is called the Road of the Crystal Palace. Perhaps it will lead to the palace of which you speak, but I have never been there." A total absence of curiosity? No, it is the feeling that he has found everything he wants and needs in the forest. Others like him have never delved into the hidden corners of the forest and still they think only of her, the forest. It is the only thing they love. The poisoned fruit of knowledge is not for them, no more than the search for a wife, a mother, or a sister. Because the forest is a woman, it fulfills all their desires. She offers them refuge from values they no longer identify as theirs.

Life cut off from society, however, does not embitter them. Never do they reject the hero when he approaches them, his strength exhausted. Never do they condemn him to wander endlessly. These hosts of the magic woods propose, to the contrary, that he rest before they send him forth on the right road. Simple is the bed, plain is the fare. A holy man does not hide this frugality from the unexpected guest: "You will have nothing less, nothing worse than what I will have. Some greens and some roots—and the bare earth for a bed."[11] It is meager indeed, but it is considerable. It is not the quantity that counts, truly, but the manner of giving and receiving. The portions are rigorously equal. And because this poor man among the poor perceives humility and gratitude in the young man, he recommends him to another hermit, an "older and wiser" man than he, the master of the winged clan.[12] And so the chain of solidarity runs through the woods. *Carbonari** and woodcutters in the

---

* EDITOR'S NOTE: "Charcoal burners," the name given to one of the secret revolutionary societies that were organized in Italy during the early nineteenth century. Guided by Christian and humanistic principles, the *carbonari* sought to overthrow Austrian domination.

Figure 3.2
Maurice Denis, *Path through the Trees* (1891). In the de-Christianized society at the end of the 19th century, only women still took the straight path to salvation. Trees eternally green, evoking coniferous trees then in full growth and spared the death that comes with autumn, shelter and guide the women.

nineteenth century will acknowledge this movement when evoking their
"brotherhood."

Living with these exceptional people enables the adolescent to complete his education. He will need it, since he is not destined to enter into
their company. The hero must take the journey to the end, that allegorical beyond, the crystal palace, the sun kingdom, or the house of glass.
The name given the place evokes time spent by innocent souls—that is,
the pure and transparent—who will be free only after Cerberus, the
dragon shooting flames, the beast with seven heads, or the colossal giant
is killed. There is always something of David in the young fighter, a distant echo of the Jewish scriptures. He alone will have to brave the supreme moment, but he will be much better equipped than before, thanks
to his encounter with the sages of the forest. They know that to return
from the land of the dead, courage and willpower are not sufficient. The
gift that transforms, for a time, the adolescent into a superman clearly
shows that these generous givers have nothing in common with ordinary
beings. Their silent arrivals and sudden disappearances, moreover,
confirm the fact. These hermits so aged that they no longer have any sign
of age, these charcoal burners so black that they no longer have a face—
are they still human? The forest is their element. They move in it like a
fish in the water and an insect in the air. Similar ease demonstrates how
precious their transmitted knowledge is. Is it not this knowledge that
reconciles man and nature?

The Transfer of Forces

The hero is indeed a man in that he is perpetually dissatisfied. He determines who he is by action, challenging—at the outset—the limits assigned to his existence: mortal, dare he not journey to the dead? His educators will not accompany him. They do no more than put him on
guard, and what they can do for him they do. Their assistance accelerates
the apprenticeship. The reckless man has to decide for himself whether
to persist in folly. "Oh dear," says the child, "how do I get through these
woods?" And he finds an old man there . . . and the old man says to him,
"To get through the woods you have to summon a crow." Which the
hero does without discussion. His mentor furnishes him not only with
advice, but also with the art of putting the powers of the air, the water,
and the earth to his own use.

Through the asceticism that the sages—his symbolic ancestors—
inculcate in the young man, everything that was once important to
him—title, fortune, pleasure (beginning with the hunt if he was noble),

his thatched cottage, his family (if he was not)—ceases for the moment
to define him. Contact with the forest has washed away the false appearances of civilization. What remains is the essential—the vigor of the
body, the agility of the spirit. Here then is the hero in his nakedness, but
he is not the Adam from before the Fall. Fear, obscurity, and hunger dog
him. He who had all becomes the most deprived of all men, and on that
point the hero of the fairy tale is different from modern heroes, although
authors have borrowed much from the mythological idea of life in the
forest. Neither the young Mowgli so dear to Rudyard Kipling nor the
bounding Tarzan from our childhood endures similar agonies. Animals
weaned them. They belong to Eden and will not stir from it. The hero
of the fairy tale, by contrast, hastens to cross it and return to his kin. In
this sense, he is more human than the products of the novelists' imagination. His mission accomplished, reconciliations are not in doubt. Eden
loses its reason for existing. Besides, this Eden, is it not the hero who created it? If he had not signed the friendship pact with the animals, how
could he have triumphed?

This pact apparently is all the more necessary to his victory given that
it runs counter to the basic actions undertaken by the hero, who may
come from either end of the social scale. Princes and woodcutters haunt
the wooded expanses, the first for having gotten too far ahead of the
game, the other for not having left the workplace before sunset. Double
sacrilege is the result: the violation of space and the violation of time,
each devolving on the natural powers. It is often this excess in pleasure
and in work that closes the jaws of the trap. The hero cannot release them
except by appeasing those powers insulted by the very arrogance of
youth. Acteon, who angers Artemis, rejoins Hubert here before his conversion. This is outside customary social restraints, and still in the realm
of the forest-desert, but under the guidance of his mentors the hero of
the fairytale, the heir of ancient mythologies and popular religious practices, renounces practices that he now finds barbarous. Perhaps this is a
pang of conscience for animal dignity.

More likely, he recognizes the animals as his brothers, brothers in
full and not brothers beneath him, now that he has lived with the ones
that have escaped his blows. It is a capital experience that makes the
language of the animals comprehensible to him. Without the capability
of communicating, is love conceivable? The hero therefore does not
dream of subduing the wild beasts. How can a dominant-dominated
relationship be imagined when the only question is that of equality
among all the creatures of God? It is a vision of paradise in which the
hermits, Saint Anthony and Saint Paul, have served as models ever since

the fourth century.[13] Each lived as a recluse in an isolated place. Each spoke with the animals. In the East, the companion par excellence was the lion. The Western adaptation to this schema saw the friends of the man recruited from among wolves, foxes, bears, and deer. The presence of the hermit in the woods even hides a refuge within a refuge, as illustrated by the life of Saint Godric, who died in 1170 in Finchale, near Durham, England. He attracted hares and rabbits fleeing the ferocity of the hunters. From the perspective of a world turned upside down, which is how everything that touches the forest is characterized, the desire for blood thus is no longer the mark of wild creatures but of impious men.

The hero of the fairy tale does not attempt to domesticate, or even to tame. Rather, he wants to serve these so-called savage animals—always this theme of inversion inseparable from the forest milieu. Little Henry announces to the wolf, the animal with the worst reputation in the peasant's bestiary, that he can go to the table: "Here, my dear sir, is the game from your forests. I cooked it as you commanded me to." The new master is not ungrateful to his kind server.[14] He sets him on his back and carries him across to the other side of a terrifying precipice. He even believes that he has not been generous enough. The payment he finds too parsimonious will be paid in full at the edge of the forest: "When you have picked the plant of life . . . mount the horse on this baton." In the forest, the trivial object can be providential—another way of expressing the reversal of values, appropriate for this setting.

This alliance between the hero and the animal permits the transfusion of specificities. One acquires capabilities he has lacked, the other the power of words. The pact gives advantage to both parties: the hero does the deed; the beast saves his life, for he knows that the one who taught him language will not kill him. Having overcome all obstacles, the adolescent demonstrates to the clan that he possesses the virtues that make him a man. Faults and failures remain in the forest. From the forest he brings back a moral treasure that his children will receive some day. The wooded space is the center of acculturation precisely because the initiation of the young plays nature against culture. The boy delivers himself in effect to a series of bloody acts culminating in blows that finish off the monster. The deed shows how his existence will be molded: hunting and war, the hunt as preparation for war. Does not the preservation of every animal demand that the male brave danger in defense of women and children? Guarding territory does not signify latent aggressiveness and gratuitous bloodshed. The men of the forest teach the hero how not to abuse his superiority. The animals of the forest make him understand that

Figure 3.3
Jean Marais in costume as the Beast in *Beauty and the Beast,* dir. Jean Cocteau (1945). The forest is a world where time is forgotten, where life is reversed, a place of spells and enchantments. Beauty stays at the castle; the Beast rediscovers his primitive instincts and rules over the inhabitants of the woods.

to bring down game for food is just but to do so for pleasure is odious. To live under the cover of the great trees is to return to instincts, certainly, but only to those that ennoble man.

The Table of Abundance

The course for women in the forest prepares them only for amorous combat. Do they not offer themselves directly to the beast who wants to have them? Doing this, these heroines fulfill their function. In every patriarchal society young women are of importance only because of their place in the strategy of the group: lands acquired, power affirmed, connections consolidated. Also, in the narratives, they are always saving some threatened parent, generally the father, by their sacrifice. The intentions of these charming characters are pure, even if their filial piety engenders risky relationships. Nevertheless, order is restored. On the wedding night, the Beast, freed from his spell, emerges from the repugnant envelope and becomes a prince of great handsomeness. Beauty, by her obedience, succeeds doubly: she receives a seductive spouse, and she offers her family a prestigious alliance.

It is worth noting that all during this liaison that is contrary to nature, which remains a secret, no work is required of her. Life in the woods appears free of all material constraints. Indeed, culinary variety and abundance figure on the menu of every fairy tale. Even when the beginnings of the repast are modest, the results are always admirable. The table surges, "magnificently served," with no need to order service. An astonishing banquet where the wishes of the dinner companions are granted before they are uttered: the table is covered with drink and food, the servers pass through the thick walls, hands lacking arms bring in each course. Nowhere is a word breathed about domestic work: lighting the fire, going for provisions, cooking the roast, taking care of the leftovers—a total absence of the drudgery that weighed heavily on the shoulders of the mistress of the house at a time when warmth came from a wood fire.

This in its own way recalls the words spoken by those living at the beginning of the twentieth century. "In the woods I was my own master. It was a beautiful life and I miss it," declared one of them. A life without obligation and without thrift, the opposite of the villager's dream. "You lived on your own. You didn't make any money," another elaborated.[15] To have everything to overflowing and no worry of the morrow, that is what defined their freedom. Villagers who worked the fields during that period remembered the shock experienced on visiting the lodgings built by the charcoal burners. One villager recounted, "I entered the hut, and I liked it very much." Another continued the point: "Oh, they were as happy as could be! They weren't cold, they didn't need fuel," which obviously they did not, "nothing at all. They were happy. . . " They certainly were, especially during times of celebration, meaning early in summer, with its long lazy evenings, and when they were paid. To an outsider, their occupation seems so pleasant: no professional hierarchy, no cares about supplies, good air, and passionate conversations. Memory for both the actors and the spectators retains only the happiness of being in the forest. To make the break and settle in is to assume the beautiful simplicity of a Robinson Crusoe leaving behind the superfluity of civilized life.

From that standpoint, why would children not love to gambol in the forest? They know the marvelous paths on which legendary heroes journey. They want to do as much, if only to show their parents that they have attained the age of independence. Adventure, that's for them. The woods then become a gigantic playground. The boulder is a toboggan; the tree is for scaling, the branches for hiding, and the hollows for disappearing into. They move about without a care, playing to the fullest. Whether the trees are deciduous, coniferous, or a mixture, whether there are different kinds of trees—oak, beech, or ash, Douglas fir, spruce, or pine—whether there are scraggly or tall trees: all this is a matter of indifference to them. Besides, they hardly know the different species, a gap that will not be filled when they reach adulthood. What matters is the totality of these elements of the forest—trees, thick and slender, tall and squat. Their specificity will be decided in their games.

The little ones reason much like their parents. For most adults the woods of today mean nothing but happy activities. It is only on reflection, and that not spontaneous, that they perceive that the woods are not just a place for pleasure. The woods also represent monetary value precisely because these trees deliver wood. Hence they must belong to someone. Harvesting trees brings on pangs of conscience, with admonitions such as, "They are cutting too many. I told them to stop!"[16] The forested space appears a delightful retreat where it is forbidden to forbid. The lively outburst of a little boy shows it when he says, "It is nice in the trees; that's because they belong to everyone." No owner! In any other place, that is not the case, and one must control one's acts, indeed, reflect on the fact that one is entering a place, formally or otherwise: Proper dress does not entitle one to be there. Nothing like that in the forest: no holding back in behavior, no holding back in words.

Perhaps the imaginary approach to the forest might yield an understanding of the infatuation with the fantastic tale, which did not fade in either the nineteenth or the twentieth century. Start with the success of the Countess of Ségur (1799–1874) with her *Nouveaux contes de fées* and the success of the Brothers Grimm (1786–1863) and their *Children's and Household Tales*. And before them, for another public to be sure, Charles Perrault's (1628–1708) *Contes de ma Mère l'Oye* (Mother Goose Stories), which were very much in vogue again during the Restoration. The apprenticeship described in the fairy tale is not exempt from fear and suffering, which only heightens interest. Little children shiver as their elders did at the same age, which proves that today's grandmothers are indeed equal to the storytellers of old. The success in the book trade of stories written down long after circulating as the spoken word cannot be explained by literary alchemy alone.

A social reality must be kept in mind. At the end of the last century, agriculture was in crisis, the rural exodus was accelerating, and scholars were hastening to collect the remnants of a dying world; Cormay (1883), Bladé (1886), Lezel (1887), Pineau (1891), Sébillot (1895), and others were collecting memories that promised great success. Looking toward the past avoided worrying about the future. Progress moved forward in spurts, the city grew, the countryside argued over memory. As for the forest, it appeared indifferent to these convulsions; it was outside of time, or at least that was the desire. The forest was affirmed as the antidote to modernity. This was as true before 1914 as it was after 1968. The same attitude was evident right after the First Empire, but in that instance it was not the basis for fixing economic dislocations: The political fits and starts that people had endured since 1789 were the only cause. In all cases, the forest was asked to provide the image of stability in periods when everything was changing.

A cult of the forest has arisen because it furnishes reference points in time for man, but—and this is precisely the point—does this cult not refer to a civilization of the tree? Today's civilization is buried under the economic and social layers of man's history. The civilization of the tree seems very distant to those who have known only running water, central heating, and that pixie we call electricity. Nevertheless, in the city as in the countryside, many signs of it are still visible. It is certainly not as remote as one might think. The memory of today thus blends the forest of dreams and the forest of reality. Nowhere can it be said that the power of the imagination will dampen the echo of what has survived.

THE HERITAGE OF A CIVILIZATION

The forest has never ceased being a universe that is at once familiar and disturbing. Familiar, for it is visited all the time: the people of France belong to, or rather were part of, this dominant cultural area in Europe until it began shrinking, although it has not vanished completely, because of the houses of stone and the coal in the earth. Disturbing, for none of the concepts and none of the methods forged and polished in the village—property, servitude, seeding, rotation of crops—completely apply. Between the world of the trees and that of the fields there exist discontinuities but also resemblances. This is, moreover, why the forest can be both a continent to be explored and a place for initiation. Every story thus has a moral that takes on weight only because the *hidden* life in the woods has validity in the *public* place. Indeed, the French have assimilated all that, from distant ancestors with long hair who occupied Gaul to our recent forefathers who exchanged the rustic smock for an urban suit. Whether it is the need to seize control of a narrow strip of land from the trees or to lament the fate of trees eaten away by acid pollution, there is always that feeling that the tree lives by a rhythm inaccessible to ordinary mortals. So man will contemplate his evolution and his struggles to master rebellious nature.

Figure 3.4
Illustration by Gustave Doré for La Fontaine, *The Forest and the Woodcutter* (1868). Under the influence of German landscape artists, the deep forest of fir trees once again gained favor. At the same time, however, the Barbizon school and its leader, Théodore Rousseau, challenged the expanded planting of conifers in the forest at Fontainebleau, undertaken to get around the difficulties of growing oak trees.

The Legacy of the Peasant

The saying "the charcoal burner is master in his own house" deserves attention, for it expresses exactly what a village dweller expects from the forest. By characterizing the forest dweller's way of life as one of total autonomy—an arguable point—the village dweller exalts it as a much-envied contrast to his own status. What the village dweller describes is in fact not so much his situation as that of his father, or at least what his father described to him.

The peasant resents community practices that curb innovation, even if as one of the underprivileged he survives thanks to collective rights. The peasant detests the seigneurial regime, synonymous with diverse stings and vexations, so much more galling if he profits from it as a well-off farmer, a farmer on the lord's domain or a tax receiver. The argument is perhaps illogical. It is no less apparent when city dwellers start feeling the weight of constraints of which the people of the woods are unaware. And even when these fetters become lighter and then lose all reality, the fantasy does not necessarily vanish. We like to think of that place where everyone organizes his day in his way and no one works with bent back because the ground is too low. There is a value judgment reflecting an attitude found throughout all society that is applied to the posture imposed by the task at hand. Writers of all kinds, starting in the mid-nineteenth century, have used the woodcutter as a symbol of protest at a time when passivity before the immutable order of fields and men is personified in the gatherer of cabbages lying in the fields.

Memory in our time registers this strong contrast. Several generations have understood the forested expanse and the cultivated field in this antinomian manner. Such a perception does not disappear even when the best pastures are overrun by brush or allowed to lie fallow to avoid agricultural surplus. France does not repudiate its agrarian past even when the smallest effort to enhance the value of the land seems to call for its counterpoint: the free disposition of virgin spaces. The patch of ground on which the farmer sweats, does he not call it the land that grows the harvest by itself? The patch of ground that the neighbor covets and that the farmer pays for with much frugality day in day out, does he not see it as an expanse to be enjoyed without spending a penny? All this is what the forest can be and, to a certain degree, has been.

The rural elders bequeathed this attitude in their genes. A true forest, in the eyes of their descendants, whether residing in town or in the country, could not be a privatized enclosure, still less a wood factory. The definition of the peasant forest is open land that is multifunctional. It thus has a varied look: different plants, hence the colors; mixed ages, hence the forms. Regularity of the stock, whatever its origin, arouses a vague repugnance. Grafting, as recently as 1945, when the National Forestry Foundation was created, has not been an acceptable procedure. People reject the foundation as a foreign body; from the hunter's point of view, it is harmful. Uniformity contrary to nature, which is used to denounce the foundation, is due to the artificiality of man-made conifer forests. Such artificiality, though disturbing, corresponds to the internal demands of contemporary silviculture, increasing the return per hectare and extracting timber and finished products. No one argues that there has not been improvement, but that bears little relationship to the traditional economy of living symbiotically with the forest.

What is astonishing is that we still feel nostalgic about the forest at a time when nothing justifies it. By unlocking remote regions, the railroad brought about a new form of speculation that does quite well without access to trees. Subsistence crops and the nourishing forest cannot be separated from each other. The alliance will last until one of the partners frees itself from the other. Was not the forest of old dedicated more to producing what agricultural exploitation required than to fabricating wood products? It is not an exaggeration to say that wood is of secondary importance when compared with other products.[17] The forest delivered kindling for the hearth, compost for the garden, forage for the cattle, and rations of sugar, fruit, and honey for people—everything that now comes from international trade. The forest used to be an annex of the farm, in fact its most precious annex, since it directly affected both building value and production potential.

Some remnants still remain of these ancient woods. They are retreating little by little, devoured by proliferating suburbs, metamorphosed into country landscapes, abandoned or taken over by owners resolutely engaged in intensive silviculture. The sole imprint of these abolished limits can best be seen in the names: for example, the extension of Montmorency Forest to the south was marked by such names as Les Brosses (brushes) near Bessancourt, Le Chêne (oak)-Boquet near Beauchamp, Les Charmilles (hedges) near Ermont, or La Belle-Rachée (stump) near Domont.[18] It is true that the elements of the rustic forest easily lead to pleasure or production, but they also can result in the forest's destruction, with vines and pavilions placed here and there as a substitute until the moment when the owner cedes the property to the developer. That does not blur the memory of the first purpose of the forest. Words remain that designate the metamorphosed spot. The forest, even when destroyed, still attracts. Nostalgia may be nothing more than that, but it still serves to sell the new housing development.

Figure 3.5
Paul Cézanne, *Mont-Sainte-Victoire Seen from the Stone Quarry of Bibemus*. A harsh panorama because the mountain is bare, no longer covered with bushes or trees. The high mountain areas are for sheep. Lower down, regions alternate between fruit trees and subsistence crops arranged in terraces.

Going to the Forest

The rustic forest offered a tangled cluster only in its center, the medieval forest with its game and tree reserve containing the most beautiful and oldest subjects. Shepherds were careful not to take the communal flock there. Often the land use charters banned them from it, and even when they did permit such intrusion, that part was too far away for the animals to return before nightfall. Axes were rarely used, for the same reasons: bringing the wood out over a great distance was difficult, and the cuttings went only to stock the master's supply. The exploitable sections of the forest were near the village, and this advantage turned into a disadvantage when it was overused. In addition, the tree populations in these sections appeared distinctly less dense and younger than those in the master's reserve.

The borders of the forest—and note how many hamlets are called Les Bordes, Les Bordières, and La Borderie [*bord* = edge, bank, side]—served as a space for all kinds of work. Men and animals moved in and out daily, which suggests both activities to thin the woods and some not-inconsequential damage that added to the destruction. Everything that could be retrieved was done without harming the growth of the forest. Dry twigs served for kindling; shoots coming up from the forest floor became solid young trees. Ferns and briars were likewise recycled. With all that there was no need for dry logs for fires or strands of hemp for rope. Feathers would be sold as down at the market. The regular clearing of

Figure 3.6
Georges Braque, *L'Estaque* (1906). The encroachment of houses on Estaque Mountain above Marseille is portrayed here at the beginning of the 20th century. This zone would soon become a suburb, and the surrounding areas, abandoned by agriculture, would return to forest. The private and communal forests are located outside the urban area and, accordingly, visited too much not to be prey to fires.

the undergrowth consumed hours of work. But this task took place only during the dead of winter, and it brought substantial savings.

All available energy went into the production of wheat. Cereal cultivation thus required all available land; plants that could be used as forage did not become a subject for discussion until the second half of the nineteenth century. To set aside parcels of land to feed cattle was for a long time considered a horrible waste. When the population grew, there was only one way to reestablish the equilibrium between the volume of grain harvested and the mouths to be fed: increase the area sown with corn, at the expense of the forested spaces. That was the case in the thirteenth century, and it began again in the first part of the sixteenth. In the last third of the eighteenth century, this good old habit sprang up yet again—the impulse stopped with the July Monarchy—although this time it was the heaths and stunted trees that bore the cost. Les Essarts, Les Essartis, Essert [*essarter* = clear off], Le Brûlis [*brûler* = burn, scorch], and l'Effrechis [*friche* = fallow land], are all names that retain the memory of stubborn men hacking their way into the forest and clearing away the trees.

In conditions of extreme precariousness—any growth in density compromises the system—the animals were forced to seek their allowance of food outside seeded areas. Only the hedges along the roadside, the abandoned stubble, and the woods were left to them. They had to have grass so that they did not destroy the bark or new growth. Grass would not

grow if vegetation grew uncontrolled, suffocating the land; hence the obligation to purge the deadwood, but no more than that if the clearing was
insufficient for it; hence the necessity of spacing the trees to let in the rays
of the sun. The yield in forage for a forest producing six hundred kilograms
a hectare when the trees are not five years old falls to a tenth of that twenty
years later—those are numbers that give pause for reflection. Cutting trees
at close intervals, five years or so, was as essential as clearings conducted
with brutality. There was no other way to assure food for animals. The forest burned less, and the animals ate better. There is no reason for surprise
that in the district of Fontenoy-le-Château (Meurthe-et-Moselle) brush-
wood not yet fifteen years old occupies 46 percent of the forested area.[19] It
is not ignorance but realistic to act in this way.

The forest thus formed bears only a distant relationship to the forest-
desert of the fairy tale. The course of its development assumes constant
reshaping: demand multiplies the number of shops or businesses that can
transform its products into shoes, shingles, pikes, poles, and so on. Empty
spaces profit from the least improvement. The forest is a place of passage,
not of gathering. Women seek medicinal herbs and collect wood. Men
busy themselves with cutting trees and with ceremonies. Boys help with
transport. Girls and old people watch the cattle and sheep. Sounds of the
axe and shouts: one is always running across people who live there. Officials know the name of every woodcutter, and everyone knows everybody. No criminal would think of going underground there, for if there
were any threat or collusion, tongues would quickly wag and denunciation would come quickly. Violence, more often verbal than physical, de-
ters talkative neighbors and nosy forest dwellers.

For this reason the forest milieu, so familiar to everyone as a welcoming refuge and shelter—as in the fairy tales—does not enjoy the
reputation one would expect. The claim is barely made. It is deplored as
a hostile environment. The local people mistrust the stranger emerging
from the woods and wind up declaring the place to be stifling and un-
wholesome. It is a godsend or an accursed place. This only appears to be
a paradox. Such expressions are not intended for the same parts of the
forest. The worries of the peasants are understandable. The massive forested areas of those days, where timber removal has left trails that are
hardly visible, conceal dense thickets in their depths. People flee there to
hide because of some misdeed. These outlaws do not resemble Robin
Hood and other men of legend, righters of wrongs whose existence gives
back hope to people skeptical about judicial impartiality. In the enclosure
of the forest these men reject social norms: they decline identity, earn
their meager fare, and raise their offspring. Time spent in the forest does
indeed represent an escape. Taboos disappear, which means that every

encounter with these solitary individuals represents a risk. They live wretchedly from hunting and theft, which caution requires them to commit far from their hiding place, just as foxes do.

During the reign of Louis XIV, carriages did not dare enter the Forest of Bondy, with its sinister memories, except under escort. This background makes clear why the Ordinance of 1669 on waters and forests devoted five articles of Title XXVII to the "useless ones" and the "vagabonds," enjoining them to leave the forest without delay. Otherwise they would taste the iron collar or prison; with a second offense they would see the inside of His Majesty's prison galleys in Toulon. The guards, noticeable with their special royal shoulder strap, could not fulfill their mission and deal with the maraudings until the king authorized them to have "pistols both for the preservation of our woods and for the safety of their persons." In every period when the central authority was in retreat, brigandage returned, with professional bandits joining with political dissidents in the imagination of town dwellers. Such people were not, however, the chief victims. Under the Directory and right up to the Restoration, it was not safe for peddlers and merchants returning from the fairs to travel through the forest at night. The perpetrators were not always trappers. With the First Empire, brigandage tended to recede, thanks to patrols by the gendarmes in search of deserters. It was totally eliminated with the highway program established by the Law of March 25, 1860. In our time, forests seem more peaceful than city sidewalks. And yet city dwellers revive the fantasies and fears of our peasant ancestors in fairy tales and cast them into their imagination, come Sunday. That is the day, never a weekday, that they go to the woods. The solitude is oppressive, and bad encounters are dreaded. Therein lies a contradiction that is resolved only by a tale of marvels. With a story, solitude proves to be beneficent and the encounters fruitful.

The War over Fire

Townspeople like to evoke brigandage, for it attracts the sympathy of the authorities, who might then lighten the tax burden. A closer look, however, reveals that such attacks were very much the exception. Judicial documents show that in those instances where the victims allege an attack, they are in fact describing a fistfight caused by two or three persons who have been banished by the community. The exaggerated comments leave no doubt. Their veracity is even arguable. For example, in October 1758, when the inhabitants of Varzy (Nièvre) reported that prowlers, wild after an evening of debauchery, had held them for ransom and departed after burning thirty-six houses and barns, it was a travesty of the facts. In reality, the attackers were a crowd of people coming from the nearby hamlets of Les Crisenons and Oudan who only wanted to loot the piles of wood.[20] The *échevins* of Varzy had forbidden these people from taking wood out of the adjacent forest that belonged to the bishop of Auxerre, citing the charter that set rights and fees. Was not the charter granted when the town had no satellite communities? An unacceptable situation for those who had left the town—hence the frequent clashes between, in this parish, the people of the center and those of the periphery. The incident underscores the capital role that the forest played in communal life. The forest was the purveyor of life-giving fire, and its stability was maintained through the *affouage*—the right to take wood annually from the communal forest.

To be sure, it was not uncommon to find mention of deadly brawls in these daily conflicts. Tensions were particularly high between local inhabitants and seasonal workers living in the woods who had been hired by merchants to produce and transport diverse goods to local markets or to the regional capital. Export necessarily meant reducing the local share. Preventing these products from leaving ensured domestic supply, and the calls to resist were frequent. But the traders rarely appeared during the sorting-out of these operational matters; they let their agents take responsibility for getting the work done. The locals vented their anger on the workers who were there day in and day out, and they in turn took whatever was at hand to defend themselves—axes, peaveys, pruning hooks—tools that became lethal weapons.

Charcoal burners and muleteers—the two are often confused—were the objects of opprobrium. Scorn and hatred summed up the various names used to welcome them on their arrival in town. They were little liked, denigrated as those "black men" or subject to imprecations of banditry in the local dialects (*tourloupes, arruchos*). For a thousand reasons: a dirty face, half hidden by the broad-brimmed leather hat that protected them from soot; their indifference to holidays, including the Lord's day, or to the night, for the task of maintaining a low fire could not be interrupted like halting a plow in a field. Their way of living was held against them, and they were resented for earning more than woodcutters, who were hired on the spot. In addition, they came from somewhere else, coming down from the upper Bourbonnais on their way to the Nivernais, moving from the Basque country to the peaks of the Couserans. Every stranger was an undesirable. A xenophobic reflex? Certainly, but not altogether. They earned reputations as braggarts, spendthrifts, and skirt chasers and left behind bad memories that did not fade. The traces of their activity were inscribed in the ground and lasted well after the craft lost all relevance.

Figure 3.7
Biringuccio, *Pyrotechnics* (1572). The technique for stacking wood to make charcoal has changed little: piling the wood in a spiral, setting up an internal chimney, covering the mound with earth, and setting the fire at the top.

Figure 3.8
The "charcoal place," an area cleared by the charcoal burners and used whenever they wanted to set up stacks of log. An area was cleared far enough from the forest cover to prevent sparks from setting the trees on fire.

True, between 1940 and 1945, the charcoal burners did reappear. They used sheet-metal ovens that could be dismantled; some rusted remains still lie scattered in the underbrush. Their ancestors are the ones who are remembered. They frightened children. They lived in the woods. They left their mark, the sites where they erected their stacks of wood. Their work started by clearing out a round area, which they made completely level. These sites, which are easily identified, were used again and again. The wood tar flowing out during the slow carbonization of the logs, known as the *charbonette,* did not allow normal plant growth to resume for long periods. These clearings are even easier to discern when the terrain is uneven. The charcoal burners did their work, then, not so much in an area already cut, but by the roads or on the ledge of a hillside. This created a vast workshop. On the road from Arleuf (Nièvre) to Haut-Folin, one of them can be spotted at Les Montarnus in a place called, naturally, La Place-au-Charbon.

Once the *charbonette* was laid, the worker—with assistance from the women and children—stacked branches around it so that in the end it formed a round stack of about fifteen cubic meters, with the *charbonette* inside in nearly vertical layers, one on top of another. At the center of the stack an opening was left to act as a chimney to draw air. After the stack was built, the worker covered it with moss and pieces of sod and then smoothed it over with damp earth, using a shovel. Once the fire was going in the chimney, the amount of air had to be regulated so that a very slow and very even combustion was obtained. To achieve this the worker did three things: he limited the air intake at ground level, sealed up every opening that might appear in this earthen dome, and made the chimney opening as small as possible. It is not too much to say that his attention was unremitting.

Combustion, varying with atmospheric conditions, took three to six days. Then the worker plugged up every opening to smother the fire. After the stack cooled, he opened it up, separating out the charcoal and putting it into huge sacks that weighed about fifty kilograms when full. It was common for a charcoal burner, with a helper, to have five stacks going at one time, either being set up, in operation, or cooling down. The process was visible from a distance: in the woods, so goes the proverb, "there is no smoke without fire." This technique requires a skill that few have today. The foundations of these structures themselves recall a way of life, a method of work, and the importance of this fuel for the city and the factory until coal ended its monopoly. That was yesterday.

Not until the 1840s did coal begin to rival wood and charcoal. Certainly, the way was prepared with lime kilns, tile factories, distilleries, and breweries, but the situation was not yet settled for steel forges. Only factories well situated with respect to the waterways could receive coal at a good price, but that in itself was not enough to induce them to convert. Without the accompanying technology, the quality of the finished product proved unsatisfactory. Coal aroused great repugnance in the home. A survey conducted in Toulouse reported, "One part of the population had used coal but abandoned it because the fuel gave off a disagreeable odor or because they could not use it to cook food." Need one point out that today a wood grill is an asset for any restaurant? Wood as fuel in its two forms thus kept its supremacy well into the nineteenth century.

Prices, which had continued to rise, soared in the last third of the eighteenth century, and the revolutionary troubles did little to calm the fever. Anything that affects the production of metal has strategic importance in times of peace; so, too, of course, in times of war. Still, sacrificing the needs of the city to the demands of Mars—the god of war—has never been possible. A shortage of wood was at least as serious in the city as that of grain, if only because it halted the baking of bread. In these circumstances, can it ever be imagined that the masters of so essential a resource of energy would not draw the maximum from it? This reasoning holds as true for the State, the heir to the monarchy and its possessions and the owner of the national forests, as it does for the large private landowners, be they aristocratic or bourgeois. The search for profit implies the extension of peasant practices favorable to long-term leases, which are the only means to curb excessive and unforeseen increases.

The villagers groaned under the same changes. They could mistreat the day workers whose intensive work produced standardized wood. They could do nothing against the triumph of the market. Their complaints, in vain, added to the anti-industrialist current developing in France in the second half of the eighteenth century, which was destined to have multiple resurgences in the years following. If they no longer had the choice of buying the wood they used to warm themselves, the popular expression is appropriate here: let them find cheaper substitutes! All across the countryside that was the question, and it found an echo in the revolutionary register of grievances that noted in one place the use of peat, in another cow dung. Judging by the registers, the fight for control of fire opposed the village to the factory, both declared enemies of the countryside.

Sharing the Fuel

Fuel consumption by urban areas and the metalworking industry ultimately did come to the attention of the authorities. Although both competed for that attention, neither seemed assured of victory. For a long time, only the needs of the town retained the attention of the authorities, which very much handicapped the cause of the metalworkers. The reason was that scarcity and cost of wood was as serious a factor in riots as was a wheat shortage. The first denunciation of the misdeeds of the metalworkers dates from the Ordinance of May 18, 1543, which cited "the great destruction and depopulation that has occurred in the woods and forests of our kingdom to maintain and supply the great number of iron forges situated near the said forests." Up to 1552, setting up a forge was prohibited in the royal forests. The pattern that held sway in the minds of the social elites—and it was a prejudice to which popular opinion would hold on tenaciously—can be summed up as follows: the forge damaged the forest that was so essential to the town. Further, there is no lack today of amateur ecologists persuaded that this applies to industry in general.

. What was intended by the Ordinance of 1543—the protection of the forest or the protection of the city? The author Jean François Belhoste seems to incline to the latter. This law claimed to be general. In fact, it continued certain specific measures, most dating back before the sixteenth century, that prohibited fuel consumption in the city. In the Dauphiné, in 1339, all the forges in the Grésivaudan, from Bellecombe to Voreppe, were demolished to ensure a monopoly by the city of Grenoble of the forests that served them: the assertion that "a furnace to make charcoal is the ruin of wood as it destroys and exterminates the forests" clearly reflected the authorities' position.[21]

In fact, while the authorities were taking steps to prevent the ironworks from harming the city, economics ensured that it did not. Excluding that industry did not require a legislative arsenal, contrary to what the inhabitants thought. A good example is the Beaumont mine that supplied Caen. Its location within the city's perimeter proved to be unfortunate. Although it supplied all the forges in the western part of lower Normandy as well, it closed down between 1465 and 1500. The iron drawn from its ore was too expensive to be competitive. The cost of fuel, charcoal, was the reason. The city of Caen, devastated in the Hundred Years' War and in the midst of reconstruction, was siphoning off all the wood in the vicinity, from Cinglais and Grimbosq. Demand exceeded supply, hence the price level. The metal industry in the hedgerow country [the *bocage*], had to resort to iron imported from a region further out near the Massif d'Halouze, where Caen had no influence. Charcoal was affordable there. The Beaumont mine did not reopen until 1875, when the importation of English coal effaced the memory of the area that was under the hegemony of wood as the source of energy.

The civilization of wood thus brought about alliances and divorces that its decline would undermine, particularly because it affected the health of businesses. Certain interregional solidarities, formed precisely to satisfy the demands for wood as a fuel, would for the most part survive without wood. The initiative belonged to the cities in this matter. Supply linkages that were fragile because of defective transport obliged city officials [*échevins*] to an extensive exploration of alternatives. It is in this light that the two measures enacted by the Hôtel de Ville of Paris should be understood. In 1416, it was made illegal to unload and store any merchandise intended for the capital before it arrived at the city gates. This was to avoid speculation in basic necessities. In 1520, owners of trees at a distance of less than six leagues from flowing water no longer could freely dispose of the wood. This was to prevent abusive clearing or exploitation of trees that would reduce the wood reserves for the capital. These efforts never did go out of fashion. The population of Paris, 150,000 in the time of Henri II, quadrupled between that time and the end of the ancien régime. And the growing demand for comfort ensured that people would no longer be content with a single fireplace in the common room. The other rooms were also heated in the second part of the eighteenth century.

From the 1720s on, the city authorities made every attempt to ensure deliveries of wood for heating that came from the south, including the forest at Orléans, from Burgundy with its branches in the Nivernais and Morvan, and through exploitation of areas well to the east on the plateau of Champagne (Argonne, Barrois, Perthois), not to mention incursions into the forests of the Eure and the Loire Valley. The municipalities in other regions behaved in similar fashion. For all the cities, energy consumption became more and more eclectic. At the beginning of the eighteenth century, people primarily burned wood that was produced in groves that were managed and aged about twenty-five years. One century later, they were using charcoal as well as smaller pieces of wood, chunks rejected for other purposes, and whitewood.[22] This evolution erased the differences separating the demands of the city from the demands of the iron industry. The forge accepted timber aged about fifteen to eighteen years.

Can one then say that the competition between these two consumers of the forest was heating up? To be sure, on more than one occasion the desire to shy away from such competition manifests itself. The archives of Meurthe-et-Moselle show this conflict gnawing away in 1787 between Metz and the forge at Moyeuvre. The city gained a point when authorized to divert for its own use the saplings originally intended for the forge by virtue of the right of *affouage*. Nancy in 1838 did the same in order to remove the threat that the forge at Chavigny posed to the community. There was no shortage of protests from the opposite side either. In 1809, it was the masters of the forges at Aubois who denounced the hunger of the capital. In 1812, the master of the forge at Arc took up the relay. And in 1820, facing a levy by Paris estimated at forty thousand cubic meters of wood, the masters of the forge at Le Rouvre decided to postpone the opening of a new blast furnace. Nevertheless, all these recriminations in the first part of the nineteenth century had the feeling of a rear-guard action.

In fact, the division of the wood harvest had already been set for at least fifty years. The observed tensions did not correspond to a permanent conflict. They were the episodic movement of two tectonic plates. Whenever there was a crisis, one of the two consumers enlarged its buying area and used abnormally high prices to encroach on that of its rival. This was not an ordinary occurrence. Most cities actually published a price list for firewood to keep merchants from manipulating the price. Fluctuations created obstacles that left no other choice but to fix the sale price. The traders retained the right to play on the cost price. Purchases could be made at a lower rate when costs of transportation were high owing to distance or difficult terrain. The limits of a city were determined at the point where the cost of cartage, barges, and other inland water transport became such that the city's merchants could offer prices lower than what the local metal industry could afford. Too far removed from its base, the metal industry needed local assistance, either reduced tariffs or improved water transport.

Each side viewed the forest as private hunting preserves. Maps were distributed beginning in the 1760s. Certain regions produced for the city, others for the forge. There were areas of friction where two systems of measure existed, when the rope to measure the wood for the urban fireplace did not have the same length as that for industry. Everywhere else there was only one system that gave clear finality to production. The difference between the two camps was de facto, as seen when metalworkers, who knew that energy represented at least two-thirds of the cost of producing the metal, moved quickly when properties seized in the Revolution were sold off. The confiscated noble lands, the *biens nationaux*, that they recovered protected their source of supply from the uncertainties of the market. For a long time in this sector, innovations targeted the fuel economy with the result that capital tied up in the forest patrimony came to finance different ventures until the sale of coal became useful to business.

Every land rich in wood has found itself caught in the same seemingly endless situation. Heavy industry rarely, if ever, follows the dictates

Figure 3.9
Claude Caron, *Traité des bois servant à tous usages* (1676). Outside the city, a vast warehouse for wood, enclosed to prevent theft. Wood arrives at the gate by boat, by floating in logs, or by light or heavy wagon depending on the size. The wood then has to be dried and put in lots for the merchants, who will finally sell it at retail as firewood or staves.

of the metropolitan area, where economic growth favors businesses involving manual labor—textiles or construction—and later the service industry. The influence of the large city begins to fade as soon as the presence of water and ore make it possible for the metal-producing industry to form clusters, crystallizing all social and cultural life around them. The broad lines of French industrial geography took shape with this division that goes back roughly to the second third of the eighteenth century. The introduction of coal did not really alter its features. The shape and form of this industry was to change only with the gamble on oil and the building of waterfronts tied to the import of raw materials.

This is another way of saying that the twentieth century inherited in large part the legacy of industry's beginnings. Urban expansion and multi-industry growth went hand in hand in the same way, alas, as did the mono-industry and what has been termed the civilization of the blast furnace. It is forgotten that the latter was first and foremost a civilization of wood. Is there any memory still left in those locales that throughout the eighteenth century were bound to the option of producing metal because they lacked the ability to compete in the capital? This was the case for the area between Bar-sur-Aube and Bar-le-Duc as well as for the Sambre-et-Meuse Valley, which extends to the present-day Belgian border. The industrial settings of the present reflect the map imposed by the past. The memory found in the large economic regions also crosses the destiny of the French forest. Memory for the large or small cities bears in it the mark of wood, not only because it was the only known fuel but also because it was found to be the best construction material—easily shaped, relatively inexpensive, and readily adaptable for the evolution of the house.

Wood in the City

Wood is the source of energy and the material for construction. In fact, anyone who strolls through the downtowns that are still intact despite bombings, fires, reformers, and developers will confirm the second use, construction, while seeing no evidence of the first, fuel for the home—which implied in any case huge storage areas. The heaviness of wood presupposes that the city and business alike will ensure the design of the storage area or the arrangement of the buildings for taking delivery. Both cases call for specific spatial organization, both for receiving the timber and for its care and use. By the end of the eighteenth century, a Parisian required nearly a ton of wood by weight per year for heating. A blast furnace devoured at least five thousand cubic meters by volume. This enormous quantity did not pass unnoticed in the countryside.

From today's perspective, imagining the size of one of these wood warehouses is a vain exercise, unless some miracle provides a quick way of classification. It was colossal. Technological progress and new ways of handling the product have generally made its size superfluous. The warehouses have therefore been torn down. One would expect instead to find in every town a timber market, along the lines of the markets built to store and sell grain, cloth, horses, and cattle. Nothing of the sort. In Dijon at the Place de la Sainte-Chapelle, in Orléans the Martrois, in Angers the Haut-du-Pilori do nothing if not recall the spot where logs and firewood were put into piles. Those markets sold only new wood,[23] meaning that the wood, brought in by cart or wagon, had not been immersed in water. The prices reflected this. Therefore well-off people took only what they needed, in small quantities and for clearly defined uses. The five places that figure on the old maps of Paris where wood entered the city were the so-called ports: La Bûcherie, l'École, the Tournelle, the Quatre Nations, and Saint-Nicolas. Coastal shipping alone justified the name of port. In addition, the surface area was laughable: half a hectare for the Place de Grève. This exiguity made the affected merchants complain. No warehouse was more than forty-five square meters. In 1746, the place was abandoned and the merchants moved to Louvier Island, opposite the Arsenal. A freeze on land would later permit the building, on the Right Bank, of the Célestins barracks, rue de Sully, and the city's municipal services buildings near the Morland barracks, on the Quai Henri-IV, across from the southern end of the Île de la Cité.

As a general rule, the architecture of these markets, in particular the covered ones, did not resist the future when there was a shift in location as in Paris or, at the end of the nineteenth century, a total loss of interest in the place for lack of work. Its very size condemned it: it was impossible to assign it any other role. At the heart of the city, available space, rare to begin with, required total demolition. And the principle of dividing land into lots meant demolition down to the foundations. The only thing left was a vague memory associated not with the actual site but with the streets that led to it: rue de la Huchette, rue de la Tonnellerie, rue de la Bûcherie. The residents there were not all dependent on wood—far from it. Their neighbors were people in the food industry, leather artisans, and members of the university. The proportion of those who worked in wood seems to have been greater than in the outskirts. In 1563, for example, on the tax list for the rue de la Bûcherie, north side, resellers of firewood; south side, carpenters. Often they moved in only when a small office—a grain grinder, a controller of weights, auctioneers of heating wood—demanded a regular presence in the marketplace. In effect, they converted dilapidated hovels into de facto factories.

The geographic mobility of these residents also explains why no one put much effort into saving these markets. The tight quarters were not a problem when the wood merchants, like their counterparts the wheat merchants, had to sell their merchandise quickly. That was no longer conceivable after the sixteenth century, when lumber was floated in and then required months of drying, attracting a growing number of foreign traders to Paris. Transactions multiplied. With all that it was not useful to move a product that weighed so much and required so much space.

So the merchants who supplied wood to the capital looked to the periphery, outside the fortifications, in space that was mostly rural because there were few roads, but close to the waterways and the markets for horses, two factors that directly affected transport. The areas in question were, to the southeast, the Quai Saint-Bernard to the Faubourg Saint-Victor; to the northwest, the Roule in the Faubourg Saint-Honoré; to the southwest, the Gros Caillou extended from Les Invalides. In these places, surrounded by high palisades and guarded night and day—theft was frequent, fire dreaded—they were finally well off. They moved in their families, workers, and night watchmen as well as their stock. Did not every work site on the Quai Saint-Bernard comprise at least five thousand square meters, more than the entire port of La Tournelle? And labor abounded: recent arrivals first of all, the day laborers, the porters, floaters of wood—all miserably poor—who had followed the Seine and its tributaries right to Paris. And the *pensionnaires,* the people who were stuffed into poorhouses or charitable establishments—they also lived there. The seventeenth century swarmed with such people. What would they not do to improve their lives?

The decision to move out, however, isolated the merchants. It cut them off from the masses, who were quickly riled up whenever rumors of price increases were circulating. It damaged an already poor image of the location of their factories. At night, these places were called a desert; during the day, they were known as seedy areas with few regular customers—in short, a place to flee. The development into real estate came only much later, although the settlements on the east and west sides did not follow the same course: on the west side the houses of the upper bourgeoisie, and on the east side a populous arrondissement, the twelfth, always open to the immigrant tradition with its "Chinatown."

In both cases, the urban fabric reveals some large gaps well before the nineteenth century: in the 1920s, not all the land parcels on the Quai d'Orsay had been built out; in the 1950s, the project for the Panhard sites would leave a gaping hole. The transformation of what would be characterized as the "parvenus' seventh" (arrondissement)—in contrast to the seventh of the Faubourg Saint-Germain—began in the second half of the eighteenth century, thanks to the expansion of the military (Champ-de-Mars, the Dupleix barracks) and continued to the end of the nineteenth century with the construction of governmental office buildings (Economic Affairs, the meteorological administration on the Quai Branly). It was carried out, using the tested model, with Le Roule during the Haussmann period. Paris from this point of view is the exception that proves the rule for the future of the lumberyards.

Developments in the Faubourg Saint-Victor followed this rule: the lumber factories became coal dumps, then opened up to the gas industry, and ended up with hydrocarbons. The growth in energy sources continued along many different lines. The same phenomenon can be observed in Strasbourg and in Rouen, in Toulouse and Toulon with the waterways, the railroad shops, and the switchyards. Space freed up by the energy revolution was not for construction but for whatever assured the dynamism of a city or a region.

Memory in Default

The forest, inestimable gift to man, cannot be sold or confiscated, actions that mark the exercise of property. On this subject, social usage of today is much the same as economic usage in the past: city dwellers going to the forest and demanding full and total use hardly differ, at bottom, from their peasant ancestors, who understood how to extract from it whatever they wanted. Through every period there runs the idea that need establishes right. Yesterday it was fuel for the fireplace and food for cattle. Today it is aesthetic pleasure and physical fitness. The certainty that going to the woods is a normal activity has not changed.

And yet, the forest belongs to someone, whether it is an individual, a local group, or the State. The forest produces a harvest that this owner moves and sells, exploits and commercializes, though rarely in person. The protection that is at all times accorded to it, with varying degrees of success, is based on these notions of ownership of capital and possession of merchandise. These ideas seem, however, to be the exact opposite of what the forest is, perhaps because by tradition no distinction is made between it and nature: both are seen to be generous and fecund.

The House of Men

In the shadow of the trees the individual feels the inner contentment of being at home. What could be worse than expulsion? The proverbs answer: "One does not cut one's roots," "The ivy dies where it clings." Comparisons are not reasons, but there is no better way of conveying the sense of the favored relations that man and the forest have maintained. These relations have an impact on the way the forest is *seen*. The forest has also become a symbol of intimacy, comfort, and wealth. Advertising makes wide use of these themes—wood, "a living substance"; wood, "like in the old days"; wood, "the noble material"—to promote everything from cleaning wax to the charm of the rustic kitchen and the aristocratic look of a wood-paneled library. Slogans have gained possession of the memories attached to the house made of wood. *Toujours la nostalgie. . .*

Still, we ought to understand what structure is under discussion. Those structures with horizontal beams forming an interior space with coffered ceilings or set vertically with crossbeams consumed a great number of trees. Those trees have to be rectilinear and very tall. This technique, found in the Slavic model in the settlements on the edge of the taiga, has been adapted to the forest products of the mountains. It was not applicable to the specimens that the forests of western Europe have provided to the plain from time immemorial. For the Carolingian period, excavations undertaken at Douai, Fécamp, Tours, and in the northeast corner of church at Saint-Denis have uncovered structures only partly of wood. The walls are a clay-straw mixture on wicker panels.[24] Stakes provided the support for the sides and the roof structure, whence the name *maison-cage* (cage house).

The process apparently lost ground quickly. From the twelfth and thirteenth centuries, the house made of stone became more common. Some towns, of course, took pride in their ancient residences with their wood panels, happily described in the guidebooks as medieval. Would they not be described as such anyway? The most venerable of them rarely dates from the fourteenth century, so to discriminate carefully means knowing whether the method of construction corresponds to the legacy of the High Middle Ages or, on the contrary, whether it represents a revival, with all that that implies for innovation and trial-and-error.

Public opinion does not understand it that way. It wants to see the first habitat of man, first in the primitive sense, imagining those huts on stilts depicted in every elementary schoolbook—no one realizes that in some areas people went from living in caves to living in stone houses—and longing for the summer cottage in the pines. The wooden house is thus confirmed as *prior* to the stone house, *more sanitary*, a *better bargain*, and *easier* to erect. Hovering about it is the poetry of illumination by candle, dark streets traversed by the night watchman, and large family reunions before the blazing hearth. Balzac in *La Maison du Chat qui pelote* and Zola in *Le Rêve* are the romantic authors par excellence on this topic,

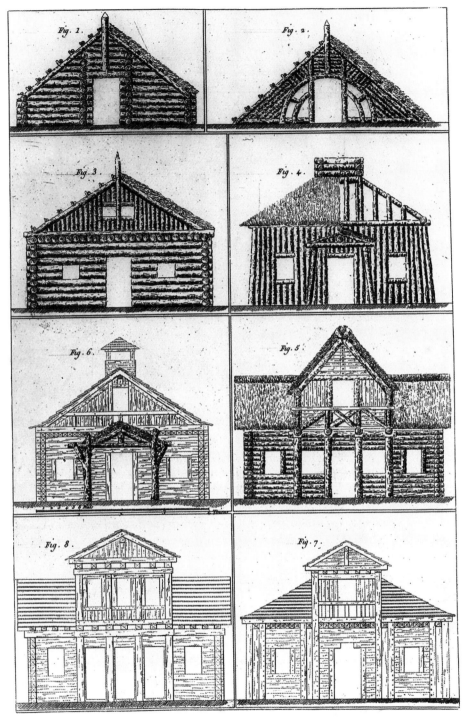

Figure 3.10
In France, where stone houses predominate, wooden houses are considered archaic, fragile, and rudimentary. The variations in structure here show that such judgments have more to do with prejudice than reality.

which is right out of the engravings from the market town of Nurem-
berg, Gustave Doré's version, along with windows resembling the bottom of a bottle, and a slate-gray décor to boot.

Nothing could be more false than this conception, according to
which the stone house, with its more sophisticated technology and
higher price, represents at once inevitable progress and the increasing
wealth of the bourgeoisie. In the eighteenth century, the wooden house
was still common, and those who placed an order to have one built did
not belong to the lower classes. They were expressing a taste that ran
counter to style, that is all. It was not a matter of a desire for economy:
working with wood was expensive and adjusting the different pieces demanded highly skilled labor and many hours of work. Contrary to what
is commonly asserted, it is stone, not wood, that lowers the bill. Stone
does not really replace wood everywhere or at the same time. Stone
never replaces wood entirely.

Similar imagery has value today only in financing the restoration of
so-called antiquities made of wood that just barely escaped the catastro-
phes that occurred in the urban milieu. Air raids blew 40 percent of the
old part of Tours to pieces. Memory here can only be refreshed using
imperfect postcards, old photographs, or flattering sketches. In Angers,
46 wooden houses remain; in Orléans, 112. They are missing something:
the fragile canopies have disappeared, leaving bare the corner holes; columns decorated with sculpted and dated ornaments have been chiseled
out for aesthetic reasons—style, once again! As for the corbels, they and
the support pillars were knocked out on the day when plans to modernize were made concrete. In many cities, the years 1730 to 1830 were not
good years for wooden houses. Today, they benefit by contrast from municipal solicitude, whereas about thirty years ago—the reversal is thus recent—their demolition for reasons of insalubrity was only a matter of
time. One has only to recall the pitiable state of the patrimony of Troyes
in the early 1970s to measure the change in attitude. What was judged an
insult to modernity finds itself suddenly invested with all the positive
values of the past.

Wood as a "living substance"? Clearly not from a physical point of
view. But it is nonetheless a living thing in peoples' imaginations. The
zeal of certain renovators testifies to that. To give the feeling of the old—
how else to express it?—means no hesitation in putting exposed beams
on every floor, carefully fitted to give the flavor of the period. But the
renovators cannot really lay claim to the distant past. Most often their efforts are limited to fitting out the "noble floor," the level above the mez-
zanine, with beams. The fact is that from the end of the seventeenth century on, most ceilings were made of a lattice covered with plaster,

The subtle harmony that this habitat offers today is cause for marvel. One can perhaps appreciate it all the better the more contemporary real estate shows such disparities in form, material, texture, and color, with a range of choices that too often turns into cacophony. This patchwork, which today lies open to criticism, was once inconceivable. The unity of the past reflected not only the limited possibilities for the materials but also the repetition in the rhythm of their use. The log served as the module for the framework of the roof, as did the plank used by masons. There was therefore a deliberate blending of measurement and merchandise that could be fabricated with corresponding quantities of wood, which held true for any wood cut the same way for industry and work.

Sawing the oak, the chestnut, and the fir tree with two-man saws shows the same approach to logs as does splitting by professional log splitters and, eventually, by others. In Champagne, for example, staves, meaning all wood split and cut up for the coopers, were sold for vine arbors.[26] This unity comprised a set number of *longailles* (pieces of wood forming the length of a barrel), *foncailles* (pieces used to make the base of the barrel), and *traversins* (pieces used to reinforce the bottom of a barrel), the quantity required to build fifty 200-liter barrels, about four cubic meters. The vine arbor basically constitutes, to use an anachronism, a standard "kit." The mechanism is identical when working with wood. The panel, in the region of the Loire Valley, has a median diameter of 0.18 meter at its two ends, from 0.22 meter and 0.32 meter, for a length of 12 meters. The house built using wood of these measurements cannot help imitating the house next to it, decorations and signs providing any differences. The panel therefore is a unit of measure and a module for construction. It exists elsewhere, but with other values that relate to other building traditions. This lasted until materials could be moved by railroad, which rendered the reference system based on wood obsolete.

Arbitrage in Question

Wood for the fireplace, wood for housing, wood for the factory, wood for shipping—how could the public authorities avoid establishing an all-powerful administration capable of supervising the populations that use and abuse wood and of directing its production? The primary objective has obviously always been to increase the volume of wood of large dimensions. If there was cause for concern, it was not because of a worldwide shortfall. In more than one region, as a matter of fact, the owners did not know what to do with fallen timber. The establishment of a forge did make a forest valuable; otherwise the owner would have been obliged to abandon all of it to the local inhabitants for their use. It even happened that those splendid logs marked for use by the navy rotted on the spot, while in the neighboring county people were complaining about the price of wood and the difficulty in obtaining it. Alas! It was impossible to think of getting the wood transferred from zones of low consumption to zones of high consumption because lack of transport was such an obstacle. The problem the authorities faced was always local.

On the eve of the Revolution, the rate of afforestation had risen to 10 percent, which is 40 percent of the current rate. The royal forests, with 925,000 hectares, occupied an area that was less than that of the ecclesiastical forests (949,000 hectares), the communal forests (1.024 million hectares), and the woods owned by individuals (3.8 million hectares). With nearly 7 million hectares of trees, the country was definitely not exposed to dearth. Did not visiting foreigners underscore their envy by saying that the France of the eighteenth century was indeed the heir of the bearded Gaul? It remained to be seen what value would be placed on the trees of the high forests, dedicated in theory to lumber production.

When peace was re-established at the beginning of Louis XIV's reign, the Administration of Waters and Forests resumed its normal administrative practices. It found that in the heart of the central plateaus, where everyday use had fallen off and was limited to the cutting of saplings, the forested areas were overgrown with old trees, some more than a hundred years old. The decision was made to get rid of them, and in the 1670s, lots from the royal domain were put on the market with the aim of finding a successful buyer to make a clean sweep. The appearance in merchant circles of important quantities of old wood during the last half of the seventeenth century lent credence to the idea that the high trees were being felled without distinction. The authorities reacted strongly, dismayed by the thought that the naval arsenals might not be supplied, because at this time they were calling for a bold naval policy. The remedy was as appalling as the malady. Their concern, far from calming down, increased. Disappointment in the natural regeneration of the high trees led to a diminution of time allowed for growth: if the reseeding could not be achieved, was it not preferable to knock down the reproductive trees, that is, the seed trees, before they lost all reproductive capacity? According to Perthuis, the reports of the grand masters of the Waters and Forests would later describe that the number of trees, 8 million in 1669, was no more than 1.6 million in 1789, signifying a density of 5 fully grown trees per hectare.

The rural areas and ecclesiastical communities bore the brunt of this modernization in the age of exploitation.[27] If there were fewer of the tall trees in the woods of the royal domain, then trees elsewhere had to be marked and well cared for to compensate. It was up to local organizations, because they were the chief owners, to bear whatever costs and inconveniences there were for growing this material. In the seventeenth century as in the eighteenth, specialists in silviculture did not doubt that the volume would increase with time. This assumption crumbled only in the second half of the nineteenth century, when the oaks at Fontainebleau that supposedly dated back to Saint Louis were closely inspected. This notion was tenaciously believed. How many oaks said to be planted in Colbert's time dated only from the Restoration? This was the case for one section of the Tronçais forest. How many lime trees were baptized "trees of liberty," planted in Year II of the Republic, even though they were actually planted, with all due solemnity, in 1848, specifically to celebrate the beginning of. . . the Second Republic!

Whatever the shortcomings of this coerced history, one has to admit that contemporaries could hardly have done without it, given the scientific data of the period. If the royal forests were entering a cycle of shortened growth, how could people compensate for the diminution of surface area for the large trees that this implied? Individual owners were indeed constrained to keep the reserved trees in their forested area, but this measure did not provide a solution: maintaining a tall-tree forest signified for them capital tied up in an unsustainable way. As for the communities, they were better positioned to support a similar freeze on assets. The demands for a change in forest management did not yet affect them: their trees were of new- or short-term growth, for heating and grazing. In return, the lack of wood created a risk in the face of financial demands. The consequence would be clear, since trees were often the single available resource for paying taxes, removing outstanding obligations, and initiating public-works projects.

The problem was thus transferred rather than resolved. Its repercussions caused much turmoil in the seventeenth century and later, and current policy on forests has not yet recovered from it.

The first consequence concerns what has been called the "forest regime," which is defined as the supervision that the Administration of Waters and Forests exercises in the public interest over the domain and communal forests, like that for repairing the dunes or reforesting the mountains.[28] That supervision contains a mute echo of measures taken at the beginning of the reign of Louis XIV. The subordinate organizations running the forests could not authorize the smallest expense without referring it to the Council of the King. The Ordinance of 1669 made the Edict of 1667 particularly restrictive. These organizations had to put one-quarter of their trees in reserve within the forest, with no hope of drawing any profit, either in cash or in kind. In 1912, in the *Statistique et atlas des fo-*

rêts, Lucien Daubrée calculated the total forested area to be 3,148,071 hectares, 38 percent of which was exploitable. At this date, 268,142 hectares were to pass under the State's control, which came to about 9 percent of what it already had. In other words, the State already controlled most of the trees. Hence the title of Gérard Buttoud's thesis, *L'État forestier.*

The second consequence dealt with the way this regime turned policy into reality. Again in 1912, the share of exploitable forest in the domain lands was 51 percent, an appreciable percentage, which was tied to the conversion of the new-growth forest into an exploitable old-growth forest that had begun at the end of the Second Empire. The sections set aside for long-term growth satisfied the demands of the Administration of Waters and Forests, which added new-growth forests next to the other when price levels permitted. By setting aside several trees of large diameter for two or more cycles, hardly more in the nineteenth century, forest officials displayed foresight. When the price of firewood fell under pressure from coal, the wood buyers became rare. Making that wood available for carpentry was a better use, even wood that split easily. Some of these trees can still be seen at the edge of the communal woods, spared by the woodcutters as they marked trees for sorting.

The third and final consequence concerned the image that these people of the Waters and Forests administration left. That they took advantage of wood taken illegally from the reserve areas to regulate surpluses, that is, new-growth wood intended for the fireplace, did not bother anyone. And by not concealing the yearly cut, the so-called ordinary, they ensured that procuring wood remained consistent from one year to the next. There was not the least recognition of this fact, but the villagers did understand that setting aside portions of the forest for the long term meant less fuel for those who enjoyed the right of *affouage.* It also reduced space for pasturage. The beginnings of the forest regime, which had basically existed from the seventeenth century, limited satisfaction of needs and freedom of action. The regime extended its authority more widely during the nineteenth century. What had concerned only the trees on the plains was then sought for the mountains. The communal areas integrated into an agropastoral system were ultimately requisitioned in the name of the public interest to check erosion and flooding. State interference was becoming more and more effective, thereby arousing the anger of local populations. The beginnings of the seventeenth century, the revolutionary period, the 1830s, the ephemeral Second Republic, the Third Republic, so shaky at its beginning—all these periods of transition and uncertainty recorded the flames of violence. When the city dweller admired the slopes of the Couserans in autumn, where the dark green of the pine trees blended with the tawny shades of

Figure 3.11
Abundance and charm, the golden age of the forest: pasturage, hunting, and gathering. Napoleon III will show his capacity for remembering by proposing the reforestation of the mountains. The peasant, the declared butcher of the forests between 1790 and 1804, a period of uncertainty in forest administration, will bear the brunt of Napoleon III's law of 1860.

Figure 3.12

Lazare Bruandet, *Road through the Low Trees.* At the beginning of the 19th century, the landscape was freed from historical and mythical constraints intended to confer a certain majesty on a genre judged to be minor. Art lovers rediscovered Dutch painting (the grand masters of which were expensive and the lesser ones rare) and turned to contemporary artists, with their modest prices and light brush. Nature seen here is without any other affectation than what the artists' talent provides.

the beech, did he know that the spruces were not there during the time of his grandfather? The fir trees planted by the Administration of Waters and Forests, so they claimed in the 1880s, did not have time to grow: their crowns were lopped off, their trunks uprooted, the saplings sawed into pieces and given to cattle or set on fire—all this was good for people wanting to repel the administration's green colonization. Yes, the Administration of Waters and Forests made itself unpopular because every program for protecting the tree populations and determining the harvests led to opposition from the peasants. There is no doubt that the peasants hated the agents of the Waters and Forests more than the tax collector.

The Refusal of Private Ownership

The 1960s saw the Administration of Waters and Forests pilloried once again: "The inadequacies of the current administration are proof that administrative rules are not suitable for a service whose basic mission is to manage state-owned property."[29] Recalling the advantages gained by the statute that converted those industries and commercial enterprises having national importance to public enterprises in electricity, coal mining, and telecommunications (Électricité de France, Charbonnages de France, Radiodiffusion-Télévision Française—or, more commonly, R.T.F.), the government of the Fifth Republic sought to extend this statute and entrust to one large administrative organization "production in the forests of the State and other public entities." The finance law of December 23, 1964, set up the administrative organization, granting it a civil personality and financial autonomy. On January 1, 1966, the Office national des forêts (O.N.F. [National Office of Forests]) began operations.[30] After some twenty years, just attending a meeting of the friends and defenders of the forest—the necessary term because it is generic—is enough to show that the resentments built up over three centuries have not entirely died out.

The misunderstanding that existed between officials of the royal administration and the peasant world still poisons relations between the O.N.F. and city dwellers without access to nature. They believe anything that does not seem modeled on the latter's definition of a true forest can only be imputed to the hereditary enemy, the dispenser of fines and evil administrator of a silviculture that has excluded any other way of using trees. The exaggerations in the debate have in the meantime burst forth more loudly today than yesterday. Yet the representatives of the forest state are far from being the only actors in the changes occurring in the forest. As early as the eve of World War I the area under their control (3,148,071 hectares) represented not quite one-third (31 percent) of the total forested area, then about 10 million hectares—9,886,701, to be exact. The changes continued, and all the while the State never stopped increasing its territory, buying back the woods at the periphery of the cities and in the zones devastated in the war, reforesting here where the shells had plowed up the fields, there where the caprices of nature were not to be trusted. The forest patrimony of the nation thus recovered 300,000 hectares, much more than was removed by those laws alienating the land that had been enacted in the nineteenth century to fill the budgetary gaps caused by the foreign occupation in 1815.

The private forest, however, advanced faster than the public forest in France. The increase since 1935 alone was estimated to be 28 percent of the already large area that existed after World War I. That area covers at present nearly 10 million hectares, as much as the total area covered by the entire French forest prior to 1914. Though divided in a more homogeneous manner than at the beginning of the twentieth century, the chief areas under private control are in central and western France.

That includes more than 1.5 million hectares in Aquitaine (98 percent of the total forested area) and exceeds three-quarters of the forest capacity in the Limousin (97 percent), the Paris region (80 percent), central France (79 percent), the Auvergne (77 percent), and the lands of the Loire (76 percent). In this France of plains and plateaus, large property holdings persist despite successors' pushing their rights to divide them.[31] This is not the case for the foothills or mountains at medium altitude, where small property holdings are the rule. This is a normal situation because capital is not interested, and the State and peasant are left alone together.

Private property of the forest assuredly owes its great resurgence to the French Revolution. Was it not based on the sale of the properties of the church and the nobles? That its dynamism did not sag during the nineteenth century is self-explanatory. The nobles groaned in vain, but they did not lose everything, quickly recovering the splendor of the past. As for the upper bourgeoisie, they wanted woods and hunting, in which they saw the crown of their social ascent. People of more modest means followed their example, taking advantage of low land prices to put together a little property. One planted and waited. After all, investment in green gold was worth more than other investments that were riskier and less pleasurable. What was extraordinary is that the extension of individual forests withstood everything. It was a crisis nonetheless. Firewood sold on the Parisian markets at 18 francs a stere in 1871, and then, at a more peaceful conjuncture in 1881—the two peaks in the curve between 1860 and 1910—did not attract any buyers at half the price in 1895. Because it never rains but it pours, to the drop in sales was added social unrest as woodcutters and loggers refused to revise their already miserable wages downward. Nothing helped. The forest that its admirers wanted to offer to everybody proliferated only if more and more areas were sectioned off. Barriers, barbed wire, traps, and signs came to delimit the innumerable units that formed the fabric of the contemporary forest.

It was an irresistible evolution in all respects: between 1960 and 1980, more than a million hectares dedicated to agricultural or pastoral purposes came back under private control. The large forested properties seemed nearly all consolidated. The number of small holdings accelerated. Properties of less than fifty hectares—57 percent of the forest surface area in private hands in 1910 (3.42 million hectares)—now occupied more than 70 percent, with 5.5 million hectares. The rural exodus caused this. Property as forest took over the mountain zones, beginning with those that already had the advantage of a tradition in materials. It has expanded today to the plain, including even the best lands. The decisions emanating from Brussels to reduce agricultural surpluses do have a bearing on it. Converting land to woods will therefore not stop soon. It remains to be seen what role this new forest can play. Its structure displeases the lovers of nature. Its appearance no longer suits them.

The Horror of the Green

In practice, the new growth and old growth forests still retain their position only in the places where there are large forested properties. Reforestations in almost all cases are done with pine trees. Plantations of conifers of less than ten years constitute, for example, 40 percent of the private forests in the department of the Meuse and 25 percent in that of the Moselle. The new forest is turning into a total production forest. A praiseworthy objective—if its proponents find the means to carry it out. Every owner has an unbelievably large number of parcels, each of which is an administrative unit. In these conditions, how can a harvest be obtained in quantities that can be commercialized? In the Vosges and Meurthe-et-Moselle, there are 3.5 parcels in one piece of property, and each parcel measures on the average 0.8 hectare! The garden forest in a way, but it is a useless garden.

Dividing and subdividing the land have thus affected the economic mobilization of privately held trees. So in 1960 an organization was set up, the Association technique pour la vulgarization forestière (A.T.V.F.) or Technical Association for the Popularization of the Forest, financed with contributions from its members, by deposits in farm savings accounts and, since 1964, by the Fonds forestier national (F.F.N.) or National Forest Fund. The A.T.V. F. seeks to increase tree production. The deficit in the commercial balance in pulp and paper justifies its actions. This industrial sector, if it is to survive, has to have abundant raw material available to it. The intensification of forest practices is the order of the day. Because the effects will be perceived better on young plantations, the spotlight is trained on rapid- growth species. In the Landes de Gascogne, for example, where the tree system was the responsibility of the papermakers, all effort goes into promoting the development of the maritime pine tree, sown in rows for easy fertilization. Nothing in this new forest recalls the forest as it was once farmed.

Nevertheless, excessively dense planting means that the F.F.N. plantations do not deliver as much small-sized lumber as they ought to, for two reasons: the lack of technical ability on the part of the owners and mediocre prices for wood intended for trituration. That in turn does not encourage crop thinning, an operation that costs more than it brings in. To bring the annual harvest of 600,000 steres to 1 million steres, the papermakers in 1975 got the State to subsidize clearings in the seventeen

Figure 3.13
The Douglas fir, intro-
duced around 1825,
combines two advan-
tages: it grows rap-
idly, and it causes less
soil acidification than
do pine and spruce
trees. A cross-section
showing the growth
rings allows the age
of the tree and the ef-
fects of weather and
meteorological events
in a given year to be
calculated.

departments where they controlled timber resources, in the Limousin, northeast France, and Aquitaine. Two years later, this assistance was put into general use. In this way a forest countryside was created that was perfectly regular—green uniformity.

What a revenge for the conifers, beginning with the fir! Once per-secuted by rural inhabitants who preferred the beech and oak groves for their multiple uses, the fir eventually became scarce on the lower slopes and was driven to the frontiers of the higher altitudes. The triumphal de-scent of the conifers to the valleys accompanied the Third Republic. It was finally admitted that above three thousand meters reforestation was impossible. This was a totally new finding, because for a long time people believed that where they could not live perennial vegetation could, since it was not handicapped by the lack of oxygen, the rigors of the cold, and little sunshine—all of which serve to define the abode of the dead. In some very mountainous and forested countries, such as Japan, the place where deceased souls wander is set, understandably, in this combat zone, the place where the tree has to adapt to survive. The vocabulary of the forest managers and the symbolic nature of plants sometimes help mem-ory in a very strange way.

The solution that brings the fir tree front and center [*mise en sapin*], an all-encompassing expression filled with contempt, disturbs because it obscures the landmarks.[32] With the Douglas fir, the spruce, the Nord-mann, or the Weymouth pine, maturity comes after fifty years, and once the trees are cleared, the area for miles around is left shorn, littered with debris, quickly fouled with thickets. Not so long ago, such an ordeal meant famine. That experience made the suffering all the greater because of the affluence that had preceded it. The best techniques must not provoke the anguish of rupture, emptiness, or shortage. Inversely, those things are adjudged detestable that may lead to an upheaval into the

Figure 3.14
Pierre Bessa, *The Pyramid Oak*, engraving by Legrand fils (ca. 1795). The race for exotic, rare, and high-priced species began with explorations in far-off lands. The passion for the park in the English style, created to highlight not only a point of view but also a subject noteworthy for its form and color, is inseparable from that search.

unknown. This trauma seems always to go hand in hand with aggressive forest production. The woods that one visits and the spectacle that one savors fleetingly maintain a fantastic emotional potential. Viewing chaos is unbearable. It reflects an attitude that adapts poorly to a system in which the harvest is an end in itself, not the promise of renewal.

Attention to the coniferous expanses and the forest wastelands also does not linger in the same fashion. Those wastelands arouse hardly any comment and no protests about wastage when the new-growth forests are left to degrade, rot, and decay: "That's not unfortunate, this massacre, they're good for nothing anyway." This sense of detachment conveys the serenity of knowing time has passed. Planting conifers, on the contrary, is seen as an intrusion, whether it is the fruit of administrative tyrants decreeing the conversion of underexploited communal areas or the result of foreigners buying up overgrown land for planting. That the truth is more complex matters little, even if those who are most critical know well that a good number of the plantings are due to local people. Everyone prefers to blame the green tide on outsiders. "Fir trees," they grumble, "they resemble a forest, but they aren't. Animals don't like them. Nature is going to disappear." The traditional forest never violated nature.

The old idea of trees rests on the notion of natural cycles, not on alternately planting and cutting.[33] For this reason the broad-leaved trees had no rivals. They could be exploited in a way that assured a permanent forest cover. At fixed intervals, the woodcutter would remove the subjects that had been marked in advance after reaching the required dimensions. The hour of the harvest did not mean slashing everything. The prying government did not rule out leaving stumps and shoots after a clean cut. It was still subject to constraints, but the peasant who was ready to bend to the necessities of the land could work within them. So that new growth was heavy, the successive operations—marking trees that were to remain, cutting, hauling, hewing—flowed into a rigorous calendar. Mars was not tamed before the tasks were done. Sap flowed in the buds. Nature resumed work, and man could not stop it. He therefore left nature alone. To act otherwise would be profanation.

The trunks that fall to the axe will return one day. The new growth will appear, not from their ashes, like the phoenix, but from their cuttings. The ground will absorb the blood that flows and childhood will flourish, imagery from the great myths of antiquity that explains the return of plants. If the forest is so treated, how could it not embody the eternal return? On two counts the tree recapitulates life—when it transcends the seasons (laid bare in winter, it turns green again in spring) and when it transcends death (cut down, it prepares the way for the change of generations). In the traditional culture of the forest, this desire to return to the mother—the word connotes bountifulness—explains the lukewarm reception given to conifers. Their somber branches evoke the funereal tradition associated with them: eternity in the abode of the dead, the longest night of the solstice. From the soil where they take root, no shoots come forth. The individual is alone and then nothing. Sterility until the owner decides to plant or lay seed. The forest of old was fertile. It still exists, but changing needs, technologies, and choices have created other trees. Profitability condemns archaism and sometimes turns its back on the "natural," which often reflects knowledge and perception carefully developed over the centuries. This applies to business, and it applies to silviculture. The lovers of the tree give in with difficulty. They see the effects of forestation when innovation finally occurs.

The Reveries of the Promenader

In the forest of legends time no longer slips by. In the forest of peasant realities, by contrast, it is present everywhere. The reason is that the former does not bear the weight of economic demand, whereas the latter is enmeshed in it. The passer-by of today strongly resembles the imaginary hero. Because the harvest is a matter of no concern to him, he goes from surprise to anger, like someone who deems aesthetic only that which his memory of distant times magnifies. But where are the trees of long ago, those that made up the forest of broad-leaved trees, the forest for exploring and searching out—the non-forest word "plundering" would fit very well—a forest where the hours may count or may count double?

City dwellers short on chlorophyll are the new users, and they are a force that will not be held back. Starting in the 1960s, visits to the Parisian forests, including the Bois de Boulogne and the Bois de Vincennes, as well as that strip of green along the Oise River with Chantilly, Compiègne, and Senlis, have now reached respectable proportions. The number of visitors exceeds 4 million. The total number of visits touches 60 million.[34] That represents, for a given year, almost as many days spent in the woods as in darkened rooms—and six times as many hours dedicated to the cult of the tree as to the monuments and curiosities of the Île-de-France! This hunger for nature did not begin in 1960, even if that date is asserted as the beginning. Similarly, the capacity for antiauthoritarian behavior does not mark the dawn of a movement. No, that date only marks the unease about transformations in plant life, transformations that at that moment have accelerated.

In fact, the wish to cement ties with the forest, that distillate of nature, which people felt had weakened, appeared around 1850. A romantic longing? The first people to frequent the forests without being forced to did not exhibit any symptoms of that so-called *mal du siècle*. To the contrary, these were extremely active people who belonged to the social elite and who therefore had the means to take advantage of all the advances that were then flowering in the Second Empire. Because of the rapid change in their lifestyle, these people, who were eccentrics and remained so until the style became public domain, sought, in the shade of the great trees, to reestablish an impaired equilibrium, meaning a new serenity and increased energy, as if the murmur of the foliage might better teach them how to master their existence. To forget about everything, breathe in the fresh air, rediscover walking and running—activities done with the conscious intent of demonstrating how untamed space helped achieve self-control—for the health of the soul and the body.

The motivations of the nineteenth century were very similar to those of the twentieth. At the core was a conservation reaction that wanted to perpetuate a past judged more harmonious than the present, whether in the quality of life or in the value of the spectacle. It is quite impossible to ignore this pressure. Every age wants to turn the forest into a keeper of memory. The forest at Marly illustrates this attitude well. At the end of the eighteenth century, nothing remained of the village of Retz but ruins. Monville, the son of a grand master in the Administration of Waters and Forests in Rouen and proprietor of the place, had a strange tower built there. With fluted columns thirteen meters high and intentionally left uncompleted, it was a false ruin next to the real ones. This curious "folly" was decorated with two hundred flowerpots and set next to a Chinese pavilion made of teak. The Administration of Fine Arts in 1939 classified this as the Desert of Retz for "its savage beauty." The roar from the superhighway is audible today. No matter! In spectacles of nature produced by man, hearing counts less than seeing.

For the visitor to enjoy the production there has to be some minimum number of points of assistance and certain other items available. The charms of a scene are better savored when one is comfortable. Since the nineteenth century, the authorities have been installing items deemed best suited for this contemplative activity. This goes for the signs indicating a remarkable place, a rare plant, the age of a tree, or those recalling a dramatic or historical incident, and for the benches set in cozy spots with baskets to collect greasy napkins as well, as picnic tables for those wanting to dine outside without ants on the menu. Such items reflect a notion very different from that represented by the magnificent stone tables that figure on the plans for the royal forests. A glance at these plans makes clear that the paths and roads served only to facilitate hunting. The intersections allow for ease of pursuit as the animal—be it a stag or a boar—twists and turns in flight. At Marly, hunting tables were built at the intersections so that there was a place to prepare trophies and food. Three of these tables are still standing, one at the last point that the Route des Princesses crosses before it meets the Route Dauphine, the second at the Carrefour Royal, and the third at the Carrefour du Chêne.

In this way the government responds to consumers' expectations about forest space. The authorities cannot, however, yield too much in their direction. Every improvement in access to the green zones and in the services offered (parking and rest areas, fitness trails, and hiking) reaps something unintentionally sown: an exponential growth in the forest clientele. In twenty years, from 1965 to 1985, just in the Île-de-France, the number of visits increased at a rate of 14 percent per year. Only since 1976 have the special management programs originally planned in 1964 for all the forests under the forest administration's authority gone into effect, and then only for a tenth of the area (barely 500,000 hectares). It was only in 1976, with the guidelines of October 20, that the demands of new users calling for productive use were included. The text affirms that "the increasingly numerous crowds seek out the woods and the forests more every year to find distraction and relaxation during their hours of leisure." The verdict, in conclusion, is: "The tamed forests have to be *open* to guests, who must be *welcomed* there and not just *tolerated*." Admittedly, but how far does one go with such pomp and circumstance?

To the degree possible, wisdom counsels holding in check the human pressure on a patrimony that is too much appreciated. Adapting to the influx of visitors by providing various types of facilities accommodates visitors' needs, which mirror in large part their social status, and protects the woods from an excess of admiration. The concept of the "zone of silence" relates to this double imperative. Spared from noise, a symbol at once of the industrial world and of active intruders, the forest then approximates what is wrongly believed to be its original state. This approach completely suits the lovers of virgin nature, the "essentialists," such as Robert Ballion. It also offers the advantage of expelling noise pollution from cars and play areas to the edge of the forest. That in turn pleases the "instrumentalists," those sedentary individuals who only flourish if they are at least a hundred meters or more from their car.

The space so ordered can then absorb most of the users coming from the cities. It constitutes a transition between the metropolis and the suburbs and nature, humanized just enough so that it is easy to get one's bearings. The bill that has to be paid is for the localized loss of forest identity, meaning 1 percent to 3 percent in the forests found in the outer suburbs of Paris, about sixty-four kilometers out, to 10 percent of those in the near suburbs. The conversion of real estate into personal property is accentuated by degree of proximity. The attack on the integrity of the

large forests remains for the moment a marginal phenomenon. That is
not because the erosion there is insidious and thus easily avoided. The
"essentialists" are too much taken with the trees to tolerate such distraction. Wild space has to be protected from any concession; a fortiori, it
cannot be a target. That is the meaning of the fight begun in 1983 against
the Asterix amusement park: its construction cut into the Plailly woods
and risked harming the Oise forests. It mattered little to the "essentialists" that not only was land cleared and money sunk into it, but also
promises were made to respect the environment. Asterix insulted nature.
They were not wrong to protest: The guarantees did not carry much
weight, and, furthermore, a business can file for bankruptcy. It all can fail,
but the park will remain a scar etched into the countryside and serving
no purpose. Besides, even if commercial success becomes the order of the
day, this park will continue being what it is: the sign that a collective
good is benefiting partisan interests, namely the financiers who financed
the operation and those curious people who pay the entrance fee.

Are the Trees Dying Out?

Actually, ever since the first third of the nineteenth century, the French
have been terrified by the possibility of losing their forests. A good number are convinced that they are already witnessing the forest's disappearance. According to them, the forest is in retreat, eaten away by urbanization, airports, and highways—not to mention devoured by the paper
industry, as if that sector did not depend on what it supplied, or ravaged
by summer fires. This pessimism is de rigueur, although never has the
forest patrimony occupied so vast an area or increased so much: more
than 14 million hectares in the 1980s, compared with less than 11 million
before 1914—a growth of 27 percent in only three generations. The forest is winning on all fronts, except for the Mediterranean coast, where
soon it will exist only as a "landscaped park," like that of Valbonne Val-
lauris (maritime Alps). Everywhere else the forest attests to its dynamism.
Here is memory caught in flagrante delicto. How is such an error in perception conceivable?

Memories become indelible only when they are fixed by the image
the mind captures, photographically speaking. What is seen is the removal of trees, and thus what comes to mind is a forest cut down right
at maturity, artificial regeneration dispensing with the need to keep a few
mature trees. What is also affected, to a lesser degree, is the forest that
keeps mature trees just long enough to assure a natural seeding and, in a
general way, all trees that large-scale projects have ripped out, leaving
behind tree trunks lying on the ground, bare stumps, and a gaping hole.

True, the spectacle will never revert to what it was. Trees, other kinds, will replace them, but very slowly. There is one other slightly tangential link to memory: the image that something irreversible has occurred.

In short, man has the fearful power to wreak havoc on the landscape. He requires a catastrophe to imagine that nature can do as much, doubtless because when talking about it he evokes only its most gentle elements. The march of vegetation seems peaceful to him because it is regular, continuous, and discreet. An abandoned space becomes a wasteland, but then the brambles take hold, along with some adjoining hazelnut trees, followed by birch trees colonizing the whole area. But here seedlings of the *Abies grandis,* the great fir trees, are developing, a selection the proprietor has made that the eye of the passerby does not even catch. Concealed by thickets, they will majestically soar over them one day, but realization of the moment will come too late. The promenader will see no more than the green tops of the trees and swear that this parcel of land has been a forest for years. The success of the one divergent fact rests on the fact that it is not "divergent." It is singular. Imagination embroiders only on what it finds disconcerting. It therefore focuses on the violated forest, never on the planted or reconstituted forest.

Numbers do not soften such feelings. Even when repeated, numbers leave the listener skeptical. The dark green uniformity that obliterates distinctive features catches the attention only of people living there. It does not reach the media. The forest attracts little thought or alarm. It is a matter of either concern or distraction. Everyone feels both the child and the master of the forest. The risk of losing or abusing it forms the two faces of a dreaded divorce. The sylvan glade may no longer be in retreat, but it could be. Because of that, anguish seeps out.

Westerners are thus alarmed almost as much by runaway taxes in the tropics as by the damaging effects of acid rain at home. In summer, what weekly magazine does not feature, with headlines, one of two themes: To what extremes will African governments go? How can we breathe without the Amazon lung? Spring comes, acid rain is the star attraction: trees are dying, with photographs of poles holding them up. To be sure, a forest is considered in decline as soon as 50 percent of the trees have been removed, and that is the case in one forest region out of 400,000 hectares in the Vosges Jura. The affected area amounts to 2.5 percent of the total![35] Images obliterate an effective approach to the phenomenon. Explanations by journalists focus on the culpability of factories and vehicle emissions. The camera remains ignorant of the connection between acidification of the land and species planted in the forest since the nineteenth century. The perception "forest antidote," so dear to new users, is played out as it sweeps away everything in its path, beginning with the "cultivated forest space." The essential thing, it must be said, is that a forest that man does not manage is neither beautiful nor productive, whatever one thinks.

Enormous trunks, roots with powerful claws, branches like talons, bark with deep cracks, foliage for the humble scientist, light that is clear or murky, and the effect of backlighting—all this underlines the prodigious vitality of nature in total decomposition or in perpetual renewal. This forest—perhaps it is the one in the fairy tales—is the one in which the peasant does not feel overwhelmed, and it is also the one seen by the painters in the Flemish golden age of the seventeenth century or in the Barbizon school of the early nineteenth century. The forest reserves at Fontainebleau, do they not correspond to underexploited and aging forest populations? Théodore Rousseau made his grandiose and tortured oaks the very marks of human passions. It is a classic connection that shows that the forest constitutes more than scenery for the visitor. Does not the forest give the measure of all that is ephemeral on earth?

The forest does not have the exclusive rights to this pedagogic role. Other paintings encapsulate the same messages: plucked fruit, dazzlingly beautiful but overripe, books with sumptuous bindings that are already losing pages, trophies of fowl and game where the resting fly announces the worm. The forest falls into this genre, its emptiness depicted in the foreground with a dead and rotting tree. The view on display contains a lesson much stronger than all those representations, for in the chaos of green growth, man, infinitely small, has his place. It is not by chance that an artist never grants his subjects the proportions they deserve. Do they not embody the necessarily precarious and laborious character of existence? It is not just a spiritual but a practical lesson: it is the Lilliputian who tames the tutelary forces present in every one of the trees in middle plane of the painting. The smallest detail conveys his constant activity: the man with the axe and the man with the saw, the hunter in the blind, the shepherd coming home with his flocks, lurking danger. Thieves and murderers, soldiers and deserters are there too.

It would be a pity to reduce these details to a philosophical leitmotif. The reversal of circumstances that occurred in the mid-eighteenth century makes still life pleasant and turns the forest into a rustic scene. That is true, but the current value of those lesser masters of the seventeenth century—de Vadder, d'Arthois, Huysmans, Baudewyns, or Coppens, following the long purgatory of the years 1730 to 1960, certainly conveys more than games for money. Nature's lesson always fills the senses.

During this eclipse, the forest came into memory through the language of sexuality and fecundity. This is the mother lode that all the

Figures 3.15 and 3.16
Mimizan (Landes) in
1959 and 1987. In
thirty years, the forest
gained ground as
mixed farming re-
treated. The communi-
cations network im-
proved. That in turn
not only affected
rapid response to fire,
but also facilitated all
activities relating to
forest maintenance
and the transport of
wood products.

writers of the nineteenth and the first part of the twentieth century exploit. Boy and girl sink into a cozy nest of green as if nature itself had prepared the drapes for the lovers. The complicity of the matchmaker is evoked, for example, in Guy de Maupassant's *Yvette*.[36] Yvette nearly loses her head and her virtue when she smells "the freshness of the damp earth wafting under the high thick branches that appeared to bear as many nightingales as leaves." Others like her succumb with less formality. Is it not in the nearby woods that the young people of Châtillonais, on the evening of April 30, seize a charm and deposit it at the door of every pretty girl lacking a husband? Intentions are not hidden, since after that date no one goes to the altar. It is the month of Mary. As Blondeau the father remarked, when the sociologist Évelyne Chaussin interviewed him, "It's good to marry the beautiful one and good to screw her." Under the foliage when the invitation is accepted, the young blades have complete hope.

Trees and sex are in truth an indissoluble unity. The custom has not disappeared, if one is to judge by the lovers seeking a spot in the Bois de Boulogne and the Sénart Forest. Anyone can consume fruits there that are elsewhere forbidden. The prostitute recruits her client there. The wife falls into adultery, unless she is imagining the forest for her most shameful fantasies in imitation of the woman in Luis Buñuel's film *Belle de jour*. In the shadow of the trees, impulses are satisfied. Likewise, popular tradition easily links the tree to the serpent, as a number of place-names reveal: Les Vipères (vipers), La Pierre-qui-siffle (the hissing stone), La Couleuvrine (the grass snake), and others. Blondeau shows the way: "Sure enough, that's done all alone, right? No need to learn to know how to do it." It is often said that one must avoid the woods between May and September because those are the months where there are no respectable chores for girls, like gathering mushrooms or filling a basket with peas. Guilty pleasures or innocent pleasures, the old-timers in town remember with some emotion as well as mischief how some husband obliged his wife to stomp on the moss. "Snakes, I never saw any, upon my word!" She was stomping, just in case, before lying down. Adventure still awaits in some corner of the woods, good or bad but always necessary for the fulfillment of life.

The memory we have of trees is in truth quite strange. The fairy tales that rock the child, the ancient myths seen again in Latin class, the slow fashioning of mentalities by a civilization that depends on that memory, distorted remembrances that old people like to relate, not to mention the marvelous discoveries made there during one's early years—all of these are memories inextricably joined together. How then can we examine these memories if we set aside cultural knowledge that has been

Figure 3.17
Forestation in 1986.
Northwest France
shows little forest
cover, whereas the
rest of France is heav-
ily wooded, some de-
partments having
more than 45% of
their total surface area
in trees. The forest
cover is particularly
high in three regions:
(1) the southeast, ex-
cepting the depart-
ment of Bouches-du-
Rhône; (2) the east,
from the department
of Doubs to the Bel-
gian and German
borders; and (3) the
southwest, with the ex-
panse of the vast for-
est in the department
of Landes making it
the first European for-
est mass. This break-
out reflects the legacy
of the second half of
the 19th century:
planting trees in the
mountains for control
of heavy rain and cre-
ating artificial forests
for turpentine and
cellulose.

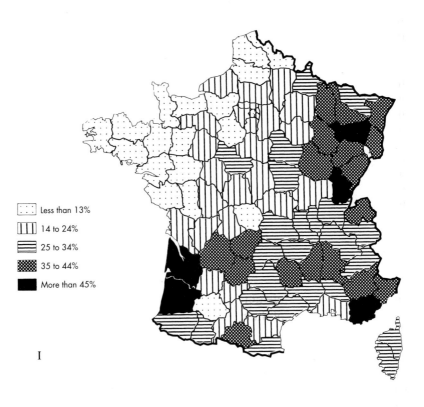

Less than 13%

14 to 24%

25 to 34%

35 to 44%

More than 45%

I

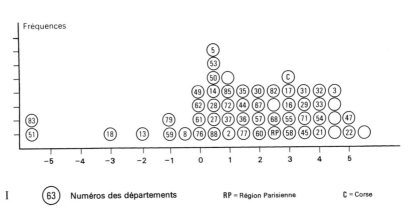

Fréquences

I   (63)   Numéros des départements   RP = Région Parisienne   C = Corse

Figure 3.18
Variations in the percentage of forestation from 1945 to 1986. This graph corrects the impression the preceding map gives that the degree of reforestation was intentional. What now becomes clear is that since World
War II, trees, desired or not, have been colonizing abandoned fields and unused pasturage. Provence in the
interior, the Massif Central and its outlying areas, and the Pyrenees region, notably the department of Ariège,
all have seen the influx of day workers, peasants with small landholdings, and people isolated in the high-
lands or living in small villages. Those remaining in the countryside are no longer controlling rural space.
They are letting the forest take over. *Note:* Numbers in circles are department numbers; PR = Paris region;
C = Corsica. From the *Grand atlas de la forêt française* (Paris: De Monza Edition, 1991). Charts drawn up
by the National Forest Inventory and the Biogeography-Ecology Laboratory of the École Normale Supérieure
at Fontenay–Saint-Cloud.

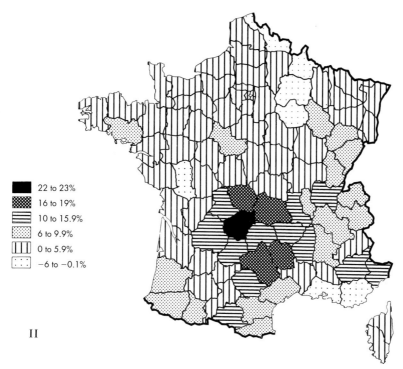

22 to 23%
16 to 19%
10 to 15.9%
6 to 9.9%
0 to 5.9%
−6 to −0.1%

II

Figure 3.19
Frequency in the percentage variation of forest cover between 1945 and 1986. The resumption of the rural exodus, interrupted during the war years, was a trend that authorities encouraged to modernize rural taxation and to reinforce the secondary and tertiary structures that affect the rural economy. The National Forest Fund was set up in 1946 to make grants of seeds and plants as well as to authorize financial subsidies to owners wishing to plant trees on one or more parcels of land. This movement, which especially benefited the southern mountain regions of France, slowed considerably after 1955. Seeding conifers on plots of land that were often minuscule has not yielded the expected returns: failure to thin the growth and do adequate clearing meant that the trees failed; failure to consolidate land holdings resulted in small lots that could not be easily sold. In the end it was recognized that turning a peasant into a forest manager was not an easy matter, and that dealing with the communes was preferable to working with individuals. From the *Grand atlas de la forêt française* (Paris: De Monza Ed., 1991). Histogram drawn up by the National Forest Inventory and the Biogeography-Ecology Laboratory of the École Normale Supérieure at Fontenay–Saint-Cloud.

stratified over time into the history of a country and the history of an individual?

Actually, in all periods the forest has counted for too much for a neutral view to be possible. Under Louis XV, the peasant felt his father lived in the golden age. According to him, no one spoke of economizing on an impoverished resource. That was the time, however, when the Colbert Code went into effect. Under Charles X, that peasant's descendants were also dreaming of the golden age, but now that paradise had slipped so far into the past that no one dared fix a time. The procedure for dividing up time functioned well before the return of the Bourbons to the throne.

It continues even down to the present. People are sorry to see open land closed off for hunting—the last step in a process that little by little has extinguished community practices, beginning with the *affouage*. Those who speak with emotion about its convivial character did not hesitate to hire mercenaries to chop down trees until even that became superfluous. The cutting areas are deserted because coal or fuel oil is used for heating. Those who criticize conifers that were brought in are the last ones to call for closures or new conifer plantings. A past that becomes more and more remote is idealized and contradictions are experienced in everyday life that underlie all these behaviors. In this there is true permanence.

Memory ratifies these expanses as lands of liberty, in the full ambivalence of the word. The liberty of others can be a threat; the liberty that I exercise is a delight. In fact, even when the harvest in wood was not a market commodity, it did become subject to the control of the authorities, a control that was sometimes only theoretical, though the idea was still there: prevent this property, which can reproduce itself, from dying out from having been bled too much. This is, moreover, the argument that residents always adduce against any stranger in the country: "The locals . . . they know it's still nature. They are relatively respectful." Nature? An implicit reference to what?

This nature is not a concept. It provides fuel for the imagination as something generous and good, and therefore it takes the shape of a tree. Induction is a matter of course today and has been so for less than two centuries; before that either the question of its image was not posed, because God inheres in all the landscape, or the question would not elicit this answer, because the expanse of the great trees was denounced as oppressive and the pleasantness of the open countryside was seen as the best way to convey nature's solicitude with respect to man. The promotion of the tree owes much to the progress of science, which in overturning assumptions about the future generated an anxiety about tomorrow and its antidote in green trees.

The intellectual elites of the nineteenth and twentieth centuries seem fascinated by the ineluctable decadence that lies in wait for humanity in thrall to the excesses of industrialization. The absence of civilization and the death of a civilization borrow the same signs to express the pain in living: There are no more signs of vegetation. The pompous painter Fernan Cormon turned to prehistory. At the center of a vast canvas [*Cain* in the Musée d'Orsay], a sad horde of fierce-looking people passes before the spectator, carrying their old as if displaying game. A hundred years later, the filmmaker Luc Besson, dealing with the same problem, conceived of a future no less sinister than Cormon's prehistory. In a film entitled *The Final Combat,* the survivors blindly fight for what they need. The expanses before them are frozen, covered in dust, a place where cannibalism is the rule. There is not a plant in sight.

The study of prehistory begins in the nineteenth century. At that time, it was unimaginable that man could have known luxuriant tropical forests, because his origins only went back four or five thousand years. It is curious to find that science fiction authors combine the future with this notion of a universe without trees to depict worlds where man no longer has a place. In the presence of trees, nature and civilization become one at last. How can we admit that these trees no longer resemble the model that generations have created over time? To do so would cut nature off from civilization.

NOTES

1. Countess de Ségur, *Ourson: Nouveaux contes de fées* (Paris: Club français du livre, n.d.), 189.

2. Maurice Maeterlinck, *Théâtre,* vol. 1, *La Princesse Maleine* (Brussels, 1903 – 5), 59.

3. Wilhelm Charles Grimm, *Contes populaires de l'Allemagne,* French translation by Max Buchon (Paris, n.d.), "Hansel et Grethel," 171.

4. Wladimir Propp, *Racines historiques du conte merveilleux* (Paris: Gallimard, 1983), chap. 17.

5. Charles Perrault, *Contes de ma Mère l'Oye: Peau d'Asne* (Paris, 1948), 89.

6. Grimm, "Les Six cygnes," in *Contes populaires,* 179.

7. Yvonne Verdier, "Chemins dans la forêt," in *Des arbres et des hommes: Actes du colloque Forêt et société, Lyon, 1979* (Arles: Actes Sud, n.d.), 344–50.

8. Évelyne Chaussin, "Les Villegeois et la forêt," in ibid., 313.

9. Perrault, *Contes,* 179.

10. F. M. Luzel, *Contes populaires de Basse-Bretagne* (Paris, 1887), vol. 1, "Le Château de Cristal," 44.

11. Luzel, ibid., "Le Corps sans âme," 427.

12. L. Pineau, *Les Contes populaires du Poitou* (Paris, 1891), 19.

13. Jacques Le Goff, "Le Désert-forêt dans l'Occident médiéval," in *Pour un autre Moyen Âge: Temps, travail et culture en Occident* (Paris: Gallimard, 1977), 67.

14. Comtesse de Ségur, "Le Petit Henri," in *Ourson,* 88.

15. Cited by Tina Jolas, "Bois communaux à Minot (Côte-d'Or)," in *Des arbres et des hommes,* 127.

16. Chaussin, "Les Villegeois et la forêt," 366.

17. Andrée Corvol, *L'Homme et l'arbre sous l'ancien régime* (Paris: Economica, 1984), 178.

18. Isabelle Flavet, "Les Forêts de Montmorency, Carnelle, L'Isle-Adam" (3rd cycle thesis, University of Paris I, n.d.).

19. J. P. Husson, "La Forêt lorraine: Étude de géographie humaine" (Ph.D. diss., University of Metz, 1989).

20. Henri Megrot, *Petite histoire de la fôret* (Paris: Nouvelles Éditions latines, 1972), 109.

21. Jean François Belhoste, "Une histoire des forges d'Allevard des origines à 1885" (3rd cycle thesis, École pratique des hautes études en sciences sociales, n.d.).

22. J. Bossière, "La Consommation parisienne de bois et les sidérurgies périphériques . . . ," in *Forges et fôrets* (Paris: L'Harmattan, 1990).

23. Bossière, ibid.

24. J. M. Pesez, "Le Bois dans les constructions de la ville médiévale: Les questions," in *Le Bois et la ville, du Moyen Âge au XXe siècle,* ed. J.-L. Biget, J. Boissière, and J.-C. Hervé (Fontenay-aux-Roses: ENS de Fontenay–Saint-Cloud, 1991).

25. J. M. Pérouse de Montclos, "Les Difficultés d'approvisionnement en grands bois et l'innovation technique en charpente (XVIe–XVIIIe siècle)," in *Le Bois et la ville, du Moyen Âge au XXe siècle,* ed. J.-L. Biget, J. Boissière, and J.-C. Hervé (Fontenay-aux-Roses: E.N.S. de Fontenay–Saint-Cloud, 1991).

26. Andrée Corvol, "La Métrologie forestière," in *Introduction à la métrologie historique* (Paris: Economica, 1989), 302–46.

27. Corvol, "Le Nouvel ordre sylvicole," *Histoire, économie, société* (1984), 53–65.

28. The expression "forest regime" first appears in the Code of 1827, articles 1–90. The wording, not the idea, was modified in the Law of December 30, 1941. Its import is still valid.

29. Raymond Lefèvre and Jean Gadant, *Les Eaux et forêts du XIIe au XXe siècle* (Paris: Éditions du Centre nationale de la recherche scientifique, 1987), 640.

30. Ibid.

31. Gérard Bouttoud, *Les Propriétaires forestiers privés* (Nancy: E.N.G.R.E.F., 1984), 86.

32. Andrée Corvol, *L'Homme aux bois* (Paris: Fayard, 1987), 300–318.

33. Chaussin, "Les Villegeois et la forêt," 313.

34. Deforpa Program, *Dépérissement des forêts à la pollution atmosphérique,* École Nationale du Génie rural des Eaux et des Forêts (Congress Palace, Nancy, February 24–26, 1988), 3 vols., typed.

35. Ibid.

36. Guy de Maupassant, *Yvette: Oeuvres complètes* (Paris: Club français du livre, n.d.), 47.

THE REGION

✿

JACQUES REVEL

It is well known that France has a complicated relationship with its unity as with its diversity, a relationship most often peremptory, sometimes offhand, and at times obsessive. The scene is all the same quickly played out by its dutiful protagonists. On the one hand, the affirmation of unity, a mixture of centralization and administrative, political, cultural, and economic standardization. The evidence for this major role in national history is scarcely discussed; at the very most its contours are suggested. On the other hand, French diversity, acknowledged from the outset as more difficult to take into account. One must give it its due, but it is difficult to say something definitive. Everything happens as though, by definition, it evades the eye and words which attempt to grasp it. The status of these two figures is unequal and hierarchical. One cannot, however, think about the one without the other.

Since at least the end of the Middle Ages, in varying ways, our representations of territory have been in keeping with the tension created by unity versus diversity. This tension, it should be noted, has not been constantly—nor even for the most part—translated into political conflicts, into demands made by the center on the periphery or, as one would rather have expected, by the periphery on the center. It has been expressed more frequently through methods of geographical description, in the wider sense of the term.[1] One could argue on this score that Vidal de La Blache and his followers, at the beginning of the twentieth century, put a very old question at the heart of their scientific

Figure 4.1
Does the region exist? The failure of the referendum of 1969 delivered an uncertain response. Poster for the region (1969).

reflection. They can be credited with having given it a new and rigorous formulation.

Nonetheless, we will not limit ourselves here to these attempts at scientific illumination. In the history of the French representations of territory, the region has a special place. It is everywhere, but it remains elusive. French memory is easily accommodated by national space, even if it means inventing an immemorial existence for it. On the other hand, it multiplies local roots, which it researches on the levels of country, countryside, and birthplace. The memory of the region is even more uncertain and difficult. It is not that such memories do not exist; on the contrary, they proliferate, but they evoke a historical and spatial reality that seems ready at any moment to dissolve before our eyes. French diversity has not given up on finding its roots, on creating a past legitimacy for itself. Far from it. But it struggles to articulate what it wants to say. Moreover, the very vocabulary is indicative of this difficulty. Before administrative and political practice imposed the term "region" during the 1950s, the expression of national feeling meant hesitating before such terms as "province," "region," and "country," among others, using one word, then another, sometimes even within the same sentence. In this essay I will preserve this instability, this indecision about language, because it translates, in its own way, the various uses and perceptions of the region. The undertaking is, in many respects, paradoxical; it seeks to understand how and why a haunting but vague memory has been formed, one that refers to a short-lived reality and which has never found its true place.

This inascribable memory was nonetheless formed at a precise time, the contradictory terms of which have left their mark. The long half-century spanning the last decades of the ancien régime, the Revolution, and the Empire (1760–1820 or thereabouts), I will argue, marks a decisive moment in the imagining of territory as well as the practices around it. It should come as no surprise that my analysis will concentrate on the Revolutionary phenomenon. Doesn't the reason seem obvious? Doesn't everything from our thought tendencies to our academic traditions conspire to link the birth of a new regime, a new society (with that, too, of the contemporary history of the nation), to the beginning of an inexorable process of centralized standardization? In common usage, the term "Jacobin" has too easily come to stand for this multifaceted transformation, which is most often perceived as univocal. It is true that the word allows for both clarification and license to do anything.[2] Overused in a very unclear way, the never-ending resort to a timeless Jacobinism was perpetuated beyond the Revolutionary years until the middle of the Fifth Republic, by which time it hid more things than it enabled one to understand. One must perhaps look to that time to find the reasons for the success of a referent in spite of its overuse. Even so, we will not deviate here from strong certainties. Instead, I will attempt to show that, beyond the official statements and obvious choices, the period under consideration is one in which the interaction between French unity and diversity was being defined in very complex as well as ambiguous ways. The connections between them were stated in a provisional manner. They would all be reformulated later. Still, for the past two centuries they have influenced our representations and memory of national space.

The last decades in France have been marked by a strong recrudescence of regionalist feeling. As was anticipated, these years also saw new and frequent recourse to history to try to retrace the developments that led up to the current situation. Conveniently, people have often explored the forms and expressions of regional identities through the transformations of a series of object markers: ethnographical traditions and scientific works; the relationship between the national language and regional languages, dialects, and patois; and religious, political, and social behaviors. These have all been used by historians who, whether professional or not, have willingly given themselves the task of reconstructing and rehabilitating the pluralist past of a lost France. Such a rediscovery is far from original in our history. Yet it has had some unique aspects, only one of which I will deal with here: without ever absolving the Revolution and Empire of the Jacobin sin, recent historiography has by and large tended to situate French centralization and standardization on a longer timeline, beginning much earlier. Did not Tocqueville, belatedly consulted during these years, suggest that one could read the Revolution as the fulfillment of the absolute monarchy's promises and anticipate by several centuries first the marginalization and then the obliteration of regional life? The diagnosis is famous: "All these differences were superficial and virtually external. France already had, in truth, only one soul. The same ideas were current from one end of the kingdom to the other. The same customs were in force there."[3]

The renewed interest in the regionalist motif is due to an abundant and uneven literature, a very important wealth of unpublished data, and substantial revisions of accepted interpretations. I will draw heavily on these. Still, one is struck by the fact that, with some exceptions, the vast majority of these works have not called into question the explanatory model of the State, the "cold monster," confronting the regions, powerless and docile entities, destined for sacrifice. Let it be understood: it would be a vain and ridiculous paradox to deny the existence of tendencies toward centralization and standardization present over the very long course of our national history. But must we accept that the State and the regions were intangible realities locked in a perpetually antagonistic relationship during two, three, or four centuries of France's history?

The reflections that follow are intended as a review of these too widely held convictions. They in no way aspire to propose a new interpretation, still less a counterinterpretation. They seek only to conform to a slightly different perspective than that which has been accepted by most up until now. We all think we know what the State is and (perhaps to a lesser degree) what the regions are. We are also convinced that we have a clear idea of their current relationship. It is from this contemporary notion that we instinctively tend to reread and interpret our history. It seems to me that one thus runs a double risk. On the one hand, acceptance of the notion that we collectively use essentialist definitions (of the State, region, etc.); on the other, dissolution of a historic process stretched out over time, the result of the very history that we are seeking to understand—a temporary process happening before our eyes. One can contrast this temptation to be anachronistic with an approach that has undoubtedly more modest and fewer immediately gratifying results. Rather than interpret the old attitudes and policies of the State with respect to regional life according to our own parameters, it seems reasonable to seek to understand the significance of these ideas for contemporaries. Beyond political choices, one can thus try to reconstruct the systems of representations that have informed and authorized these choices, and, at the same time, to question the pertinence and uses of the ideas that we will encounter in this essay.[4]

As it happens, the period spanning the last years of the ancien régime, Revolution, and Empire constituted, beyond the disruptions and political shifts, a moment of intense theoretical reflection and practical experimentation concerning the diversity of French space. How can we conceptualize this diversity? That is, how can we recognize it? How can we explain it? And, finally, what can we do with it?

Let us now focus on the situation during the last decades of the absolute monarchy, since it was during these years that the problem was conceptually constructed at the same time its stakes were being defined. At the onset, two contradictory observations stand out.

The kingdom was a mosaic of particularisms, imperfectly fitted together and blended. Around the former royal domain, progressively enlarged, a certain number of territorial communities were brought under the kingdom's jurisdiction at widely varying times and through widely varying means, linked in a contractual type of relationship. The affirmation of their identity was perpetuated by the existence, more or less deeply rooted, of special rules of law (customs) and institutions (in particular the provincial estates) that represented the provincial authorities to the king. Even so, let us be aware that the contractual relationship was not unique to the regional bodies; it was based on the privileges claimed by cities, seigneuries, and simple communities of residents or professions at the heart of a corporate society [*société de corps*]. Such a heterogeneity of statuses was the common rule until the end of the ancien régime, which explains the classic formula of Mirabeau, who saw France as an "unformed aggregate of disunited people." The multiplicity of rights was increased and complicated even more by a de facto plurality, based on how recent the date of integration into the realm was, the relative distance from centers of command and control (the court, ministries, and bureaus), and the future proximity of rival hubs across the borders. Different linguistic customs were also factors that reinforced regional variegation. This state of affairs had nourished the nostalgia of reactionary thought for two centuries, from Joseph de Maistre to Charles Maurras, who saw the former monarchy as the political form most capable of respecting and strengthening the individual identities of organic communities, the essential base of social organizations. A conservative historiography, which remains active to this day, has for a long time intensified and sometimes propped up these analyses.[5]

But this picture has another side with completely opposite features, because the French monarchy, since at least the fourteenth or fifteenth century and especially after the seventeenth, had been the agent and primary beneficiary of a powerful movement of centralization and leveling on which it had essentially based its power. It is unnecessary to recall here the details of a cumulative evolution from Philip the Fair to Louis XIV, from Colbert to Maupeou, from the edict of Villers-Cotterêts (1539) to the institution of intendants through the litany of great royal decrees. This history is known and has been written about several times.[6] It leads one to believe that the ancien régime set itself the essential task of imposing a coherent whole on the different components of the kingdom and placing restrictions through common rules in matters of power, administration, law, belief, and culture.

Both these perspectives are accurate. Later, every historian will tend, of course, to continue to insist on one of the two aspects according to his own investments or his need to prove his argument. But it seems important to hold up both ends of the chain here and not to sacrifice one perspective to the other. France at the end of the eighteenth century was at once a relatively disparate assembly and a State highly aware of its unity, which had long withstood powerful ambitions to standardize. It was precisely from this tension between two contradictory positions that a multifaceted reflection on differentiations of national space was born.

It is not a given that, during the last years of the ancien régime, this reflection was the product of an awareness of any special relevance within a "regional" framework. What are we talking about, anyway, and what word was agreed upon to designate a haunting—if elusive—reality? The historian's difficulty today is evidence of the uncertainty of the old vocabulary. In the 1920s, at the end of a meticulous survey, G. Dupont-Ferrier concluded that there was no single term, but rather a constellation of terms (province, region, nation, country, language) in administrative language as in common usage.[7] Each of these, in its diverse uses, could cover some part of what the notion of region and the provincial mindset evoke for us today. None expresses it completely or in an unequivocal way. Moreover, did not a deputy from the ranks of the nobility, the comte de Tracy, during the debates of the autumn of 1789, propose that the constituents make it a priority to "define what one means by the word *province,* before dealing with the new administrative partitioning"?[8]

The lacuna indicated by these words was found in part on the level of practice. The number, name, administrative boundaries, and composition of provincial bodies varied considerably from one geographer to another, not even taking into account the texts of the last forty years of the monarchy.[9] The definition of "province" in the 1762 edition labored over by the academy's *Dictionnaire* is, in spite of all this, marked by its imprecision: "A considerable stretch of land, which is part of a large State and which is composed of several cities, towns, villages, usually under the same government." It accepted the idea that a certain size described the province and chose to privilege the political connections that linked communities of settlements to the State, an approach that has nothing, or almost nothing, in common with what we would read into the notion. The reality of provincial life did not have a meaning as such here; it only existed, as Thierry Gasnier reminds us, in order to refer to the territory as a whole.

Let us try to take this further. There existed, in the history of the absolute monarchy, a relatively old tradition of texts that set themselves the task of describing the kingdom. The origin and motives for this could have been diverse. It all went back to the plan to acquire a better understanding of the resources, the means and, occasionally, difficulties of governing. The texts were meant to provide information to a central administration—which was becoming ever more demanding, especially from the mid-seventeenth century onward—or even to educate the prince. For example, such was the case of the famous survey prepared between 1697 and 1700 by Louis XIV's intendants under the aegis of the duc de Beauvilliers, to "serve to instruct Monseigneur the duc de Bourgogne," that is, the heir to the throne. The reports that resulted were quite uneven in quality. But in reading them, one is struck most by the lukewarm interest they show in pinpointing and analyzing "regional" or "provincial" specifics, even though they were intended to introduce the dauphin to the diversity of his subjects. In truth, the particularisms seem to have been taken into consideration only in the legal and fiscal ordering of privileges. Nonetheless, the investigative plan addressed to the intendants advised them to characterize the people in their areas: "Men: their nature, lively or grave, industrious or lazy, their inclinations, their customs." It was, amid a set of primarily administrative and economic concerns, an invitation to comment on the dispositions of the subjects and even to observe them. In fact, the answers hardly showed any such effort. Some were content to repeat the same terms used in the question. Most of them referred back to a hardy regional characterology, pertaining to the wisdom of nations, which academic instruction had spread widely.[10] What is there, in most cases, is conventional portraits. "There is, generally speaking, more good sense and staunch spirit [*solidité d'esprit*] than refinement and liveliness. The most common and normal characteristic is slowness and inaction." The Normans are "attached to their interests, one leads them by letting them glimpse some profit. They have prudence and good sense." The Provençaux are "brave enough, but inconstant, two-faced, one cannot be certain of their good faith," while people from Languedoc, "as a group are full of spirit, activity, industry," "sparing no attention or pains to get what they want." Those surveyed were usually content to repeat some simple beliefs, which held that the towns (and areas in the south) had more spirit and vices, and the countryside more hard obstinacy. Beyond these sketches, which hold no real surprises, one is struck by the inability of most of the intendants to pinpoint and define regional distinctions: not only because, from one place to another, one encounters the same reliance on oppositions such as "lazy" and "industrious," "docile" and "undisciplined." The point of the investigation was to acquaint the prince with "the nature of the inhabitants of his various provinces, their important customs." The research proved to be incapable, in fact, of considering the distinctive features of places and appreciating them in an articulate way.[11] Of course, everything contrasted the province with the court and the city. But the former was apprehended only through a schema that tended to simplify and unify or, on the contrary, through vague and elusive detail about local

characteristics, never organized into a coherent description or explanatory model.

One finds a similar lack of accommodation in the observations made
about French space by some privileged observers in the second half of
the eighteenth century. They too were more concerned with better
assessing the kingdom's resources and improving their use. The case of
two groups—of two schools, one should say—well analyzed by Roger
Chartier is illuminating.[12]

The physiocrats devoted themselves to placing spatial distributions in
economic categories. So, too, their "pinpointing of space [owed] nothing either to history or to the picturesque"; it was entirely based on a
central clash between countries with greater culture [*pays de grande culture*] and countries with lesser culture [*pays de petite culture*]. This distinction enabled them to divide France between a minority composed of a
productive elite and a majority of social rejects. This hierarchical distribution is subject to one observation: it can be understood in terms of
economic analysis; it never goes back to the specific evolution of a ter-
ritory-based community whose forms would explain the particular
characteristics. As for the political arithmeticians, they multiplied the criteria that would allow them to classify the demographic realities they
were studying at the same time. They at least agreed on the existence of
a sort of national gradient, which, from north to south, contrasted an urban, dense France, producing and consuming goods, with a rural France,
thinly populated and economically backward. This major contrast—
which, on the detailed level of local situations, was really expressed
through a whole series of gradations—did not accord any particular relevance to the reality of the region. This viewpoint was carried beyond
the kingdom's borders and applied much more widely to European
space, for which France offered, within its legitimate boundaries, a striking example. Everything happened as though observers were only capable of conceptualizing national space in terms of often abstract macro-
divisions, totally indifferent to the existence of territorial realities,
however old and deeply rooted.

Besides the observers who could only ponder on the larger whole,
others existed, during these same years, whose outlook seemed afflicted
by the opposite problem and who proved to be incapable of going beyond the particulars of local situations. These were the doctors, mid-level
administrators, geographers, travelers, sometimes mere amateurs (more
or less educated), often mere notables. For the most part, we owe to them
the rediscovery of grassroots France, which marked the last decades of
the ancien régime. For them—and, incidentally, in very diverse works—
description and analysis had to be resolved into the infinitely smallest

part, as though the reduction in scale was a definitive guarantee of the sincerity and truth of the observation. Let us take, for example, the network of doctors corresponding with the Société royale de médecine, who, from the heart of the provinces, sent to Paris information they had gathered in their area. They proved to be uncompromising about the exceptional nature of their territory, even as they took part in a vast national survey. They were convinced, along with other local observers, that each canton was a monad, an indivisible atom in natural and social fact, the product of a unique combination of factors controlled by an environment: one soil, climate, vegetation, water system—in short, an ecology that was chiefly responsible for determining the specific forms of social organization. It was the ordering of these different elements, most often governed by analogy, that defined the specifics of a place. A neo-Hippocratic vision, in which one perceives a unifying force in topographies and medical field notes alike, but even more widely in a huge range of texts intended to explain the unique aspects of each spatial unit.[13] Inventorying these inestimable differences was a whole other peripheral side of the Enlightenment. The word "province," among many other words, here served only to express this reduction in scale, which allowed an organic picture to be drawn of specific characteristics usually considered to be insignificant. The geographer Darluc, who devoted himself to discovering those of Provence, says so plainly at the beginning of the 1780s:

> The natural history of a province, which would have as its goal the mere cataloguing of its fossils, the description of its mountains, that of its climate and its products, could not do more than satisfy curiosity. That which would, on the contrary, link all these different parts together, and try to use them to make inductions about mankind and relate them back, insofar as possible, to public utility . . . would be much more precious.[14]

Both the farsighted and the nearsighted vision symmetrically fail to see provincial existence as a historical, social, and cultural reality. This is not to say, of course, that it did not exist, but rather that it was not obvious, and rarely pondered. If one wanted to encounter it as an issue at the close of the ancien régime, one had to seek it among the social and cultural elites—at the heart of the provincial academies, for example, which seemed to rediscover, during the years 1740–50, pride in local history and undertakings.

This shift was not, however, obvious. The oft-repeated references to the pomp of the Burgundian court and the Renaissance in Toulouse were not enough to mask the national—that is, Parisian—culture's unwillingness to make a place for regional cultures in the days of the absolute monarchy. Against the strongest reasoning, it refused to recognize them as regional cultures; at best, it referred to them as a vague other. The regions were the collective, still inchoate expression of the "people," an uncertain protagonist, which for a long time did not correspond to any precise social designation and was defined only by its otherness.[15] The compilers of proverbs in the sixteenth century and the collectors of superstitions in the seventeenth and eighteenth centuries proved to be, at heart, not very attentive to the deep-rootedness of the works they were recording. To be precise, in their eyes, provincial versions were viewed only from the angle of diversity and variation. They found their place at the center of an inorganic continuum, without markers or limits, unified only by their contrast to legitimate culture.[16]

Things changed, however, in the middle of the eighteenth century. Provincial academicians no doubt continued to gather everything they could about local curiosities and rarities. Among this learned bric-a-brac, history held a new place, the importance, limits, and complexity of which have been demonstrated by Daniel Roche.[17] It maintained its predilection for "charters and objects," for the noble periods of antiquity and the Middle Ages, and rarely ventured into later periods. But it did not hesitate from then on to be mindful of the reality of provincial life and to accord it a new dignity. It no longer saw a patent contradiction nor an irreconcilable difference between the national and local: "It is provincial in its scholarly leanings, it aspires to be patriotic and philosophical by privileging the study of great men who promoted first regional, then national, civicism."[18] Through regional history projects that were then multiplying, a provincial consciousness was being expressed and finding support. Daniel Roche sees in this the obliteration of a long-standing inferiority complex vis-à-vis Parisian institutions. Some were going even further: in Nîmes, people based demands for local liberties on historical experience; in Bordeaux, the history of the academy was seen as "the school of the true citizen. . . . It is in the history of his region that he will learn, perhaps without even knowing it, his most real duties."

In any event, history was not the only means by which this new consciousness expressed itself. Cartography also lent itself to similar investments. At the moment when the immense and interminable undertakings of the Cassinis seemed to be getting bogged down in financial and political difficulties, critics were cropping up all over. The national map was blamed for having sacrificed topography to geometry and for being barely usable when it came to details. Above all, the information did not meet the expectations of users. The provinces were particularly dissatisfied. They believed themselves to be as poorly represented geographically as they were with respect to their interests. They did more than just complain: at the same time Cassini's map was being produced, they undertook to give themselves their own cartography. The states of Burgundy, from the 1760s onward, and those of Languedoc in the 1770s, entrusted some engineer-geographers with the task of improving the regional plates of the national map. In Guyenne, an entirely new project was begun by Belleyme in 1761 (but it remained unfinished). This was also the case in Provence, Artois, and Brittany. Administrative concern and the weight of economic interests favored the assertion of provincial identity, which nonetheless remained discreet and usually practical.[19]

We will not, however, overestimate this evolution during the second half of the eighteenth century. First of all, because it was only happening among the learned elite and, to a lesser degree, among those with political power. The academic archipelago was rare and was irregularly represented in the kingdom, as were political bodies and the courts, moreover, unequally active. But, beyond this, the role of these elites was by definition ambiguous, as was their position as intermediaries.

Before political power became interested in local language, monuments, and history, or its particular set of interests, the enlightened province had to begin by getting recognition. And it only knew how to do this at the price of a prior submission to the rules and values dictated by the center (which were all the more easily imposed given their reception by provincial elites with conflicts of interest). The culture restored by the notables' efforts was, to a large degree, a reconstruction that had to be able to satisfy both Parisian expectations and the new taste and need for provincial identity. It came to legitimize the intermediary position of a restricted group that was itself seeking a double recognition. The vogue for "Provençalism," which arose at the end of the eighteenth century, could have taken on the appearance of local patriotism and nostalgia; however, it was expressed in terms that could have been welcomed anywhere and obviously had very little in common with the daily habits of most people.[20]

The record of the ancien régime is thus ambiguous. The monarchy, during its absolutist phase, was really a political and legal form tolerant of provincial personalities and particularisms. It put up with them as long as taxes were coming in, public order was guaranteed, and loyalty to the crown was not in question. On the other hand, it hardly cared to give them any status, still less to grant them anything more than formal legitimacy. On the face of it, the approach remained discreet for a long time

Figure 4.2

Map of Burgundy. The text in the title cartouche reads: "Map specific to the duchy of Burgundy geometrically drawn by order of Messiers the Generals Elect of the Province as a result of the Decree of the States of 1751, divided by Diocese, Bailiwicks, and Subdelegations. . . . Drawn up and executed by Séguin, engineer and geographer to the King in 1763."

and was poorly maintained by the end of the eighteenth century. This was because the State was not the only one implicated in this long-standing reluctance. The belated consciousness that took hold of some groups of notables was not enough to make the province as such exist. Although Brittany was destined to have a good future as regards the affirmation of identity and stereotyping, Catherine Bertho estimates that before the Revolution "no one noticed anything that later was to nourish contemporary collective representations: neither a coherent group of authors, nor support for specialized literature, nor even a genre of choice" (one is tempted to add, nor a public). "As for the writings of administrators . . . and travel narratives, they touched on Brittany's geography and economy; they did not write exclusively about Brittany's geography and economy."[21]

Does the province exist? Territorially, its definition is ultimately vague. Where can one squarely situate it in the maze of administrative, legal, and political districts sedimented over the course of centuries? The monarchy's administrators, from Vauban to those of the Enlightenment, continually denounced an organizational structure of the kingdom that they considered to be anarchic and inefficient. To its proponents, it posed no fewer problems; and, in multiplying its membership, it undoubtedly did not make obvious or easy the relationship, so familiar to us, between the consciousness of a particularism and identification with a region. This additional difficulty helps us to understand why resorting to history may have seemed a surer and more useful solution. In any case, it is useful to go back to the ancien régime itself to understand "France's particular difficulty in conceptualizing regional differences," as Mona Ozouf has quite rightly put it.[22]

The Revolution drastically changed the conditions of experience. From the outset it considered the empirical compromise on which the monarchical order had been based for so long to be unacceptable. It saw its first mission as the realization of the building of the nation. In the eyes of the men of 1789, this goal had to undergo political redefinition, but it demanded throughout the establishment of a fundamental transparence, removing political and administrative barriers, which was thenceforth to govern relations between citizens. This, among other things, was the significance of the Night of August 4, which ended feudal privilege. In the dismantling of privileges, the province found an unexpected dimension. Whatever its real shape, the province embodied par excellence distinctive features and irregularity, from then on both equally intolerable. So it is not surprising that its definitive suppression was determined. "A national constitution and public liberty being more advantageous to the provinces than the privileges enjoyed by some, and the sacrifice of which is necessary to the intimate unity of all the parts of the Empire, it is decreed that all the special privileges of provinces, principalities, regions [*pays*], cantons, towns, and communities with residents whether financial, or of any other nature, be abolished without reversion and will live by the natural law of all the French" (decree of August 11, 1789, article 10).

But in thus affirming the absolute priority of national unity, and in effecting legal means to achieve it, the Revolution invented, in a way, the regional problem; or, rather, it brought the problem to light and made it, potentially, an obstacle that could not be ignored. Nevertheless, it is interesting to note that, in the text just quoted, the "province" is not considered an exceptional phenomenon; it is only one of the examples of fundamental irregularity that had until then marred the relationship between the parts and the whole. It appeared among other bodies and communities governed by privilege or claiming to be so. It was not the province's special features as such that were targeted by the decree of August 1789, but one of the methods of the former order; it was not the identity of a territorial community, but the aspiration of a part to impose its law on the whole. The perspective here is not that of a centralization that sought from the outset to deny differences and characters; it is that of a legal standardization, which was to serve as the base for new social relations.

⚜

The country was, however, only on the brink of a transformation of greater magnitude. Far from being disregarded, the common question of the nature and importance of provincial roots came to center stage in the months that followed, owing to preparations being made for a new administrative division of the kingdom.[23]

On first reading, the plan is obviously radical. Sièyes very early on summed it up: "It is only by eliminating the provinces' boundaries that we will succeed in destroying all these local privileges, conveniently reclaimed when we were without a constitution, and which will continue to be defended by the provinces even when they are only obstacles to the establishment of social unity. . . . I do not know a more powerful or immediate method of making, without unrest, all the parts of France into a single body and all the peoples that divide it into one Nation."[24] The reasons for the undertaking were in fact more complex. To the already old concern, if one recalls, for simplification and rationalization of administrative organization was added imperative urgency, linked to the Revolutionary movement itself. It was not only a matter of trying to get the State mechanism going again (and, first off, the treasury), but most important, to define as quickly as possible the territorial basis of political representation. This immense program, successfully completed in the months between September 1789 and March 1790, was inseparable from an even greater ambition to revolutionize the French space—that is, to make it one of the instruments of national regeneration. Certainly, there is a big difference between the initial geometrical and utopian projects and the actual solutions, negotiated over a long time, that would be kept in the end. The fact remains that those who worked on the partition plan, those who tried to modify it, and those whom it concerned were all convinced that reorganizing territory in fact led one to redefine the conditions of social and political interplay.

In the debate that was thus opened, the regional level held a decisive place. Its existence, during the last years of the ancien régime, was discreet, as we have seen. But the plan to divide the kingdom suddenly gave it a new cast. It became something to be eliminated. The last attempt of the absolute monarchy to reform its administrative and political position, around the issue of provincial assemblies, had been the occasion for a sort of general rehearsal. In its contradictions, a text by Condorcet from 1788 displayed the full measure of the problem that had to be confronted henceforth. In his *Essai sur la Constitution et les fonctions des assemblées provinciales,* he announced: "We have assumed that this Constitution had to be the same for all the Provinces because it was impossible for us to imagine a real motive for establishing any differences between them." But he immediately made it clear that "following this, we will seek to eradicate the overly large inequality between the Provinces and districts, their overly irregular or elongated form, their overlappings, but seeking first to reconcile these changes with local preferences regarding customs, certain local habits, and the form of taxation, until such time as uniformity can be reestablished."[25] It was really the reform plan itself that constituted the provincial problem. It raised an obstacle in the path of progress and, by the same token, had to produce the means of overcoming it. It also set this tension in a history. The province, hardly fixed, was from the outset situated in a past whose weight the reasonable Condorcet knew he had to accept provisionally.

The Revolution raised the stakes because it expected more of the future that it had just opened up. Sieyès declared the political urgency of the new division of territory: "If we let this occasion go by, it will not come again and the Provinces might keep their *esprit de corps,* their privileges, their claims, their jealousies." In point of fact, in the autumn of 1789 the revolutionary course was already in full swing and real resistance from the assembly and the country was feared. On November 3, Thouret, a lawyer from Rouen and spokesman for the Constitutional

Committee, hardened the tone even more. He opened the parliamentary debate by prophesying the day when "the entire French people, joined together in one family, having only one law, and one kind of government, will abjure all the prejudices of the particularistic and local group mindset [*esprit de corporation*]."[26]

One would be wrong, however, to interpret this unification plan in terms of centralization. In 1789, equalizing, regularizing, and standardizing the distribution of territory in no way implied that privilege be reserved for the capital. On the contrary, it meant guaranteeing the same possibilities to parties within a larger whole. The operation meant both the definition of an egalitarian basis for political representation and an optimal redistribution of power between the center and the peripheries. It was necessary, in a word, to determine the right territorial unit that would make possible the best integration of the kingdom; in a word, "divide to unite." It was a very ambitious—as well as abstract—project, which hoped to create the conditions for a balance between special interests and the nation's interests. Even its abstraction, for that matter, left little room for the reality of the province; it was the principle of diversity, not de facto diversity, with which the constituents were confronted. The existence of regional districts was not, as such, threatening, since they were busy creating new ones. But it happened that those bequeathed by the ancien régime, because of their history and structure, generated disorder.

The long negotiations that began in the autumn of 1789 nevertheless witnessed the affirmation of a new provincial—or, to use an anachronistic term, regionalist—feeling. It encompassed very diverse intentions and interests, as we shall see. But everything happened as though the promise of imminent disappearance gave old monarchical districts a new reality and importance. Several months earlier, many *cahiers de doléances* had protested the vagueness and complexity of administrative boundaries and the kingdom's abysmal architecture, even though some already evinced, on the eve of the great national payback [*échéance*], an unexpected sensitivity to tradition and provincial affiliation.[27] But the debate on the creation of departments was another thing entirely. Provincial identity then became an argument and a stake.

It comes as no surprise that the leaders of the resistance to the plan to create departments were those who spoke in the name of peripheral provinces and areas of the State. Some of these territories had only recently been joined to the kingdom; others kept their distinct linguistic and cultural particularisms and sometimes maintained strong ties of solidarity to areas lying beyond their borders. None was ready to give up administrative and tax privileges that benefited it. Brittany, Artois,

Franche-Comté, the Dauphiné, Provence, and Béarn were included in this group. Their interests went no further than the conservation of already-acquired advantages, as one would expect. On the other hand, what is more surprising was the affirmation of the indissoluble character of provincial affiliation. The baron de Jessé put it in a striking way: "How can one vanquish the feeling that ties the provincial inhabitant to the name of his land as much as to the land itself? They might say that we must merge our spirits; but such a trial for the body politic should only be attempted when it is healthy and strong enough to withstand this operation. I conclude that [there must be] conservation of the division of provinces."[28] Still, Jessé did not rule out the future possibility. Mirabeau, who for many reasons was made the herald of the provincialist party, held that the partition plan called into question a natural order and intangible solidarities: "I well know that they would break up neither houses nor steeples, but they would slice through that which is most inseparable, they would slice through all the ties that have for so long bound together mores, customs, products, and language."[29] The invocation of nature and the organicist theme were both destined for a beautiful future in the plea for regionalisms by the Left as well as the Right. They were rooted no doubt in the geographical thought of the Enlightenment but also went back—in a much vaguer and seemingly more effective way—to the vision of an inseparably physical, historical, and social order. The province thus came to put itself in the way of revolutionary voluntarism.

But we will not linger on these overly general reasons. A multiplicity of local interests rushed into the open breach. Marie-Vic Ozouf-Marignier has closely studied the intervention and arguments of the Comité de division. For the representatives of towns—that is, institutions, notables, economic lobbies—it was a matter, of course, of getting the best part of the new deal. The safeguarding of ancient privileges and the pursuit of new profits could not, however, be displayed in an egotistical way. People had to speak in the language of the Revolution, which was that of the general interest. Nature and history were once again cited as proof.

This was also true when referring to the provinces; usually one did not appeal to clearly defined entities with an explicit historical identity, but rather, once again, to a principle based on balance. It is this that, in a timeless way, has guaranteed the fortunate presence of human activities on the land; it is also this that has made possible their happy complementarity, which nothing today can call into question. The department's rational functionalism was contrasted with the country's providential functionalism. It gave birth to a quasi-spontaneous anthropology, which sought to convince the legislator that the most favorable division was objectively the best. If one had to liberate Saint-Quentin from the tutelage of its rival, Cambrai, it was because there was, forty kilometers away, "such a marked difference in the way of thinking, mores, customs that perhaps it would be dangerous to make it the administrative center of our area." The same reasons were more often used in the opposite way and argued for a given territory's annexation, for an increased power to command. The reality of regional life took shape; it nourished convictions that in turn strengthened it. Of course, the departments were created in 1790. But with them their doubles or phantoms came into being. Not only because the initial utopian plans were succeeded by a division that was more sensitive to the prior economic, institutional, and social landscape, but because the construction of the departments transformed the perception of French space.[30]

The controversy over departments was only the first instance of a two-sided and contradictory affirmation. The federative, then federalist, moment was another, when the lines of force were not being superimposed on previous ones, and the meaning of which shifted greatly according to the Revolutionary dynamic between 1790 and 1793. Let us recall its general characteristics, as laid out by Mona Ozouf.[31] The federations were initially associations for defense and solidarity that were organized, little by little, into a national network. There was no trace of particularism in their program or in the conviction they sustained; their activity was completely dominated by a dream of unity, of fusion, grandiosely orchestrated into the Parisian celebration of July 14, 1790. In spatial terms, it occurred in a France that was from then on totally transparent to itself and in which each citizen and each collective was at home everywhere. People were enthusiastic about the return of the federative banner: "The municipality, the district of Angers and the other districts and neighboring municipalities cannot contain their excitement; they fly before it. The municipality does not in the least consider whether or not it is advancing outside its territory? Does today's patriotism admit these lines of demarcation that arrogance and pettiness had drawn in the past?"[32]

Between the outburst of 1790 and the "federalist" insurrection of 1793, the sense of continuity was ambiguous, to say the least. Three years of the system of departments had no doubt given the new districting its own texture and raised expectations, although they had not called into question the republic's unity. There is no expression of provincial feeling in the texts that accompanied the movement, and still less indication of a separatist plan. Moreover, large sections of provincial France hated Paris; it reproached Paris for having, by virtue of its abuses and authoritarianism, jeopardized the equality that was supposed to govern the different parts of the territory. It was Paris and the Montagnard speeches, moreover, that imputed to the Girondist insurrection the plan to dismantle the nation and demonized "federalism." In this asymmetrical confrontation, the regional problem was scarcely considered as such. It served as a tool for polemical argument, but not as the foundation for specific demands.

This is not necessarily to say that the regional issue was absent from debate—quite the opposite. It was used by its defenders. The tougher stance of Parisian politics also took the form of exasperated intolerance toward all the variations of the actual France. Nothing makes this clearer than the emphasis placed, during these years, on the Revolution's linguistic policy.[33] In the schema of national regeneration, the realm's diversity of languages posed a real problem: how could one be understood, teach new values, or bring men together who so often could not understand one another? A two-tiered answer was found in 1790, which argued that time was needed to set in motion educational methods to instill conviction. A policy of public instruction was to imprint on the collective soul of the citizens "new feelings, new mores, new customs." But this was a long-term project. In the meantime, it seemed wiser to translate decrees into the realm's main regional language of communication, either in Paris or in some bureaus in the departments.

Several months later, in August 1790, the Abbé Grégoire sent the provinces "a series of questions relating to the patois and the customs of country people." The investigation was to last nearly four years. It showed a genuine interest in real life, about which it sought to bring together both general and specific data, even as it confessed its real long-term goal. The twenty-eighth question asked: "Have you noticed that [patois] is gradually becoming similar to the French idiom, that certain words are disappearing, and since when?" The next question was even more explicit: "What would be the religious and political significance of completely destroying patois?" And finally: "What would be the means of doing this?" But when Grégoire presented the results of this collective labor before the Convention in Prairial year II (May–June 1794), it was in the abbreviated form of a *Rapport sur la nécessité et les moyens d'anéantir les patois et d'universaliser l'usage de la langue française,* which, although not recommending any use of force, scarcely left waiting as a solution. In the meantime, trouble was building and suspicion was aroused. In Pluviôse (January–February), did not Barrère, in his *Rapport sur les idiomes,* attribute the dangers that threatened to "plotting by ignorance and despotism"? "Federalism and superstition speak low Breton; emigration and hatred for the Republic speak German; the counterrevolution speaks Italian, and fanaticism speaks Basque."[34]

In 1793–94, diversity was suspect everywhere. Public safety demanded that people close ranks, and Revolutionary educational practices became stricter. But long before and after the Montagnard dictatorship, one encountered the widely held conviction that history and the national plan were going in the direction of the obliteration of differences—political and social differences, of course, but also cultural differences—between men. In the general trend of statutes that were being imposed, the regional character was looked on as a relic consigned to oblivion, even in the eyes of those who, by virtue of their profession, ought to have been the most attentive to it. In 1792, the geographer Mentelle thought to record the benefits of the new direction: "Would it not be ridiculous to answer, being almost in Dunkirk, when someone was asking people: are you Flemish? No, sir, we are Walloons. In Dieppe, in Caudebec, you are true Normans; no, sir, we are from the Caux region. In truth, we say: we are brothers."[35] At the same time, visiting the Oise region in their *Voyages dans les départements de la France,* Lavallée and Brion went even further and prophesied the coming of an age without distinctions:

> It is to be hoped that sooner or later the Revolution will introduce the benefit of a national costume and that the traveler, going from one department to another, will no longer believe himself to be among different peoples. To see the inhabitants of the department of Bouches-du-Rhône next to the inhabitants of the department of the Nord, those of Finistère beside those of the Bas-Rhin, those of the Seine-Inférieure next to those of the Var, could one believe they belonged to the same nation?[36]

A France first united, then unified. This leveling of the countryside, however, only revealed one aspect of Revolutionary territory. It had another side, which presents a contrasting picture in almost every way. At a time when, in Paris, people wished to see only one France, France extended its resources, revealing its multiplicity and complexity. The invention of departments had suddenly made the strength of provincial roots felt. The plan for national leveling imposed, in the eyes of even those who were given the task of effecting it, a sense of the contrasts within the real country. Things had, it is true, begun well before the Revolution. We have already had cause to refer to this collective movement, which, at root, had begun to uncover the distinctive features of grassroots France during the years 1750–60. It was most often the work of men in the field: provincial administrators, local scholars, travelers, and doctors, whose accounts became part of a large and disparate corpus. They had in common, however, the experience of being confronted with real life in the kingdom. They had detailed knowledge of it and let themselves be captivated by it—to the point of vertigo. These men of the Enlightenment found in the ambient neo-Hippocratism reasons to accord a new importance to that which defined the distinctive features of each place, and they strove to think of these differences as part of a system.

But this topographic obsession was not closed in on itself. It was part of the much larger perspective of a first cultural anthropology that, from the 1760s until the Empire, stood out as the main methodology for a science of man, the contours of which the Enlightenment attempted to define. It rested on a simple conviction, that of the unity of mankind, which it sought to demonstrate even amid the unlimited variety of its strange expressions. He who chose to gather and describe the details of local life was no longer content just to take note of their uncompromising originality, but had to situate them in the general picture of humanity. Between the observer and the object of observation, between "us" and "them," the relationship up until then had been one of exteriority and often exclusion. It was thenceforth reformulated in the name of a very strong awareness of identity, which in principle assumed the unity of the specific forms of human societies. It is advisable to pay attention to the many attempts, often modest and improvised, of the great theoreticians of the century, by Rousseau as well as Buffon, to reconstruct the social and cultural genealogy of men. All these efforts were made in order to reconstruct the whole picture, which would restore a forgotten coherence to the contributions and histories of those societies. This was because each piece of a lost culture, each local characteristic was henceforth perceived as the relic of an older state, like the eyewitness account of a past that had to be restored. Archaism, a term readily applied to popular and provincial cultures, changed in meaning; it was no longer the heinous mark of a bygone past, but the inestimable sign of a history the comprehension of which was necessary to understand the present.

The very thing that had resisted standardization and assimilation was becoming, by the same token, the main object of attention and study. Until then a cultivated traveler knew the provincial areas, towns, monuments that were vestiges of an already-formed "great history." From then on it followed an entirely different course. It was in the years between 1770 and 1780, according to Michel Vovelle, that visitors to Provence became curious and began to explore its interior [*profondeurs*] more systematically. They turned their attention to those places where no obvious monument remained, no visible history: side routes, out-of-the-way places, mountains.[37] In these same years, similar motivations led Ramond de Carbonnières through the Alps and the Pyrenees, Legrand d'Aussy to Auvergne, Cambry to the Finistère, Grasset Saint-Sauveur through the

Landes, and Grégoire through the Vosges. This exoticism of the interior
was both a return to origins and an exploration of social issues. A little
later, during the heyday of Ideology, de Gérando was to give this approach a perfectly explicit theoretical justification: "The traveler/philos-
opher, who sails to the ends of the earth, crosses the succession of the
ages; he journeys in the past; each step that he takes is a century crossed.
These unknown islands that he reaches are for him the cradle of human
society."[38] These unknown spaces were also, for the inventors of French
ethnography, the interiors of our provinces.

All the remote places were like scattered pieces of an immense puzzle that had to be put back together. Such a universalist image obviously
did not encourage one to accord importance to the regional framework
as such. It was perceived only as a localized feature in a broader system.

We can also observe the degree to which the anthropological project, rooted in the Enlightenment, was deeply associated with a political
agenda. This became obvious, of course, with the Revolution and the
deliberate and willful construction of the French nation, but it was already present in the last decades of the eighteenth century. A good part
of this literature, which uncovered, inventoried, studied, and classified
accounts of local culture, was, as has been said, the work of isolated investigators or else associated with larger undertakings. Compared to the
older literature dealing with administrative description, their texts—incidentally, incomparably more numerous and richer—innovated out of
an explicit desire for social intervention and practical efficiency. Most of
them raised a central question: how could a better knowledge of the terrain allow for a better management of society? How could one pave the
way for the Enlightenment and innovation?

But the urge to innovate too often clashed, they thought, with resistance from tradition: from the repeated complaints in physiocratic literature that deplored the inertia of peasant behavior, to the answer to
François de Neufchâteau's surveys concerning "public spirit" in provincial France in the time of the Directory. Echoing the concerns of the
Abbé Grégoire about the actual penetration of Revolutionary conviction
and values in the countryside, the administrators of the Enlightenment,
both Parisian and provincial, continued to see behaviors and mentalities
as an obstacle. They were undoubtedly not the first to see regional France
as the very symbol of social opacity and cultural inertia, the world that
resisted their beneficial undertakings par excellence. But they no longer
knew how to be satisfied with this acknowledgment. Much more than

VUE DU ROCHER DE CORNILLON,
et d'une partie du Cours de la Romanche.
Le Soleil paroissant coucher très-fort derrière la Montagne a certaine joute de l'année à l'heure
"" Rolance à l'échelle   A.P.D.R.   N.º   "" Balin de Violant.

Figure 4.3
*Picturesque travels
through France with
descriptions of all her
provinces.* "National
work dedicated to the
King and embellished
with a large number
of engravings exe-
cuted with the greatest
care, and drawings
by the best artists of
the capital by a soci-
ety of men of letters."
View of the Rocher de
Cornillon, engraved
by Fessard after Balin.

Figure 4.4
Montbard, department of the Côte-d'Or, in J. B. Lavallée, J. B. Breton, and L. Brion, *Voyages dans les
départements de la France enrichis de tableaux géographiques* (1792). Landscapes and depth: it is the
task of natural history and all the sciences of observation to take note of the variations in the actual
country.

their predecessors, they were concerned with practical efficiency. Administrative rationalization was thus required to be coupled with an educational method. It supposed, moreover, that people knew how to pinpoint and explain that which, in provincial France, encouraged the obstinate refusal of beneficial progress; instead of considering customs as erratic expressions of a fundamental inferiority, they sought to understand their coherence in order to break them up better. This is what made it a system. In other words, this is what, in the representations common to all these pioneers of regional ethnography, enabled the association of the interior with the same explanatory picture of geographical determinations, forms of human settlement, rules of sociability, distinctive physiology, and unchanging psychological features, all characteristics whose interaction, in the final analysis, was supposed to allow one to realize the backwardness of minds and social and political blockage.

✳

The Revolution was thus a paradoxical moment that combined the will to unify with the discovery of regional differences, each supporting the other. Nonetheless, from the ground, observers of France were faced with de facto situations that could be very unequally contrasted. Certain provincial groups were quite distinctive, such as Alsace, Brittany, Roussillon, and, to a lesser degree, the Franche-Comté; others, such as Gascony and Burgundy, stemmed from old political alliances, conscious of their glorious past but deeply altered by the kingdom's administrative and political framework. Still others were no more than meaningless structures. The existence of a distinct linguistic community, the demand for lost (and sometimes forgotten) privileges, a more or less expressed resistance to the movement at the core of French centralization, the attraction of centrifugal forces, the rallying of local elites to the monarchy and then to the Revolution—all these elements shaped provincial characters, made them unevenly sensitive as well as unequally aware.[39] These were the concrete differences that the Enlightenment's intellectual system was least prepared to understand, obsessed as it was by an anthropology of generalization.

By contrast, observers during the Revolutionary years perceived these differences, but their approach was marked even more by the principle that differentiation infinitely fragmented the nation's territory. Most of them were the transmitters, agents, sometimes the executors of a Parisian policy of which they approved. But they also had contact with real life and resistance. The descriptions they delivered on demand rarely conformed to what the government and committees expected from them, without one necessarily being able to call into question their loyalty to, or confidence in, the Revolutionary schema. They were caught between two levels, two scales of perception and analysis that fit poorly together and often contradicted one another. These were the distinctive features that most persistently hampered the integration of French society, which was their most highly valued goal. It was thus all-important to pinpoint, describe, them, and, as much as possible, understand these differences.

From this tension a long-winded, often contradictory, and invaluable literature was born. The description of the real France, which was at least as much rural as regional, was that of nature. The men of the Enlightenment not only readily described geographical nature—mountains versus plains, the Mediterranean climate versus the temperate climate—but also an organically linked complex of local characteristics that could not be deconstructed. The "facts" of society and culture were, in their minds, inseparable from a particular stage of mankind. Grégoire's questionnaire had already invited such deep examinations by multiplying the requests for information about the mores and activities of dialect-speaking French people. The answers sent to the abbé probably surpassed his expectations, painting a picture that refuted in advance the possibility of a harmonious and spontaneous linguistic integration. To suppress dialects, did one not have to "destroy the sun, the coolness of nights, the type of foods, the water quality, man entirely"?

Of course, some were ready to concede that "patois each day was becoming gradually more like French," as they were invited to say, but it can scarcely be expected that these sound convictions would be backed up with evidence. The Abbé Fonvielhe, a priest of Saint-Amand-de-Boisse and a member of the Société des amis de la Constitution de Bergerac, speaking about the elimination of regional speech, was sure that "its political as well as religious importance is obvious." But he did not hesitate to state that "patois brings men together, unites them, it is a language of brothers and friends."[40] The informants who were supposed to make provincial opacity understandable ended up making it an insurmountable obstacle. The nature of patois went back to an innate ordering of the social bond linked to a place; it touched on innate emotions and native solidarities. It was a reminder that something deeper existed in the heart of the people, not identified with the dreadful time of feudalism, that the new political society still did not know how to dissolve or replace.

This contradiction on the part of observers was even more noticeable, if that is possible, during the immense undertaking to collect statistics from the departments, sketched out by François de Neufchâteau in year VI and then systematically organized by Chaptal between year IX and 1804.[41] Yet it consisted of a centralized project with an approach directed, supervised, and commented on by Paris. It was in keeping with the new framework of the department and thus broke, from the beginning, the solidarities of the former France. It was, moreover, less inclined to take stock of the past than the future. As Marie-Noëlle Bourguet has correctly observed, the investigation was to be used to set up a "basic index of the present day," to fix "the image of France in 1800 like a cornerstone necessary for the establishment of all later accounting"[42]—that is, worthy of future advances in national unity. Chaptal suggested this in the instructions he addressed to the prefects on 19 Germinal year IX telling them to devote themselves to "know[ing] France" better: "The Revolution no doubt influenced all parts of France; it did not affect every place the same way. It produced different effects on people in the Vendée than in the departments of the east, in those of the interior than those in the Midi."[43] The thorough investigation was rigorous and coherent from the start, and it benefited methods of local administration. The paradoxical result is that statistician prefects, such convenient symbols of Jacobin centralization, and their collaborators definitely recognized the proliferation of French diversity. The census of men, resources, and opinions was always straying into ethnographical description (already part, it is true, of the questionnaire that directed the gathering of facts). Space in the department, at once too abstract and too vast, was fragmented into smaller units—cantons, regions [*pays*], a town, an area [*terroir*]—each endowed with an absolute, an irreducible originality. Only nuance, difference, the intractable feature mattered from then on. The game of explanatory hypotheses was increasing. It became more complex seen from up close, so much did France's details discourage the usual readings. Worse, the Revolution's effects on this repertory of differences were not univocal; it got to the point that they even reinforced them instead of blurring them.[44] Descriptive statistics, by their very nature, encouraged the production of data that were hard to fit together. But, from Thermidor to the Empire, they revealed the pieces of a puzzle the piecing together of which seemed to be unthinkable. It was up to ethnographical imagination and the abilities of another discipline, anthropology, the objectives of which were being defined at the same time, to come back to the task of finding the key. At the turn of the century, the Société des Observateurs de l'Homme and later the Académie celtique were to work on the problem.[45]

This outcome was not immediately realized. In the first years of the Empire, the statistical plan was modified in terms of a stricter centralization and, above all, a more rigorous standardization of data. The department was to cease to be the setting for a discovery of France in favor of becoming that for local accounting destined to become part of a national summary. The Napoleonic takeover led to the establishment, thirty years later, of a Statistique générale de la France.[46] Administrators were henceforth urged to renounce, as Montalivet, minister of the interior, said in 1813, "overly broad views" cluttered with "too many details." The figure took precedence over description, the sum over a detailed list. But Napoleonic statistics were not solely implicated here. When, under the restored monarchy and at the beginning of the July Monarchy, one wondered about the unevenness [dénivellations] of French space, it was in entirely different terms that would scarcely accord any more importance to the regional level. From the baron Dupin to d'Angeville, the major distributions that appeared on the map of the two Frances as a result of the work of the so-called moral statistics were compiled at the national level and on the basis of standardized information from the departments; they did not spend much time pinpointing specific regional features, still less on their interpretation.

Everybody knew that it was the department that emerged triumphant from the Revolution and for a long time after. It was not until the last third of the nineteenth century that the debate on France's territorial organization brought the regional theme to the foreground again in sociological terms by Le Play, whose La Réforme sociale (1864) sought to correct the imbalances linked to urbanization through a better distribution of power and suggested the creation of thirteen provinces (without any relation, incidentally, to the ancien régime's districts). It was also grounded in geographical terms through the exploitation of "natural" units confirmed by history, identified by Élisée Reclus and later Pierre Foncin; and in administrative and economic terms, at the turn of the century, with the ambition on the part of certain business circles to reorganize regional balances and powers. The logic that inspired them was, of course, that of interests, and regional memory did not have a central role in it.[47] Moreover, in the series of plans for territorial reorganization promoted by Le Play, by Clémentel in 1917, under the Vichy régime in 1941, and, lastly, on the definition of twenty-one (later twenty-two) regions between 1956 and 1970, is it not significant that it was the unit of the department that, imperturbably, served as the basis of the constitution of "regional" units of larger size?

It is noteworthy as well that the nineteenth century also saw the affirmation of powerful regionalist feelings, even if they remained unequal from one provincial group to another. Cultural regionalisms, for the most part, were rediscovering—or reinventing—the power of local tradition. From within and without the interior, it was this time of provincial stereotyping that, to a large degree, was responsible for the characterology of French regions as we still know them today,[48] even if it was partially reformulated with more recent conflicts in the 1970s. This regionalist creation took many different routes. In Brittany, it took the form of a rediscovery of a historic, archaeological, and literary heritage that, in the nineteenth century, came to positively support the feeling of identity. In the neighboring Vendée, it was a completely different case: the conflicting tricks of memory came to give consistency and character to the territory of the war of 1793 and then the insurrection of 1799. The provincial character of Provence, in spite of the region's antiquity and titles, in spite of the blossoming of Félibrige,[49] remained flexible enough to be deeply redefined when it chose to recognize, in the mid–nineteenth century, Africa's disturbing proximity rather than the classical values inherited from Greece and Rome.

The region exists and does not succeed in existing—such is the ambiguous legacy of the Revolution. Everything attests to this in-between situation, this contradictory status. The departments had sought to obliterate even the traces of the old provincial districts and their memory from territory. They succeeded to the degree that they became dense, full realities, the locus of real investments in very diverse ways. And yet they were never emancipated from the old forms they had come to replace. Not only because in the end their borders had to conform, more often than had been envisioned, to their former outlines or because they would continue to call themselves—and to feel—Breton, Alsatian, Gascon, or from the Auvergne, but rather because the department was no longer being perceived as antagonistic to the province. The department, in some way, had given life to the regional space that encompassed it, the significance of which came to be recognized at the close of the twentieth century. Lavallée and Brion witnessed this in the course of their *Voyages* in 1796, rediscovering the continuities in natural and social landscapes: "The department [the Cher] we are visiting has boundless analogies with that of the Indre, through which we have just traveled. This will seem natural, if one recalls that we have already noted that both were part of the same province previously known by the name Berri. Same character of inhabitants, just about the same kind of culture, and a sort of unity in the products of nature as well as the soil."[50] All through the nineteenth century, from the Joanne guides to the *Tour de la France par deux enfants* (1877),[51] the description of France would thus operate simultaneously on two levels of reference.

The Revolution did not invent the region, which still uneasily exists today. It did something else. In its very dynamics, it defined the terms of a regionalist nostalgia that struggled to find expression. The word for region itself was not imposed much more forcefully in 1820 than in 1789.

What it evoked was divided among a series of realities that did not always overlap: the province, region [*pays*], place, the hardened opposition between center and periphery with remarkable histories, which you will find in this volume. What was by and large imposed, on the contrary, was a sharper, more sensitive, "dramatized, politicized"[52] perception of diversity and French identities. Also imposed was the conviction that the latter translated the profound shifts of national history into space: the advances, retreats, reasons to hope and, even more, to be concerned. This unfinished, contradictory, unhappy formulation even today affects representations of France's territory. The region has still to be invented, but we can henceforth no longer ignore it. The Revolutionary moment was the time of this uncomfortable discovery.

NOTES

1. Daniel Nordman and Jacques Revel, "La Formation de l'espace français," in *L'Espace français: Histoire de la France,* vol. 1, ed. André Burguière and Jacques Revel (Paris: Éditions du Seuil, 1989), 29–169, esp. 34–37.

2. I found Mona Ozouf, "'Jacobin': Fortune et infortune d'un mot," *Le Débat* 13 (1981): 28–39, to be a useful study of the uses of the word and translation; see also, in the same issue, the reflections of Maurice Agulhon, "Plaidoyer pour les jacobins: La gauche, l'État et la région dans la tradition historique français," 55–65.

3. Alexis de Tocqueville, *The Old Regime and the Revolution,* vol. 1: *The Complete Text,* ed. François Furet and Françoise Mélonio, trans. Alan S. Kahan (Chicago: University of Chicago Press, 1998), 59. Note that this oft-cited judgment is nuanced and clarified elsewhere: "Not only do the provinces resemble one another more and more, but in each province men of different classes, at least those who are positioned apart from the people, are becoming more and more similar, despite particularisms of rank" (143).

4. Cf. the reasonable remarks of Christophe Charle, "Région et conscience régionale en France: Questions à propos d'un colloque," *Actes de la recherche en sciences sociales* 35 (1980): 37–43. The article is a reflection on the proceedings of the 1974 conference, *Régions et régionalisme en France du XVIIe siècle à nos jours* (Paris: P.U.F., 1978).

5. Charles Maurras, *Enquête sur la monarchie* (Paris, 1900), gives a good synopsis of this tradition of thought. A recent historical interpretation can be found in Yves Durand, *Vivre au pays au XVIIIe siècle: Essai sur la notion de pays dans l'ouest de la France* (Paris: P.U.F., 1984), with a preface by Pierre Chaunu; or, still more discreet, better argued, and less explicitly political, in Yves Castan, *Honnêteté et relations sociales en Languedoc au XVIIe siècle* (Paris: Plon, 1974), as well as Nicole and Yves Castan, *Vivre ensemble: Ordre et désordre en Languedoc (XVIIe–XVIIIe siècle)* (Paris: Gallimard/Julliard, 1981).

6. The latest is by R. Descimon and A. Guéry, who have strongly nuanced the reasons; see "Un état des temps modernes," in *L'État et les pouvoirs,* ed. Jacques Le Goff, vol. 2 of *Histoire de la France* (Paris, 1989), 181–356.

7. Gustave Dupont-Ferrier, "Sur l'emploi du mot 'province,' notamment dans la langue administrative de l'ancienne France," *Revue historique* (1929): 241–67, 278–303.The only rigorous uses of the term "province" were ecclesiastical and medieval. As for its administrative—and more generally secular—meaning, it had a belated success with the edict of June 1787.

8. Cited by Ferdinand Brunot, *Histoire de la langue française depuis les origines à nos jours,* vol. 9, part 2, *La Révolution et l'Empire* (Paris, 1937), 1015.

9. I rely here on the results of an unpublished D.E.A. dissertation by Thierry Gasnier, prepared under the supervision of Pierre Nora, École des hautes études en sciences sociales, 1987. I thank Thierry Gasnier for giving me permission to use this excellent work. See in particular Appendix 1. For the corpus studied, see Pierre Doisy, *Le Royaume de France et les états de Lorraine, par ordre alphabétique,* 2nd ed. (Paris, 1753); Brion de la Tour, *Coup d'oeil général sur la France* (Paris, 1765); Antoine Augustin Bruzen de la Martinière, *Le Grand dictionnaire géographique et critique* (Paris, 1768); R. de Hesseln, *Dictionnaire universel de la France* (Paris, 1771); *Almanach royal* (Paris, 1789).

10. François de Dainville, "Les Français vus par leurs intendants," *Études* (1954): 60–74; Louis Trénard, *Les Mémoires des intendants pour l'instruction du duc de Bourgogne (1698): Introduction générale* (Paris: Bibliothèque nationale, 1975).

11. Cf. *La Découverte de la France au XVIIIe siècle,* proceedings of the ninth conference organized by the Centre méridional de rencontres sur le XVIIe siècle (Paris, 1980).

12. Roger Chartier, "Les Deux France: Histoire d'une géographie," *Cahiers d'histoire* 4 (1978): 393–415.

13. Mona Ozouf, "La Révolution et la perception de l'espace national: Fédération, fédéralisme et stéréotypes régionaux," in *L'École de la France: Essais sur la Révolution, l'utopie et l'enseignement* (Paris: Gallimard, 1984), 27–54. This article is essential for the subject.

14. Darluc, *Histoire naturelle de la Provence* (1782), vii, cited by Numa Broc, *La Géographie des philosophes: Géographes et voyageurs français au XVIIIe siècle* (Paris: Ophrys, 1975), 407.

15. Jacques Revel, "Forms of Expertise: Intellectuals and 'Popular' Culture in France (1650–1800)," in *Understanding Popular Culture: Europe from the Middle Ages to the 19th Century,* ed. Steven L. Kaplan (Berlin and New York: Mouton, 1984), 255–73.

16. It is true that in the sixteenth century an explicit interest was shown in certain forms of popular culture, some characteristic features of which scholars were beginning to gather. In the face of clerical culture, it was a matter of defending and illustrating the resources of French, enriched by some of its regional nuances. Words and expressions were collected, as well as proverbs, to which Erasmus gave new dignity: were they not the beginning of a common language between men as well as the expression of a wisdom that spanned the ages? The collections, which then multiplied and drew on provincial collections, nonetheless accorded scarcely any importance to the local roots of proverbial formulations and no more to their specific purposes. "Popular," "gallican," or "common" proverbs really belonged to another culture, the details—still less the diversity—of which no one felt compelled to explore. Could they be known anyway? Charles de Bouelles, author of two of these compilations in 1531 and 1557, seemed to doubt it: "There are at present in France as many human customs and languages as peoples, regions, and towns." The collected documents were published in French (often in Latin as well) without any special care

for either their wording or their original context. The same indifference is evident in Jean Nicot, *Thrésor de la langue françoyse* (Paris, 1606), which collects the lexicographical work of the preceding century and yet gives a reasoned welcome to provincial meanings, the origins of which he often points out. It is completed, among other appendixes, by two collections of proverbs: the first, arranged in alphabetical order, gives without any commentary the French wording and its Latin translation; the second offers explanations in the vernacular for some sentences but almost never bothers to indicate their origins.

From this relative indifference, one finds, a century later, a counterpart in the immense effort undertaken by Jean-Baptiste Thiers to gather superstitions. Aside from his famous *Traité des superstitions* (1679; much expanded in 1702 and republished many times in the eighteenth century), he was the author of innumerable lampoons, essays, and theses, all of which were devoted to denouncing false beliefs, pointless practices, and the corrupted exercise of religion. This parish curé, linked to a network of Jansenist priests, unhappy with his relations with the ecclesiastical hierarchy, was, in spite of his university credentials and torrential learning, a grassroots man whose pastoral concerns necessitated the theologian's militant vigilance. A man of the grass roots, not the land: even though he practiced as a minister in country parishes, his knowledge was drawn entirely from books. Through his correspondence, we see him exchanging cards, bibliographical references, hardly ever looking around him. "When he got it into his head to write he always chose extraordinary or bizarre subjects, rummaging through all the tables in his books, among which he had a goodly number of fairly rare ones, and went searching in good libraries or among his friends, to provide for his designs, and threw his discoveries on paper." Let us not be astonished not to find ethnographical concerns on the part of an author whom ethnohistorians today have made much of: that was most certainly not his plan. Thiers was exclusively motivated by the concern to oppose the particularity of popular beliefs with the Catholicism of the religious norm. In his lack of interest in concrete observation one senses even more than a strictly intellectual choice: an instinctive reply to the proliferation of reality that would threaten to go beyond the scope of his undertaking to identify, describe, classify. He was prepared to separate the true from the false, but he was not definitely capable of mastering the multiplicity of real practices whose significance and coherence he never sought to either clarify or understand.

17. Daniel Roche, *Le Siècle des lumières en province: Académies et académiciens provinciaux,* 2 vols. (Paris and La Haye: Mouton and Éditions de l'École des hautes études en sciences sociales, 1978), 1:342–55 (academic competitions), 366–84 (works of academicians).

18. Roche, *Le Siècle des lumières,* 1:350. For the multiplication of provincial histories started or finished, see Roche, *Le Siècle des lumières,* 2:186, n. 160.

19. Cf. Broc, *La Géographie des philosophes,* 417–19, which relies on F. de Dainville's works.

20. François-Xavier Emmanuelli, "De la conscience politique à la naissance du 'provençalisme' dans la généralité d'Aix à la fin du XVIIIe siècle," in *Régions et régionalismes,* 117–38.

21. Catherine Bertho, "L'Invention de la Bretagne: Genèse sociale d'un stéréotype," *Actes de la recherche en sciences sociales* 35 (1980): 45–62; see also, to gauge the contrast between the eighteenth and nineteenth centuries, Bertho, "Les

Enseignements d'une bibliographie: Les livres consacrés à la Bretagne au XIXe siècle," *Revue française d'histoire du livre* 20 (1978): 6–33.

22. Ozouf, "La Révolution et la perception de l'espace national," 27.

23. Marie-Vic Ozouf-Marignier, *La Formation des départements: La représentation du territoire national à la fin du XVIIIe siècle* (Paris: Éditions de l'E.H.E.S.S., 1989); Mona Ozouf, "Département," in *Dictionnaire critique de la Révolution française,* ed. François Furet and Mona Ozouf (Paris: Flammarion, 1989); Marcel Roncayolo, "The Department," below in this volume.

24. Emmanuel Joseph Sieyès, *Instructions envoyées par M. le duc d'Orléans pour les personnes étrangères de Sa procuration aux assemblées de bailliages relatives aux États généraux* (1789), 43–44.

25. Condorcet, *Essai sur la constitution et les fonctions des assemblées provinciales* (1788), 188–90, cited in Ozouf-Marignier, *La Formation des départements,* 28.

26. *Archives parlementaires,* ser. 1 (1789–99), 9:656.

27. Ozouf, "La Révolution et la perception de l'espace national," 31–32. But the author rejects the thesis of a "federalism in the *cahiers*" and emphasizes what prevailed, "the feeling of the omnipotence of the contract and the desire for unity."

28. *Archives parlementaires,* 9:461, cited by Ozouf-Marignier, *La Formation des départements,* 48.

29. *Archives parlementaires,* 9:660.

30. One will find the expression of this solidarity in the system of double nomination used for a long time ("department X, in the former province Y"), but in a much more significant way in the fact that the lists of departments were presented not at all according to the abstract convention of alphabetical order, as one would have expected, but grouped by provinces (cf. Gasnier, 16–17).

31. I use here the very solid analysis of Ozouf, "La Révolution et la perception de l'espace national," 37–45.

32. F. Uzureau, "Les Fêtes de la féderation à Angers," *Andegaviana* 3 (1905), cited in Ozouf, "La Révolution et la perception de l'espace national," 38. See also Uzureau, *La Fête révolutionnaire, 1789–1799* (Paris: Gallimard, 1976), 44–74.

33. Michel de Certeau, Dominique Julia, and Jacques Revel, *Une politique de la langue: La Révolution française et les patois; L'enquête de Grégoire* (Paris: Gallimard, 1975).

34. *Archives parlementaires,* ser. 1, 83:715.

35. E. Mentelle, *Méthode courte et facile pour apprendre aisément et retenir sans peine la nouvelle géographie de la France* (Paris, 1791), 4.

36. J. Lavallée, J.-B. Breton, and L. and L. Brion, *Voyages dans les départements de la France, enrichis de tableaux géographiques et d'estampes* (1792–1802), "Oise," 5.

37. Michel Vovelle, "La Découverte en Provence, ou les primitifs de l'ethnographie provençale," in *De la cave au grenier: Un itinéraire de Provence au XVIIIe siècle* (Québec: Serge Fleury, 1980), 407–35.

38. J.-M. de Gérando, *Considérations sur les diverses méthodes à suivre dans l'observation des peuples sauvages* (Paris, 1800).

39. Bertho, "L'Invention de la Bretagne"; as well as the contributions of Albert Soboul and, above all, in the same collection, of L. Trénard (the French Netherlands), M. Gresset (Franche-Comté), A. Marcet (Roussillon), F.-X. Emmanuelli (Provence), and M. Bordes (Gascony), *Régions et régionalismes,* 25–154.

40. Certeau, Julia, and Revel, *Une politique de la langue,* 146–47, 206–7.

41. See Marie-Noëlle Bourguet, *Déchiffrer la France: La statistique départementale à l'époque napoléonienne* (Paris: Éd. des archives contemporaines, 1988). Cf. also Ozouf, "La Révolution et la perception de l'espace national." For the epistemological agenda of descriptive statistics, see Jean-Claude Perrot, *L'Âge d'or de la statistique régionale française (an IV–1804)* (Paris: Clavreuil, 1977).

42. Bourguet, *Déchiffrer la France,* 76.

43. Chaptal, *Circulaire du Ministre de l'Intérieur aux préfets des départements,* 19 Germinal year IX, notes for chap. 2.

44. Ozouf, "La Révolution et la perception de l'espace national," 50–53; Bourguet, *Déchiffrer la France,* chap. 7; Certeau, Julia, and Revel, *Une politique de la langue,* chap. 6.

45. J. Jamin, "Naissance de l'observation anthropologique: La Société des Observateurs de l'Homme (1799–1805)," *Cahiers internationaux de sociologie* 67 (1980): 313–35; Ozouf, "L'Invention de l'ethnographie française: Le questionnaire de l'Académie celtique," in *L'École de la France,* 349–77.

46. See Hervé Le Bras, "The Government Bureau of Statistics," in *Rethinking France: Les Lieux de Mémoire,* under the direction of Pierre Nora, vol. 1 (Chicago: University of Chicago Press, 2001), 361–400.

47. Marcel Roncayolo, "L'Aménagement du territoire, XVIIIe–XXe siècle," in Revel, *L'Espace français,* 509–643.

48. Some recent studies have demonstrated well the diversity and complexity of regional experiences. For Brittany, besides Bertho, "L'Invention de la Bretagne," see henceforth Jean-Yves Guiomar, *Le Bretonisme: Les historiens bretons au XIXe siècle* (Mayenne: Société d'histoire et d'archéologie de la Bretagne, 1987). For the Vendée, see Jean-Clément Martin, *La Vendée et la France* (Paris: Éditions du Seuil, 1987); Jean-Clément Martin, "The Vendée, Region of Memory: The Blue and the White," below in this volume. For Provence, Jean-Claude Chamboredon and A. Méjean, "Styles de voyage, modes de perception du paysage, stéréotypes régionaux dans les récits de voyage et les guides touristiques: L'exemple de la Provence (fin XVIIIe–début XXe siècle); Essai de sociologie de la perception touristique," in *Territoires,* 2 (Paris: Presses de l'École normale supérieure, 1985).

49. See Philippe Martel, "Le Félibrige," in *Les Lieux de mémoire,* under the direction of Pierre Nora, 3 vols. in 7 (Paris: Gallimard, 1984–92), vol. 3, book 2, 566–611.

50. Lavallée and Brion, *Voyages dans les départements: Cher,* 12. In 1807 the *Tableaux comparatifs de l'ancienne et de la nouvelle division de la France* clarified this interdependent and ambiguous connection by reminding the reader that the former districts "will live on always in the imperishable pages of history, of which the accounts would be unintelligible for those who only know the departments shaped since the Revolution. Did not the Emperor often say: 'my peoples of Champagne, my Norman battalions'"? Cited by Gasnier, 25.

51. See Daniel Nordman, "Les Guides-Joanne," in *Les Lieux de mémoire,* vol. 2, book 1, 529–567, and Jacques and Mona Ozouf, "Le *Tour de la France par deux enfants,*" vol. 2, part 1, 291–321.

52. Ozouf, "La Révolution et la perception de l'espace national," 54.

CHAPTER 5

THE DEPARTMENT

༜

MARCEL RONCAYOLO

In 1911, Henri Mettrier introduced his monograph on the formation of the department of the Haute-Marne in these terms:

> Today, one is generally of the opinion that the departmental division no longer responds to the needs of our epoch. . . . In the presence of the unexpected rapidity currently enjoyed by communication and transportation, the maintenance of departments that are too small, too weak, seems a shocking anomaly. Geographers reproach them for not taking into account the natural divisions of the countryside;* historians, for not recognizing the old provincial groupings, which recall the progressive formation of French territory. All agree in seeing the departmental organization established in France as a hastily conceived and insufficiently planned experiment, offering proofs at each step of the arbitrary method by which this change was accomplished.[1]

The case waged against the department around 1900 is well summarized in Mettrier's quotation. The department is attacked for two symmetrical reasons: it does not look toward the future and is therefore already obsolete in its dimensions and its boundaries; and it betrays the past

---

* In this chapter I have translated *pays* as "country" when it refers to France or the French nation, and as "countryside" when it refers to land or territory, as opposed to urban areas. I have also often translated *territoire* as "countryside," again to mark the opposition between countryside and city. TRANS.

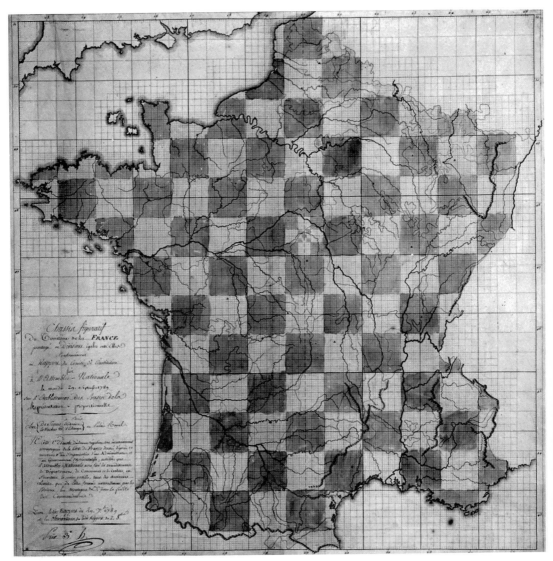

Figure 5.1

When geometry establishes equality: orthogonal sectioning. This "ideally regular sketch," presented to the assembly on September 29, 1789, illustrates a principle: equality among territorial divisions is a requirement for a rational government. But it was achieved "by deviating as little as possible both from the former boundaries and from those created naturally by rivers and mountains and for ease of communications."

while at the same time neglecting nature, history, and culture. It is an abstract, artificial space, which suits neither the living administration of the country—the department serves only the bureaucracy—nor the maintenance and the activity of the territorial memory of France. A useless division, which, if one accepts the indictments of the prosecutors of the

time, would not figure among the *lieux de mémoire*. At best, it would deserve to be included episodically, as one very sketchy scene of a history
confined to the nineteenth century.

Paradoxically, this critique grew louder, beginning with the centennial of the French Revolution in 1889, going so far as to suggest projects
for administrative reform in the middle of a world war. Every celebration undoubtedly necessitates the sacrifice of an expiatory victim. The
second centennial (1989) occurred after the battle was over: regions were
constituted, given an elected assembly and executive, situated in a policy
of decentralization. The departments are still there, as pieces composing
the regions—a more or less satisfying patchwork.

Are the departments a simple phenomenon of inertia, on the surface
of our society? After all, phenomena of inertia also depend on our memory and our representations; they do not simply express the imaginative
laziness of politicians and administrators. It is thus necessary to reevaluate
the department, across this observation of its duration: is it the consciousness of residents or the very texture of places? Three pieces of the dossier
will be examined: first, the formation of the departments. In the beginning, this division and the subdivisions that it ordered were born of a revolutionary act, a voluntary "antimemory"; but their reality is much more
ambiguous. The second stage is the consolidation of the department under the reestablished monarchy, which then became "liberal." The "best
proof of the utility or, to be more exact, of the excellence of this reform,
is that for a century it has traversed our revolutions without suffering serious attacks. The departments are still standing,"[2] wrote the *Revue de géographie* in 1889—at the moment, however, when the happy effects of the
beginning of the century were fading, when opinion was shifting. The
third stage is the resistance of the departmental division to the double criticism—irrelevance, obsolescence—that animated the movements for reform or transformation. But the territorial division was not the principal
target; the department regained legitimacy with each of these tests. Games
of memory, which in sum express the relative flexibility of the institution,
its capacity to erect a tradition—or, rather, a relay of traditions. What follows is not a hagiography of the department, but only an attempt to explain the duration and even the growth that one observes.

THE FORMATION OF THE DEPARTMENTS: LIMITS OF ANTIMEMORY

The department as antimemory?[3] How could one doubt the reality of
this intention? The members of the Constituent Assembly (1791–92),
mostly men of law, educated in or influenced by the philosophy of the

Enlightenment, dreamed of a rational State and of a definitive unification of the French nation. It was necessary to prolong the work of simplification undertaken by the absolute monarchy, with more audacity; to eliminate consequently the obstacles that had kept it from reforming the provincial assemblies and taxes; and therefore to impact the very principles of disparities, privileges, and individual statutes, whether they applied to men or to territories. The creation of the departments lengthened the Night of August 4. It was an egalitarian reform, the first equality being to submit all Frenchmen to the same law; but at the same time to establish, throughout the country, at each echelon of responsibility, the same representative regime.

It is easier to understand the urgency of the reform if one considers that the new division of the territory was imposed by electoral commissions charged with creating the image of the country—of the legal country, at least—even before providing a geographical framework for its administration. This mission implied the *invention* of a conscription map: indeed, the inheritance of the ancien régime was heterogeneous, impractical from this point of view. The majority of the provinces had long ago lost their juridical and political role (except when there existed *parlements* and Estates); at bottom, the labyrinth of jurisdictions and domains blurred positions. The break was inscribed as much in facts as in ideology, and Jacques-Guillaume Thouret, director of the Committee of Division, could declare without too much exaggeration: "A plan for the division of a great Empire is almost unto itself the Constitution."[4] The reproach that one would later make against the department, that it was the best instrument for centralization, is only a belated repetition of this compliment.

Truth be told, the will to centralize is disputable. It has been the object of long debates in French historiography, often along ideological lines. The Constituents were divided, undoubtedly, between and within themselves. The work has two faces: looked at from the side of local collectivities, from municipalities to departmental institutions, the election orders everything in the Constituent's proposal, assemblies as well as executives. An experiment in self-government comes to mind. But the unity and the authority of the State remain whole in principle. We are far from the idea of confederation or even of federation, despite the name given several months later to the second celebration of July 14 (the *fête de la fédération*). It was better to ensure unity that the administration drew closer to the citizen. The territorial cells must not reconstitute the corps of the ancien régime, which were capable of challenging the homogeneity of the nation. Every deputy spoke in the name of the French people; the departments were only fractions of a unitary territory. "Divide to unite," Marie-Vic Ozouf-Marignier eloquently said of the Constituent's intentions.[5] Fragile equilibrium—which, as one would later see, poorly resisted the revolutionary jolts. But the departmental division—outside the institutional games of 1790—durably imposed its design.

What scandalized people, maybe still today, was the committee's initial proposal: a purely geometrical division, in the manner of a division of scarcely inhabited territories, already imagined in 1780 by Robert de Hesseln,[6] and obeying the rule of multiples of nine for the entire country down to its subdivisions. In other words, eighty departments (plus Paris), themselves subdivided into nine districts, and each district into nine cantons. Intellectually the proposal was highly satisfactory; this arithmetical law imposed equality of size on the departments, which seemed hardly compatible with geography. But this model was not without justification: it replaced the utopian with the practical. Three hundred twenty-four square leagues for a department (some 6,500 square kilometers): this is what, for the Committee of Division, "offers a moderate area that is appropriate for direct electoral districts, that is even more appropriate for administrative districts, and that could be appropriate, in the future, for similarly dividing the exercise of public powers."[7] Arithmetic thus justified itself by convenience—that of the elector of primary assemblies (at the district level), of the administrator, of the member of a jurisdiction. Division and participation demanded this constraint of proximity. Several days later more concrete information was provided, in terms of accessibility. The size of every department should permit each citizen "to arrive from every point of this territory at an administrative center, within one day of travel,"[8] which grounds the hypothesis of approximately eighty departments. Departmental territory might thus be *known* by its administrators and its notables—particularly the redistribution of landed property.

The new division thus corresponded to a model of collective life. Was it capable of avoiding the two major risks that one feared at the end of 1789—the federalist temptation (if the districts were too large, too few in number) and anarchy (if the division was excessive)? Critics arose against geometry, against the consideration of surface area only. Why not search for more real equilibriums in population and wealth, since it was a question of populated territories and not of vast spaces to clear? On the one hand, people imagined concentrating the departments into forty districts, in principle weighing each one (plus Paris) according to its population. Mirabeau, on the contrary, proposed bringing powers and population closer together by reducing the hierarchy to two levels: 120 departments, 720 municipalities. This was something that would satisfy many urban ambitions while retaining the old envelope of the provinces.

Figure 5.2
The ecclesiastical map of France at issue: 83 dioceses, redrawn within departmental boundaries, as opposed to 136 on the eve of the Revolution. A spatial organization, hierarchies of function and prestige, revenues threatened.

The Committee of Division resisted and insisted on accessibility, equilibrium between town and countryside, and organization on three or four levels.

The idea of a tabula rasa was, however, seriously compromised by a whole series of concessions. In the end, the departmental division was accomplished out of the former provincial borders, with corrections made on the margins to balance territories. The local deputies were invited to undertake this task themselves by negotiating with their colleagues in neighboring provinces. The Committee of Division simply imposed the number of districts and intervened only as a last resort. In short, nothing purely abstract or artificial; but it was easier to decompose than to re-compose, with each territorial cell looking out for its own interests. Reading the departmental monographs, one sees a sort of Erector set of hundreds of pieces variously put together, according to the ambitions of one or the other department. The political goal remained: it was a ques-tion of dissociating administrative competence from the jurisdiction of the old provinces, the exercise of powers from a historical inheritance that compromised unity. This mission accomplished, the particularism of daily life presented less of a danger. The break was thus in large part sym-bolic. In baptizing the departments, one wiped away every memory of the old provinces, as well as every town name that established and ac-centuated urban domination. If one referred to geographical accidents, it was only to found the new division on natural coherence. This argument was not essential. It was made especially to localize the departments, in the most precise and neutral way possible with regard to history: a form of coordinates. In sum, one took the departments for what they were supposed to be, functional spaces.

We may thus imagine departments with other borders, another de-sign. If the dividing line of water played a significant role, if rivers split or oriented territories, it was a question of intellectual habit rather than of well-defined strategy. The eighteenth century was impassioned by hy-draulics, and maps were often traced in the style of Buache.[9] If forests and swamps—which traditionally separated the cells of the French interior (from the Gallic cities to the dioceses, for example)—seem to be respected here and neglected elsewhere, it was the result of detailed negotiations, in-dividual agreements, the effect of inertia, or the replay of real discontinu-ities. Thus forests still separated the departments that were inheritors of Normandy (Manche or Orne) from the Sarthe and the Mayenne. Between Pas-de-Calais and Somme, one repeated the uncertain divisions between the Artois and the Picardy. But the "inventors" of the Haute-Marne did not hesitate to annex all of the Vallage, to the extent that it was the eco-nomic complement to Saint-Dizier. No solution appeared to be illogical, if it could "work" in practice. In other words, the geographical realism that the department transmits was not founded on a recognized and reasoned priority of natural divisions. Much more often, it corresponds to what the Constituents called "conventions" [convenances]: in a word, to custom.

It is in this context that one may situate the veritable back-and-forth movement between rational utopia and reality; abstract reflection drove the Constituents and notably the members of the Committee of Division to conceive a model and a type of administrative division. Division could hardly occur without knowledge of the terrain: local deputies and notables thus intervened. But knowledge and individual interests went hand in hand. If the number of departments was fixed a priori, the game was reopened when it became a question of defining geographical limits—the subdivisions (in particular the districts, the next lower echelon), the departmental centers—in other words, of building a hierarchy that was both administrative and urban. A fierce battle hence broke out, less between abstract spaces (the limits of the department themselves mobilized opinion very little) as between towns of flesh and of stone, very concrete places of collective action, agitated if not powerful. Rational arguments, more or less inflected, were not lacking: accessibility depended on the naive and geometric notion of centrality. But easily opposed to it was the other centrality, that of practices, conventions, real actions, which, it is implicitly admitted, did not conceal the first centrality.

The task was in effect enormous, although the Committee of Division had thought to decentralize the decision as much as possible, by entrusting it to local deputies or primary assemblies. The correspondence received by the assembly added up the demands and denunciations of towns, boroughs, sometimes even ambitious villages. Certain ones tried to defend or to improve on an old administrative, judicial, or religious position, others to sneak among the beneficiaries of the new organization. One thus cannot take the content of this polemic at face value. But, taking these reservations into account in a precise and attentive reading of it, Marie-Vic Ozouf-Marignier provides us with a veritable tableau of the representation of urban France at the end of the ancien régime: *the memory of a debate rather than of a condition.*

First, the extent of the struggle, proportional to what was at stake. Jean-Claude Perrot, according to the *Dictionnaire de la République* of 1794,[10] identified 83 large cities, 686 towns—which corresponded to the consolidated part of the urban infrastructure, exceeding in general 3,000 inhabitants—and more than 1,000 small towns and boroughs, floating on the outer limits of the urban world. More than 2,000 able candidates, on average about 20 per department. More than half of them (about 1,300) had previously exercised more or less prestigious functions. Bernard Lepetit[11] counted 699 governor subdelegations in 1789, which already ensured a territorial framework more regular than that of medieval institutions; add to that 400 to 500 bailiwick and presidial seats, which did not necessarily correspond to those just cited and which were particularly numerous in the former jurisdiction of the Parlement de Paris, more rare in the former domains of the Estates; plus bishops and their ecclesiastical seats, which were dense in the south of France. Also to be counted, with varying influence, were military governments [*gouvernements militaires*], masters of the waters and forests [*maîtrises d'eaux et forêts*], salt suppliers [*greniers à sel*], and seigneurial judges [*justices seigneuriales*]. This dispersal of functions, unequally sown, did not accord well with the Constituent Assembly's desire for rationalization. In the end, there were 546 district centers in 1790, of which 83 coincided with the center of the department. Of course, one reserved the right to leave such and such religious or judicial institution at a particular urban site: respect for tradition or a compensatory scheme. But this was a concession and not the rule. Thus the majority of towns were menaced with demotion. Those that played a principal role in the organization of the ancien régime feared the realignment: at best they would fall among the 83 departmental centers. *Diminutio capitis* was implied by the very choice of the departmental model and the political sense of the reform. The most modest towns became rivals, over the course of a strict sorting operation: in 1790, 40 percent of the former subdelegate centers preserved the title only of district heads. It was necessary to demote here, where towns with administrative traditions were redundant; to promote there, where the urban infrastructure had until then been very weak.

The paradox is that, in order to justify their propositions or their decisions, the Constituent Assembly, the Committee of Division, and the various arbitrators essentially invoked the interest of the countryside— by dint of physiocratic ideology, which made the town a place of income consumption, of territorial enclosure, even of moral perversion, more than a motor for the creation of riches. The city-countryside relationship that lies at the heart of the departmental organization draws its particular characteristics from this ideology. The agricultural argument, moreover, serves every meaning; it suits every rhetorical turn. The partisans of vast districts (because they favor several opulent centers) argue for the necessity of associating the town with a vast countryside, which would have at least equal weight in the local assemblies. The partisans of small, numerous districts (and therefore of a maximum quantity of centers, an essential advantage for the majority of towns) judge that if the area of the district is too vast, the deep countryside will not participate much in political and administrative life. In any case, the ideology of the Enlightenment dominated the conscience of the Constituents, inspiring distrust with regard to urban concentration, excessive accumulation of functions, impoverishment of the network of small towns. The country's territorial framework did not necessarily appear compatible with other vocations, with big commerce, or with extensive maritime projects. Urban rivalries? Without a doubt. But one may also conclude that, through them,

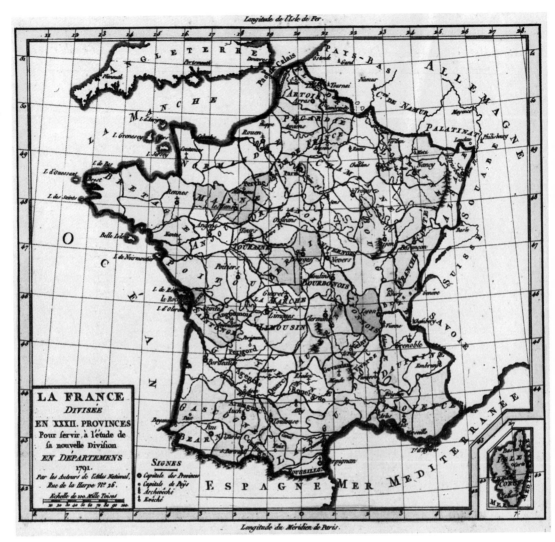

Figure 5.3
A historical reference: map of the provinces, drawn in 1791 for the *Atlas national*. The earlier divisions were known not to have always corresponded to similar historical origins, nor to administrative reality at the end of the ancien régime. A notion that went beyond these frameworks: that of a "capital of the land."

the two Frances imagined by the historian Edward Whiting Fox could enter into conflict.[12] The formation of the departments thus brings us back to these more long-term, more stable realities concealed in the urban infrastructure.

First of all, at the summit of the urban pyramid, outside of Paris: the great ports and the interior crossroads of Lyon, linked to the great extra-national networks. The possibility of creating specific departments for

Lyon, Marseille, Bordeaux, Rouen, or Nantes was proposed before the National Assembly. Each one of these towns would find this advantageous, according to Marseille's representative, Sinety:

> It is impossible ever to hope that the operations of great commercial towns and their interests can be directed and put into action by a superior administration of the towns and the agricultural areas to whose authority one wants to subordinate them. Either the superior administration will be composed of a greater number of active citizens from the commercial towns and thus the interest of commerce will dominate the interest of agriculture, or the agricultural citizens will be of a greater number and in this case commerce will be poorly represented and sacrificed. Let us avoid putting men and interests in opposition.[13]

The Marseillais, who sought especially to prevent the supremacy of Aix, was understood perfectly by the representatives of the Forez and the upper Vivarais, who were attempting to escape the Lyonnais administration for the same reason.[14] This debate spread to more modest echelons: in choosing between towns with administrative or commercial traditions, the directors of the reform (whether on the local or national level) tended most often to respect the first, which often held more prestigious memories, and to leave the second to its own devices. The warehouse town, linked to heavy transportation or interior navigation and therefore "extroverted," was sharply distinguished from small local capitals, whose activities, from administration to commerce, all depended in the end on the directions that they gave and on the personnel whose living they provided. The people of Clermont did not hesitate to claim, against the ambitions of Riom: "Our town is lost. One speaks of its commerce; commerce does not create, does not form the town. It is the maintenance of our town that can sustain commerce."[15]

The administrative town, by avoiding overly risky or obscure specializations in controlling its territory, remained for the Constituents the safe choice, the keystone to the vault of the edifice, just as the department was perceived in principle as a town-countryside ensemble, associating and balancing activities and social groups. On this point, the reform did not aim at a real rupture; on the contrary, by means of rational arguments, it took up the baton to maintain the oldest modes of relation. Active memory, if one likes. In the name of this same principle, the urban department (except that of Paris, limited to a narrow suburb) was rejected. One often established boundaries in favor of the town "of the agricultural countryside" rather than the most dynamic center, that which assured distant relations or aimed at wider markets; Saintes won out over La Rochelle, in spite of that town's past and its well-constructed argument;[16] Laon was chosen over Soissons and Saint-Quentin, after multiple manipulations between Aisne and Seine-et-Marne; Aix was favored over Marseille, Douai over Lille; on a more modest level, Chaumont won out over Langres, though the latter was full of history; and Saint-Flour was picked over Aurillac. Reims, an archbishopric but also a great center of industry, had to bend before Châlons-sur-Marne; Chalon-sur-Saône, an important site for inland shipping and interior transactions, ended by ceding to Mâcon, which, it was said, had only commerce in wines. Geometric centrality—for better or worse, and often assisted by variations in departmental boundaries (as in the case of the Haute-Marne)—was often invoked to carry or justify such decisions. Even more, the functions of a district center were attributed, often as compensation, to this type of locality, something that often led a town to descend to rather humble rungs in the demographic hierarchy. The necessity of rather regularly dividing the surface of a territory of very unequal activity, density, and urbanization had the same effect: the promotion or the maintenance, thanks to the administration, of many small towns. The Revolution did not manage to preserve the same attributions, the same chances, for all of them: rationalization had its costs. But, thanks to this division, it presented itself as the conservator of a certain urban type.

In fact, the decisions—whether they came from local arbitrators, ratified by the assembly, or from the Committee of Division (which often proposed alternation, compensation, or the postponement of a definitive choice)—did not obey a single logic. Poorly fitted garments, they were crafted as things happened, negotiated between contradictory arguments. Often one had to bend before the evidence: the domination of several principal, inevitable towns. The twenty or so cities that found themselves at the head of the classifications established by Bernard Lepetit (according to three criteria—demographic, administrative, fiscal)[17] at the end of the ancien régime were difficult to dispute as candidates. Neither Bordeaux, nor Rouen, nor Lyon considered themselves enclaves, despite their external horizons. On the contrary, they affirmed their empire over the interior, through the exchange of agricultural products, the possession of land, or the diffusion of industrial work. On this point, the dispersed organization of manufacturing, dear to the eighteenth century, came to the aid of other towns such as Le Mans or Laval,[18] which disposed, moreover, of other assets: but the borders of the department seemed curiously to coincide in this case with those of the distribution of textile work.

This diversity of choices was not linked solely to the existence of established capitals or particular economic phenomena. Even in the rural

departments—the most numerous—every classificatory rule ran up
against the absence of regularity and homogeneity in the inheritance.
Regional modes of the urban infrastructure: it suffices to think of the
Mediterranean south or Alsace; of the role of the coasts, which blurred
the maps, deviated from the notion of centrality, and managed to stay out
of the way of administrative divisions—but even more of the superposi-
tion of different strata. At the end of the eighteenth century, urban
France did not obey a single model, and everything was not the result of
delays in the imposition of a single pattern for unification. There was no
neat hierarchy, graduated according to an explanation that applied to the
ensemble: big cities, unequally rooted, floating more or less above a rural France. Towns that were heavily agricultural, organized hierarchically
here, juxtaposed there, without any geographical order providing the
reasons for this disparity. How to divide the Aisne among Soissons, Saint-
Quentin, Laon, and even Château-Thierry—a zone, however, of heavy
agriculture, of dense circulation, and well equipped, ready to foster an
organized urban network? One in fact ended up, between Seine and
Aisne, with the coexistence of small "capitals" of five thousand to ten
thousand inhabitants. An effect of the proximity of Paris, or even of
Amiens or Reims? Likewise, in Saône-et-Loire, rivalries on the inside of
a composite infrastructure: Mâcon, Chalon, Autun. The magnetic poles
were less obvious than one would think; those marking the principal
stages of river navigation did not coincide with those resting on access to
vast homogeneous lands. In the face of this imbroglio, there remained
only random solutions: manipulation or delay tactics. Manipulation,
when, by a boomerang effect, the choice of a center determined the district boundaries. Prudence, when functions were divided between rival
towns or, even more, when they were alternated between them. Transi-
tory episodes, in general. In less than one generation, the real hierarchies
corrected the pattern: Marseille, Lille, La Rochelle reacquired the departmental administrative bodies. As for the districts, which the Convention Assembly (the successor to the Constituent) considered too numerous and a source of anarchy and which it therefore sacrificed, they
were reestablished, under the name of arrondissements, but they en-
gendered new and drastic cuts: 240 centers flanked the 88 Napoleonic
prefectures.

What was entailed in these changes? Antimemory in relation to the
provinces and their ultimate esprit de corps, the departments bear them,
down to our day, the mark of this condition of French towns at the end
of the eighteenth century. Memory of a moment in history, of a meeting between the logics and the generations of cities—a bit in the manner of a family photograph, associating different ages and characters in

one privileged instant. The most serious upheavals of the economy came only later, with the railroads and heavy industry. The urban fabric, fixed, selected, hierarchized by the departmental organization, still belongs to the economic ancien régime. The reality of the department, this functional space, lies not, properly speaking, in geographical division, but rather in procedure, in the concrete society that embodies it and to which it is destined. It is the urban elites who thought up these town-countryside ensembles, on the scale of their experience and their interests. An affair of the educated, of magistrates, of big landowners whose clientele came essentially from the countryside and who constructed the administrative space of a society dominated by landed property. The department is a close relative of the land register and the Napoleonic Code. Of course, the relations between town and countryside and between the proprietor and the exploited were not identical across France: by restricting the area of districts in relation to provincial customs, the department underlined the external and internal contrasts. The administrative reform gave a general *form* to this game of disparities, most often identified after the fact. At the risk of often slicing in the counter-direction, the multiple authors of the new map of France undoubtedly neglected the countryside and homogeneity; they were interested, for better or worse, in flux, but essentially in those changes that could hence be mastered, translated into a durable organization of space, in those changes that affected the administration. The division was partial; it was neither abstract (in relation to its objective) nor artificial—except for the fact that it certainly was a construction.

CONSOLIDATION: KNOWLEDGE AND POWER

Until the Second Empire, the organization and the division of the French territory into departments did not arouse any true hostility from governments or public opinion. The First Consul, Bonaparte, made the department the most efficient instrument of centrality, thanks to the establishment of prefects and subprefects, reinforcing the tutelage of the State, utilizing the hierarchy of spaces and towns. The restored monarchy, more liberal, prudently made a few concessions to local assemblies, administrators, and notables without renouncing its right to oversee them. In short, the institution, reinterpreted in 1800, consolidated and enrooted itself; something that is paradoxical across so many changes of political regime. But against the department there then existed only provincial nostalgia, irresistibly turned toward the past, or utopian projects dreaming of a more egalitarian or more libertarian territorial organization. Frame of reference for knowledge, district for economic action, site for the establishment of a society of tax-paying electors: the Constituents' invention acquired these three functions.

Nothing seemed to destine the department for this first object: to conserve and to order knowledge, including its most scientific aspects; it seemed to respond primarily to political demands and to opportunistic arguments. However, if France has a memory, alongside the great national foundations or institutions charged with preserving it, and alongside the capital, the department is definitely the site of its conservation, both natural and symbolic. This was a normal consequence of the territorial organization that, after ten or so years of chaos or improvisation, placed in each center representatives of the State—directors of technical corps; the Napoleonic university, that key institution; the *lycée*—and made all of these the permanent echelon of political life, whether divided into arrondissements or not. The departmental archives constituted one of the great state services: they modeled, according to their norms and eventually their presuppositions, a vision of the past that went back in time to 1790.

Between the countryside's new divisions and territorial knowledge, there existed more than just occasional affinities. The administrative organization was part of a larger current of knowledge, that of the Enlightenment: universalist, but concerned with drawing laws of physical or human nature from the multiplicity of its manifestations. The administration of the territory and, first of all, its description were part of this field of exploration, which, beginning at the end of the ancien régime, was illustrated by a taste for memoirs or topographies, whether they came from travelers, doctors, or engineers. The departments were created, we know, without too much concern for geography; but this concern became important after the fact. To make the territorial institutions function meant above all taking account of the real resources of the district, its geography, and the mentality of its population. The unification of the administration or of the territorial grid soon led to an adaptation of this apparent functional simplicity according to the characteristics of the countryside. Expelling particularisms from the institutional construction only meant encountering them again later as something to be dealt with.[19] Paradoxically, until the institution of the Empire, the progress of centralization, the very organization of administrators or of missionaries coming from elsewhere, moving from one post to another, implied the acquisition of a knowledge that was often transmitted in the form of recipes between the successive possessors of authority. The central power itself increased and revealed its interests: measuring revolutionary changes (including the redistribution of property), opinion polls, development projects, more classical information on subsistence and resources and the

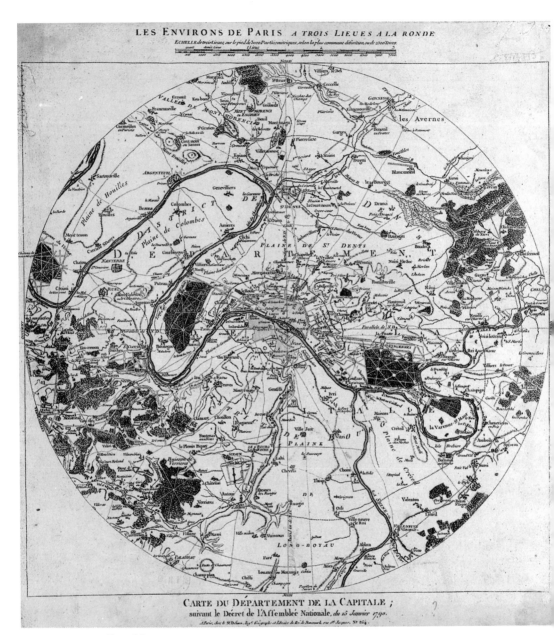

Figure 5.4

A department for Paris. The capital was not subject to the constraints of territorial equality. Its department was inscribed within a narrow suburb, with an area of less than three leagues, comprised of silty plains and landscaped forests. A desire to limit the demographic weight of the department (doubtful. . .) or to maintain the exceptional nature of Paris? In any event, plans for an "urban" department for other large cities were abandoned. Forty-eight thousand hectares for the department of the Seine; that was twelve to thirteen times less than the average department.

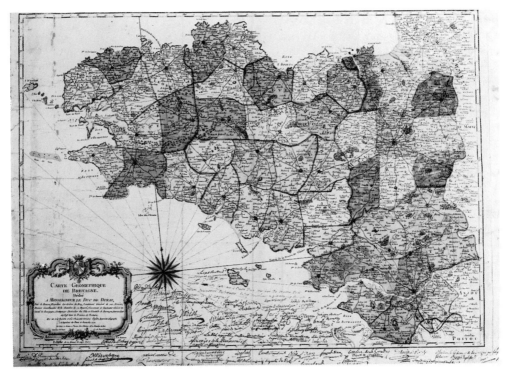

Figure 5.5
Divisions within the French provinces. . . . This map of Brittany, drawn before the Revolution, was used as a working document by the provincial deputies, who were called upon to define new districts. A preliminary map that was later to be used to establish the administrative hierarchy; the connected divisions appear to be organized around a series of small towns.

moral situation of the population. Knowledge, power—one now understands the inferences.

From investigations or revolutionary reports (often produced on the spot) to imperial statistics, an inventory of the territory and its inhabitants was undertaken, across the grid of the new divisions. This "Golden Age" of territorial knowledge was part of a fascination that remained encyclopedic.[20] From François de Neufchâteau to Coquebert de Montbret,[21] the departmental statistics aimed to be both collections of memory and guides to action. One now knows the advantages and the disadvantages of this; one also knows how the offices of the administration informed and deformed the project, sniggered over the sometimes mythical literature that came across their desks, tended rapidly toward the closed questionnaire and the statistical yearbook. A work of reduction, but also of formation, which led in the 1830s to the creation of the Statistique générale de la France (General Statistics Office of France). The department tended to become a line (or several lines when one

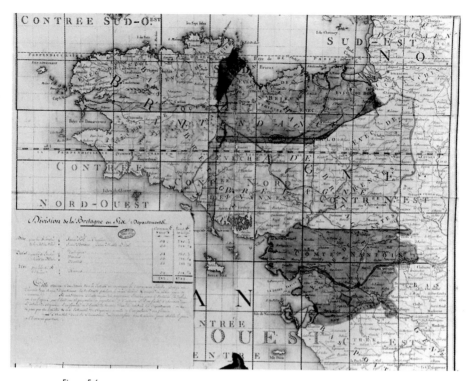

Figure 5.6

. . . And departmental divisions. The division of Brittany into six departments was related to the earlier ecclesiastical organization and in the end revolved around the cities that were capable of fulfilling the role of administrative center: Saint-Pol and Saint-Brieuc, Quimper, Vannes and Nantes, and last, Rennes. But legitimacy was sought through other aspects: "These divisions will reconcile all interests by respecting local customs, since they will gather together in each department inhabitants who speak the same language and are engaged in the same type of business. If these divisions differ somewhat from those established for the territory, what they lose in terms of land is compensated for by a proportionate increase in their populations," says the caption.

broke it down into arrondissements) in a recitation of numbers; alphabetical order won out handily over geographical contingencies. Although the case against norms is easy to make, let us not critique too harshly this alignment between order and questions; after all, it was perhaps reductive of differences, but it also established the possibility of a common language and, in an even more elementary fashion, the framework for every comparison across space and time. The continuity of the departmental division ensured information its place in a chronological series: a sort of permanence. Go ahead and play with the numbers, in districts that vary geographically! The departmental echelon thus became the conservator of a series of givens; the department, with the help of imagination, acquired part of its own image here. The composition of numbers, often slow to change, the correlations that one established

between them—from the simple juxtaposition of maps to more sophisticated analyses—sketched bit by bit the traits of a personality, at the risk
of blurring internal differences and of falling into the trap of the mean.
The department thus imposed itself as a collective of thought—for the
researcher, the politician, or the traveling salesman. Each drew from it his
or her own colors, the representation of a temperament.

The logic of administrative or technical agents thus made the department serve as a form for disciplines that were completely foreign to
it. Mining engineers, beginning in the first decade of the 1800s, established the bases of a geological description of France within administrative borders.[22] Naturalists discovered and explained a "departmental
flora" and left a record of it in herbariums or museums. What the provincial haze veiled or drowned in pervasive particularism, the clear and
apparently neutral demarcation of the departmental divisions highlighted: contrasts within departments and between them, contrasts that
were connected to the landscape (forest, plain, hedged farmland, mountain, foreland), to the habitat, to cultural traits. France decomposed and
recomposed itself, starting from this crossroads-echelon. A malicious
spirit might suggest that the notion of the countryside took shape only
after the departmental inventory, thanks to this capacity of surveillance
and of analysis acquired from studying the new divisions. This was scientific culture, but also popular culture. The "picturesque" voyages of
Captain Hugo in departmental statistics, the national atlases, the guides
and monographs of Adolphe Joanne, launched at the end of the 1860s,
inscribed themselves in this logic. France learned communally, according
to a litany: departments, prefectures and subprefectures, rivers that
crossed them—a framework in which diverse knowledge, often barely
coherent, was subsequently reclassified. Geography teachers, preco-
ciously concerned with the immediate environment, discovered in the
department the intermediate step between close, direct knowledge and
knowledge of distant spaces, of the nation or the world. A long tradition,
anterior to the school of Jules Ferry: I refer to the instructions for teachers of 1857[23] and to the ambitious program constructed by Levasseur in
1872, in the aftermath of the French defeat by Germany,[24] in the line of
"intellectual reforms." It was inheritance that made the departmental
litany—a tidbit as classic as the multiplication table—obligatory in the
republican school.

The scholarly image of the department was created during the era of
the constitutional monarchy—perhaps the true golden age for this type
of knowledge—because departmental statistics did not end when they
encountered the hostility of imperial offices and Montalivet. The prudent revival attempted under the Restoration found a more efficient

Figure 5.7
Creating a map of France: the work of a dynasty. Dominique Cassini (1625–1712), an astronomer from Nice who was trained in Italy, set out to define the meridian from Paris. His grandson, César, used that geodesic research to begin having the map of France drawn, a project that would last fifty years. This portrait of Dominique Cassini is the work of his great-grandson. It is dated 1798, the year that monumental project was completed.

agent: the interest of local institutions and of notables, who had too often failed at the consular and imperial enterprise. Two model monographs inaugurated this second phase: that of the baron Trouvé for the Aude and that of the prefect Villeneuve-Bargemon for the Bouches-du-Rhône. These works, just as encyclopedic as those of the preceding generation but more profound, more informed by contemporary concerns, were achieved and published, in spite of the withdrawal of government subsidies, by subscription. Statistics renewed their ties with a social milieu. They were rooted in the tax-paying class, between the possessors of property and the possessors of intelligence. From 1815 to 1830, only a dozen monographs were completed; between 1830 and 1848, some thirty departments benefited from studies of this genre, eighteen for the first time.[25] What were the characteristics of this production? An encyclopedic knowledge, joining historical relics (often the most fragile), natural sciences (plants, rocks, and animals were enumerated and classified, with abundant descriptions), agronomy (traditional practices and current or potential improvements), initial attempts at statistics on local demography, the social and moral condition of the district, local works in the style of Villermé. This line of questioning was generally accompanied by a review of improvement projects. It was the era of hydraulics, of public works, soon of railroads. All of this knowledge supposed the direct or indirect collaboration of inspirers, informers, sometimes investigators: a team that might extend from the prefect to general councilors, from engineers in territorial positions to *lycée* professors or to erudites of learned societies. Statistics became the creator of a social bond, sometimes the bearer of a project, in the best cases.

This phenomenon is confirmed by a parallel movement, the diffusion of scientific societies. Certain of these societies were created to undertake or extend the publication of statistics through complementary works. Thus the Société statistique de Marseille, founded in 1827, or the Commision spéciale created by the general council of the Rhône in 1831. In fact, the movement was both more widespread and more restrained. The learned societies benefited primarily from the renaissance of the ancien régime's provincial academies, beginning in the Consulate.[26] Under the July Monarchy, a second push: the country's erudite framework was multiplied, notably under the action of the prefects. It demarcated the departmental infrastructure: present in the prefectoral centers, it was also installed in the arrondissement centers that were most important or had an intellectual tradition. The 1870s were the last phase of the creation of this type of society. There is nothing exceptional in this conjuncture: the 1830s, the end of the 1860s, and the 1870s correspond to periods of activity, of rising consciousness, of demands on the part of provincial notables. This rhythm was also found in political life, the critique of centralization, the economic initiative, or even the litigation against business monopolies. We can count 605 societies concerned partially or principally with natural sciences. Fifty-three were established between 1830 and 1839, seventy-two in the decade of the 1870s. The societies, in the same manner as the compilers of statistics, sought to associate knowledge and action: natural sciences were mixed with history, archaeology, or fine arts, but also, in good physiocratic tradition, with agriculture. Divisions of the departmental type: the 605 societies counted were located in 243 towns. Around 1880, a third of these societies carried the name of the center, more than a quarter that of the department, while less than a sixth evoked the name of a province. For a department, the dispersion among different localities increased only in a few cases, where the magnetism of the center was weak or contested, where the urban infrastructure was divided rather than hierarchized: notably in the Aisne, the Manche, the Saône-et-Loire, or the Pas-de-Calais. This movement declined in the last quarter of the nineteenth century and was henceforth organized upon new foundations. The societies became more specialized rather than emphasizing their multiple concerns. Anthropology or natural sciences became autonomous; agriculture, less interesting to the minority, was marginalized. At the same time, the range of abilities changed: The movement became regional with the appearance of societies beyond the department level. There thus existed a "departmental" episode in this mobilization of erudition, which accompanied the consolidation of the "new divisions" emerging from the Revolution. The administrative structure inserted itself into society and its dominant representations.

The field of participants remained too narrow to lead to the affirmation of departmental identities. Erudition broke the public and its interests down into separate operations. On the contrary, the project unified and contributed to the creation of a new memory. The department appeared—notably in the 1830s—as a district of economic action, if one may risk this anachronism. It was no longer only a division for the exercise of the State's tutelage. Maybe this beginning of the nineteenth century is in the end too close for us to recognize the importance of minor, local decisions, which made a relatively coherent unity out of the department designed or proposed at the moment of the Revolution. Try to imagine—while taking regional differences into account—a countryside in which moving about was difficult: relatively close connections were perhaps less easily made than long-distance ones, which benefited from the network of royal (or national) highways. The department suffered less from being cut, sometimes with some capriciousness, out of the former provinces than from a lack of internal cohesion, of unity between its parts. Infrastructure was secondary to the establishment of the administration and political life. It arrived after the fact in the nineteenth century, in gradual steps, notably in the July Monarchy.[27]

The Revolution was born in large part from fiscal crisis. The new organization of the territory aimed at responding to this. The growing departmental consciousness seems to me to begin using fiscal issues to sweep individual interests aside. Two of the principal taxes—on landed and movable property—obeyed the system of redivision. The law attributed to each department an annual contingent, according to a key that was not easy to modify. The first contingents were established under the Revolution, from more or less questionable estimates, drawn from the fiscal returns of the ancien régime and from an illusion of the stability of territorial revenues. In the nineteenth century, the administration in vain sought the means of making adjustments and of following geographical variations in wealth. As for the local assemblies, at each level they had to divide sums that did not come from their jurisdiction between arrondissements and communes. The department was the hinge of the system, the place where the State passed its problems on to the elected representatives of collectivities. Identities thus defined themselves through litigation, the demands of some (the overtaxed); and through the defense system of others. Around 1830, the commentaries went further: to the inequality of burdens was added an inequality of public spending and subsidies. Captain Hugo, in his *France pittoresque,* found an economic distribution that was no longer at all accidental but that split the countryside into vast slices. The deficient departments (those that paid more in taxes than they received in budgetary attributions) were situated to the west of the Saint-Malo–Rhône line, a new variation on the theme launched by the baron Dupin. Around Paris, the expenditures made in the capital compensated, by their indirect effects, for smaller deficits. On the borders, military or maritime expenditures reversed things; finally, some departments were significant beneficiaries of the system: commercial and urban departments, active in the extreme, as if fiscal advantages contributed to wealth. This was, of course, true of Paris, but also of the Gironde, the Loire-Inférieure, the Rhône, the Nord, the Bas-Rhin, the Bouches-du-Rhône, and Brittany—Bretagne most curiously. Let us not dispute these evaluations, however capricious. It is the reasoning that counts: "In our opinion, it results from what precedes; one need not look elsewhere for the cause of ignorance or lack of industry in the departments than in the current fashion of dividing the taxes and the expenditures of the State."[28] From the outset, the department entered into the polemic on territorial inequalities.

This polemic often seems naive, but it underlines how a consciousness of inequalities grafted itself onto the departmental institution; the department was no longer only a statistical entity in a series but a territory with real reference and membership. Contrary to the arguments of the Constituents, the burdens were not quite the same on both sides of the interior frontiers. Instead, the idea developed of augmenting the autonomy of local assemblies, counseled and controlled by the state bureaucracies, in the area of public spending and investment. A mechanism that seemed stalled after the disappearance of the Estates, existing in several provinces of the ancien régime. With the July Monarchy, the departmental assembly's responsibilities grew in the domain of infrastructure, something that went hand in hand with the concern for restraining political ambitions. The general councilors were henceforth elected, according to the rules of tax-based suffrage, with each canton having an elected representative. The legal country was thus engaged, across its entire geographical expanse, in the decisions of the council. The council became a veritable site of arbitration, voting on the budget and complementary resources, additional taxes, possibly loans. In short, under the tutelage of the State, it was able to define an infrastructure policy. The law of 1836 on byways provided the opportunity: communal roads but also more heavily used roads, veritable departmental highways, constructed and managed by the departmental authority and not by the Department of Bridges and Roads, which would open up communications. According to Michel Chevalier, beginning in 1836, the year the law was voted on, eighty-two general councils decreed the classification of roads and the ordering of public works; he concluded, moreover, not without enthusiasm: "A royal highway is a free gift of the State; a departmental highway is a present that a department gives to itself, at its own expense. It is certain that one can summarize the ideas for improvement with which a department or at least a general council (including the prefect) is animated by the number and the proper order of the departmental highways."[29] The territorial organization created in 1789–90 thus discovered after the fact the infrastructure that justified it and ensured its total functioning. Taking into account the diversity of inherited traffic conditions, it was through this investment effort that the administrative map transformed itself into geographical reality. A work requiring much endurance, taken up again after 1870 with the construction of the departmental railroads. For Étienne Juillard, who had studied the example of the Sarthe, the magnetic attraction of economic and social life to a town center was truly accomplished only with the construction of this network.[30]

One could conduct similar analyses with regard to other parts of the infrastructure: swamp draining, canals, irrigation. Rooted in memories of the eighteenth century, a veritable imaginary program entered into the representation of the departments. The role of "statistics" consisted in part in upholding this discourse. For all that, everything was not immediately realized. Hydraulic improvements might be in fashion, even during the July Monarchy or the Second Empire; but they also became a stake in struggles between urban interests and networks, between users whose expectations were opposed. The example of the Bouches-du-Rhône, with the Camargue, the irrigations of the Comtat, and the "mythical" project of the Provence Canal would alone provide an anthology. The Durance Canal, a partial version of the great Provence Canal, was initially confiscated by the city of Marseille, but as part of a project with multiple objectives: irrigation of the land, supply of water for the city, dredging of the port, provision of mechanical energy. But the Provence Canal would have to wait more than a century for its completion, owing to the tardiness of the agreement between two departments and several big cities. The memory of the department is also this collection of projects, works and studies, deliberations and diagrams, that accompanies the maturation of great ideas, which threaten, after so long a wait, to fall into oblivion.

Agricultural improvement is at the heart of the departmental institution. In this sense, the motivating idea of the Constituents, an urban and administrative infrastructure at the service of a land-based economy, was not betrayed. The department, the general council, the society of notables were poorly adapted to industrial development, whose demands were both more localized and linked to larger and more indeterminate networks. For the organization of large railroad lines, the department carried less weight than economic interests and their representatives, the chambers of commerce. The recurring theme, on the contrary, was agricultural progress, whether it was a question of investments, cultivation techniques, specialization, or soil improvement. The agricultural fair thus entered into this new folklore of the French province: leaving the general council a great deal of autonomy, the government preferred to entrust relatively free associations (rather than elected bodies) with the responsibility of informing cultivators and rewarding merit. The *Grand Larousse du XIXe siècle* accorded a certain significance to these fairs, some of whose foundations were laid at the end of the eighteenth century and which, after 1815, were dispersed according to the web of the departmental organization—from the prefecture to the cantonal center: "Since 1830, the institution has undergone considerable development; today they number 584. There are only four departments that are deprived of one, and the good the fairs accomplish makes one hope that before long, not only each department but each arrondissement will possess its own." Five hundred eighty-four sites: that was already a remarkable result, one that recalls, more than the sum of department and arrondissement centers in the nineteenth century, the urban infrastructure of the end of the eighteenth century. Rural democracy? In a France whose geographical variety of modes of exploitation is well known, the fair expressed especially the continuity of the class of landowners, of the rural bourgeoisie, and of the proprietors of great estates, of noble or common origin. At the summit of the departmental hierarchy, the general council mediated between the various interests of this semirural world—something that was a way of integrating the countryside and that, in spite of the variety of the land, often gave the departments a more simplified, sometimes specialized image. Alain Guillemin, in a study on the Manche,[31] underlines the role of the departmental assembly, "whose innovative action in the area of agriculture helped to open up the small regions." He evokes "the more or less complete restructuring of an administrative space into a relatively homogeneous economic and social space." A trajectory that is undoubtedly unique to this department, which, by successive contagions, transformed itself into a prairie, at the risk of imposing on the small peasantry a social cost that is difficult to evaluate. But elsewhere, under other forms, with other objectives, agricultural innovation used the same agents—societies of agriculture and societies for the encouragement of agriculture, fairs, the first chambers of agriculture—at the behest of prefects and general councilors. Agricultural improvement constituted, from this point of view, the site of action of a relatively restrained local society, hardly different in the majority of French departments (all things considered) from the "legal country" of the constitutional monarchy.

The department, by a mirror effect, thus reflected for almost a century the image of the society that had created it. Faithful, so to speak, to groups of notables, whose social authority and eventually whose political promotion it ensured. Government tutelage was inscribed in the texts; but the department was something besides the jurisdictional district of a bureaucracy. It established a certain type of power and constituted elites, an area of action, by making use of intermediaries (the cascade from district centers down to city hall). The department thus created a sort of common reference between social groups, which continued to distinguish themselves far into the nineteenth century. These groups entered into communication, combined their interests—in spite of ideological oppositions. The department with its institutions thus became the site of negotiation par excellence; between landed notables—from the legitimate aristocracy to the propertied bourgeoisie—and the possessors of intelligence, an instance of confrontation, of encounter. Let us look once more at the Manche: Guillemin recalls that, beginning in the July Monarchy, the middle bourgeoisie, and notably the representatives of the liberal professions, participated in large numbers alongside the aristocracy in the general council, which the assembly made less a "closed field" than a "court of conflicts." "Homogenization of the directing classes," without a doubt, but this also gave local powers a certain flexibility, an ability to open up to new notables. This version of the history of France perhaps hides other conflicts, which revealed themselves during national crises and upheavals (1848–49). But the department also reminds us of the slow maturations or substitutions that characterized this history. Moreover, the sometimes bitter memory has been preserved of conflicts between notables and representatives of the State, prefects, directors of important bodies. This is to neglect the mass of more discreet collaborations, the amalgamation that most often occurred between functionaries and local elites. "The prefect and his notables,"[32] to borrow the analysis of Jean-Pierre Worms, was also a reality of the nineteenth century, perhaps blurred during the Second Empire and therefore overly neglected. Let us evoke the case of the engineer de Montricher in Marseille: engineer for the Department of Bridges and Roads, builder of the Durance Canal, (unfortunate) designer of a Marseille–Avignon line that was more sensitive to departmental interests than the line that was ultimately chosen, very able director of the national workshops of 1848, general engineer for the Department of Maritime Works (and hence designer of the new port), agricultural innovator (setting the example of irrigation), and

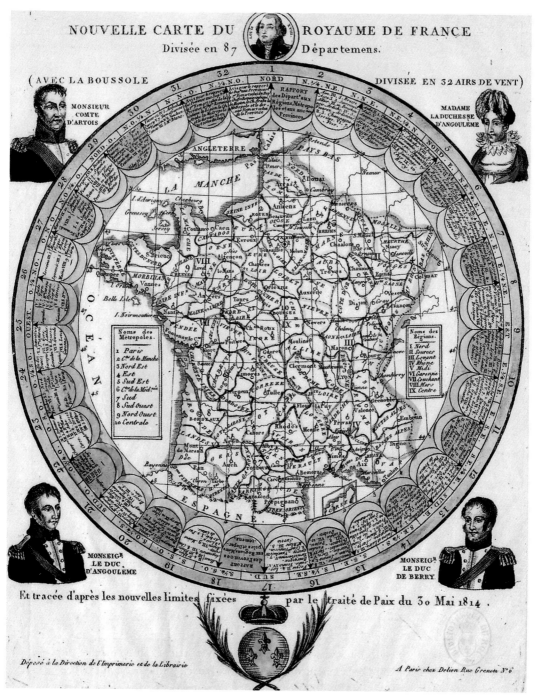

Figure 5.8

Resistance of the department (1814–15). The territorial division of France survived imperial tradition; eighty-seven departments were inscribed within the borders of the country, referring back *grosso modo* to the divisions of 1792. But the departments were reclassified geographically as cities and regions, without any administrative reality.

privileged expert on the great public works of Marseille, from the end of the 1850s until his premature death.[33] Notable or functionary? Only the peasant remained distant and sometimes "invented" on this scene of local interests, which was reserved in spite of everything to an elite.

The educational institution occupied a large place in this formation of elites. Despite the strength of religious establishments, the State *lycée,* the *grand lycée,* generally established in a department's center, structured these tightly controlled mechanisms of unification and openness. This educational geography was destined to last: in 1936–37, there were still only about 120 public *lycées* in France, all dependent on the State, privileged sites of a collective memory; only a few duplicates in districts that were more populated or had a great cultural tradition; a few distortions, sacrificing their ancien régime inheritance (in Ardèche, the *lycée* was established at Tournon, site of a famous *collège*). It was indeed the grid of 1790 that ordered transmission of knowledge and selection by merit.

The *lycée* was thus added—and it was not the least active force of all those that worked toward the concentration of this society of notables, established or aspiring. Except in several departments lacking a magnetic center, which we have already cited, the mechanism functioned indisputably to the benefit of the district center. Beginning in 1789–90, the pleas of the towns figuring in the Constituent's correspondence testify to the residence of the most prominent citizens.[34] Wealth was associated with the idea of ability and measured the capacity of towns to exercise an administrative function. Before being commercial or institutional, centrality aimed at being social. Curiously, the new administration, willingly "functionalist," resurrected the old criteria of the town as site of culture. Even in sleepy small prefectures, which were laughed at in Paris, this image dominated into the nineteenth century: perhaps it is what fueled the daydreams of the regulator of weights and measures in Jean Giraudoux's play *Intermezzo* (1933). With the help of more certain information, one may evaluate the tendency of the richest individuals, first of all, toward agglomeration in the department center: the lists of the Empire's notability and different studies on notables in the middle of the nineteenth century confirm these residential choices,[35] which generally accompanied an advantageous demographic increase.

It is more difficult to draw conclusions about the cohort of arrondissement centers, which were so disparate. To what extent were they stifled by the reinforcement of prefecture-towns, often accumulating motives for expansion, or were they tied to the institutions, functions, and inhabitants that were left to them? Let us hold on to this idea: the departmental organization remained capable of establishing an urban life, and for better or worse it preserved ancient forms and dignities. The selection of 1789–90, and the even stricter one of 1800, provided a chance to alleviate the outward sputterings of industrialization and to resist the menace of urban exodus. Remains of an outdated civilization? Our century often follows old paths. Maybe it is necessary to find reason for indulgence in these manifestations of duration, consolidated by the administrative task and all that accompanies it. In the population censuses published around 1900, particularly in 1911,[36] the General Statistics Office of France listed every town that had at least five thousand inhabitants, whatever its administrative status. A complementary list included towns with a more modest population, if they exercised the function of a department or arrondissement center. Good awareness on the part of the bureaucracy or implicit judgment of the urban nature of these localities and the irreversible character of their dignity? In any case, beyond the period of majority cohesion (which seems to us to be the July Monarchy), the nineteenth century in France operated according to this framework of knowledge and power and the physical matrix designed under the Revolution.

CRISIS, RESISTANCE, AND CHANGE: THE DEPARTMENT, CONSERVATIVE OR MODERATE?

It was at the end of the Second Empire that the first serious criticisms were lodged against the department. Henri Mettrier summarized them in one sentence: "There needed to be a scientific revolution without historical precedent, which modified old habits, shook up economic life, considerably shortened distances; there needed to be the excesses of centralization that, with the rise of the imperial regime, had become stronger than ever, in order for one to conceive doubts about the value of the divisions created in 1790."[37] But in the last quarter of the nineteenth century, things moved quickly, at least in writing. In 1871, the notables, disappointed, condemned this "best instrument" of centralization; a reduction in the number of districts was envisaged, from which a stronger resistance to Parisian influence and the development of "literary and scientific centers" in the provinces were anticipated.[38] Gambetta, at the beginning of his great ministry, proposed a reform of the administrative map. Goblet, in 1887, suggested correcting the departmental model by taking into account the new distance that one could cover in six hours, thanks to the railroads. In 1894, there was a new push for administrative reform projects, accompanied by an idea for university reform.[39] In 1898, an article by Pierre Foncin, based on the works of geographers, latched onto the department as a more modern level of economic and social life, between the "countrysides," considered most authentic, and the regions.[40] In 1907, the learned societies themselves meditated—without putting too much of a brake on criticism—on the obsolescence of their privileged space. Parliamentary projects accumulated in the assemblies, an echo effect of the regionalist movement, also contemporaneous with the perspectives of urbanism. Certain names marked these relationships, among them Beauquier, Siegfried, and Cornudet.[41] The agitation culminated on the eve of World War I with the Hennessy bill, which condemned the departmental organization, and the Ribot bill, which proposed to accord more autonomy to the districts. In the middle of the war, the deputy Clémentel, the minister of commerce, issued a text, based on the study of experts, on the formation of economic regions (1918).[42] The "memory" of the department, like its possibilities for adjustment, like the meaning of the resistance to it, emerges more clearly from the analysis of this crisis, which foreshadowed later debates—at the time of the fall of the Third Republic, and again in the 1950s and 1960s, when territorial improvement was taking place. The idea of administrative reform and of decentralization thus opened the debate on regionalism.

There would be, moreover, the issue of regions. But regionalism supposed a certain number of conditions. First the search for an "objective," durable, noncapricious division. The old provinces, although they had regained their honor through local erudition, most often through the departmental framework, seemed "outdated," too, even if their vague prestige and their name were exploited. Regionalism also implied cultural foundations: the linguistic and ethnological revival of French diversity at the end of the nineteenth century is a familiar story. But over against the department—this artificial division, hardly authentic— regionalism tended especially to construct a scientific and practical legitimacy.

The works of the French geographers of 1900 provided the scientific backing; it was openly invoked in the exposé of the motivations behind the legislative proposals, and the name of Vidal de La Blache seemed to sponsor the reform, probably beyond the master's intentions, as in the happiest times of an active geography. However, the geographical production of the epoch—except for several articles, including Pierre Foncin's in the very well known *Revue de Paris*—prudently advanced the principles of the new divisions, more than it directly inspired the reformers. It aimed especially at marking itself off from historical geography and from the scholastic geography (that of enumerations and litanies) inherited from the nineteenth century. It strove to distinguish administrative divisions, more or less capricious, from more authentic divisions of the territory emerging from nature or human relations. On one side, the countryside: invented or rediscovered by geologists, in their description of outcroppings. The *Revue de géographie* still expressed this affiliation in 1889 by reporting on a rather dated book, *La Géologie en chemin de fer* by Lapparent. The work has the merit of describing "these divisions traced in the surface of the soil by nature herself: it is to these divisions that it [the book] intends to restore the name so true—so dear and so gentle—of countryside, whose absence it regrets in almost all of our geography books, as on almost all of our maps."[43] The geographers made up for lost time, however, by making these "natural" unities the cells of peasant life and of human relations. Élisée Reclus, a good Communard, suspicious of the State, defender of elementary communities, launched the theme in 1881: "Groups of communes—cantons, arrondissements, and departments—of about the same size have their contours traced in an arbitrary manner. This division of France into departments, of about the same size, is not at all natural. Thus the true limits of the natural countryside, which are in many places the same as those of the old *pagi minores* of the Gallo-Romans, have not ceased to be recognized by their inhabitants, in spite of all the changes in feudal and administrative borders."[44] The department had been created in 1789, it was said, in opposition to the province; a century later the countryside was reinvented in opposition to the department. In the legislative proposals contemporaneous with World War I, Vidal de La Blache was called to the rescue as a defender of the arrondissements, closer to the countryside, against the departmental organization.[45]

On the other hand, in contrast to the department was the region, the modern region, centered on a capital, sometimes associated with the hinterland of a port and an influential bank: a phenomenon no longer anchored by the stagecoach. Élisée Reclus anticipated it, yet again:

> Thanks to accelerated means of communication, France is narrowed, so to speak, from the standpoint of distance; the territory is therefore seven times less long and seven times less wide than it was two generations ago. The populations of the towns are not only nearer in fact, they also live a communal life, thanks to the incessant exchange of books, letters, telegrams. They thus acquire a sort of ubiquity.[46]

It is not certain that the geographers and, even more, their commentators were totally clear in negotiating between the countryside, expressing a desire for eternity (or almost), and the modernism of communication. At each of these levels, they strove to reconcile the principles of homogeneity and of polarity, which were often confused—the one with natural geography, the other with economic geography. Thus the necessary lesson given by Gallois, refusing to question the departmental experiment in the name of geography, even if it could be considered sterile, as long as it led to the natural division of the territory.[47]

The debate would have echoed only the discreet resonance of epistemological and academic conflicts, if it did not respond to other realities. Toward 1900, the economy undertook a new experiment with spontaneous regionalism, simply following the march of affairs and the constraints of new techniques: new or reinforced regional banking networks (centered on Lyon, Lille, Nancy, Grenoble, and even Marseille, traditionally little inclined to this type of concern); and the creation of production and distribution networks for electricity in the Alps, on the Mediterranean coast, around coal basins, in the Parisian agglomeration. The big agglomerations, to fulfill the needs of their own consumption and financial equilibrium, strove to organize larger spaces, on a scale allowing for transportation (of electrical energy, for example). The Clémental project very explicitly evoked these facts, by founding the region of the Alps around Grenoble on the banking capacity of this town and the exploitation of hydroelectricity: similarly, the boundaries of the future Marseillaise region were designed around the zone of activity of the Energie électrique du littoral méditerranéen (Electrical Energy Association of the Mediterranean Coast). A movement headed by an idea, almost a regional lobby, pushed for these accomplishments and hoped to make them the basis of a political and administrative reform. "Industrial societies," more or less established (as in the Mulhouse tradition, Nancy or Lille), societies for the encouragement of business, chambers of commerce regrouped into regional entities: these were the most active participants in this movement.[48] The stake was not only geographical. What was in question, in reality, was not only the departmental division, but the definition of territorial collectivities and the selection of their directors.

Since the nineteenth century, in fact, two risks were combined in the life of the department: that of a political excess, with the establishment of universal suffrage; that of an archaism emerging from the former seat of notables. The regionalist offensive took hold early on, in 1864, in Frédéric Le Play's project for "social reform."[49] Le Play revisited the classical argument: the departments were too numerous and therefore could not constitute more autonomous entities with respect to Paris. One would not find, even in eighty-nine attempts [then the number of departments], the skills needed to give them life. His proposal was to concentrate provincial power in thirteen regions. Suppress the department? Le Play remarked that districts of the same size worked well in other European countries (the British county, for example). What was dangerous was the confusion of rural interests and urban agglomerations. He denounced "the false assimilation that has submitted rural districts and urban agglomerations to the same law, by confusing interests that, with all peoples and in our own tradition, have been not only different, but independent from each other."[50] He thought to give urban communes their autonomy, but at the same time to limit their rights "locally": "Communal life must grow in the towns and come to an end in the countryside." The department would receive, on the contrary, the responsibility for administering the countryside under the authority of proprietors: "To resolve the problem of local government, it is necessary to attribute to the resident proprietors chosen by the sovereign both the administration of the department and the exercise of local judicial power."[51] Swimming against the current of urban polarities, the countryside would thus be protected from the political contagions of the towns and from the "abuse" of electoral power. The territorial organization would combat the risks of universal suffrage. Le Play, simultaneously an official actor in the Empire, commissary general of the world fairs, ethnographer, and conservative philanthropist, strove in his own manner to reconcile technical progress and stability of the social body.

The Republic, on the contrary, remained attached to the submission of both town and countryside to the same law, whether it was a question of identical status for all communes or of a hierarchy of districts, which, from the canton to the department, encompassed countryside, boroughs, and towns in the same grouping. This measure, in 1790 and during the entire period of property qualifications for voting, seemed to accentuate the domination of urban elites. In the second half of the century, with universal suffrage, it became a potential avenue of change.

The offensive was of another order around 1900. Behind the region, which had lost its archaic references, one saw an attempt by entrepreneurs, men of industry or commerce, to acquire local power at the level that suited them, that of territorial groupings organized by the modern economy and painted in their own hues. The ambiguity that persisted until 1917 between administrative reform (which was also political) and the creation of economic regions (a sort of enlarged chamber of commerce) partly camouflaged this ambition. The deliberations of the Association industrielle, commerciale et agricole de Lyon (Industrial, Commercial, and Agricultural Association of Lyon), among so many others, revealed the significance of these plans in 1918:

> The great idea is administrative reform, that is to say decongestion of the central power by the clear division of public services currently entangled between general offices of the State, regional offices in the provinces, and communal offices. . . . The corollary is the creation,

via the path of elimination, of a Council of Authorized Representatives, chosen among the unions of employers and workers, the organizations of capitalists and merchants, of professors and engineers, a
council which is capable of speaking loudly and strongly, of acting
efficiently and quickly, of putting the collective interest first, without
however neglecting individual interests.[52]

The proposal by the deputy Hennessy (1915) uncontestably targeted the
whole of the administrative system: it reinforced the arrondissement, a
level of proximity, suppressed the department, and constituted a restricted number of regions—sixteen to eighteen. At the head of each one
of them, it placed an elected assembly. But the mode of election was revealing: the citizens could enroll themselves either on a general list (normally composed of people lacking a profession), or on professional lists
that included both "salary-givers" [*salariants*] and "salary-receivers"
[*salariés*] of the same branch or sector, the elected representatives being
split equally between these two categories.[53] According to one's perspective, one can see in these propositions a touch of modernity—the invention of socioprofessionals, which are so important in our time—or
the expression of a corporatism, of which other regimes were the fore-
runner. This countercurrent persisted in the last twenty years of the
Third Republic, deflected in part by the useful and inoffensive creation,
on the national level, of an Economic Council.

On the contrary, the Republic remained attached to an exclusively
territorial electoral system. Universal suffrage established no other divisions between citizens than those of voting residence. The department
supplied the geographical matrix of this political system, whether for local
elections or general elections (and whether the ballot was for the department or arrondissement). Born of a restrictive conception of the legal
country—the property qualification system—it became a line of defense
for classical, territorial, universal suffrage, at the risk of moderating the effects on the real redivision of the population, through the habitual tardiness of electoral division. France had until then steered clear of any proportional system that would redistribute seats on the national or even the
regional level. Let us look even closer, at the 1969 referendum that condemned the Senate and instituted the regions: the departmental representatives were not the least significant adversaries of this project.

Conservatism, sense of continuity, preparation for necessary evolu-
tions? The department contains in its memory all of these characteristics,
sometimes in opposition to the supposed shaking and balancing of French
politics. The department, depository of a certain idea of the republic,
expresses the search for an eternity, reinforcing the social and the terri-

torial, the one by the other. It is seen sometimes as an excess of conservatism, sometimes as a useful means of controlling progressivism, without real rupture, with only surface changes. In this manner, too, the departments, whatever they are, form a sort of resistance to the capital: that of another temperament imposing itself, in spite of centralization. The two readings, order and movement, are not incompatible.

On the conservative side, the department kept alive an administrative organization that a Cartesian mind might judge absurd. Thirty-six thousand communes, defined according to a single model, although two-thirds of them did not exceed 500 inhabitants and although the most populous, aside from Paris and Marseille, had between 250,000 and 500,000 inhabitants. Some three thousand cantons, of an extremely variable caliber, especially if one looks at population and wealth. But one knows how attached the French are to the most humble echelon, maybe the most solid in a democracy, and the hostility that proposals for reunification and concentration ordinarily excite.[54] The same goes for the canton: disliked or ignored in the big agglomerations, without administrative function, given only an elected representation making up the general councils of the departments, the canton remained, for the modest cells, the expression of common interests, rediscovered with generalized urbanization. In relation to this elementary world of districts, it is the department that, through tradition, custom, memory, still plays its initial role: site of information, of mediation, of the arbitration of conflicts, of the redistribution of financial resources. In our day, it comfortably occupies a place in the decentralization experiment, which here modifies not so much the range of abilities as the procedures. Across that, one may glimpse the portrait of a ritual France; a France in which rural values have long been privileged, where the countryside is overrepresented (even if it was really represented by urban notables). A significant case is the Senate, whose existence, then survival, in sum symbolizes this collective choice. "Grand Council of the Communes of France," Gambetta used to say. But elections pass through the department because of indirect suffrage. They are negotiated in the departmental center, even if each important department tries to attain an equilibrium in its composition between the "urbans" (that is, the representatives of significant agglomerations) and the "rurals." The political gesture thus takes on another value. The Senate, progressively deprived of any real role in the functioning of the Third Republic, resisted the establishment of the Fourth, then of the Fifth, in the referendum of 1969, and it still seeks rejuvenation today. Representing territory more than men, it provides cause for reflection. A conservative Senate is attentive to the preservation of principles—and particularly to that of property. A glance at the history of urbanism suffices to confirm this assertion.

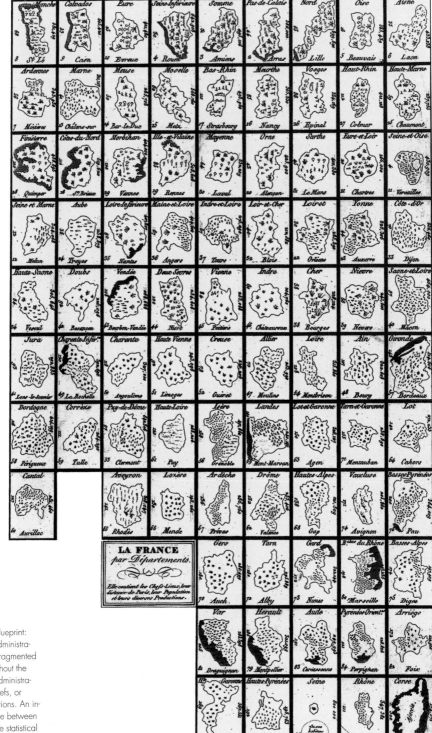

Figure 5.9

Departmental blueprint: physical and administrative layouts. A fragmented geography, without the placement of administrative centers, reliefs, or specific orientations. An intermediary stage between the map and the statistical series; *La France par départements* (1824).

Do we have here a pure conservatism, the simple (and often active) memory of French archaisms? A debatable conclusion. First of all, our age, curiously taking up a debate started by the Constituents of 1789–90, restores a certain value to the countryside, a rather abstract surface but also a concrete environment. It is wary of unqualifiedly endorsing the production of wealth and human densities as the only criteria. Just as the commune, whatever the size of its population, ensures (not without difficulty) a sort of minimal guaranteed framework for the territory, the department divides the soil. It is not out of simple corporate interest that all the bodies attached to the surveillance and the maintenance of the natural domain seem to show a predilection for this echelon, neither too close nor too far away. Let us look closer: everything does not move in the direction of a concentration of services and facilities, which one often confuses with the reinforcement of the metropolises.[55]

The department has even remedied certain deficiencies of the territorial organization linked to urbanization. Think of the interwar episode in the Parisian region. Greater Paris then gave form to the department of the Seine. Henri Sellier and the general council dreamed of "departmentalizing" a part of the Parisian and communal services and of thus obtaining a better redivision of means and responsibilities.[56] The departmental envelope around Paris was, however, rapidly surpassed. But, paradoxically, in 1964 new departmental divisions were cut in the agglomeration: always the argument of proximity, which was appeased only in part by the district, then the region, and which in the end left the Parisian agglomeration more divided. Paris thus reinforced its particularism: becoming once again a commune with full powers, it rose at the same time to the level of department.

Elsewhere, the old formula of the department sometimes compensated for the absence of the urban community. Nothing unequivocally said that the geographical borders traced two centuries ago were still legitimate; but how to change the framework? The most absurd departmental line, that which divided the agglomeration of Lyon between Rhône and Isère, resisted every attempt at rationalization. The urban community intervened here as a corrective. In other cases, the acquired, historical boundary continued to influence the current representation of phenomena more than one would have thought. The metropolitan area of Marseille provides a good example. Economic logic assuredly attracted Marseille to the Rhône region. This was already the form given to the department of Provence-Occidentale in 1790; but it preserved, from this very fact, a more abnormal asymmetry in the age of the metropolis, abating on the east the old frontier between Bouches-du-Rhône and the Var.

The department inscribes itself, finally, in another point of view, which is not pure conservatism. This division of the territory, it is seen, was based on the notables and exuded notability—a sort of genetic function, which did not exclude change: long substitutions, begun with the parliamentary monarchy, prolonged with the Republics, even the Empire, and the rise of "new [social] layers" [*couches nouvelles*]. The form of notability persisted, in spite of serious social or ideological modifications. In particular, the department acquired functions connected to schooling and selected new elites or at least new settings: first of all, the *écoles normales primaires,* departmental by definition, founded in principle in the departmental centers beginning in the July Monarchy: there followed the awarding of scholarships, then the establishment of the *écoles primaires supérieures* and of the *collèges,* even if they arose out of municipal initiatives in most cases. But this denser educational fabric more or less faithfully mirrored the administrative hierarchies, and more rarely (in technical instruction) the industrial map. The trajectories of promotion via school are departmental until the baccalaureate.

On another side, the department, through its institutions and notably the elective hierarchy that it implies, is even more directly a machine for creating new types of notables. A theme to analyze would be the level of radicalism needed to ensure the succession of more classical generations of notables in this or that region of France (the basin of the Garonne, certain departments forming the "crown" outside of Paris). Alongside reproduction, change plays a role: the radical, then socialist, teacher; the small businessman; the former unionist now become mayor and general councilor; even the organizers of "red" municipalities end up, along the pathway of honors, being admitted to a game that "naturalizes" them somewhat. The department thus becomes a sort of machine for social and political acculturation, more than national institutions. The type of relation evolves only slowly, undoubtedly more slowly than recruitment: relations among notables themselves and, before decentralization, relations between the prefect and his notables. Did decentralization essentially target this inherited form of complicity or more recent interferences between the local level and Parisian offices, carried by the very change in political personnel? In any case, a social and political memory was thus constituted in counterpoint to the great events—a memory which is that of the French territory.

✴

The department deserves to be called a *territorial form* for several reasons. First, because it has the physical characteristics of one; it is delimited, circumscribed, fixed. The a priori legitimacy of its border (whether

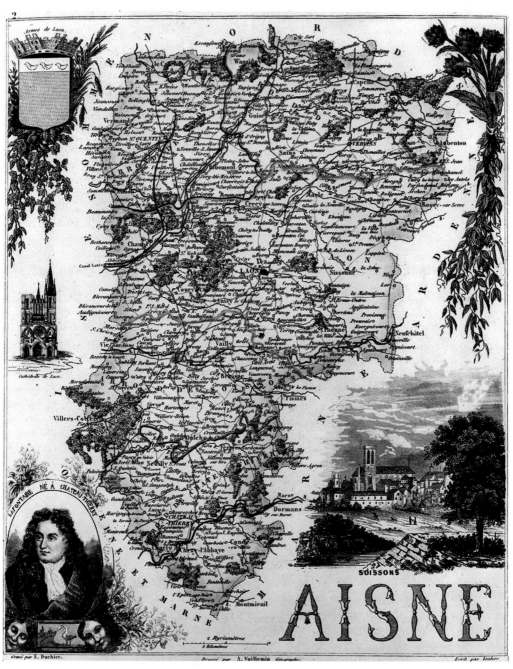

Figure 5.10
Remembrance of places and *lieux de mémoire*. Map plates and atlases drawn for each department in the middle of the 19th century combine the precise details of the locations and the symbolic images that were associated with them. The department of the Aisne, as seen by the cartographer Vuillemin, *Nouvel atlas illustré* (1852).

FRANCE.

D. Comment Divise t'on la France ?

ANGLETERRE

LONDRES

Commerce
étendu.

Manche

Nombreuses
manufac-
tures.

PAYS-BAS

Riches
produits.

Sol fertile

ESPAGNE

MÉDITERRANÉE

Corse

Brillante
armée

Vaillance

Nobles
souvenirs

6 **RÉPONSE.**

La **FRANCE** se divise en quatre-vingt-six départements, qui tirent leurs noms des rivières qui les
arrosent, ou des montagnes qui s'y trouvent. Ses
principales montagnes sont : les Pyrénées, les Alpes
et les Cévennes. Ses principales rivières sont : la
Loire, le Rhône, la Seine, la Saône, la Garonne, la
Meuse, le Rhin, la Somme, la Dordogne et la Charente.
La France est bornée au nord par la Manche et
la Hollande; à l'est, par le Rhin qui la sépare de
l'Allemagne, par la Suisse et les Alpes qui la séparent
de l'Italie; au sud, par la Méditerranée et les monts
Pyrénées, qui la séparent de l'Espagne; et à l'ouest,
par l'Océan. Son étendue est de 250 lieues en lon-
gueur, sur une largeur de 215. Sa population est
de 34,000,000 d'habitants.
Paris, une des villes les plus célèbres du monde,
est la capitale du royaume; son étendue, sa richesse,
sa population, son commerce, ses monuments, tout
en fait un objet d'admiration pour les étrangers qui
y viennent admirer tout ce que les arts et le génie
ont créé de plus beau. Le Français est vif, spirituel,
confiant, intrépide; il aime tous les genres de gloire.
Le gouvernement est une monarchie constitu-
tionnelle, où la couronne est héréditaire. La religion
catholique est celle de l'État; tous les autres cultes y
sont tolérés.
Les colonies de la France sont : en Afrique, le
royaume d'Alger, l'île Bourbon, le Sénégal; en
Asie, Pondichéry, Chandernagor; en Amérique, la
Martinique, la Guadeloupe, Cayenne.

Figures 5.11 and 5.12
The catechism of the
territory. Departmental
divisions, as the first
article of knowledge
of the country; H.
Duru, *Géographie il-
lustrée* (1841).

it comes from geography, economy, or culture) is less important than its acquired legitimacy. One thus understands how an administrative and political projection becomes a geographical construction. A form, more-over, because it envelops realities, functions, and activities that change. The department has the capacity to give shape to a knowledge, a con-sciousness of the French territory. Without a doubt, people have been slow to measure this rediscovery or discovery of France that is occurring, through the norms of modern science (that of the nineteenth century, es-pecially) and thanks to the departmental grid and to the needs—more or less direct—of its administration. The renaissance of regional cultures, paradoxically, only occurred after the fact, as an *effect* of this knowledge or this folkloric interest.

Certainly, the departmental model is hardly suited to the dimensions of economic activity since the end of the nineteenth century. But was it ever suited to them? In the beginning, the clothes were a bit large for the banal level of relations in rural France. The new district (despite its reduced size, in relation to the provinces and governorships) was an in-vitation, the sign of an opening, more than a result of the level of daily exchanges, which perhaps explains the state of grace in which the department lived from the Consulate to the Second Empire. It was a motivational form. Everything was later shaken up, under the effect of social or political fears, then realities, leading up to the great offensive of the early 1900s. The Clémentel report, a masterwork of political subtlety, demonstrated that the region was the new horizon of affairs, but that, by contrast, the boundaries of the department were fluid, changing, uncertain, depending on competition, conjunctures, sectors of activity, even manipulations (railroad or port taxes). The economy could not by itself constitute the basis of a territorial division; it designated poles, not limits. In short, it was a question not only of changing dimensions, but of imagining space differently—something that corresponded poorly with the daily demands of administrative life.

This was even more so because regional identity was difficult to restore, despite the cultural foundations that could prop it up. A recurrent argument is that the majority of supporters of reform wanted to distinguish the regions (of a more or less economic inspiration) from the heritage of the provinces and pure tradition. On the contrary, the department—below the regions—curiously managed to preserve itself, to deal with rivalries and demands. It persisted as a strong component of identity, although it seemed poorly adapted to the economy; nearby administration and facilities are less negligible than one might think—but beyond that, it is the remarkable resistance of the departmental conscience that one must admire.

What does all this mean, finally? One must call attention to what remains active on the level of the department: associations, unions, political and educational life, among other things. More profoundly, one must call attention to the place held by small cities, mid-sized cities, or even the second tier of big cities (those of 100,000 to 200,000 inhabitants) in the departmental structure. We know that, alongside the growth of metropolises (not always the most brilliant), the rapid urbanization of France since the 1950s has been achieved on this level: departmental identities and urban identities combine their effects.

Although the department sometimes plays the role of substitute in the management of great agglomerations, when other federative organisms do not exist, the threat comes from the metropolises. They form another geographical structure; they possess strong identities, but, like the economic regions, without precise boundaries. A focused image, a diffuse territorial presence. The crisis of the department signifies something other than the maladjustment of a model or a boundary: it is a crisis of the old forms of territoriality, which no longer work. The end of the territory, squeezed between micro-local roots and the abstraction of economic exchange, would perhaps be more than an administrative or

Figure 5.13
Pedagogy of the Republic. The departments as an educational tool used in elementary instruction: holders of
national images and remembrances. Cover to a magnetic question-and-answer game (ca. 1880).

social change. It would be the end of a memory, of which the department was not the only depository, but an active conservator and creator.
From this point of view, departments and cities find their destiny connected in the French heritage.

NOTES

1. Henri Mettrier, *La Formation du département de la Haute-Marne: Étude de
géographie politique* (Chaumont, 1911), introduction, 3. This is the most important
work of the second generation of monographs aiming to offer a scientific response to
the criticisms lodged against the division and the institution of the departments
around 1900. The first generation, around 1870, was contemporary with the revolt of
notables against the Empire and the beginnings of cultural regionalism. The debate
became reanimated in the 1930s and 1940s, when, once again, the structures of the
Republic were called into question. The reflections that accompanied the

improvement of the territory and the search for a more rational urban hierarchy revived curiosity at the end of the 1950s.

Among the works that directly or indirectly approach the formation of the departments and the explanation of their durability, and that were consulted for this essay at the time it was written (1990), we will cite primarily the works (originally university theses) by Marie-Noëlle Bourguet, *Déchiffrer la France: La statistique départementale à l'époque napoléonienne* (Paris: Éditions des archives contemporaines, 1988); Marie-Vic Ozouf-Marignier, who has particularly inspired this work, *La Formation des départements: La représentation du territoire français à la fin du XVIIIe siècle* (Paris: Éditions de l'E.H.E.S.S., 1989); and finally the substantial work by Bernard Lepetit, *The Pre-industrial Urban System: France, 1740–1840* [1988], trans. Godfrey Rogers (Cambridge: Cambridge University Press, 1994). We cannot forget two older studies: F. Steevelberg, *Contribution à l'étude de l'armature urbaine préindustrielle française: Essai sur les rapports spatiaux d'après le découpage en départements, 1789–1790* (Paris: E.H.E.S.S., 1977), and Patricia Rodriguez Ochoa, *Les Rapports entre l'évolution de la structure administrative et le réseau urbain de la France, 1789–1856* (Paris: E.H.E.S.S., 1976), as well as Thierry Gasnier's first works.

2. "Patriae Amans" and "Les Départements français: Étude de géographie administrative," *Revue de géographie* 24 (1889): 401ff.

3. After several concessions on practical matters, the strong-man of the Committee of Division, Thouret, remained faithful to this objective of symbolic rupture: "And when would that be? would it not be desirable for the assembly to be able to accomplish this imaginary evil that one criticizes in the Committee's plan . . . , in order to destroy the provincial spirit which, in the State, is only an individual spirit, enemy of the true national spirit?" Discourse of November 7, 1789.

4. Intervention of Thouret, Reporter of the Committee of Division, Discourse of November 11, 1789, cited in "Patriae Amans," *Revue de géographie,* and Ozouf-Marignier, *La Formation des départements.*

5. Marie-Vic Ozouf-Marignier, "De l'universalisme constituant aux intérêts locaux: Le débat sur la formation des départements en France, 1789–1790," *Annales E.S.C.* (November–December 1986): 1193ff.

6. Robert de Hesseln, *Nouvelle topographie ou description détaillée de la France divisée par des carrés uniformes* (Paris, 1780).

7. Report by Thouret, which presented the proposal for the "geometrical" division of the realm to the Constitutional Committee, November 3, 1789.

8. Target, Intervention of November 11, 1789. Ozouf-Marignier insists on the fact that economic accessibility was not the principal argument, but that it was a question rather of the dimensions (and the distances) appropriate "to the physical form of the assemblies of the department, district, and canton" and to the *sufficient* and *restrained* number of subdivisions that was necessary in each department.

Verifying this argument for the department of the Sarthe, Étienne Juillard observed that in the beginning of the nineteenth century, "the forty-five to fifty kilometers that separated Le Mans from the peripheral communities represented, via a good highway on the plain, some five hours in the coach and, taking into account the often steep slopes created by an undulating relief, more like six or seven hours"; Juillard, "Espace et temps dans l'évolution des Cadres régionaux," in *Études de géographie tropicale offertes à Pierre Gourou* (Paris-La Haye: Mouton, 1972), 29ff.

9. Buache, a geographer who died in 1773, published an *Atlas physique de la France* that divided the country into hydrographic basins, separated by a water divide. A scientific vision of the territory, which often dominated cartographic representation until the beginning of the nineteenth century. It responded in part to the conception of "connecting canals" [*canaux de junction*], with which engineers were obsessed.

10. Jean-Claude Perrot, "Les Villes françaises en 1794," *Recherches et travaux, Institut d'histoire économique et sociale de Paris,* bull. 9 (October 1980): 1ff.

11. Bernard Lepetit, "Armature urbaine et organisation de l'espace dans la France préindustrielle, 1740–1840" (thesis, University of Paris I, 1987); published under the title *Les Villes dans la France moderne, 1740–1840* (Paris: Albin Michel, 1988), published in English as *The Pre-Industrial Urban System: France, 1740–1840,* trans. Godfrey Rogers (Cambridge: Cambridge University Press, 1994).

12. Edward Whiting Fox, *History in Geographic Perspective: The Other France* (New York: Norton, 1971), an argument undoubtedly excessive in its developments, but whose premises remain interesting: the division between a maritime France, open to outside influences, more "liberal," and a landed France, more agrarian, dominated by the administrative "framework," from the monarchy to the Republic.

13. Cited in Ozouf-Marignier, *La Formation des départements,* 115–16.

14. Charles Jolivet, *La Révolution dans l'Ardèche, 1788–1795* (Paris, 1930).

15. Cited in Ozouf-Marignier, *La Formation des départements,* 232.

16. From the pen of the defenders of La Rochelle, one may read the most lucid and pertinent definition of "conventions" [*convenances*].

17. Among the fifty-eight ancien régime towns classified at the top of the scale, forty-five were retained as departmental centers. Thirteen, mostly ports and "industrial" towns, failed to achieve this status. Lepetit, *The Pre-Industrial Urban System.*

18. For Laval, René Musset revealed the importance of redistributing the work of the "manufacturer" in *Le Bas-Maine: Étude géographique* (Paris, 1917), 20. For Le Mans, see Juillard, "Espace et temps."

19. See Bourguet, *Déchiffrer la France,* and Thierry Gasnier, "Une géographie en Révolution: Les catégories de perception de l'espace, 1770–1810" (D.E.A. thesis, University of Paris, 1987).

20. Jean-Claude Perrot, "L'Âge d'or de la statistique régionale, an IV–1804," *Annales historiques de la Révolution française* (April–June 1976): 215ff.

21. Cf. Lucien Gallois, *Régions naturelles et noms de pays* (Paris, 1908); Bourguet, *Déchiffrer la France;* and Marcel Roncayolo, "The Landscape of the Scholar," below in this volume.

22. Gallois, *Régions naturelles.*

23. Instruction given to the rectors in a circular of 1857: "One must supplement primary education with very simple notions of geography, by taking as a point of departure the village, the canton, the *arrondissement,* the department. . . . It is most useful to know the remarkable places, productions, and things of our country. . . . Thus we must regret, in spite of the numerous publications destined for schoolchildren, that a special book on the geography of each department does not exist." Cited by Gérard Gley, *Géographie physique et historique des Vosges* (Épinal, 1870).

24. É. Levasseur, *L'Étude et l'enseignement de la géographie* (Paris, 1872).

25. The list is established in the *Encylopédie des Bouches-du-Rhône,* general preface by P. Masson (Marseille, 1932), 1: L–LXIV.

26. See here the general bibliography of historical and archaeological works published by the *sociétés savantes* since 1864; in particular, Y. Laissus, "Les Sociétés savantes et l'avancement des sciences naturelles," in *Actes du 100e congrès des Sociétés savantes* (Paris, 1975), 41–68.

27. Michel Chevalier, *Des intérêts matériels en France* (Bruxelles, 1838).

28. A. Hugo, *La France pittoresque ou description pittoresque, topographique et statistique des départements et des colonies,* Tables on Fiscal Matters (Paris, n.d.), 97–100.

29. Chevalier, *Des intérêts matériels en France.*

30. Juillard, "Espace et temps."

31. Alain Guillemin, "Le Conseil général, l'innovation agricole et la constitution de l'identité départementale dans la Manche au XIXe siècle," in *Actes du colloque de Rennes, Association pour l'étude du fait départemental* (Rennes, 1982).

32. Jean-Pierre Worms, "Le Préfet et ses notables," *Sociologie du travail* 3 (1966).

33. *Encyclopédie départementale des Bouches-du-Rhône,* vol. 9, *Le Commerce* (1922); vol. 11, *Biographies* (1922); municipal archives of Marseille and archives of the Chambre de commerce, divers fonds.

34. Ozouf-Marignier, *La Formation des départements.*

35. Lepetit, *The Pre-industrial Urban System;* see also the investigation, directed by Louis Bergeron, titled *Masses de granit: Cent mille notables du premier Empire* (Paris, 1979), 240ff.

36. For example, *Résultats statistiques du recensement général de la population effectué le 5 mars 1911,* vol. 1 (Paris: Imprimerie nationale, 1913–17), 60–74, table 1.

37. Mettrier, *La Formation du département,* 228.

38. *Sociétés savantes,* 1907, session of April 4: Charles Beauquier's brief on the territorial districts in France recalls earlier reform projects.

39. Ibid.: "Fossard, Bechard, Vinier, Reynaud, hauts fonctionnaires en retraite, demandant que l'on rétablit le trajet de 6 h entre le chef-lieu et les sous-préfectures . . . mais 6 h accomplies en chemin de fer" (1887); Ribot report to the National Assembly, 1894. In 1890, the rector Liard launched his university reform project (affecting in particular the relations between universities and their regional milieu).

40. Pierre Foncin, "Les Pays de France," *Revue de Paris* 2 (1898): 737ff.

41. *Sociétés savantes,* 1907, session of April 4, report already cited; Statement of Beauquier, Intervention of Charles Brun, general delegate to the Regionalist Federation; note sent by Mazel, more prudent, in the following style: "It is necessary to preserve the departments, but to regroup them."

42. The elements of this campaign are recounted in a bulletin of the association: Association industrielle, commerciale et agricole de Lyon et Grenoble [Industrial, Commercial, and Agricultural Association of Lyon and Grenoble], *Chronique de l'association* (July 1918). See also, regarding the expectations for the project, "Projet de division de la France en régions économiques," presented by the Ministry of Commerce, Industry, Postal Services, and Telegraphs, submitted first to the chambers of commerce (Paris, 1917). Among the writers of this proposal was a historian, Henri Hauser.

43. *Revue de géographie,* geographical works, old books (1789), new books (1889), 359–60.

44. Élisée Reclus, *Nouvelle géographie universelle,* vol. 2, *La France* (Paris, 1881), 722.

45. Mettrier is much more critical with regard to the notion of countryside [*pays*]. He shows how the notion of countryside was smothered (at the end of the ancien régime) "under the extraordinary assemblage of districts and jurisdictions, which, by superposing themselves on each other over the course of centuries, without either method or plan for the ensemble, had finished by creating a monstrous labyrinth." The geographers of the seventeenth and eighteenth centuries had tried to establish order here, but "the confusion that frequently occurs between historical names and popular names for countrysides has led to numerous misunderstandings. . . . The coincidence between the two types of natural and public divisions has almost never been realized," Mettrier, *La Formation du département,* introduction.

46. Reclus, *Nouvelle géographie universelle,* 723.

47. Gallois, *Régions naturelles et noms de pays.*

48. See Association industrielle, commerciale et agricole de Lyon et Grenoble, *Chronique de l'association.*

49. Frédéric Le Play, *La Réforme sociale en Europe* (Paris, 1864).

50. Ibid., 437.

51. Ibid., 419.

52. I. Izart, "Rapport sommaire sur le régionalisme," in Association industrielle, commerciale et agricole de Lyon et Grenoble, *Chronique de l'association.*

53. Analysis of the Hennessy proposal, in Association industrielle, commerciale et agricole de Lyon et Grenoble, *Chronique de l'association,* 28, 29.

54. Henri Mendras, *The Vanishing Peasant: Innovation and Change in French Agriculture,* trans. Jean Lerner (Cambridge, Mass.: MIT Press, 1970).

55. See, in *Association pour l'étude du fait départemental,* the articles on the intercommunal redistribution of fiscal resources by L. Laurent, "L'Effet chef-lieu dans l'évolution des districts scolaires," 241ff.; and the articles by M. Bordes on Auch, by R. Béteille on Rodez, and by M. Genty on Périgueux.

56. Henri Sellier, *Les Banlieus urbanisées et la réorganisation administrative de la Seine* (Paris: Librairie Marcel Rivière, 1920).

Figure 6.1
The National Confederation in Paris, July 14, 1790, or how to make one with many.

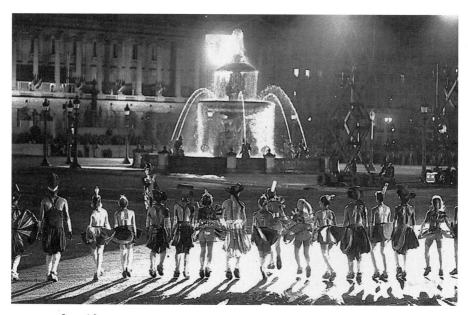

Figure 6.2
The parade of the Marseillaise by Jean Paul Goude: the provinces of France on the Place de la Concorde, July 14, 1989, or how to make many with one.

CHAPTER 6

THE LOCAL

One and Divisible

❧

THIERRY GASNIER

"A country that has two hundred and sixty-five kinds of cheeses
cannot be conquered." — "It cannot even be governed."

That dialogue between Churchill and De Gaulle, authentic or not, is
only one of the many commonplaces expressing the identity of
France: how to be at once completely one and also infinitely divisible?
Since the Third Republic at least, the tension between the one and the
many, the universal and the particular, forms the basis for all approaches
to France.

Territory reveals this organizing pattern most distinctly. Traditionally, the best access to France has been the deliberate examination of
those images that reveal the diverse ways France extends into space:
wines and cheeses, shapes of church towers and types of habitat, costume
and cuisine, temperaments, languages, and landscapes. That comparable
diversity exists within neighboring countries is irrelevant. Alphonse
Dupront has shown that the "making" of France is its constituent element. France is a territorial achievement constantly starting afresh.[1]

In this system local space plays an essential role. Whether it involves
an administrative or ecclesiastical district or a geographical or historical
entity, all divisions of French space may furnish a setting for displaying
local distinctiveness. The smallest parcel of French territory thus shares
in the fact of France by its very specificity and demonstrates its vitality.
From Michelet to Braudel, France is a continuous miracle and everywhere visible because it is rooted everywhere.

In today's world, the basic dogma of unity and diversity is becoming outdated. The unifying fact of nationhood has been weakened by the retreat of France to the ranks of a second-rate power and by decolonization and has been diluted in the process of constructing Europe; this defining feature has further blurred in the debates over immigration. The capacity of France to be *one* is henceforth the problem. The theme is not really new: One could find similar questions after 1870 or in the 1930s. With the disintegration of the national model inherited from the nineteenth century, the overall perception of France as a territory is shattered. That is what is important here.

The indicators of this change are abundant. The resurgence of provincial names, the return of accents, especially in southern France, the multiplicity of sometimes improbable names for "country," and the very recent transition of "local" to a noun express the increased vitality of the local fact as much as the vote for the decentralization law in 1982 and the central role of local notables in political life. The confluence of standardized lifestyles, the changing values of a society in crisis, and the development of tourism and the promotion industry all contribute to the rise in value of the particular and the fragmentary. Nothing showed that better than the parade on the night of July 14, 1989, when plurality became the determinative way of representing France.

It could be said that this is only a case of gimmicks or fading nostalgia. Yet the evolution just described is accompanied by a massive increase in local memories. The multiplication of historical spectacles, folklore groups, and local events of all sorts testifies to this. The last thirty years have seen a spectacular revival of learned societies: of those 674 listed in 1975, 161 were created between 1960 and 1975, against 146 created between 1914 and 1960. The same tally included 180 societies for local studies. Finally, if one could speak of "1,000 museums of France" in 1962, today the count is over 1,700. To the new creations for memory may be added the many redevelopment and revitalization projects.[2]

Local space has likewise been constituted as a place of memory. In fact, since the time of the Revolution, which invented local space, such space has been the place and object of an ongoing production of an increasingly dense body of knowledge alongside efforts to generate knowledge about the nation. Every division of French territory has therefore been literally stuffed with history and traditions, the constituent parts of local patrimonies. At the same time that local knowledge has been rediscovered, the current period is unearthing and updating the practices that produced that knowledge.[3] Local memory thus includes the history of its production and its producers.

Far from being a spontaneously produced and motionless tradition, whose origins might disappear into the night of time, local space was erected during the nineteenth and twentieth centuries as the space for memory. Moments, places, issues concerning its formation, the layers within local patrimonies, and the customs to which they gave place are the objects of this analysis.

THE MEMORY OF PLACES

Beginning with the Revolution, representations of French space, the whole that it formed and the parts that composed it, were organized around two opposing yet complementary terms—the general and the particular, the local and the national. The history of these representations was, to be sure, not linear. Whether the question refers to modalities of territorial organization or to ways of describing France as space, two antithetical positions came about during the revolutionary decade, and they alternate constantly. The one poses the indivisibility of the territory as a principle and imposes it for uniformity. The other, in opposite fashion, starts from the fundamental heterogeneity of the same territory. Local space stands at the center of these two opposing positions, which offer two divergent definitions based on the recognition or negation of the significance of memory for places. I will seek to show the formation of these two competing models and their inexorable growth during the nineteenth century.

The Revolution: The Local as Memory

Right from its early days, the Revolution affirmed itself as a territorial as well as a political activity. The remolding of the territory and its representations was, in the eyes of the men of 1789, the preferred way of constructing the nation. The process of creating the departments and the movement of the federations, which signaled the same desire, give evidence of this activity. Through the fusion of differences, anchored in the soil or imposed by history, the nation constructed itself.[4] It thereby affirmed itself as a reality greater than the sum of its parts. Positioned at the outset as universal and homogeneous, it triggered the association of the fragmentary and the particular.

That did not mean that before 1789 perceptions of French space ignored local spaces. Rather, the lists of the provinces and the *pays* into which they were subdivided, as the preferred way of displaying the geography of the time, reproduced the fundamental diversity of the kingdom conceived as a succession of annexations. The kingdom was a composite territory, understandable only through enumeration. It is at this point that the Revolution caused a fundamental break by establishing a difference in kind between the whole and its parts. Local space, up to then limited by its particularity alone, was henceforth defined by the nation that included and surpassed it.[5]

The general and the particular. The organization of powers resulting from the municipal elections of 1789 accounts perfectly for this detachment of the local and the national perfectly. The Law of September 14, 1789, assigned to municipal governments "two kinds of functions: the first appropriate to municipal power, the other to general administration of the State and delegates to the municipalities." In the first months of the Revolution, France experienced a totally new organization of its territory based on extreme decentralization. Not only the municipal executives but also the representatives of the State to the commune were elected by the active citizens. For the first time, and the last, "the organ that represented the central government was not under the control of the central government."[6] The Constitution of 1791, which sharply separated the areas of competence of the State from those of local authority, confirmed this arrangement. The demand for local autonomy, which persisted through the last decades of the ancien régime, found its culmination here.[7] French space was henceforth organized according to two separate and complementary categories: the local and the national.

The two were not quite on an equal footing. With the nation facing not only pressure for unity but also a need for definition, its construction banished the particular to a now superseded past. Not that this was anything new. Reports from the end of the eighteenth century insist at every possible opportunity on the archaic and retrograde character of local particularities, terminated by the growing homogenization of the French territory. The Revolution only hardened already formed views. The division of time caused by 1789 also cut across the field of spatial representations: the local was the national in infancy.[8]

This system was put to a severe test in 1793. The radicalization of political debate and the increasingly well-founded dread of seeing the recent territorial unity burst apart set the two categories of 1789 in opposition. One key event in this change occurred during the federalist episode when, by turns, Paris and the departments disputed the right to speak in the name of the nation.[9] The cohesion of the national territory being the condition of survival for the Revolution, any affirmation of particularity threatened mortal danger to the entire nation. This theme, constantly reinforced by the increase in local resistance, was central in the arguments over the "inexplicable Vendée" during the debates of the

Convention in March 1793.[10] The revolt was the sign of the persistence of the ancien régime and of a history believed to be definitively concluded. Particularity was becoming an obstacle to the course of the Revolution. It attested to the persistence of shadows in a space believed to be totally transparent.[11] It meant the end of the utopia of 1789, when the nation was realized in the spontaneous fusion of differences and in the renunciation by localities of their particularity. The local is the reverse of the national, its opposite, and it had to be not just suppressed but crushed.

The same shift can be read in the "policy on language" initiated by Abbé Grégoire's inquiry in 1790. Whereas the inquiry banked on the spontaneous and continuing disappearance of local dialects, the speech by Bertrand Barrère, a member of the Committee of Public Safety, in January 1794 put the particular outside of the nation: "Emigration and hatred of the Republic speak German [in Alsace]." The "necessity of crushing the dialects" is obvious, proclaimed Abbé Grégoire in May 1794.[12] The local is the antithesis of the national, itself taken over by the capital. The opposition of the center and the peripheries redoubled and reinforced the opposition between the general and the particular.

This concept, subsequently described as "Jacobin," is at the heart of the administrative reorganization of 1799 and 1802. While the local councils continued to be elected bodies, the mayors were henceforth to be nominated by the central government in the same capacity as the prefects. These new agents of Parisian authority did nothing more than replace the central government's agents and representatives on assignment, who had gone out in large numbers into local spaces during the revolutionary decade. The Revolution was completed through the transformation of the departments, arrondissements, and communes into administrative districts. The "Jacobin" local space thereby rediscovered the administrative districts of the late monarchy, though it was henceforth the field of action for a State that ignored particularity.[13]

The Jacobin and the antiquary. At the same moment, the considerable quantity of travel narratives in France (557 titles during the revolutionary decade) and statistical descriptions reflected an image perceptibly different from that diffused by the new geographies of France. Whereas the latter were quietly carving up the territory into departments, arrondissements, and communes, the former were conjuring up the infinitely diverse experiences of work and celebration, languages everywhere, varied customs and practices right in the heart of the departments. By means of the local cultures, the diversity that prevailed before 1789 and that departmental rearrangements had just excluded from the territorial order was reintroduced into the descriptions of French space.[14] But this return of differences was not carried out in the same way in each case. The texts of the revolutionary period, as Mona Ozouf has shown from the example of festivals, give a totally new status to cultural particularities.[15]

These cultural particularities were, first of all, subject to a systematic inventory, whereas the authors of the travel narratives at the end of the ancien régime accorded them only sporadic attention, classifying them under the convenient rubric of "curiosity" or "remarkable thing." Later descriptions were much more neutral, omitting the sarcastic remarks about the credulity and naiveté of the people that were widespread in the texts prior to the Revolution. Finally, whereas these texts were systematically written in the imperfect tense, as if to signify the inevitable disappearance of the festivals being described, the narratives of the revolutionary period were just as systematically written in the present tense.

These multiple changes in tonality are easily explained. Not content with resisting the successive assaults of measures aimed at making such particularities disappear, local cultures blossomed at a time when the framework that sustained them (the Gregorian calendar, administrative districts of the monarchy) had disappeared. The essential determination that they were irreducibly permanent brought about a decisive change. Revolutionary texts in large numbers abandoned the hypothesis about the superficial character of local culture that underlay their prior descriptions. Permanence constrained observers to see in them the products of a milieu in which they reflected the characteristics or ancient traditions anchored from time immemorial in the customs of the inhabitants. Off on a discovery of a very young people in a very old territory, the authors of these travel narratives and the compilers of statistics caused the emergence of a very old people in the very new territory of the department. The immutability of the particular is explained by the depth of its roots.

From these descriptions there arose the France of tiny pieces, a vast multiplicity of irreducibly particular spaces. The Revolution, at the moment when it closed on the triumph of "Jacobin" space, discovered the overwhelming weight of the memory of places. The "Jacobin" point of view found its double in the antiquary's.[16]

Nevertheless, it is not useful to exaggerate the distance that separates them. Apart from the fact that the same men adopted, in turn, one or the other approach, the "antiquarian" approach rested largely on the foundations that went back to the "Jacobin" approach. Sensitivity to conditions posed by the environment is supported by the anthropological views about the primitive, forged on other continents and extended to the departments. The multiple faces of the particular connote, through their differences, the first state of humanity taken as a whole. In the same way, the conversion of local cultures into traditions dating from the dawn of history is strongly supported by a vogue for all things Celtic. Reemerging in the second half of the eighteenth century, it gave France origins that were distinct from Greco-Latin antiquity. In particular, it conferred on it, beyond the diversity of the present, a long-standing unity.[17] Indeed, in 1805 the Académie celtique was established as part of the Musée des Monuments français. Its promoters launched a program of systematically collecting customs and dialects that achieved the level of materials serving the history of the nation.[18] The differences were constantly thought of in terms of identity.

The "Jacobin" and the "antiquarian" approaches are thus much more complementary than opposing. The local is a vestige of the ancien régime with a present unity or the trace of the original unity. Placed at the confluence of these two methodologies, local space is a space of memory, since it organizes the relations of France to its past.

The territory of the particular. Local space was not just torn in two for a Jacobin present and antiquarian memorials. The revolutionary period imposed on it two different territorial realities as well. Whereas the department furnished a convenient grid for stating the present reality of the nation within the totality of French space, all manifestations of particularity converged on the province. The latter, however, was considered an old idea in the last decades of the eighteenth century. So it was the division into departments that basically formed the territory of the ancien régime. Because it was at once the symbol of privileges, and therefore to be destroyed, and the expression of natural as well as human realities, and thus to be preserved, the province was in the end retained as the base for the new division.[19] After their limits had been set, the provinces were split into departments. The list of new administrative districts made the province and the department complementary. A total continuity was thus established. The province legitimized the existence of the department, which came to reflect the past of the ancien régime. During the entire Revolution, the persistence of provincial names, preceded by the ritual *ci-devant* (former), fixed the province as the past of the department. It occupied the void left by the disappearance of the monarchical districts, the customary framework for description before 1789.

But the rupture of the departmental frameworks caused by the antiquarian view gave rise to contrasts that the province could not take into account. *Le pays*, that "small natural region," became the framework of description, enabling the particularity to be linked to the imperious laws of soil and climate.[20] Likewise, extolling the Celts caused the sudden resurgence of Gallic *civitates* in the departments. Thus, the specificity of the Cher department is explained because of the Avariques, that of the Isère department by the Allobroges.[21] Provinces, *pays*, and *civitates* allowed the proliferation of the particular to be rationalized.

From One Tableau, *the Other*

It is possible, after having shown that France emerged from the Revolution as both completely one and irreducibly divisible, to lay out the stages that highlight this pattern. Basically, there are really only two, in the form of two *Tableaux*, one by Michelet, which appeared in 1833, and the other by Vidal de La Blache, which opened Lavisse's *Histoire de France* in 1903. Between these two dates, the significance of the particular grew considerably, with the portrayal of the territorial indispensable to any presentation of France.[22]

This frame does not take into account the incompatibility of the Jacobin and antiquarian points of view during the Empire and continuing during the nineteenth century. The key events for this new change are easily identified. Among these are the law for the official publication of departmental statistics in 1805 and the completion of work by the Académie celtique in 1812. The hypothesis for the common Celtic origin of France extinguished, by its fragility revealed in experience, the research to which it had given rise.[23] As for the Napoleonic state, which based its existence on the exclusion of particularities, this was a matter on which it could not back down.[24] Finally, the regimes after 1815 did not question this attitude. The Restoration kept centralization intact and maintained the powers of the prefects, just as it reserved for the central authority the right to nominate local officials.[25]

Nevertheless, a real culture of decentralization existed that penetrated the entire political class of the period. It was fact for the ultras, who demanded the reestablishment of the local liberties of a mythic ancien régime, an extension of aristocratic demands from the end of the eighteenth century. In contrast to this provincialism of the Right, for whom the chief demand was the establishment of locally elected assemblies, there was the tradition of 1789. For the liberals, local liberties were the necessary counterweight to the omnipotence of the central government.[26] These two traditions, reinforced by a common opposition to the Empire, did not lead to any evolution in administrative structures after 1815. The Martignac project of 1829, which provided for the election of local officials, was torpedoed by the Left, which judged it insufficient, and by the Right, for whom it excessively diminished the powers of the state. Weakly supported by Charles X, it was withdrawn.[27] The decentralizing laws of the July Monarchy, which brought about elections to municipal councils, maintained the central government's right to nominate mayors and establish the powers of the prefects. The Jacobin tradition penetrated all political families. Centralization became the necessary condition for the functioning of the State, and the demand for decentralization a point of the opposition, whether it was from the Right or the Left. This was the case right up to the Nancy Program of 1865, when all the factions realigned in opposition to the Second Empire. For this reason, the entire nineteenth century was one long period of Jacobin predominance over the antiquarian going hand in hand with the recovery of the local by the national.

Michelet. No text shows this better than the *Tableau de la France*, the first chapter of book 3 of Michelet's *Histoire de France*.[28] The belated insertion of the *Tableau* (it precedes the history of feudal France and follows the accession of Hugh Capet) can be explained, according to Michelet, by the predominance of the racial factor in history up to the year 1000. It is not until that date that France appears as space. "For the first time, it occurs in its geographical form. When the wind blew away that sterile and formless fog with which the German empire had covered and obscured everything, the country appeared in all its local diversity, drawn on a background of its mountains and rivers" (185). Prior to history, it was geography that produced divisions.

Here is where Michelet created something novel with respect to previous histories and geographies. The monarchical tradition was based on the description of different parts of the kingdom, itself the product of successive annexations. Each province was an extension of the totality of the territory, itself inscribed in the totality that prefigured the kingdom. The history of France is a puzzle that one has to put back together. The historiography coming out of the Revolution did not modify this pattern. The divisions of the national territory were the heirs of previous administrative districts. The perdurability of unity was based on the permanence of the elementary divisions of France.[29]

The *Tableau* introduces a different pattern. In the permanence of the divisions, which he used for his own purposes, Michelet sees the proof of the miracle that is France. It is not fate. It is division: "Let us contemplate France and see it divide of itself" (186). Bursting the feudal origins is the point of departure for history, the meaning of which is the realization of unity. For the traditional theme of the puzzle Michelet substituted alchemy:

Thus was formed the general and universal spirit of the country. The local spirit disappeared every day; the influence of soil, climate, and race yielded to social and political action. *The inevitability of places has been conquered.* Man has escaped the tyranny of material circumstances. . . . Society and liberty have overcome nature. History has erased geography. In this marvelous transformation the spirit has triumphed over the material, the general over the particular, and the idea over the real. (227)

History taken as a whole, which the *Tableau* sums up, is thus organized around the systematic opposition of two complementary poles: the nation, which is universal, since it is a work of the spirit; and the local, by necessity particular, since it is a product of nature. This reuse of categories from the Revolution is put to the service of an entirely new history. The fragmentary and the local become the foundations for a history of unity: "Liberty is strong in the civilized periods, nature in the barbarian times. So the inevitability of the local is all powerful, and simple geography is one history" (183). The unfolding of a homogeneous historical process would henceforth be based on the fusion of particularities: "The more one delves into ancient times, the more one moves away from the pure and noble expansion of the modern spirit. The barbarian epochs present almost nothing but the local, the particular, and the material" (227). Michelet reproduces the utopia of federations on the scale of the history of France. The mystique of fusion serves as a philosophy of history.[30]

"To diminish, and not destroy, local and particular ways of living in favor of a common and general way of living—that is the problem for human sociability" (226). It is also the major problem posed by the *Tableau*. For, far from respecting the model showing fusion of differences, unity is achieved by centralization, by "the annihilation of any local spirit of any provinciality," orchestrated by the center, "which is known and knows what is to come," where "the general has dominion"(224). All history, then, sways between two organizing principles. The final structure, built according to a strict hierarchy, is imposed on a prior geography, based on the equality of its parts. "The hardy and warlike force and the virtue of action are at the extreme ends, intelligence at the center." Which is to say, France is summed up in Paris ("Who says Paris says all of France" [224]), which apportions a role and a function to every province. Transcending particularity means marginalizing it.

Since then, the meaning of the description of France has been radically modified. Using predictions about the contribution of each province to the formation of France as a starting point, the historian can only trace and explain a sequence of unfulfilled destinies. The provinces become fields of ruins where collecting the vestiges of an unfinished history is the only thing possible.

The *Tableau* takes the reader to twenty-four different places, each described in an identical manner. It begins by showing how nature defines and circumscribes the province: "Brittany, hard and poor, spreads out over fields of quartz and schist" (187); the Auvergne, "a vast extinguished fire" (197); the Rouergue, "an enormous mound of coal, iron, copper, and lead" (198). The physical traits determine the unique local character: "nature expires [and] humanity becomes gloomy and cold"—Pointe du Raz, on the coast of Brittany (189); "the Limousin where so many rivers pour forth . . . its vast forest of chestnut trees that nourish a virtuous population that is also oafish, timid, and awkward through indecision" (197). The suitability of men to the land culminates in the presentation of characters that the province gave to the history of France. Every one of them bears the mark of soil, the climate, and their place of origin.

But in parallel, the environment is shown to account for the failure of the province. Provence is the most telling example:

> Provence, in its imperfect destiny and in its incomplete form, seems to me to be a song of the troubadours, a *canzone* by Petrarch with more fervor than impact. The African vegetation of its coasts is soon met by the glacial wind from the Alps. The Rhône runs to the sea but never arrives. (207, 208)

Michelet thus reduces the accumulated knowledge of each province to a unique system: the people, the landscapes, and the customs and practices are all vestiges that explain their own ruin. Local space is closed in on itself and, by its own particularity, made sterile. It contains but the dead memories of France.

The Jacobin predominance. The *Tableau* sums up the problem in the connection of the local to the national during the nineteenth century. The local is situated in the general economy of the *Histoire de France*, but only parenthetically, giving way to the unfolding of a history that is purely national. With the Empire, a dominant representation of France is established that marginalizes the particular.

The long promotion of the theme of France as two countries, separated by a line from Saint-Malo to Geneva, testifies to this.[31] From baron Dupin, who "conceived" the theme in 1826, to Adolphe d'Angeville, who applied it systematically, all the variables concerning French space were subject to economic indicators valid for the entire territory of

Figure 6.3
Space converted into memory. Nodier, Taylor, and Cailleux, *Voyages pittoresques et romantiques dans l'ancienne France* (1829), *L'Auvergne*. At the center, volcanoes; above, Christianity comes to the province; below, the great men in the history of the Auvergne.

France. Spatial differences were converted into delays occurring at different times in development. By this means a chronological measurement was superimposed on a spatial measurement. Particularities were eliminated from the description of France.

The creation in 1835 of the Statistique générale de la France (General Statistics Office of France) led to an extension of this perspective. Statistics, henceforth purely arithmetical, knew only neutral and undifferentiated space, in which quantified and homogeneous series were easily integrated. The functioning of the State rested on the fiction of a smooth national territory where perceptible differences were nothing more than slight distortions.[32]

The distance that separates the prolific epoch of the July Monarchy and the revolutionary period can be measured with the publication in 1835 of *La France pittoresque*. This work, by Abel Hugo, splits the statistical perception of France in two. The subtitle shows the ambivalence: "Picturesque, topographical, and statistical description of France . . . accompanied by the Statistique générale de la France." The latter occupies the first part and is totally separate from descriptions of the departments that derive from statistics from the Revolution. The same exercise does not apply when he describes France and presents its parts. The departmental reports themselves fall into one of two categories—descriptive (history up to the annexation, antiquities, customs and characteristics, illustrious men, topography, climatology) and quantitative, found at the end of the record.[33] In Hugo there are two types of local space within the departmental framework: one is the particular, which sets the description; the other is of general interest, open to quantification. The strict division of their presentation clearly means that no continuity is possible between them. The local comes across as an excess in the description of the department.

The department stands out as the preferred point of entry to the nation. The century sees the "triumph of the department," for which the schools in the prefectures and subprefectures and the prolific number of departmental geographies were the most effective agents. The appearance in 1868 of the *Géographie de la France*, by Jules Verne, was the high point.[34] Quite obviously inspired by Hugo's text, the descriptions of the departments systematically brought the particular back into the administrative framework at a time, 1835, when the latter already seemed too large. Local particularities were becoming stereotypical vignettes of the departments.

One final illustration of this tendency to marginalize the particular can be found in the policies pursued by Guizot when he served in the Ministère de l'Instruction publique (Ministry of Public Instruction) between 1832 and 1837. The creation of the Société de l'histoire de France

(Society for the History of France) in 1833 and of the Comité des Travaux historiques (Committee of Historical Works) in the following year had the same goal, furnishing the nation with sources and original documents of its history. The important point here was the organization of a network of local correspondents, eighty-nine by 1834, charged with forwarding to the committee documents for publication. Coordinating the production of historical knowledge, of which the reorganization of the departmental archives was another essential feature, depended on the strict centralization of activities. That meant eliminating any history that had the potential for particularity and removing any localism from the history of France. When the Comité des Travaux historiques et des sociétés savantes (Committee of Historical Works and Learned Societies) was created in 1858, the prominent role of the State in defining what was national was confirmed. The committee was to publish "the most remarkable of the local societies' works."[35] Local history thus became an implicit division of national history that had only two categories: "everywhere and nowhere."[36]

The nineteenth century sees the two complementary figures of the puzzle and homogeneous space become reality, thereby illustrating the marginalization of the local in the national. This double "Jacobin" approach was particularly visible in the two inquiries on dialects: In the first, launched in 1807, the Ministry of the Interior asked the prefects to have the parable of the prodigal son translated in their departments. In the second, departmental surveys were requested in 1863 by the Ministry of Public Instruction to learn the ratio of those speaking dialect to those speaking French.[37] The first sought to reconstitute the puzzle of deviations from the model, the other, to quantify cultural backwardness. Between the two, local space was emptied of any particular content.

On the fringe of this process, one practice of the local space held steady and preserved its status of space for the particularity. This was the narrative and notebook of the romantic journey, which emerged as literary genres, in addition to the antiquarian journeys of the Revolution. The most representative type, not to say the model, was furnished by the *Voyages pittoresques et romantiques dans l'ancienne France*, the publication of which began in 1820. Its aims were defined by Charles Nodier in the introduction to the first volume, devoted to Normandy:

> It is not as scientists that we travel through France, but as travelers caring about interesting features and eager for memories. Shall I say which tendency, easier to feel than to define, circumscribes this voyage into the ruins of ancient France? Some melancholic disposition, some involuntary predilection for the poetical customs and arts of our

ancestors, the feeling of some decadent or ill-fated community or other among these old buildings and the generation that came to an end. . . .

This voyage is therefore not a voyage of discovery. It is a voyage of impressions, if it may thus be so expressed. We are not walking in the tracks of history. We are only calling upon it to contribute to our emotions as much as it fortifies by its serious evidence and augments by some narrative the majesty of the monuments.[38]

No better statement about local space as the conservatory of sentiment about the past could be made. It is the favored point of entry for what Nodier later calls "sensitive and living history." The marginalization of the particular makes the voyage into the memory of France possible.

The Discourse of the Particular

Travel literature is far from being the only source for the preservation of particularity in the representations of France. During the nineteenth century, the province continued the discourse of the particular. Whether it was easily located in the province did not mean that it was exclusively represented there. In the same way that the antiquarian viewpoint survived in the capital, the province did not exclude the Jacobin approach. The question is how to identify the clearest indications of examples where conceptualized local space reintroduced particularity.

The dissipation of sources of knowledge. One example of the introduction by the local of the particular is certainly the increase in the number of learned societies in the provincial cities. This development has not yet been made the subject of a general study that would allow us to grasp its size and extent. One must be content with lists and directories from the period. Incomplete as they are, they do allow for significant observations. From the list drawn up in 1862 by the Committee of Historical Works to the notebooks of Henri Delaunay in 1903, these groups increase from 204 to 915, the last representing the highest point in the movement when these societies were established. World War I interrupted this movement and brought about a noticeable decline in their number. The Tassy and Léris directory shows 627 societies in 1921. It does not include the local sections of the French Alpine Club and the horticultural societies shown in the Delaunay list. The number grew in layers because the first societies established did not disappear. Three-quarters of the societies listed in 1862 still existed in 1921.[39]

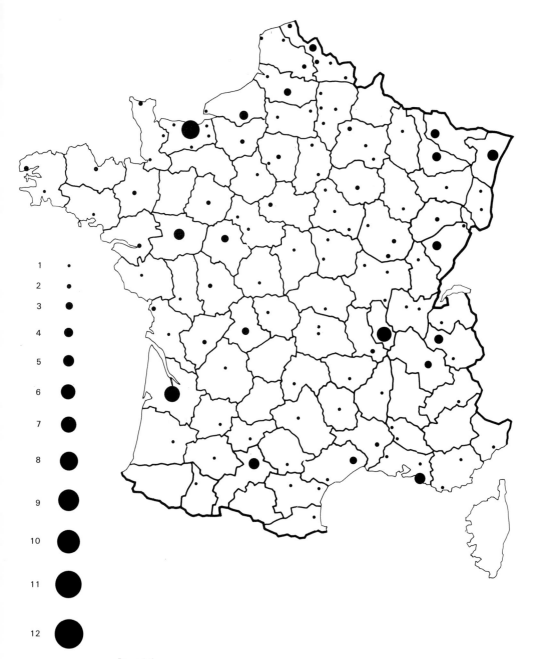

Figure 6.4
Learned societies in the provinces, 1862. Based on the *Liste des sociétés savants de province*, drawn up by the Comité des Travaux historiques (Paris, 1862).

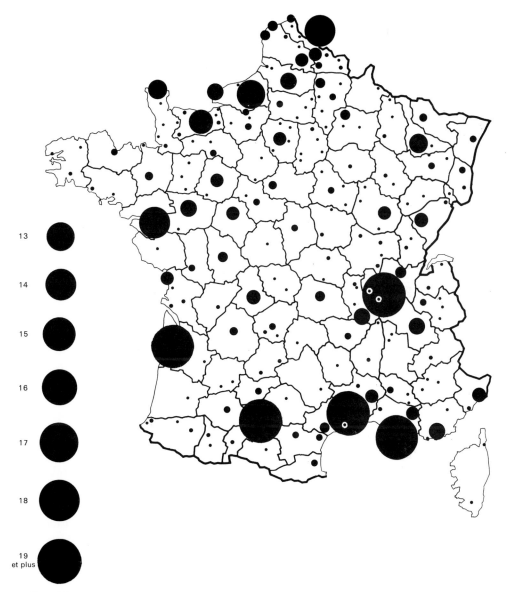

13

14

15

16

17

18

19
et plus

Figure 6.5
Learned societies in the provinces, 1921. Based on E. Tassy and P. Léris, *Les Ressources du travail intellectuel en France* (Paris, 1921).

The increase in the number of these societies did not lead to their uniform distribution across France. For one thing, they developed chiefly in the large cities. The top twenty concentrations of societies represented 40 percent of the total in 1862. In 1921 it was 39 percent, while the total number had tripled. Their establishment moved much more quickly than did their localization: 124 villages shared 204 societies in 1862. Their distribution obeyed the double logic of concentration at the summit of the urban hierarchy and limited diffusion at the base. For another thing, the regional divisions evolved slowly. The areas of initial highest density remained throughout the century. A veritable "fertile crescent" from the lower valley of the Loire to the Alpine regions stood in contrast to a "quasi-desert" in 1862. The same strong points are found again in 1921: the Nord and Pas-de-Calais departments with 34 and 17 societies, respectively, along with the neighboring departments of Picardy, represent 13 percent of the total. The departments in the Rhône Valley (Rhône, Isère, Saône-et-Loire, Côte-d'Or) had 62 societies, of which 24 were in Lyon. The five departments of Normandy had 70 societies, 11 percent of the total. These three areas had a combined total of one-third of the provincial societies. The 1921 map, in addition, shows a high concentration of societies along the Mediterranean coast: 23 in Marseille and 19 in Montpellier, extending to Toulouse with 20 and Bordeaux with 19.

To these extreme inequalities in geography may be added profound disparities of focus and dynamism in the organizations already highlighted. The Société des antiquaires in Normandy, founded in 1824, published thirty-four volumes of memoirs and forty-three bulletins, whereas some societies, like those of Guéret and Montauban, published nothing the entire century. Likewise, the Société historique et archéologique des Vans (Ardèche), a private organization that had only 25 members in 1903, cannot be put in the same rank as the Société des antiquaires de l'Ouest, which numbered 228 members that same year. Finally, what primarily should be kept in mind for each society are the periods of activity, punctuated by long periods of lethargy. For all these reasons, it is difficult to consider the learned societies' movement as a uniform whole.[40] It is nevertheless possible to extract the general import.

This massive and continuous movement to create and preserve these societies was the product of several factors. The initiative to start one came from the government, which encouraged or pushed for the formation of agricultural and competitive societies during the Revolution and archaeological societies beginning with the Restoration, and from private groups. Arcisse de Caumont and the societies in Caen, as well as the Société française d'archéologie and the Institut des provinces de

France, played a predominant role in pushing and coordinating private initiatives.

Whether spontaneously created or encouraged, societies—and this constitutes a second reason for their growth—evolved in two directions. The field of knowledge covered by their activities widened considerably. The re-creation of the old academies, beginning in 1796, saw the reappearance of the classics (letters, arts, and sciences), to which were added, depending on the situation, agriculture, commerce, and industry. Societies with a general or "polymath" bent represented 38 percent of the total number of societies in 1862, but only 24 percent in 1921. Competition from the growing number of societies focusing on a single discipline was the reason: History, creeping in under the general names for 2.5 percent of the societies in 1862, was the exclusive activity of 23 percent of them by 1921. Medicine (13 percent of the societies) and natural science (7 percent) were the other strong points in the growing movement toward specialization in the nineteenth century. This movement was pushed the farthest in the large urban areas. Bordeaux counted two generalist and four specialist societies in 1862, and seventeen specialized societies out of a total of nineteen in 1921. The breakdown into disciplines covered the relative geographic dispersion.

The triumph of localism. The creation of learned societies was the result of another logical development: 73 percent of the societies listed in 1862 were set up in the administrative center of the department. That was still the case for 65 percent of them in 1921. This regression occurred at the expense of the administrative centers of the arrondissement, its share reaching 27 percent of the total in 1921, when all the prefectures were equipped with a learned society. The geography of such societies tended to reproduce the administrative geography. The increased number of societies in the important towns perpetuated, at the level of the department or arrondissement, the practices of the old academies at the provincial level. The often decisive role of the prefect, the governor of the department, and the local functionaries in the creation or functioning of the societies showed, in the new administrative divisions, the close ties of interdependence between agents of the State and local notables. And while the laws of 1831–33 and those of 1871 and 1884 were expanding the participation of local notables in municipal and departmental affairs, the powers of the prefects were growing in parallel from 1800 to 1852. The learned societies were the product of the "power of the periphery," analyzed by Pierre Grémion, within which the local production of knowledge played an essential role.[41] They were the preferred instrument for acceding to notability or the confirmation

thereof. The administrative framework fostered learned activity. The example that comes to mind here is that of the Société belfortaine d'émulation (Belfort Competitive Society), created one year after the department.

From the mid-nineteenth century on, the creation of societies fit neatly into the newly drawn up administrative districts. The study conducted by Jean-Paul Nardy on the Société d'émulation du Jura (Competitive Society of the Jura) shows that its activities went up to the departmental boundaries and systematically ignored everything beyond them. Agriculture, transportation, and history were seen only in terms of the Jura, doubly defined not just through its boundaries but also through its intrinsic qualities yet to be developed. Thus, the members of the societies reproduced the eighteenth-century academicians' approach to space.[42] The department became a close and homogeneous space where local differences were treated as good or bad *pays*. Local space was closely tied to the organizing perceptions of the center.

In every case, local space itself became an object of inquiry. Publications by the learned societies, however, were only the most visible aspect of the discourse on the particular, immeasurably greater through the increase in sources. Departmental directories, guides for use by "foreigners," histories, and local descriptions piled up, doubling whatever Paris

Figure 6.6
The Congress of
Learned Societies at
Dunkirk, 1907.

produced. This was particularly evident with the second wave of statistics that got under way during the Restoration. In contrast to memoirs of the Directory and the Consulate, these were systematically published at the local level. Drafted by the prefect, by the secretary or archivist of the prefecture, by a society, or by a single author, they illustrated most completely the vast movement by the provinces in producing knowledge about places.

We can see the premises of this movement within the milieu of the universities and the *parlements* of the ancien régime when it appeared in the eighteenth century in the descriptions and histories of local origin. Likewise, the production of local maps, on the initiative of the *parlements*, accompanied the drafting of the Cassini map.[43] The ability to describe local space was a major focus for provincial elites. The phenomenon spread over a large area and expanded, thanks to the Revolution. The creation of the departments made knowledge about places imperative to the extent that such knowledge could be the basis for a city's claim to acceding to the rank of administrative center. Especially during the Directory and Consulate, as the inquiries multiplied, they sparked the creation of a world of investigators and informers closely tied to the representatives of the central government.[44] Their body of knowledge became totally autonomous because it had no relevance for the nation after the law on large statistical collections was enacted. As a result, each district was likely to produce a body of knowledge the purposes of which were locally confined. Scholars and learned societies prolonged the France "of fragments," conjured up by the prefects' statistics.

The end of the nineteenth century and, even more, the twentieth century saw federal agencies put in place that did not reconstitute a national framework. Congresses, which multiplied at the end of the century, were strictly regional—for example, the congresses of learned societies of Provence (Marseille, 1906) and of the departments of the Nord and Pas-de-Calais (Dunkirk, 1907). The federations that appeared primarily after World War II had the same territorial base. The association of learned societies in Burgundy included sixty societies from six departments. The Fédération des sociétés savantes du Centre stretched over ten departments. This movement extended to the regional level and included Languedoc, the southwest, the Île-de-France, and Alsace. These regional groupings were most often carried out through a regional university. Some regional groupings occurred in the Aisne, the Ardennes, and the Maine-et-Loire. Taken as a whole, these structures, with each society acting independently, preserved the fragmentation of knowledge.[45]

At the end of this process, local space constitutes French space as much as it sets itself apart from it. It is at once the framework for State action and, based on this fact, for the generic division of the national territory and a particular fragment thereof, the intrinsic qualities of which irreducibly distinguish it from other fragments.

THE LOCAL REGISTRIES

Because it allows for the dilution of the particularity or its reduction to stereotype at the same time that it authorizes its affirmation, local space acts doubly as a framework for memory. Local notables, situated as they are between the national and local, are the principal beneficiaries of this double status. They also produce the local memory.

The Local Patrimonies

The increase in the number of museums in provincial towns, which began during the Revolution, was the clearest manifestation of these investments in memory. In 1814, thirty-four provincial towns shared some 40 museums existing at that time. In 1907, Henri Lapauze counted 255 towns with museums. There were 802 in 1982.[46] The history of these

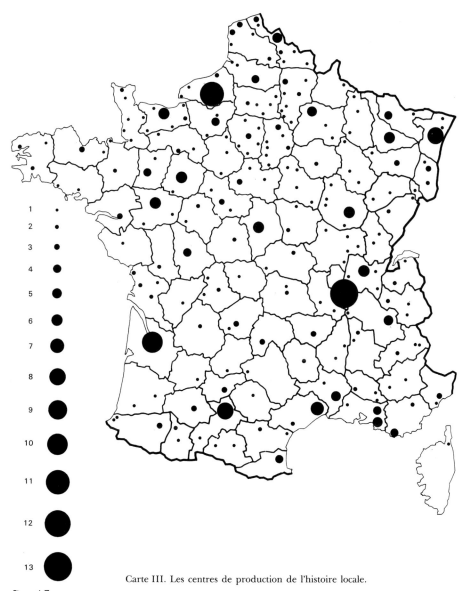

Carte III. Les centres de production de l'histoire locale.

Figure 6.7
The centers of production for local history. Historical publications of municipal learned societies up to 1914, drawn from Robert de Lasteyrie, *Bibliographie générale des travaux historiques et archéologiques publiés par les sociétés de la France* (Paris, 1888–1904); *Supplément 1886–1900* (Paris, 1911–18) and *Bibliographie annuelle des travaux historiques et archéologiques des sociétés de la France* (Paris, 1909–14); and René Gandilhon and Charles Samaran, *Bibliographie générale des travaux historiques et archéologiques des sociétés de la France, période 1910–1940* (Paris, 1944–61).

Figure 6.8
The Cacault Museum in Clisson. One of the Cacault brothers gave the town collections he had brought back from Italy. The *Statistique du département de la Loire-Inférieure* mentions it as the richest collection in the province.

institutions allows us not only to elucidate the process by which they were established but also to uncover the layers of local memory.

The producers of local memory. The seizures of aristocratic and ecclesiastical properties during the Revolution undeniably formed the first collection for a great many museums. That was especially true for the towns where there had existed, before the Revolution, schools of drawing and academies of painting where the staff immediately took charge of the newly created public collections.[47] In other cases, the seizures broke up collections already open to the public. This was notably the case in Arles, where the collections of inscriptions were dispersed. In 1814, there were only about forty museums, of which twelve were created by the State. The law of 14 Fructidor year IX (September 1, 1801) established museums in fifteen provincial towns: Lyon, Marseille, Toulouse, Bordeaux, Nantes, Rennes, Caen, Rouen, Lille, Nancy, Strasbourg, Dijon, Mainz, Geneva, and Brussels. The fifteen most important collections, beginning with the mass of artistic treasures accumulated in the capital, were scattered among the administrative centers.[48] This operation, however, was short-lived. Except for Tours, in 1803, and Montpellier, in 1806, the central government no longer intervened to establish

Figure 6.9
The public museum of ancient monuments in Arles, by Advinent (1784).

provincial museums. This state of affairs continued throughout the entire
nineteenth century, even though the Second Empire did establish a limited number, for example the Museum of Alise-Sainte-Reine, containing discoveries organized by Napoleon III from the Alesia site, and the
Museum of Napoleon in Auxonne.

The great increase in the number of museums occurred after 1815.
The process is difficult to reconstruct, so great is the uncertainty that
surrounds the dates of establishment of a good number of them. It is nevertheless possible to highlight the trends. Starting with the Restoration,
when about twenty were founded, the rhythm began to intensify. There
were between three and four museums created annually, on average,
from 1830 to 1860, and between four and five annually from 1860 to
1910. The war was only a momentary interruption. Between 1921 and
1930, seventy-five new museums can be identified, another ninety-two
between 1930 and 1941.[49]

The widespread increase occurred in a totally unsystematic way because of the absence of the State. The departments played only a limited
role in the matter except for a few museums, those in Cahors, Épinal,
Rouen, and Troyes. The driving force came from the communes, representing the extreme dispersion of any initiative.

Figure 6.10
The ceiling of the exhibition hall for drawings in the Bonnat Museum in Bayonne, by Noël Bouton. The muse is holding a miniature of the museum in her hand.

The increase in the number of museums during the nineteenth century, however, cannot be explained by municipal politics alone. The period saw the emergence and extension of the network of collectors that had been disrupted by the seizures occurring during the Revolution. In 1908, a census of collectors was taken showing 16,489 in France, of which 11,000 were in the provinces.[50] Private collections often played a decisive role in the establishment of a local museum. The documentation found in the catalog of Germaine Barnaud allows the conclusion that at least a third of the museums established in the nineteenth century were created through individual initiatives, which could take the form of a bequest or a donation to the commune of the private collection, or even a building that became the museum, or both at the same time. In other cases, money bequeathed to the town allowed for the realization of a museum. Taken together, these initiatives reveal the massive development of a strictly municipal patronage. On the occasion of gifts, the love of the little *patrie* was abundantly proclaimed.[51]

Figure 6.11
The centenary medal
of the Calvet Museum
in Avignon.

The typology of the donors brings out the constituent elements of the milieu that they formed. First of all, they were political elites. The establishment of the museum in Le Puy, in 1820, was due to the initiative of the vicomte de Becdelièvre, who had obtained the patronage of the duchesse de Berry. The change in government personnel in the second half of the nineteenth century did not impede the continuation of the movement. Under the Second Empire, the decisive action of Achille Jubinal, deputy from the department of the Hautes-Pyrénées, in setting up museums in Bagnères-de-Bigorre in 1852, and in Tarbes between 1859 and 1861; and, under the Third Republic, the same with Sarrien, a senator, for the museum in Bourbon Lancy, or with Vincent Auriol, for the Clément Ader de Muret museum—all provide evidence of the movement's continuation. The cases are more numerous where the mayor played a central role.

To this first type may be added the economic elites: industrialists such as Caumartin (in Chalon-sur-Saône) and Crozatier (in Le Puy) bequeathed their collections to municipal museums. Physicians such as Esprit Calvet (in Avignon) and Philadephe Thomas (in Gaillac) and architects such as Antoine Vivenel (in Compiègne) can also be included. Generally speaking, groups of founders were drawn from the ranks of artists and scientists. The most outstanding figure was Boucher de Perthes, who took a direct part in setting up the two museums in Abbeville. There were also naturalists (Emmanuel Liais in Cholet) and especially local painters (Léon Bonnat in Bayonne, Just Veillat in

Châteauroux, and Alexandre Dubourg in Honfleur).[52] Local notables from all levels were to be found whenever a museum was established.

Their activity was taken up and expanded by the learned societies, which played a double role in the establishment of their own museums and in the establishment of the municipal museums. These societies as a result established some fifty museums between 1830 and 1870, and another fifty-three between 1871 and 1914. The twentieth century saw the high point of their activity, with 183 additional museums established between 1918 and 1971. In sum, one-fifth of the provincial museums are due to the learned societies.[53]

The action of the municipalities, societies, and individuals was not limited to erecting structures. Once established, the museum experienced spectacular growth, through successive bequests and donations, in a real course of patronage. The State did not intervene in the process except in a limited and intermittent way, when it brought unending negotiations to a close, with its deputies and prefects acting as intermediaries.[54]

Because it was situated at the juncture of individual, collective, and local initiatives, the museum was the perfect indicator of local memory. Analysis of this memory has to take into account certain obvious limits. The growing number of museums obscured a considerable number of disparities, notably in the wealth of the collections. Further, most of the provincial museums did not suffer comparison with the museums in Paris.[55] Finally, during a great part of their existence, museums lived in a rarified atmosphere. Their exiguity, poverty, and infrequent visitors were recurrent themes in Stendhal's *Mémoires d'un touriste* or Taine's *Notes sur la province.* The *Rapport sur les musées de province,* drawn up by Henri Lapauze in 1907, at every possible opportunity pointed to the deficiencies of most of them and on the negligence of the municipal authorities,[56] as if the formation and existence of a collection stood apart from its presentation. Provincial museums, furthermore, were all the product of an unsystematic accumulation of successive gifts, which turned the places into shambles, improbable jumbles of the most diverse materials, in which the worst only exceptionally encountered the best.

The strata of local memory. Only by going back to the chronology of these accumulated layers of collections that are local memory is it possible to elucidate the successive stages. Most of the museums established in the nineteenth century were museums of the fine arts and, here and there, a museum of natural history. Thus occurred the idea of patrimony liberated by the Revolution. The museum had the pedagogical task of presenting the progress of the human spirit. This was true for the museums created by the State in 1801 and for the municipal museums, the exclusive depositories of individual collections after the Revolution. The local museum was not originally intended to be the conservator of the memory of places. This idea lasted throughout the nineteenth century. The collections bequeathed by Cardinal Fesch to Ajaccio in Corsica allowed the visitor to "follow the history of painting from its rebirth up to its completion without the paintings leaving the gallery."[57]

Very soon afterward, another definition of patrimony was grafted onto collections of this sort, which were common to almost all new museums in the nineteenth century. It appears after the Restoration, with the establishment of museums of archaeology, distinct from the fine arts museums. Some of these collections came from individual collections that existed before the Revolution, as in Dijon, Arles, Autun, or Bordeaux. More often, these museums were the result of actions taken by local archaeological societies as in Périgueux (1836), Niort (the same year), and Angoulême (1844). The museum's mission was changing—its new task, to gather all the scattered debris of the past of a particular place. A strictly local definition of patrimony was being superimposed onto the definition accepted from the Revolution. Their juxtaposition clearly appeared in the numerous cases of museums in which art *and* archaeology were combined. Thus, the museum of Chalon-sur-Saône, established in 1819 and enriched in 1829 by a collection of paintings by Carbillet, became a totally different museum in 1866 when it integrated the collections from the local society of history and archaeology.[58]

This separation of two kinds of patrimony did not exclude the persistence and the expansion of nonlocal collections. Witness the increase in the collections of art and exotic ethnography, built up in provincial museums and expanded through the extension of the Empire. Local memory was constructed at the intersection of two types of patrimony developing simultaneously. The growing importance attached to local interests becomes quite apparent in the collections. Collections devoted to natural history tended to integrate the local flora, fauna, and minerals. The fine arts experienced the same evolution with the appearance of collections of paintings from specific regions.

As the century progressed, archaeology increasingly lost significance for local collections, even though it had played a decisive transitional role. The museum gradually covered the totality of local history with the aim of establishing a perfect continuity between the most remote and most recent periods. The best examples of this evolution are seen in the establishment of the Musée breton in Quimper in 1846 and the Musée lorrain in Nancy in 1848.[59]

Another feature of this evolution becomes perceptible with the development, in the twentieth century, of ethnographic museums. There were twenty-four in the provinces when the Musée national des Arts et Traditions populaires opened in Paris in 1937. The first among these was the Museon Arlaten in Arles, founded by Mistral in 1896. By the end of the century, collections of popular arts and traditions were investing the patrimony of local areas. Here again, in numerous cases these museums came about because of a connection to an older collection. The museum of Auch, which had become the Musée d'Art et d'Archéologie when the holdings of the Société historique of Gascony were added, received an important collection of Gascon ethnography in 1948.[60] By juxtaposing these layers, museums became conservators of an immeasurably extended past in which local memory took root.

This course of events reached its final stage in the twentieth century with the implementation of regional museums distinct from museums for the fine arts. Beginning in 1906, Grenoble built a museum with collections that brought together the archaeology, history, and traditions of the Dauphiné. Other regional museums were set up in Limoges (1911) and Nantes (1926). This trend grew after World War II, with new museums established in Amiens (1945), Rennes (1959), and Lille (1962). Significantly, the gemological museum in Bordeaux disappeared in 1945, to the benefit of the Musée d'Aquitaine.[61] The trend can be found even at the most reduced scale. The interwar period saw this wave of museums dedicated to the past of a city or the development of an urban area. The museums of Old Montmartre, Old Toulon, and Old Chinon were established in 1886, 1905, and 1907 respectively. By 1939, there were thirty-five museums of this type, set up by associations.[62]

These freely evolving trends obviously did not exclude the profound disparities from one town to another. Rather, they clarify this process of sedimentation, found everywhere, that makes the local patrimony understood. The most recent construction of museums, chiefly in very small towns, was very often done at the expense of history and archaeology for the sake of granting as much space as possible to popular arts and traditions.

The most recent periods saw the development of museums dedicated to one activity anchored in the town's past. The Mulhouse industrialists (Musée du Dessin industriel [Museum of Industrial Design], founded in 1858) were the pioneers. Not surprisingly, there are museums devoted to tobacco in Bergerac, to the pipe in Saint-Claude, and to shoemaking in Romans. Likewise, from the 1930s on, fourteen museums of wine appeared, each recreating a history of winemaking and doubling as an ethnographic collection that reconstructs the environment.[63]

This local patrimony, more and more inclusive, also integrated the most outstanding figures from the history of the locality. Museums early on developed commemorative collections. Thus, in 1866 materials relat-

ing to Nicéphore Niépce, one of the first inventors of photographic devices, began to enter the Chalon-sur-Saône museum. The founding of
museums dedicated to individuals is of even more recent origin. There,
the departments acted as precursors, but rarely as instigators. The department of the Vosges, in 1818, bought Joan of Arc's house in Dom-
remy. It was the general council of Corsica that took the initiative for the
Pascal-Paoli de Morosaglia museum and the general council of the department of Seine-Inférieure for the Pierre Corneille du Petit-Couronne
museum. The historical figures most commonly found in museums are
Napoleon (fourteen museums) and Joan of Arc (five museums). The
justification for these museums is sometimes laborious. Louis Pasteur is
spread out among three museums—in Arbois (museum of the house of
Pasteur's father), Dole (museum of the house where he was born), and
Bollène (the Pasteur museum).[64] Much more common are the museums
that celebrate someone born locally, integrated into the local patrimony,
who enjoyed national importance. The great man places local memory
in the bosom of the nation.

The memory that counted was the memory of those who produced.
Memory originating from a restricted circle of notables gets dispersed, as
will be seen, far beyond the museum. Memory does indeed propel great
men into public space, through statues and the names of streets, and rel-
egates the "organic" memories of places to the background. The museum is the laboratory for the memory of the notables.

A Past Takes Root

Within the process of the formation of local patrimonies, the local production of history plays a determinative role. This occurred during the
nineteenth century and coincided with the development of national history. Building on previous histories, it considerably expanded in volume.
The inventorying worked out by Robert de Lastyrie led to a dizzying
132,235 articles dedicated to history by learned societies up to 1901. In
the last decade of the century, this already considerable mass grew by another 42,612 articles.[65] And still these numbers represent only the most
visible part of a historical activity that to a large extent surpasses the
learned societies.

The invasion of retrospective. This flood is the product of the ever-
increasing number of sources of historical knowledge produced during
the nineteenth century. From the creation of the Commission des antiquités de la Seine-Inférieure in 1818 to that of the Société historique du
Calaisis in 1914, 184 societies were formed in the provinces for an ex-

pressly historical purpose. An examination of the names clearly shows the steps in their creation. Three-quarters of the societies created between 1818 and 1850 had the word "archaeology" in the name. This predilection is explained by the interaction of several factors.

The thrust in Normandy to create societies appears in the first rank (of the first five created in the nineteenth century, two were in Caen, one in Rouen, and one in Dieppe). Normandy benefited from influences from Great Britain. On the initiative of Arcisse de Caumont, Caen became one of two centers encouraging archaeology. In 1834, the Société française d'archéologie was established, followed by the Institut des provinces in 1839, forming a network of correspondents blanketing all the departments. The Société des antiquaires de Picardie (1836) and the Association bretonne (1843), among others, had their origin in Caen's example.[66] The second center was in Paris. In 1838, the Comité des Travaux historiques sent an archaeological questionnaire to the departments. Under the Second Empire, the same committee launched a *Répertoire archéologique* and a *Dictionnaire topographique* by department, of which the first volumes began appearing in 1861.[67] This impulse can be explained by other causes as well, not the least of which were the increase in land development, imposed by urban growth, and the great construction projects, such as the railroads, that increased the possibility that vestiges of the remote past would come to light. Finally, there was that persistent style of a romanticized Middle Ages, seen in the success of Nodier's *Voyages,* that helped orient research of the past to even more distant epochs.

After 1850, the names of the societies show that their activities extended to the entire past of the locality. If archaeology still represented 20 percent of the total, it was in most cases—one-third of the societies established from 1850 to 1900—tied to history. As for the societies that were strictly historical, during this same time period they represented one-fifth of those established.

But those societies doing history exceeded an already large circle of specialized societies. Over the course of the century, most of the non-specialized societies felt the importance of history increase, to the detriment of their other activities. A sampling of nineteen societies, done by Charles Olivier Carbonell, shows that between 1830 and 1870 history was the principal activity of thirteen of them. History represented the subject of less than a quarter of the publications until 1840, and more than a third thereafter. The predominance of retrospective stands out especially after 1860. The Société d'émulation du Jura only occasionally involved itself with history prior to the 1850s. Restructured in 1864, after a decade of inaction, it focused its activities thereafter exclusively on history. To a lesser degree, the same tendency is found in several other cases: for the Société nivernaise [Nevers] des sciences, lettres et arts, history represents 78 percent of works produced between 1851 and 1871. The trend was at times subtle: The Société philomatique de Perpignan apportioned only 23 percent of its works to history between 1866 and 1875. We see exactly the opposite movement elsewhere, as with the Académie de Reims.[68]

Robert de Lasteyrie's inventory lists 412 societies that produced histories of 226 cities between the Restoration and 1914. The map for these centers of production, which brings together all the work done during the nineteenth century, reveals again already-noted disparities for the general movement of learned societies. It also confirms the importance of northern and eastern regions and the influence of the administrative centers of the department, which accounted for 60 percent of total production.

The spatial dissemination of producing history refers to the great expansion in the number of historians. The enrollment for the Société d'émulation du Doubs (Competitive Society of the Doubs) went from 60 to 530 members between 1840 and 1875. The congresses of the Institut des provinces were able to assemble between 800 and 2,000 people.[69] Although the Revolution broke up the networks of professionals in local history, first and foremost the Benedictines of the Abbey of Saint Maur, the nineteenth century saw the circles of amateur historians expanding. History appears as the favorite activity of these groups of notables. Their growth was selective. Access was subject to a contribution, and recruitment to very strict conditions (the Société des antiquaires de Picardie admitted a teacher to its ranks only in 1909). The very possibility of exercising scholarly activity made producing history one of the criteria given priority for the definition of notability.[70]

Amateurs practicing history did not necessarily mean that producing history had no purpose. The emergence of "Bretonism," studied by Jean-Yves Guiomar, in the societies of Brittany was the starting point for a total redefinition of the society, which to a large extent went beyond the history of the province. Likewise, Jean-Clément Martin has shown that the prolific literature devoted to the wars of the Vendée in 1793 cannot be separated from political attachments. Finally, the great number of clerics from the region of the Franche-Comté engaging in historical research coincided with debates troubling the church, in particular the imposition of the Roman rite in the mass and, even more so, conflicts during the Third Republic.[71] These matters prolonged the "rapid emergence of local history" in the provincial academic and legal milieus at the end of the eighteenth century.[72] Political rifts stimulated an increase in the number of circles of production. In Colmar, the clearly liberal focus of the *Revue d'Alsace,* established in 1850, led to the creation of the *Revue catholique d'Alsace* in 1859. In most of the administrative centers where there was a society of the "Right," there was a corresponding society to the "Left." Dunkirk experienced clashes at the end of the century between the liberal Société dunkerquoise pour l'encouragement des sciences, des lettres et des arts and the conservative Union Faulconnier.[73] The local production of history was the principal source of legitimacy, for an organization and in political debate.

The territory of the historian. Because local notables were the ones producing history, their work strongly reflected their perceptions of local space. In the Aisne, the activities of the Société archéologique de Soissons only in exceptional cases went beyond the borders of the arrondissement, whereas those of the Société académique de Laon—focused in part on the environs of the town—also extended to include the department. In 1851, the Société d'émulation du Jura was corresponding with forty-seven societies, but it only focused on the department. Studies not dealing with Brittany represented only 8 percent of what the Breton societies produced.[74] Historical research extended investigation into the past various societies were pursuing in the present.

If the first societies most often took the department or the arrondissement as the frame of reference, the end of the century saw the number of provincial names increase, particularly when the department was already "covered." Some societies, moreover, established themselves using a town or an urban area for their frame of reference. After the Société du Vieux Montmartre (Society of Old Montmartre), there appeared the Société du Vieil Arles (Society of Old Arles) (1903), the Société du Vieux Chinon (1905), and the Société de Vieux Fécamp (1909). Adding another scale of use for the same place turned into another trend. The department of the Côte-d'Or saw one activity after another superimposed: first, the academy of Dijon (reestablished in 1798), followed by the Commission des antiquités de la Côte-d'Or (founded in 1831), the Société bourguignonne de géographie et d'histoire (Burgundian Society of Geography and History) (started in 1881), and the Comité d'Histoire et d'Archéologie religieuses (Committee of Religious History and Archaeology) of the diocese of Dijon (started in 1882). The societies of Beaune, Semur, and Montbard—all in the same region—could also be added to this list. Thanks to political rivalries and competition between cities, the number of groups that produced history multiplied.

All this activity presupposed applying the resources for investigation to the past. If the nineteenth century was the golden age of antiquaries, so too was it for the bibliophile. The Société des sciences historiques et naturelles de l'Yonne (Society of Natural and Historical Sciences of the Yonne) took as its task to "do a bibliography or literary study of works written by all authors born in the department."[75] More common was the reprinting, at the local level, of works that had been produced about the local area in previous centuries. From the first histories to statistics of the seventeenth and eighteenth centuries, the totality of knowledge accumulated on the scene was systematically mobilized again. Groups of bibliophiles were formed. The first was the Société des archéologues et bibliophiles Lyonnais (Society of Archaeologists and Bibliophiles of Lyon), founded in 1846 (it disappeared the following year). More lasting were those established in the 1860s, in Rouen (Société des bibliophiles normands, in 1863) and Bordeaux (Société des bibliophiles de Guyenne, in 1866). Lastly, it was the love of books that fed the continued growth, through bequests and donations, of public libraries.

The same trend saw the systematic utilization of departmental and communal archives. Local history in this instance expanded the national history that was being developed concurrently in Paris through the Société de l'histoire de France and the Comité des Travaux historiques (Committee of Historic Works). The first inventories and summaries of archives were completed. Archivists acting in the same capacity as librarians became central in a network of local historians and were by far the most productive participants. Here, too, specialized societies in the publication of archival documents appeared. The Société des archives historiques de Guyenne (Society of the Historical Archives of Guyenne) was established in 1858; in 1874, in Saintes, the Société des archives historiques de la Saintonge et de l'Aunis (Society of Historical Archives of the Saintonge and the Aunis) was formed.[76]

The work of the scholarly amateur. Local history is first of all the history of the territory. It allows for two different approaches. The Société d'émulation du Jura held a competition in 1826 proposing the history of the department "from Julius Caesar to the present," and the archaeological program of the Société des sciences historiques et naturelles de l'Yonne proposed bringing to light "the division of the department during the epoch of the Gauls . . . the trace of the Roman roads that traversed it . . . the ecclesiastical divisions of the dioceses of Auxerre, Sens, Autun, and Langres on the points they once occupied in the department."[77] In one case territory is the framework for restoring the continuity of the past; in another it served to restore the very material of this past. The first approach expanded upon the scholarly histories of the seventeenth and eighteenth centuries. The documentary base amassed by the Benedictines was put into a departmental framework and expanded by the exploitation of the archives over the century. The second approach aimed at establishing a complete inventory of the vestiges of the past found in the territory of the department. By systematizing, it built on the activities of the antiquaries from prior centuries. These in fact were not two different approaches but rather extensions of each other. In 1781, volume 4 of the Benedictine history of Burgundy opens thus: "It has long been recognized that we will never have a general history of France so long as the individual history of its provinces is not laid before the public."[78] In 1864, the preface to *Monographies communales* of the department of the Tarn takes up this program and moves it one step further: "Therefore it has to be recognized [and] asserted that we will only have a good, complete, and serious history of France when all of its provinces have [a history] of their own. . . . Similarly, the history of a province or a department has to be the sum of the history of its communes and cantons. No locality, even the smallest, dare be left out."[79]

It would be overstating the case to define the smallest parcel of local space as a conservator of the past. The nineteenth century saw the high point of the monographic genre that restored the history of a town, a village, or a building based on the traces left behind. The past of a department, a province, or a diocese, in other words, was rooted in the many places of its unfolding history that only the dictionaries and directories can reassemble. Local history becomes a sequence of retrospective chorographies or depictions, done in alphabetical order.

Because it seeks to restore the past of a place in its totality, the production of local history to a large degree transcends the boundaries of traditional history, even if political and religious history remains the principal field of investigation. At the edges of this activity some totally new themes make their appearance. The works of Charles de Robillard de Beaurepaire, departmental archivist for the Seine-Inférieure, are a good example. In addition to the works he devoted to the estates of Normandy, the principal figures in the history of Rouen, and the royal visits to the city, his mammoth work includes studies about its poorhouses, prisons, and houses of charity. Extending the traditional limits of history led him both to "the state of the countryside in Upper Normandy during the late Middle Ages" and to the taverns of Rouen in the sixteenth century.[80]

Edouard Husson Fleury best illustrates this encyclopedic tendency to which local history leads. He devoted all of his scholarly activity to the history of the Aisne in general and to Laon in particular. His prodigious work, completed between 1849 and 1882, included Belgian Gaul, the *bailliage* of Vermandois, and the department of the Aisne as well as the cities of Laon and Saint-Quentin. It covered, moreover, a long chronology, going from antiquity (*La Civilisation et l'art des Romains dans la Gaule Belgique*), to the Merovingian times (in passing), to the prolific writing about the Revolution, down to the *Éphémérides de la guerre de 1870–1871 dans l'Aisne*. Fleury's historical writing covered a vast subject matter: to his monumental monographs and studies on episodes in religious and political history may be added an *Essai sur l'histoire de la musique,* based on representations of musical instruments on monuments of the Middle Ages, and several studies on underground habitats. All the territories, all the epochs, and all subject matter from the past are the territory of the historian.[81]

The writing of local history was not separate from historical study aimed at preserving vestiges of the past. In Laon, Étienne Midoux, the general secretary of the Société académique, was both the author of a study on the stained glass of the cathedral and the organizer of its rescue. It is true that local historians were excluded from any power of decision on this matter with the establishment of the Inspection des monuments historiques in 1830. Still, during this same time, they did play a major role in providing the initiative and impulse. It was the Société polymathique du Morbihan that prompted the intervention of public authorities to preserve the megaliths of Carnac.[82]

Likewise, scholarly activity during the nineteenth century was not separate from artistic creation. Here, the case of Léo Drouyn from Bordeaux is the best example. His historical and archaeological work doubled his considerable activity as an engraver. Archaeological landscapes were an extension of his vast monographs.[83]

The past immeasurably extended. The study of local practices and languages remained, at least for the first half of the century, more often the activity of social observers and compilers of departmental statistics than of scholars. The place that texts from the time of the July Monarchy granted to such study, nevertheless, grew noticeably. The statistical survey for Villeneuve has ninety pages devoted to mores, customs, and practices of the inhabitants of the Bouches-du-Rhône, many more than the moral and psychological observations, often hastily done, found in memoirs during the Consulate. But even if their influence grew in the descriptions of local space, local customs occupied a place that had long been marginal.[84]

Customs were not altogether excluded, however. The study of dialects in particular was used to determine the traces of the boundaries of "cities" in Gaul. Using the same perspective, Antoine Passy showed, in an article appearing in *Recueil des travaux* of the Société libre d'agriculture, sciences, arts

Figure 6.12
Pierre de Belay, *The Blue Horse* (1943).

et belles-lettres of the Eure and made famous by Lucien Gallois, that the names of the natural regions "obviously belonged to the Celtic language." That language provided an access to the early times in the history of the territory.[85] These widely varied examples show the persistence of the initial hypothesis of the Académie celtique, which showed the convergence of customs with ruins from the very distant past. The same "archaic" orientation is found in the Vedic hypothesis, even more extreme, that underlies several works on traditions, and especially those by Désiré Monnier on the Franche-Comté. According to this hypothesis, local traditions taken as a whole "irrefutably go back to a common point of departure, the mountains in Asia."[86]

These premises aside, these works show the progression of a territorial conception of languages and local practices. In 1844, the Commission historique du département du Nord (Historical Commission of the Department of the Nord) published a map showing the extent of the French and Flemish languages. Traditions tended to become favored indicators of a territory defined by its most distant past.[87]

This trend is easily identified in Brittany, where collections of traditions increased between 1820 and 1850. After Aymar de Blois, who

Figure 6.13
The republican restoration of local memory: 19th-century Brittany in brief. Jules Benoît-Levy, *Brittany*, Salon of 1911.

collected the first popular poems around 1820, Hersart de La Villemarqué published the *Barzaz-Breiz* in 1839 (analyzed by Yves Guiomar). *La Galerie armoricaine,* by Hippolyte Lalaisse, presents local costumes down to the last detail. Lastly, the traditions and practices of the Bretons form the material for works by Souvestre and the *Breiz Izel* by Perrin. Brittany had the advantage of both that which belonged to the Celtic style and that which belonged to literary and historical romanticism, which turned the people into actors wholly apart from history. The study of its traditions and its practices opens the way to seeing the personality of the province. Émile Souvestre makes this objective explicit in the first pages of *Le Foyer breton,* which he dedicated to Michelet: "If history is the complete revelation of the existence of a people, how to write it without knowing what is most characteristic in its existence? Do you not see that these indications concerning the intimate life of a nation are chiefly found in popular traditions?"[88]

At least up to 1850, Brittany remained an isolated case. Indeed, during the first half of the century, collecting traditions was limited to "remote worlds," Corsica, the Pyrenees, and in general the marshy and mountainous areas of the country. Elsewhere the study of local customs was stifled by the enduring dark image of the peasantry, seen particularly in Balzac's *Les Paysans* and reinforced by the menacing Breton. Such images were pervasive at this time.[89]

It was only after the middle of the century that studies of local customs began to proliferate. The June Days of the Revolution of 1848 marked a change in the image of the peasant (the evolution in the Breton stereotype accounts for this in part): the image of Brittany goes from the ferocious peasant to the young girl dressed all in white.[90] At a time when the dark legend of the rural world persisted as described at the end of the century in Zola's *The Earth,* a new theme appears in literature that turns that same world into the conservator of the social order in its confrontation with the ever more threatening city. In this movement, which produced 478 novels with a rustic theme between 1860 and 1925, George Sand was one of the first figures.[91] By producing novels that drew heavily on the customs of the Berry, she promoted the study of the area. *Croyances et légendes du centre de la France* by Laisnel de la Salle appeared in 1875.[92]

The Franco-Prussian War of 1870 accelerated the integration of customs and popular traditions into the local patrimony. In many respects, the first war on French territory since 1814 played a major role in raising the awareness, in urban elites, of the disintegration of rural communities brought about by the rural exodus. All regions of France were affected, even those parts of the territory spared by the invasion.[93] The period from 1870 to 1914 saw a massive development in regional ethnographies. Historical societies increased the number of questionnaires and appeared as the first specialized institutions. The Société dauphinoise d'ethnologie et d'anthropologie (Dauphiné Society of Ethnology and Anthropology) was established in Grenoble in 1894, the Société d'ethnographie et d'art populaire du bas Limousin (Society of Ethnography and Popular Art of the Lower Limousin) in Tulle in 1899. In particular, physicians, teachers, and curates were the principal actors in expanding the number of studies on local customs.[94] Collecting to a large degree went beyond languages, oral traditions, and customs held in common. Through the text as well as through photography, collecting came to include all aspects of rural life, converted into traditional civilization. Ethnographic space extended the plunge into the past of local history.

Writers about the past only rarely gave way to popularization. The study done by Gonzague Tierny on the learned societies of the Somme shows that initiatives on this point remained extremely isolated examples. Produced by notables, the local past was intended for their consumption. Archaeological or naturalist promenades enjoyed, beginning in 1840, an enduring popularity. Likewise, the regional schools of painting that were developing around the societies of the friends of the arts (the first one, it

appears, was established in Douai in 1821) took as their theme the patrimony of monuments and the landscapes of the countryside.[95] Privilege
for a narrow elite, local memory was constructed at the intersection of
two spaces, of two times, and of two cultures.

The Uses of the Particular

The advent of the Third Republic opened a period in which a profound
change occurred in the way local space came to be represented in French
space. By all indications, prominence was given to this shift. The local
became the basis for defining France; the newly installed Republic anchored its functions and rituals in it; and it became finally one of the
commonplaces of the dominant culture. Any approach to France passes
through the inventory of its infinite diversity.

One, Yet Divisible

The long predominance of the national and the consequent marginalization of the local in the definition of France make this reversal at the end
of the century all the more striking. The formation of a French school
of geography, the reemergence of an ethnography of France, and the
publication of the *Revue de synthèse* are the principal elements in the
undertaking to redefine the connections of the local and the national,
which began after 1870.

The Vidalian synthesis. The *Histoire de France* by Lavisse, published in
1903, opens with the *Tableau de la géographie de la France*. The overall description is based on the prominence given the diversity of landscapes and
lifestyles as they reveal the fundamental heterogeneity of the morphology
of France. That heterogeneity appears in the unending division created
when each of its parts is broken down into the smallest component. One
can read France to identify the natural regions and areas of France, conceived as the basic cells of French actuality. That approach enables the geographer to grasp the intimacy that unites a territory and a group of
people. Anchoring the differences more firmly in the soil does not necessarily lead to shattering the whole. It leads, rather, to the prominence
of solidarity among the parts. France is situated at the intersection of the
differences in the elements that compose it. Local space becomes the
cornerstone for identifying the actuality of France. It permits what is
"fixed and permanent" in France to be grasped. It also allows for an
understanding of its history, conceived as a sequence of developing

potentialities contained in its infinite diversity. France is perpetually transforming itself.[96]

Such a break with the past obviously proceeds from new questions being raised, the starting point being the defeat of 1870. Indeed, the annexation of Alsace-Lorraine makes borders the question that defines the nation and, by the same token, blurs the line of separation between the local and the national that the Revolution raised.

This aspect of the "German crisis in French thought" appears in the waning arguments regarding the question of provinces in the centralized State. The last embers of the debate died out in the monarchist assembly of 1871. Even though Maurras and others tried to keep the dispute alive, the regionalist idea relegated it to the fringe. Brought forth in the Second Empire by Le Play's research, this idea represents the demand for decentralized powers of the State and, at the same time, for newly defined territorial unities that could overcome the deficiencies of the department. It marked the moment when the idea of the nation, taken as universal, and the territory, presumed homogeneous, fell into disrepute among the entire political class.[97] The French school of geography was the pivot of this vast enterprise to redefine the nation around local spaces.

The redefinition of the geography of France, beginning with the individualization of its fundamental units, leads to yet another rearrangement. Since research about France includes the study of relationships between territory and population, it necessarily fixes on their most tangible expression. The attention given to landscapes, products of human activity, and the lifestyles as well as those interactions between men and environment pushes observers to look at rural space:

> So we think that the great changes to which we have been witness will not touch what is essential in our national temperament. The robust constitution of the countryside that climate and soil give to our country is a fact cemented by nature and weather. It is an expression of the number of homeowners, which is nowhere equaled. A certain stability rests on that, perhaps encountered in no other country to the same degree as in ours, a French solidity.[98]

The rural material of France, visible in the plenitude of its local spaces, is thus placed at the center of every definition of France.

The same "ruralist" orientation reinforced in 1870 by the discredited urban modernism of the Second Empire and the double shock of the war and the Commune simultaneously gave rise to a movement for the systematic collection of local traditions. New publications had made this apparent already in 1870 with the *Revue celtique* and then with *Romania* in 1872 and *Mélusine* in 1877. The last named was meant to be, according to its promoters, Henri Gaidiz and Eugène Rolland, the standard for memoirs published by the Académie celtique, as well as for the repertory of popular literature and of traditions from the provinces of France. In 1886, Paul Sébillot founded the Société des traditions populaires and the *Revue* of the same name. These efforts were all focused on the vernacular languages and literatures as well as common customs. In 1895, the establishment of the Société d'ethnographie nationale et d'art populaire added for inclusion collections on every aspect of material life. The 1880s likewise saw the beginnings of research by the Comité du Travaux historiques (Committee on Historic Works) into rural housing, results of which started appearing in print in 1894. The emerging prominence in the diversity of the rural patrimony was accompanied in 1888 by putting into the Musée d'ethnographie a *salle de France* featuring costumes and reconstructions of habitats from the different provinces.[99] Lastly, between 1904 and 1907 a four-volume study appeared titled *Le Folklore de la France*.[100] Starting with the considerable mass of local monographs, Sébillot had produced a "picture of the French ethnography" by interweaving the rural memories of its parts.

The fragmentation of history. History finally enters this movement through the *Revue de synthèse,* a journal that started in 1900. Based on, among other things, local history, the first volume contained two programmatic articles: "Reflexions sur l'histoire provinciale" by Henri Berr and "Introduction à l'étude des régions et des pays de France" by Pierre Foncin. Both articles drew from the considerable mass of information collected by scholars and learned societies and assigned to the journal the task of providing the synthesis. At issue was the task of collecting the scattered pieces of a local past for the purpose of creating "a very precise psychology of our France" (Berr) and "building in some way a temple to France and its regions" (Foncin). The project came to fruition, beginning in 1903, with the publication of a series of monographs. The first was dedicated to Gascony and followed by nine others, including ones by Marc Bloch and Lucien Febvre.[101] In the general introduction to the series, Henri Berr stated that the divisions were left to each author. Such discretion stood in contrast to the much more ambitious project defined by Paul Lorquet in the second volume. By posing the problem of a principle of division that would "reconcile the data from geography and history," he was led to reject both natural regions

Figure 6.14
The provincial ordering: the Burgundian pantheon in the great hall of the Dijon *hôtel de ville*. Henri Lévy, *Les Gloires de la Bourgogne* (1896). Seen here are Bossuet, Saint Bernard, Philip II ("the Bold"), Charles the Rash, Lazare Carnot, Lamartine, and, seated on the throne, France.

and historical provinces. Through successive elimination, he arrives at the commune and then at the quarter:

> These are the elementary units, and as moral persons, these first collective units, these parcels that are distinct from the soil and populated by distinct fractions of the nation, must be analyzed at the very outset if a fair and serious synthesis of the small *pays,* in particular its historical and natural subdivisions, is to be obtained. These partial syntheses may never be definitive but at least they will approach that point and eventually combine in a general synthesis.[102]

In the very recomposition of its historical material, so very much fragmented, France would become apparent.

In Praise of Diversity

Gambetta dramatically provided the starting point in 1871, when he embodied the will to resist provincial apathy. The *tour de France* by the republican committees, which he undertook in 1872, was a magnificent break directed to the future, in comparison to the previous Republics. From its establishment until the Boulangist crisis in 1889, the Republic more and more based its institutions and its functions on local space. The definitive integration into the republican tradition of voting according to arrondissement, after the unhappy attempt in 1885 to vote by departmental list, sanctioned the influence of local notables. Similarly, the Senate, seen up to that point as the bastion of conservatism and suspect because of the indirect nature of its recruitment, became, to use the republican terms, "the great council of the communes of France." In a parallel fashion, a republican agrarianism took shape, the chief features of which were the establishment of the Ministry of Agriculture in 1880 and the creation of an award, the Mérite agricole, by Méline. The Republic exalted "the eternal order of the fields" and identified itself with a democracy of small proprietors.[103]

   This evolution is easily explained by the memory of the defeats suffered by the Second Republic, and even more by the results of the February 1871 election, which confirmed the influence of the provinces and rural areas. The majority in those localities, favorable to the monarchists, had been the principal support of the Empire for twenty years. These events revealed the urgent necessity of giving the Republic other foundations than proclamations from the balcony of the *hôtel de ville* in Paris and the republican fervor of the capital. This was especially the case when in the 1880s public opinion in Paris began furnishing large battalions of

antirepublican nationalists and socialists. After 1885, the regime turned
into the Republic of local committees, where the deputy of the arrondissement, backed by a dense network of republican notables (every
mayor elected after the laws of 1871 and 1884), was the pivot of the
political life of the nation.[104] The Republic of the radicals only
confirmed this movement that, with Jules Ferry's government, solidified
the political fortunes of provincial notables: Ferry was from the Vosges;
Combes began his career as a municipal councilor in Pons (Charente) and
Fallières as mayor of Nérac.

Republican ritual strictly adhered to this evolving pattern. Because
it was by definition a regime by local notables, the Republic could do
nothing less than organize, on the occasion of the Universal Exposition,
a banquet for the mayors from departments' administrative centers. The
government of the Defense of the Republic repeated the gesture in
1900, at which time the mayor of every commune (36,172 total) was invited to the banquet preceding the exposition; 20,777 attended.[105] Republican folklore, at which banquets played an essential role and which
one finds on a smaller scale in the departments, attests to the fact that the
regime was sinking deeper and deeper roots into the plenitude of local
space.

One finds the same tendency in the rebirth of the presidential tour
when the newly elected presidents, Sadi Carnot and Félix Faure, went to
the Élysée Palace. Napoleon III had been the pioneer in this "rediscovery of the territory." His trips, begun during his presidency and
expanded after 1852, aimed at consolidating his personal power.[106]
MacMahon and Grévy remained in the tradition of Parisian power, continuing the "imprisonment" at Versailles, but their successors, by contrast, made multiple journeys into the provinces. In the space of ten years,
Reims hosted three presidents of the Republic. To be sure, it had the advantage of a monarchical past incorporated into the memory of the nation and status as a required stop in military maneuvers. By turns, Carnot
in 1891, Faure in 1895, and Loubet in 1901 made the trip to Reims.[107]
Every visit became an opportunity to affirm the strength of the government and to glorify pride in the locality.

The Republic never stopped encountering various local initiatives
designed to bring forth a slice of the past of a particular place. The 1860s
and 1870s were the starting point for the vogue in historical spectacles.
Very often they were organized by the local scholarly society for the
purpose of celebrating the great moments and prosperous times of the
locality. At the same time, these festivities had the additional effect of
placing the local past in the past of the nation. Beginning in 1863, Caen
organized a cavalcade, the principal theme of which was the entry of

Figure 6.15
Celebrating France
through its provinces:
allegories. Postcard
for the 50th anniver-
sary of the annexation
of Savoy to France,
1910.

GROUPE ALLÉGORIQUE du CINQUANTENAIRE
De l'Annexion de la SAVOIE à la FRANCE
— 1860-1910 —

«... nos cœurs vont où coulent nos
[rivières »

Figure 6.15
Celebrating France through its provinces: allegories. Postcard for the 50th anniversary of the annexation of Savoy to France, 1910.

Francis I into the city. In 1866, Nancy held a four-day celebration of the centenary when Lorraine became part of France. Two parades illustrated the past and present of the province. Other demonstrations were more extensive. For instance, the cortege that filed across Carcassonne on May 23, 1876, showed Princess Galeswinthe, daughter of Athanagilde, king of the Visigoths, on her way to Rouen to marry Chilperic, king of Neustria. The town was celebrating the moment when the alliance between northern and southern France was sealed.[108] The vogue of commemorations did not diminish in later decades. In fact, it grew in size at the local level with events celebrating the centenary of the Revolution. Reims indulged in two celebrations, one after the other—one for 1789 and the other for 1792. Chambéry and Avignon were content with modest centenary celebrations of their unification to France, while other urban plunges into the past were vastly more impressive. In 1896, Reims commemorated the 1,400th anniversary of the baptism of Clovis. Marseille, three years later, celebrated with much pomp the 2,000th anniversary of its founding.[109]

The same trend also had more durable results. The period from 1870 to 1914 was marked by a surge in commemorative statuary in public

Figure 6.16
Celebrating France through its provinces: rituals. Speech by the mayor of Rennes at the unveiling of the monument commemorating the union of Brittany with France, 1911.

places that had begun during the Restoration, when several counterrevolutionary monuments in western France were constructed. The trend continued during the July Monarchy with patriotic monuments. In the Second Empire and even more in the Third Republic, official patriotic themes were used to support and provide the framework for local celebrations, which began with recent memories, the Franco-Prussian War of 1870, before going back in time. The towns of Belfort, Bayonne, and Roanne first erected monuments to the dead of 1870 and then monuments to the resistance to the invasion of 1814. Jemmapes, Valenciennes, and Hondschoote started at the same point but went back to celebrate battles of the Revolution. Certain towns went even further. Saint-Quentin, through two successive monuments, first honored its dead from 1870 and then resistance to the Spanish in 1557. Along those same lines, Formigny in Normandy acquired a monument in 1903 recalling the battle of 1450.[110] Bouvines, lastly, obtained an obelisk in 1845 and commemorative stained glass for its church in 1879. Through these undertakings the patriotism of the parish nourished patriotism to the

Republic. This last became steadily more apparent in local celebrations as the risk of war with Germany grew. In July 1914, the 700th anniversary of the battle of Bouvines* turned into the French counterpart of German celebrations of the battle of Leipzig the previous year.[111]

The field of statuary provides the most spectacular illustration of this movement aimed at promoting local patrimonies. As Maurice Agulhon has shown, public spaces began to fill up with the glories of the locality during the July Monarchy. Local political rivalries and competition among those towns likely to receive the effigy of a hero were the engines of this movement. But it was the Empire and especially the Republic that really drove this mania for statues.[112] The role played by subsidies from the Direction des beaux-arts was decisive. If Angers owned a statue of King René in 1855, it then sought and obtained a succession of statues: first David d'Angers (1880), then Beaurepaire (1889), Chevreul (1893), Monseigneur Frepel (1899), and finally Marguerite d'Anjou (1902).[113] To the already classic political and military glories may be added literary, scientific, and artistic celebrities. These examples could be multiplied without end, so widespread was the movement that reached right down to the most humble commune. For most of them the enthusiasm for commemoration rested on nothing more than glories known but to a few. Some towns were better endowed. Nolay (Côte-d'Or) was able to honor Sadi Carnot: Mont-sous-Vaudrey, Jules Grévy. Local memory was thereby joined to the memory of the nation at the moment when republican aesthetics were spreading into all the communes. The mixed monuments were the most evocative of this juncture. In Dôle, the statue to Jules Grévy was accompanied by the female allegory of the Republic.[114]

Patriotic pedagogy, on the theme of the lost provinces, inspired numerous towns to erect statues to Joan of Arc, who up to then was honored only in Orléans. After 1880, in France she became the person of whom the most statues were erected. Republican patriotism also led to the erection of monuments distinctly marginal to the past of many localities. Vercingetorix, normally honored at Alésia by Napoleon III and at Clermont Ferrand by the Republic (the two places where the Gauls inflicted defeat on the Romans), made his presence felt in Bordeaux and Saint-Denis.[115] Broadly speaking, statues allowed the importance of local space in the history of France to be celebrated. The ceremony of the unveiling, enhanced

---

* EDITOR'S NOTE: In 1214, Philip II, with support from Emperor Frederick II, defeated an anti-Capetian alliance comprising the English, a rival German emperor, and most of the feudality of Flanders, Belgium, and Lorraine. The victory put the French monarchy into the first rank of European powers.

at times by the presence of the undersecretary of state for the fine arts, became one of the powerful moments of republican folklore.

Over and above these mixed historical civic celebrations, the period
experienced the parallel development, especially pronounced in the west
and the south, of regional cultural movements. The Félibrige in Provence
was the first of these organizations pushing to preserve local traditions.
Their number increased after 1870. The Breton Regionalist Union was
founded in 1888 and the Escola lemouzina (Limousin) in 1893. Their
chief focus was the defense and illustration of local language with the
compilation of dictionaries (Mistral published *Le Trésor du Félibrige* in
1877) and the promotion of literary works in the region's vernacular. But
beyond that, these movements developed or revived the entire panoply
of local tradition. The Bleun Brug expanded the number of festivals in
Brittany. The Félibrige rallied in 1894 for the defense of the "liberty of
the bullfight." Mistral standardized Provençal dress.[116] Putting these
movements into action was the task urban groups set for themselves, with
municipalities and organizations taking charge of organizing local events.
Festivals such as the Visscherbende in Dunkirk and the Festival of the
Gayants in Douai became new emblems of the city.[117]

These multiple affirmations of identity, focusing on fragments of
memory of a city or a province, connected to republican themes more than
they opposed them. The Republic kept the centralization of the State intact while developing an official regionalism. The best proof of this is the
fate of the *Tableau de la France* under the Republic. An expanded edition
with Michelet's travel accounts, done by his wife and published under the
title *Notre France,* began a long career as a schoolbook, starting in 1886. By
1922, it had gone through fifteen editions.[118] Regionalism invaded the political life of the times as well when the Féderation régionaliste française,
founded in 1900, held a place of central importance. The organization, of
which Jean Charles-Brun was the general director for life, brought the advocates of provincialism together with official regionalism. During the
radical Republic, the regional idea served as the "ideological crossroads."[119] It even became a centerpiece of the republican consensus. In
1920, the very official *Histoire de la nation française* opens with a work by
Jean Brunhes, entitled *La Géographie humaine de la France,* that is one long
accolade to the infinite diversity of local regions.[120]

A Culture of Local Space

A complete redefinition of the representations of France and its political
ways cannot be separated from the actualities of local cultural practices.
In the increasingly homogeneous space that is France, local space and the

features it developed during the nineteenth century became the commonplaces of culture for the Belle Époque.

The diffusion of knowledge about places. The diffusion of knowledge about places saw its beginnings in a wave of novels with a regional theme that swept over the French book market until 1940. Anne-Marie Thiesse's study of this phenomenon revealed that during this period thousands of titles with "regionalist" titles appeared. Because these works so completely entered the rural world and invariably presented a negative image of the city, this production of books furthered the rustic novel. But they differed from that genre in their ability to reveal the landscape and its people. The use of local dialects—with translations at the bottom of the page—and the precise descriptions of material conditions stood in sharp contrast to the generic provinciality upheld, with some exceptions, by this rustic literature.[121]

The prior period was not short on regional literature. The successes in Paris of Jasmin, Mistral, or Erckmann-Chatrian testify to that. The chronology of these successes in fact extended throughout the century, falling into successive "regional" styles. The Belle Époque was remarkable precisely because authors from different regions enjoyed contemporaneous success. Right before World War I, the Société des écrivains de province (Society for Writers of the Province) was formed. Parisian publishers produced specialized collections (*Pays de France,* published by Nouvelle Librairie française; *Le Roman des provinces de France,* published by Ollendorf). In 1907, Émile Moselly received the Goncourt Prize for *Terres lorraines,* and three years later, it was Louis Pergaud's turn for *De Goupil à Margot.* Six Femina prizes and five grand prizes in literature from the Académie française crowned regional novels between 1910 and 1937.[122]

The success of the regional genre in literature finds an exact parallel in tourist customs using the province as the setting. Daniel Nordman has shown that the Guides-Joanne, starting in 1880, dropped the formula of the itinerary in favor of the province.[123] Tourist activity up to that time was closely dependent on the main railroad lines. The completion of the branch lines and the development of more flexible ways of moving about, such as the velocipede and automobile (The Touring Club of France, initially for velocipede riders, was founded in 1890), allowed for a systematic exploration of local space.[124] Guidebooks, which multiplied after 1900, included everything. They reproduced the customs and practices of the space of the local notables. The collection launched by Masson at the beginning of the century, moreover, was entitled *Les Guides du touriste, du naturaliste et de l'archéologue.*[125] Products for the tourist showed great homogeneity in content. After a summary presentation of the local space, there followed a list of its localities. Then came a summary description of the chief public buildings and traces of the past still evident.

During the same period, local tourist offices took up where those in Paris left off. Between 1889 and 1913, 231 tourist offices were set up, the first in Grenoble. Put together by interests and by scholarly societies at the municipal, departmental, or regional level, these associations continued, through their own publications, the volume of tourist products, without adding anything original.[126]

The movement to diffuse the contents of local space was expanded, beginning in 1889, by the generalized usage of the illustrated postcard. The studies by Adeline Ripert show that the number of postcard publishers grew rapidly even in the smallest locality. In Fontainebleau, Parisian publishers completely dominated the market up to 1900. Two years later, three local publishers were selling postcards with some 350 different subjects. Further, a study of the Bergeret house in Nancy reveals in detail the range of subjects used by local publishers.

The cards, for the most part, have a very strong local focus (except for "artistic" cards, which are a totally different category). Three large groupings can be distinguished: First, views of the city, with monuments to the patrimony passing in review. These include public buildings. Next come the great events that happened in local life and, finally, different aspects of the area's rural folklore. Organized in series by municipality, department, or province, postcards came to be the preferred way of representing localities. They supplanted lithographic production, which had been expanding all during the century. With that a trend came to an end that had given predominance to visual elements in representations of places.[127]

Space as pretext. The Belle Époque, which saw the increasing "consumption" of local space through literature, tourism, and pictures, was also the time of a declining production of local knowledge. Yves Lequin has shown that at the turn of the century, the notables were turning away from the "local" signs of traditional notability. Their economic activities, like their social practices, all tended toward homogenization from one end of France to the other. As evidence, the number of members in the Norman Association in Caen declined sharply between 1861 and 1897 from 288 to 52.[128] The same tendency affected all the scholarly societies, with some important exceptions. It is explained in part by the decline in the economic, social, and political influence of traditional elites, along with the marginalization of their scholarly activity. Beginning in the

Figure 6.17

Celebrating France through its provinces: pedagogical lessons. Frontispiece by J. P. Pinchon, *Les Provinces de France illustrées* (1927). The text printed within the map of France reads: "Note by the Editor. We wish to offer children and grownups an attractive and instructive publication and to present at the same time geographical documentation relating to the former provinces of France and their division into departments, which will enable children to learn while having fun and grownups to recall that very important part of the geography of our country.

"Before 1790, France comprised 33 major provinces. The division into departments, through the decree of January 15, 1790, by the Constituent Assembly, did not abolish a tradition that retained the original names of our old provinces.

"Particularly from the tourist's point of view, custom has retained for most of the regions of France their beautiful names from centuries past."

1890s, amateur historians were increasingly finding themselves in competition, on their own ground, with the professionals in history at the regional universities. Scientific history and regional universities removed from the scholarly societies the privilege of producing history. Marginalized, their history became what the French call *petite histoire*. The period that followed World War I did nothing but confirm the fact that the formation of local patrimonies had slowed down. The declining number of scholarly societies after 1914 illustrates the point.[129]

Because of this, local spaces became "space as the pretext" for increasingly undifferentiated tourist activities.[130] One of the signs of this

Figure 6.18
Celebrating France through its provinces: stereotypes. J. P. Pinchon, *Burgundy* (1927).

evolution might be the development, at the fringes of already established practices, of gastronomic tourism. The literature devoted to cuisine and regional specialties grew tremendously after the 1920s. In 1933, Curnonsky, the great gastronome, and Austin de Croze came out with the first index of regional specialties. In the *Trésor gastronomique de la France*, dishes and specialties presented as extensions of the land competed with history and traditions as the distinctive signs of the locality.[131] The locality had indeed become the object of a thriving industry in memory. The potteries of Quimper began producing their decorative wares in 1878. In Carcassone, where commercial inscriptions in Gothic letters began to proliferate, local legends were converted into souvenirs or pastries. This ultimate transfiguration of the local past would receive its finishing touch with the development of mass tourism, which in the Vendée turned the *chouan*, the counterrevolutionary rebel of the 1790s, into junk jewelry and pork products.[132]

The history of stereotypes still remains to be written. Clearly all during the nineteenth century, the range was considerably expanded by new visual elements that were added to traditional literary stereotypes. Catherine Bertho has shown how, from 1835 to 1935, from *La France pittoresque* of Hugo to *Provinces de France illustrées*, images describing local space were brought into a system of simplified signs attached to a territory.[133] Studies carried out on regional dress show that this is a process of extension, with symbols of one area turning into symbols for the whole region. Thus, the dress of Arles becomes the dress of Provence. But the progression could go in reverse. The knot in the headdress for women in Alsace, the Franche-Comté, and southwest Germany became the Alsatian headdress between 1870 and 1918.[134] In the diffusion of these stereotypes, tourism played an essential role. Posters for the railroads as well as local tourist offices devoted most of their space to these stereotypes right up to the 1930s.[135] To this might be added advertising for food, the production of postcards, and regional art schools. Pierre Pasquini has shown that this last played an important role in fixing and diffusing the principal features of an eternal and simplified Provence.[136]

After World War I, official imagery took charge of these stereotyped local spaces. The first stamps using the feminine allegory of Marianne to represent the Third Republic in 1870, and required in that year, did not appear until 1917. Beginning in 1929, a series of five "sites and monuments" was printed showing the Arch of Triumph, the cathedral of Reims, Mont-Saint-Michel, the port of La Rochelle, and the Pont du Gard. In 1931, a remarkable series of stamps showed the headdresses from the different parts of France: Arles, Boulogne, Alsace, and Brittany.[137] In one series after another, the images of towns and provinces from the four corners of France were established as official representations. The Universal Exposition of 1937 merely confirmed the fact. France was represented by a "regional center" that adjoined a "rural center."[138] That same year, the Musée national des Arts et Traditions populaires was built.

These events ended a trend that had begun with the Revolution, turning the divisibility of the territory into the preferred vector of identification for France. But just as official regionalism was reaching its culmination, it was deprived of the foundations that had supported it up to 1914. In 1928, the celebration of Carcassonne at 2,000 years, managed by the authorities, did not arouse any particular fervor in the town.[139] Integrated into the Republic, regionalism, like official agrarianism, appeared as the recourse for a society in crisis. The Republic that was about to end was playing regional diversity against social and political tensions.[140]

To this long decline during the 1930s may be added the disrepute of Vichy's cultural project. Christian Faure has shown that provincialism and local memories, reemphasized through new historical and ethnographic research, became the elements of a real politics of memory and were aimed at mobilizing the elites for Vichy's national revolution. The revitalization of the province—the honoring of local languages, costumes, and local festivals; the establishment of regional models of architecture and furnishings—are among the many elements of official folklore that blossomed in 1940. But this reimplantation of local memories quickly turned into a failure. Precisely in 1941, it found itself marginalized in the very culture of the French state.[141] The fall of the regime only confirmed a decline already long under way.

Throughout this process, which we have just scanned, the beginnings of the Third Republic appear as the special moment when the two approaches to France emerging from the Revolution join together. During this short period, France came to be, completely and at the same time, one and infinitely divisible. Thereby it linked the far distant past of each local area to the present of the Republic. Considerable traces remain from this exceptional period, compared with the ones preceding and following. Even if the urban spaces have not all kept the monuments with which they have been stocked, local memories remain. The small numbers of learned notables who created these memories for their own use fashioned durable representations as well as practices for all local spaces.

NOTES

1. Alphonse Dupront, "Du Sentiment national," in Michel François et al., *La France et les français* (Paris: Gallimard, Encyclopédie de la Pléiade, 1972), 1423–75.

2. Jacques Thuillier and Jean Vergnet-Ruiz, "Les Mille musées de France," *Arts de France* 2 (1962): 7–22; Pierre Cabanne, *Guide des musées de France* (Paris: Bordas, 1984).

3. O. Benoit-Guilbot, R. Cabanes, G. Caussade, et al., *L'Esprit des lieux: Localités et changement social en France* (Paris: Éd. du C.N.R.S., 1986).

4. Marie-Vic Ozouf-Marignier, *La Formation des départements: La représentation du territoire français à la fin du XVIIIe siècle* (Paris: Éd. de l' E.H.E.S.S., 1989); Mona Ozouf, "La Révolution française et la perception de l'espace national: Fédérations, fédéralisme et stéréotypes régionaux," in *L'École de la France* (Paris: Gallimard, 1984); Mona Ozouf, "Fédération," in *Dictionnaire critique de la Révolution française*, under the direction of François Furet and Mona Ozouf (Paris: Flammarion, 1988).

5. Daniel Nordman and Jacques Revel, "La Formation de l'espace français," in *Histoire de la France*, vol. 1, *L'Espace français*, under the direction of André Burguière and Jacques Revel (Paris: Éd. du Seuil, 1989).

6. Jean-Luc Pinol, "Les Formes de l'État," in *Histoire des français, XIXe–XXe siècles*, vol. 3, *Les Citoyens et la démocratie*, under the direction of Yves Lequin (Paris: Armand Colin, 1984).

7. *Les Constitutions de la France depuis 1789* (Paris: Flammarion, 1972); Jacques Godechot, *Les Institutions de la France sous la Révolution et l'empire* (Paris:

P.U.F., 1968); Jean-Yves Guiomar, *La Nation entre l'histoire et la raison* (Paris: La Découverte, 1990).

8. Ozouf, "La Révolution française."

9. Ibid.

10. Jean-Clément Martin, "The Vendée: Region of Memory," below in this volume.

11. Ozouf, "La Révolution française."

12. Michel de Certeau, Dominique Julia, and Jacques Revel, *Une politique de la langue: La Révolution française et les patois* (Paris: Gallimard, 1975).

13. Guiomar, *La Nation*.

14. Jean-Claude Perrot, *L'Âge d'or de la statistique régionale française (an IV–1804)* (Paris: Société d'Études robespierristes, 1977); Marie-Noëlle Bourguet, *Déchiffrer la France: La statistique départementale à l'époque napoléonienne* (Paris: Éd. des Archives contemporaines, 1988).

15. André Burguière, "Les Pratiques matrimoniales"; Mona Ozouf, "La Fête"; and Marie-Noëlle Bourguet, "La Région" and "Naissance d'une ethnographie de la France," in *Objets et méthodes de l'histoire de la culture*, under the direction of Jacques Le Goff and Bela Kopeczi (Budapest and Paris: Éd. du C.N.R.S, 1982).

16. *Objets et méthodes de l'histoire de la culture;* Mona Ozouf, "Passé, présent et avenir à travers les textes administratifs de l'époque révolutionnaire," in *L'École de la France.*

17. Bourguet, *Déchiffrer la France.*

18. Nicole Belmont, "L'Académie celtique et George Sand, "*Romantisme 9* (1975): 29–38.

19. Ozouf-Marignier, *La Formation des départements.*

20. Bourguet, *Déchiffrer la France.*

21. Numerous notations of this kind can be seen in the administrative reports found in the departmental series F1 CIII of the National Archives.

22. Jean-Yves Guiomar, "Le Désir d'un tableau," *Le Débat* 24 (March 1983): 91–106.

23. Mona Ozouf, "L'Invention de l'ethnographie de la France: Le questionnaire de l'Académie celtique," *Annales E.S.C.* 36, no. 2 (March–April 1981); reprinted in *L'École de la France.*

24. Perrot, *L'Âge d'or.*

25. Guillaume Bertier de Sauvigny, *La Restauration* (Paris: Flammarion, 1955).

26. Rudolf von Thadden, *La Centralisation contestée* (Arles: Actes Sud, 1989).

27. Bertier de Sauvigny, *La Restauration.*

28. Jules Michelet, *Le Tableau de la France* (Paris: Olivier Orban, 1987). Page references are drawn from *Moyen Âge* (Paris: Robert Laffont, coll. Bouquins, 1981).

29. Guiomar, "Le Désir d'un tableau."

30. Roland Barthes, *Michelet* (Paris: Éd. du Seuil, coll. Écrivains de toujours, 1954).

31. See Roger Chartier, "La Ligne Saint-Malo–Genève," in *Les Lieux de mémoire*, under the direction of Pierre Nora, 3 vols. in 7 (Paris: Gallimard, 1984–92), vol. 3, book 1, 738–75.

32. Roger Chartier, "Les Deux France: Histoire d'une géographie," *Cahiers d'histoire* 18 (1978): 393–415; Yves Lequin, "La France, une et indivisible?" in *Histoire des Français, XIXe–XXe siècles*, vol. 1, *Un peuple et son pays*, under the direction of Yves Lequin (Paris: Armand Colin, 1984).

33. Abel Hugo, *La France pittoresque* (Paris: Delloye, 1835).

34. Jules Verne, *Géographie illustrée de la France et ses colonies* (Paris, 1867); Nordman and Revel, "La Formation de l'espace français."

35. Françoise Bercé, "Arcisse de Caumont et les sociétés savantes," in *Les Lieux de mémoire*, vol. 2, book 2, 532–67.

36. Lequin, "La France, une et indivisible?"

37. Nordman and Revel, "La Formation de l'espace français." The results of the survey of 1863 can be found in Eugen Weber, *Peasants into Frenchmen: The Modernization of Rural France, 1870–1914* (Stanford: Stanford University Press, 1976).

38. Charles Nodier, Justin Taylor, and Alphonse de Cailleux, *Voyages pittoresques et romantiques dans l'ancienne France*, 23 vols. (Paris, 1820–78). For a typology of the journeys, see Jean-Claude Chamboredon and Annie Méjean, "Styles de voyages, modes de perception du paysage et stéréotypes régionaux dans les récits de voyages et les guides touristiques: Essai de sociologie de la perception touristique," in *Récits de voyages et perception du territoire: La Provence, XVIIIe–XXe siècles*, Territoires 2 (Paris: Presses de l'École normale supérieure, 1985).

39. *Liste des sociétés savantes de province* (Paris: Comité des Travaux historiques, 1862). Henri Delaunay, *Les Sociétés de France* (Paris, 1902); Edme Tassy and Pierre Léris, *Les Ressources du travail intellectuel en France* (Paris, 1921).

40. Dominique Julia and Daniel Milo, "Les Ressources culturelles," in *Histoire de la France*, vol. 1, *L'Espace français*; Bercé, "Arcisse de Caumont."

41. Pierre Grémion, *Le Pouvoir périphérique: Bureaucrates et notables dans le système politique français* (Paris: Éd. du Seuil, 1976).

42. Jean-Paul Nardy, "Perceptions d'un espace régional: La Société d'émulation du Jura et la Franche-Comté (1818–1898)," in Daniel Mathieu, Jean-Paul Nardy, and André Robert, *La Franche-Comté à la recherche de son territoire*, Annales littéraires de l'Université (Paris: Les Belles Lettres, 1985).

43. Numa Broc, *La Géographie des philosophes, géographes et voyageurs français au XVIIIe siècle* (Paris: Ophrys, 1975); Michel Vovelle, "La Découverte de la Provence, ou les primitifs de l'ethnographie provençale," in *De la cave au grenier* (Québec: Serge Fleury éditeur, 1980).

44. Ozouf-Marignier, *La Formation des départements;* Bourguet, *Déchiffrer la France.*

45. Robert-Henri Bautier, "La Coopération des sociétés savantes," in *Colloque interdisciplinaire sur les sociétés savantes: Actes du 100e congrès des Sociétés savantes, 1975* (Paris, 1976).

46. Julia and Milo, "Les Ressources culturelles"; Henri Lapauze, *Les Musées de province* (Paris, 1908); Germaine Barnaud, *Répertoire des musées et collections publiques de France* (Paris: Éd. de la Réunion des musées nationaux, 1982).

47. Édouard Pommier, "Naissance des musées de province," in *Les Lieux de mémoire*, vol. 2, book 2, 451–95; Julia and Milo, "Les Ressources culturelles."

48. Thuillier and Vergnet-Ruiz, "Les Mille musées de France."

49. The number established is based on information contained in Barnaud, *Répertoire*.

50. *Répertoire général des collectionneurs*, drawn up by E. Renart, bookstore expert (Paris, 1908), cited in Thuillier and Vergnet-Ruiz, "Les Mille musées de France."

51. Ibid.

52. This information can be found in Barnaud, *Répertoire*.

53. P. Marot, "Les Musées des sociétés savantes," cf. n. 44.

54. Pierre Angrand, *Histoire des musées de province au XIXe siècle*, 5 vols. (Les Sables d'Olonne: Le Cercle d'Or, 1984–88).

55. Thuillier and Vergnet-Ruiz, "Les Mille musées de France."

56. Stendhal, *Mémoires d'un touriste* (Paris, 1838); Hippolyte Taine, *Carnets de voyage: Notes sur la province, 1863–1865* (Paris, 1897); H. Lapauze, *Les Musées*.

57. J. Thuillier and Vergnet-Ruiz, "Les Mille musées de France"; André Chastel, "La Notion de patrimoine," in *Les Lieux de mémoire*, vol. 2, book 2, 405–50.

58. Barnaud, *Répertoire*.

59. Ibid.

60. Ibid. A map of these museums may be found in *Hier pour demain: Arts, traditions, patrimoine*, the catalog for the exposition at the Grand Palais, June 13 to September 1, 1980.

61. Barnaud, *Répertoire*.

62. Marot, "Les Musées des sociétés savantes," cf. n. 44.

63. Barnaud, *Répertoire*; Cabanne, *Guide des musées de France*.

64. Ibid.

65. Numbers furnished by Charles Du Bos, "L'Avenir des sociétés savantes," *Revue de l'histoire de l'Église de France* 7 (1921): 30–39, 252–266; Robert de Lasteyrie, *Bibliographie générale des travaux historiques et archéologiques publiés par les sociétés savantes de la France*, 4 vols. (Paris, 1888–1904); Lasteyrie, *Supplément 1886–1900*, 2 vols. (Paris, 1911–18); Lasteyrie, *Bibliographie annuelle des travaux historiques et archéologiques des sociétés savantes de la France*, 3 vols. (Paris, 1909–14); René Gandilhon and Charles Samaran, *Bibliographie générale des travaux historiques et archéologiques des sociétés savantes de la France, période 1910–1940*, 4 vols. (Paris, 1944–61).

66. Bercé, "Arcisse de Caumont"; Jean-Yves Guiomar, *Le Bretonisme: Les historiens Bretons au XIXe siècle* (Rennes: Société d'histoire et d'archéologie de la Bretagne, 1987); Gonzague Tierny, *Les Sociétés savantes du département de la Somme de 1870 à 1914* (Paris: Éd. du Comité des Travaux historiques et scientifiques, 1987).

67. *Répertoire archéologique de la France*, 8 vols. (Published by order of the Ministry of Public Instruction and under the direction of the Comité des Travaux historiques et des Sociétés savantes, 1861–88); *Dictionnaire topographique de la France*, comprising the ancient and modern names of places, 35 vols. (Published by order of the Ministry of Public Instruction, and under the direction of Comité des Travaux historiques et des Sociétés savantes, 1861–).

68. Charles-Olivier Carbonell, *Histoire et historiens: Une mutation idéologique des historiens français, 1865–1885* (Toulouse: Privat, 1976); Nardy, "Perceptions d'un espace régional."

69. *La Franche-Comté à la recherche de son histoire, 1800–1914*, Annales littéraires de l'université de Besançon (Paris: Les Belles Lettres, 1982); Bercé, "Arcisse de Caumont."

70. *Histoire d'Amiens*, under the direction of Ronald Hubscher (Toulouse: Privat, series "Pays et villes de France," 1986).

71. Guiomar, *Le Bretonisme;* Jean-Clément Martin, *La Vendée de la mémoire, 1800–1900* (Paris: Éd. du Seuil, 1989); *La Franche-Comté.*

72. Vovelle, "La Découverte de la Provence."

73. *Histoire de Colmar*, under the direction of Georges Livet (Toulouse: Privat, series "Pays et villes de France," 1983); *Histoire de Dunkerque*, under the direction of Alain Cabantous (Toulouse: Privat, series "Pays et villes de France," 1983).

74. Nardy, "Perceptions d'un espace régional"; Guiomar, *Le Bretonisme.*

75. "Programme d'études historiques et archéologiques," *Bulletin de la Société des sciences historiques et naturelles de l'Yonne* 1 (1847).

76. Robert Henri Bautier, "L'Apport des sociétés savantes à la publication des sources documentaires," in *Colloque interdisciplinaire sur les sociétés savantes.*

77. Nardy, "Perceptions d'un espace régional"; "Programme d'études historiques et archéologiques."

78. *Histoire générale et particulière de la Bourgogne*, vol. 4, 1781.

79. *Monographies communales, ou étude statistique, historique et monumentale du département du Tarn* (Toulouse, 1864).

80. Charles-Auguste de Robillard de Beaurepaire, *Répertoire bibliographique des travaux de Charles de Robillard de Beaurepaire* (Rouen, 1901).

81. *Histoire de Laon*, under the direction of Michel Bur (Toulouse: Privat, collection Pays et villes de France, 1987).

82. Ibid. Henri Marseille, "Origines et orientations de la société polymathique du Morbihan," in *Colloque interdisciplinaire sur les sociétés savantes*, 121–132.

83. *Bordeaux au XIXe siècle*, under the direction of Louis Desgraves and Georges Dupeux, in *Histoire de Bordeaux* (Bordeaux: Fédération historique du Sud-Ouest, 1969); François Portelli, "Un paysagiste archéologue bordelais," *Annales du Midi* (1967): 409–27.

84. Vovelle, "La Découverte de la Provence."

85. For example, Dr. Vincent, "Étude sur les patois de la Creuse: Limites des Lemovices, des Bituriges et des Arvernes retrouvées dans les limites de leurs dialectes," *Bulletin de la Société des sciences historiques et naturelles de la Creuse* 5: 226–316; Antoine Passy, "Essai sur les contrées naturelles de la France," *Recueil des travaux de la Société libre d'agriculture, sciences, arts et belles-lettres de l'Eure*, 3rd ser., 5: 129–50.

86. Désiré Monnier, *Croyances et traditions populaires, recueillis dans la Franche-Comté, le Lyonnais, la Bresse et le Bugey* (Lyon, 1874).

87. Nordman and Revel, "La Formation de l'espace français."

88. Émile Souvestre, *Le Foyer Breton: Traditions populaires* (Paris, 1845). On the ethnographic collections in Brittany, see "Le Mouvement des traditions populaires," in *Hier pour demain.*

89. Ronald Hubscher, "La France paysanne: Réalités et mythologies," in *Histoire des Français, XIXe–XXe siècles*, vol. 2, *La Société*, under the direction of Yves Lequin (Paris: Armand Colin, 1983); Catherine Bertho, "L'Invention de la

Bretagne: Genèse sociale d'un stéréotype," *Actes de la recherche en sciences sociales* 35 (1980): 45–62.

90. Ibid.

91. Paul Vernois, *Le Roman rustique de George Sand à Ramuz, ses tendances, son évolution* (Paris, 1962).

92. Belmont, "L'Académie celtique et George Sand."

93. Weber, *Peasants into Frenchmen*.

94. Gérard Cholvy, "Clercs érudits et prêtres régionalistes," *Revue de l'histoire de l'Église de France* (1985): 5–12.

95. Tierny, *Les Sociétés savantes; Histoire de Douai*, under the direction of Michel Rouche (Lille: Éd. des Beffois, coll. Histoire des villes du Nord-Pas-de-Calais, 1955).

96. Jean-Yves Guiomar, "Le *Tableau de la géographie de la France* de Vidal de La Blache," in *Les Lieux de mémoire*, vol. 2, book 1, 569–97.

97. Nordman and Revel, "La Formation de l'espace français"; Vincent Berdoulay, *La Formation de l'école française de géographie, 1870–1914* (Paris: Comité des Travaux historiques et scientifiques, Bibliothèque nationale, 1981).

98. Paul Vidal de La Blache, *Tableau de la géographie de la France*, vol. 1 of Ernest Lavisse, *Histoire de la France* (Paris: Hachette, 1902).

99. "Le Mouvement des traditions populaires," in *Hier pour demain*; Alfred de Foville, *Enquête sur les conditions de l'habitat en France* (Paris, 1894–99); *Habitat et espace dans le monde rural* (Paris: Éd. de la Maison des sciences de l'homme, 1988).

100. Paul Sébillot, *Le Folklore de la France*, 4 vols. (Paris, 1904–7).

101. Krzysztof Pomian, "L'Heure des *Annales*," in *Les Lieux de memoire*, vol. 2, book 1, 377–429.

102. Paul Lorquet, "Quels cadres choisir pour l'étude pyschologique de la France?" *Revue de synthèse* 2 (1901).

103. Maurice Agulhon, "Les Paysans dans la vie politique," in *Histoire de la France rurale*, under the direction of Armand Wallon and Georges Duby, vol. 3, *Apogée et crise de la civilisation paysanne, de 1789 à 1914*, under the direction of Étienne Juillard (Paris: Éd. de Seuil, 1976); Hubscher, "Modèle et antimodèle paysan."

104. Agulhon, "Les Paysans dans la vie politique."

105. Ibid.

106. Nordman and Revel, "La Formation de l'espace français."

107. M. Agulhon, "Les Citadins et la politique," in *Histoire de la France urbaine*, under the direction of Georges Duby, vol. 4, *La Ville de l'âge industriel*, under the direction of Maurice Agulhon (Paris: Éd. du Seuil, 1983).

108. *Histoire de Caen*, under the direction of Gabriel Désert (Toulouse: Privat, coll. Pays et villes de France, 1981); *Histoire de Carcassonne*, under the direction of Jean Guilaine and Daniel Fabre (Toulouse: Privat, coll. Pays et villes de France, 1984); Maurice Crubellier, in collaboration with Maurice Agulhon, "Les Citadins et leurs cultures," in *Histoire de la France urbaine*, vol. 4, see n. 106.

109. Crubellier, "Les Citadins et leurs cultures." [The monument commemorated the defeat of the English in the Hundred Years' War, a defeat that led to the English withdrawal from Normandy. TRANS.]

110. Ibid. Maurice Agulhon, "Imagerie civique et décor urbain," *Ethnologie française* 5, no. 1 (1975); reprinted in *Histoire vagabonde*, vol. 1, *Ethnologie et politique dans la France contemporaine* (Paris: Gallimard, 1988), 101–36; M. Agulhon, *Marianne au pouvoir: L'imagerie et la symbolique républicaines de 1880 à 1914* (Paris: Flammarion, 1989).

111. Georges Duby, *Le Dimanche de Bouvines* (Paris: Gallimard, 1973).

112. Maurice Agulhon, "La 'Statuomanie' et l'histoire," *Ethnographie française* 8, no. 1 (1978); reprinted in *Histoire vagabonde*, 137–85; Agulhon, *Marianne au pouvoir*.

113. *Histoire d'Angers*, under the direction of François LeBrun (Toulouse: Privat, coll. Univers de la France, 1975).

114. Agulhon, *Marianne au pouvoir*.

115. Ibid.

116. Lequin, "La France, une et indivisible?" Pierre Pasquini, "Le Félibrige et les traditions," *Ethnologie française* 18, no. 3 (1988). On the Félibrige, see in the same volume Philippe Martel, "Poètes et paysans: Les écrivains paysans dans le Félibrige."

117. Crubellier, "Les Citadins et leurs cultures."

118. Jules Michelet, *Notre France, sa géographie, son histoire* (Paris, 1886).

119. Thiébault Flory, *Le Mouvement régionaliste français: Sources et développements* (Paris: P.U.F., 1966).

120. "The remarkable thing in the history of France was to turn all of these accumulated fragments of population into a single people, and the most homogeneous people in the world, and also to make this land into a single land." Jean Brunhes, *La Géographie humaine de la France*, vol. 1 of *Histoire de la nation française*, under the direction of Gabriel Hanotaux (Paris, 1920).

121. Anne-Marie Thiesse, "Le Mouvement littéraire régionaliste," *Ethnologie française* 18, no. 3 (1988).

122. Ibid.

123. Daniel Nordman, "Les Guides-Joanne," in *Les Lieux de mémoire*, vol. 2, book 1, 529–67.

124. Paul Goujon, *Cent ans de tourisme en France* (Paris: Le Cherche-Midi, 1989).

125. Among others, Armand Vire, *Le Lot, Padirac, Rocamadour, Lacave* (Paris, 1907).

126. Nordman, "Les Guides-Joanne"; Goujon, *Cent ans de tourisme*.

127. Adeline Ripert, *La Carte postale: Son histoire, sa fonction sociale* (Lyon: Presses universitaires de Lyon, C.N.R.S., 1983).

128. Lequin, "Les Citadins, les classes et les luttes sociales"; *Histoire de Caen*.

129. *La Franche-Comté à la recherche de son histoire*.

130. Lequin, "La France, une et indivisible?"

131. Curnonsky and Austin de Croze, *Le Trésor gastronomique de la France* (Paris, 1933). Complete directory of the specialties from thirty-two provinces in France.

132. Guilaine and Fabre, *Histoire de Carcassonne;* Martin, *La Vendée de la mémoire*.

133. Catherine Bertho, "La Géographie symbolique des provinces françaises de la monarchie de Juillet à l'entre-deux-guerres," *Ethnologie française* 18, no. 3 (1988).

134. H. Toullier-Feyerabend, "Les Usages publicitaires," in *Costume, coutume*, catalog of the March–June 1987 Exposition at the Grand Palais (Paris).

135. *Cent ans d'affiches des chemins de fer* (Paris: La Vie du rail, 1980).

136. Pasquini, "Le Félibrige et les traditions."

137. *Catalogue spécialisé des timbres de France* (Paris: Amicus-Yvert et Tellier, 1975).

138. *Le Livre des expositions universelles, 1851–1989* (Paris: Éd. des Arts décoratifs, 1983).

139. Guilaine and Fabre, *Histoire de Carcassonne.*

140. Thiesse, "Le Mouvement littéraire régionaliste."

141. Christian Faure, *Le Projet culturel de Vichy: Folklore et révolution nationale* (Lyon: Presses universitaires de Lyon, C.N.R.S., 1989).

CHAPTER 7

THE PAINTER'S LANDSCAPE

❧

FRANÇOISE CACHIN

Close your eyes. Conjure up the French landscape. Pictures go by: private recollections, scenes from films, paintings. Filing past at random you have wheat fields, riverbanks, a cow standing by a pond, a canal with a passing barge, a cabbage patch, a road lined with trees, a steeple seen through branches, a cliff at Étretat, Antibes in the mist. Images inspired, pell-mell, by the paintings of Sisley, Cézanne, Pissarro, Corot, Courbet, and Monet, by the films of Jean Vigo, and by holiday memories. There are no archetypal images. Yet turn the kaleidoscope of memory slightly about the notion "typically French," and a sort of cliché forms: a gently undulating landscape with a winding road, a village steeple in the background, and a meadow behind a half-drawn curtain of trees. A picture that might be set anywhere in two-thirds of France, in the north or southwest. In the comforting, earthy resonance of that picture, the collective unconscious can find a symbol of peaceful togetherness, the setting for tradition. An edifying picture, a picture for an electoral campaign: it is no accident that the winner of the 1981 French presidential elections should have used it on his posters.[1] It brings to mind other clichés, verbal ones, such as "bien de chez nous" (there's no place like home), "la terre ne ment pas" (the earth doesn't lie), "la France à l'heure de son clocher" (France at the hour of its [village] steeple), which have a Pétainist and, as it were, after-dinner flavor to them. These, moreover, are the associations of ideas that television advertisements wish to conjure up when making use of undulating wheat fields and lowing cattle to sell cheese and sausage, or Mère Denis to promote some household appliance. The more industrial the product, the more archaic the image.

In the public memory of a people long predominantly rural and today urbanized, the painted landscape conjures up a distant family past. Even after several generations as city dwellers, many of us have heard of a mythical forebear so hale and hearty that she gave birth only after she had mown the field of clover or milked the cow. In folk songs and sayings, the landscape is where lovers take their afternoon nap, "couchés dans le foin / avec le soleil pour témoin" (lying in the hay / with the sun for witness), as well as one's final resting place: Mandrin's last glance, as he is about to be hanged, is at the countryside—"du haut de ma potence / je regardais la France" (from my high gallows / I looked upon France). Finally, our landscape covers us once and for all when we "mange les pissenlits par la racine" (eat dandelions by the roots)!

All these images clearly conjure up a rural past, and precisely at a time when the latter was no more than a place of remembrance; the enormous popularity of painted landscapes coincided with the mass urbanization of the nineteenth century. The triumph of the Barbizon school of landscape painters, and later the omnipresence of the theme in impressionist works during the last third of the century, were contemporary with the first great waves of rural drift and the development of the railroads. The fad for painted landscapes seems clearly linked to a twofold movement: the drift from the countryside to the cities in one direction, and, in the other, the growth of tourism and ease of transport.

The emergence and success of representations of the French landscape is likewise tied up with the growth of regionalist movements, first launched in literature by George Sand and given expression throughout the provinces in the last third of the century, from Mistral's Félibrige to Gaugin's "Britannizing" clogs—movements that were institutionalized by the first regionalist congress in 1883.

Now, the key question is to ask why specifically in France the national landscape in its painted form only really worked its way into the sensibility so long after its neighbors, in particular its northern neighbors. There would seem to be two obvious reasons for this. To begin with, a nation with such a long-standing peasant tradition, steeped in the day-to-day reality of the countryside, was unable to conceive of an emblematic landscape, especially since the extreme diversity of the French landscape makes it difficult, a priori, to symbolize the country by a single image. One's mental image of France is, first and foremost, abstract, historical, allegorical. After all, the colored map, the contours of which have changed relatively little in the course of time, has been the face of France for generations of schoolchildren. It presents a convincing form in which all differences—of climate, vegetation, physical type, language, mentality, sky color—are unified by an outline that is geometric, balanced, pleasing to the mind for being concentrated (though not without one or two fidgety and mischievous cut-outs in the northwest), and closed like a fist in which all its disconcerting variety is contained. The geographers' hexagon overlaps nicely with a demand for unity.

The painted images of the French landscape would be slow to acquire an identity; radiating out little by little from the centralizing heart of Paris and the Île-de-France—and, more broadly speaking, from the Loire to the English Channel—they would only be charged with signals of recognition once they were able to present a unifying image through the actual view of the country they provided. It is as though the most representative landscape was the setting that allowed the country to endure, to put down strong chronological roots, on those very sites that lie at the heart of national history, where nature is interwoven with the marks of time.

This crystallization of the French landscape occurred very late in Europe. There was a German landscape by the fifteenth century—the forest—and a Dutch one by the sixteenth century—a road, a windmill, a seascape, all under the same boundless sky. There was also an English landscape that was national in feeling: tall trees above inimitably green grass, a nature cultivated for its beauty and not for its yield, and seen through the eyes, not of the peasant, but of the squire. Is this because the latter were nations of burghers, merchants, navigators, and landed gentry, whereas the classical order and the royal power had impressed on France, from the Renaissance to the late eighteenth century, a centralizing, ideal model, steeped in classical antiquity? An aesthetic based on court life and sociability will favor portrait and history painting. Landscape, as a mirror of the country, could be conceived, as in the Netherlands or England, only in a universe that was more democratic, more homogeneous ethnically and geographically, and less bound to the ideal of reason. Nature and origins divide and individualize; ever since the Renaissance, the French moral and aesthetic model had been built on all that transcended differences, spreading its influence outward from the court.

In France, nature would long be tolerated only in an idealized form, refined by distance or time. Classical French landscape painters, such as Poussin or Le Lorrain, painted Italy or an ideal landscape based on the Roman *campagna*. The triumph of this rationalized landscape is the garden of Versailles, where a divine order and picturesque symbolic mythology organize a nature that is controlled, civilized, and strictly regulated.

Figure 7.1
"Follow me! Keep your confidence in the eternal France." Poster by Villemot for Philippe Pétain, 1940.

The painted French landscape appeared at precisely the same moment that this "French-style" garden, which imposed order on nature, disappeared. It was in the late eighteenth century, at a time when England was passing on to us a taste for the "natural" landscape garden, that an idyllic and "sensitive" new image of the countryside appeared: it was no longer the place where the peasant's labors attached themselves to the soil, nor the woodland setting where hunts went by, but a countryside "for dreaming," the countryside of an enlightened Third Estate, midway between the rustic universe of the farmer and the ideal cosmos of the landscape garden in the manner of Le Nôtre. This sociological "recycling," as it were, of the French landscape, which gave rise to the great age of national landscape painting, would blossom in the early nineteenth century, when Italy and the classical model were overtaken, in the French sensibility, by the culture of the north, and the royal model by the democratic ideal.

Indeed, French landscape painting took on a dominant role in the history of art only with the "realist" movement and the democratic aesthetic of the nineteenth century, at the very moment a national history aiming to be that of a people and a place, rather than of a king and a heaven, was developing. Its rapid growth is very closely bound up with the movement of contemporary ideas, as the determination to paint a real landscape that was both a mirror of daily life and a place where one put down roots gradually (between the late eighteenth century and the 1830s) replaced the idealized, "historical" model and the metaphorical framework previously furnished by scenes from the Bible or mythology. Freed from the spell, the French landscape became a natural environment that was in itself a motif of lyricism and meditation, a school of truth and modesty, and a source of refreshment on which national continuity could draw. Barbizon had replaced Versailles.

The link between national identity and landscape art was crucial, or structural, for a relatively short period, roughly from the Barbizon school to Bonnard, reaching a peak with impressionism and postimpressionism—broadly speaking, from the 1830s and 1840s to the early twentieth century. These dates, however, correspond to a key moment in the crystallization of an identity. The contemporary movement in painting was one of its forms, and not merely, as it is traditionally seen to be, from Barbizon to the impressionists, an impulsive transcription of reality by individual sensibilities.

This link, of which the artists involved were certainly unaware, is not the only one they kept with history. Even if, for the time being, they were misunderstood, they were in line with the major movements of ideas of their day and, like the latter, did not come about, as romantic criticism and the modern cult of the artist might lead us to believe, through spontaneous generation. They were equally attached, both in what they rejected and in what they inherited, to a tradition—if only by fits and starts.

THE FRENCH LANDSCAPE: ITS EMERGENCE AND ECLIPSE

For a long time in medieval France there were doubtless only two images of landscape: the place where you lived and which gave you your livelihood—the land of subsistence; and then a transcended landscape, the image of an ideal nature with which you no longer struggled—the earthly paradise.

Images of nature could, of course, be found at the time, but they acted as scenery: forests for hunting,[2] walled gardens for paying court, or metaphorical landscapes that provided settings for scenes from the Bible. For a long time, both in miniatures and medieval mysteries, reality was

coded: a rock meant a mountain, a tree the countryside, two trees a
forest. And it was thanks to artists from the north that the French
landscape briefly made an appearance before going into a partial eclipse
for three centuries.

The circumstances were both particular and unique. The national
landscape arose in the early fifteenth century when northern practitioners received large commissions from the aristocracy. Chronologically, the
first real French landscape appeared, it seems, in the *Heures du maréchal de
Boucicaut* (1405–8).[3] A few years later, the Limbourg brothers were entrusted by their patron, the duc de Berry—who was narcissistically com-
missioning portrait after portrait of his own person and possessions, including his dogs and crockery—with illustrating his book of hours with
pictures of his châteaus surrounded by his estates: he asked the Limbourg
brothers for a portrait gallery of his residences. Glorifying and didactic,
it was the first in a long series of topographic commissions by the central powers that can be followed down over the years to the ports of
France commissioned by the marquis de Marigny in the eighteenth century or the photographic reports instigated by large nineteenth-century
companies—that, for example, of the new French landscape, transformed
by railway architecture, commissioned in 1855 by the Chemins de Fer
du Nord.[4]

These miniatures, like Fouquet's *Heures d'Étienne Chevalier* forty
years later, immediately brought together themes that would each have a
destiny of its own in French painting: a Bible scene (developed in history
painting); a recent construction—château, church, or walled town (destined for topographic painting); a seasonal image (in its historical form
leading to Poussin, in its naturalistic form to impressionism), and an image of rural labor, whose belated offshoots would be Millet, Jules Breton,
Bastien Lepage, or even Van Gogh. Before each pictorial genre had been
determined everything was concentrated here with genius and naiveté,
in an attempt at naturalism that would shortly, with the coming of court
society and a centralizing monarchy, be pulverized by the Renaissance,
humanism, the codification of genres, and Italian supremacy.

It is interesting to observe in this connection the extent to which the
historiography of French art under the Third Republic stressed the national character of Fouquet and the master of Moulins when compared
with painters from the north, such as the Limbourgs or Van Eyck, and
sought native origins for the French landscape: "Fouquet will make do
with a landscape in the Cher with its humble little valley, its peaceful
river," whereas in the work of the Limbourgs, who were Flemish, there
is "no genuine emotion when faced with truth that is perfectly straight-
forward and naive, no hint of that respect in the presence of a patch of

Figure 7.2
"Calm Strength. President François Mitterand." Poster by the Roux-Séguéla Agency, 1981.

nature that one finds in the work of the master of Moulins, [who was] reserved, restrained, modest, and as it were humble when confronted with the tiniest blade of grass. . . . One senses that the Frenchmen are deeply imbued with recipes imagined at home answering to a need for calm, tact, and good taste."[5] In short, it's Fouquet and the master of Moulins, viewed like the "bonhomme Corot" around 1900. We will not dispute the stylistic and historical veracity of these remarks: Fouquet had been through Italy, and what the author describes could equally be applied to the pictures painted by the Flemish Limbourg brothers, even if they were still colored by Gothic taste. They testify, however, to the republican canonization of fifteenth-century landscape painters by nineteenth-century sensibilities.

Moreover, whatever their sources, the miniatures of the *Très riches heures* exert their fascination to this day. To begin with, through the charm of a naive and accurate historical report, on the banks of the Loire or the Île-de-France, in which lords and serfs are presented side by side as models of different views of history, one focused on kings and events, the other on humble folk and attitudes of mind; ancestors painted, moreover, under the same light as ours and in sites that have changed, certainly, but are familiar, being dominated by "our" châteaus and "our" cathedrals. These miniatures conjure up a delicious sense both of distance in time and of continuity, giving a visual perspective to our sense of belonging historically to French territory. Here, seasonal farm work—plowing, seeding, grape picking, harvesting—is described without the kind of underlying edifying commentary one finds in nineteenth-century representations of the rural world. Our own rural past is present, but suffused with a sort of serene grace in a cosmos whose upper part— the cosmic calendar—ensures eternity. The grapes that are to produce "our" Saumur wine are shown being harvested outside the château (it was with the aid of this miniature, moreover, that the château was partially reconstructed in 1932).[6] A meadow is being mown outside the Île de la Cité, opposite a Sainte-Chapelle that is unchanged.[7] Our national heritage sites are also situated in a religious eternity: Saint Michael struggles with the dragon before Mont-Saint-Michel; Fouquet portrays Job with his dung heap outside the dungeon of Vincennes and Saint Martin in front of the bridge of Notre-Dame, while the magi of the Limbourg brothers meet on the square there.[8] Other miniaturists locate their symbolic scenes in landscapes that are always familiar, such as the country footpath where "Coeur" and "Humble Requête" meet on horseback in the work of the master of the *Coeur d'amour épris*.[9]

Appealing to a public memory that unites the rural past, religious beliefs, and historical sites that are still visible to this day, it is not surprising that these miniatures should always have been accorded, independently of any artistic considerations, a particular place in our imagery—a place, moreover, that has been given a new lease on life by cinematic reconstructions such as *Les Visiteurs du soir* or Laurence Olivier's *Henry V.*

Besides, for quite some time these were the only paintings to provide us with an image of our country. Indeed, the "French" landscape as an image of national identity and memory later disappeared for nearly three centuries. As a result of the supremacy of the artistic model established by the Italian Renaissance, which was to dominate French taste from the early fifteenth century on, landscape was very low in the hierarchy of genres. Let us recall the crushing irony with which Michelangelo spoke of Flemish landscape painting: "nothing but rags, hovels, fields of greenery, shadows of trees, and bridges, and rivers, that they call landscapes, and lots of figures here, and lots of figures there."[10] After the Carracci, the ideal landscape was at last established in all its grandeur by the Frenchmen Poussin and Le Lorrain, Frenchmen from Rome painting "Roman" landscapes that had been recomposed, idealized. Before long,

Figure 7.3
Pol de Limbourg (15th century), The Château of Saumur, from the *Très riches heures du duc de Berry*.

landscape would be codified into two major genres, the heroic style and the rural or pastoral style. Roger de Piles very clearly defined the basic elements of the classical landscape to be used by French painters: in the heroic style, "if nature is not expressed as we happen to see it every day, it is at least represented there as one imagines it ought to be"; in the rural

Figure 7.4
Master of the Coeur d'amour épris (15th century), *Meeting of Heart and Humble Request.*

style, "the various regions are represented [in such a way that they] appear not so much cultivated as abandoned to the vagaries of nature alone."[11] Whatever the genre, landscape should be subordinated to the representation of figures, the rural style to the heroic style, color to design, and landscape painting to history painting: in short, the real to the ideal. The subsequent history of French national landscape painting would be determined in great part in opposition to these definitions, as the vision of truth—a truth made up precisely of chance and vagaries—came to supplant an order imposed upon the world.

Whenever a landscape painter was needed to paint "backgrounds" or scenery for battles, a Flemish painter such as van der Meulen would be called in. And when Poussin painted *L'Été* (Louvre), he portrayed it as a deified field in which costumed models with noble gestures are inscribed within an ideal, geometric landscape, the image of a higher order applying to divine greatness: trees of paradise, classical constructions, *fabriques* that situate a metaphorical harvest in a timeless order.

Figure 7.5
Jean Fouquet (1415–1481), Saint Marguerite and Olibrius, from the *Heures d'Étienne Chevalier*.

The landscapes of Poussin and Le Lorrain would dictate the model to be followed until halfway through the eighteenth century. Taught at the École des Beaux-Arts, historical landscape painting would be pursued under their tutelage throughout the nineteenth century, while resisting the realist trend. So powerful was their model that techniques were invented to help landscape painters impose this ideal vision on their gaze: the famous "Lorrain glass," which enabled a landscape to be seen through the gilded varnishings of Claude, then a box the painter would use to frame a section of countryside that lent itself to the ideal model of the Roman *campagna*.[12] By the nineteenth century, this canonical landscape was no more than an academic cliché, and it wasn't until the end of the century that the avant-garde—in particular, Seurat and Cézanne—were able to recover the spirituality of Poussin's compositions in the observed French landscape. It was indeed to Poussin and the great tradition that these two artists referred when, after the concrete realism of the Barbizon artists or the impressionists, they sought to recover a conceptual grandeur that mere imitation kept strictly confined to the level of sensations. The genius of Cézanne lay in his ability to reconcile very faithful images of his native countryside with an ideal reconstruction—which, in his case, no longer entailed transformations imposed on natural reality, but were his way of bringing out their "cosmic" and abstract structure—a kind of ideal essence, as it were. Moreover, his declared aim was "to do Poussin after nature" and make impressionism into "something sturdy, like the art of museums."[13] This was also, using other means, the "scientific" and metaphysical ambition of Seurat's landscapes. In each case—the countryside around Aix for the one, for the other the Channel ports—the almost obsessive loyalty to place is very striking to the contemporary eye. This makes the transfiguration all the more noticeable. The metaphysical image has no need of church or parable any more: nature itself is spiritual and an expression of eternity.

NATIONAL NATURE AND HISTORY

What the painted landscape was to become for nineteenth-century France was heralded by the novel in the early seventeenth century, and under circumstances that suggest analogies. *L'Astrée* associates a particular French landscape—the Forez—with the national identity, at a time when royal power—Henri IV—had undertaken to unify the country. As with the Barbizon school in the nineteenth century, the countryside is held up as an antidote to the corrupting life of town and court, and the favored territory of historical roots. The enclosed space in which the novel is set, in a mythical Gaul, has enabled its inhabitants to resist "the extreme tyranny of the Romans, not only over possessions, but over souls."[14] Recourse to origins and national identity involves being faithful to a place and refusing Italianness, just as it would, in a different form, in the history of painting two centuries later.

Indeed, the same ideas turn up in the mid-nineteenth century—for example, when the Goncourts cite landscape painting as a source of refreshment on which the nation can draw:

> Landscape is the victory of modern art, it is the honor of nineteenth-century painting . . . yes, the Old World is looking back at its childhood, at the green and blue cradle in which its heroic soul once wailed. Weighed down by the centuries, it is returning to all these lovely things, to this heavenly theater where it now performs . . . the

epic poem of its nomadic, agricultural, and warlike youth . . . at a
time when a path through the meadows was the road . . . and God
the general forestry commissioner.[15]

Admittedly, between Honoré d'Urfé and the Goncourts the image
of the national territory had had time to appear—very gradually—in
French art, and to confer the stamp of respectability on the observation
of nature.

The titles of landscape paintings exhibited in the Salons from the
time they first opened is very interesting in this respect, and Monet's
famous *Impression, soleil levant,* which gave its name to the impressionist movement in 1874, is simply a new form of the titles traditionally
found in Salon catalogs, albeit the subject is no longer, as it was in historical landscape painting, the biblical or mythological scenes once depicted there. The subtitle "painted after nature" appears as early as the
eighteenth century.[16] Before long, the precise moment would be indicated: for example, "on a moonlit night,"[17] or even "the time of day is
morning."[18] Next came "effects," at the turn of the century, at the time
of a living, preromantic nature. Not long after that, to details of locality,
hour, or weather, "study after nature" would be added, at a time when
it was not yet self-evident.[19] It is, of course, obvious that landscape
painters paint from nature, even if, up until the middle of the century,
the final painting was made in the studio. As early as the first quarter of
the nineteenth century, landscapes entitled "recollections" of such and
such a place began to appear in the Salons,[20] indicating the work of
reconstruction that had been done from sketches made from life. Not
long after, Corot would turn these landscapes that had been observed,
then recreated through memory, into archetypes, such as the famous
Souvenir de Mortefontaine in the Louvre, which is a synthetic reverie of
the Île-de-France. The Salon titles make fairly clear the attitude toward
landscape, the moment at which it ceases to be a piece of scenery, a "fantasy country," and becomes a definite place, part of the inhabited
world. Slowly, over a century and a half, the French landscape became
a motif that gained in definition ("seen from"), then surrendered definition to that of the artist, who conveyed the effects it made on his
sensibility ("effects"), memory ("recollection"), and finally sensation
("impression").

Let us briefly call to mind some of the stages that marked the shifts
in sensibility, taste, and memory in the way French people saw their landscapes, from the latter part of the eighteenth century to the crucial years
of crystallization, 1820 to 1830.

Even if most landscape paintings up until 1830 or thereabouts belong to the "historical," "heroic," or "ideal" genre, a spectacular increase can be observed in the subject from the latter part of the eighteenth century on. Statistics for the Salon between 1759 and 1781 show that, for a total number of exhibited works that had nearly doubled in twenty years (124 to 232), history painting had increased proportionately (from 34 to 83), portrait painting and still lifes had declined (from 41 to 37 and from 16 to 12, respectively), and landscape painting had risen (from 11 to 68).[21] The increase was spectacular and would continue during the Revolution and under the Empire, despite the official neoclassical ideology.[22] All painting was doing here was following that general shift in eighteenth-century sensibility of which Jean-Jacques Rousseau had been the triumphant expression. Whether literary or painted, landscape at the time was the embodiment of the natural state of the world, a privileged setting for the emotions. Needless to say, like the child or the good savage, landscape represented that good nature as against bad culture that, by osmosis and effusiveness, constitutes a source of inner refreshment.[23]

It's the "mood" landscape dear to Diderot, Rousseau, and, in some ways, Chateaubriand, who would be the first to transcribe painted landscapes in literature: in *Mémoires d'outre-tombe,* the images of a Breton Atlantic awash with his own ego, or of the shores of the Mediterranean haunted by Napoleon, are paintings by Joseph Vernet.

But in the eighteenth century, the landscape in which you dreamed, collected plants, or immersed yourself in the childhood of the world was not the only type of landscape that existed. In the age of the *Encyclopédie* there was a landscape made up of knowledge, landmarks, and voyages, notably in France itself. An entire poetic rhetoric based on the England of Thompson and Young was already celebrating national nature: Bernis's *Les Géorgiques françaises,* Delille's *Les Jardins,* and Saint-Lambert's *Les Saisons.*[24] By the turn of the century, a genuine topographic catalog of France was in the making; the earliest systematic publications of *Voyages pittoresques*—"hydrographic, picturesque, physics, historical, moral, political, and literary paintings"—were set in motion by Louis XV's first *valet de chambre,* Jean-Joseph de Laborde. After a project on Italy, he undertook the *Voyage pittoresque de la France, ouvrage national dédié au roi,* of which only four volumes, illustrated by regional topographic artists (1780–92), appeared of the twelve announced, the undertaking cut short by the Revolution.

The landscapes of Joseph Vernet and Hubert Robert gave expression to these two different trends. On the one hand, we have "Rousseauist" nature painting; on the other, landscape painting as a spatial and historical inventory of France—sometimes in different paintings destined for a specific market, but sometimes in the self-same canvas. For example, a landscape with ruins is both a definite place and the stuff of dreams.

At the head of the category "inventory of France" may be classed the ports of France series (1754–65) commissioned from Joseph Vernet by the marquis de Marigny, a report extolling the activities of the kingdom. In this portrait of a maritime France, the composition and grouping of figures indicate calm, prosperity, economic activity, and strategic strength. These harbor portraits are nothing if not taken from life and portray a carefully detailed variety (regional costumes, activities peculiar to each port) that is nonetheless unified in somewhat similar compositions depicting places and moments related to the grandeur of France as it faces the open sea.

Now, what could only have been a work of royal commission was immediately a great public success. The series was circulated widely in the form of engravings in the latter part of the eighteenth century and regularly thereafter through the chalcography practiced at the Louvre, whose reproductions, constantly reprinted, would decorate for a century—and still do to this day—the walls of numerous second homes, like "family portraits" of a common topographic past.[25] Though somewhat disdained by critics and theoreticians, from Roger de Piles in the early eighteenth century to Diderot later on, a great many regional painters—the French equivalents of Italian *vedutisti* such as Guardi or Panini—reflected an interest and a local market for "paintings of views." Let us cite, by way of example, Boissieu in Aix, or Lacroix in Marseilles.

Realism of vision was increasingly appreciated. Diderot was enchanted by an illusionist painting: "Look . . . with a glass which shuts out the edge [i.e., the frame], and forgetting suddenly that you are examining part of a painting, you cry out, as though you were placed on the top of a mountain, spectators of nature itself: O what a beautiful view!"[26] This taste for the reconstructed picturesque obviously required on-the-spot observation and sketches after nature, but this was not something new; Poussin, Watteau, Le Lorrain, Boucher, all worked in this way. "On Sundays and holidays," a contemporary of Boucher's tells us, "his main pastime was to go to the forest of Saint-Germain, to Chantilly, to the Bois de Boulogne, and study landscape, tree trunks, plants, stormy skies, horizons."[27] Late-eighteenth-century France reveled in displays of weather, a taste introduced from Flanders and the Netherlands and even exported to England since Loutherbourg, one of the star landscape painters of Diderot's Salons, went to London in the 1790s and founded "a small theater without actors called Eidophusikon [display of nature], depicting landscapes set in motion mechanically. The aim of the operation was to present nature's atmospheric transformations on the stage"; the method caused a sensation in London and was imitated by Gainsborough.[28] It is amusing to note, moreover, that the fashion for "marvelous clouds" and changing skies then crossed back over the channel at the turn of the century, with the vogue for Bonnington in Paris around 1824–26, before blossoming out with Boudin and Monet.

In the eighteenth and early nineteenth centuries, of course, these life studies of trees and skies were merely working models on which the final composition was based. In his famous manual of landscape painting, published in the year VIII, the historical landscape painter Valenciennes encouraged all forms of life study as a catalog for the studio. At the time, even the most traditionalist of painters would urge students at the École des Beaux-Arts to study after nature: "Let them take their beggar's pouch, a staff, and a box of colors and, after giving the arid white powder of the School in the rue des Petits-Augustins a good shake, go round France and Italy working."[29]

Little by little, these "preliminary notes" rose in the hierarchy of taste and ultimately culminated in impressionism; the latter, according to a study typical of a revisionist movement in contemporary art history that tends to upgrade academic art, merely transposed onto the "finished" painting the sketch made by landscape painters trained at the École.[30] In short, the "sketch" had undergone a sea change and evolved into the work.

The reform of the Concours de Rome shows that the very structures of the academy had evolved in response to a growing interest in landscape: in 1817, a Grand Prix de Rome was set up for historical landscape, then, from 1821, a new competitive exam (every four years) for "the landscape sketch." The latter broke down into two parts, one for trees and one for the landscape sketch proper.[31] Despite these efforts, the mediocrity of the winners of the Prix de Rome was becoming so apparent that the competitive exam for sketches was dropped in 1863. As we shall see, by this time the talented landscape painters were elsewhere.

Before long, the pressure of surrounding taste was such that even the staunchest upholders of historical landscape painting gave in: at the Salon of 1839, the Ingrist Paul Flandrin had exhibited a landscape in the manner of Poussin, *Adieu d'un proscrit à sa famille;* in 1852, he showed it again, unchanged (getting round Salon regulations, which did not allow you to exhibit the same work twice), calling it this time round *Les Montagnes des Sabines* and thereby transforming an image from antiquity into nothing more than a landscape of the Roman countryside.[32] What had taken place in French art over this period that even a Flandrin should clamber down from the country of the gods to that of the tourist?

NORTH AGAINST SOUTH

While landscape painting, albeit "historical," was being accorded more and more importance in the teaching at the École des Beaux-Arts, shaping whole generations of artists (Aligny, Desgoffes, Paul Flandrin, Français, and Michallon, among others) who Musset once said seemed "to have carried over into landscape, a modern invention, the love of modeling dear to Antiquity,"[33] a movement in landscape painting, at once romantic and realist, was developing out of the various eighteenth-century trends.

In this dichotomy between historical and realist landscape painters something of the quarrel between Homericists and Shakespeareans in the literary movement of the day can be found. The opposition involved a rift not only between ancients and moderns, but also between the culture of the south and that of the north. There can be no question that, little by little around the turn of the century, after the neoclassical movement, the fall of the Empire, and the return of peaceful relations between England and France, the artistic climate changed—not only in respect of Delacroix, who took his themes from works by Byron and Shakespeare, but also in respect of those new French landscape painters who, for the sake of convenience, were called "romantics," then "realists," and were characterized by their attachment to nature and the French territory.

These young artists were no longer necessarily trained in Rome and came increasingly to admire northern models of landscape painting—historical models in the case of Flemish and Dutch painters, and contemporary models from England—who led them to observe nature without having recourse to convention.

This new interest in northern art is marked by a few well-known facts. In Paris itself, the tradition of the English topographic artists was maintained by travel books and prints portraying French sites, which were widely sold in studios.[34] The biggest illustrated publishing program of the period was *Voyages pittoresques et romantiques dans l'ancienne France,* which published nearly three thousand lithographs between the 1820s and 1878, and the title of which shows how intimately related the growth of national tourism and the quest for the past were at the time. It was a Franco-English venture, as it were, since the publisher was the famous Baron Taylor, an Englishman from Paris and friend to the entire romantic generation.[35] All the famous romantic painters took part in these illustrated reports, French and English alike: Isabey, Eugène Lami, and, above all, the young landscape painter Bonington, whose work played a major role among French artists of the 1820s and paved the way for the huge success of Constable's landscapes at the Salon of 1824, which focused the interest of young landscape painters of the romantic generation once and for all on his own source of inspiration: Flemish and Dutch painting.

In fact, the great landscape painters of these seventeenth-century northern schools had been an underlying presence ever since the eighteenth century. In the representation of a rural scene, even a localized one, not only the model but even the method employed and the arrangement of the various iconographic elements were of northern convention: Oudry's *La Ferme* was subtitled "in the Flemish taste." Pillement and Loutherbourg imitated Berghem and Dujardin, and Fragonard's landscapes between 1770 and 1780 or thereabouts were clearly inspired by Ruysdael, reproductions of northern works having long been widely circulated in the form of engravings.[36] In the early nineteenth century, not only could this stock of engravings still be found in plentiful supply in studios and in the homes of art lovers, but historical circumstances themselves led to a renewed interest in those specialties of northern art, genre scenes and landscapes. In particular, let us remember that, from 1793 to 1813, Paris was home to the Musée Napoléon, the contents of which had been plundered by the imperial troops from collections in Antwerp, Brussels, Berlin, Potsdam, Cassel, the stadhouder of Holland, and elsewhere before being returned in 1815.[37] An entire generation of artists had felt the shock of these collections, and the influence of this realist "northern" art had since been maintained by innumerable engraved reproductions and pedagogic landscape-painting manuals offering Dutch-style motifs in the countryside around Paris.[38]

Two artists trained in the late eighteenth century and today largely forgotten would carry over into France Dutch and Flemish conceptions of landscape as the forerunners of a new vision: Demarne and Georges Michel. Neither of them studied at the academy, but although Demarne presented varied images of the national territory that were always enlivened by a genre scene of northern inspiration, Georges Michel devoted his life to representing what at the time were the immediate outskirts of Paris: Montmartre, the Saint-Denis plain, and so forth, modest sites lacking in picturesque qualities, the beauties of which Gérard de Nerval was celebrating at exactly the same period.[39]

Like Renoir at the turn of the century mocking Gauguin for leaving for Tahiti—"One paints so well at the Batignolles!"—Georges Michel had found, in a restricted part of the Île-de-France, in its quarries, wastelands, and gloomy little hills dotted with windmills, a national translation of the Dutch landscape of Ruysdael and Rembrandt and was developing his theory of local rootedness: "The man who can't spend his entire life painting on four leagues of space is nothing but a blunderer in search of a mandrake and will never find anything but void."[40] It is an attitude at once modest and ambitious and, all things considered, was the one adopted by Corot, Pissarro, and Cézanne, and even by Bonnard in the twentieth century. The romantic critics were perfectly aware that the national image involved drawing on the northern model: "History should not be relinquished, but there can be no doubt that *we will only be in full possession of our genius* through genre painting,"[41] that is to say, landscape in particular. The critic Thoré, a patriot, republican, and defender of the landscape painters of Barbizon, held up the northern model *against* the Italian model: "The greatest painters of all ages and countries are precisely those who never went to Italy . . . imitation of Italy has always been harmful to all foreign works. Everywhere it has killed off the initial inspiration, poetic sentiment, individual style . . . it is good to be French in France, German in Germany, and so on."[42]

It was thus with the northern model in mind that, even before 1830, a whole new generation of young artists would seek inspiration on the outskirts of Paris, at Saint-Cloud, Sèvres, and, above all, Fontainebleau: Corot, prior to his stay in Rome (Corot, moreover, along with Daubigny, was one of the few landscape painters of that generation for whom the Italian countryside counted, though his vision was that of a realist), Huet, Diaz, Barye, Dupré, Charles Jacques, and Théodore Rousseau.

LANDSCAPE AS *LIEU DE MÉMOIRE*

The years around 1830, when for the first time the native French landscape came powerfully to the fore, coincided with the growth of the democratic "Sunday in the country" and the sentimental tourism of the romantic age. Think of the amorous escapades of George Sand and Musset among the rocks of Fontainebleau, or of Rosanette and Frédéric in Marlotte in *L'Éducation sentimentale*. Fontainebleau at the time was an accessible spot where bohemians from Paris could flourish in a "natural" setting that lent itself to fits of rapture and melancholy alike. These lovers' retreats were like a realization of the outpourings of Diderot, for whom landscapes were "magical mirrors," inviting us to muse not only on the passing of time but on absent love: "Why am I alone here? Why is there no one to share the charm and beauty of this spot with me?" he had cried on contemplating the bucolic scenes of Vernet.[43]

Figure 7.6
Joseph Vernet (1714–1789), *Port of la Rochelle* (1763).

The rural reveries of the early French romantics—Chateaubriand, Amiel, and Senancour, for example—were an echo of this. But if Fontainebleau, that "coarse, mute patchwork of small plains of heather, little ravines, and petty rocks,"[44] was hardly an ideal setting for these lovers of raging torrents and impassioned headlands, it was precisely on its simplicity, its more secret eloquence, that the painters of the 1830s would draw in formulating an image of the country that one might begin to call "national."

Indeed, for the founders of French landscape painting in 1820–30, Fontainebleau, which for romantic bohemians had been a place in which to get tipsy "acting out" the gentle reveries of Diderot, was something more essential: a *lieu de mémoire*. Huet, a landscape painter of the French Sturm und Drang who painted tempests and was enormously successful in his day, gave expression to the great tides of human emotion. The Barbizon painters, on the other hand, painted landscapes imbued with historical emotion. The French countryside they chose to portray, more distant from Paris than that of Georges Michel, was also more "primitive," a countryside of forests, moors, and marshland—the countryside of a "deep France," of a forested Gaul. All of a sudden, we are far re-

Figure 7.7
François Boucher (1703–1770), *The Fisherman* (ca. 1750).

moved from the rustic picturesque of the late eighteenth century but strikingly in tune with contemporary ideas.

Take the case of Théodore Rousseau, doubtless the best example and the finest of them all. His career was fairly typical of the great nineteenth-century landscape painters: a relatively humble background, early studies with an academic landscape painter that he soon abandoned, copies of Dutch paintings, rapturous wanderings in forests on the outskirts of Paris. Then, in 1830, he stayed in the Haute Auvergne, in "the reputedly wild, authentic country of the Arverni . . . where nature is in the same state of upheaval as in the early days of the world."[45] A friend of Gérard de Nerval and George Sand, Rousseau would always be attracted to landscapes that seemed to recall the origins of the world, France as it was before France existed. The age, moreover, was fascinated by natural sites suggestive of a remote past: Rousseau's famous *Allée de châtaigniers* was seen by critics either as a "druidic temple," or—after Chateaubriand—as a gothic vault,[46] but in either case as an allusion to the national past, whether Gallic or medieval. Rousseau himself, when painting a village,

Figure 7.8
Hubert Robert (1733–1808), *View from Marly near Saint-Germain-en-Laye* (ca. 1780).

was aware that he wanted to make a "painting of primitive customs."[47] Being close to Paris, the forest of Fontainebleau enabled him to present a fierce nature suggestive of the ancestral land from a time before the great clearings and the Roman occupation. It was this "Celtic" and Gallic France, this France as it was at the beginning, that at exactly the same period historians such as the Thierry brothers (above all Amédée, whose *Histoire des Gaulois* was a huge success in 1828) and the young Michelet, of course, were seeking to uncover and turn to good account.[48]

Though no particular text proves this (we know very little, unfortunately, about the reading habits of the artists in this group), it is clear that the painters of what is called the Barbizon school sought to express a nature inhabited by time and to set a new grandeur, natural and national, against the ideal nobility of the "historical landscape."

A fascinating to-and-fro of sensibilities was at work between 1820 and 1830, when painting was putting down roots in a landscape inhabited by time, and when history, with Michelet, was becoming a visualization of the French territory and a pictorial description. Michelet's *Tableau de*

Figure 7.9
Jean-Honoré Fragonard (1732–1806), *The Celebration at Saint-Cloud* (ca. 1777).

France is a panoramic, whirlwind view of the varieties of national land-scape—"history is above all geographic"—that, at the end of the chapter, comes lightly to rest, as it were, in the north of France, where "strong life" is to be found and "the great surge of nations has occurred."[49]

This convergence could also be found elsewhere at the same period. In 1829, Delecluze, a defender of historical landscape painting, presented students at the École des Beaux-Arts with a new method for elevating the art of observation to the dignity of history painting: "*The whole of nature is a setting for history* . . . the plains of Poitiers, the field of Agincourt, the villages of Marengo, of Tours, of Waterloo."[50]

Yet it was not so much battlefields that prompted the historical reveries of the great landscape painters of the time as sites "haunted" by an ancestral mythology and a tradition older even than the Greco-Roman-Italian culture of the academy.

The landscapes of Millet—a Norman peasant, not trained at Rome and associated with the Barbizon group in the 1840s—are inhabited by the peasants of his day. But he has stripped them of the folklore that would have turned his paintings into merely outmoded genre scenes and has conferred something timeless on them. The silhouettes of his figures, whose faces are generally concealed, are those of the eternal French peasant and even less individualized than those of Le Nain, who is part of the landscape and time. One only has to compare Millet's work with some of the rustic scenes being painted at the time in Germany, Italy, or even Russia—or with those, so popular in their day, of other French painters of nineteenth-century rural life (Rosa Bonheur, then Jules Breton, Lhermitte, and so on)—to feel in his work an iconography that has emerged from the "depths of time."

In their own way, Courbet's landscapes also have their roots in time. His series *Grandes vagues* (1869, Louvre; 1870, Berlin) can be considered alongside contemporary writings by Michelet and Hugo (*La Mer*, 1861, *Les Travailleurs de la mer*, 1866). The seascape becomes a spectacle whose lyrical aspect, new in painting, carries us off not only into the savagery of the elements but into their archaism; Cézanne rightly sensed that "his tide emerges from the depths of time."[51] His accumulations of rocks on the outskirts of Ornans appeal to geological continuity, and his *Chêne de Flagey*, also known as *Chêne de Vercingétorix* (Philadelphia), illustrates a folklore that, by the middle of the nineteenth century, was soon to turn national.[52] His oppressive undergrowth shows an all-pervasive nature that has nothing in common with the traditional view. Distance is abolished between the painter and the portion of nature that he sections off with his gaze. There is no longer any perspective, no longer any "viewpoint"; the painter plunges in, nature *is* the painter and gives expression to its fearsome "ego." It is not immaterial that the very center of Courbet's great allegorical composition, *L'Atelier*, should be a landscape of Ornans that the artist is in the process of painting with a brush pointed like the finger of God or a fairy's wand: it is the very heart of the painting, at once a manifesto of the artist's roots and an icon of realist landscape painting triumphant.

In mid-nineteenth-century France, painting as a portrait of one's native soil had indeed become a major genre in the Salon. In 1857, one of the best critics of the day, Castagnary, put forward a historical explanation for this all-pervading success: "Eclogues and idylls have nearly always been the indirect result of social unrest . . . the resurrection of landscape painting is largely due to this. To this current of ideas we owe *La Mare au diable, Jeanne* and *Les Paysans;* in art: Rousseau, Troyon, Daubigny, and Rosa Bonheur. It would seem that, swamped with violent emotions, disgusted by its own corruption, society has turned right back to the true . . . it has caught a glimpse, far from the loathsome cities . . . of rural life, its works and its pleasures. . . . It has recalled the path lost in corn, the windmill turning in the wind."[53] As if the sheep painted by

Troyon and Charles Jacque were forerunners of the consoling flocks of the communities founded in the Cévennes after 1968!

Some critics were more bitter and saw the success of landscape painting in the mid-nineteenth century—not long before impressionism—as a sign of the decadence of French art:

> How can you expect an era that is shriveled, positive, wholly given over to the appetites, lacking in virility, lacking in passion, and lacking in belief, to produce a powerful art capable of moving people! . . . Today, the sky is empty . . . God himself is made man . . . Jupiter is on the run . . . everything holds together, everything connects; little citizens, little literature, little apartments, little paintings. We no longer believe in gods and martyrs and heroes, but we still take pleasure in seeing the clear water flowing beneath the willows and we willingly contemplate the cows returning to their byres. That is the kind of painting we are fit for.[54]

The allusion to "little apartments" unfailingly calls to mind scenes such as that that in Maupassant's *Bel-Ami,* when his hero, who has just begun to rise in society, goes to dinner at his employer's home: after looking up, for want of something to do, at the wall, he hears M. Walter saying in the distance, visibly eager to show his possessions off to their best advantage: "'You're looking at *my* paintings!' . . . 'Let me show them to you.' And he picked up a lamp, so that we could make out all the details. 'Over here are the landscapes,' he said."[55]

The huge success enjoyed by French landscape painting in nineteenth-century society can, of course, be put down in part to "bourgeois" and democratic taste, comparable in the influence it exerted to the vogue for landscape paintings in seventeenth-century Dutch interiors. Here, too, in these ponds, these gusts of wind, these seascapes, and these riversides, something of one's roots and one's identity can be found. It is France in all its depth and variety that is possessed and tamed in these compartments, where nature is imprisoned in heavy, gilded, stuccoed frames placed edge to edge. In this respect, collections such as those of Chauchard and Thomy-Thiery, bequeathed in their entirety to the Louvre and hung there in several rows, are very revealing about the late-nineteenth-century fondness for "visual libraries" of this kind, machines for dreaming your country into a state of nature on the cozy walls of your apartment.

It might seem surprising today that the great collectors of this enlightened and well-to-do bourgeoisie should have held out against the impressionists until the turn of the century, when the latter's themes—all in all rather similar to those of Boudin or Corot—corresponded perfectly to their desires. This would be to overlook the novelty, shocking at the time, of their technique, and the unofficial channels through which, excluded from the Salon, they became known. Yet it was to the same circles that, in Europe and on the other side of the Atlantic, they would owe their success with succeeding generations. Apart from the fact that the extravagant prices paid for them give them the status of relics, in the twentieth century impressionist landscapes acquired the importance that religious paintings or historical parables had up until the nineteenth century. As a result of a shift in values, the sacred is now mediated through nature; the flickering lights of Renoir, the implacable structures of Cézanne, the hallucinatory water lilies of Monet all give a new shape, at once vague and pantheistic, to man's metaphysical longings and his ponderings on the mysteries of the world and time.

Landscape and Passing Time

In the nineteenth century, there was a gradual shift away from a more stagelike viewpoint to the very heart of landscape; we merge into the scenery, as it were. Trees, which ever since the seventeenth century had been placed to either side of the view like the two uprights in a theater, suddenly look familiar. They are there, they form part of the landscape, they are no longer props. In Corot's *Église de Marissol* (1866, Louvre), Pissarro's *Toits rouges* (Orsay). or Monet's *Printemps à travers les branches* (1858, Marmottan), for example, they act as a curtain between ourselves and the background—sometimes distant, sometimes near—formed by a village, a church, or passing clouds. They are portions of countryside captured by a person walking, and no longer picturesque "viewpoints" held up to the stationary traveler. Henceforth, we are merely passing through—going faster and faster, in fact, with impressionism, our senses more alert now that new sensations have been added to that of vision: we are sensitive to the wind, to smells even, in the glittering seascapes and leafy gardens of impressionism.

Historiography under the Third Republic was unanimous in viewing Corot, a painter who is crucial to our argument, as the most "French" of painters, if harmony, proportion, and "common sense" are to be considered national qualities. Corot's France is modest, peaceful, dignified, restrained. His vision is that of a peasant-bourgeois contemplating with wistful serenity an earthly estate where there is always something to conjure up his past, his passing. Corot is all about the grandeur of his "sweetheart France," a France that is earthy and alive, and if Baudelaire felt "he [didn't] have enough of the devil in him"—that he lacked imagination, in other words—he nonetheless recognized in Corot "a clear tone of voice that is at the same time modest and harmonious,"[56] a naiveté and love of nature that made him the ideal mouthpiece for the countryside of northern France, where the harmony of past and present is achieved quite naturally in a light at once subtle and precise. Take a look at *La Cathédrale de Chartres* (Louvre), for example. The facade stands quietly and without hierarchy beside two rather scrawny trees, and behind an embankment and a heap of stones indicating work in progress. Everything is on the same level, the timeless and the provisional, in the total unity of what he himself called his "little music."[57] In Corot's work, as in the work of all the best nineteenth-century French landscape painters, including the impressionists, painting from life, using a technique that was to become progressively more simplified and allusive, coincides with a modernity of vision and the "rendering," as it were, of something timeless. The landscapes of these painters express both the eternal and the familiar, so that for anyone who contemplates them today they evoke mixed feelings of belonging and melancholy. And the more precise the moment in time—a certain lighting, the wind blowing from this or that direction, the suggestion of such and such a temperature—the more the scene conjures up the everlasting cycle of the hours and seasons, the more aware we become of our attachment to the places being described, and the more reassuring these fleeting glimpses become. This vision of a gust of wind at sea by Monet, a humble copse by Pissarro, a rather gloomy sunset by Dupré or Rousseau, a curtain of trees by Corot, or the Mont-Sainte-Victoire by Cézanne is something we have felt, it has something of ourselves in it, it "feels like home." We have recovered these places and moments thanks to these artists, and, at the same time, we *see* our landscape through the image they have given us: this is how it was a century ago; these instants have outlived the painter and will outlive us. But this reassuring impression can also make us feel uneasy. "Vanitas under an open sky,"[58] landscape paintings are implacable memento mori, all the more so since the universe they describe is a familiar one.

The nineteenth century no longer needed ruins to conjure up the passing of time. In the eighteenth century, when Hubert Robert painted the arenas of Nîmes or the Pont du Gard, it was both a national image and an image of his own historical past. We know how successful this "poetics" of ruins was and the influence it had on the sensibility of its day: "Things get destroyed, are gone, will soon be gone. . . . We anticipate the ravages of time, and our imagination scatters over the earth the very edifices we inhabit . . . we are all that remains of a nation which has ceased to exist."[59] In Diderot's day, landscapes of ruins inspired philosophical reveries but did not cause bitterness or anxiety. In the mid-nineteenth century, however, there were times when even green nature itself was seen as that deathly, barren place where Baudelaire's "stupid plant-life" grew: "We go to the country with Saint-Victor, like shop assistants," wrote the Goncourts; "we walked along the Seine, in Bougival . . . we at last found a spot where there [was] neither a landscape painter sitting painting, nor a melon rib that someone had left behind. . . . To me nature is hostile; and the countryside seems a mortuary. This green earth seems to me like a huge cemetery, waiting. This grass grazes on man. . . . Trees, sky, water, it all reminds me of a ten-year plot."[60]

As a source of reveries that wound or soothe, the French landscape, particularly that celebrated by the impressionists and their successors, is precisely a sublimation of this countryside around Paris which, from Bougival to Asnières, haunted "shop assistants," the employees of Maupassant, and the *petite bourgeoisie* of Labiche.

PORTRAITS OF FRANCE AND POPULAR IMAGES

What is so French, then, about a French landscape?

If one tries to put together an Identikit picture made up of elements common to representative paintings from the late eighteenth century to the last third of the nineteenth century—from Boucher or Oudry, say, to Monet and Cézanne, and taking in the Barbizon school, Courbet, and Corot along the way—one ends up with a few recurring elements that help define what is specific to the national landscape, whatever corner of France it was painted in.

Let us first of all see what it is not. It is not sublime, and it is not picturesque. Nature is not dramatized: it is not a grand opera, it's a little ditty. It does not inspire sublime emotions in the way that mountains, waterfalls, natural curios, and grandiose sites do. After all, the national landscape might have immortalized "our" Alps and Pyrenees; it did not.

In other countries in the nineteenth century, nationalism liked to represent itself in spatial form—in Denmark, for example, from the turn of the century on, or in Russia, where landscape painters were associated precisely with the Old Russia nationalist movement. But it was the smallest and largest nations that between them produced "sublime" images of their country in the nineteenth century: Switzerland and the United States, whose landscapes are lyrical in themselves—the conquest of the sky and the conquest of the Far West.

Nothing of the kind exists in France. The landscape has long been domesticated and is characterized precisely by a harmonious and

Figure 7.10
Georges Michel (1763–1843), *Country Road.*

indissociable blend of culture and nature. There are even stereotypes of "natural" images that are traps, what appears to be countryside in reality being cultivated land—whether the forest of the blue line of the Vosges celebrated by Barrès, in fact planted in the late fifteenth century, or the cypress tree, the "natural" flame of Van Gogh's landscape around Arles, planted during the Second Empire.[61]

French landscape painting also implies a modesty, a vision that is comfortably enclosed. This is likewise true of the formats it employs. It is difficult to know whether this fondness for small canvases was determined by their appropriateness to the subject or in response to market demand: from Barbizon to the impressionists, paintings were made for apartments, no longer for châteaus or churches, and not yet directly for museums.

Figure 7.11
Turpin de Crissé (1782–1859), *Landscape* (1806).

The "archetypal" landscape is rustic, cultivated, under crop, enlivened by footfalls, the sound of bells, and, before long, the echo of a railway line. "Ah, my friend, how beautiful nature is in this little canton!" Diderot had proclaimed in his day.[62] It was still *nature put to use,* as celebrated in the *Encyclopédie,* submissive and transformed by human industry. What remains of "natural nature" is channeled, humanized, inhabited, haunted; even the "raw" nature of the Barbizon painters is not innocent but alludes to a remote cultural past. The French landscape perpetuates the image of a world that is old but carefully wrought, in which everyone can find visual recollections and a scenery that is theirs by inheritance. That the singularity and grandeur of the French landscape resides in the fact that it expresses, by virtue of its very limits, a principle of reality and endurance is felt more keenly perhaps by a foreign traveler. Thus Scott Fitzgerald, nostalgically contrasting before the Swiss Alps "the sense he had in finite French lanes that there was nothing more. . . . The Alpine lands . . . were not a being

Figure 7.12
Théodore Rousseau (1812–1867), *The Pond.*

here, as in France, with French vines growing over one's feet on the ground."[63]

This sense of continuity and belonging can be found in a minor but significant style of popular imagery such that it can be followed down from the pictures used in the late eighteenth century in almanacs—originally known as cabinet almanacs, then postal almanacs, then postal calendars—through the illustrations used for engraved vignettes and color lithographs, to the photographs that come with modern office calendars. Apart from the odd year when events or fashion briefly gave rise to new subjects (for example, a troubadour in 1824, the Paris–Versailles railway in 1847, or battle scenes during World War I), the same imagery can be found in calendars from the turn of the nineteenth century to the late 1960s, when landscapes were replaced by animals.[64] The return to landscape would seem to be of very recent date and to involve

Figure 7.13
François Millet (1814–1875), *Angelus* (1859), detail.

Figure 7.14
Gustave Courbet (1819–1877), *The Oak of Flagey* or *The Oak of Vercingetorix* (1864).

painting, since it turns up again in 1985 in the reproduction of a painting by Sisley.

In the nineteenth century, these images make repetitive use of rural scenes depicting farmers at work in the fields, lovers walking in the
country, riders going by, hunters, and anglers. The same vignettes and
pastoral scenes, moreover, can be found in such industrial products
as Liberty print fabrics, porcelain decoration, and wallpaper. Throughout the nineteenth century, these bucolic images would be framed by
tall trees in a scaled-down, popular version of the presentation used
for classical landscapes, the foreground being permanently occupied by
footpaths and gently sloping hills, the background by a windmill or a
church. The grove would remain the traditional image up until about

Figure 7.15
Gustave Courbet (1819–1877), *The Painter's Studio* (1855), detail.

Figure 7.16
Camille Corot (1796–1875), *The Cathedral of Chartres* (1830).

1835 and sometimes featured a walled country estate with English-style grounds.

These romantic calendars show the countryside that surrounds you and the one you possess, walled grounds being the domesticated countryside of the wealthy. During the same period, Balzac gave a very good description in *Les Paysans* of the inner and outer landscape represented by countryside and grounds; it is the same countryside, only put to different use.

In the early 1850s, calendar landscapes became more accurate and topographic, depicting "views" of towns in France and Europe. Henceforth, people were on the move, as the world opened up to the train. Similar imagery occurs in the same period in the forerunners to the cartoon strip, where four basic scenes are repeated over and over: an outing in the country, a boat in tow, a hunt in the marshes, a village fete. Many of the same motifs can be found in the color lithographs and photographs of early-twentieth-century calendars, which are more concerned with local character than unity. The French countryside is shown in all its diversity and folklore; since the 1930s, there has been no shortage of Breton women in traditional headdress or views of the walls of Carcassonne. Continuity in popular imagery is ensured, as it was a century earlier, by hunting and fishing; the theme is obsessive from the 1920s to the 1960s and takes up the same little figures used in the old almanacs, now seen at close quarters wearing modern dress and rubber boots. There is no end of fishermen standing watch in a torrent or sitting patiently in a boat or on a landing stage; no end of hunters lying in wait or proudly sporting their catch. From medieval tapestries to postal calendars, the unity of the French landscape seems to be bound up, in time-honored fashion, with hunting and fishing.

Similar remarks could be made concerning postcards over a shorter period. Though the images are unpretentious and often naive, their wide circulation has certainly played a role in making people aware of the multifariousness of national identity. As a rule, they are composed like paintings, the only reservation being that they depict famous regional sites—precisely those sites that landscape painters in the nineteenth century were generally loath to paint. In fact, they are nearly always urban landscapes in which the civic setting—town hall or war memorial—is altogether present. They, too, form part of the catalog of public memory and today provide French collectors less wealthy than those who acquire paintings with testimonies in situ of a recent past.

These popular images of the French landscape, found in calendars and postcards and redolent of the Third Republic, raise certain questions about the relations French landscape painters enjoyed with the Republic, even if ties of this kind were more often evoked by critics than by the painters themselves, with the exception, of course, of Courbet and Pissarro.

LANDSCAPE, REPUBLIC, NATION

Under the Restoration and the Second Empire, Philippe Burty tells us, "the label of realist was indistinguishable from that of Republican."[65] At the time, the realist painter was contrasted with the history painter, the painter of ideas; landscape painters, of course, were classed among the former. In fact, they were felt at the time to be painters of democratic outlook, as much for the models on which they drew as for the success they enjoyed, above all with a nonaristocratic public.

It is highly significant, moreover, that the successive fads in France for landscape painting were the work of an urban "Third Estate": from as early as the eighteenth century, the period that saw the official triumph of religious and history painting, "death inventories in bourgeois homes reveal[ed] increasing numbers of small landscape paintings."[66] The great majority of these, no doubt, were imported from and modeled on Flanders and Holland and may be an indication of city taste compared with that of the court.

The same unbroken thread that opposed realist art—genre and landscape painting—to the major genres of history painting and the painting of ideas supported by critics such as Delecluze, or modern painting of the imagination and the marvelous as defended by Baudelaire (for whom landscape was a poor source of inspiration, as it was for the century's leading lights, Ingres and Delacroix), can be found in the nineteenth century. Landscape painting as a mirror of French reality was supported and even guided by critics such as Burty, Champfleury, Castagnary, Planche, and Thoré, who all had in common the fact that they were republicans, revolutionaries of 1848, then opponents of the Empire.

It comes as no surprise that realist landscape painters (the Barbizon school, Courbet) should have received special support from one Republic after another. That of 1848, for example, commissioned large landscapes from painters turned down by the Salon under Louis-Philippe and, under the impetus of Charles Blanc, had large-format landscapes such as Rousseau's *Forêt de Fontainebleau,* Rosa Bonheur's *Labourage nivernais,* and Daubigny's *Les Bords de Seine* admitted into the Louvre.[67]

The government of the Third Republic, though it did not specially support the impressionists, nevertheless associated landscape painting, and especially open-air painting, with a hard-won liberty in which it saw analogies with its own new-found political freedom.[68] In his manifesto on the ties between the republican government and the fine arts in 1879, Jules Ferry praised—although posthumously, it is true—Théodore Rousseau, and, from the new school system, "an entire generation of artists [who are] pursuing a truth [that was] more fugitive but also more intimate, more difficult to grasp, but for that very reason more striking, and today known as open-air truth."[69]

The years 1880 to 1900 would be marked by important State or municipal commissions to decorate the walls of railway stations and town halls, with growing numbers of representations of local landscapes appearing alongside allegories and historical subjects.[70] Unfortunately, these commissions went more or less systematically to semiofficial painters or those from the "right background," those very painters who were to give more academic form to the discoveries of impressionist and postimpressionist painting, such as Gervex, Henri Martin, and Albert Besnard, painters Degas once described as "stand[ing] on our own two feet."

Of course, some of these decorations in which a localized landscape appears are of high quality—those of Puvis de Chavannes on Paris, for example, in the cycle devoted to Saint Geneviève in the Pantheon. But Manet is said to have offered in vain in 1879 to decorate the new town hall with scenes "portraying, to use an expression . . . that gives a good picture of what I have in mind: 'the belly of Paris,' with the different trades going about their business, the public and commercial life of our day. I would have Paris—Markets, Paris—Railways, Paris—Port, Paris—Undergrounds, Paris—Racetracks and Gardens."[71] Most of the decorations painted for official buildings under the Third Republic were historical or allegorical; topographical landscapes began to appear in town halls only gradually over the last fifteen years of the century. It was the age in which the painted ceiling of the restaurant in the Gare de Lyon displayed urban and maritime landscapes of places served by the Paris–Lyon–Marseilles line, in response to the regionalist program of the Third Republic to which the "mustachioed" parliamentary eloquence of the time bears witness:

> What other land in the world, for historical memories, living traces
> of the past, monuments of all styles, is more worthy than France of
> the admiration of genuine artists, and what favored land affords the
> most charming and the most grandiose displays of nature to the same
> degree as our old Gaul, where, from the misty hills of Armorica to
> the sunlit mountains of Provence, from the Vosges to the Pyrenees,
> and from the Pyrenees to the Alps, the most different climates, the
> most sundry aspects, the most characteristic sites, and the most varied

colorings are to be found. Let us see to it that our dear homeland is known and appreciated, not only by strangers, for whom Paris seems to be the sole attraction, but by the great many Frenchmen who are not really familiar with it, or don't appreciate it enough.[72]

This patriotic program for a France of "moderate hillsides," which would soon prove dear to Albert Thibaudet and the ideal framework for a Center-Left mythology, had its roots in the realist ideology of the mid-nineteenth century. Certain artists, such as Courbet, were very conscious of the will to paint and glorify their country: "Don't these people have a country, then? . . . To paint a country you have to know it. I know my country, I paint it . . . go and see, you'll recognize all my paintings."[73] At the same moment, critics were theorizing about this artistic patriotism: "Through landscape painting, art becomes national . . . it takes possession of France, of the soil, the air, the sky, and the landscape of France. This earth that has borne us up, this air we breathe, this harmonious and gentle whole which constitutes as it were the face of our mother country, we carry it in our soul."[74] Nor is this all: the landscape painter not only expresses a national truth, but works on behalf of national memory: "To paint what exists, at the moment you observe it, is not only to satisfy the aesthetic demands of your contemporaries, it is to write history for your future descendants."[75]

THE ECLIPSE AND TRIUMPH OF FRENCH LANDSCAPE PAINTING

Castagnary's text, written in 1867, which actually concerns the Barbizon painters, anticipates the huge success enjoyed today by the following generation of painters, the impressionists. This success, which has grown over the last few years, coincides with a new, more sociological approach to Monet, Sisley, Pissarro, and company, such as it is defined, after Meyer Schapiro, by contemporary English and American historians of impressionism.[76] Going beyond the technical novelties and expressions of individuality that caused the scandal at the time and the success enjoyed by the movement at the turn of the century and even as late as the 1960s, the current perspective tends to treat the impressionists more as witnesses than revolutionaries, more as makers of pictures than creators of form and style. It is as though, over time, now that the technical daring has been fully digested and overlaid by all the other stylistic inventions of one avant-garde movement after another, we have grown more attached today to the iconography of these works, which have shaped our vision to such a degree that this or that bank of the Seine in the Île-de-France, such and such a view of the Normandy coast or a Parisian boulevard seen

Figure 7.17
Camille Pissarro (1830–1903), *Entrance to the Town of Voisins* (1872).

from above in a certain light have created archetypes underlying the way we actually see these places today.

Impressionism is our best ambassador: "The world knows more about France through their vision than it knows from experience of this country. Impressionist landscapes have become the universal touchstone of the general public's taste, supplanting the work of Raphael, Leonardo, and Michelangelo in the universal public imagination."[77]

Even in twentieth-century France, landscape painting from the last century has little by little become part of the national imagery while gradually disappearing from living art. A French landscape tradition was perpetuated between the two wars by artists of unequal quality, such as the former Fauves Derain and Vlaminck or younger artists, "Montparnassians" of the soil such as La Patellière, Lhote, Segonzac, and company,

Figure 7.18
Claude Monet (1840–1926), *Spring through the Branches* (1878).

who, in the 1920s and 1930s, satisfied a prevailing nationalist and regionalist taste that was often rather backward-looking in inspiration. After the internationalist outbursts of the turn of the century, French art at
the time was in the midst of a "return to order," a jingoistic falling-back
brought about by the war. The regional populist movement in painting
saw landscape as the expression of a particular "French quality" centered
on tradition: Derain saw himself as the heir to Corot, Courbet, and the
seventeenth-century landscape painters, Vlaminck was forever painting
his stereotype of a village street in a storm or the snow, Utrillo his side-
streets. Meanwhile, younger artists such as La Patellière, Lhote, and La
Fresnaye painted rural effigies by altering and smoothing down cubist devices. All formed part of the same movement. Studying their leitmotifs,
their commercial triumphs, and the critics who extolled their French

Figure 7.19
Paul Cézanne (1839–1906), *View of Auvers-sur-Oise* (1873).

qualities, then placing them in the sociocultural and literary context of their day, would greatly contribute to the history of national attitudes of mind between the two wars.[78] The fact remains, however, that their short-lived success was bound up with events of the day and has not left a mark on public memory.

At the same time, very few of the "leading lights" in art showed any interest in the French landscape. And those that did either developed an iconography and style derived from impressionism (Dufy in his beach views, Marquet and Signac in ports of France or views of Paris), or, as in the case of the greatest creators, subordinated the landscape to their own vision, keeping it at arm's length, as it were. The landscapes of Bonnard, Vernonnet, and Cannet are viewed from a terrace or a window; the Mediterranean gardens of Matisse are glimpsed from a window, between

Figure 7.20
Pierre Bonnard (1867–1947), *Country Dining Room* (1913).

shutters, or filtered through a curtain. In all these works, it is significant that nature is shot from an interior, as though the landscape no longer existed in its own right, as though it had become nothing more than a pretext for painting, a high-angle shot taken from the studio or from an opening in the wall. The window sections off a "framed landscape" that is already a painted object. The outside world is once more seen from the studio, to which, after an escapade of little more than half a century, we have returned for good.

In actual fact, landscape painting as a national genre disappeared after World War I, when, on the one hand, modern art became an international style, and, on the other, the reality deemed worthy of interest was no longer the spectacle of nature as such but its movement (Futurism), structure (Cubism), infinitesimal mystery (Klee), or what lay behind appearances (Surrealism), and so forth, to say nothing of abstract art, which only took on national importance in France after World War II.

But just at the time French landscape painting was becoming a moribund genre in living art, its images were working their way into public taste and memory, with an outlook already rooted in the past and echoing with dead formulas. Countless more or less humble artists and spare-time painters would persist in portraying open-air landscapes: "legions of easels are scattered throughout the woods and countryside, parasols flower in all the fields, blow as the mistral might . . . the easels stand firm . . . neither dust in the eyes, nor the harsh glare, prevents thousands of Frenchmen from going about their touching labors: dabbing away at a canvas stretched like a snare for pictures."[79]

That open-air painting as a national sport much like angling reflects a need for roots and simple pleasures is borne out today by the popularity of exhibitions and the many illustrated publications devoted to impressionism. Since around the 1950s, the painted French landscape, whose chronological limits we have seen, along with the powerful ties it enjoyed with the country's history, appears to have been no more than an object of remembrance, and no longer a motif for creation and identification. The success of such exhibitions as the *Centenaire de l'impressionisme* in 1974, or, ten years later, *L'Impressionisme et le paysage français* has rightly been put down in large part to nostalgia (in which environmentalism has a share), to the evocative power of images portraying places at once familiar and remote, and to the setting of the lost paradise our own national garden may once have been. Visitors stood about for hours in order to leaf through the family album of public memory and rediscover a landscape inhabited by time and, beneath the greenery, a little of their history.

NOTES

1. The same motif was also used on a poster for Valéry Giscard d'Estaing, which in the end was not chosen. The design was already being used in 1940 in the poster of Pétain with a village in the background: "Follow me, remain confident in an everlasting France."

2. The fresco of the bird catchers (ca. 1343), for example, in the Palais des Papes in Avignon, as well as all *mille fleurs* tapestries and those with landscapes in the background over the following centuries.

3. In the Musée Jacquemart-André. See Millard Meiss, *French Painting in the Time of Jean de Berri*, vol. 1, *The Boucicaut Master* (London: Phaidon, 1974), xx.

4. Françoise Heilbrun, "Le Paysage dans la photographie française au XIXe siècle," in *L'Impressionisme et le paysage français* [exhibition catalog] (Paris, 1985), 373.

5. Henri Bouchot, "Le Paysage chez les primitifs," lecture given at the École des Hautes Études, 1905–6, in Henri Marcel et al., *Histoire du paysage en France* (Paris, 1908), 120.

6. Pol de Limbourg and Jean Colombe, *Septembre*, in *Très riches heures du duc de Berry*, Musée de Chantilly, no. 547.

7. Pol de Limbourg, *Juin*, in *Très riches heures*, no. 544.

8. Jean de Limbourg, *Très riches heures*, no. 597; Fouquet, *Heures d'Étienne Chevalier; Très riches heures*, fol. 51v.

9. Master of the *Coeur d'amour épris*, Vienna, Library, cod. 2597, fol. 31v.

10. Quoted in Francisco de Hollanda, *Quatre dialogues sur la peinture* (Paris, 1911), 28–30.

11. Roger de Piles, *Cours de peinture par principe* (1708). Often quoted, in particular by Marcel, *Histoire du paysage*, 140.

12. Kenneth Clark, *Landscape into Art* (London: John Murray, 1949), 108.

13. Joachim Gasquet, *Cézanne*, quoted in *Conversations avec Cézanne*, ed. P.-M. Doran (Paris: Macula, 1978), 122; second quotation from Maurice Denis, *Théories* (Paris, 1912), 242.

14. Honoré d'Urfé, *L'Astrée*, ed. Jean Lafond (Paris: Gallimard, coll. Folio, 1984), 25.

15. Jean and Edmond de Goncourt, *La Peinture à l'Exposition universelle de 1855*, reprinted in *L'Art du XVIIIe siècle*, ed. J.-P. Bouillon (Paris: Hermann, 1967), 214.

16. Oudry, *Un petit paysage où apparaît une grosse tour, d'après nature*, 1737, private collection, *Oudry* [exhibition catalog] (Paris, 1982–83), no. 89; Boucher, *Un paysage d'après nature des environs de Beauvais* (Salon of 1742).

17. *La Nuit par un clair de lune:* title of a painting (1762) by Joseph Vernet, Musée National du Château de Versailles.

18. Loutherbourg, *Paysage avec figure et animaux* (1763), Liverpool Museum.

19. Mongin, *Le Curieux, étude d'après nature*, in *De David à Delacroix* [exhibition catalogue] (1974–75), no. 132.

20. I have only been able to trace titles back as far as 1824 and Bidauld's *Souvenir des bords de l'Isère* (no. 144). Detailed research into the titles of works remains a rich field for investigation that to my knowledge has not been exploited.

21. V. van de Sandt, "Le Salon de l'Académie de 1759 à 1781," in *Diderot et l'art de Boucher à David* [exhibition catalogue] (1985), 83.

22. Antoine Schnapper, in *De David à Delacroix* [exhibition catalog], 113–14.

23. See D.-G. Charlton, *New Images of the Natural in France* (London: Cambridge University Press, 1984).

24. Cardinal de Bernis, *Les Géorgiques françaises* (1763); Abbé Delille, *Les Jardins* (1767); Jean-François de Saint-Lambert, *Les Saisons* (1767).

25. By Cochin and Lebas.

26. *Salon de 1763*, quoted in *Diderot* [exhibition catalog], 300.

27. Gougenout, *Mémoires inédits* (1761), 2:365, quoted by L. Deshairs, "Le Paysage en France après Watteau," in Marcel, *Histoire du paysage*, 155–56.

28. Rüdigger Joppien, catalog entry on Louthenbourg, in *Diderot* [exhibition catalog], 314.

29. Delecluze, *Salon de 1825,* quoted in Philippe Grunchec, *Le Grand Prix de peinture: Les concours de Rome de 1797 à 1863* (Paris: École Nationale des Beaux-Arts, 1984), 380.

30. Albert Boime, *The Academy and French Painting in the Nineteenth Century* (New York, Oxford: Phaidon, 1971), 121.

31. Grunchec, *Le Grand Prix,* 98.

32. Geneviève Lacambre, *Le Musée du Luxembourg en 1874* [exhibition catalog] (1974), no. 82.

33. Alfred de Musset, review of the Salon of 1836, *Revue des deux mondes,* April 15, 1836, 151.

34. By Girtin in 1803, Cotman Pugin and Gendall in 1821, Hardity and Burnet in 1835, and, of course, Turner in 1837. Cf. Robert Herbert, *Barbizon Revisited* (Boston: Museum of Boston, 1962), 16–17.

35. On illustrated works published by Baron Taylor, see Michel Melot, *L'Illustration* (Geneva: Skira, 1984), 136.

36. See Jacques Foucart, "Les Paysagistes de la première moitié du XIXe siècle et l'art néerlandais" (postgraduate diss., 1963); and Petra ten Doeschate Chu, *French Realism and the Dutch Masters* (Utrecht, 1974).

37. H. van der Tuin, *Les Vieux Peintres des Pays-Bas et la critique artistique en France de la première moitié du XIXe siècle* (Paris: Vrin, 1948), 12–16.

38. Seven hundred and twenty plates of works from the Musée Napoléon were reproduced in Filhol's album; some ten thousand copper plates were constantly being reprinted by the print-seller *veuve* Jean; *Manuel* of the *époux* Marchand, 1813; cf. Foucard, *Les Paysagistes,* 38ff.

39. Gérard de Nerval, *Promenades et souvenirs* (Paris: Gallimard, Bibliothèque de la Pléiade), 122ff.

40. Quoted in Alfred Sencier, *Georges Michel* (Paris, 1873), 21.

41. Anonymous review in *Globe,* November 17, 1824, quoted by van der Tuin, *Les Vieux Peintres,* 61.

42. Thoré, *Le Magasin pittoresque,* 1847–48, vol. 11, 214–16, quoted in van der Tuin, *Les Vieux peintres,* 85.

43. Diderot, apropos Vernet, *La Source abondante,* etc., in *Diderot* [exhibition catalog], 408.

44. Senancour, *Oberman,* letter XXV. Cf. *Les Plus belles pages de Senancour,* ed. Jean Grenier (Paris: Mercure de France, 1968), 122.

45. Alfred Sencier, *Théodore Rousseau* (Paris, 1872), 18.

46. Ibid., 153.

47. Letter from Th. Rousseau, quoted by Sencier, ibid., 277.

48. See *Nos ancêtres les Gaulois,* Proceedings of the International Symposium of Clermond-Ferrand, ed. Paul Viallaneix and A. Ehrard (Clermont-Ferrand, 1982).

49. Jules Michelet, *Tableau de la France,* in *Oeuvres complètes* (Paris: Flammarion, 1974), 4:332–33.

50. Delecluze, *Salon de 1829,* quoted in Grunchec, *Le Grand Prix,* 384.

51. Cézanne to Gasquet, in Doran, *Conversations avec Cézanne,* 144.

52. Cf. Hélène Toussaint, in *Gustave Courbet* [exhibition catalog] (Paris, 1977), no. 76; Linda Nochlin, quoted in Gabriel Weisberg, *The Realist Tradition* (Cleveland: Cleveland Museum of Art, 1980), 182.

53. Castagnary, "Philosophie du Salon de 1857," in *Salons,* Paris: Bibliothèque-Charpentier, 1892.

54. Henri de la Madeleine, "Les Beaux-arts à l'exposition universelle," in *Paris-guide 1867,* 2031–32.

55. Guy de Maupassant, *Bel-Ami* (Paris: Gallimard, coll. Folio, 1973), 161.

56. Charles Baudelaire, "Salon de 1859," in *Oeuvres complètes* (Paris: Gallimard, Bibliothèque de la Pléiade, 1976), 663.

57. Alfred Sencier, *Corot* (Paris, 1871).

58. Jean Starobinski, in *Diderot,* 20.

59. Denis Diderot, "Salon de 1767," apropos Hubert Robert in *Salons* (Paris, 1983), 118, 227.

60. Jules and Edmond de Goncourt, Sunday, June 8, 1862, vol. 1, 1085.

61. Jean-Robert Pitte, *Histoire du paysage français* (Paris: Tallandier, 1984), 1:110, 2:89.

62. In "Salon de 1763" (on Loutherbourg).

63. Scott Fitzgerald, *Tender Is the Night* (London: Everyman, 1996), 124.

64. It was precisely in 1806, at any rate, that the collection preserved at the Musée des Arts et Traditions Populaires was begun (inv. 75587–81; 735393ff.; 763127ff.). For the 1960s, calendar imagery faithfully reflects the steady increase in household pets in France: thirty-six million, according to the statistics, more than in any other European country. It is as though being close to nature was more a question of domestic animals than of one's vision of landscape.

65. Ph. Burty, in *Léon Bonvin, l'aquarelliste,* quoted in Pierre Vaisse, "La IIIe République et les peintres" (Ph.D. diss., University of Paris IV, 1980), 153.

66. Jacques Thuillier, "Le Paysage dans la peinture française du XVIIe siècle," *Cahiers de l'Association internationale d'études françaises* 29 (1977): 50.

67. See Herbert, *Barbizon Revisited,* 39; on artistic policy, see Timothy Clark, *The Absolute Bourgeois* (London: Thames and Husdson, 1973), chap. II.

68. Prize-giving speech for the Salon of 1879, published in *Le Salon de 1880,* VI.

69. Ibid., VI, VII.

70. See Vaisse, *La IIIe République,* and Thérèse Burollet, F. Folliot, and Daniel Imbert, *Grands Décors parisiens (hôtel de ville, mairies), 1870–1914* [exhibition catalog] (Paris, 1986).

71. Letter published in Bazire, *Édouard Manet* (Paris, 1884), 142; cf. *Manet* [exhibition catalog] (1983), 516.

72. Maurice Faure, speech delivered before the assembly in 1898, quoted in Vaisse, *La IIIe République,* 156.

73. Quoted in André Fermigier, *Courbet* (Geneva: Skira, 1971), 16.

74. Castagnary, "Salon de 1867," in *Salons,* 235.

75. Ibid., 242.

76. Cf. Meyer Schapiro, "Nature of Abstract Art," *Marxist Quarterly* (January–March 1937): 77–98; Robert Herbert, *The Social Iconography of Impressionism,* Slade Lectures (Oxford, 1978); Paul H. Tucker, *Monet at Argenteuil* (New Haven: Yale University Press, 1982); R. Brettel, S. Schaeffer, and S. Patin, in *L'Impressionisme et le paysage français* [exhibition catalog] (1985).

77. R. Brettel and S. Schaeffer, ibid., 15.

78. Romy Golan, *Modernity and Nostalgia: Art and Politics in France between the Wars* (New Haven: Yale University Press, 1995).

79. André Lhote, *Traité du paysage* (Paris, 1939), 12.

CHAPTER 8

THE SCHOLAR'S LANDSCAPE

MARCEL RONCAYOLO

The memory of locations and landscapes is most assuredly part of the nation's memories. Physical landmarks emerge from that memory. Classical psychology, we know, gives such material signs the capacity of localizing places of remembrance and calling memories forth. This memory acts in several ways: first, as a collective appropriation, through image and representations, of a geographic unity that goes beyond individual experience. The landscape is an object of memory, a mental map. Another way in which it acts is to serve as a source of knowledge, an archive of living and material things: land use and development contain the traces of a distant and eventful history, on the scale both of geological time and of societies. It is an inheritance to discover, make over, and comb through when it does not quite lie in full view of the experienced observer. Thus, whether we look to the land and the soil for extractable wealth or productive use, evidence of development or values or symbolic attachments, the knowledge of the land in its concrete forms and places, without arbitrary demarcations, parallels national history and even the nation's development. In the United States, the photographic and scientific exploration of the west was a key episode in the formation of the nation. In France, the correspondences are exact: the ordeal of 1870 led to a renaissance in the teaching of geography, which became in a short time a central piece in republican pedagogy.[1] Knowledge of the land and knowledge of the national history appeared to come together and reach their peak in the monumental work to which the geographer Vidal de La

Blache lent his assistance, Ernest Lavisse's *Histoire de France,* and which opened the twentieth century.[2]

This experience of the nation's landscape certainly does not depend on scientific learning. Representations and other means of dissemination often meet the demand. Nevertheless, the scientific reading of places penetrates and modifies the most common forms of knowledge. The awareness and appreciation of one's territory passes through the most sophisticated tests, technical clarifications, the formation of disciplines, and the divisions of learning. Still, this epistemological task is not discharged by study of the national terrain alone. The explorations across the planet and, in certain cases, colonization and penetration ultimately gave geography its universal validity. The nineteenth century was the time of universal geographies, if one goes by the French editions like the kind done by Malte-Brun (whose *Précis* was published for the first time in 1810–11)[3] or by Élisée Reclus (the first volume of whose *Géographie universelle,* called new, came out in 1876),[4] or with the project launched a few decades later by the Vidal team. National geographies are often only a means to self-understanding that is refined, enriched, and objective. In this respect the colonial adventure, following the experience of the great explorers, such as Humboldt, had a decisive impact, fueling the epistemological debate.

Scholarly study, to be sure, does not occur outside of society. Past and present, forms and events, landscapes and historical movements send back their reflections, like a hall of mirrors. We therefore have to go beyond the various disciplines. Actors in history or a work of society about itself (Michelet evokes "the powerful work of the self on self where France as it advances ultimately transforms all of its raw elements") will be conceptualized in ways that are necessarily ideological. Introducing social connections or historical authenticity constantly comes into question when interpretations are given to physical forms and landscapes. If we stay with the idea of landscape for a moment, we see it floating among multiple categories. Scholarly examination does not exclude aesthetics, stereotypes about travel or exotic discoveries, or the development of the landscape into a spectacle or an object of consumption. Neither does it exclude the creation and perception of images. The rise of photography and then aerial imaging, the use of photogrammetry, messages from satellites—thanks to the power of such tools to see things in their totality, ambition is rekindled. Finally, it does not exclude very recent concerns about the environment. Roger Dion's *Essai sur la formation du paysage rural français* (1934) was republished fifty years later under the auspices of the Direction de l'urbanisme et des paysages.

This tangle of viewpoints that goes from epistemology to the history of taste and sensibilities and the representation of society cannot easily be unwound. If we simply highlight the changes that have taken place in the interpretation of landscapes (the notion of space is an even larger idea and applies to totally different realities), three distinct periods should be noted. The first period comes with the publication of the *Encyclopédie** in the eighteenth century and its legacy, which informs the division of scientific views and which is open-ended and incomplete: statistics, cartography, geology—and, in a certain measure, history, if one heeds the call of Jules Michelet—are in this way placed and defined as branches of knowledge. Indeed, there are as many landscape "disciplines," but they are far from covering the entire field. The image of the territory is appropriated in a parallel manner, without strict rules, through a diverse literature. The second period, which goes back to the 1870s, is the establishment of the Vidal school of geography. This approach does not burst on the scene like a thunderclap. Rather, it emerges from multiple sources with the express purpose of founding a science of places and landscapes. Yet in showing the necessity of integrating explanations of nature and history, it constantly runs the risk of naturalism. The third period comes about through the particular yet representative idea of the *rural landscape,* which—although a scientific object for the historian and the geographer—leads to the first "decomposition" of the landscape, the science preceding or underscoring the very evolution of society. This is the period that we would like to chart, with the understanding that intellectual habits, and even more their diffusion and instruction, are neither quickly acquired nor easily abandoned.

FROM THE *ENCYCLOPÉDIE* TO THE DIVISION OF DISCIPLINES: KNOWLEDGE OF THE COUNTRYSIDE FRAGMENTED

Encyclopedic Opacity

Legacies and experiences have to be sought outside of a specific literature and, at times, beyond French territory. First, the travel narratives and the guides—among them the devotees of the Grand Tour to Italy—were at once the originators and the users diffusing the model. To draw up a balance sheet on this tradition, limited to the seventeenth and eighteenth centuries, reveals certain types of voyages and interests. But at this stage

---

* EDITOR'S NOTE: *Encyclopédie, ou Dictionnaire raisonné des sciences, des arts et des métiers,* one of the most important intellectual and publishing ventures of the age, often characterized as the embodiment of the fundamental ideas of the French Enlightenment, was published between 1751 and 1772. Edited and inspired by Denis Diderot and Jean d'Alembert, who wrote some of its most important articles, the massive collective work was in seventeen large volumes, supplemented by eleven additional volumes of plates.

an encyclopedic curiosity prevails and with it the respect for antiquities, the knowledge of monuments and places marked by history, and a taste for the marvels of nature and impressive landscapes: in short, natural history. Thus was established an inventory of things to see that had no borders. A meticulous description, on the other hand, was tied to each parcel of curiosity. The general sense of the physiognomy of a country was neglected. Rarely was the backdrop fully illuminated. It furnished the context for personalities and events in the past or present—much like a painting—and it was relegated to the shade, an almost neutral space connecting exceptional places.

Jean-Claude Perrot has shown how, parallel to this general curiosity and at times directly tied to it, there developed in the second half of the eighteenth century the field of statistics inspired by the desire for knowledge and the measure of the public interest.[5] (The effort was oriented toward the great debate on tax reform, which was understood as territorial.) One work of the time, which dealt with the Angoumois, had a title that recapitulated the multiple targets of these memories: *Essai d'une méthode générale propre à étendre les connaissances des voyageurs, ou Recueil d'observations relatives à la culture des terres: le tout appuyé sur des faits exacts et enrichi d'expériences utiles* (1777 [Essay for the General Method Appropriate for Expanding the Knowledge of Travelers, or Collection of Observations Relating to the Distribution of Taxes, Commerce, the Sciences and the Arts, and to the Cultivation of the Land: The Entirety Backed Up by Exact Facts Enriched by Useful Experiences]). The author was an inspector of bridges and roads. Topography, geographical description, natural history, and often even the most anecdotal history thus come into close contact with statistics. For its part, statistics wavers between very abstract arithmetic, as applied to population and resources, and numeric description. The emergence of such memories, in short, constitutes, through geographical fragments, a first look at the territory and brings together the sometimes naive knowledge of local elites. Other efforts come from more specific professional groups, particularly physicians. From the perspective of a medical discipline converted to neo-Hippocratism (i.e., the decisive role of the environment), the investigation of one's surroundings lies at the heart of every concern. A new approach was born: medical topography, which over several decades had expanded provincial studies to include the towns. Official encouragement came from the Société royale de médecine, which in 1776 launched a major questionnaire aimed at describing the kingdom.

The journey of the agronomists assumes another dimension, one that is more firmly fixed on its object, the very disparate competences of the authors notwithstanding. The doctrines of the physiocrats are on this

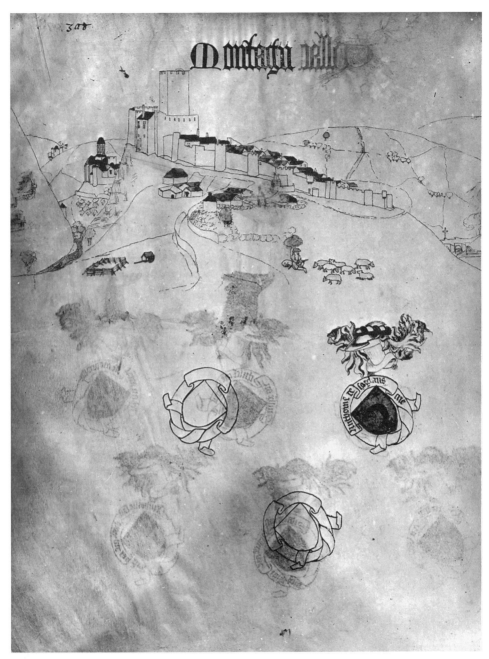

Figure 8.1
A visual and simplified image of the landscape: Montaigut-le-Blanc (Puy-de-Dôme). Castle of Guillaume Revel (second half of the 15th century). The distinctive features of the landscape are depicted in perspective: the fortified village, dominated by a dungeon; a monastery; hamlets with animal pens and flocks of sheep; pastures and fields, here and there planted with trees, shown in relief. A "qualitative" description more than a complete picture.

point multifaceted: respectful of natural phenomena and concerned about the growth of resources that improvements in technology and agricultural economics alone can obtain. The agronomists were without a doubt the first to develop the pattern for a scientific reading of the landscape, which included the two often conflicting interpretations that divided it. In his *Essai,* which did not take into account the criticisms of Arthur's Young's work,[6] Roger Dion referred to the official report based on investigations that the ancien régime toward the end initiated concerning open pasture and land closure taxes. "Arthur Young's text only increases in value in our eyes. It reveals to us, in its schematic simplicity, primitive realities that are not so clearly perceptible in the countryside of today as they were in his time." Young's account is valuable precisely because it is more real than nature, because it is based on features he chose, sorted—the open or enclosed field, the density and kind of cover, the opposition between large and small landholdings—and related more or less explicitly to agricultural practices. According to Dion, in research on the past and investigation into the great divisions in the French landscapes, such testimony came to replace the direct observation of what was a very blurred panorama. It was indeed through texts of this kind that the landscape as found not only in nature but also in the conditions of production, work, and tools, as well as land management by social groups, takes on a different character.

From Statistics to the Bureau of Statistics

The "statistics" ordered by the administrations of the Directory and the Empire drew inspiration from this legacy. It was a true inventory comparing the situation before and after revolutionary events and changes, and its statistics were a response, in the first days, to the "encyclopedic" curiosity, the wide-ranging inquiry into the natural, topographical, and human conditions of life and activity in the new departments, the concern with giving "numbers" to population and production data and with establishing "interconnections." They were to establish the level of prosperity, understood in a context that took into account geographical diversity. Despite the collaboration of enlightened circles in the provinces, this ambition only resulted in a few miscellaneous in-depth works of uneven quality. Beginning in 1806, the Bureau of Statistics lopped off the curiosities, concentrating rather on the construction of quantitative data that were solid, prepared with regularity and by sector as well. The geographical picture turned into a performance indicator. From the end of the Empire on, this pattern marked the increasingly specific requests from departments of the central administration (the Bureau of Statistics, which was becoming too independent, was dissolved in 1811) as well as the definition of a particular branch of knowledge: quantitative statistics that were rigorous and oriented toward the mathematics of economics and the construction of regular series. A specialization that was surely effective and already laid out in certain works of the eighteenth century, it heralded the creation of the General Statistics of France in the 1830s.[7]

The fact remains that detaching one branch to allow it to flourish might not necessarily benefit the whole. As a result, the general view of territorial economics would suffer over the course of the nineteenth century. The opacity in the encyclopedists' descriptions could not be structured or set apart from the anecdotal tradition. The landscape risked losing its connection to production and social practices. The compilation of delayed "statistics" expressed this regret and difficulty simultaneously. Let us take the example of one of the richest collections, known as the De Villeneuve, which dealt with the department of Bouches-du-Rhône,[8] a source that is still worthy of great interest. This statistical study criticizes the already available descriptive literature and dossiers prepared during the time of Chaptal* for "details too hastily drawn up and too minute, and for the gaps that had to be filled in by essays that more or less echo the views of the author."[9] Over against fantasy used as information, the author claims the rigors of observation. This careful description, bringing together written sources, oral information, and studies of the terrain, is summed up by the key word *topography*. The first two books of the work bear an inscription: "Physical topography, which is the subject of the first book, makes known places; administrative topography describes housing for us. Thus, first one sees develop a country that nature alone has taken care to embellish. Then this same country is presented covered with cities, towns, villages, and hamlets."[10] History is read through the topography of settlements and the remains of monuments. Topography, more than landscape? The former lays claim to objectivity and rules; it corresponds to a trade and a variety of tools. It is closely associated with cartography, more than at first glance. Landscapes belong to artists, topography to engineers and scholars.

"Statistics" were confirmed in this way by the purpose inherited from the physiocrats, from the agronomists in their explorations, and from political economy. Knowledge was collected only "to deduce from it, in a word, those facts that might propagate the means to improve

---

★ EDITOR'S NOTE: Jean-Antoine Chaptal (1756–1832) was a chemist and political figure who gave his name to a process for adding sugar to wine at the beginning of fermentation, opened the first factory to produce chemical products in France, and served as Napoleon's minister of the interior (1800–1804).

everything."[11] The description of nature or the social state of the country was meant for progress in methods and resources: "To make known nature and the needs of different areas of the departments, to discuss the difficulties and advantages of proposed projects, thereby to show capitalists an equally honorable and useful application of their funds and, at the same time, bring down upon the country all the benefits to which it might be susceptible."[12] Statistics were thus transformed into a kind of guide for development, oriented to investment and production, with agriculture topping the list. These priorities led to a certain disequilibrium: despite the unusual care taken by the authors of these statistics to keep an even accounting of what natural and human history each contributed (only with rare exception would there be found such interest applied to systems of cultivation, tools, and agricultural practices or to the social status of the land or even to conditions in which progress in agriculture occurs), the physical milieu assumed a particular explanatory value. "In the first volume of this work we gave some very exact details concerning the soil in different valleys, plains, and basins, concerning the waters that flow through them, and concerning the meteorological events that are seen there . . . we have nothing more to do, in the books that follow, but *deduce consequences and make useful application of them for the prosperity of country*" (italics added).[13]

The example of these "departmental statistics" furnishes some food for thought. Rhetoric without a doubt provides cover for the fragility of scientific reasoning, often limited to a banal environmentalism. But the reader of today is more sensitive to the descriptive quality of detail (the urban landscapes, soils, waters, vegetative covering) and to technology. Here is a store of ethnographic wealth, while physical anthropology remains anecdotal. One can see in all this what the exhaustion of the genre has led to: the real inventories of local erudition and curiosities from folklore are relegated to stores for the picturesque. The technical and ethnographic dimensions find no place at first sight in any of the "specialties" that have been established: cartography, geology, and even history. Economics and general statistics are left to themselves. When all is said and done, the landscape becomes dehumanized.

A Scientific and Codified Cartography

Cartography thus became detached as a special branch through the compilation of maps, particularly maps on a mean scale.[14] It had long been recognized that the ancien régime in its waning days made a great contribution to France with the magnificent collection of Cassini maps, done on a 1:86,400 scale. Long attributed to some monarchical caprice, the compilation of this map seemed to be part of a more general move-ment to do reconnaissance on a described territory. The quality of the work, which was ahead of its time, could not hide its limitations: a work born of a dynasty of astronomers, the Cassinis, and with a concern for "mathematical" geography (the calculation of the meridian of Paris and the attempt that followed to triangulate the territory were the scientific foundation), this map *fixed* places more than it *described* them. Started in the 1750s (the triangle map was completed in 1744), the map was prac-tically finished in 1789, with surveys and drawings. Revolutionary events and perhaps military prudence led to a delay in the publication of the last sheets until the return of peace in 1815. The work suffered, without doubt, from archaic equipment, inexact measurements, and the enduring ignorance, in the eighteenth century, of the topography of the country. Taking another look at the *Statistique des Bouches-du-Rhône* shows us how, around 1810, the reconnaissance of the terrain was carried out by geodesic points, land surveys, and connecting links to Cassini's triangles. By that time, instruments and methods had evolved: the experience of the corps of engineers and geographers at the end of the eighteenth cen-tury and then during the revolutionary and imperial years was consider-able. The conquered and occupied lands furnished good terrain for prac-tice. Along with the military incentive came another of a different sort from the land registries. Determining the physical state and property lim-its functioned as one of the fundamental myths of the society that emerged from the Revolution. The desire was to put the work of local surveyors and chorographers into a vast and coordinated complex. The basics and principles of Cassini's map, therefore, had to be revisited. Starting in 1802, the Dépôt de la guerre envisaged the idea of drawing up a new topographical map and defining the general rules of this art—a true effort to codify: absolute separation between a bird's-eye view of things and geometric projections, scale ratios, systems of signs, and de-piction of land in relief (contour lines and hachures). It was only in the course of long, delayed discussions, from 1817 to 1824, that the plan was defined: separate cadastral operations and topographical maps (a victory for administrative particularism), adoption of the scale of 1 : 80,000 for maps and 1 : 20,000 and 1 : 40,000 for surveys, and use of hachures for indicating slopes. The Dépôt de la guerre was put in charge of executing the plan.

The projects took over forty years and caused problems in rank-ing according to priority. The suppression of the corps of engineers-geographers in 1831 illustrated the uncertainties. The needs expressed by the launching of the great public works (canals, then railroads), followed by tourism, supported publication in any case. Only in the aftermath of

1870 could the publication be brought to completion at a time when the oldest maps, published under the July Monarchy, required revision. Cartography thus experienced before it was invented this debate over stability versus change, which would be at the center of the difficulties facing landscape geography in the second half of the nineteenth century. Émile Levasseur pointed to the inadequate distribution and the "confidential" aspect of this discovery of the landscape through maps: "The map itself was little used by officials finding its price too high and by cartographers retreating before the painful work of simplification."[15]

Geology and Naturalism

The 1 : 80,000 map would serve after 1870 (a delay to be sure) to establish the geological map of France.

The movement began with the first works of location and geological surveys. Curiosity about the natural sciences and the desire to draw up an inventory of natural resources converged, starting with the Revolution and the Empire, with the Corps of Mining Engineers coming to support the "amateur" scholars along the lines of the encyclopedists.[16] Drawing up the geological map was to be part of the ideology of improving, managing, and exploiting natural reserves. Lucien Gallois was the one, in his critical work *Régions naturelles et noms de pays,*[17] who analyzed this current and, going from a topographical description to an examination of geological outcrops and a definition of the physical environment, developed a new way of explaining the French landscape. Whether one examines the first efforts to draw up a geographical map, undertaken in 1810 by Omalius d'Halloy, a young Belgian geologist recruited by the Committee of Mines, or those by Caumont or Antoine Passy, or even the comments written in the margins of the 1 : 500,000 map by the engineers Dufrénoy and Élie de Beaumont in 1840,[18] the landscape became a facade, a manifestation of the disposition of the subsoil and nature of the rocks.

> Can one profitably travel who does not possess any idea of geology? Whether he wanders through Switzerland, the Auvergne, Normandy, or any other *pays,* he indeed sees mountains, plains, varied sites, but within this assemblage he will discern only a confusing pile of stones, the aspect of which he will only be able to enjoy mechanically. How many unnoticed circumstances will, by contrast, charm him if he is able to recognize the nature of the terrain and determine their geological level! He will see each butte, each valley, with a pleasure that can only be fully understood by those who have experienced it.[19]

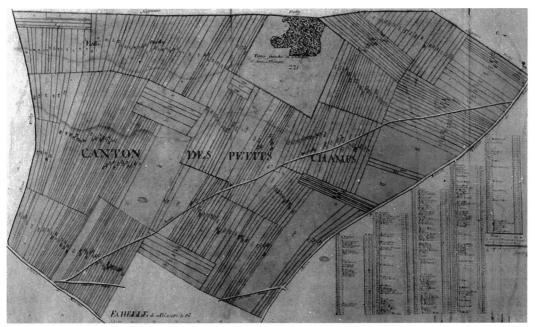

Figure 8.2
Social uses and formation of the land: the seigneury of Puiseaux, village of Burcy, in Beauce (Loiret). This land map represents the division of the inheritance, rights, and fees due the seigneur. Open fields are laid out in strips in the northern plains of France. This geometric plan from the 18th century sacrifices all other descriptive elements to precision of measurements and the survey, demonstrating the primacy of the social function.

This reconciliation of aesthetics, the understanding of things, and natural history, itself transformed, provides the key. Geology does not just constitute a "scientific reading" of the landscape; it is the *way* to read it. Topography and administrative divisions, which are arbitrary, were replaced by an idea that defined *natural regions* as a principle for analyzing geographic reality: "These mineralogical or geological differences, as they used to say, have as corollaries changes in the aspect of the country, vegetation, culture, the style of the houses, and whether they stand isolated or in groups. It is these dispositions that are given the name of natural regions."[20] Defined here is what amounts to a general field of interpretive study that orders the understanding of the natural landscape as well as the products of the soil and practical knowledge. The marking out of "natural regions" was organized into more or less clearly defined interlocking "layers" that fit into basic units, namely "countries," which were to become an object of geographical curiosity. On the scale of a country, this method finds a sort of legitimacy in popular consensus. Toponymy would confirm that these units are not only the creations of

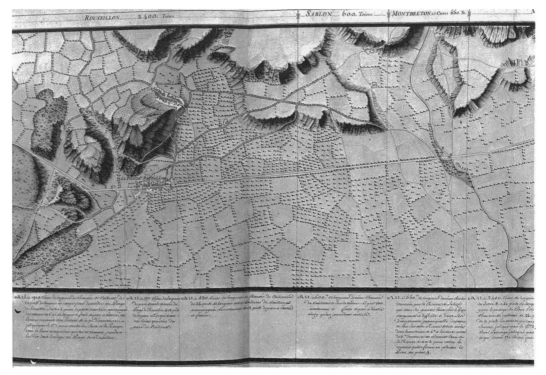

Figure 8.3
Circulation and land reconnaissance: map of the road from Lyon to Provence (ca. 1750). Work begun for the construction and maintenance of the bridges and highways provided an impetus for mapping land areas in the 18th century. Here, the outline of the irregular fields of the south, filled with or surrounded by trees (Péage-de-Roussillon region), is drawn with care, with relief lines heavily underscored.

detached science but the perceptions of society, particularly of peasant societies. Again, it is Antoine Passy who provides the best explanation:

> We have to characterize geologically and agriculturally the physical divisions of our territory, which are more ancient than the divisions accepted during the time of the Romans and the Middle Ages. The names do not correspond to ecclesiastical, feudal, or administrative divisions prevailing in the world of officialdom. They remain fixed through the centuries in the everyday language of the inhabitants. . . . Based on their physical characteristics and their individual aspect, the diverse parts of our territory each obtained a specific name and that name was usually joined to the communities of which they were a part to distinguish them from their homonyms located in another region.[21]

Without a doubt, this version of landscapes frees scientific inquiry from purely archival work in geographical history and from the primacy of institutions. One senses the long term in rural societies as well as the archaeological function of the landscape, supported to a greater or lesser degree by the names and ancestral memory of peoples. But by telescoping natural geography and the perception that the inhabitants have of their surroundings, the action of societies disappears. Geology becomes the factor for transparency. "Naturalization" comes not from the importance given to the soil or the climate, but from the implicit negation of history by the discovery of an "eternal" order of the fields and of peasant wisdom, always one and the same thing. The decisive contribution of geologists bequeathed this ambiguity to geography. At the outset the result was obviously a cultural and professional distortion, but its success merits a different explanation. Levasseur, moreover, applied this lesson without criticism to the names of the parts of France in his 1872 program.[22]

The generation of Vidal de La Blache was without doubt confronted by an international movement that affected the discipline, coming from the study of plant life that Humboldt taught or the philosophic approach that Ritter inspired on the connections between man and nature. Through their numerous writings the geologists discreetly exercised their pedagogical role and set the course for the advocates of a new discipline. It is curious that Lucien Gallois was the only one to deal with the history of this discipline, and that with the limited objective of a critique about names. It is as if the newly arrived science had thrown a veil over its origins.

Land and History

For many purposes, national history draws from the same sources: The *Tableau de la France* by Jules Michelet,[23] which overflows with dazzling concepts, examines the diversity of French lands and regions for the principle of unity and of success. Therein is found aesthetic satisfaction: "The strength and beauty of the whole coexist in the reciprocity of mutual assistance, in the solidarity of the parts, in the distribution of the functions, and in the division of work in society." According to Augustin Thierry, the work can be criticized as both insufficiently spiritual and insufficiently materialistic: "Material conditions, the race, and the people who perpetuate it all seem to me to require first a good strong base—the earth that bears and nourishes them. Without a geographical base, the people as historical actor will seem to walk in the air like in Chinese paintings where the ground is missing." This early yet mature text of Michelet (1833) combines a certain naiveté with profound views on changes in society within its geographical differences. Naiveté? More like an excessive desire to reconcile the physical divisions with the historical ones that goes well beyond the caution of agronomists and geologists. "The infinite variations of the feudal world, the multiplicity of objects that strains the eyes and exhausts the mind, is nothing less than the revelation of what is France. For the first time, France appears in its geographical form. . . . Political divisions here correspond to physical divisions." But the ecological postulate, widespread at that time and serving here as a reference, more directly introduces history's part. "It nevertheless is not enough to trace the geographic form of these diverse countries. More than anything they are explained by their fruits, by which I mean to say by the men and events that their history offers." Places and men seem to call to each other by a kind of echo, an identity that the very art of Michelet suggests when he blends moral and physical attributes and invokes the spirit of places when talking about a country. The result is that this tableau of France is the evocation of moral landscapes as much as it is a vast territorial description. With all this, one is then quite close to the report drawn up by the municipality of Paris in its charge to study the cholera epidemic: "This is a truth for all times and for all places that constantly has to be repeated because it is constantly forgotten—namely, there exists between man and all that surrounds him hidden ties and mysterious connections, the influence of which is constant and profound." Work and the environment are also invoked to explain *a contrario* the mysticism of the great industrial cities. The historical action more clearly reasserts its place and autonomy, however, when Michelet is dealing with cities, especially with the centrality of Paris. National awareness is born not from the countryside, but from experience: "The barbarian periods present almost nothing but the local, the individual, and material conditions. Man still holds to the soil, he is committed to it, he seems to be a part of it. History then looks at the land and even race itself, which is so powerfully influenced by the land. Little by little the strength inherent in man will free him and uproot him from this land."

The intuitions and lyricism of Michelet are not sufficient to create a scientific history of the landscape. But they did invite meditation on this possibility, especially when they were compared with the hesitations of a romantic geography,[24] so little sure of its rules. Next to the specialized fields of scholars and with a rather restricted circulation that had just been tabulated, this approach reestablishes (or seeks to reestablish) a global view of landscapes. In reality it was the connection to diversity that was renewed, without which no planning and public interest objectives can be developed as clearly as in the time of imperial "statistics." A return to the past as such, sentiments about nature, and a resurrection of the grand deeds and celebrated men were mixed together in this romantic bric-a-brac. The *Voyages pittoresques et romantiques de l'ancienne France,* collected in the 1820s by Nodier, Taylor, and Cailleux and published in 1833, did not escape this nostalgic look, but the authors did provide a new generation of recitals and travel impressions that collected the best signatures— Stendhal, Théophile Gautier, and even Alexandre Dumas. The texts themselves were supported by lavish illustration as lithography had come to support works in a popular edition meant for wide distribution. Photography entered the scene in the 1830s, bearing its own witness to truth. The technique was difficult, since photographs were not immediately reproducible. First there was the drawing, then the engraving, and finally the photo plate to complete the circuit for transmitting an image.[25] Around 1880, the *Géographie universelle* of Reclus was still illustrated using drawings and wood engravings, based primarily on photographs. But, starting in 1850 with the beginnings of photoengraving, systematic efforts were made to photograph landscapes (Blanquart-Évrard, for example). From all these disparate sources a generation of atlases was born. The series,[26] based most often on divisions by department, together with a focus on relief and nomenclature maps, combined symbolic representations, architectural or landscapist views, commentaries, and statistical information and by this marriage of illustration and text, in a play of condensed images, summarized a knowledge of space. In short, the most ambitious of those works renewed the association of the picturesque, topography, and statistics.[27] Departmental monographs published by Adolphe Joanne on the eve of the Franco-Prussian War were in several ways close to this perspective and served as pedagogical documents, though barely attached to a discipline. Thus was composed, in a chaotic mix, elements of knowledge that benefited from a large circulation and contributed to the formation of perceptions on the national scale and thereby to the construction of stereotypes.

A Science of Places and Landscapes? The Vidal School

The maturation of geography was therefore not that of a discipline or the result of an internal logic. Rather, its renewal, or the overhauling of its foundation, was inherent in certain powerful trends in the early nineteenth century that were announced in the progress and specialization of scientific work as if it were an ideology (the ecological postulate or national consciousness). It was the combination of these strata that explains, most probably, how French geography, developing parallel to German geography, emerged almost in spite of Humboldt and Ritter as a national discipline, defined more as a cultural manifestation than as a science imposing identical rules everywhere. At the same time, however, it inherited multiple interests, lines of concurrent interpretation, and practices that were themselves restrictive. Through this legacy it inherited the idea of *paysage* or landscape, a notion with little definition because it had been subordinated within its apparent "reality" to different approaches. Sometimes it was a collection of objects, forms, and tangible traces from among which the scholar chose the materials for reconstructing the past or making a demonstration. Sometimes it was the overall view in which the meaning, never immediate, implied an appeal to individual fields of knowledge. It was an impossible synthesis and risked, by contrast, turning into a confused play of echoes and analogies that hardly made any distinction between natural history and the actions and creations of humanity, themselves more or less naturalized. This situation did not mar the success of Vidalian geography, in particular with respect to historical geography, which was too exclusively oriented to the reconstruction of political, juridical, and political boundaries, or with regard to a history centered on institutions and political events. The contrast between the German and French interpretations of the discipline is also understandable: in a country like Germany, in search of its political unity, geography tends to be used to link the State with the soil. In a country where unity is affirmed through the nation and the political existence of the nation (except for the problem of frontiers) is not in question, geography tends to be a means of discovering, behind the facade of institutions and the history of governments and princes, the concrete conditions of the material and national culture. Is this another form of legitimating or another horizon on society, with its connections to the land?

Vidal de La Blache brought to this task his talent and the diversity of his education: a remarkable master of language (the classical education), more archaeologist than historian (the School of Athens), and concerned about basing the scientific character of geography on natural history. The landscape is present everywhere in his writings, whether he is describing the diversity of the country (the *Tableau de la géographie de la France*) or speculating about the inequalities in population and density (the *membra disjecta* assembled in *Principes de géographie humaine* after his death). It is astonishing, then, that an author who tried to combine evocation, research into trace amounts of evidence, and comprehensive interpretation did not make the landscape an object of methodological reflection. The originality of geography compared with, for example, social morphology meant not paying too much attention to epistemology. That originality does not prevent a "philosophical" or explanatory discourse on the relationship between man and nature or the geographic setting and society, nor on lifestyles, a key idea and mediating principle in Vidal's thought.

But on landscapes, as a means of approach to be constantly used, there is very little. Even the word does not occur: landscape, country, physiognomy (which comes from botany), language stops short. Even in the late-appearing article in which Vidal (when considering habitat) outlined very clearly the definition of rural landscapes—"The village is a well-defined organism, distinct, having its own life and personality, that expresses itself in the landscape"[28]—landscape was not constructed; it was considered an immediate given, a substance that was made part of the central focus of his investigations. Vidal maintained a degree of uncertainty: "A city, a village, houses—all are descriptive elements; whether one examines their form or construction materials, their adaptation to a style of life that is rural or urban, farming or pasture, they throw light on the relationship between man and the soil."[29] Thus, demonstration necessarily rests more on collecting examples than on the rigorous definition of the nature of phenomena. On this point Vidal recalls at times the almost mythic uncertainties of the ecological postulate. It is that way for the word *pays* (in English, "country"): "*Pays* as an expression has the characteristic that it is applicable to inhabitants almost as much as to the soil."

It would be absurd to transform a thought into something rigid and to deny all the nuances, the corrections, and the variations in shading by which the work of Vidal is enriched. But I do not wish to oppose a Vidal-Jekyll to a Vidal-Hyde as other commentators do, each choosing which Vidal is the good one. The permanent contradiction in the work and its presuppositions no doubt comes from the difficulty of distinguishing natural history from social facts, difficulties present at the outset and in the very reasons for the success of this geography. The Vidal of the "human clusters" is without doubt closer to social morphology than the representatives of those two currents think. The Vidal of the *Tableau* follows more easily the larger trend represented by the naturalist interpretation.

It is first a rule of the genre: Jules Michelet had boldly situated his tableau of France *historically* at the beginning of the feudal era. Vidal's *Tableau* comes, in a way, *before history* to describe its place and conditions. Naturalism, however, does not stem from the place necessarily granted to physical elements—relief, climate, and water—nor from the geographical situation, even if that means extending the inventory and analysis of movements to plants and people. It is not enough to affirm that "man has been with us the longtime faithful disciple of the soil" and that "the study of the soil will therefore contribute to illuminating the character, the customs, and tendencies of the inhabitants."[30] Here we see a recognizable expression of the classical postulate. What Vidal brought

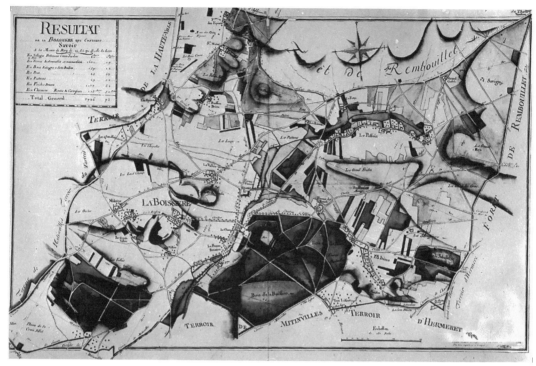

Figure 8.4
Announcement of the land survey: the territory of La Boissière, near Rambouillet, *intendant's* plan (1785–86). The *intendant's* plans, which were proposed for raising local land taxes based on better information, represented a preliminary draft of the land registry. The distribution of cultivated land by size is indicated in the box labeled "Résultat."

was a new point of view on the relationship concerning the beginnings of history. The important thing, in this new form of naturalism, was not the interest in geology or botany seen through landscape. It was the analogy with living things or the image of germination. Through that, place became, in a manner of speaking, a historical actor: ferment and germination were inscribed in the soil; they guided history through their own development. Nature and past were merged. As for Paris, Vidal defined the function of the tableau: "We do not have to follow it in its historic development. . . . Geography is assuredly not uninterested, but it no longer plays the key role. It is enough for us to have studied where and how the seed of future beings was deposited, how a *perennial plant* grows that cannot be uprooted by any storm and to have shown in this *vitality* a powerful and imposing force from the *soil* makes itself felt and the intertwining roots pushing out all directions, roots that one cannot rip up or cut out" (italics added).[31] The archaeological role of the landscape was left behind: the geographer was seeking a principle of explanation, not

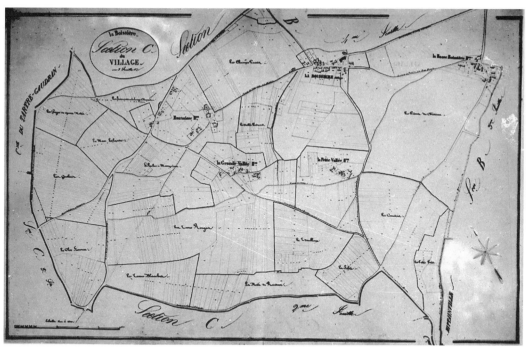

Figure 8.5
The first land survey: section map for the commune of La Boissière (1820).

material traces, by going back to a time that is more or less indeterminate. The urban network of Flanders gave Vidal the opportunity to go back to the image of the seed: "There was actually in the reciprocity of needs and the possibilities of transportation the seed of a rich development in urban life. But the roots from which was born this fecund and exuberant urban foliation go much deeper into the past."[32] The site and the situation were no longer opportunities, but the preponderant factors for explanation—for the beginnings and over the long term. In the urban landscapes (the photographic commentaries stress this), how something took root can be read in the topography, materials, and so on. Thus, a genuine "transparency" was established between the landscape seen over the long term, beginning with still extant signs, and the interpretation that was given to it. In contrast to Michelet, always the "demiurge," Vidal never escaped the illusion of legibility, the look given to the long term and material culture—an obvious enrichment—ending in some negation of the history and nature of social facts. The prestige of style often made up for the deficit of analysis. Substituting "physical" materials for the archive constitutes an incontestable advance, with which all history, as science and memory, is very pleased today. But the material in question is raw, and it had sufficiently rubbed up against critique from other sources.

A Vidalian caprice? He emerged in an intellectual and social configuration of circumstances. The fertile soil was not negligible, and the connections were many. First, there was the success of natural history and of experimental research right at the end of the nineteenth century, which placed reflection into a series of debates with powerful ideological echoes:[33] the Pasteur revolution and the academic (almost political) struggle about spontaneous generation and fermentation; then Darwinism; and, finally, the rebirth of vitalism, if only in the philosophic form that Bergson gave to it. These tendencies were not quite contemporary with each other. If they surfaced in Vidal's thought, it was not just for reasons that were local or accidental (direct links or school ties). Vidal did not try to reconstruct them in a coherent manner. They were a play of images and analogies, a real "collage," reflecting one aspect of the natural sciences to the other, as the comment about Paris illustrates. The process resulted in a rich and composite language more than a lesson in method.

This view of the French landscape fits well with movements in society that were more autonomous with regard to scientific and academic scruple (e.g., travel accounts and guides). The genre was modified as a function of the clientele: tourists less concerned about encyclopedic knowledge and social utility than about exotic trifles, views, and spectacles. The consumer landscape was designed in the second half of the nineteenth century, validating the journey, homogeneity, the brand image for the entire country. Jean-Claude Chamboredon studied the "creation," the "invention," of the Provençal landscape intended for social uses that diverged from production and social realities. One image of the natural landscape was generalized as the general physiognomy of the country: "In this landscape plant life in its luxuriance and strangeness expressed the country's physical qualities. . . . The geographical descriptions concerning the Moors expressed this new law of the landscape."[34] That is, if the landscape did actually exist in relation to forms of production, and otherwise for the outside observer, the landscape's function did indeed change. "Its naturalization, notably because it effaces the image of a cluster of profitable and productive uses, allows leisure space to be purchased for speculation (subdivisions) and natural space to be turned into museums (reserves and parks)."[35] Through painting, another approach to the landscape, Chamboredon showed how the description of the French peasant was transformed through the work of Jean-François Millet.

> In a paradoxical fashion, it was the peasant utopia invented by Millet that would provide the image of the morality of humble folk. Thus,

for the sake of the new urban classes and a widely diversified peasantry, the morality of an independent ancient peasantry would be proposed. At the moment of industrialization, the image of work as eternal and immutable labor would be offered. During the time of mechanization, ancestral techniques and tools would be offered as a quasi-ritual practice.[36]

Turning the peasant into folklore doubles the naturalization of the landscape and makes it part of the scene's unchanged character in the tableau.

Geography therefore intersects with these movements that are nourished by the economic and social history of the country, history that is more or less transposed into sensitivity or strategy. How can we be astonished when the products—even more the social practices (and divisions)—of the soil were blurred in the *Tableau* that opens the history, republican and progressivist as it was, by Ernest Lavisse? The rural areas of France seemed, in this last third of the nineteenth century, to come close to a kind of stationary state. Politically, they were no longer the place of lively conflict among those dividing up property. Social conflicts came to life only as a function of new stakes, in the wine-making areas of the Midi and at the beginning of the twentieth century. The analysis offered by Marx in *The Eighteenth Brumaire of Louis Napoleon* turns out to be exactly right, in retrospect, given the outcome of 1871. The great depression, which particularly affected agricultural products, shed light on the world of small producers. Paradoxically, for about twenty years, rural emigration slowed down. The great tax levies partially and sometimes completely emptied the countryside of a surplus population of day workers and workers paid in kind, and especially of artisans and cottage workers. Once reduced and purged, the countryside closed up again on the peasant world of farmers and landowners. The evolution of this social simplification was grasped in the great geographical works of the early 1900s, of Jules Sion and Albert Demangeon in particular.[37] But even then agriculture clearly did not lack for manpower. Agricultural capitalism, which still depended on labor and the reserve of day and seasonal workers, felt this demographic situation and, reacting as if to a drop in prices, let the pressure subside that it had exerted since the beginning of the century in several regions. This affected the ideology of land development and improvement. We therefore seem to be actually coming close to this peasant utopia founded on small and medium property. The stationary state would express above all social stability. Let us pause a moment. The peasantry, like the landscape, seemed to regain or find a truth, that of a long-term equilibrium between the upheavals that surged during the first part of the twentieth century and the needs of modernization, which still remain uncertain. Of course, the question is an image, and geographers take a sly pleasure in measuring the gaps between one region and another or between opposite movements. Nevertheless, the standard has been set. After all, the dispute between the conservatives and the progressives involves this peasantry in the context of a republic that is generally accepted.

The tendency to turn things into tradition includes rivalries and defensive policies. Conservative regionalism, driven, for example, by the Société des agriculteurs de France, does not significantly differ from the "progressivism" that inspired the communal monographs of the *instituteurs* (schoolteachers for the lower grades). Geography, often enlisted by republicans and often heir to the *instituteur* culture, did not mechanically reproduce all these social phenomena and strategies. But a "synchronous" logic did reinforce its choices and gave them an ideological resonance, of which the neutral and apparently objective landscape provided justification. To that may be added, for the years 1890 through 1900, the feeling of an asymptotic evolution, as if reaching the point where the rural and urban populations were equal constituted the end of one history and allowed for a state of ideal equilibrium.

The time of the Vidal school must not be imagined as a time of dogma. The absence of rules, in the Durkheim sense of the word, and the taste for the topic fed the most involved students' arguments, which on other occasions could have been interpreted as trenchant criticisms. I see three that deal mainly with the major risks of naturalization. The first comes from Lucien Gallois, a most analytic and rigorous spirit. Gallois recognized the existence of natural regions, of "countries" [*pays*], and even the geography's vocation in detecting them. Nevertheless, preoccupied with territorial divisions more than landscapes, he never confused what pertained to natural conditions and what pertained to man. "How can we discern what is an act of man from what is an act of nature if we start off putting the work of men and natural conditions in the same categories?"[38] The best demonstration consists of breaking apart the accepted connection between natural geography and the peasant consciousness as typified in area names. Based on a critique of geographical nomenclature that skillfully married the traditional practices of historical geography and the sense of the terrain, Gallois calls into question the heterogeneity of this so-called class of names. Jules Sion joins in this critical work by studying the names of the areas in eastern Normandy, but he goes even further: he pushes the meaning of landscapes from the natural domain into the arena of human affairs. The structure of farms, cultivation practices, and the presence or absence of domestic industry make each area original and underlie the consciousness that the peasants have about it: "Today, the farmer points out especially the expanse of the farms that at times have a hundred or two hundred hectares under the direction of the *gros messieurs*. The size of the farms, the fecundity of the soil— such are for him the essential characteristics of the Vexin."[39] What distinguishes Normandy from Picardy is not the natural landscape. "It is not or is no longer its methods of cultivation; it is rather its language, its social state."[40] On the Picard side it is the "multitude of small proprietors" and a "strong rural democracy." On the Normand side it is the manorial houses. Lucien Febvre takes up this idea more generally in *La Terre et l'évolution humaine*. A difficult book and often badly understood, it shows that profound affinities and rejection of systems make of this arbitrage between Vidalian geography, German geography, and social morphology a defense and illustration of Vidal's approach. Yet at the same time, this historian refuses the naturalization of social facts and without question defines a new orientation of geography and analysis of landscapes, as seen in this nearly forgotten passage, which at the same time skirts the ecological postulate:

> Whoever studies the action of geographical conditions on the structure of social groups runs the risk of getting confused. . . . He risks seeing in it "the cause" of a certain social structure, the ubiquity of which he seems to be ignorant. But whoever reverses the terms and asks . . . *what features of a given landscape,* of a geographical grouping directly understood or historically reconstituted, are explained or can be explained the *continuous action, positive or negative, of a certain group or a certain form of social organization* . . . [,] that person, if he is cautious, will risk no error, no confusion nor abusive generalization. (Italics added.)[41]

The idea could not be better expressed that the landscape, if it is accepted as an object of research, must be constructed and that its appearance is the product of man's action more than a kind of antecedent. What can therefore be observed through these lines is the effort to orient geography to a social geography that says the opposite of "naturalization." At the same time, the age of certain perceived or detected developments risks putting the origin of the most significant contrasts back in time out of memory. The return to history will not take place straightaway. When he reissued his *Essai* of 1934, Roger Dion went back to the central idea:

> This opposition between two modes of rural landscape is not a necessary effect of the composition of the soil. It is an action that is purely human and goes back to prehistory. When the agricultural revolution

of the nineteenth century took place, putting land that was once left fallow into forage crops, nothing had as yet threatened this primitive contrast. We still observe today striking remnants of it in the way rural dwellings are spread out and in the look of the cultivated lands themselves.[42]

THE PART PLAYED BY GEOGRAPHY AND THE PART PLAYED BY HISTORY: THE CRITICAL ANALYSIS OF THE LANDSCAPE

Clarification emerged during research on the rural landscape, although it did not take place immediately.[43] These studies did not really penetrate in France until the 1930s, when economic and social history converged with renewed themes and sources as well as a more self-critical return of geography. The parallel interventions of Marc Bloch (*Les Caractères originaux de l'histoire rurale française* [1931]) and Roger Dion (the *Essai* of 1934) revived debates on rural history and traditional civilizations that until then were not widespread in France. Earlier, Meitzen had sought to bring together opposing views on the agrarian systems of "races" that had shared Europe. Marc Bloch considered this "beginning" phase as one step. "Truly, we have to be able to go further back to the anonymous populations of prehistory, the creators of our lands. But let us not speak of races or peoples—nothing more obscure than the idea of ethnography. It is better to say 'types of civilizations.'"[44] A great part of French literary geography had been focused on more modest subjects, linking the forms of population, groupings, and dispersion of settlements with the natural conditions and notably with the permeability or impermeability of the subsoil. There, too, failure was certain. Yet from these two sides the game of hypotheses (and their destruction) was launched. Thereby the idea of the rural landscape was freed as something quite distinct from that of the ambiguous idea of landscape, since the latter notion expressed neither its totality nor its autonomy. Among certain repeated elements of the landscape—the groupings of the settlements, the design and delimitation of the fields, the disposition of the woods and forests, the role of fallow lands—the "inventors" of the rural landscape established a system of more or less stable relationships. This landscape, taken apart, analyzed, and sorted, was itself confronted with techniques of cultivation, use of tools, ways of feeding animals (which did not always leave legible traces in the landscape), social organization, collective practices here and there, and customs that were on the order of relationships among men. Even if reflection comes from concrete data and remains subject to multiple tests of coherence about the land, the question still remains about setting up a scientific objective that is not involved with

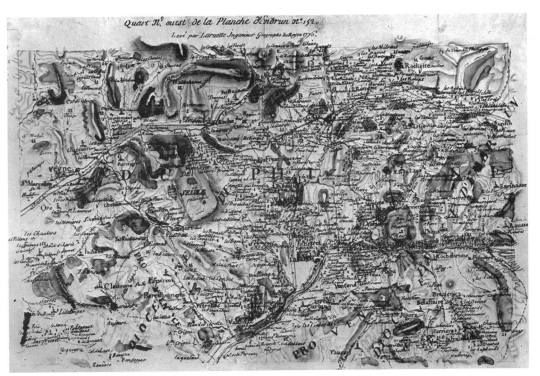

Figure 8.6
The Cassini map, excerpt of the minutes of the map of Embrun, surveyed in 1776. Drawn on a scale of
1 : 86,400, the Cassini map, the first complete depiction of French territory, still mingled techniques and
modes of representation. Relief and topography are indicated in a manner that is more expressive than exact.
"These beautiful maps . . . are only 'geometrical.' . . . They are not based on any measurement of altitude,
nor do they try to represent the real shape of the land" (*Dictionnaire de géographie*, 1970).

the traditional way of dividing up domains and sources of history or
with the division between the visible and nonvisible. Roger Dion described this effort well in the 1981 edition of the *Essai:* "These facts are
not the kind that are immediately perceived. If we are to grasp them, we
have to forget views that are close together and aspects of detail that in
every landscape fix and retain our attention."[45] The landscape of the
scholar is another landscape.

Progress consists of disassembling and reassembling the toy. Marc
Bloch and Roger Dion were the first critics of the arguments, which they
spelled out in full, that there are two kinds of rural civilization that stand
in contrast to each other through these developments: the rural economy
of the north, with its communal practices, and the rural economy of the
south, with its freedom to close off and plant; the land of the open field
and the land of the enclosed field; the land of the *charrue* (a heavy plow,
pulled by two or more animals, used to turn the soil and often having a

front axle with two wheels) and the land of the *araire* (a light or "scratch" plow, drawn by one animal, and used to push the soil to either side of the furrow to cover the seeds). Any exception, contradiction, or simple discrepancy between the elements of the landscape goes up in value more or less according to the scale. Remote enclaves allow more for pondering, especially if it is recognized that they show similarities only in the slight differences in tools, social organization, and forms of habitation.

Thus, on the scale of France as a whole, including neighboring countries, Dion is able to set aside the old problematic of countries and reinsert geology, or more precisely the detailed interpretation of the features of rocks in their place. But he admits that the contrasts in terrain and climate generally reinforced the progression of a "Nordic" style of development on the fertile and silt-laden plains of northern France, whereas the climatic irregularity and topographical contrasts encouraged agrarian individualism and the distinction between the *ager* (arable land belonging to the community) and the *saltus* (woodlands or uncultivated land used for pasture). Marc Bloch gave further nuance to this dichotomy when he argued that if we take a close look at the agrarian landscape and organization, a tripartite division should be noted: regular and open fields in the north, where collective servitude and triennial rotation were the rule; irregular and open fields in the heavily populated agricultural zones of the south, where collective constraints were less powerful and the rotations more varied, based on the "biennial" model; and zones of enclosure, which by contrast were the rule in the less attractive regions because of the discontinuity in arable soil, the extent of woods and moors, the age of the population and the clearings, and the social context of this conquest. This articulation of natural geography and history is what Roger Dion reemphasized when he undertook to expand the *Essai* into a detailed study of the "rural settlement" (the term preferred over "landscape") of the Parisian basin.[46]

This more heightened sensitivity to geographical differences must not conceal the principal tendency, which is a return to history and a progression from a relatively uncertain anthropology to a more precise analysis of the conditions and actors in each period. The return to history is based on multiple observations, the chief one in that telling criticism that the system that integrates social organization and landscapes was not constructed all at once. Ultimately phases can be discerned. Even if we admit that collective practices, the division into extended fields, and the annual reallocation of lands have existed for a long time, the consolidation of settlements, the strengthening of the village community, and restrictive customs only recently took on their systematic character, beginning in the twelfth and thirteenth centuries. Expanding on Marc

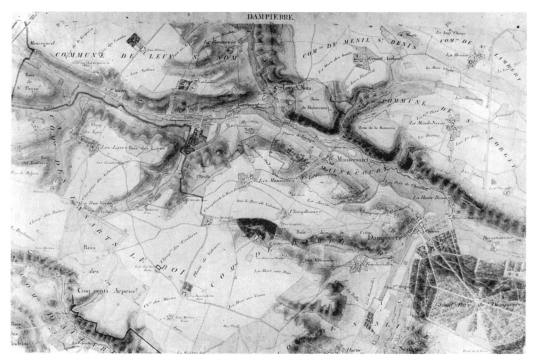

Figure 8.7
The cartographic memory of France: the map of the general staff. The first series of maps, which showed Paris, Melun, and Beauvais, was prepared in 1818–23. The surveys, which were drawn on a scale of 1 : 100,000, represented objects according to their shape and "true" dimension. Work showing topography (relief represented in hachures) and planimetry was done in ink and enhanced by colors. Minutes of the map of Melun, reduced to 1 : 80,000.

Bloch, Dion explained how the domain villa of the High Middle Ages became the "village land." In parallel there were the ever-increasing collective constraints (imposition of the triennial rotation, which extended to existing lands under cultivation in northern France), and the expansion of the village into the surrounding areas. "The large landowner, who had once been the head of the farming operation in search of manpower, became a rentier in search of revenues, the importance of which grew with the number of people who paid him dues."[47] This way of living from the *cens* (a feudal obligation in the form of a fixed tax that the possessor of a parcel of land paid the seigneur of a fief), together with the functioning of the farm community, creates the rural landscape, in a fashion. In the same way, starting in the fifteenth century with the less populated lands and under the impact of economic changes (income became more attractive than the *cens*), the domain became attractive again for the seigneurs and then for the bourgeois citizen. This was a reversal of the current in favor of one form of agrarian individualism, contested to

be sure by the most powerful peasants. Let us omit the debates about the
details that this reassessment provoked. In any case, the rural landscape no
longer appeared to have been set from the beginning; it was posed as a
historical problem even if the effect of the natural qualities of the soils
and climate was that these actions and their impact might show geographical differences. The mediations, then, were numerous, whether or
not they involved the resistance and fragility of the populations, the possibility or impossibility of modifying agricultural techniques and investing in a change of agricultural techniques and tools. Going beyond Vidal, "scholarly" reasoning returned to the reasoning used by the imperial
statisticians and agronomists.

This return to history—and more precisely to a history of social relationships and the conflicts that derive from them—Roger Dion, who
admittedly never departed from a Marxist vantage point, stated with clar-
ity in 1951 when he drew up a balance sheet of a generation of works
(and notably one of his most recent achievements, Derruau's study La
Grande limagne).

> One is thus led to recognize that in this outline many features, per-
> haps most of them, have neither the antiquity nor the fixity that was
> first ascribed to them. One finds oneself in the presence of the fact
> that in the history of agrarian arrangements, the modern and con-
> temporary period, the one we see the best, is dominated by an antag-
> onism that is definitely not that of two civilizations, still less that of
> two races, but, more modestly, that of two social classes: the peas-
> antry on the one hand, and the landed bourgeois on the other. The
> control over cultivated land by peasants and bourgeois was expressed
> in the different patterns of the land parcels, the respective extension
> of which grew or declined as economic, demographic, or political
> circumstances dictated. The explication of a rural landscape or, bet-
> ter, the agrarian structure of which this landscape is the picturesque
> expression must, in large part, come from the history of those social
> classes to which the current owners of the land belong.[48]

For a contrary view, Dion recalls "the excesses of an opposing conception which, in the interpretation of this same landscape, denies any
efficiency to tradition as well as, in a general way, to collective attitudes
independent of immediate economic necessities." Let us delineate the
consequences of this return to history and to social relationships. The
transparency and coherence of landscapes do not emerge strengthened.
The problem is no longer, when looking at certain evidence, finding nature or man again. The dialectic is artificial, should such be the case, or

too global. The problem is elsewhere: identify experiences in the course of which the natural data can intervene as a factor. These successive experiences leave, in varying degrees, traces in the landscape—some are "alive," others are adhesions or fossils. In one sense, hardly any importance can be accorded to a vague frontier between what the landscape reveals and what it conceals. Between the practiced eye of the specialist (or skill in chemical analysis) who gives the alert to such and such a form, land division, or alignment through aerial photography, and the work in the laboratory, the search, the technique will take the principal place. Let us also not forget that to establish or locate is not to explain: forms, recognized patterns can preserve usefulness or a social or symbolic value (land parcels, limits of fields, outlines of roads) at a time when the reasons for their establishment have disappeared. For example, rural divisions and the division of property do not necessarily coincide at a predetermined moment. The image of the fields as they appear in photographs, in color or in shades of gray evoking the different kinds of plants and the varied advance of agricultural work, does not faithfully reproduce the land registry.

The countryside must be interpreted as a palimpsest. The commentators on "Haussmanization" (the work of destruction is proper for uncovering old structures) borrowed this comparison.* The idea is also applicable to rural landscapes. On this point, British curiosity has by far preceded French "science." Both the historian and the weekend archaeologist at the beginning of the twentieth century sought, in the landscape of enclosures, the structures of open-field villages predating this powerful agrarian revolution, which began in the fifteenth and sixteenth centuries. They found below the open field the signs of previous developments, networks of ditches and embankments that belonged to the "partitioned lands," which resemble what has been found in Cornwall and Wales. In his 1934 *Essai,* Roger Dion, still faithful to the ethnic argument, showed an interest in these archaeological discoveries:

> La Beauce, though subject to the collective restrictions that
> characterize the northern agricultural milieu, contains, at least in the
> southern part, more hamlets than large villages. And it is precisely in
> a community in this region, Villexanton (Loir-et-Cher), that an
> archaeologist, to whom we already owe the explanation of the

---

* EDITOR'S NOTE: "Haussmanization," a nineteenth-century coinage, was inspired by the work of Georges-Eugène Haussmann, prefect of the Seine under Napoleon III, who transformed Paris from a medieval to a modern city. Vast neighborhoods of old Paris, most notably the Île de la Cité, were demolished in the process.

"curtains" of Picardy, quite recently recognized a network of tiny
land parcels, following the custom of the north, and vestiges of an
early land division into fields that were larger and less narrow.[49]

In Lorraine and in Cambrésis, regions that had a settlement characteristic of the open field, land research has brought to light traces of fields
bordered by land embankments and an ancient division of the settlement,
verified at least up to the end of the Gallo-Roman period. Recovery of
ancient civilizations or ethnic groups? The image of the front or the frontier, varying according to the ebb and flow of peoples—is it always convincing in similar cases? Ethnography risks "naturalizing" in its turn
agrarian developments through global or excessive contrasts. No doubt
explanations must be sought in the waning or growing, sometimes unstable, ascendancy of men, which varies according to density, demographic pressure, and the capacity of groups or masters of the soil to provide for orderly land use.

The representation given today of the rural landscape of the High
Middle Ages,[50] for both southern and northern France, differs from the
classic image of the Merovingian villa and the village community domi-
nating the surrounding area. A question about the continuity of inhabited sites has been raised. Described instead for these remote times is a
population that hangs over the territory like a loose piece of clothing.
The peasant population lived in puny hamlets, constructed with flimsy
materials, that could be abandoned whenever they moved on to cultivate
new lands. Land use did not ultimately divide the land into an *ager* or a
saltus. Rather, people changed fields according to temporary practices as
they moved about, leaving behind fields that had lost their fertility. These
are images that are closer to African agriculture than to those arrangements deemed of time immemorial that formerly and until quite recently
had been ascribed to our countryside. The organization of lands into
fixed cells, the distinction between the *ager* and the *saltus,* the construction of a dwelling as something more permanent, and the organization of
the village community and parish are later developments. When we
reflect on this change, the significance of the combination of agricultural
techniques and methods of organizing the land (and people) that Pierre
Gourou has shown seems illuminating: it certainly applies to the historic
role of the seigneury. That parallels, in the following centuries with the
great land clearings, with the other mobility in habitat. Hamlets and
other new communities, more fragile and less populated, participated in
the improvement of marginal areas or a forested no-man's-land. These
were not all meant as a way to withstand the rationalization of the land,
the crises of the fourteenth century, or simply the accidents of farm life,

Figures 8.8 and 8.9
The rural landscape
seen from an air-
plane: the commune
of Ouarville (Eure) in
1949 and 1964.
That there is a chrono-
logical correspon-
dence between the
use of aerial photo-
graphy and the ad-
vance of research on
the rural landscape no
longer appears acci-
dental. The meridian
view reveals orderings
and arrangements
not so visible from the
ground. Seeing one
parcel, we can better
grasp the usages and
evolution over the
long term.

where the return on the land was uncertain. If, as in a movie, the images of this rural history were accelerated, the rural landscape would appear as a series of twitches. Unless critically examined, representations of the landscape as "fixed" or references to rural civilizations as a dichotomy pose a trap.

Likewise, the idea of "reading" has always had something passive about it. While it may be conceded that the landscape—examined, observed, or dealt with through the intermediary of technical means—reveals signs and suggests hypotheses, any attempt to explain and to recreate its history must mobilize other tools, with a battery of "models." It was archaeology, first of all, that, after the detection of several sites allowed us to make sense of the *Wüstungen* (deserted villages)[51] and undercut the apparent continuities and the "fixed" arguments. The study of the vegetation then followed. An examination of the limits of the forests was undertaken by Vidal de La Blache, Camille Jullian, and Roger Dion. Another step had to be taken to consider plant groups as they relate to the history of this carpet of trees and agriculture and to find the traces of the oldest clearings. Plants also have their archaeology, but one that is not without mediation, starting with the soils and remains of fossil plants (charred tree trunks, for example). In brief, more and more sophisticated models have been used in the analysis of objects in the landscape that are less and less visible, just as the chemical treatment of aerial views and messages launched by satellite and converted to numbers or colors create genuine interpretations that are more than "readings."

If one changes the point of view and seeks, in the history of the French countryside and society, explanations of this interplay of questions about the rural landscape and the break between Vidal's generation and Dion's, which one can appreciate in retrospect, hypotheses spring to mind, perhaps too easily. The impression of equilibrium, along with the tendency to restructure the countryside and turn it into a piece of folklore, is in part shattered by the mobility of rural society. In negative terms first of all, it was thought, up to 1900, that the agricultural world would become visible, freed from the dross and debris as well as the clusters of groups that had accumulated in the countryside at the margins of agricultural activity. The war, more than any other event, created gaps in the active population; the rebuilding led to some attempts to reassemble land parcels; the economic disasters shook the markets even before the 1930s; and the rural exodus magnified by the crisis thrust this world into a history of menace that had no continuity. The spasms were for the short term, part of the experience lasting up to the more serious and perhaps more positive upheavals that followed World War II. Turning everything into folklore in a period during which the lines of "destructuring" could already be detected too easily takes on the allure of the ideology of rejection or ignorance. In conditions yet to be elucidated, epistemology will once again meet up with social history.

The hypothesis is overly marked by "sociologism." It should inspire criticism. But let us reread Roger Dion's conclusion to his 1946 article: he based it on a forecast that was wrong in its content but yet confirmed the hypothesis. Reflection on land development accompanied the return to history.

> This agrarian individualism to which the elite of rural society aspired so passionately in the hundred years from 1750 to 1850 gradually began to fade under the pressures of mechanization. After just ten years, necessity would make itself felt when pieces of arable land were marked out according to the exigencies of these machines, and from that moment on, our agrarian schools were studying the means of constraining the exploiters of small family farms to group their holdings into large tracts of land required by this mode of plowing. We would then see the reappearance, in new form, of the disciplines of crop rotation and communal obligation.[52]

For this period, another assessment should give rise to further reflection. The idea of the rural landscape's expressing a certain tension between the fixed theses and the meaning of agrarian changes developed at the moment when the urban landscape, which had just emerged from the phases of simple description and "naturalist" reminders of the Vidalian period, was blurring, with the city appearing, without doubt, as the particular place of change and odd ideas. Raoul Blanchard put the explanation for the urban landscape in the location and the situation more than in the articulations of building morphology and society. Advances in these studies were identified first with demography, with economic data, with the definition of functions and their possible transformation. The landscape was set up as mediation for the understanding of the countryside. It swung between an aesthetic judgment and a simple picture, in the approach to the city. Geography in this domain was transformed into economics. Urban history, as affirmed by the Institut d'urbanisme de Paris through Marcel Poële and Henri Lavedan, was exclusively interested in forms, almost to excess, but rediscovered the slope of a certain naturalism in growth (close to that of Vidal) and floated among the disciplines. Nevertheless, through this history, and even more through the criticisms that it aroused, a certain idea of the landscape was created as a minor theme.

This text has not sought to draw together a complete history of the landscape, which ought to be based in any case on perception and sensibility. Nor is it even a complete picture of the manner by which scientific disciplines have made use of the landscape. What matters is even less the state of the question on current trends in research. It is rather more an attempt to establish in what conditions this idea, quite vague at the outset and always rich in ambiguity, could correspond to scientific subjects. An economic history of the idea might be created for imperial statistics (the period of the topographies) or an agrarian history or a geography in the tradition of Marc Bloch and Roger Dion.

It is clear that the truth of the landscape does not lie in the landscape. As in a work of art or in contemplating a natural spectacle, the eye of the observer does everything and provides a meaning to the relationships that we try to establish between nature, history, and development. Put simply, the observer is armed, whether he says so or not, with hypotheses, instruments of detection, and a concern for verification. Hence the curious place of Vidal de La Blache, who arrives on the scene after a series of analytical studies posing connections of nature and human developments (notably the work of the geologists), but he is also there at the origin of a movement that by means of an idea of agrarian civilization cautiously reintroduces social facts or history as explanatory factors. For reasons of education, context, and even overlapping national circumstances, naturalism remains the predominant view in expression, approach, and in reasoning, even if it means naturalizing humanity through ethnicity and folklore. It is the idea of rural landscape that, in the successive critical studies it provoked, offers the most complete and useful way of obtaining a cumulative impression. It is the richest moment of this adventure—rich through an intentionally incomplete vision of what a landscape is. But this episode confirms what is already known and what Pierre Gourou forcefully reminds us of:

> To come to useful conclusions on such a vast subject, it seems appropriate to recall that the landscape in its entirety is not a structured system. To be sure, the physical landscape is in large measure structure (in large measure, but not entirely). . . . But the physical elements and the human elements of the landscapes do not form a truly structured entity. Within the interior of the landscape, human elements are not closely tied to each other. To find a structured system, you have to go back to civilization. . . . Again, this must not be exaggerated. If there exists at the level of civilization a certain interdependence of techniques, that interdependence is not rigorous.[53]

This view is incomplete and biased. We are less astonished that modern geographers, trained in ecology, consider that "the tradition inaugurated by P. Vidal de La Blache has been lost to view." This is a new phase in the course of which man or society is replaced in nature and not subject to an analysis of different factors. The landscape again becomes a new synthesis. The progress in instrumentation (aerial views and then satellite photos, information manipulated by chemistry and computers) promises ways not only of understanding groupings, structures, and organizing them by networks, but also, as a result of work in ecological history, of grasping the models that better define the connections between physical and human data. The concepts of the French word *charge* recall the old debates of the eighteenth century, with very precise variables in theory. Does this method, for all that, account for the diversity of development and the capacity of societies to control their territory? Landscape without a real actor always poses a problem even if one reaches the point of refining a theoretical or numerical apprehension of phenomenological interactions. Let us cut to the core: this method until now has been useful for suggesting classifications and a conceptualized description. But in such and such a concrete interpretation, referring to the succession of kinds of exploitation and social conditions for improvement, the method does not appear, except for language, to produce many novelties, compared, for example, with Roger Dion's essay of 1946. It remains an open question.

Another open question: the revival of interest in the subjective landscape has reentered, in a completely normal fashion, the core of scientific studies. The time is favorable for psychoanalysis, with permanent possible ambiguities between the archetypes (which nevertheless comes close to being the individual) and a more confused "social" psychoanalysis. The time and the promptings of the present, if one admits that the current urban crisis seen in the destruction of the regular landscapes, the widespread ugliness and anguish, relate back to the landscape. Raising the question of urbanism is based in any case on this new look at the physiognomy of urban and rural areas. The inherited landscapes therefore become our inheritance and conservation the style. On this point (and on this point alone), the lesson learned by studying the rural landscape allows for a certain distance. Retaining ways of development and skills, admitting that these skills conform to a wisdom and deep knowledge of the conditions of the environment—that is a task that seems indispensable, noble, and useful. We are aware of the collective inconveniences and the biological imbalances that the destruction of the *bocage* in Brittany (large hedgerows or thickets, common in western France) brought about. So be it. But is it from the moment when the landscape conceals the succession of developments and from the moment where the best way is not necessarily indicated in the physiognomy of things? Is the landscape that is to be preserved or some form of development better adjusted to our social, technical, and biological knowledge and to fixed objects? Otherwise, one risks continually hesitating between an arbitrary conservation of what exists (in the name of the "fixed" arguments) and the transformation of the landscape into a museum, collecting for the instruction of the young images of different developments—the Gaul's hut, the villa, the hamlet of the High Middle Ages, the village. To preserve a heritage does not mean becoming a victim of a superficial reading of landscapes and their transparency, the fragility of which we have tried to establish. The first rule for a desirable conservation policy is to respect the multiplicity of history. It is not surprising that the reassuring spectacle value of the land-scape then regains all its rights, and all things considered aesthetic judg-ment (more than biological necessity) prevails in the choice.

> We are attached to the beautiful rural landscapes of Western Europe and allowed to hope that the landscapes of the *bocage* and mixed cul-ture, which are particularly charming, will be kept. This does mean preserving the human and not the natural landscapes. . . . I personally would prefer to keep the latter as it is the most threatened (and prac-tically speaking it has disappeared in France). But am I right? And do others have a different opinion?[54]

Was not the "scholarly" reading only a transition? And is that not a sign of an entirely "urbanized" society, even if it cultivates the charm of a "country" residence?

Compared with the miscellaneous lot of impressions, pieces of in-formation, and narratives more or less researched, Vidalian geography left an effective and purified description of landscapes and territory of France. Reflections on the original diversity of the country avoided the excesses of finalism. Images assumed an unquestionable social consis-tency through teaching and geographical readings, to the point that one could ask what the true nature of this discipline was: science or peda-gogy. But at the same time, this "reading" did not eliminate the preju-dices inherited from Enlightenment philosophy and, beyond that, the wisdom of nations, in particular the ecological postulate. If one there-fore discerns a series of scientific approaches that brought more rigor and fragments of explanation to knowledge of the landscape and the na-tional space, the hiatus or discrepancy remains: the lesson about re-searching the rural landscape shows that beyond factual knowledge and some necessary representations it is indispensable to define a scientific objective. Landscape becomes the objective only when it is subject to close scrutiny.

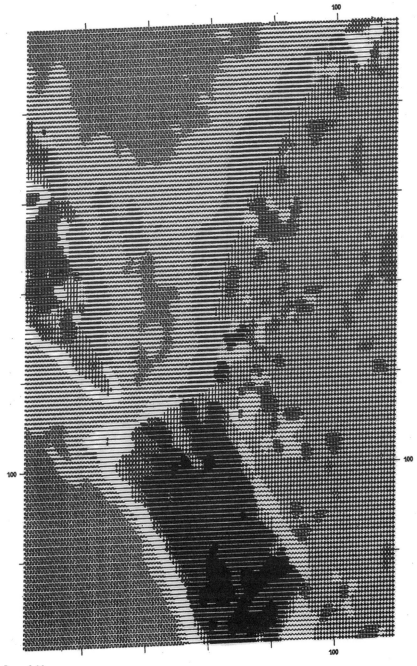

Figure 8.10

An abstract reading of the landscape: the Fromentine region seen digitally from the Landsat 1 satellite. Instruments using remote sensing technology record physical phenomena, in particular the energy that objects reflect. Digital information is converted into automated maps with "false" colors. Then the meaning of the forms and structures has to be uncovered.

NOTES

1. Émile Levasseur, *L'Étude et l'enseignement de la géographie* (Paris, 1872).

2. *Tableau de la géographie de la France,* vol. 1 of E. Lavisse, *Histoire de France* (1903); republished as a separate work (Paris, 1908).

3. Konrad Malte-Brun, *Précis de géographie universelle* (1st ed., 1810−11; later eds., 1841, 1852).

4. Élisée Reclus, *Géographie universelle* (1876−); the volume dedicated to France is dated 1881.

5. Jean-Claude Perrot, *L'Âge d'or de la statistique régionale française (an IV 1804)* (Paris: Société des études robespierristes, 1977).

6. Arthur Young, *Travels during the years 1787, 1788, & 1789, undertaken more particularly with a view of ascertaining the cultivation, wealth, resources, and national prosperity of the Kingdom of France* (London, 1794).

7. See Perrot, *L'Âge d'or,* and Stuart Woolf, "Contribution à l'histoire des origines de la statistique: France, 1789−15," *La Statistique en France à l'époque napoléonienne* (Brussels, 1981). In 1810, J. Peuchet and P.-G. Chanlaine drew up the first synthesis of these memoirs in *Description topographique et statistique de la France . . . ,* 3 vols. (Paris, 1810).

8. De Villeneuve, *Statistique du département des Bouches-du-Rhône,* 4 vols. (Marseille, 1821−29).

9. De Villeneuve, "Discours préliminaire," in ibid., 1:XV.

10. Ibid., LXIII, LXXIII.

11. Ibid., XXV.

12. Ibid., XXXIII.

13. Ibid., IV:39.

14. On the Cassini map and the origins of the map, known as the État-major or staff map, at the scale 1 : 80,000, see Colonel Berthaut, *La Carte de France, 1750−1898,* 2 vols. (Paris, 1898); F. de Dainville, *Le Langage des géographes* (Paris: A. et J. Picard, 1964); and the catalog, *Cartes et figures de la Terre* (Paris: Centre Georges-Pompidou, 1980).

15. Levasseur, *L'Étude et l'enseignement de la géographie,* 4.

16. The *Journal des mines* was created in 1794 under the direction of Coquebert de Montbret, a diplomat and scientist, who also directed the Bureau of Statistics from 1803 to 1806. The common inspiration focused on "statistical" projects and applied geology, the first studies of which were published in the journal.

17. Lucien Gallois, *Régions naturelles et noms de pays* (Paris, 1908).

18. Between 1830 and 1835, Dufrénoy and Élie de Beaumont drew up a "geological map of France" on a scale of 1 : 500,000. It was not printed until 1840. In 1841, they began publication of the three volumes of the *Explication de la carte géologique de la France* (Paris, 1841−73). Lucien Gallois recalled that the decision to draw up a geological map on a scale of 1 : 80.000 was taken in 1868; the map was begun in 1870 and finished at the beginning of the twentieth century.

19. De Caumont, *Essai sur la topographie géognostique du département du Calvados* (Caen, 1828), cited in Gallois, *Régions naturelles,* 23, 24.

20. Antoine Passy, *Description géologique du département de la Seine-Inférieure* (Rouen, 1832), cited in Gallois, *Régions naturelles,* 25.

21. Antoine Passy, *Essai sur les contrées naturelles de la France* (1857), cited in Gallois, *Régions naturelles,* 47.

22. Levasseur, *L'Étude et l'enseignement de la géographie,* 27. "Dufrénoy and Élie de Beaumont noted the close connection that exists between the geological layers of our France and regions such as Beauce, Brie, Vexin, Bray, and Sologne. These regions were never administrative divisions, and yet, in the language of countryside, their names have survived the changes in districts because they are in general founded in the nature of cultivation, which itself is a consequence of the nature of the terrain."

23. Jules Michelet, *Histoire de France,* vol. 2, book 3, *Tableau de la France* (Librairie Internationale, A. Lacroix, 1876), 1–83. The text dates from 1833.

24. An excellent work by Alain Delissen, "Géographie romantique: La cartographie illustrée de la France au XIXe siècle" (master's thesis, University of Paris IV, 1985), takes this as its focus.

25. Jean-François Chevrier, "La Photographie dans la culture du paysage," supplement to the review *Photographies,* bull. 2, photographic mission of the D.A.T.A.R., in which the importance of the heliographic mission of 1851 is noted.

26. These were studied by Delissen, "Géographie romantique," in particular, V. Levasseur and A. M. Perrot, *Atlas national illustré* (eds. of 1842, 1854, 1861), and A. Vuillemin, *Nouvel Atlas illustré* (eds. of 1844, 1855, 1874). To this may be added popular dictionaries, for example, Décembre-Allonier, *Dictionnaire populaire illustré d'histoire et de géographie* (Paris, 1864).

27. Along the same lines as the departmental statistics, let us note the work of a former staff officer, A. Hugo, *La France pittoresque ou description pittoresque, topographique et statistique des départements et colonies de la France* (1835), which included economic as well as judicial, moral, and medical data from the *Statistique générale de la France.*

28. Paul Vidal de La Blache, *Principes de géographie humaine* (Paris, 1921).

29. Vidal de La Blache, ibid., 182.

30. Vidal de La Blache, *Tableau géographique,* introduction.

31. Ibid., 133.

32. Ibid., 70.

33. Some chronological elements should be recalled here. Paul Vidal de La Blache was a student at the École normale supérieure from 1863 to 1867. From 1857 to 1866, Pasteur was the director of scientific studies at this school. The principal works on fermentation date from 1863 to 1868 and were more or less contemporary with the great ideological and academic debate from 1860 to 1865 on spontaneous generation (Pasteur, *Mémoire sur les corpuscules organisés qui existent dans l'atmosphère* [1861]). Bergson was a student at the École normale at the time when Vidal de La Blache was exercising his functions as assistant director (dissertation accepted 1878). He published *Matière et mémoire* in 1896 and *L'Évolution créatrice* in 1907.

34. Jean-Claude Chamboredon and Annie Méjean, *Territoires,* No. 2, P.E.N.S. (Paris, 1986).

35. Chamboredon and Méjean, 57.

36. Jean-Claude Chamboredon, "Peinture des rapports sociaux et invention de l'éternel paysan: les deux manières de Jean-François Millet," in *Actes de la recherche,* no. 17–18 (Paris, 1977), 28.

37. Albert Demangeon, *La Plaine picarde* (Paris, 1905), and Jules Sion, *Les Paysans de la Normandie orientale* (Paris, 1908), attached great importance to the rural domestic economy. See also *Histoire de la France rurale,* vol. 3, under the direction of Maurice Agulhon (Paris: Éditions du Seuil, 1975–77). On the "peasant" ideology, see Francine Muel, "Les Instituteurs, les paysans et l'ordre républicain," in *Actes de la recherche,* no. 17–18 (Paris, 1977), 37ff.

38. Gallois, *Régions naturelles,* 224.

39. Sion, *Les Paysans,* 9.

40. Ibid., 14.

41. Lucien Febvre, *La Terre et l'évolution humaine* (Paris, 1922), 76, 77.

42. Roger Dion, *Essai sur la formation du paysage rural* (1934; reprint, Paris, 1981).

43. For another perspective, see the recent synthesis by Jean-Robert Pitte, *Histoire du paysage français,* 2 vols. (Paris: Tallandier, 1983).

44. Marc Bloch, *Les Caractères originaux de l'histoire rurale française* (Paris, 1931; reprint, 1952), 64.

45. Dion, *Essai* (1981).

46. Roger Dion, "La Part de la géographie et celle de l'histoire dans l'explication de l'habitat rural du Bassin parisien," in *Société de géographie de Lille* (Lille, 1946).

47. Ibid., 26.

48. Dion, "Réflexions de méthode, à propos de *La Grande limagne* de Max Derruau," *Annales de géographie* (January–February 1951): 27, 31.

49. Dion, *Essai* (1934), 150, 151.

50. J. Chapelot and Robert Fossier, *Le Village et la maison au Moyen Âge* (Paris: Hachette, 1980), and Robert Fossier, *Enfance de l'Europe: Aspects économiques et sociaux,* 2 vols. (Paris: P.U.F., 1982), have enabled us to examine more closely the characteristics of this "revolution in the year 1000."

51. Collective work, *Villages désertés et histoire économique, Xe–XVIIIe siècle* (Paris: S.E.V.P.E.N., 1965).

52. Dion, "La Part de la géographie," 80.

53. Pierre Gourou, *Pour une géographie humaine* (Paris: Flammarion, 1973), 362, 363.

54. Ibid., 374.

THE VENDÉE, REGION OF MEMORY

The Blue and the White

❧

JEAN-CLÉMENT MARTIN

ixing a precise place for the Vendée in all the traces, sediments, and crystallizations left behind by the French Revolution is never easy. The symmetry between the counterrevolution and the Revolution is too obvious, at best only a lure. As if the entire counterrevolution could be reduced to a provincial appendage of western France! When it was triumphant in the nineteenth century and still quite alive in the twentieth. As if popular protest against the Revolution in the Vendée and in the neighboring departments could be ascribed exclusively to the counterrevolution! As if the Vendée were definitively formed after this epoch! These are fundamental ambiguities, which were and still are filled with misunderstandings.[1]

Yet it was during the French Revolution, and in opposition to it, that the Vendée defined and revealed itself, following a series of wars on its soil from 1793 to 1796. It kept the image it acquired at that time, with its inhabitants preserving and transmitting memories of battles and massacres. Established at this time were the foundations of a tradition that made the Vendée a special region, marked by those recollections and by the memory of that war.

Over the years, the connections between these recollections and the region became more and more complex. Collected, organized, and refined, they coalesced to form a collective memory that shaped the people of the Vendée and ultimately gave the region its unique status of "region of memory." To be sure, objects, movements, writings, and common assumptions do not of themselves account for the endurance of the wars of 1793 in the region's mentality. All of these things combined into networks, which created a strictly defined space and thereby provided it with meaning. Simply recalling the wars of the Vendée does not make the creation of this region intelligible. The region is the result of a complex process of assimilation and incorporation of the effects of those wars. It is this unique phenomenon that has to be described, in its origins and developments, if we are to understand in what sense and to what point it is legitimate to see in the Vendée a true region of memory.

The particularity of the Vendée is not buried in some tribal memory or found in a set of customs about life and death that are separate from the events and historical facts that go back beyond two or three generations.[2] The Vendée—and this is what makes it profoundly unique—draws its identity from a historical memory that is precise, decipherable, and even haunting.[3] Indeed, the vitality of the idea of the Vendée attests to this uniqueness.[4] The name itself refers to a region that owed nothing to administrative arrangements or to a distant beginning. The borders of the Vendée correspond to the area in revolt in 1793, specifically several departments—the upper two-thirds of the Vendée (areas known as the Bocage, the Breton Marais, and the Chantonay basin), the northeast part of the Deux-Sèvres (the Bressuire *bocage,* the area around the Argenton chateau), the western part of Maine-et-Loire (the Mauges), and the southern part of Loire-Atlantique (Loroux, the *pays* of Retz, Maine, and Sèvre rivers). The area excludes the Loire Valley and the Atlantic Coast. Taken together, these places had little coherence. The economy of the area was different: there were those who worked the poor land of the Bocage and the Gâtine marsh while their neighbors benefited from the somewhat more prosperous lands of the Mauges, the vineyards of the Clissonais, and the solid lands of the Marais and of Retz. The types of people were different: those known as the *bocains, maraichains,* and *paydrets,* with their different habits scorned their neighbors, the artisans and textile workers, who formed a significant part of the rural population of the Mauges and the lower Bocage, who had their own customs that were unknown elsewhere. From a political and administrative point of view there was even less coherence. The provinces of Brittany, Anjou, and Poitou joined at a border in complex, overlapping ways that in the past had given rise to conflicting laws and regulations for people living right next to each other.[5]

Despite all this, the people in the rebel armies, identified as the "brigands of the Vendée" at the time of the repression, always demanded to be known afterward as the people of the Vendée. Those from the Mauges, first of all, who gave the insurrection its first commander, Jacques Cathelineau, claimed to be the heart of the Vendée, but so did those from Retz, where François Athanase Charette lived. Then in 1818, Fontenay-le-Comte, an important center of resistance to the Republic, claimed to be the true Vendée; soon it was imitated by other towns, so much did the prestige and fame of the militant Vendée and of the Catholic and royal armies eclipse any other reference. Today the reason for these claims is understood. This region known as the Vendée now finds confirmation of its existence in tourist signs. Cholet now claims to have been the capital of Vendée in arms, forgetting its revolutionary stance and opposition to the Vendéens in 1793. The logo of the department of the Vendée is a double heart, inspired by the one the insurgents of 1793 wore. No doubt these official markers make for shabby points of reference and displays of mediocrity, but they assure and reinforce those sentiments of belonging to the region. If these feelings find little outward expression, they are nevertheless widespread and accepted.

THE ORGANIZING EVENT

The Presence of the Dead

One of the original features of this region, and one of the differences that sharply divides it from its neighbors, lies in the proliferation of reminders of the wars of 1793. No sooner had the fighting ended than survivors started putting up crosses and arches, grateful for having escaped death or desirous of preserving the memory of fallen family members.[6] But this ripple of private commemoration was nothing compared to the wave of commemorations that poured forth during the first Restoration. There is the monument to Charles Artus, marquis de Bonchamps, at Saint-Florent-le-Vieil, the statue and chapel at Lege to the memory of Charette, the Cathelineau monument at Le Pin-en-Mauges, the Torfou column—one of the biggest battles in 1793 was fought at Torfou—and others. The memory of the wars became the first order of business during visits by the high nobility (the duc and duchesse d'Angoulême, the duchesse de Berry), which were celebrated in the presence of the "veterans." Such occasions always left behind new projects for monuments, so in 1830, the great leaders and principal places were put into durable form for the public's recollection. For a more restricted audience, memory took the form of paintings, done at the command of Louis XVIII for his palace at St. Cloud, that represented twelve Vendée and Chouan generals.[7] Memory also lived on in innumerable publications.[*]

Despite the July Monarchy, which obliterated inscriptions and smashed monuments, the effort to keep memory alive in monuments continued, surging to its greatest expansion in the last half of the nineteenth century. The high point was reached in the years 1880 to 1910, when to recall the wars of the Vendée had immediate political significance at the national level. For example, two leaders were commemorated—Henri de La Rochejaquelein, with a statue erected at Saint-Aubin-de-Baubigné, and Charette, with a cross erected at La Chabotterie. During this same period too, in countless places around the region, crosses, stained glass, and even plaques recalled the massacres suffered by the simple country folk. Much later, though the current had slowed considerably, it did not entirely stop, as seen in the completion of the Mont des Alouettes chapel, blessed in March of 1968, 140 years after the first stone was laid. This current still maintains existing monuments and adds to the stock of places marked for remembrance at a rate of three or four per year. Thus is formed, with links of different size to be sure, the chain connecting the places of memory.

A similar movement became an institution with the formation of teams of specialists. At the beginning of the nineteenth century, these groups were composed of nobles who supported the royalist cause. By the end of the century, they were scholars, politicians, and priests. Their mission was to defend and pass on memory. Today, various associations numbering about 2,500 to 3,000 individuals have picked up the baton.[8] If the result of these activities cannot be precisely determined, at least memory has been maintained without interruption for two centuries. In fact, it has been popularized and diffused to the extent that everyone

---

[*] EDITOR'S NOTE: "Chouan" refers to the *chouannerie,* the massive peasant uprising that spread across much of western France. Resistance took the form of guerrilla attacks and pillage. It died out during the Consulate. The Chouans later became the great heroes of the royalist tradition. The *chouannerie* generally does not include the insurrection of the Vendée, which had the character of a genuine war with pitched battles. The wars of the Vendée were fought over a much more limited area and ended in military defeat in 1793 and execution of the Vendée leaders in 1794. Both, nevertheless, were a reaction to the coercive de-Christianization mounted by the republican government, when priests were required in 1791 to take an oath to the Civil Constitution of the Clergy, and to forced conscription into the republican army. The *chouannerie* also had a decided economic bent: the intense resentment of the countryside first against the bourgeois, for appropriating the *biens nationaux* (property, often ecclesiastical, confiscated by the revolutionary government), and then against the government, for letting them take a share.

Figure 9.1
The Chapel of the Martyrs in the forest of Vézins, built by a group called Souvenir Vendéen (1950). In front of it is another chapel, built by Count de Maulevrier and blessed in 1863.

enjoys a piece of it. The choice of street names over the last ten years in the towns and villages of the Vendée bears witness to this. For nearly all of the localities where battles took place, citing a hero or a prominent event is to be expected. By contrast, no one who wore the blue uniform of the national government, with the exception of a few moderates, has the honor of a plaque. Local figures—humble combatants or victims, whose names mean nothing outside the locality—are the ones who get mentioned.[9] The principal leaders—Charette, Cathelineau, La Roche-jaquelein—are present in communes that were once long ago under their authority, like the *pays* of Retz, Mauges, and the Bressuirais. Finally to be noted is the local square of the martyrs or the street of the Salve Regina, which commemorates the massacres that threw those communities into mourning.[10] In sum, these choices are not made to give vague satisfaction to the demands for some kind of retrospective. Rather, they are made as a way to communicate with the depths of a local history that is always known and always assumed.

Networks of Remembering

Perhaps the essential power of this remembering is its ability to hook together the smallest facts and the humblest personalities, and to impregnate everyday life with these special memories. Several reasons explain why this memory is so powerful: First, it was mediated through a prodigious mass of objects, images, narratives, publications. The wars themselves, because of their duration, their popular character, and their limited area, left behind many weapons as well as ammunition, even clothes, cult objects, and emblems. Royal recompense during the Restoration in the form of rifles, swords, decorations, and pensions had already been added before 1828 when the duchesse de Berry, that patron saint of collectors, paid a visit showering clothes, shoes, and little pieces of silverware on her relations. Finally, there was a desire to get back at the authorities, a taste for history, or quite simply the lure of profit, all of which resulted in the commercialization of little objects recalling the wars: pipes with the heads of Charette or Henri de La Rochejaquelein, statuettes, and, most notably, lithographs, prints, and later on photographs and postcards, not to mention the souvenir Vendée hearts made out of all possible materials. So many of these objects were given a prominent place in the homes of Vendée families that the presence of the past was assured. The oral tradition only completed the process for many families. Thus it is possible at the end of the twentieth century, without too much searching, to encounter individuals who can give a recitation of events of the wars that has not been written down.[11]

Figure 9.2
The places of remembrance drawn in the style of the romantics and listed in Tom Drake, *Album Vendéen* (1856–1860). Here the monument erected at Nuaille to the memory of La Rochejaquelein.

While it is true that it is easier to hear narrations of published texts that date back only one or two generations, even this unauthentic oral tradition attests to the durability of interest in these wars and the status vested in the most anecdotal episodes.

This points to the second reason for the permanence of memory. The war was profoundly popular. The leaders, who were noble, could exert command only with the assent of the parish captains, who were rural men appointed by their peers, neighbors, and allies. Later, both by political calculation (to keep the people opposed to the Revolution) and by necessity (to accommodate an unmanageable and armed populace), these peasants, descendants of the combatants of 1793, were given honors by the region's notables. In that way the local culture and its oral traditions suffered no scorn. Quite the contrary, interest in these humble heroes never waned. The nobility of these rustic illiterates was constantly praised. They were the guardians of the best in French tradition. Scorn came only from political adversaries and had only the effect of authenticating the rural world and memory all the more. This was the way the histories of these peasant soldiers were transmitted, the best example being Jacques Cathelineau.

Family traditions persisted—and this is the third reason—for these traditions were powerfully helped by the sporadic continuation of the wars that affected the region. While the wars of the Vendée properly speaking ended with the death of the leaders, Charette and Jean Nicolas Stofflet, in 1796, the last fires of revolt burned until 1799. They would flame up again in 1815 and in 1832. At the time of Napoleon's return for the period known as the One Hundred Days, the local Vendée leaders, under the command of Louis de La Rochejaquelein, brother of Henri, tried to organize the Vendée into a royalist bastion. It was a way of prolonging the first uprising and giving it meaning. They succeeded, but not without difficulty. They did recruit peasants in the area that was part of the original insurgency, but the lack of preparation, which was their real weakness, and the fear by the peasants when recalling the repression of twenty years before resulted in the collapse of the movement before Waterloo. Seventeen years later, the duchesse de Berry, coveting the throne of France for her son, resolved to stir up revolt in the Vendée against the reigning monarch, Louis Philippe. In the name of 1793, she sought to win the Vendée to her cause, declaring it to be the land of loyalty. The outcome and defeat are well known. Here again memories played their part. Auguste de La Rochejaquelein and Athanase de Charette commanded peasants who were brothers, sons, or nephews of the fighters of 1793. Yet memory belongs to everyone, as the leaders quickly learned. Most of the peasants had not forgotten the insurrection, nor had their

Figure 9.3

Stained glass as history and the way of the cross, here showing Christ and at his side the papal Zouaves carrying the banner of the Sacred Heart, General Charette de la Contrie, and an unnamed Vendée leader from 1793. Stained-glass window in Beaune, Maine-et-Loire (19th century).

adversaries when they had to fight in the Bocage and the Marais. These fifty years of war, even if the extent of the battles varied, forged attitudes and traditions and froze images. The people of the Vendée became fearless defenders of throne and altar, something their leaders would draw on in siding with the legitimate kings of Portugal and Spain when under attack by the liberals. Later they would organize into a corps of papal Zouaves in defense of the temporal power of the pope. With General Juchault Lamoricière from Nantes and then baron General Charette de la Contrie at the head of this force, the papal Zouaves attracted a good number of peasants from the western departments that made up the Vendée, clearly demonstrating their connection to the combatants of 1793, whom they claimed as their own. They also became a volunteer unit against the Prussians in 1870.

It is also understandable—and this is a fourth reason—that the political and ideological adversaries likewise remember the Vendée. They make continual reference to the wars of 1793. They distrust the region, hence the tight surveillance imposed by Napoleon and Louis Philippe. The latter took the step of hacking through terrain called the *bocage,* as distinguished from the area of the same name, to build strategic roads linking the principal towns. Hence the suspicion of republican governments after 1877 that led to the establishment of a network of gendarmes and schoolmasters to gather information. The Vendée is thus constantly confronted with what it was in 1793 and is called on to conform to that image.

The Desire for Enclosure

This consecration of the Vendée by its adversaries is not to be underestimated. They were the first to designate this region the land of the counterrevolution and the ancien régime. During the first months of the First Republic (1793), a wave of peasant revolts broke out from Alsace to Provence. Troubles were likewise reported in the departments of Deux-Sèvres, Maine-et-Loire, and Loire-Inférieure. Yet it was the Vendée, unknown until that point, that became the common term for counterrevolution and the ancien régime after March 19, 1793. On that date, the first regular army forces sent to the area suffered a rout. That event overturned assumptions about the insurrections and turned the Vendée into the flag bearer of the counterrevolution. At the time it occurred, the émigrés and their allies knew little or nothing about the revolt and the rebels, whom they scorned.[12] The republicans completed this consecration of the region by portraying it as turned to the past, frozen in traditions, the image of early France. The people of the Vendée, guided by nobles and priests, became a caricature of reaction. It was not just the countryside and its impenetrable *bocage,* with its lack of roads or towns, that underscored the isolation and therefore the backwardness of the region. The Vendée was already a region of memory in 1793, a museum of oppressed times. This image of a nostalgic region was indeed that of a vanished golden age, which the partisans of the Vendée would exalt in later years. Accordingly, the memoirs of the marquise de La Roche-jaquelein open with a chapter dedicated to "the description of the *bocage*. Customs of the inhabitants, first effects of the Revolution. The period that preceded the War of the Vendée," in which the people of the Vendée from before the wars of the Vendée are described as exceptional beings, peasants worthy of pastoral bliss, wise, pious, respectful of customs and of their masters, no doubt sullen, even superstitious, but all in all the last witnesses of a people before corruption. This idyllic tableau was a theme repeated by most works composed later by authors favorable to the Vendée.[13] Historical truth obviously counted for less than the polemical intent contained in descriptions of the Vendée before the error of revolution. The region thus became a daughter of the past, turning its back to the France of the Revolution. A simplistic and Manichean vision, to be sure, but one that had the advantage of being perfectly reversible at the wish of each person's judgment and values.

We might agree that this literature is not to be taken too seriously, but its historical interest cannot be denied. The description of a bucolic Vendée gathered around its pastors under the protection of its nobles was more a premonitory dream than a realistic picture. It is this ideal Vendée that its elites wanted to bring about when the region found itself on the fringe of republican France at the end of the nineteenth century. During that period, the region affirmed more than ever the inalterability of its choices despite the rest of the country. Its representatives to the national government belonged to the monarchist Right, or on occasion, to the clerical Right. This was the time when the regions of the Bressuire elected Julien de La Rochejaquelein, a royalist aristocrat, and the Marais, the marquis de Baudry d'Asson, one of the last royalists of the Third Republic, celebrated for his virulent opposition to Emile Combes, an anticlericalist minister in the government (as minister of education, Combes rigorously enforced the law of 1901 requiring religious institutions to have government authorization. As *président du conseil*, he abolished religious education and initiated policies to separate church and State). The political opinions that crystallized in this impressive bloc were first described by André Siegfried.[14] Leaving its evolution aside, Siegfried emphasized the changes produced by the election of clerical deputies who were not monarchists. He rightly noted: "In reality, whether under the royalist or the Catholic flag, the Vendée basically stayed exactly the same."[15]

More recent times have confirmed Siegfried's observation. Royalist sentiments have little currency now, but that does not mean that the political unity of the region has been weakened, as the massive and repeated victories of the French Right demonstrate to this day.[16] The Vendée's attachment to the Catholic religion demonstrates even more the tenacity of the region's identity. The religious fervor affecting Christianity in the nineteenth century found particularly fertile soil in the Vendée. Whatever dissensions there were between the pastors and their flocks before 1793, the extreme antireligious measures of the Revolution welded the people together in their Catholicism. Indeed, they provoked religious fervor. The clergy who were sympathetic to the Concordat of 1801 between France and the papacy that reestablished the church in France responded to this popular piety by creating new orders. The memories of the period were thus transcribed into religious language, with the people of the Vendée compared to the Maccabees of the early church and the Revolution identified with the Prince of Darkness. Finally, in the last year of the nineteenth century, the bishop of Luçon called forth a quest to find martyrs to the faith, specifically those priests who died during the wars of the Vendée, with an aim to their beatification. This accord between remembrance of the wars and religious sentiment explains the creation of churches, crosses, and grottoes, similar to that of Lourdes, that covered the region. Religious sentiment kept the region's seminaries filled with priests who would be sent to all areas of France, and nearly all the population crowded into church every Sunday. Thus was established a Vendéen community, faithful to its ancestors of 1793 and to the principles they were deemed to embody. It was a community so intolerant of contrary ideas that the only outside elements capable of resisting over the long run were the police and schoolteachers.

The region thus closed itself off to the outside world—politically, ideologically, and demographically. In fact, the countryside of the Vendée became overcrowded at a time when industry was calling for more and more workers. To go to the city was to enter a place of perdition. The small farms responded by welcoming families of fifteen to twenty people. Impoverished day laborers put off marriage.[17] Eventually the breaking point was reached, but only at the end of the nineteenth century. Emigration began, not just to nearby towns, but to areas like the Charente and the entire Aquitainian southwest (called the Garonne), already emptied by an earlier exodus. The nobility and the clergy condemned these migrations, which actually involved only a small part of the population, the people who were in the extremes of misery and misfortune. The Vendée thus set itself apart through systematic opposition to progress and its rejection of any outside influence.[18]

The dangers that demographic pressure put on society and on the social system it represented eventually pushed certain of the elites to create and guarantee the economic changes necessary to keep the rural masses in the countryside. So under the guidance of reactionary priests there arose workshops and even factories that changed the modes of culture and the relationships to the land.[19] In an area called the "foggy Cholet," a manufacturing center was established that remains one of the most original and extensive examples of decentralized industry in a rural environment. Humble people have been promoted to heads of businesses there. They are the dynamic peasants who did not remain inactive after getting a good start in the rough school of the farm syndicates and lay organizations of the Catholic church. They replaced traditional elites in every field of activity.

This change was not a rupture. The past continued in another form. There was no mental upheaval to validate a popular initiative, in a region where a teamster had been commander in chief and where personal choices conformed to the will of the community and the will of God. There was hardly any conflict in the factories subject to the Sunday rest and to a patriarchal spirit. Besides, the workshops, absorbing the excess labor from the peasant farms and dwellings, enabled the previous demographic equilibrium to be maintained and with it the political and religious balance. The region thus remained itself, preserving the unity acquired and recognized in 1793.

It is certain that the preservation of memories as found today could occur only in the continued presence of a stable, homogeneous society that respected its own culture. Without this undeniable economic success, memory would only exist in pieces. Inversely, it is the presence of memory as an organizing force, flowing into the conscious life of the individual, that gives vitality to the region. And if it is possible to imagine that the memories of the wars of the Vendée risk gradually fading from the consciousness of the Vendéen people, the collective habits they forged in the region will still remain. These characteristics today identify the people of the Vendée in relation to the rest of the French population and single out Vendéens living elsewhere. The trauma of the wars did indeed give the region its mode of discourse and its definitions.

Les Curés soulèvent les paysans.

Figure 9.4

"The priests incite the peasants." Illustration by L. Dumon, engraved by Andrieux, in Eugène Bonnemère, *Les Guerres de la Vendée* (Paris: Martin, 1884).

UN PRÈTRE DONNANT
L'ABSOLUTION
AVANT
LE
COMBAT

Figure 9.5
The same picture as in fig. 9.4, but with a radically different caption: "A priest giving absolution before battle." Illustration by L. Dumon, engraved by Andrieux, in M. Crétineau-Joly, *Histoire de la Vendée militaire*, illustrated ed. (Paris: Maison de la Bonne Presse, 1895–96).

DIALECTIC OF MEMORY

To present the Vendée in this way is, let us hope, to furnish an explanation that can give a scientific account of the reality of the region. Nevertheless, it would be fruitless not to think of using this explanation as a key with a variety of other explanatory elements without which this key would be useless; moreover, it is particularly effective with them. Is it not presumptuous to speak of a region of memory if this memory is revealed to be only a moment in a longer memory, if one is ignorant of the role played in the creation of memory by deliberate choice and contrived experiments, and if one does not appreciate its importance in daily life and in the habits of thought found in the people of the Vendée?[20]

What, then, is the tie that links memory and the Vendée together? Was the region defined and structured by the memory born in the war of 1793, or were this and the event that was its pretext only moments in the long evolution of the region? One thing is certain: the wars of the Vendée played the role of "decisive event" like that played by the *chouannerie* in the department of the Sarthe. The *chouannerie* brought into the open conflicts and divisions that up to then had only been latent.[21] In the Vendée two different communities existed next to each other—on one side, the rural, with peasants and textile workers, and on the other, the urban, known as the *bourgadins,* who were the property owners, the bourgeois, and merchants. There were powerful tensions between the two right up to the end of the ancien régime, but changes sought by the revolutionary government led to political and military confrontations that unified the towns and thereby the entire Vendée.[22]

Memory Predisposed

Yet, the regional structures established by 1793 could already be seen, apparently, in the sixteenth century, if not before, as the conflicts between the Bocage, the Marches, and the Mauges, on one side, and the towns in the surrounding plain, on the other, seem to demonstrate. The piety of the inhabitants in the Bocage and the Mauges had nothing in common with religious sentiments in the other area.[23] During the Wars of Religion, Protestantism, vigorous in the plain, failed in the Mauges and only penetrated the industrial Gâtine of the lower Bocage through the urbanized textile workers. That provoked violent armed clashes.[24] The soldiers of the Catholic and royal armies two centuries later would have had no trouble espousing the same cause as had their ancestors. Thus the same structures were in the same places; only the modalities—the attitudes and conflicts—were different. Previous attitudes and conflicts had changed. In the same way the Vendée of the Catholic League was around Vitré during the Wars of Religion, the Chouans were in 1794, while the descendants of the Protestants are the republicans.[25] And in the twentieth century, even if the correlation does not work perfectly, in one department, Ille-et-Vilaine, those who fought in the Resistance came from the region of the Blues, while the region once dominated by the Whites remained impervious to calls to join.[26] Similar connections can also be shown in Lower Brittany, where the revolt of 1793 was almost a perfect reflection of the area of insurgency in 1675 during the Revolt of the Red Hats (*Bonnets rouges*) against a tax edict.[27] In short, did the year 1793 reveal a new region, or did it only put fresh attire on an immutable landscape? The academic debate continues largely unresolved and serves as a pretext for countless partisan hack writers who, in their obstinate fanaticism, have been tearing each other to pieces for two centuries with their pens. It seems possible to advance some hypotheses that could shed light on this irreducible duality.

First of all, there do not appear to be any essential differences between the causes of the wars of the Vendée and the origins of the *chouanneries*. The Chouans of the Sarthe department may have been more prosperous than the people of the Vendée,[28] but that distinction is not so clear-cut elsewhere.[29] What led to the outbreak of the Chouan revolts was the accumulation of frustrations felt by rural communities; they were especially antagonized by the enforcement of the Civil Constitution of the Clergy.[30] We know that from 1790 to 1793 the west was the theater of multiple confrontations between the urban National Guard and rural communities over the religious issue. In 1793, the entire region was affected by armed revolts occurring at the same time that had no connection with each other. There had been conspiracies among Breton landowners (*hobereaux*), but they had fizzled out. Up to that point, then, the same causes had produced the same effects. As the Revolution pushed its religious policy, it came increasingly into conflict with people of the rural communities, who felt their religion was at stake. Religion became the center and the pretext for a specific rural identity. Let us also note that the duality between the believers in the Bocage and the Mauges and the nonbelievers in the municipalities of the plain had dimmed over the course of time, and opposition between the two regions was less than at the beginning of the eighteenth century.[31] It took the brutality of the Revolution on the sensitive question of religion to create a new reality. In that, the event truly did appear to be the cause of a structure, created then and recreated over the years, and its justification.

Memory Bestowed

The Vendée and the *chouanneries* soon ceased to have the same destiny. The region of the Vendée would be defined by a homogeneous territory. The parishes in revolt were exclusively rural. Numbering about 480, they formed the area surrounding several small towns and municipalities that were loyal to the central government (Les Herbiers, Cholet, and others). These islands of resistance were at first submerged and then integrated into the Vendée of the Whites. A totally different situation existed for the *chouanneries*. This insurgency had the look of a leopard skin: the dispersed communes in revolt never linked up. The creation of the Vendée, by contrast, had occurred in the single year of 1793.

The vicissitudes of the war in part account for this situation. From April to October 1793, the Vendéens operated in a territory subject almost entirely to their authority and ruled by the main council at Châtillon. Their local adversaries had disappeared: they were refugees in the republican zones, prisoners watched by the Whites, or they were killed in combat. This military situation seems more the result of chance than of the particular disposition of the region. Everywhere else, moreover, the regular armies were present and sufficiently strong to nip revolts in the bud. That was the case in Vannes in 1791 and especially in the department of the Morbihan in 1793, likewise in the Léon area at the celebrated bridge of Kerguidu. The most compromised or the most stubborn insurgents joined up with the Vendée to continue the fight, such as Cadoudal and groups from the defeated town of Segré.[32] The Vendée did not suffer similar repression. When the regular troops were sent, the region inflicted defeats on them thanks to their lack of preparation and ineptness. The arrival of troops from Mainz under the command of General Kléber soon reversed this situation.

That is why the Vendée is important, and why it is surely responsible for its formation as a particular region. The Vendée became the gravest internal threat to the Revolution, to the point that it quickly became the generic term for all the other insurrections. It came to be the counterrevolution incarnate. It thus played the role of traitor in the revolutionary tragedy, confirming and justifying the installation of the "rule of suspicion."[33] The struggle against the Vendée then assumed a symbolic dimension, which led logically to exceptional measures. "Destroy the brigands of the Vendée" was the policy pursued, for it was the source of all the ills in the Republic even if it must be recalled that destruction—in principle or in reality—was brought to Lyon and Marseille and to the village of Bédouin in the Vaucluse, and that Basques in several villages were deported en masse. Nothing less would suffice. This decision, taken by the convention following a celebrated speech by Barrère, was implemented by mobile army columns that systematically destroyed anyone they met, whether they were partisans of the Vendée or of the Republic, ignoring the decrees of August and October 1793 that stipulated protection for women, children, old people, and even unarmed men. They were all on the same "infamous soil," as someone described it. The brutal reality was covered by expressions of the principles that the Thermidorians, or the victims of the Terror, enunciated in their descriptions when the "conventional language" was abandoned after the fall of Robespierre. Today that reality remains misunderstood and misrepresented.

Repression had two results: on the one hand, it deeply marked the surviving terrified populations, and, on the other, it brought the Vendée to the attention of all the enemies of the Republic, émigrés and crowned heads. Thus were born two different but concordant traditions. First, the image of the Vendée was definitively fixed in the political consciousness of its friends and enemies. Next, repression became anchored in local memory from one generation to the next. Also, the Vendée became the common ground, on territory defined by insurrection and massacre, for a population that had gone through the same irrefutable hardships. These hardships were given ideological representation and attributed to the entire region. The result was a specific memory that the zones of the *chouanneries* do not possess.

At issue is imposed memory, first by the republicans and then by the royalists. This is the way that the many interventions in the Vendée by the clergy and upper class at the end of the nineteenth century must be understood. The actions of the republicans must also be understood in the same way, although they did not realize that in their zeal they were responding to a Vendée that once was. The originality of the Vendée is found in the echo that these operations had in the popular mind. By contrast, in the Chouan areas, the popular view held to the image of the Chouans as highway robbers, and upper classes never sought to identify themselves with the insurgents.[34] Memory was therefore fabricated. But the Vendéen of legend, denounced regularly by kind souls in search of "demythification," was not the only one responsible. He was only one

Figure 9.6
"All the Vendée is there, its epic, its work, the faith of its people." Maxime Real del Sarte, *The Vendéen* (1935).

part of a mental and social framework that extended beyond him. Thus, neither the event nor the structures prior to it carry memory forward. It is rather the image of that event and the actions taken in response to it that serve to engrain memory in a society.

Memory Accomplished

It is fitting, finally, to evaluate the place of memory in the society of the Vendée. Obviously the memories of the wars of the Vendée did not negate or completely replace other memories, preoccupations, and interests. This is evident in the continued autonomy of the different groups that make up the society of the Vendée. No fusion ever took place between the inhabitants of the Mauges, the Gâtines, and the Marais. Each kept its own identity. Clearly there are enduring traditions that remained despite the lack of any tie to the wars of the Vendée. Religious beliefs and superstitions remained part of life after the wars and remained long afterward. In fact, up to the beginning of this century, wolves and werewolves still roamed the countryside at night. Clearly, too, all the practices of everyday life and all the customs of the community that codified the moments of the great events of life—birth, baptism, death—persisted. Similarly, memories remain that date from the Wars of Religion,[35] and some of these have become entwined with those of the wars of the Vendée.

So it was that the memories of the wars were considerably altered and many of them slowly forgotten. Shame over the event, a wish to forget, neglect pure and simple—by the end of the nineteenth century, many massacres were remembered by only a few people until the clergy recalled the events to the collective memory. For example, the massacre committed at Petit Luc fell into silence for nearly seventy years.[36] Then the carnage of World War I, of which the Vendéens were very much a part, noticeably diminished the evocations of those wars, then seen as too remote and not so awful. Last, social and economic transformations in the second half of the twentieth century have had the further effect of minimizing the value of the narratives about these events, all the more suspect because they are associated with social traditions and arrangements that are losing influence. Since the 1990s, however, interest in these memories has assumed new vigor.[37]

The memories were, and still are, largely dependent on the actions of mediators and intermediaries without whom they would have dissipated, indeed disappeared, but because of whom they are skewed in particular ways. Thus, the work and activities of the church provided the memories with the coloration of sacrifice, with the ultimate defeat of the

Vendéens making the victim more majestic, the cause of the peasant soldiers being likened to a crusade, and the victims of the massacres, especially the children, deserving of beatification.* Putting the events in the light of religion in no small measure gave an orientation to the memories that made them acceptable to the large mass of people in the countryside, who had always balked at confronting memories that were too political. At this point we must be specific about the impact these actions had on the collective mind. The frequent reference to the wars, the unity of the region, and the influence of the elites did not preclude the continuation of tensions and conflicts. Submission to the noble landowners did not suppress every gesture of resistance by the peasants seen when they voted for the priest's candidate, formed little groups, engaged in deception, or quite simply left.[38] Nor did religious directives suffice to suppress the daily deviations that have led to widespread alcoholism[39] or the custom of *maraîchinage,* a local term for intimate premarital relations.[40] Finally, rivalry between the towns, between the inhabitants of villages, and especially between town and country never did stop, even when the Vendée was faced with the necessity of staying united.[41]

Remembrance was therefore limited by the many habits and conflicts that made it continually evolve, subject to many delays. Its social and economic consequences, on the one hand, and the focus of memory on great men and important places, supported by local examples, on the other, were what counted the most. What was happening was that a people was slowly fashioned and deep structures that are largely unknown today were put in place, all of which represent the memories of the wars of the Vendée and give full meaning to the expression "region of memory."

The Vendée enjoys a mental, social, and economic framework that is a true infrastructure. Little by little, memory evolved along the lines of prior structures and in response to the shock of events and conflicts. Understanding this beginning makes the presence of the region less unusual for the rest of the country, since we can see that the region has not turned its back on what is going on in the contemporary world and that it has not forgotten that the most brutal adaptations succeed all the more when they are tied to the deepest structures.

---

* In 1994, one hundred religious and lay people executed in 1794 were beatified as "martyrs of the Revolution."

NOTES

1. Michel Denis, *Les Royalistes de la Mayenne et le monde moderne* (Paris: Klinksieck, 1977), illustrates this ambiguity for the Mayenne. See pp. 111–43. See also Jean Tulard, director, "Présentation de la contre-révolution en symétrie avec la Révolution," *La Contre-révolution: Doctrine et action* (Paris: Perrin, 1990), and Jacques Godechot, *La Contre-révolution* (Paris: Presses Universitaires de France, 1984) [an earlier edition trans. by Salvator Attanasio, *The Counter-Revolution: Doctrine and Action, 1789–1804* (New York: H. Fertig, 1971)]. For an introduction to the complexity of the movements in opposition to the Revolution, see François Lebrun and Roger Dupuy, directors, *Résistances à la Révolution: Actes du colloque de Rennes (Sept. 17–21, 1985)* (Paris: Imago, 1987).

2. For example, Françoise Zonabend, *La Mémoire longue* (Paris: Presses Universitaires de France, 1980) [trans. by Anthony Forster as *The Enduring Memory: Time and History in a French Village* (Manchester: Manchester University Press, 1985)], and Pierre-Jakez Hélias, *Le Cheval d'orgueil* (Paris: Plon, 1975) [trans. by June Guichanaud as *The Horse of Pride: Life in a Breton Village* (New Haven: Yale University Press, 1978)].

See also studies by Jean-Clément Martin: *La Vendée et la France* (Paris: Éditions du Seuil, 1987), in particular for the war of 1793–1800; *La Vendée de la mémoire, 1800–1900* (Paris: Éditions du Seuil, 1980), for the transformation of memories; *Une guerre interminable: La Vendée deux cents ans après* (Nantes: Reflets du Passé, 1985), for the period 1980–85; *Une région nommée Vendée entre politique et mémoire, XVIIIe siècle–XXe siècle* (La Crèche [Deux-Sèvres]: Geste Éditions, 1996), for the social and political mechanisms that ensured regional continuity; *Les Vendéens de la Garonne* (Vauchrétien [Maine-et-Loire]: Y. Davy, ed., 1989), for the ways Vendéens emigrating to southwest France maintained their identity; *Le Puy-du-Fou en Vendée: L'histoire mise en scène* (Paris: L'Harmatan, 1996), coauthored with Charles Suaud, for the effect in the Vendée during the 1990s of the show produced by Philippe de Villiers.

3. Philippe Joutard, *La Légende des Camisards* (Paris: Gallimard, 1977), presents a "long memory" based on a literary tradition.

4. The distinction between insurgent Vendée (all the communes and parishes in revolt) and Vendée at war (theater of operations) will not be discussed here.

5. Father Louis Pérouas, *Le Diocèse de La Rochelle de 1648 à 1724* (Paris: S.E.V.P.E.N., 1963), 79–119; and Claude Petitfrère, *Blancs et bleus d'Anjou, 1789–1793* (Paris-Lille: Atelier réproduction des thèses, Université de Lille III, 1979), 1:485ff.

6. There are numerous examples; the most celebrated was the work done by the parish of La Gaubretière, department of the Vendée. See also François Lebrun, *Paroles de Dieu et Révolution: Les sermons d'un curé angevin avant et pendant la guerre de Vendée* (Paris: Imago, 1989). The monuments erected in Brittany after the *chouannerie* were not granted the same significance. See Michel Lagrée and Jehanne Roche, *Les Tombes de la mémoire: La dévotion populaire aux victimes de la Révolution dans l'Ouest* (Rennes: Apogée, 1993).

7. Josette Bottineau, "Les Portraits des généraux Vendéens," *La Gazette des beaux-arts* (May–June 1975): 175–92.

8. Among the associations, for example, there are the Souvenir Vendéen, which publishes a review of the same name, and Vendée Militaire, which publishes the review *Savoir*.

9. For example, rue de l'Abbé-Voyneau in Lucs-sur-Boulogne.

10. Numerous examples: Chavagnes-en-Paillers, Lucs-sur-Boulogne, Noirmoûtier-en-l'Île, Melay, Saint-Laurent-sur-Sèvre, Turquant. Jean-Clément Martin, "Du champ de bataille au vitrail, la guerre de Vendée, guerre de l'image et de l'imaginaire," in *La Revue des pays de la Loire: Recherches et création,* no. 303 (Nantes, 1986), 8–19.

11. The work of Dominique Gauvrit and Michel Gautier is a good example. *Une autre Vendée: Temoignage d'une culture opprimée* (Les Sables-d'Olonne: Cercle d'Or, 1980), 158–63.

12. Jean-Clément Martin, "La Vendée," *Le Monde,* June 26, 1983; Claudy Valin, "La bataille inaugurale dite de Pont-Charrault, réalité et résonance," in Jean-Clément Martin, director, "La Vendée et le monde," in *Enquêtes et documents* (Nantes:Ouest-Éditions et Université de Nantes, 1993), no. 20, 35–64.

13. For example, Abbé Félix Deniau, *Histoire de la Vendée* (Angers: Siraudeau, 1876), vol. 1.

14. André Siegfried, *Tableau politique de la France de l'Ouest sous la Troisième République* (Paris: A. Colin, 1913; reprint, Geneva-Paris: Slatkine, 1980), 29–36.

15. Ibid., 30–31.

16. Jean-Luc Sarrazin et al., *La Vendée* (Saint-Jean-d'Angély, 1982), 410ff.; Jean Renard, *Géopolitique des pays de la Loire* (Nantes: ACL-Crocus, 1988); Martin, *Une région nommée Vendée,* 157–77.

17. Yves Durand, "Les Structures familiales dans les marais atlantiques au XIXe siècle," in *Enquête et documents* (Nantes, 1978), 118–25, and Jean-Clément Martin, "Chavagnes-en-Paillers, immobile à grands pas," *Les Cahiers nantais* 19 (1981): 5–52.

18. P. Hohenberg, "L'Exode rural en France au XIXe siècle," *Annales E. S. C.* 1 (1974): 466; Jean-Clément Martin, "Les Vendéens dans la Garonne, ou les permanences limitées d'une culture collective," *Annales de Bretagne et des Pays d'Ouest* 4 (1988): 361–68; Martin, *Les Vendéens de la Garonne.*

19. Jean-Clément Martin, "Les Réactionnaires progressistes de l'Ouest," *Le Monde,* February 15, 1982; "Le Clergé vendéen face à l'industrialisation," *Annales de Bretagne P. O.* 3 (1982): 357–68; "Aux origines de l'industrie vendéenne," *Les Cahiers nantais* 22 (1983): 37–49; Martin, *Une région nommée Vendée;* Guy Minguet, *Naissance de l'Anjou industriel des Pays de l'Ouest: Entreprise et société locale à Angers et dans le Charlotais* (Paris: L'Harmattan, 1985).

20. Jean-Clément Martin and Charles Suaud, *Le Puy du Fou, en Vendée* (Paris: L'Harmattan, 1996), show the shifts in this regional dynamism for the years 1980–90.

21. Paul Bois, *Paysans de l'Ouest: Des structures économiques et sociales aux options politiques depuis l'époque révolutionnaire dans la Sarthe* (Paris: Mouton, 1960), and Emmanuel Le Roy Ladurie, "Événement et longue durée dans l'histoire sociale: L'exemple chouan," in *Le Territoire de l'historien* (Paris: Gallimard, 1973), 168–87 [trans. by Ben Reynolds and Sian Reynolds as "The 'Event' and the 'Long Term' in

Social History: The Case of the Chouan Uprising," in *The Territory of the Historian* (Chicago: University of Chicago Press, 1979), 111–31].

22. Marcel Faucheux, *L'Insurrection vendéenne de 1793: Aspects économiques et sociaux* (Paris: Imprimerie nationale, 1964), and Charles Tilly, *The Vendée* (Cambridge: Harvard University Press, 1964).

23. Pérouas, *Le Diocèse de La Rochelle,* 198–99.

24. Roger Joxe, *Les Protestants du comte de Nantes au seizième siècle et au début du dix-septième siècle* (Marseille: J. Lafitte, 1982); and F. Baudry, *Le Protestantisme au XVIIIe siècle* (Paris, 1922), 311.

25. Michel Lagrée, "La structure pérenne, événement et histoire en Bretagne orientale, XVIe et XXe siècles," *Revue d'histoire moderne et contemporaine* 23 (1976): 384–407.

26. Jacqueline Sainclivier, "Chouannerie et résistance en Ille-et-Vilaine," *Échange, Vendée-Chouannerie* (Nantes: 1981), 211–21.

27. Alain Pennec, "La Chouannerie en Basse-Bretagne," in *Échange: Vendée-Chouannerie* (Nantes, 1981), 93–109.

28. Faucheux, op. cit.

29. Petitfrère, *Blancs et bleus d'Anjou,* 1:622–713.

30. Donald Sutherland, *The Chouans: The Social Origins of Popular Counter-Revolution in Upper Brittany, 1770–1796* (Oxford: Oxford University Press, 1982) and Roger Dupuy, *De la Révolution à la Chouannerie* (Paris: Flammarion, 1988).

31. Pérouas, *Le Diocèse de La Rochelle,* 460–65.

32. Petitfrère, *Blancs et bleus d'Anjou,* 1:101ff.

33. Jean Starobinski, *1789: Les emblèmes de la raison* (Paris: Flammarion, 1979), 45–48 [trans. by Barbara Bray as *1789: The Emblems of Reason* (Charlottesville: University Press of Virginia, 1982)].

34. The word "Chouan" has had a pejorative connotation, even in the Vendée, since the early nineteenth century. The Chouans were sometimes seen as nothing more than bandits.

35. As noted in Michel Ragon, *L'Accent de ma mère* (Paris: Albin-Michel, 1980), 240. On the destruction see Jean-Clément Martin and Xavier Lardière, *Le Massacre des Lucs: La Vendée, 1794* (La Crèche: Geste Éditions, 1992), and *L'Histoire* (April 1994): 176; Jean-Clément Martin, "Vendée: Les criminels de guerre devant leurs juges," *L'Histoire* 209 (April 1997): 52–57, and "Sur le traité de La Jaunaye, février 1795," *Annales de Bretagne et des pays d'Ouest* 104 (1996): 69–88.

36. Jean-Clément Martin, "Résonances pour un massacre, paysans et politique," *Annales de Bretagne et des pays d'Ouest* 2 (1982): 247–57, and Jean-Clément Martin and Xavier Lardière, *Le Massacre des Lucs.*

37. The bicentenary of the Revolution sparked considerable polemics. One of the first to assess this situation was Steven Laurence Kaplan, *Farewell Revolution: Disputed Legacies, 1789–1989* (Ithaca and London: Cornell University Press, 1995), 84–111.

38. Henri Pitaud, *Le Pain de la terre* (Paris: Lattès, 1982).

39. Fernand Boulard, "Aspects de la pratique religieuse en France, 1802–1939: L'exemple des pays de la Loire," *Annales E.S.C.* 4 (1976): 761–802.

40. Marcel Baudoin, *Le Maraîchinage: Coutume du pays de monts* (Paris: P. Bossuet, 1932). For a perspective dealing with the problem on a large scale see Jean-Clément Martin, "Violences sexuelles, discours et histoire," *Annales, sciences sociales* 3 (1996): 643–61.

41. Alain Chauvet, "Les Facteurs de la réussite de l'industrialisation du Nord-Est Vendéen," *Les Cahiers nantais* 22 (1983): 48–62. Michel Denis, *Les Royalistes de la Mayenne et le monde moderne* (Paris: Klinksieck, 1977), illustrates this ambiguity for the Mayenne. See 111–43.

CHAPTER 10

A FRONTIER MEMORY

Alsace

❧

JEAN-MARIE MAYEUR

A survey published by the weekly *Le Point* in February 1985 well illus-trates Alsace's position—unusual in several respects—in relation to the other regions of France. In response to a question on the strength of feelings about regional identity, 92.3 percent of the inhabitants of Alsace said those feelings were intense, as compared with 85.5 percent for Brit-tany, 64.5 percent for the Limousin, and less than 50 percent for most of the rest of France. People sense that Alsace has its own powerful individ-uality, which implies that the sense of memory there is different from that of France "away from the borders," despite everything all regions have in common, and reflects characteristics that cannot fail to strike even the most inattentive visitor. To begin with, there is the coexistence of two lan-guages, French and a dialect of German, which can be heard in the streets of its cities and especially in the countryside, and seen everywhere on the signs for wine stores. Then, there is the coexistence of several religious communities. Catholicism faces a Protestantism, primarily Lutheran, that has endured without interruption since the middle of the sixteenth cen-tury. In addition, the visible signs of a deeply rooted Judaism go back fur-ther in Alsace's past than in that of most other areas of France. Finally—although one could go on indefinitely—there is the coexistence of vineyards originally from the Mediterranean and breweries rooted deep in the local past, of mustard and cumin, of *bifteck* and sauerkraut.

Is it necessary to add to these concrete details data not so visible? The persistence of local law that, notably in social matters, preserved the

Figure 10.1
View of Strasbourg:
the cathedral and the
covered bridges.

contributions of the Bismarckian empire; the preservation, in the matter of church–state relations, of the system of government as defined by the Concordat of 1801, which reestablished the Catholic church after its defeats in the French Revolution, and the "organic articles," which Napoleon enacted as an addendum to the concordat to ensure ecclesiastical subservience and public order; and the preservation, in academic matters, of the denominational or interdenominational school system, publicly funded thanks to the Falloux Law of 1850, which, by eliminating most statutory requirements, permitted any group to open a school.

In the countryside, with its particular moral climate, Alsace appears at first glance to be filled with memories of hurtling back and forth between France and Germany, and by those memories of a frontier that reflect the great moments and tragic events of all European history since the Middle Ages. It is indeed a paradox that this land, which owes so much to German culture, now affirms its attachment to France with such intensity. Another paradox: in recent history, several provinces have witnessed the intensification of regionalist demands to the point that the sense of belonging to the nation almost became a real issue, but Alsace experienced no comparable movement. Regionalism does not lack vitality in Alsace, but it has never taken a radical form, except for some marginal currents.

These are the paradoxes of a "frontier memory" that might disintegrate if it did not constantly create a bridge between components of memory that are specifically Alsatian and those that are French. These components coexist at the high moments of Alsace's history and in the complexities of its political memory. Indeed, is it not the tension between them that explains the exceptional symbolic charge the national imagination attaches to this bridge?

The Historical Memory

Strasbourg: almost immediately a strolling visitor will discover marked in stone all the traces of this long memory.

First, there is the cathedral built on the ruins of the sanctuary that occupied the center of the Roman *castellum* (fortified town). Few monuments in Europe crystallize memories of religious and national passions as intense as those elicited by this edifice of rose-colored sandstone. The sandstone was drawn from the quarries of Kronthal, located between Marlenheim and Wasselonne. The intricate rose window was done by Erwin;[1] the building's single spire was completed in 1439. For Aeneas Silvius Piccolomini, the humanist scholar and future Pius II (1458–64), that spire "hides its head in the clouds." The nave was influenced by the grandeur of Reims. A relief showing the workshop of Chartres decorates the "Pillar of the Angels." The memory of the Holy Roman Empire is perpetuated in the stained glass in the north aisle. In tunic and cloak, carrying scepter and orb, the emperors "peer down at the faithful with iconic glance."[2] We see the Holy Roman Emperors of the Ottonian dynasty of the tenth through twelfth centuries, who so closely united in themselves the spiritual and the temporal; and Frederick Barbarossa, the Hohenstaufen emperor renowned as the incarnation of the chivalric ideal, who in December 1187 received the delegates from Pope Gregory VII in Strasbourg on a mission to recruit for the Crusades.

From 1524, when the Mass was said in the vernacular for the first time—an act demonstrating the break between the city and Roman Catholicism—to 1681, when Strasbourg was annexed to France by Louis XIV, the cathedral was a place of Protestant worship. When His Most Christian Majesty Louis XIV, to use his religious title, entered Strasbourg on October 23, 1681, a Te Deum was celebrated in the cathedral, once again Catholic.

In 1771, an admiring visitor, the great German poet Goethe (1749–1832), discovered in the cathedral an example of "Gothic and German art" built in times truly German by a master whose name bespoke his German origins. Goethe set down his observations in a pamphlet significantly titled *Über die deutsche Baukunst* (On German Architecture). The patriotic German lesson that Goethe drew from his visits to the cathedral would be heard by his fellow Germans only at the beginning of the nineteenth century. That lesson would have a lasting influence.

During the Nazi annexation, the cathedral lost all religious character. Adolf Hitler visited it in the summer of 1940. Once it became a secularized monument, it was featured in newsreels as a high point in Teutonic culture, set to the muted sounds of a folksong dear to the hearts of Alsatian autonomists: "O Strassburg, Strassburg, du wunderschöne Stadt" (O Strasbourg, Strasbourg, you marvelously beautiful city).[3] Some months later, at the Koufra oasis in the heart of the Libyan desert, General Philippe Leclerc, commander of a Free French division in Africa, called upon his men to take an oath "not to lay down their arms until our colors, our beautiful flag, flies over the cathedral of Strasbourg." On the day after the liberation of the city, November 23, 1944, General LeClerc, then head of the 2nd Armored Division, issued a "Proclamation to the Inhabitants of Strasbourg" that declared: "During the gigantic struggle led these last four years by General de Gaulle, the spire of our cathedral has remained our obsession." Many others, Free French and Resistance, could have made the same statement.

The cathedral remained inseparable from French national sentiment during the period of its two annexations to Germany. At the moment of the Franco-German reconciliation in 1956, its religious dimension was recognized, and its significance as a important place for Christians was invoked in the stained glass done by the artist Max Ingrand and presented by the nations of the Council of Europe. The glass showed a Virgin Mary with arms outstretched.

In just a short distance from the cathedral we come to the Lycée Fustel-de-Coulanges, with its modern neoclassical facade. Built by Joseph Massol, the *lycée* was formerly a Jesuit seminary. It bears the name of the eminent French historian Numa Denis Fustel-de-Coulanges, a professor of ancient history who taught there until 1870. After the annexation, he shifted the focus of research and wrote a six-volume study of feudalism attacking the generally held idea that feudalism was of German origin. He once told Theodor Mommsen, "Perhaps after all Alsace is German by race and language. But by nationality and patriotic sentiment it is French."* To the right of the *lycée* we see the Rohan Palace, another building by Joseph Massol. It fairly "shouts France,"[4] declared one French historian, Lucien Febvre, as do the grand eighteenth-century *hôtels* located on the Place Broglie.

Let us cross the river Ill and go to the Place de la République, a legacy of town planning from the time of the first annexation. The Palace of the Rhine is the former imperial palace, which in turn is an imitation of the palace in Mantua. Just opposite are two neoclassical buildings, the university library and the conservatory. From 1911 to 1918, the legislature, called the Landtag, met in the conservatory. This was the period when the German Empire granted a certain degree of autonomy to the Reichsland, the imperial designation of Alsace and Lorraine. A statue of the German kaiser, Wilhelm II, once stood in the square. In his largely autobiographical trilogy *November 1918,* the German novelist Alfred Döblin described the crowd tearing down the statue during the revolutionary days of November 1918. Döblin, an army doctor in 1918, wrote the novel during his stay in France in 1937 after fleeing Nazi Germany.

Let us look again at the broad perspective afforded by the Place de la République. On the Place de l'Université is a statue to the poet Goethe, without doubt the university's most illustrious student in the eighteenth century. The facade of the palace of the university displays stone reliefs honoring the great figures of humanism, the Renaissance, and the Reformation. Several of these individuals visited or resided in Strasbourg. This building, another result of urban planning and of the cultural

---

★ EDITOR'S NOTE: Mommsen (1817–1903) was a distinguished Roman historian, medievalist, and Nobel Prize winner for literature in 1902. The passion of German militarism always dismayed him. His major work on Roman provinces, *Die Provinzen, von Caesar bis Diocletian,* was published in 1885.

ambitions of the German Empire, was the place where eminent German scholars taught—the jurist Paul Laband, the sociologist Gregor Simmel, the historian Friedrich Meinecke.[5] After 1918, French scholars, such as the historians Lucien Febvre and Marc Bloch, were the ones who commanded attention, along with the sociologist Maurice Halbwachs; the legal historian and canonist Gabriel Le Bras; and the jurists Marcel Prélot, Raymond Carré de Malberg, and René Capitant—all famous in their time.

We resume our path along the Ill River to get back to the old city. The Quai des Bateliers (Boatmen's Wharf) and the Quai des Pêcheurs (Fishermen's Wharf) point to one of the sources of the city's prosperity—the place where the Ill and Rhine meet. Here the Rhine turns from a raging torrent into a navigable river. Beyond the Place du Corbeau we find the Alsace Museum, not just an outstanding museum of the arts and regional traditions, but one that brings the entire history of Alsace together in one place. A little farther on stands the austere mass of the Church of Saint Thomas, an important center for Lutheranism in Alsace. For the Reformers it was a revered place. The religious traditions of Alsace, though, are not just Catholic or Protestant. Some of the most moving galleries in the Alsace Museum and the names of certain old streets remind us that Judaism, too, had its place in the city's multiconfessional history.

Other towns besides Strasbourg could also serve as an introduction to Alsace. Wissembourg, inseparable from the memories of the Wars of the Revolution and the defeats of 1870—General Hoche in Geisberg shouting "Landau or death!" In 1792, Hoche, commanding the Army of the Rhine, led the attack on the Prussians at Wissembourg, forcing them to lift the siege at Landau—the rout of the Turcos on August 4, 1870, in the Franco-Prussian War, and the death of their commander, General Abel Douay. The Turcos were Algerian colonial troops. Colmar has the Unterlinden Museum and the altarpiece of the late-fifteenth-century painter Mathias Grünewald, that masterpiece of Rhenish art commissioned for the convent of the Antonins of Issenheim. In the town of Selestat the former wheat market contains, almost intact, the library of the first humanist school in south Germany, which numbered among its students Jacob Wimpheling and Beatus Rhenanus. The latter was a friend of Martin Luther and his contemporary, Europe's most illustrious humanist, Desiderius Erasmus.

Something else, even older than the ruins of Roman towns, can introduce us to the memory of Alsace: the Rhine River. The name echoes a prehistoric past, and its banks carry traces of agricultural activity dating back centuries. The Rhine, dotted by one marvelous archaeological find after another, was the shortest route between the plains of the Po River

Figure 10.2
Saint Thomas, the Lutheran church in Strasbourg.

Figure 10.3
The Jewish cemetery of Rosenwiller.

in northern Italy and the lands of northern Europe. According to Julius Caesar, the Gauls considered the Rhine to be the frontier of Gaul. The Roman legions built *castra* (camps) along its banks as a line of defense against Germania. In times of peace the Rhine became a hyphen linking the two shores, but in times of war a ditch made impassable by each side.

Certain theorists over the centuries have contended that the Rhine was a "natural frontier" that France had to control in order to guarantee the security of the kingdom. This idea was based on arguments drawn from ancient authors: Caesar and his contemporary Strabo, the noted Greek historian and geographer, who saw the Rhine in terms of borders. By defining it as such, they legitimized the river as the border of Gaul. The theory of "natural frontiers" does not, of course, explain the policies of the monarchy. Historians such as Georges Pagès put an end to that notion.[6] Faced with possible invasion from Germany, Cardinal Richelieu, Louis XIII's chief minister from the mid-1620s until his death in 1642, was preoccupied with defense and the desire for the monarchy to have "gates" and "to advance to Strasbourg, if it is possible, and secure an entrance into Germany" (as he wrote in his *avis* to the king, January 1629). Circumstances in Germany during the Thirty Years' War, specifically the menace of the Habsburg Imperial Army, which did in fact invade eastern France, explain the actions of Richelieu and the subsequent defensive moves into Alsace undertaken by his successor, Cardinal Mazarin.

Nevertheless the theory was used as a means of justification. A medal struck in 1683 after the "capitulation" of Strasbourg and the construction of the citadel by Vauban proclaimed, "Clausa Germanis Gallia" (France is closed to the Germans). Nourished in classical culture, the men of the French Revolution adhered to the same concepts. "It is in vain for us to fear extending the Republic too far," cried Danton, a revolutionary who aspired to spread republican ideas and institutions across Europe by force. "Its limits are set by nature. We will reach those limits at the horizon, at the banks of the Rhine, at the shores of the ocean, and at the Pyrenees and the Alps. That is where the limits of France are to be found. No human power will be able to prevent us from attaining them. No power will be able to get us to cross them."[7]

The German romantics contested the French view of the Rhine border from the beginning of the nineteenth century. "Der Rhein Teutschlands Strom aber nicht Teutschlands Grenze" (The Rhine Germany's River but not Germany's Border), declared Ernst Moritz Arndt in a celebrated pamphlet of the same name, which he wrote in 1813 during what the Germans called the "Wars of Liberation" from the occupying French army. Arndt was an ardent nationalist poet and professor of history: "I understand by this title," the author explained, "that the two sides of the Rhine and the surrounding countryside have to be German as they were once before and that the people and the land that were taken from us must be won back. Without the Rhine German liberty cannot exist."[8] In 1840, when national passions were at fever pitch, a town clerk in Cologne, Nicolas Becker, wrote a poem called *Rheinlied,* directed against the French:

> They will not possess the free German Rhine
> Until the waters have buried the bones of the last man on earth.

Figure 10.4
"Clausa Germanis Gallia" (Gaul is closed to the Germans), medal struck in 1683 after Vauban's construction of the citadel at Strasbourg and the port of Kehl. Vauban was the Louis XIV's chief military engineer.

To which the author and poet Alfred de Musset replied:

> We have got your German Rhine
> There it has remained in our glass.

A number of authors, including the young Friedrich Engels, constantly used the theme of the German Rhine. For them the Rhine crystallized a new concept of Germany as an integrated state with borders that coincided with the boundaries of German dialects.

A fantastic and picturesque Rhine nourished the imagination of the nineteenth-century French romantics, from Gérard Nerval, who translated Goethe's poems into French, and Victor Hugo, the renowned author of *Les Misérables,* to the engraver Gustave Doré and the prolific novelist Emile Erckmann-Chatrian. The Rhine, however, did not become in France, as it did in Germany, "a myth for the masses."[9] Rather, it was imported picturesque material. It was "the pretext for romantic travel narratives . . . a literary theme for the initiate." Furthermore, the Rhine was never a part of French national feeling the way it was in Germany. The Rhine of the French romantics, tourists, and travelers (the first Baedeker appeared in 1832; the Joanne guide, which described both sides of the Rhine, in 1863) was above all the Rhine of the "heroic gap" cut into shale rock—not the Rhine from Basel to Wissembourg, which was an Alpine torrent bordered by insalubrious forests, an inhospitable area infested with mosquitoes.

The Vosges Mountains in Alsace, with their somber forests, their deep lakes, and their ruins, all played their part in the romantic myths of the Germans, but their towns did not. The giants of Nideck Castle, immortalized by the early-nineteenth-century German poet Adelbert Chamisso, the water nymphs in the mist of the waterfalls, the gnomes from the mines, and the sleeping knights like Emperor Friedrich Barbarossa were awaiting the time to go forth and restore German greatness, all part of the folklore influenced by the Grimm Brothers and popularized by August Stoeber in the1840s.[10] Onto this folklore were grafted the legends of Alsace.

No doubt few passers-by on the Place de la République in Strasbourg know that the Rhine Palace has served as the Central Commission for the Navigation of the Rhine since 1919 and that this commission is the oldest European agency still in existence. It evolved from the Magistracy of the Rhine, an agency Napoleon installed in Strasbourg in 1808 to have jurisdiction over matters relating to river navigation. After the Treaty of Vienna in 1815, which ended the Napoleonic Wars, the magistracy was transferred to Mainz and then to Mannheim. It was responsible for introducing freedom of navigation on the Rhine in 1868.[11]

The choice of Strasbourg as the present seat of this commission was, of course, a consequence of France's victory over Germany in 1918. It was also a recognition of the city's evolving importance in commerce on the Rhine. Strasbourg as a city of roads on one side of a river and on a bend between two branches of another has been a center of Rhine riverboat traffic ever since the Middle Ages. The prosperity of the riverboat guild, from the fourteenth to the fifteenth centuries, and the story of the gift of a pot of hot porridge brought by the city fathers of Zurich on June 20, 1576, illustrate this history. For all that, starting in the seventeenth century, commerce on the Rhine sank into a period of mediocrity owing to increased tolls, competition on the river, and haulage by road.

The *Strombau,* the German term used to describe the harnessing of the river through a system of dikes, began in the nineteenth century and made navigation upstream from Karlsruhe much more difficult. The work to control the river downstream from Strasbourg was begun early in the twentieth century and completed in 1924. The next step was the construction of the Alsace Canal between 1928 and 1977, which in turn was tied to the construction of hydroelectric dams. With the completion of these projects, traffic at the port of Strasbourg increased dramatically, and navigation became possible up to Basel. At that moment, the medieval tradition came to life again.

The cities, the river, and even the weather from earliest times to the nineteenth century were all realities the memory of which did not disappear until the present time. The land too has created a memory. The expanse of the fields, with their even waves of tilled earth [*Ackerberge*] bear witness to more than a millennium of the constant work of plows on soil so rich in loess. The very name of Alsace, which appeared for the first time in the seventh century, preserves the memory of a duchy established at that time. The present-day borders between the departments of Haut-Rhin and Bas-Rhin, that is, upper and lower Alsace, follow the *Landgraben* (ancient trenches that marked territorial boundaries). The *Landgraben* between Selastat and Colmar go back to Neolithic times, and during the Carolingian era, they separated the two counties of Nordgau and Sundgau.

After the disintegration of the duchy, Alsace remained a "geographical expression" for centuries, a collection of principalities, seigneuries, and free towns belonging to the Holy Roman Empire. The power of the urban bourgeoisie in the towns prevented the bishops of Strasbourg from establishing another ecclesiastical state like those of Trier, Mainz, and Cologne.[12] An active center of the humanist movement and the Reformation, Alsace had turned into a mosaic of denominations, governed according to the formula *cujus regio, ejus religio* (whoever rules determines the religion), by the end of the Wars of Religion in the sixteenth century.

By the end of the sixteenth century, there were two Alsaces, marked by the ancient boundaries, facing each other. The north, meaning Lower Alsace, was profoundly affected by Lutheranism. The Catholic areas felt strongly the influence of Rhenish Catholicism. The southern part of Alsace was predominately Catholic except for an island of Protestantism at Mulhouse. Catholicism there assumed a baroque face, with its religious structures resembling those in southern Germany or Upper Austria.[13]

After 1648 and the end of the Thirty Years' War, Alsace passed under the control of the kingdom of France. Little by little the royal government turned it into a unified province. The comment by the nineteenth-century French historian Ernest Lavisse still fits: until the French arrived, Alsace "was . . . a geographic place as disordered as Old Germany. We molded it into a country." In the eighteenth century, the elite of Alsatian society came under the growing influence of French culture, as shown by the architecture and portraits of the period.

Then came the Revolution, with its profound consequences. Rouget de Lisle, a captain in the French army, composed the "Song of the Army of the Rhine" in the drawing room of the mayor of Strasbourg, Friedrich Dietrich. Rouget de Lisle hoped to inspire his companions-in-arms, who were about to march against the Prussians who had invaded France to crush the Revolution. We know the song, of course, as the "Marseillaise." The Revolutionaries affixed the inscription "Here begins the country of liberty" on the entry gate to the bridge between Strasbourg and Kehl. Other images engraved in the national memory no doubt hid a reality that was deeply shared, as evidenced by the hostility to the de-Christianization policies imposed by the Revolutionary government and the support given "refractory priests," those who refused to swear the constitutional oaths. Yet with the Revolution a heartfelt patriotism of the people, particularly in the cities and the towns, emerged and along with it a desire to be part of France.

The creation of the two departments, Bas-Rhin and Haut-Rhin, brought administrative unification. The customs border was extended to the Rhine. The city of Mulhouse, a free city in the Holy Roman Empire, entered into the French Republic. The Concordat of 1801, which brought peace between France and the papacy, simplified ecclesiastical geography. The diocese of Strasbourg now corresponded to the two departments. Up to that time, Wissembourg belonged to the jurisdiction of the diocese of Speyer in Germany and upper Alsace to the diocese of Basel in Switzerland, while the diocese of Strasbourg extended across the Rhine into Germany.

The Napoleonic Empire, a guarantee of authority and order based on the principles of 1789 and economic prosperity, found a favorable reception in the population of Alsace. The part played by soldiers and officers from Alsace—no fewer than seventy generals—in the Napoleonic epic, which was an opportunity for social promotion and glory, gave Alsatian patriotism an enduring military coloration. At the same time, patriotism transformed the Napoleonic legend into another component of memory for Alsace. The Second Empire would have no difficulty gaining popular sympathy. Imperceptibly, from the beginning of the century, the knowledge of French spread, thanks to the perseverance of successive administrations and to the growing integration of Alsace into national life.

Integration left intact the religious memory of the region. On this point, Alsace continued to be an extraordinary land of contacts. The twentieth-century French historian Lucien Febvre characterized Meister Eckhart, the famed fourteenth-century mystic, as "a man from Thuringia who did his studies in Paris, preached in Strasbourg, [and] taught at Cologne," and his student, the Dominican Johannes Tauler, as "a man from Strasbourg who preached in Cologne and died in Strasbourg."[14] Tauler, also a mystic, was much admired by sixteenth-century reformers. Half a millennium later, Alsace again played the role of hyphen in religious matters concerning France and Germany. An Alsatian by the name of Joseph Louis Colmar was the first to hold the episcopal seat at Mainz after the Revolution. He founded a seminary where another Alsatian, André Raess, bishop of Strasbourg from 1842 to 1887, taught from 1811 to 1830. In Mainz Raess founded the review *Der Katholik,* which brought Joseph de Maistre and Robert de Lamennais to the German public. (Both were outspoken Catholic apologists actively fighting for, among other things, universal acceptance of papal authority.) This school was to play an important role in the religious revival in Germany in the first half of the nineteenth century.[15]

Are examples needed from the history of Protestantism? We need only mention Edouard Reuss, who earned his doctorate at the University of Göttingen and taught at the faculty of Protestant theology in Strasbourg for thirty-six years. Let us also note the establishment in Strasbourg in 1850 of the *Revue de théologie et de philosophie chrétienne,* which introduced liberal Protestant German exegesis and theology to France.

Deeply embedded in the history of Alsace since the Middle Ages, sometimes tolerated and other times victimized during anti-Semitic fevers, Alsatian Judaism before the emancipation evoked the shtetls of Central and Eastern Europe.[16] It was part of that Jewish world in the Rhineland whose influence reached as far as Prague and Warsaw, Lithuania and Galicia. An extraordinary cultural intermediary, Alsatian Judaism displayed very specific features: a sense of reality that did not allow for mysticism, intense patriotism, and a sense of gratitude to the "Great Nation [France] as Emancipator."

No one did a better job at bringing to life a rabbi from the first part of the nineteenth century than Erckmann-Chatrian with his old Reb in *L'Ami Fritz.*[17] The great-grandfather of Robert Debré was supposed to have been the model for the old Reb. The rabbinate could be shown, like the pastorate in the Protestant world, as a door opening the way to an intellectual career. Robert Debré, born in 1865 in Selestat, was the son of a rabbi and the historian of the republican party of France. These examples suggest the importance in contemporary French history of Jewish emigration from the annexed provinces of Alsace and Lorraine.

POLITICAL MEMORY

The Time of Annexation

The Franco-Prussian War (1870–71) brought back tragic scenes of war and of memories that had never disappeared: the Peasants' War (1524) in the early years of the Reformation, the Thirty Years' War, the wars of Louis XIV, the invasion of 1814 by Germans and Russians, annexation in 1871, the return to France in 1918, another annexation in 1940—a person who was eighty years old in 1945, who had been born during the German Empire, would have seen himself tossed from one country to another four times during his lifetime. The stakes were always Alsace. It is not necessary to review this well-known history.[18] However, debates and innumerable second thoughts, which the fate of Alsace has prompted, oblige us to sift through the various ideas about its destiny and reexamine the readings drawn from its political memory.

A few isolated personalities did call for autonomy to create some kind of buffer state, the embryo of some new Austrasia, between France and Germany. The proposal was only an abstract idea formulated around 1870 by some academics, but it proved to be useful in later circumstances—at the end of World War I, between the two wars, and even during World War II. Joseph Rossé, one of the leaders of the autonomist wing of the Union populaire républicaine, the Catholic party, brought up this idea in his contacts with the German Resistance and President Roosevelt.

At the beginning of the twentieth century, after protests had ended, near-total agreement was reached for status as a confederated state within the German Empire. It was, to be sure, an arrangement imposed by necessity originating in the Treaty of Frankfurt in 1871, which confirmed the cession of Alsace and Lorraine to Germany. Let us now go beyond the political controversies and take a close look at the various conceptions of autonomy. A certain consensus existed that regarded autonomy as the point of departure for a rapprochement between France and Germany. This group affirmed loyalty to Germany and included the "nationalists," as the ardent Francophiles were called. Yet nearly everyone affirmed "sentiments of piety" toward France, to use the words of one German academic, Werner Wittich, a professor of political economy at the University of Strasbourg. It would be inaccurate to see in this attachment only the "nationalists" when, in fact, they included a number of adversaries—Catholic centrists, democrats, and socialists such as Georges Weill and Jacques

Peirotes, who also asserted their loyalty to French culture and traditions. The sisters of Georges Weill were professors in France. Peirotes was a printer and a great-grandson of a soldier in Napoleon's army.

Autonomy, a widely held desire at the beginning of the twentieth century, was actually an ambiguous notion. For some, it was the "legal form of protest," a last line of defense, wrapped in a halo of protest. It was fundamentally French, according to Pierre Bucher, the editor of the *Revue alsacienne illustrée,* which did so much in the early part of this century to affirm French traditions in Alsace. Abbé Wetterlé and the democrat Blumenthal from Colmar, who were leaders of a group called the Union nationale, professed this concept of autonomy.

They were a minority, which was opposed by another minority for whom autonomy was a necessary condition to a progressive acceptance of the fait accompli of 1871. For this group a certain attachment to the German Empire grew out of devotion to the little fatherland of Alsace, which they called their *Heimat* (homeland). This attitude was present in that part of the Lutheran world that looked to Wittenberg, Leipzig, Berlin, and Tübingen—the centers of Lutheran thought in the German Empire. The young Albert Schweitzer, while a student of theology, belonged to this world. Schweitzer (1875–1965), a noted humanitarian, musician, and scholar, received the Nobel Peace Prize in 1952.

The same concept of autonomy, envisaged as a step toward progressive integration, became the majority view for those priests and militant Catholics who looked to Mönchen-Gladbach, the center of the Volksverein, the leading Catholic organization, or to Cologne, where the main newspaper of the Association populaire catholique (Catholic Center Party), the *Kölnische Volkszeitung,* was published, or to the faculties of theology at Wurzburg and Munich.

For most people, however, autonomy was at best a hypothesis imposed by the Treaty of Frankfurt, a formula that allowed Alsatians to escape their undefined nationality and accept the new status quo without an all-or-nothing choice. They were not compelled to prejudge the future or sacrifice loyalties or traditions.

Thus we see that autonomy as a political demand involved the different ways of viewing the connections that Alsace had with France and Germany, and especially the different ways of understanding Alsatian particularism. Particularism drew on diverse cultural sources and carried in it several memories. Various groups evoked the Alsace of the Middle Ages and the Reformation. Catholics were nostalgic for the Holy Roman Empire and the organic harmony of medieval Christianity. The Lutherans found nourishment in the history of the German Reformation. Both were bearers of a memory going back centuries, to a time when Alsace was tied to the destiny of the German world. Indeed, the monuments the German Empire built in Alsace, from the train station in Colmar to the post office in Strasbourg and the reconstruction of the Haut-Koenigsberg chateau during Wilhelm II's reign, all aimed at giving life to memories of the Middle Ages.

Other parts of the Alsace elite favored the French cultural patrimony, with its memories of Alsace in the eighteenth century, the Enlightenment, the Revolution, and the Napoleonic era. Pierre Bucher, professor and model for the hero in the novel *Au service de l'Allemagne* (In the Service of Germany) by the nationalist author Maurice Barrès, sought to affirm the loyalty of Alsace "to the land and to the dead." He attacked the "uprooted," who, "making of necessity a virtue[,] posed as despisers of times past." Taking aim at the Hohenstaufen emperors, who had made Haguenau one of their favorite residences, he declared that "the exploits of a dynasty that ended in the thirteenth century after Jesus Christ today exercise an influence less powerful than the deeds of the 'ancien régime,' which perfected the unity of Alsace and of the Revolution. It was the Revolution that revealed to Alsatians their true political and social affinities."[19] This text illustrates the selectiveness of memory, which conceals on the one hand and on the other extols certain aspects of the past.

The interpretation of Alsatian history made by the illustrator Jean-Jacques Waltz, better known as Hansi, displays the same characteristic.[20] Hansi set up a contrast between eternal pan-Germanism, severely caricaturized in his *Professor Knatschke,*[21] and the France of the Revolution, with its message of liberty and the country of the good life and traditional values, as opposed to brutal Germany, caught up in the Industrial Revolution. Yet without doubt the best evidence for this Francophile memory is the monument erected on October 17, 1909, in Wissembourg on the initiative of one Auguste Spinner, with the assistance of the group Souvenir français, to the French soldiers killed in the battle of Wissembourg in 1870. The obelisk is decorated with plaques that commemorate the wars of the ancien régime, the Revolution, the Empire, and the Franco-Prussian War of 1870–71.

In sum, there was an Alsatian particularism that built its own foundation. The "little *patrie*" does not resemble the "large *patrie*" of either France or Germany. It is simply the *patrie.** Given the religious and cultural values of Alsace, a true national sentiment for Alsace did eventually assert itself. Those of the generation who became part of the intellectual and political life at the turn of the century were very representative of this state of mind. A personality such as Abbé Haegy, who played a significant role in

---

* EDITOR'S NOTE: The French speak of the natal region, province, even city, as *ma patrie.*

Après les « bombances » de ce genre, on éprouve souvent le besoin d'une émotion plus élevée, on recherche les endroits où l'on puisse communier avec l'âme de notre pays. Et pour cela, rien de plus sûr que de retourner à nos champs de bataille. Oh! il ne s'agit pas d'aller passer en revue les marbres et les bronzes colossaux, ornés d'aigles féroces, de lions grimaçants, pour y rencontrer toujours quelque société de vétérans d'outre-Rhin fêtant bruyamment un anniversaire quelconque; mais il faut aller voir les stèles, les petites croix qui marquent les places où les soldats de France ont fini par succomber. Là, pas d'orateurs, d'orphéons, ni de bannières, pas de couronnes de zinc ou de verroterie. Ceux qui ont voulu grouper les deuils autour de ces tombes ont été condamnés ou obligés de s'exiler. Mais vous y trouverez très souvent quelque enfant du pays, tout ému, qui s'éloigne discrètement à votre approche, en laissant sur la tombe un bouquet d'humbles fleurs des champs. Et nous, quand vers le soir, nous arrivons devant le monument français élevé sur cette terre où par trois fois les nôtres se sont battus contre l'envahisseur, alors une profonde émotion nous étreint. Les derniers rayons du couchant viennent dorer le fier coq de bronze, il semble s'animer et à son appel on croit voir accourir du fond de l'horizon les escadrons de sabreurs héroïques...

Cela, c'est une fête du cœur que nul gouvernement ne pourra nous empêcher de célébrer.

Figure 10.5
Illustration by Hansi (Jean-Jacques Waltz, 1873–1951) in *Mon village*. The war monument and tomb at Wissembourg, the hills and a vision of the French army in glory are depicted.

Alsatian Catholicism, embodied this kind of particularism, which was an exaltation of *Elsässertum* ("Alsaceness"). In the close partnership he established between the "small *patrie*" and the Catholic religion, he was like priests of the late nineteenth century in Slovakia, Flanders, and the Basque country who affirmed, in their opposition to the national state, the rights of a "people" whose destiny was inseparable from that of the church. During the interwar period, the Alsatian desire for autonomy, with its clerical roots, was imprinted with this image of Alsace, and this image became a regular feature in the journal *Heimat,* founded by Abbé Haegy in 1921. Haegy defined himself at one time as "a Catholic first and then an Alsatian." He had "defended the interests of God, the church, and the Christian people of Alsace within their German state with respect to the German state." He would try, "with respect to the French state," to render the same service to the "small *patrie*" of Alsace within France.[22]

Autonomy and Regionalism between the Two World Wars

The origin of the "Alsatian malaise" and the autonomist crisis of the 1920s are well known.[23] A climate of patriotic enthusiasm, confirmed by much evidence, accompanied the return to the mother country. But very soon, there appeared economic and administrative problems growing out of the reintegration into France: psychological blunders, on the one hand, and a difficult entry into an intellectual and cultural universe to which Alsace had been a stranger for half a century, on the other. The image each partner had of the other did not completely conform to what had been imagined. In 1924, the cartel of the French Left pushing for secular assimilation sought to abolish the religion and school statute in the reintegrated departments. The attempt put a match to the powder. Faced with a storm of protest, the government abandoned the project, while the autonomist movement used the opportunity to assert its position. On June 8, 1926, the *Heimatbund* (Union for the Homeland) issued a manifesto with the demand that the "people of Alsace-Lorraine" obtain, in order to ensure the protection of their rights, "complete autonomy as a national minority within France."

The term autonomism, in fact, comprised different realities: the clerical autonomism of a Rossé or Haegy; lay autonomism; and, in the democratic tradition of a Dahlet, communist autonomism, which in the name of the international proletariat denounced French imperialism and until 1934 enjoyed the support of the Parti communiste français. The situation was similar to the period before 1914 but was inverted, so that we must sketch a scale of attitudes if we are to discern the different images about the destiny of Alsace.

A small fringe group was made up of Germanophiles for whom autonomy was but a preliminary expedient to a return to Germany, of whose culture Alsace had been an intimate part. In relation to some Alsatians, these men were deeply integrated into German culture, and in 1918, they left for Germany at the same time the German immigrants in Alsace were expelled. Among the former was the Catholic theologian Joseph Schmidlin, professor of church history and missions at Mönchen-Gladbach.[24] Others included several Protestant pastors, such as Gustav-Adolph Anrich, son of a pastor, who as professor of theology at Bonn and later Tübingen began serving as president of the Wissenschaftliches Institut der Elsass-Lothringer im Reich in 1924. There was Robert Ernst,[25] also the son of an Alsatian pastor as well as an officer in World War I. During the first years of the Weimar Republic he was the driving force behind Alsatian irredentist organizations in Germany and presided over efforts to assist certain Alsatian autonomist groups whose goals were allegedly cultural. The only political organization that was openly Germanophile was the Autonomistische Landespartei (Autonomous State Party), headed by Karl Roos.[26] Later, as the Unabhängige Landespartei (Independent State Party), it experienced only modest success, notably in certain Lutheran areas in the northern part of Alsace. The Nazi myth of *Blut und Boden* (blood and soil) was very seductive to these clearly "separatist" circles.

True autonomists like Ricklin, Rossé, and Dahlet (all members of the French parliament—the first two from the Catholic party, the third a democratic Radical) turned their attention first to Alsace, not to Germany or France. They affirmed their loyalty to Alsace in the same way they had to the Reich before 1914. This autonomism, for which Abbé Haegy was the chief theorist, enjoyed wide and noticeable support. Indeed, at certain times, it was able to outmaneuver the Union populaire républicaine (UPR), the Catholic party.

Reexamining this distant political history, which once aroused so many passions, is indispensable for illuminating the attitudes of that age. The regionalists were in fact the dominant force in the UPR. These regionalists included Michel Walter, Thomas Seltz, and Henri Meck. This last was a member of parliament in three republics. For them loyalty to the French *patrie* converged with devotion to the identity of Alsace. They were very representative of a popular social Christianity that had sprung from German culture in Alsace and from the *Volksverein* (People's Association), which had sought and found welcome in the institutions of French social Catholicism, and to which Henri Meck as late as the Fifth Republic (the present government of France) made reference. Depending on the individual and the moment, the Union populaire républicaine emphasized either the national or the regional pole of this double loyalty.

In 1926, those Catholics who disapproved of the UPR's apparent uncertain policy toward the autonomists founded the Action populaire nationale d'Alsace (APNA, or People's National Action for Alsace). APNA
wanted to be connected to the religious and academic structures of Alsace and to its regional identity, though their patriotism still had nationalist overtones. They were truly representative of that brand of Alsatian
patriotism that was nourished by military memories, all the more ardent
because it was the patriotism of a frontier province. With the exception
of an autonomist minority, the popular Christians of the UPR were no
less patriotic, but it was a different kind of patriotism, one with an Alsatian specificity, which they vigorously affirmed. We might add that the
national Catholics of APNA were liberal conservatives with a touch of
Gallicanism (Gallicanism was a long-standing French tradition of resistance to papal authority). The UPR, by contrast, was made up of
Catholics who adhered to Christian social teachings and ultramontane
doctrine. They were rooted in the Catholic traditions of Alsace at their
most profound, which, since the beginning of the nineteenth century
had taken its cue from Rome.

The Weight of World War II

World War II was the last ordeal of the drama that began in 1870. Even
today, its tragic memories still weigh in people's memories—the brutal
defeat of France, de facto annexation by Germany, the feeling of aban-
donment by the Vichy government, Nazification, and incorporation into
a totalitarian regime. One publication appeared during the Occupation
that described the mechanics of the Nazi system. Entitled *Témoignage
Chrétien, Alsace et Lorraine terres françaises* (Christian Witness, Alsace and
Lorraine French Lands), it was written by a professor of philosophy,
Emile Baas, and Abbé Pierre Bockel, then the archpriest of the cathedral
of Strasbourg. Once again, the Alsatians faced tragic choices, and once
again Alsatians were wearing uniforms of the opposing sides. Some were
forced into the German army. They saw combat chiefly on the Russian
front. Others were volunteers in the Free French Forces or in the Alsace-
Lorraine Brigade formed in southwest France that fought in the Resistance under the command of Colonel Berger, otherwise known as André Malraux. Malraux was later minister of information and minister of
cultural affairs during General de Gaulle's presidency.

The consequences of the conflict for the Alsatian conscience were
tremendous. Certain memories were without doubt repressed: the drama
of enforced incorporation into Germany or some horrible experience
under the totalitarian regime.[27] Certain autonomist leaders, the former

communist J.-P. Mourer, or H. Bickler, the senior official responsible for
the youth organizations in the Unabhängige Landespartei (Independent
State Party), made common cause with the Nazis. Others on the autonomist wing of the UPR—Rossé, Keppi, Sturmel—were incarcerated by
French authorities at the beginning of the war. In June 1940, at the time
of the French defeat, they signed the "Manifeste des Trois Épis" at the
urging of Robert Ernst. The manifesto was their request for integration
into the Third Reich. Without doubt, faithful to their unchanging line,
they were hoping to preserve thereby the originality of Alsace and the
freedom of the church within a victorious Germany.

    Double illusion. Hitler attached Alsace to the Oberrhein Gau (Nazi
adminstrative district) and the Moselle to the Saarland and the Palatinate
to form the Westmark Gau, the capital of which was Saarbrucken. That
put an end to the myth of Alsace-Lorraine. Hitler wanted to destroy
German particularism of whatever sort. Far from being a step on the way
to Germanization, Alsatian particularism was considered to be a barrier
that had to be struck down. The Nazis mistrusted clerical autonomists,
several of whom, such as Rossé, had made contact with the German resistance. But they did reward irredentist leaders such as Ernst, whom they
made commissioner of Strasbourg.

    In the meantime, the population was stunned by the defeat and at
first wavered between a wait-and-see attitude, hostile resignation, and a
refusal to cooperate that soon developed into a resolute hostility. In a report severely critical of the policies implemented by the gauleiter, the
mayor of Stuttgart in July 1943 related a little joke going around in Alsace: "What the French could not accomplish in twenty years, the Germans are completing—turning the Alsatians into Frenchmen."[28] Faced
with Nazi oppression, the tribulations of the Jacobin Republic seemed
minor. The idea of autonomy, though not regionalism, was irretrievably
shattered by the extensive or occasional collaboration of the autonomist
leaders with Nazism. This is the main reason there has not been any
resurgence of Alsatian autonomism since 1945.

    For all that, the conscience of Alsace was not exorcised, as is evident
from the brutal but brief fever provoked by the Oradour affair eight years
after the war. In January 1953, thirteen French nationals who had been
conscripted into the German military and were implicated in the
Oradour-sur-Glane massacre were brought before the tribunal at Bordeaux along with members of the S.S. division Das Reich. The men from
Alsace were condemned to terms ranging from five years' imprisonment
to eight years of forced labor.

    The news provoked "sad astonishment among some, vehement in-
dignation for others," according to the analysis done by one of the most

penetrating observers of Alsace, Émile Baas.[29] Opinion "rose up in a true
ground swell." Flags were lowered to half-mast, bells rang, monuments to
the dead were draped in mourning, decorations were solemnly returned,
reserve officers resigned, municipal councils issued protests. On February 16, General de Gaulle issued a formal statement: "What Frenchman
cannot understand the anger and pain of Alsace? Brutally annexed by the
enemy following the capitulation by Vichy, having undergone the terrible experience of seeing many of its young men conscripted by force into
the ranks of the German army, it now passionately rejects the conclusion
of a trial which seems to the people of Alsace to be outrageous." Two days
later, at the urging of the *président du conseil,* René Pleven, the National Assembly voted an amnesty law, which quickly restored calm.

Opinion had risen up against the lack of understanding concerning
the issue of forced conscription. A complex of injured emotions had burst
into broad daylight, and the loudest protests came from the most patriotic
elements in the population. It was as if, through this trial, a suspicion had
been raised about the patriotism of Alsace during the annexation. The humiliation of incorporation by force had come out into broad daylight and
along with it the place of Alsace in the French community, because that
too had come into question. The intensity of the reaction revealed, buried
deep in the psyche of the region, memories that time alone could make
less painful. That intensity recalled the old lesson drawn by a bureaucrat in
the ancien régime: "Do not touch the customs of Alsace."

Symbolic Memory

Of all the frontier regions of France, without doubt none has more pow-
erfully gripped the popular imagination over the last century than Alsace.
The annexation of 1870 united in one destiny the two departments of
Alsace, minus Belfort, and sections of the departments of Meurthe,
Moselle, and Vosges.[30] These areas constituted what was once part of the
Holy Roman Empire. Even now Alsace and Lorraine are one in the na-
tional memory. The drama of defeat and territorial amputation caused
French nationalism to reaffirm its foundations, with Alsace becoming the
heart of France.

Let us return to that symbolic moment of the Declaration of Bordeaux on March 1, 1871. The National Assembly had convened in Bordeaux. The German army still occupied much of northern France and
the environs of Paris. The government had ratified the preliminary peace
terms imposed by the Germans at Frankfurt and accepted the annexation.
On that day, the deputy from the department of the Haut-Rhin read the
protest of the deputies from Alsace and Lorraine. Leon Gambetta, deputy

from the Haut-Rhin, was a leading author. Earlier in Paris, he had organized the government of national defense against the Germans. Soon he
would be playing a major role in shaping the Third Republic. The declaration read:

> In contempt of all justice and by an odious abuse of force and deliv-
> ered to the domination of the foreigner, we have one last duty to
> perform.
>   We declare once again null and void a pact which disposes of us
> without our consent.
>   The demand for our rights will exist forever in the form that our
> conscience dictates to each and every one of us.

In its ending phrase, which owed much to Frederick Hartmann, an
industrialist and mayor of Munster, a town near Colmar, the manifesto
reserved freedom of action for all interested parties in the future. Its major significance was the affirmation of a principle, destined to be constantly repeated: the right by law to oppose constraint. In other words,
the manifesto was a solemn proclamation that consent alone established
nationality, as the historians Fustel de Coulanges and Ernst Renan would
later assert in response to German historians. It was also a declaration that
the wound could never be closed and that protest in some form would
sound forever.

The Declaration of Bordeaux ended on a double affirmation of faith
in the destiny of France and loyalty to the *patrie:*

> We wait with total confidence in the future for a regenerated France
> to take up again the course of its great destiny.
>   Your brothers in Alsace-Lorraine, separated at this moment from
> the common family, will preserve a filial affection for the France that
> is absent from their homes until the moment comes when France
> resumes its place by the fireside.

From that moment on, French nationalism, or more precisely republican patriotism, was inseparable from the memory of the lost provinces. The painting of Jean-Jacques Henner, presented by the women of
Alsace to Gambetta in 1871, shows a pensive Alsatian woman dressed in
a black hat with a small tricolor rosette; it is entitled "She Waits."

We need not pause here to recite a history punctuated by the many
episodes that became part of the republican legend. To cite only two:
Gambetta said, "Always think about it, never speak of it." And Jules
Ferry, united by so many ties as a student at Strasbourg in his youth and

through his marriage, expressed the desire in his will, drawn up in 1890, to rest facing "that blue line of the Vosges whence arise to my loyal heart the moving cries of the conquered." Ferry had served with Gambetta in the government of national defense and was later minister of education and twice premier in 1881 and 1883.

Let us also note the short story "The Last Class: the Story of a Little Alsatian Boy," found in the *Contes de lundi* (Monday's Tales), written in 1873 by Alphonse Daudet. When it was included in widely used children's textbooks, its long success was guaranteed. How many people for the rest of their life retained the image of a schoolteacher writing silently at the blackboard "France-Alsace—Alsace-France"? Another image—the young heroes in *Le Tour de la France par deux enfants* (Two Children Tour France) go to Phalsbourg and sneak across the border in the Vosges Mountains.

Phalsbourg was a small fortified town in annexed Lorraine near the Alsatian border, and thanks to books written by Erckmann-Chatrian toward the end of the Second Empire the town became in its way a symbol of Alsace-Lorraine. The extraordinary popular success of his "national novels," such as *Le Conscrit de 1813, L'Invasion,* and *Waterloo,* all had the effect of combining the images of Alsace and Lorraine with patriotic feelings and the republican idea. An entire literature of romance and adventure, of which *Les Oberlé* of René Bazin provided one of the most remarkable examples, helped reawaken the memory of the two lost provinces as did the surveys and travel narratives about trips to the annexed lands. Other works written after 1871 by Erckmann-Chatrian, such as *Le Brigadier Frédéric* (Corporal Frederick) or *Le Banni* (The Banished) evoked the tragic fate that befell the exiles.

Emigration from Alsace and Lorraine in the years following the defeat reached significant proportions. As stipulated by the terms of the Treaty of Frankfurt, this option affected nearly 40,000 people in the Bas-Rhin department and 93,000 in the Haut-Rhin. A thin trickle of emigration began as a result, fed notably by young men who did not want to fulfill their military obligations in Germany. Those emigrating were often from the elite.[31] They were university educated,[32] high officials, officers, and at times members of the liberal and industrial professions.

Those *optants,* as they were called, played a part in keeping alive the memory of the annexed lands in the clubs formed in France by people from Alsace and Lorraine. One of these was Robert Debré, the son of an *optant* who had been a student at the rabbinical school that transferred to the rue Vauquelin in Paris from Metz. At the Winter Circus one year, he evoked the traditional Christmas tree of Alsace-Lorraine before an audience that included Mme. Ferry, wife of the former premier. When Erckmann-Chatrian's words to the song "Dis-moi quel est ton pays" (Tell

Figure 10.6
J.-J. Henner, *She Waits*, painting (1871).

Me What Is Your Country) were sung, the audience took up the refrain with "C'est la vieille et loyale Alsace" (It is the old and loyal Alsace).

In October 1873, thanks to pedagogical reforms initiated after the defeat, the Alsatian school was established in Paris. The school owed its beginnings to the efforts of several individuals educated in the Protestant gymnasium founded in 1538 by the humanist Johannes Sturm.[33] The list of benefactors and professors includes Frédéric Rieder, son of the pastor of Temple Neuf in Strasbourg, former professor at the *lycée* in Strasbourg, and director of the Alsatian School from 1874 to 1891. The list of these supporters and teachers attests to the spirit of this free school, located at 92, rue d'Assas in Paris, that was so profoundly marked by the presence of Alsace.

Without doubt this memory and this presence of Alsace, which burned in the French consciousness with varying intensity between the annexation and the eve of World War I, created a vision of Alsace that was somewhat inexact. The vision did not match the changes that Alsace had undergone as Reichsland. The contradictions between the French image of Alsace and the particular reality of Alsace caused many misunderstandings and constituted one of the reasons for the Alsatian "malaise" between the two world wars. The Alsace "restored" in 1918 was not fully identical to the memory of the "old" Alsace. The Germanist Charles Andler, born in Strasbourg in 1866 and the son of the founder of the Man of Iron pharmacy on the Place Kleber, referred to this distance between image and reality in his biography of Lucien Herr, the celebrated librarian from the École normale, who had played such an important role in the Dreyfus affair and in the development of French socialism. Herr too was an Alsatian, born at Altkirch in the district of Sundgau. In the eyes of Alsatians, the liberal Alsace as portrayed by Erckmann-Chatrian had become a "clerical" Alsace oriented to the Rhine, which they called the "street of the priests."

A number of essays on Alsace, such as "Psychanalyse de l'Alsace" (Pyschoanalysis of Alsace), which caused such an uproar after World War II, were dominated by the image of an Alsace tossed between two worlds, given up to dismemberment, still uncertain and dissatisfied with its destiny. The myth of *Hans im Schnogeloch* (Hans in the Mosquito Hole),[34] never happy with his lot, aspiring to something else, served to explain the entire psychology of Alsace. Over the years, shows at bilingual cabarets, offered to Alsatians by the songwriter Germain Muller, harked back to similar visions. The image was partly true, but over time less and less faithful to the reality. In fact, the situation in Alsace had already evolved in ways that contemporaries were not immediately aware of, and these

Figure 10.7
World War I: Marshal
Foch entering Stras-
bourg.

changes attenuated the latent contradictions of the province's cultural and
political memory. This evolution depended on two sets of phenomena
coming together: Alsace's growing integration into the French community as it affected regional particularities and the rapprochement between
France and Germany.

The caution of the political leaders after 1945, the growth in the
economy in contrast to the stagnation of the interwar period, and the
standardization in living styles and ways of thinking have all played a
significant role. To that must be added the role of the republican movement and Gaullism in the integration of Alsace into the national political
culture. When the Christian Democratic coalition was born during the
liberation, its leaders had friends in Alsace who wanted to avoid the re-
creation of a regional party like the one formed between the two wars.
In 1945, they succeeded in imposing their views on the former leaders of
the Union populaire républicaine, the regional Catholic party, who accepted integration into a national organization. The Mouvement républicain populaire, dominated by veterans of the Resistance, assumed the
task of defending Alsace's peculiar traditions in Paris. One of its leaders
was Robert Schuman, in whom the Catholic movement in the Moselle

Figure 10.8
World War II: Libera-
tion of Strasbourg,
November 1944; sol-
diers from General
Leclerc's 2nd Armored
Division in front of the
cathedral.

region before 1914 had placed so much hope. Did he not play a major policy role at the beginning of the Fourth Republic and later in the conduct of foreign affairs? There was a young MRP deputy from the department of Bas-Rhin by the name of Pierre Pflamlin. Did he not quickly become a government minister? In the new France born in the liberation, the popular Christian tradition, so powerful in Alsace and Lorraine from before 1914, thus was incorporated into a large national party. Continuity in change was thereby affirmed.

Gaullism too played a powerful integrating role. Need we recall that General de Gaulle and the other liberators of 1944–45 were quickly placed in the pantheon of Alsatian patriotism after the last offensive in Alsace? They joined the ranks of those who had gone on before in military glory—Napoleon's generals and the liberators of 1918. The portraits of Generals de Gaulle, Leclerc, and De Lattre hung for many years in the shops and homes of Alsace.

When on April 7, 1947, the second anniversary of the total liberation of Alsace, de Gaulle chose Strasbourg to announce from the balcony of the *hôtel de ville* the establishment of a new political coalition, the Rassemblement du peuple français (Assembly of the French People), he won considerable support from those Alsatians sympathetic both to authority and to democracy. His remarks aroused feelings of patriotism and distrust when he touched upon the possibility of some autonomy. Alsace served once more to revive, within a nationalist framework, a memory that was both national and regional. After the return to power of General de Gaulle and the Fifth Republic, Alsace became a bastion of Gaullism for many years. Regardless of any memory of the political landscape from the preceding half century, the political culture of Alsace had indeed lost some of its specificity.

The French-German rapprochement radically altered the problem of Alsace. Its slopes and frontier were no longer disputed space in Europe between national antagonists. Alsace had retrieved its former glory by becoming the bridge and crossroads, as it had been several times in its history. The Rhine could again "become . . . a link for the West," in words spoken by General de Gaulle in Strasbourg on October 5, 1945, when he was head of the provisional government. The symbolic charge of Strasbourg has not diminished in intensity. It has only changed direction. The city that had embodied confrontation between France and Germany and whose cathedral spire symbolized uniquely for the city the humiliation of 1871 was chosen by common agreement as the seat of the European parliament. It became again the city where roads crossed and cultures met under the sign of the "genius of the Rhine," just as the author Barrès had once dreamed. The broken memory of Alsace rediscovered its connections and ties to its entire history.

That history is perhaps symbolized in Mont-Sainte-Odile, a promontory that directly overlooks the Alsatian plain. The remains of a Celtic fortress known as the "pagan wall" attest to the antiquity of human habitation on this privileged spot. It was here in the seventh century that either Odile, the daughter of the duc d'Alsace, Aldaric, or Eticho founded the Hohenburg monastery. Here, in the times of the Hohenstaufen emperors in the twelfth century, the Abbess Herrad composed *Hortus Deliciarum* (The Garden of Delights), an illuminated manuscript, which was destroyed during the siege of 1870 when the library of Strasbourg was burned. The abbey, which was under the protection of Saint Odile, was a celebrated pilgrimage site for the entire Holy Roman Empire. The emperor Charles IV in 1354 had a bone of the saint's forearm given as a relic to the cathedral in Prague.[35]

The heart of Catholic Alsace, this sacred place embodied after 1871 the double devotion both to the church and to France. It was here in the difficult hours of 1968 that de Gaulle sought to collect his thoughts and meet with the heads of the French army stationed in Germany. Another place had witnessed something similar: the Rock of Dabo. It is located at

Figure 10.9
Mont-Sainte-Odile and Saint-Nabor.

the border between Alsace and Lorraine, a cathedral of sandstone high over the surrounding fir trees, with a little chapel dedicated to the memory of Bruno d'Eguisheim, later Pope Leo IX, the only pope from Alsace and an early force in the Gregorian Reform in the middle of the eleventh century. It was at this high location that Chancellor Kohl, who is from the Rhineland, expressed his wish to meet the president of the Fifth Republic.

NOTES

1. Known as Erwin von Steinbach in the sixteenth century, he was believed by the romantics to be the sole builder. His role, truly considerable but not unique, spanned the years from 1284 to 1318. His son succeeded him from 1318 to 1339. Hans Haug et al., *La Cathédrale de Strasbourg,* Editions des dernières nouvelles d'Alsace (Strasbourg: 1957).

2. Francis Rapp, *Route des prêtres, route des empereurs: Une histoire du Rhin* (Paris: Ramsay, 1981).

3. This revealing extract from Nazi newsreels appears in Marcel Ophuls's 1970 film *Le Chagrin et la pitié* [*The Sorrow and the Pity*].

4. Lucien Febvre and Albert Demangeon, *Le Rhin: Problèmes d'histoire et d'économie* (Paris: Armand Colin, 1935).

5. Cf. "Au berceau des annales: Le milieu strasbourgeois," in *L'Histoire en France au début du XXe siècle: Actes du colloque de Strasbourg, 11–13 octobre, 1979,* published under the direction of Charles-Oliver Carbonell and Georges Livet (Toulouse: Presses de l'I.E.P., 1983); John Craig, *Scholarship and Nation Building: The Universities of Strasbourg and Alsatian Society, 1870–1939* (Chicago: University of Chicago Press, 1984).

6. Cf. Georges Pagès, *La Guerre de Trente Ans 1618–1648* (Paris: Payot, 1939). The Jesuit Pierre Labbé, in the *Testamentum Politicum,* which he lent to Cardinal Richelieu, had the cardinal say that he wanted to "restituere Galliae limites quos natura proefixit" (restore to Gaul the limits which nature has set). This text is cited by Louis André in his introduction to the critical edition of the real *Testament politique du cardinal de Richelieu* (Paris: Lafont, 1947), 66.

7. Danton, speech to the convention, January 31, 1793.

8. E. M. Arndt, *Arndts Werke: Auswahl in zwölf Teilen,* ed. Wilhelm Steffnes, Kleine Schriften 2 (Berlin: Deutsches Verlaghaus Bong, [1912?]), 39–82. Alfred Fierro-Domenech, in his interesting work *Le Pré Carré: Géographie historique de la France* (Paris: Robert Lafont, 1986), 24, notes that this idea had already been expressed by Sebastian Münster in the French edition of his *Cosmographie* (1552), but that the absence of a German state made it impossible for the idea to gain acceptance until the dawn of the nineteenth century.

9. Robert Minder, *Allemagnes et allemands* (Paris: Éditions du Seuil, 1948), 172.

10. Cf. the introduction by Pierre Schmitt in *Histoires et légendes de l'Alsace mystérieuse* (Paris: Tchou, 1969).

11. Jean-Claude Ailleret, "La Liberté de navigation," in *Une histoire du Rhin* (Paris: J.-P. Ramsay, 1981), 375–83.

12. Jean de Pange insists on this point in a book now forgotten but rich in cultural descriptions, *Les Libertés rhénanes: Pays rhénans, Sarre, Alsace* (Paris: Perrin, 1922), 22ff.

13. These are the conclusions of Louis Chatellier, *Histoire du diocèse de Strasbourg* (Paris: Beauchesne, 1982).

14. Febvre and Demangeon, 93.

15. The books of Georges Goyau are the classic study of religious Germany, e.g, *L'Allemagne religieuse* (Paris: Perrin, 1908–11).

16. Cf. Freddy Raphaël and Robert Weyl, *Juifs en Alsace: Culture, société, histoire* (Toulouse: Privat, 1977). The "emancipation" refers to the lifting of government restrictions on Jews in France, Austria, Germany, and elsewhere in the early nineteenth century.

17. Cf. Freddy Raphaël, "Présence du Juif dans l'oeuvre d'Erckmann-Chatrian," *Revue des sciences sociales de la France de l'Est* 5 (1976): 81–142.

18. General works of synthesis include François-Georges Dreyfus, *Histoire de l'Alsace* (Paris: Hachette, 1979); Philippe Dollinger, ed., *Histoire de l'Alsace* (Toulouse:

Privat, 1970); and Dollinger, ed., *L'Alsace depuis 1900*. Works on specific topics include Christian Baechler, *Le Parti catholique alsacien, 1890–1939* (Strasbourg: University of Strasbourg, 1982); François-Georges Dreyfus, *La Vie politique en Alsace, 1919–1936* (Paris: F.N.S.P., 1969); and Jean-Marie Mayeur, *Autonomie et politique en Alsace: La Constitution de 1911* (Paris: Armand Colin, 1970).

19. *Cahiers alsaciens* (January 1912).

20. See his albums *Histoire d'Alsace* (1912) and *Mon village* (1913).

21. In 1909.

22. Christian Baechler, "L'Abbé Haegy, 1870–1932: Une politique au service de l'Eglise et du peuple alsacien," *Archives de l'Eglise d'Alsace* (1984): 287–339. The letter is cited on p. 327.

23. This is the title of a book written in 1929 by the essayist René Gillouin.

24. A victim of the Nazis, he did not survive deportation to the concentration camp at Struthof.

25. See esp. Lothar Kettenacker, *La Politique de nazification en Alsace,* Saisons d'Alsace, 2 vols. (Strasbourg, 1978).

26. Convicted of espionage, he was shot at Nancy in the autumn of 1939.

27. Cf. Geneviève Herberich-Marx and Freddy Raphaël, "Les Incorporés de force Alsaciens: Déni, convocation, et provocation de la mémoire," *Vingtième siècle* (April 1985), and elaboration by Pierre Barral, "La Tragédie des 'Malgré-Nous,'" *L'Histoire* 80 (1985): 120–24.

28. Cited by Fernand L'Huillier in *Libération de l'Alsace* (Paris: Hachette, 1975), 32.

29. *Saisons d'Alsace* (Strasbourg, 1953), 69–72. At the time of the liberation Emile Baas published a *Situation de l'Alsace* (1946), written during the war. The Oradour trial was the subject of a recent article by Jean-Pierre Rioux, "Le Procès d'Oradour," *L'Histoire* 64 (1984): 6–17.

30. The arrondissements of Château-Salins and Sarrebourg for the department of the Meurthe; and those of Metz, Sarreguemines, and Thionville for the department of the Moselle and the cantons of Saales and Schirmeck in the Vosges, respectively.

31. Alfred Wahl has shown in his 3rd cycle thesis that the very high numbers given by Paris take into account people from Alsace and Lorraine who had settled in France before 1870 and who had chosen French nationality.

32. Christophe Charles, in his thesis "Intellectuels et élites en France, 1880–1900," shows the influence of individuals of Alsatian origin in higher education and in the civil service.

33. Georges Hacquard, *Histoire d'une institution française: L'école alsacienne; Naissance d'une école libre, 1870–1891* (Paris: J.-J. Pauvert et Garnier, 1982).

34. At the end of *Bürger und Soldaten* (1918), Alfred Döblin describes a scene that takes place just as German domination is collapsing. A crowd stands at the Place Broglie singing "Hans im Schnogeloch," accompanied by an orchestra made up of firemen.

35. Christian Pfister, *Pages alsaciennes,* Publications de la Faculté des Lettres de l'Université de Strasbourg, fasc. 40 (Paris: Société d'édition, les Belles Lettres; London and New York: Oxford University Press, 1927), 111.

CHAPTER ONE

Figure 1.1   Samuel Mours, *Les Églises réformées de France,* Librairie Protestante.

CHAPTER TWO

Figure 2.1   Naval map of Western Europe in G. de Brouscon du Conquet, *Manuel de pilotage à l'usage des pilotes bretons* (1548). Bibliothèque nationale, Paris. Photo © Bibliothèque nationale.

Figure 2.2   *Naufrage de Virginie,* an engraving by Roger, based on Prud'hon, in Bernardin de Saint-Pierre, *Paul et Virginie* (1806). Bibliothèque nationale, Paris. Photo © Bibliothèque nationale.

Figure 2.3   *Orante sur le littoral,* 1803 thanksgiving plaque, Saint Paul Church, Hyères. Photo © Jean Lepage/Musée de la Marine, Paris.

Figure 2.4   Ouessant, the island sentinel with its many lighthouses. Photo © Françoise Péron.

Figure 2.5   Honfleur. Photo © Actualitat/Rapho.

Figure 2.6   Fécamp—The basin at mid-tide. Photo © Léonard de Selva/Tapabor.

Figure 2.7   The Corderie at Rochefort in the 18th century, designed by Ozanne and engraved by Le Gouax, Bibliothèque nationale, Paris. Photo © Bibliothèque nationale.

Figure 2.8   The Corderie at Rochefort in 1979, in ruins. Photo © Centre international de la mer, Rochefort.

Figure 2.9   The Corderie at Rochefort in 1991, restored. Photo © Centre international de la mer, Rochefort.

Figure 2.10   The inlet of the Brest harbor. E. Petit, *Carte topographique de Brest* (1640). Musée de la Marine, Paris.

Figure 2.11   The harbor of Toulon. *Carte topographique de la rade et du port de Toulon* (1703). Musée de la Marine, Paris.

Figure 2.12   *Le Borda, École navale: l'arrivée des professeurs,* engraving after a drawing by P. Renouard from *Le Journal universel* (September 26, 1885). Musée de la Marine, Paris.

Figure 2.13   The triumphal arrival of the *France* in New York after its maiden voyage across the Atlantic, 1962. Photo © Keystone.

Figure 2.14   The *Jeanne d'Arc* with all flags flying, New York, 1986. Photo ©
S.I.R.P.A./E.C.P.A.

Figure 2.15   Joseph Vernet, *Vue du port de La Rochelle vu de la petite rive* (1762),
detail. Musée de la Marine, Paris. Photo © Réunion des Musées
nationaux.

Figure 2.16   Géricault, *Le Radeau de la* Méduse, sketch. Musée du Louvre, Paris.
Photo © Bulloz.

Figure 2.17   Géricault, *Le Radeau de la* Méduse (1819). Musée du Louvre, Paris.
Photo © Bulloz.

Figure 2.18   Cordouan lighthouse, watercolor (18th century). Bibliothèque de
l'Arsenal, Paris. Photo © Jean-Loup Charmet.

Figure 2.19   Ouessant, crosses of *proëlla*. Photo © Françoise Péron.

CHAPTER THREE

Figure 3.1   Illustration by Théophile Schuler for Erckmann-Chatrian, *La Maison
forestière* (Paris: Hetzel, 1866–67). Bibliothèque nationale, Paris.
Photo © Bibliothèque nationale.

Figure 3.2   Maurice Denis, *Chemin dans les arbres* (1891). Musée du Prieuré,
Saint-Germain-en-Laye.

Figure 3.3   Jean Marais in Jean Cocteau's *La Belle et la bête* (1945). Photo ©
Christophe L.

Figure 3.4   Illustration by Gustave Doré for La Fontaine, *La Forêt et le bûcheron*
(1868). Coll. part. Photo © Jean-Loup Charmet.

Figure 3.5   Paul Cézanne, *La Montagne Sainte-Victoire vue de la carrière de Bibemus*.
Baltimore Museum of Art. Photo © Bulloz.

Figure 3.6   Georges Braque, *L'Estaque* (1906). Coll. part. Photo © Giraudon ©
SPADEM, 1992.

Figure 3.7   Biringuccio, *Pyrotechnie* (1572). Photo © Kharbine-Tapabor.

Figure 3.8   France, Center, miner's work. Photo © Jean-Dominique Lajoux.

Figure 3.9   Claude Caron, *Traité des bois servant à tous usages* (Paris, 1676). Bibliothèque nationale, Paris. Photo © Jean-Loup Charmet.

Figure 3.10   Primitive wood structures, 19th century. Photo © Bulloz.

Figure 3.11   *La France régénérée vous demande à recréer cette belle nature sur toute sa surface,* drawn and engraved by Monnet (ca. 1804). Musée Carnavalet,
Paris. Photo © Jean-Loup Charmet.

Figure 3.12   Lazare Bruandet, *Route en sous-bois* (19th century). Musée des
Beaux-Arts, Tours. Photo © Arsicaud.

Figure 3.13   Douglas fir. Photo © Exposition "Bois à coeur ouvert," 1990,
Musée d'histoire naturelle.

Figure 3.14   *Le Chêne pyramidal,* engraving by Legrand fils, after Bessa (ca.
1795). Bibliothèque nationale, Paris. Photo © Bibliothèque
nationale.

Figure 3.15   Map of Mimizan in 1959. Photo © I.G.N.

Figure 3.16   Map of Mimizan in 1987. Photo © I.G.N.

CHAPTER FOUR

Figure 4.1   Poster for the Region, 1969. Photo © Alain Gesgon/C.I.R.I.P.

Figure 4.2   *Carte particulière du duché de Bourgogne . . . dressée et execute par Séguin, ingénieur géographe du Roi, en 1763.* Bibliothèque nationale, Paris. Photo © Bibliothèque nationale.

Figure 4.3   *Voyage pittoresque de la France avec la description de toutes ses provinces . . . Vue du rocher de Cornillon,* engraved by Fessard after Balin. Bibliothèque nationale, Paris. Photo © Bibliothèque nationale.

Figure 4.4   *Montbard,* department of the Côte-d'Or, in J. B. Lavallée, J. B. Breton, and L. Brion, *Voyages dans les départements de la France enrichis de tableaux géographiques* (1792). Bibliothèque nationale, Paris. Photo © Bibliothèque nationale.

CHAPTER FIVE

Figure 5.1   Map of orthogonal sectioning of France, 1789. Archives nationales, Paris. Photo © Jean-Loup Charmet.

Figure 5.2   *Doléances du clergé ou les metamorphoses du diocèse* (1790). Cabinet des Dessins, Coll. Ed. de Rothschild, Musée du Louvre, Paris. Photo © Hubert Josse.

Figure 5.3   *La France divisée en XXXII provinces pour server à l'étude de sa nouvelle division en départements* (1791). Musée de la Poste, Paris.

Figure 5.4   *Les Environs de Paris à trois lieues à la ronde,* map of the capital's department following the National Assembly's decree of January 15, 1790. Bibliothèque nationale, Paris. Photo © Bibliothèque nationale.

Figure 5.5   Geometric map of Bretagne (1789). Archives nationales, Paris. Photo © Jean-Loup Charmet.

Figure 5.6   *Division de la Bretagne en six départements* (ca. 1789). Archives nationales, Paris. Photo © Jean-Loup Charmet.

Figure 5.7   Dominique Cassini, drawn by Henri Cassini (1789). Bibliothèque nationale, Paris. Photo © Bibliothèque nationale.

Figure 5.8   *Nouvelle Carte du royaume de France en 87 départments . . . d'après les nouvelles limites fixées par le traité de paix du 30 mai 1814.* Bibliothèque nationale, Paris. Photo © Bibliothèque nationale.

Figure 5.9   *La France par départements* (1824). Bibliothèque nationale, Paris. Photo © Bibliothèque nationale.

Figure 5.10   Map of the department of the Aisne in the *Atlas* of Vuillemin (1852). Bibliothèque nationale, Paris. Photo © Roger-Viollet.

Figures 5.11 H. Duru, *Géographie illustrée,* in the form of a card game (1841).
and 5.12.   Bibliothèque nationale, Paris. Photo © Bibliothèque nationale.

Figure 5.13   *Les Départements de la France,* cover to a magnetic game of questions and answers (ca. 1880). Photo © I.N.R.P., Musée national de l'Éducation.

CHAPTER SIX

Figure 6.1   The National Confederation in Paris, July 14, 1790. Anonymous engraving. Musée Carnavalet, Paris. Photo © Bulloz.

Figure 6.2   The French provinces as seen by Jean-Paul Goude at the bicentennial celebration of the French Revolution, 1989. Photo © Laurent Rousseau/Rapho.

Figure 6.3   Nodier, Taylor, and Cailleux, *Voyages pittoresques dans l'ancienne France: L'Auvergne,* vol. I (1829), frontispiece. Bibliothèque nationale, Paris. Photo © Bibliothèque nationale.

Figure 6.6   The Congrès des sociétés savantes à Dunkerque, 1907. Municipal archives of Dunkirk.

Figure 6.8   Cambry, *Voyage dans la Vendée: Vue du musée Cacault à Clisson.* Bibliothèque nationale, Paris. Photo © Bibliothèque nationale.

Figure 6.9   The public museum of ancient monuments in Arles, by Advinent (1784). Bibliothèque nationale, Paris. Photo © Bibliothèque nationale.

Figure 6.10   Noël Bouton, *Muse portant dans ses mains l'édifice du musée* (1901). Ceiling of the exhibition hall for drawings. Musée Bonnat, Bayonne.

Figure 6.11   The centenary medal of the musée Calvet by F. Charpentier, commissioned by the administration of the Calvet Museum in 1911. Musée Calvet, Avignon.

Figure 6.12   Pierre de Belay, *Le Cheval bleu* (1943). Musée des Beaux-Arts, Quimper.

Figure 6.13   Jules Benoît-Lévy, *La Bretagne,* Salon of 1911. Photo © N.D.-Viollet.

Figure 6.14   Henri Lévy, *Les Gloires de la Bourgogne* (1896). Photo © Roger-Viollet.

Figure 6.15   "Groupe allégorique du cinquantenaire. . . ." 1910 postcard. Photo © Kharbine/Tapabor.

Figure 6.16   Celebration commemorating the union of Brittany with France, October 29, 1911. Photo © Roger-Viollet.

Figure 6.17   J.-P. Pinchon, *Les Provinces de France illustrées* (1927). Frontispiece. Bibliothèque nationale, Paris. Photo © Bibliothèque nationale.

Figure 6.18   J.-P. Pinchon, *Les Provinces de France illustrées* (1927). *Bourgogne, Nivernais.* Bibliothèque nationale, Paris. Photo © Bibliothèque nationale.

CHAPTER SEVEN

Figure 7.1   "Suivez-moi! gardez votre confiance dans la France éternelle," Philippe Pétain, 1940, poster by Villemot. Photo © Collection Viollet © S.P.A.D.E.M., 1986.

Figure 7.2   "La force tranquille. François Mitterand président," 1981, poster of the Roux-Séguéla Agency. Photo © Jacques Delaborde/Explorer.

Figure 7.3   Pol de Limbourg (15th century), *Très Riches Heures du duc de Berry, le château de Saumur.* Musée Condé, Chantilly, photo © Giraudon.

Figure 7.4   Master of the Coeur d'amour épris (15th century), *La Rencontre de Coeur et d'humble requête.* Photo © Osterreische national Bibliothek, Vienna.

Figure 7.5   Jean Fouquet (1415–1481), *Heures d'Étienne Chevalier, Sainte Marguerite et Olibrius.* Musée du Louvre, Paris, photo © Lauros-Giraudon.

Figure 7.6   Joseph Vernet (1714–1789), *Le Port de la Rochelle,* 1763. Musée de la Marine, Paris.

Figure 7.7   François Boucher (1703–1770), *Le Pêcheur,* drawing (ca. 1750). The Art Institute of Chicago.

Figure 7.8   Hubert Robert (1733–1808), *Vue prise de Marly vers Saint-Germain-en-Laye* (ca. 1780). Collection Léonino, photo © Bulloz.

Figure 7.9   Jean-Honoré Fragonard (1732–1806), *La Fête à Saint-Cloud* (ca. 1777). Banque de France, Paris, photo © Giraudon.

Figure 7.10   Georges Michel (1763–1843), *La Route de campagne.* Musée du Havre, photo © Bulloz.

Figure 7.11   Turpin de Crissé (1782–1859), *Paysage* (1806). Musée Marmottan, Paris, photo © Studio Lourmel/Georges Routhier.

Figure 7.12   Théodore Rousseau (1812–1867), *La Mare.* Musée Mesdag, La Haye, © Fondation Johan Maurits Van Nassau, Mauritshuis, photo © A. Dingjan.

Figure 7.13   François Millet (1814–1875), *L'Angélus* (1859), detail. Musée d'Orsay, Paris, photo © Musées nationaux.

Figure 7.14   Gustave Courbet (1819–1877), *Le Chêne de Flagey* or *Chêne de Vercingétorix* (1864). The Pennsylvania Academy of Fine Arts, Philadelphia.

Figure 7.15   Gustave Courbet (1819–1877), *L'Atelier du peintre* (1855), detail. Musée d'Orsay, Paris, photo © Lauros-Giraudon.

Figure 7.16   Camille Corot (1796–1875), *La Cathédrale de Chartres* (1830). Musée du Louvre, Paris, photo © Lauros-Giraudon.

Figure 7.17   Camille Pissarro (1830–1903), *L'Entrée du village de Voisins* (1872). Musée d'Orsay, Paris, photo © Lauros-Giraudon.

Figure 7.18   Claude Monet (1840–1926), *Le Printemps à travers les branches* (1878). Musée Marmottan, Paris, photo © Studio Lourmel/Georges Routhier © S.P.A.D.E.M., 1986.

Figure 7.19   Paul Cézanne (1839–1906), *Vue d'Auvers-sur-Oise* (1873). The Art Institute of Chicago, photo © Giraudon.

Figure 7.20   Pierre Bonnard (1867–1947), *La Salle à manger à la campagne* (1913). The Minneapolis Museum of Arts, photo © Lauros-Giraudon © S.P.A.D.E.M., 1986 © A.D.A.G.P., 1986.

CHAPTER EIGHT

Figure 8.1   Castle of Guillaume Revel: Montaigut-le-Blanc (now Puy-de Dôme) (second half of the 15th century). Bibliothèque nationale, Paris. Photo © Bibliothèque nationale.

Figure 8.2   Land map of the seigneury de Puiseaux, land of Avrilmond (commonly Burcy, now Loiret) (1754). Archives nationales, Paris, photo Jean-Loup Charmet © Gallimard.

Figure 8.3   Road from Lyon to Provence (near Péage-de-Roussillon, now Isère) (ca. 1750). Archives nationales, Paris, photo Jean-Loup Charmet © Gallimard.

Figure 8.4   Map of La Boissière's attendant, prepared by Berthier de Sauvigny (1785–86). Archives départementales des Yvelines, photo © Archives départementales des Yvelines.

Figure 8.5   Land survey of La Boissière, section C, Rambouillet canton (ca. 1820). Archives départementales des Yvelines, photo © Archives départementales des Yvelines.

Figure 8.6   Minutes of Cassini: Embrun (now Hautes-Alpes) (1776). Institut géographique national, photo Jean-Loup Charmet © Gallimard.

Figure 8.7   Map of the Seine-et-Oise department drawn to 1 : 10,000. Institut géographique national, photo Jean-Loup Charmet © Gallimard.

Figure 8.8   Voves, commune of Ouarville (Eure), aerial photograph (1949). Photo © Institut géographique national.

Figure 8.9   Mamers-Voves, commune of Ouarville (Eure), aerial photograph (1964). Photo © Institut géographique national.

Figure 8.10   Map of the Fromentine region, seen digitally from Landsat 2, July 29, 1975. Classification FRACAM, cartography FRACARTO.

CHAPTER NINE

Figure 9.1   The Martyrs Chapel built behind the chapel blessed by Count Colbert de Laulévrier in 1825 in the Vézins forest, Maine-et-Loire. Photo © Jean-Clément Martin.

Figure 9.2   *Album vendéen,* illustrated by Tom Drake (1856–60). Monument to the memory of Maurice de La Rochejaquelein in Nuaillé. Coll. part., photo © Écomusée de la Vendée.

Figure 9.3   Stained glass window of Baune, Maine-et-Loire (19th century). Consecration of Sacré-Coeur of the father of Jesus of the Colombière, June 21, 1875. The papal Zouaves carry the banner of the Sacred Heart, General Charette, and a Vendée leader from 1793 are represented at the side of Christ among other people. Photo © Écomusée de la Vendée.

Figure 9.4   *Les Curés coulèvent les paysans,* illustration by L. Dumon, engraved by Andrieux for Bonnemère's *Les Guerres de la Vendée* (Paris: Martin, 1884). Coll. part. © Écomusée de la Vendée.

Figure 9.5   *Un Prêtre donnant l'absolution avant le combat,* illlustration by Dumon, engraved by Andrieux in Crétineau-Joly's *Histoire de la Vendée militaire* (Paris: Maison de la Bonne Presse, 1895–96). Coll. part. © Écomusée de la Vendée.

Figure 9.6   *Le Vendéen,* original plaster of the monument found in Cholet, by Maxime Real del Sarte (1935). Collection Souvenir vendéen at the

Écomusée de la Vendée, photo © Écomusée de la Vendée, © Spadem, 1984.

CHAPTER TEN

Figure 10.1	View of Strasbourg. Photo © Alain Perceval/Photair.
Figure 10.2	Saint Thomas Church, Strasbourg. Photo © Archives Éditions Arthaud, Paris.
Figure 10.3	The Jewish cemetery of Rosenwiller (Bas-Rhin). Photo © Archives Éditions Arthaud, Paris.
Figure 10.4	"Clausa Germania Gallia," medal (1683). Bibliothèque nationale, photo © Bibliothèque nationale, Paris.
Figure 10.5	Hansi (Jean-Jacques Waltz), *Mon village*. Bibliothèque nationale, Paris, photo Bibliothèque nationale © S.P.A.D.E.M., 1986.

The text at the upper right of the figure reads: "After revelries of this kind, we often feel the need for a more elevated emotion. We seek the places where we might commune with the soul of our country. And the surest way to do that is to return to our fields of battle. Oh! it is not a question of passing in review before the colossal bronze and marble monuments adorned with fierce eagles and growling lions and there encountering some group of veterans from the other side of the Rhine who are noisily celebrating some anniversary or other. Rather we must go see the columns and the small crosses that mark the places where the soldiers of France died at the end of their struggle. No orators or choirs there, nor do we find banners or crowns of zinc or glass. Those who wanted to gather in mourning around these tombs were forced into exile. But there you will find a child in tears who will quietly withdraw upon your approach after leaving a bouquet of simple flowers on the tomb. Toward the evening, when we come before the French monument erected on that earth where three times our forces fought against the invader, a profound emotion grips us. The last rays of the setting sun cover the proud bronze cock in gold. He seems to come alive and at his call we believe we see the heroic cavalrymen approaching from the horizon. . .

"That truly causes our hearts to rejoice, and no government can stop us from celebrating."

Figure 10.6	J.-J. Henner, *Elle attend* (1871). Musée Henner, photo © Dominique Fontanarosa.
Figure 10.7	The entry of Foch into Strasbourg. Photo © Harlingue-Viollet.
Figure 10.8	Liberation of Strasbourg, November 1944. Photo © Roger-Viollet.
Figure 10.9	Mont-Sainte-Odile and Saint-Nabor, aerial view. Photo © Roger-Viollet.

Chapters translated in published or projected volumes of *Rethinking France* can be found in *Les Lieux de mémoire* as follows.

VOLUME 1: *THE STATE* (2001)

Chapter 1   Alain Guéry, "The State: The Tool of the Common Good" / "L'État," in volume 3, book 3, page 818

Chapter 2   Maurice Agulhon, "The Center and the Periphery" / "Le Centre et la périphérie," in volume 3, book 1, page 824

Chapter 3   Bernard Guenée, "From Feudal Boundaries to Political Borders" / "Des limites féodales aux frontières politiques," in volume 2, book 2, page 11

Chapter 4   Daniel Nordman, "From the Boundaries of the State to National Borders" / "Des limites d'État aux frontières nationales," in volume 2, book 2, page 35

Chapter 5   Robert Morrissey, "Charlemagne" / "Charlemagne," in volume 3, book 3, page 630

Chapter 6   Alain Boureau, "The King" / "Le Roi," in volume 3, book 3, page 784

Chapter 7   Anne-Marie Lecoq, "The Symbolism of the State: The Images of the Monarchy from the Early Valois Kings to Louis XIV" / "La Symbolique de L'État," in volume 2, book 2, page 145

Chapter 8   Hélène Himelfarb, "Versailles: Functions and Legends" / "Versailles, fonctions et légendes," in volume 2, book 2, page 235

Chapter 9   Jean Carbonnier, "The French Civil Code" / "Le Code civil," in volume 2, book 2, page 293

Chapter 10 Hervé Le Bras, "The Government Bureau of Statistics: La Statistique Générale de la France " / "La Statistique générale de la France," in volume 2, book 2, page 317

Chapter 11 Pierre Nora, "Memoirs of Men of State: From Commynes to de Gaulle" / "Les Mémoires d'État," in volume 2, book 2, page 355

VOLUME 2: *SPACE* (2006)

Chapter 1   "North–South," by Emmanuel Le Roy Ladurie: "Nord–Sud" in volume 2, book 2, page 117

Chapter 2   Michel Mollat du Jourdin, "France, the Coast, and the Sea" / "Le Front de mer," in volume 3, book 1, page 616

Chapter 3   Andrée Corvol, "The Forest" / "La Forêt," in volume 3, book 1, page 672

Chapter 4   Jacques Revel, "The Region" / "La Région," in volume 3, book 1, page 850

Chapter 5   Marcel Roncayolo, "The Department" / "Le Département" in volume 3, book 1, page 884

Chapter 6   Thierry Gasnier, "The Local: One and Divisible" / "Le Local" in volume 3, book 2, page 462

Chapter 7   Françoise Cachin, "The Painter's Landscape" / "Le Paysage du peintre," in volume 2, book 1, page 435

Chapter 8   Marcel Roncayolo, "The Scholar's Landscape" / "Le Paysage du savant," in volume 2, book 1, page 487

Chapter 9   Jean-Clément Martin, "The Vendée, Region of Memory: The Blue and the White" / "La Vendée, region-mémoire," in volume 1, page 595

Chapter 10   Jean-Marie Mayeur, "A Frontier Memory: Alsace" / "Une mémoire-frontière: L'Alsace," in volume 2, book 2, page 63

VOLUME 3: *CULTURES AND TRADITIONS*

André Chastel, "La notion de patrimoine," volume 2, book 2, page 405

Philippe Boutry, "Le clocher," volume 3, book 2, page 56

Yves Lequin, "Le métier," volume 3, book 2, page 376

Louis Bergeron, "L'âge industriel," volume 3, book 3, page 130

Daniel Fabre, "Proverbes, contes et chansons," volume 3, book 2, page 612

Georges Durand, "La vigne et le vin," volume 3, book 2, page 784

Noémi Hepp, "La galanterie," volume 3, book 2, page 744

Marc Fumaroli, "La conversation," volume 3, book 2, page 678

Benoît Lecoq, "Le café," volume 3, book 2, page 854

Alain Erlande-Brandenburg, "Notre-Dame de Paris," volume 3, book 3, page 358

François Loyer, "Le Sacré-Coeur de Montmartre," volume 3, book 3, page 450

Christophe Charle, "Le Collège de France," volume 2, book 3, page 389

VOLUME 4: *HISTORIOGRAPHY*

Bernard Guenée, "Chancelleries et monastères," volume 2, book 1, page 5

Krzysztof Pomian, "Les archives," volume 3, book 3, page 162

Dominique Poulot, "Alexandre Lenoir et les musées des Monuments français," volume 2, book 2, page 497

Laurent Theis, "Guizot et les institutions de mémoire," volume 2, book 2, page 569

Thomas W. Gaehtgens, "Le musée historique de Versailles," volume 2, book 3, page 143

Pascal Ory, "Le *Grand Dictionnaire* de Pierre Larousse," volume I, book 1, page 229

Bernard Guenée, "Les *Grandes Chroniques de France,*" volume 2, book 1, page 189

Corrado Vivanti, "*Les Recherches de la France* d'Étienne Pasquier," volume 2, book 1, page 215

Marcel Gauchet, "Les *Lettres sur l'histoire de France* d'Augustin Thierry," volume 2, book 1, page 247

Pierre Nora, "L'*Histoire de France* de Lavisse," volume 2, book 1, page 317

Krzysztof Pomian, "L'heure des *Annales,*" volume 2, book 1, page 377

abstract art, 337–38
Académie celtique, 175, 237, 238, 268
Académie de Marine, 65
Académie de Reims, 263
Académie française, prizes in literature, 282
Academy of Dijon, 264
Academy of Sciences, 35
Action populaire nationale d'Alsace (APNA), 430
Adieu d'un proscrit à sa famille (Flandrin), 310
Administration of Waters and Forests, 123, 125–29
administrative division of 1789. *See* Committee of Division; departmental division
administrative reform, 215; of 1799 and 1802, 235; in the last quarter of the nineteenth century, 211; opened the debate on regionalism, 212
administrative towns, 193
adoptianism, 8
adoption, and inheritance, 22
aerial imaging, 344, 373f, 374, 377
afforestation, 125
affouage (right to take wood from communal forest), 107, 112, 127, 146
African agriculture, 372
Agen, 15
ager (arable land), 368, 372
agnations, 22
agrarian individualism, 368, 369
agrarian revolution, 371
agricultural capitalism, 363
agricultural fair, 207
agriculture: arrival in the "French" north, 7; cereal cultivation, 104; im-
provement, 206–8; in north and south in 1850s, 3–4, 5
agronomists, 346, 348, 349
Agulhon, Maurice, 280
Aigle (fort), 52
Aigues-Mortes (port), 36, 42
Ailly Point (lighthouse), 69
Aisne, department of, 221f
Aix, 15
Aix-en-Provence, 19
Albigensian Crusade, 1, 10
Albigeois, 10
Albret, 12, 19
Albret-Navarre dynasty, 11
Aldaric, 439
Alembert, Jean d', 345
Alet ruins, 41
Algerian immigrants, 17
Allé de châtaigniers (Rousseau), 315
allegories, 278f
almanacs, 325, 330
Alsace, xii, 4; attached to the Oberrhein Gau, 431; autonomy and regionalism between the two world wars, 428–30, 431; as bastion of Gaullism, 439; Catholicism, 428; as center of humanist movement and the Reformation, 421; coexistence of several religions, 409, 415; coexistence of two languages, 409; under control of the kingdom of France, 421–22; historical memory, 412–24; irredentist organizations in Germany, 429; Judaism, 423; under Napoleonic Empire, 422; particularism, 425–28, 431; political memory, 424–40; regional identity, 409–12; in the Revolution, 422; symbolic memory, 432–40;

Alsace (*continued*)
time of annexation, 424–28; World
War II, 430–32
Alsace Canal, 421
Alsace-Lorraine, annexation of, 272.
See also Lorraine
Alsace-Lorraine Brigade, 430
Alsatian malaise, 428, 436
Alsatian school, 436
Amiel, Henri Frédéric, 314
Ancein régime. See monarchy
Andler, Charles, 436
Andromeda, 89
Angelus (Millet), 326f
Angers, 121
Angers, David d', 280
Angeville, Adolphe d', 1, 2, 241
Anglo-Norman islands, 38
Ango, Jean, 43
Angoulême, 43
Angoumois, 346
Anjou, Marguerite d', 280
Annuaire des officiers d'active de la Marine
(Directory of Active Naval Officers),
59
Anrich, Gustav-Adolph, 429
Anthony, Saint, 94
anthropology, 171, 203
Antibes, 42
anti-Bonapartist societies, 87
Antifer, lighthouse at, 71
anti-industrialism, in second half of
eighteenth century, 110
Antilles, 45
antimemory, department as, 185, 195
Aotourou, 65
Apollinaris Sidonius, 8
Aquitania and Aquitanians, 8, 13
Aragon, 10
araire (light plow), 368
archaeological societies, 262
archaeology, 374
archaism, 170
Archéonaute (ship), 46
archives, 265; Archives de l'Outre-Mer
(overseas archives), 34; departmental,
197; maritime, 34–36; Service des
archives et bibliothèques (Archive
and Library Service), 34

Arcisse de Caumont, 248
Ardennes, 3
areas (*terroir*), 175
Argenton chateau, 384
Argot Baille, 57, 60
Arianism, 8
Arles, 8, 255f
Armagnac, 12
Ar Men, 71
Armorica, 63
Arndt, Ernst Moritz, 418
arrondissement centers, 210, 211
art: collecting, 256, 270, 368; Flemish
intimist painting, 31; historical land-
scape painting, 305; history painting,
304, 331; miniatures, 300–302; mod-
ern, 337; open-air painting, 331, 338;
painting of ideas, 331; portrait painting, 308; regional schools of painting,
270; Romanesque, 10; Romantic
painters, 311–12; under the Third
Reich, 300. *See also* landscape painting, French
Arthois 'd, Jacques, 141
Artois, Comte de, 165
Artus, Charles, 385
Association bretonne, 262
Association industrielle, commerciale et
agricole de Lyon (Industrial, Com-
mercial, and Agricultural Association
of Lyon), 215–16
Association populaire catholique (Catho-
lic Center Party), 425
Association technique pour la vulgariza-
tion forestière (A.T.V.F.) [Technical
Association for the Popularization of
the Forest], 132
Asterix amusement park, 139
Atelier, L' (Courbet), 306, 318
atlases, 357
Aubigné 'd, Agrippa, 15
Aubois, forges at, 113
Auguste, Philippe, 18, 27
Auriol, Vincent, 257
Au service de l'Allemagne (In the
Service of Germany) (Barrès),
426
Ausonius, 8, 9
autonomism, 428, 429

Autonomistische Landespartei (Autonomous State Party), 429
Auvergnat Grégoire "of Tours," 8
Auvergne, 11
Avignon, 15

Baas, Émile, 430, 432
Balaguier Tower, 55
Baleines (lighthouse), 69
Ballion, Robert, 138
Balzac, Honoré de: *Les Paysans,* 270, 330
bandits, 106
Bannes harbor, 41
Banni, Le (The Banished) (Erckmann-Chatrian), 434
banquets, 277
barbarian invasions, 8
Barbarossa, Frederick, 413
Barbizon school, 100f, 296, 299, 306, 313, 314, 316, 317, 324, 331
Bar-le-Duc, 115
Barnaud, Germaine, 256
Barrère, Bertrand, 168, 235, 401
Barrès, Maurice, 36, 323, 426
Bar-sur-Aube, 115
Bart, Jean, 44
Barye, Antoine-Louis, 313
Barzaz-Breiz, 269
Bas Maine, ix
Basques, 401
Bas-Rhin, 421, 422, 434
Basville (intendant of Montpellier), 15
Bateau ivre, Le (Rimbaud), 28
Baudelaire, Charles, 320–21, 322, 331
Baudewyns, Adriaen Frans, 141
Baudry d'Asson, Marquis de, 393
Bayonne, 42
Bazin, René, 434
Béarn, 11, 166
Beaumont, Élie de, 352, 380n.16, 381n.22
Beaumont mine, 111
Beaurepaire, Nicolas Joseph, 280
Beauty and the Beast, 89, 96f
Beauvilliers, Duc de, 156
Becdelièvre, Vicomte de, 257
Becker, Nicolas, 418–19
Bégon (intendant of Rochefort), 51
Bel-Ami (Maupassant), 319

Belem (ship), 45
Belhoste, Jean François, 111
Belle de jour, 143
Belle Époque, 282, 283
Belle-Île Island, 38
Belle Puule (schooner), 57
Benedictines, 266
Berger, Colonel (André Malraux), 430
Berghem, Claes, 312
Bergson, Henri, 362, 381n.33
Bernard, Jacques, 27
Bernières, M. de, 73
Berr, Henri, 273
Berry, Duc de, 300
Berry, Duchesse de, 66, 257, 388, 390
Berry region, 2
Bertho, Catherine, 162, 285–86
Besnard, Albert, 332
Bessa, Pierre, 134f
Besson, Luc, 146
Béziers, 15
bibliophiles, 265
Bickler, H., 431
biennial model, 368
biens nationaux (confiscated noble lands), 113
Black Prince, 69
Blanc, Charles, 331
Blanchard, Raoul, 375
Blanquart-Évrard, Louis-Désiré, 357
Blavet River, 52
Bleun Brug, 281
Bloch, Marc, 273, 366, 367, 368, 415
Blois, Aymar de, 268–69
Blut und Boden (blood and soil), 429
bocage (hedgerows), 377, 384, 392, 393, 398
bocains, 384
Bockel, Abbé Pierre, 430
Boétie, Étienne de la, 15
Bois de Boulogne, 136, 143
Bois de Vincennes, 136
Bonheur, Rosa, 318
Bonifacio, 42
Bonnard, Pierre, 299, 313, 336, 337f
Bonnat, Léon, 257
Bonnat Museum, Bayonne, 256f
Bonnemère, Eugène, 396f
Bonnington, Richard, 310, 312

Borda, Jean-Charles, 57
Borda (naval academy), 57, 58f, 65, 69
bordache (naval cadet), 57
Bordeaux, 11, 15, 19, 45
Bords de Seine, Les (Daubigny), 331
Boucher, François, 309, 315f
Bouchot, Henri
Boudin, Eugène-Louis, 310, 320
Boudriot, Jean, 53
Bouelles, Charles de, 179n.16
Bougainville, Louis, 33, 65
Boulogne-sur-Mer, 42
bourgadins (property owners), 398
Bourguet, Marie-Noëlle, 175
Bouton, Noël, 256f
Bouvier, Gilles le, viii
Bouvines, battle of, 280
Brantôme, Seigneur de, 15
Braudel, Fernand, 27, 55
Bréhat, 37
Breiz Izel (Perrin), 269
Brest: college of surgery, 52; harbor, 54f;
    maritime patrimony, 48; as military
    port, 53–56; Recouvrance quarter,
    56; rue de Siam, 56; topography, 55
Breton, Jules, 300, 318
Breton Marais, 384
Breton Regionalist Union, 281
Brigadier Frédéric, Le (Corporal Freder-
    ick) (Erckmann-Chatrian), 434
brigandage, 106
Brittany: affirmation of identity and
    stereotyping, 162; rediscovery of a
    historic, archaeological, and literary
    heritage, 177; resistance to plan to
    create departments, 165; studies of
    local customs, 269–70; unification
    with the French kingdom, 53
Brosses, Les (brushes), 102
Brouage, 36, 49
Bruandet, Lazare, 129f
Brueys, David-Augustin de, 15
Brunhes, Jean, 281
Buache, Philippe, 189, 227n.8
Bucher, Pierre, 425, 426
Bûcherie, La, 116
Buffon, Comte de, 170
Buñuel, Luis, 143
Bureau Veritas, 35

Burgundy, 112, 160; map of, 161f
Burty, Philippe, 331
Buttoud, Gérard, 127

cabinet almanacs, 325
Cacault Museum, Clisson, 254f
Caen, Beaumont mine, 111
Cahingt, Henri, 32
Cailleux, Joseph-Marie-Auguste, 357
calendar landscapes, 325, 327, 330,
    341n.64
Calvet, Esprit, 257
Calvet Museum, Avignon, centenary
    medal of, 257f
Calvi, 42
Campagnie des Indes, 52–53
Canal du Midi, 15
Cantons, 175, 217
Cape Brun, 55
Cape Cépet, 55
Cape Fréhel (lighthouse), 69
Cape Horn, 45
Capet, Hugh, viii, 239
Capetian State, 9, 11
Capitant, René, 415
Carbillet, Jean-Baptiste, 259
carbonari (charcoal burners), 91
Carbonell, Charles Olivier, 262
Carbonnières, Ramond de, 170
Carnot, Sadi, 277, 280
Cartier, Jacques, 40, 66
cartography, 159, 350–52
Casabianca (submarine), 32
Cassini map, x, 159, 160, 251, 350–51
Castagnary, Jules, 318, 331, 333
Catalonia, 8, 10
"Cathar" period, 10
Cathédrale de Chartres, La (Corot), 321,
    329f
Cathelineau, Jacques, 385, 388, 390
Catholic Alsace, 439
Catholic League, 399
Caumont, Arcisse de, 262, 352
Cazalès, Jacques de, 23
Celebration of Saint-Cloud, The (Frago-
    nard), 317f
Célestins barracks, 116
Celtic vogue, 237
cens (tax), 369

Centenaire de l'impressionisme (exhibition), 338

Central Commission for the Navigation of the Rhine, 420

Centralization, 15, 152, 154, 238

Cereal cultivation, 104

"C'est la vieille et loyale Alsace" (It is the old and loyal Alsace), 436

Cézanne, Paul, 103f, 305, 306, 313, 318, 336f

chalcography, 309

Chamboredon, Jean-Claude, 362

Chamisso, Adelbert, 420

Champagne, plateau of, 112

Champfleury, 331

Champlain, Samuel de, 37

Chantonay basin, 384

Chapel of the Martyrs, 387f

Chaptal, Jean-Antoine, 174, 175, 349

charbonette, 109

charcoal burners, 91, 97, 107–9

Charcot, Jean-Martin, 32

Charente, 394

Charette, François Athanase, 385, 386, 388, 390

charge, 377

Chargeurs Réunis, 35

Charles-Brun, Jean, 281

Charles IV (king of France), 439

Charles V (king of France), 55, 76

Charles VII (king of France), viii

Charles VIII (king of France), 55

Charles X (king of France), 239

Charrue, 367

Chartier, Roger, 1, 157

Chassiron (lighthouse), 69

Chateaubriand, René de, 28, 31, 41, 56–57, 308, 314

Château of Saumur, The (Pol de Limbourg), 303f

Chaussin, Évelyne, 90, 143

chefs-lieux, 15

Chemins de Fer du Nord, 300

Chêne de Flagey (also Chêne de Vercingétorix) (Courbet), 318

Cherbourg: dike, 49; maritime patrimony, 48

Chevalier, Michel, 205–6

Chevreul, Michel-Eugène, 280

children, emancipation of, 22

Children's and Household Tales (Grimm), 98

Cholet, 385

chouanneries, 386, 398, 399, 400

Chouans, 285, 386, 399, 401

Churchill, Winston, 231

Cicero, 7

Cimetière marin, Le (Valéry), 29

cities: in the departmental structure, 224; fuel demands, 112–13

Civil Constitution of the Clergy, 399

civitates, 238

"Clausa Germanis Gallia" (Gaul is closed to the Germans), medal, 418, 419f

Clémentel, Etienne, 176, 212, 214, 224

cloth manufacturers, 15

Clovis, 8

coal, 109–10, 115

coastal traffic, 40–44

coastline, rarely attracted attention of historians of France's borders, 27

"Coast of Grace," 40

Cochon-Dupuy, Jean, 51

Coeur d'amour épris, 302

Colbert, Jean-Baptiste, 34, 49, 52, 59, 63, 66, 76, 154; Colbert Code, 145; Ordonnance of 1681, 73

collecting, 256, 270, 368

collèges, 220

Collioure, 42

Colmar, Joseph Louis, 415, 421, 423

Combes, Emile, 277, 393

Comité des Travaux historiques (Committee of Historical Works), 244, 245, 262, 265, 273

Comité d'Histoire et d'Archéologie religieuses, 264

Commandant-de-Kerhallet (naval exhibition), 74

commemorative statuary, 278–81

commerce, 44–47

commercial ships, 45

Commission des antiquités de la Côte-d'Or, 264

Commission des antiquités de la Seine-Inférieure, 261

Commission historique du département du Nord, 268

Committee of Division, 166, 186, 187, 188, 189, 190, 191
common language, possibility of, 200
communal forests, 125
commune, Paris as, 219
communitarian family, 19
Compagnie des Indes Orientales (East India Company), 52–53
Compagnie des Salins du Midi, 36
Compagnie générale maritime, 35
Company of the Suez Canal, 35
Comtat, 11
Concarneau harbor, 41
Concordat of 1801, 394, 412, 422
Concours de Rome, 310
Condorcet, Marquis de, 164
Conflans, Antoine de, 55
Congress of Learned Societies of Dunkirk, 1907, 250–51f
Conrad, Joseph, 45
Conscrit de 1813, Le (Erckmann-Chatrian), 434
conservation policy, 378
conservative historiography, 154
conservative regionalism, 364
Constable, John, 312
Constituent Assembly, 185, 191
Constitutional Committee, 164
Constitution of 1791, 234
consulats, 10, 251
consumer landscape, 362
Contes de lundi (Monday's Tales) (Daudet), 434
Contes de ma Mère l'Oye (Mother Goose Stories) (Perrault), 98
Continental Blockade, 76
Contrie, baron General Charette de la, 392
Convention Assembly, 195; in March 1793, 235; in Prairial year II, 168
Coppens, Augustin, 141
Corderie royale (ropeworks), Rochefort, 49–51, 50f
Cordouan (lighthouse), 69, 70f, 71
Cormon, Fernan, 146
Corot, Camille, 307, 313, 320–21, 329f
corporate society (société de corps), 154, 216

Corps of Mining Engineers, 352
Corrèze, 3
Cortète, François de, 15
Couédic, Charles du, 63
Coulanges, Fustel de, 433
counterrevolution, 87
Country Dining Room (Bonnard), 337f
"country," multiplicity of names for, 232
Country Road (Michel), 323f
Coeur, Jacques, 36, 72
Courbet, Gustave, 318, 327f, 328f, 331, 333
Crabe-tambour, Le (The Crab Drum), 44
Creac'h lighthouse, 71, 72
Crétineau-Joly, M., 397f
Crissé, Turpin de, 324f
croquants tardifs, 13
Croyances et légendes du centre de la France (Salle), 270
Croze, Austin de, 285
Cubism, 337
cultural genealogy, 170
cultural regionalisms, 176
Curnonsky (Maurice Edmond Sailland), 285
custom (consuetudo), 19, 20

Danton, Georges-Jacques, 418
Darluc (geographer), 158
Darwinism, 362
Daubigny, Charles-François, 313, 318
Daubrée, Lucien, 127
Daudet, Alphonse, 22, 28, 434
Débat des hérauts d'armes, 76
Debré, Robert, 423, 434
Decazes, Élie, 16
decentralization, 234, 238, 239
decentralization law of 1982, 232
decentralizing laws, 232, 239
Declaration of Bordeaux, 432–33
decolonization, 232
Decree of August 11, 1789, 163
Degas, Edgar, 332
De Gaulle, Charles, 231, 430, 432, 438–39
Delacroix, Eugène, 311, 331
Delaunay, Henri, 245
Delescluze, Louis-Charles, 317, 331
Demangeon, Albert, 363

Demarne, Jean, 312
democratic aesthetic, 299, 319
demography, 375
Demonet, Michel, 3
Denis, Maurice, 92f
departmental assembly: infrastructure,
    205–6; innovative action in agricul-
    ture, 207
departmental blueprint, 218f
departmental centers: ancien régime
    towns as, 227n.17; wealth concen-
    trated in, 210
departmental division, 163–67, 185–96,
    200f, 222–23f; accomplished out of
    the former provincial borders, 188–
    89, 237; creation of a new memory,
    204; gives shape to a consciousness of
    French territory, 223; no single logic,
    194–95; political goal of, 189; resis-
    tance to plan for, 165–67; response
    to fiscal crisis, 204; sought to obliter-
    ate traces of the old provincial dis-
    tricts, 177
Department of the Haute-Marne, 183
departments: administrative organiza-
    tion, 217; archives, 197; case waged
    against around 1900, 183–85; and
    city-countryside relationship, 191;
    conservatism, 216–17; consolidation
    under reestablished monarchy, 196–
    211; created a common reference
    between social groups, 208; double
    nomination, 181n.30; gave life to re-
    gional space, 177; geographies, 243;
    highways, 205–6; machine for creat-
    ing new types of notables, 220;
    monographs offering a scientific re-
    sponse to the criticisms lodged
    against, 225; of Paris, 198f; railroads,
    206; resistance of, 209f; resistance to
    criticism, 211–20; scholarly image
    of, 201–4; schooling functions, 220,
    225f; statistics, 199; as a strong com-
    ponent of identity, 169, 224; as a ter-
    ritorial form, 220; transformed the
    perception of French space, 167;
    undertaking to collect statistics from,
    174–75
Depository of Maps and Plans, 33

Dépôt de la guerre, 351
Derain, André, 334, 335
Desert of Retz, 137
Deux-Sèvres, 384
de Vadder, Lodewijck, 141
dialects, 152, 267
dialectal literature, 15
Diaz de la Peña, Narcisse-Virgile, 313
dictionaires, 281
Dictionnaire de la République of 1794, 190
Dictionnaire topographique, 262
Diderot, Denis, 65, 308, 309, 313, 314,
    321, 324, 345
Dieppe, 33, 43
Dietrich, Friedrich, 422
Dion, Roger, 27, 368, 369, 370, 374,
    375. See also Essai d'une méthode
    générale propre à étendre les connaissances
    des voyageurs
Direction des beaux-arts, 280
Direction des recherches archéologiques
    sous-marines (DRASM), 46
"Dis-moi quel est ton pays" (Tell me
    what is your country), 434, 436
diversity: of French space, 153; inter-
    action with unity, 149, 152–53, 231;
    suspect in 1793-94, 169
"divide to unite," 165, 186–87
Döblin, Alfred, 414
Donkey Skin, 87–88
Doré, Gustave, 100f, 121, 420
Douarnenez, 44
Douay, Abel, 415
Douglas fir, 133f
dowry system, 22
Drake, Tom: Album Vendéen, 389f
Dreyfus affair, 436
Drouyn, Léo, 267
Drummond Castle (ship), 73
Dubourg, Alexandre, 258
Dufrénoy, Charles-Alphonse, 352,
    380n.16, 381n.22
Dufy, Raoul, 336
Duguay-Trouin (ship), 47, 57
Dujardin, Édouard-Emile-Louis, 312
Dumas, Alexandre, 357
Dunkirk, 44, 264
Dupin, Baron, 1, 241
Dupont-Ferrier, G., 155

Dupré, Jules, 313
Dupront, Alphonse, 231
Durance Canal, 206, 208
Durkheim, Émile, 364
Dutch landscape, 297

Earth, The (Zola), 270
easements, 21
ecclesiastical forests, 125
ecclesiastical map of France, 188f
Eckhart, Meister, 423
Eckmühl (lighthouse), 69
École, l', 116
École de santé de la marine et des
    colonies (School of Health for the
    Navy and the Colonies), 52
École des Beaux-Arts, 305, 310, 311,
    317
ecological postulate, 356, 357, 359, 378
economic regions, creation of, 215
Edict of 1667, 126
Edict of Nantes, revocation of, 2, 15–16
educational institutions, 210, 220
Éducation sentimentale, l', 313
Église de Marissol (Corot), 320
Eidophuskon, 309–10
Eighteenth Brumaire of Louis Napoleon, The
    (Marx), 363
Eleanor of Aquitaine, 10
electricity, production and distribution
    networks for, 214
enclosures, 371
*Encyclopédie, ou Dictionnaire raisonné des
    sciences, des arts et des métiers*, 308, 324,
    345
Energie électrique du littoral méditer-
    ranéen (Electrical Energy Association
    of the Mediterranean Coast), 214
Engels, Friedrich, 419
English landscape, 297
engravings, 357
Entrance to the Town of Voisins (Pissarro),
    334f
Entrecasteau, Chevalier d', 65
Erasmus, Desiderius, 415
Erckmann-Chatrian, Emile, 420, 434,
    436
Ernst, Robert, 429, 431
Escola lemouzina (Limousin), 281

*Essai d'une méthode générale propre à étendre
    les connaissances des voyageurs, ou Re-
    cueil d'observations relatives à la culture
    des terres: le tout appuyé sur des faits ex-
    acts et enrichi d'expériences utiles* (Essay
    for the General Method Appropriate
    for Expanding the Knowledge of
    Travelers, or Collection of Observa-
    tions Relating to the Distribution of
    Taxes, Commerce, the Sciences and
    the Arts, and to the Cultivation of
    the Land: The Entirety Backed Up
    by Exact Facts Enriched by Useful
    Experiences, 1777), 344, 346, 348,
    365–66, 367, 371–72, 377
*Essai sur la Constitution et les fonctions des
    assemblées provinciales* (Condorcet),
    164
essentialism, 138, 139, 153
Estaing, Valéry Giscard d', 338n.1
Estates (legislative body), 11, 12
Établissement national des invalides de la
    Marine (National Institution for the
    Disabled of the Merchant Marine), 59
État forestier, L' (Buttoud), 127
État-major, x
Été, L' (Poussin), 304
ethnographical traditions, 152
ethnographic museums, 259–60
Eticho, 439
Étiemble, Rene, 28
Étoile (schooner), 57
Eugene of Savoy, 55
Eure River, 112

Faiz de navigaige (Deeds of Navigation)
    (Conflans), 55
Fallières, Clément-Armand, 277
Falloux Law of 1850, 412
Farrère, Claude, 31
Faubourg Saint-Germain, 117
Faure, Christian, 286
Faure, Félix, 277
Febvre, Lucien, 273, 414, 415, 423; *La
    Terre et l'évolution humaine*, 365
Fécamp, 43f
"Federalist" insurrection of 1793, 167
Fédération des sociétés savantes du
    Centre, 252

Fédération régionaliste française, 281
Federations, 167, 252
Félibrige, 17, 177, 281, 296
Femina prizes, 282
feminism, 9, 22
Ferme, La (Oudry), 312
fermentation, 362, 381n.33
Ferry, Jules, 2, 277, 332, 433–34
Fesch, Cardinal, 259
Festival of the Gayants, 281
Fête de la fédération, 186
feudal privilege, dismantling of, 162
Feydeau Island, 45
Final Combat, The, 146–47
Finance law of 1904, 130
firewood, war over, 106–10
First Republic, peasant revolts, 392
fir trees, 132, 133, 140
Fisherman, The (Boucher), 315f
fishing, 40–44
fistots, 57
Fitzgerald, F. Scott, 324–25
Flandrin, Paul, 310
Flemish intimist painting, 31
Fleury, Edouard Husson, 266–67
Foch, Marshal, entering Strasbourg, 437f
Foix, Louis de, 12, 69
Folklore de la France, La, 273–76
Foncailles, 124
Foncin, Pierre, 176, 211, 212, 273
Fonds forestier national (F.F.N.)
    (National Forest Fund), 132
Fontainebleau, 313, 314, 316; forest
    reserves at, 141; oaks at, 126
Fontenoy-le-Château (Meurth-et-
    Moselle), 105, 385
Fonvielhe, Abbé, 174
Forçats de l'océan, Les (Ocean Convicts)
    (Martin), 44
forest, 374; as annex of farm, 102; as the
    antidote to modernity, 99; borders of,
    103; brigandage in, 106; communal,
    125; converting land to, 131–32; as
    cultivated space, 83; cult of, 99;
    dwellers of, 101–2; fear of disappear-
    ance, 139–40; frequency in the per-
    centage variation of between 1945
    and 1986, 145f; going to, 103–6;
    golden age of, 128f; government re-
sponse to consumers' expectations
    about, 137–38; management, 125–
    29, 132–36; man-made conifer, 102;
    Medieval, 103; Oise, 139; owned
    by individuals, 125; percentage of
    France, 85; as a place of passage, 105;
    private, 130–31; purging of dead-
    wood, 105; purveyor of life-giving
    fire, 107; role in communal life, 107;
    symbol of intimacy, comfort, and
    wealth, 119; total production, 132;
    traditional culture of, 135–36
Forest and the Woodcutter, The (Doré),
    100f
forest antidote, 140
forestation: in 1986, 144f; variations in
    the percentage of from 1945 to 1986,
    144f
forest myths, 85–99; forest tale as a his-
    tory of an aborted metamorphosis,
    89; love of others, 90–93; mystery
    forest, 87–90; path through the
    woods, 86–87; primacy of instinct,
    88–90; table of abundance, 96–99;
    transfer of forces, 93–96; women in
    the forest, 96–99
Forest of Bondy, 106
forest regime, 126–29
Forêt de Fontainebleau (Rousseau), 331
Forez, 306
Fort Lamalgue, 55
Fort L'Éguillette, 55
Fortunatus, 8
fossil plants, 374
Foucart, Jacques
Fouquet, Jean, 300, 301, 302, 305f
Fox, Edward Whiting, 192
Foyer breton, La (Souvestre), 269
Fragonard, Jean-Honoré, 312, 317f
framed landscape, 337
Français d'oïl, 8
France, 46–47; triumphal arrival of in
    New York after its maiden boyage
    across the Atlantic, 1962, 58f
France pittoresque, La (Hugo), 243
Franche-Comté, 166
Francis I, 45, 76
Franco-German reconciliation of 1956,
    414, 439

Franco-Prussian War, 270, 279, 415, 424
Franco-Russian alliance, 56
Franklin, Benjamin, 65
Franks, 8
Free French Forces, 430
freeholds: in the Midi, 20; more numerous in the south than in the north, 12
French Alpine Club, 245
French Left, 428
French Revolution. *See* Revolution of 1789
French social Catholicism, 429
French-style garden, 297–98
Frepel, Monseigneur, 280
Fresnel lens, 69
Froissart, Jean, 27
Fromentin, Eugène, 69
Fromverur, Fromrust (currents), 38
fuel consumption, by urban areas and the metalworking industry, 110–15
Furet, François, 1
Fustel-de-Coulanges, Numa Denis, 414
Futurism, 337

Gabriel, Jacques Charles, 48, 53
Gaidiz, Henri, 273
Gainsborough, Thomas, 310
Gai Savoir, 12
Galerie armoricaine, La (Lalaisse), 269
Gallia Narbonensis, 7
Gallicanism, 430
Gallic *civitates,* 238
Gallois, Lucien, 213, 268, 352, 355, 364, 380n.16
Gambetta, Leon, 211, 217, 276, 432–33
Garonne, 394
Garonne Valley, 6
Gascogne, 13
Gascons (Vascons), 8
Gasnier, Thierry, 155
gastronomic tourism, 285
Gate to the Ocean, 45
Gâtine, 398
Gatteville (lighthouse), 69
Gauguin, Paul, 296, 312
Gaul, viii, 8
Gaullism, 438
Gautier, Théophile, 357
Génie de la mer, 56

Genouilly, Admiral Rigault de, 73
geographical nomenclature, 364
Géographie de la France (Verne), 243
Géographie humaine de la France, La (Brunhes), 281
Géographie universelle (Reclus), 357
geography: formation of a French school of, 271–73, 357; historical, 358; literary, 366; romantic, 356; social, 365. *See also* Vidal de La Blache, Paul
geological map of France, 380n.16
geological mapping, 352–55
Géologie en chemin de fer, La (Lapparent), 213
geology, 352–55, 368
Géorgiques françaises, Les (Bernis), 308
Gérando, Joseph Marie de, 171
Géricault, Théodore, 66
Germany: attack on Toulon, 55; geography, 358; landscape, 297; particularism, 431; romantics, 418
germination, 360
Gervex, Henri, 332
Gévaudan, 10
ghost harbors, 36
Giraudoux, Jean, *Intermezzo,* 210
Gironde, 4
Girondist insurrection, 168
Giscardian Right, 17
Gloires de la Bourgogne, Les (Lévy), 274f
Glosssaire nautique (Jal), 63
Gneisenau, 31
Godric, Saint, 95
Goethe, Johann Wolfgang von, 413, 414
"Golden Age" of territorial knowledge, 199
Goncourt, Edmond de, 306–7, 322
Goncourt, Jean de, 306–7, 322
Goncourt Prize for *Terres lorraines,* 282
Gonneville ("The Brazilian"), 40
Gothicism, 10
Goude, Jean Paul, 230f
Goupil à Margot, De, 282
Gourou, Pierre, 372, 376
grafting, 102
Grand Bé Island, 41
Grandes vagues (Courbet), 318
Grand métier, Le (The Grand Profession) (Recher), 44

Grand Prix de Rome, 310
Grand routtier, 34
Grasset Saint-Sauveur, Jacques, 170
Grassroots France, 157, 169
graving dock, 49
great depression, 363
Grégoire, Abbé, 168, 171, 174, 235
Gregory VII, Pope, 413
Grémion, Pierre, 249
Grenoble parlements, 19
Grésivaudan, 111
Grévy, Jules, 277, 280
Grimm Brothers, 98, 420
Groix Island, 38, 40, 52
Grünewald, Mathias, 415
Guerres de la Vendée, Les (Bonnemère), 396f
Guesclin, Bertrand du, 55
Guides du touriste, du naturaliste et de l'archéologue, Les, 282
Guides-Joanne, 177, 282, 420
Guidon de la mer, 63
Guillemin, Alain, 207, 208
Guiomar, Jean-Yves, 263
Guizot, Françoise-Pierre-Guillaume, 243
Gulf of Morbihan, 44
Gutenberg, Johannes, 12
Guyot-Jeannin, Olivier, 44

Habsburg Imperial Army, 418
Habsburg Wars, 66
Haegy, Abbé, 426–27, 428, 429
Halbwachs, Maurice, 415
Halloy, Omalius d', 352
Hansel and Gretel, 87
Hansi (Jean-Jacques Waltz), 427f
Hans im Schnogeloch (Hans in the Mosquito Hole), 436
Hartmann, Frederick, 433
Haudrère, Philippe, 53
Haussmanization, 371
Haussmann, Georges-Eugène, 371
Haut-Rhin, 421, 422, 434
hedgerow country, 111
Heimat (journal), 428
Heimatbund (Union for the Homeland), 428
Hellenism, 7

Henner, Jean-Jacques, 433, 435f
Hennessy bill, 212
Henri II (king of France), 20
Henri IV (king of France), 11, 12, 13, 52, 306
Henry V. (film), 302
heroic style, 303, 304
Herr, Lucien, 436
Herrad, Abbess: *Hortus Deliciarum* (The Garden of Delights), 439
Hesseln, Robert de, 187
Heures d'Étienne Chevalier, 300, 305f
Heures du maréchal de Boucicaut, 300
Hève, La (lighthouse), 69
Histoire de France (Lavisse), x, 271
Histoire de France (Michelet), 239–41
Histoire de la nation française, 281
Histoire de la Vendée militaire (Crétineau-Joly), 397f
Histoire des Gaulois (Thierry), 316
historical geography, 358
historical landscape painting, 305
historical spectacles, 277–78
history, fragmentation of, 273–76
history painting, 304, 331
Hitler, Adolf, 413, 431
Hoche, Louis-Lazare, 415
Hohenstaufen emperors, 439
Homme et la mer, L' (Baudelaire), 28
Honfleur, 40, 41f
horticultural societies, 245
Hospitalers of Saint John, 10
Hôtel de Crillon, 48
Hôtel de la Marine, Paris, 48
Hôtel des Invalides, Paris, 51
Hôtel de Ville, Paris, 112, 276
Huet, Paul, 313, 314
Hugo, Abel, 243, 381n.27
Hugo, Captain: *France pittoresque,* 204–5
Hugo, Victor, 28, 71, 318, 419
Huguenots, 13, 42
Humboldt, Alexander von, 344, 355, 357
Hundred Years' War, 11, 27, 37, 43, 55, 66, 75
Huysmans, Cornelius, 141
hydraulics, 189, 202, 206
hydroelectricity, 214
hydrography, schools of, 59
Hyères (island), 37

ideal nature, image of, 299
ideology, 171
Île-de-France, 46; customs favored
    women's interests in succession, 22;
    property crimes, 3
Île Longue, 55
Ille-et-Vilaine, 399
Illuminations, Les (Rimbaud), 28
illusionist painting, 309
illustrated postcards, 283
Impératrice-Eugénie, 46
Impression, soleil levant (Monet), 307
Impressionism, 299, 306, 307, 310, 319–
    20, 333
Impressionisme et la paysage français, L',
    338
industrial fishing, 44
industrial societies, 214
infrastructure, 205–6
Infreville, Leroux d', 76
Ingrand, Max, 414
Ingres, Jean-Auguste-Dominque, 331
inheritance, in north vs. south, 22, 23
Institut des provinces de France, 248–
    49, 262
Institut d'urbanisme de Paris, 375
instituteurs, 364
Instructions nautiques, 34
Instruction sur le cérémonial dans la Marine
    (Directive for Ceremony in the
    Navy), 60, 62
intendants de généralités (provincial admin-
    istrators), 15
interior, exoticism of, 170–71
Intrépide (ship), 57
Invasion, L' (Erckmann-Chatrian), 434
Iroise Sea reefs, 38
iron industry, 111, 112–13
Isabey, Jean-Baptiste, 312
islands, 37–40
Isle of Sein lighthouse, 71
Italian Renaissance, 302
Italian *vedutisti,* 309

Jacobin, 151, 235; and the antiquary,
    236–37, 239; predominance, 241–45;
    and recovery of the local by the na-
    tional, 239
Jacque, Charles, 313, 319

Jacques-Cartier, 59
Jal, Augustin, 56–57, 63
Jardin de Bérénice, Le (Barrès), 36
Jardins, Les (Delille), 308
Jeanne'd'Arc, 57, 61f
Jessé, baron de, 166
Jeu Floraux, 12
Joanne, Adolphe, 201, 357
Joanne guides, 177, 282, 420
Joan of Arc: museums, 261; statues to,
    280
Journal des mines, 380n.16
Joybert, Admiral, 48
Jubinal, Achille, 257
Judaism, 409, 415
Juillard, Étienne, 206, 226n.8
Julius Caesar, viii
Jullian, Camille, 374
July Monarchy, 104, 176, 203, 204, 205;
    decentralizing laws of, 239; obliter-
    ated inscriptions and smashed monu-
    ments, 386; patriotic monuments, 279
Jument lighthouse, 71
June Days, Revolution of 1848, 270
jus soli, 25

Katholik, Der, 423
Keppi, Jean, 431
Kéréon lighthouse, 71
Keroman, 53
kingdom of France, as a composite
    territory, 233–34
Kléber, General, 400
Klee, Paul, 337
Knights of Malta, 62
Knights Templar, 10
Kohl, Chancellor, 440
Kölnische Volkszeitung, 425
Kronstadt pier, 56

Laband, Paul, 415
La Belle-Rachée, 102
Laborde, Jean-Joseph de, 308
Labourage nivernais (Bonheur), 331
Lackland, John, 38
Lafont, Robert, 17
La Fresnaye, Roger de, 335
La Grande limagne (Derruau), 370
Lake Leman, 2

Lalaisse, Hippolyte, 269

Lamennais, Robert de, 423

Lami, Eugène, 312

L'Ami Fritz, 423

Lamoricière, Juchault, 392

land: and history, 355–57; ideology of development and improvement, 363; land use charters, 103; reconnaissance, 354f; registries, 196, 351; research, 371–72; social uses and formation of, 353f

Landau, 415

Landerneau harbor, 41

Landgraben, 421

landlord absenteeism, 21

landscape, French: abstract reading of, 379f; changes in interpretation of, 345; Classical French, 303–4; critical analysis of, 366–79; "decomposition" of, 345; "fixed" arguments, 372, 374; as museum, 378; as an object of memory, 343–44; as a source of knowledge, 343–44; subjective, 377; two images of in Medieval France, 299–300

Landscape (Crissé), 324f

landscape painting, French: in 1820-30, 314; archetypal landscape, 324; blend of culture and nature, 323; classical, 297; dichotomy between historical and realist painters, 311; disappeared as a national genre after World War I, 337; in the early fifteenth century, 300–302; eclipse and triumph of, 333–38; emergence and eclipse of, 299–306; "heroic" or "ideal" genre, 308; historical, 305; increase in latter part of eighteenth century, 308; as *lieu de mémoire,* 313–20; link with national identity, 299; modesty, 323; motif of lyricism and meditation, 299; national nature and history, 306–11; north against south, 311–13; and passing time, 320–22; popularity of coincided with the mass urbanization of the nineteenth century, 296; portraits of France and popular images, 322–31; ports of France series, 309; realist, 331; and the Republic,

331–33; of ruins, 321–22; "sensitive" new image of the countryside, 298; slow crystallization of, 297; as a spatial and historical inventory of France, 308; state or municipal commissions, 332; success in nineteenth-century society, 319; titles of, 307

land use charters, 103

language: common, possibility of, 200; dialects, 152, 267; policy on, 235; progression of a territorial conception of, 268; reinforces regional variegation, 154; return of accents, 232; of the sea, 63

Languedoc, 5, 11, 13; efforts to improve the regional plates of the national map, 160; independent functioning in eighth century, 8; states of guided by the local bishops, 16; "true" property taxes, 20

langue d'oc, 10, 17

Lannion, 55

Lanterne, 42

La Patellière, 334, 335

Lapauze, Henri, 252, 258

La Rochejaquelein, Auguste de, 390

La Rochejaquelein, Henri de, 386, 388

La Rochejaquelein, Julian de, 393

La Rochejaquelein, Louis de, 390

La Rochelle (port), 37, 41–42

"La Royale, " 80n.49

La Seyne, 55

Lasteyrie, Robert de, 261, 263

Latte Fort, La, Cape Fréhel, 41

La Varende, Jean de, 31

Lavedan, Henri, 375

Lavisse, Ernest, x, 363, 422; *Histoire de France,* 238, 344

law. *See* Roman law

Law of 14 Fructidor year IX (September 1, 1801), 254

Law of September 14, 1789, 234

laws, decentralizing, 232, 239

learned societies: archaeological, 262; geography of tended to reproduce administrative geography, 249–50; historical, 262–64; horticultural, 245; for local studies, 232, 250–51; in the provinces, 245, 246f, 247f; in the pro-

learned societies (*continued*)
  vincial cities, 245–52; regional, 248; replaced by scientific history and regional universities, 283–84; revival of, 232; role in establishment of societal and municipal museums, 258; scientific, 203–4
Le Bras, Gabriel, 415
Lecat, Jean-Phillippe, 44
Le Chêne-Boquet, 102
Leclerc, Philippe, 413, 438
Le Conquet, 33, 41
Le Conquet Island, 55
Le Croisic harbor, 41
legal standardization, 163
légitime, 23
Legrand d'Aussy, 170
Le Havre, 44–45, 73, 74, 76
leisure space, 362
Le Nôtre, 298
Leo IX, Pope, 440
Léon, Seigneur du, 72
Lepage, Bastien, 300
Lepetit, Bernard, 190, 194
Le Play, Frédéric, project for social reform, 176, 214–15
Le Poulmic, 55
Lequin, Yves, 283
Le Rouvre forge, 113
Les Crisenons, 107
Les Heaux de Bréhat, lighthouse at, 71
Lesueur collection, 33
Levant (Mediterranean fleet), 75
Levasseur, Émile, 201, 352, 355
Lévy, Henri, 274f
Leygues, Georges, 57
Lhermitte, Françoise, 318
Lhote, André, 334, 335
Liais, Emmanuel, 257
Lieu de mémoire, xi, xii, xiii, 314
lifeboat stations, 72, 73
lighthouses, 68–72
Limbourg brothers, 300–301, 302
lineal power, 21
lineal reserve, 23
Lisle, Rouget de, 422
literary geography, 366
literature: dialectal, 15; regional, 282–83; in the south, 15

Little Pink Books, 31
Little Red Riding Hood, 87
livestock, 5
livestock breeding, 3–4
Livre de la description des pays (Bouvier), viii
local assemblies, 204, 205
local cultures: explained by the depth of their roots, 236; reintroduction, 235
local dialects, 235, 244
local history, 266; centers of production for, 253f
local memory: increase in, 232; producers of, 254–58; republican restoration of, 269f
local patrimonies, 252, 260–61
local registries, 252–61
local space, 237; customs, 267; development of in nineteenth century, 281–87; distinctiveness, 231; invented by Revolution of 1789, 232; "Jacobin," 235; marginalization of, 241–45; as an obstacle to the course of the Revolution, 234–35; as a place of memory, 232–33; preservation of in the representations of France, 245–52; as space as pretext, 284–87; upon advent of the Third Republic, 271; view of as archaic and retrograde, 234. *See also* regionalism; regions; space, French
local studies, societies for, 232
Loc Péran, 52
Locronan, 37
logs, 124
Loire-Atlantique, 384
Loire valley, 4, 112
Longailles, 124
Lorient, 48, 52–53
Loroux, 384
Lorquet, Paul, 273
Lorraine, 297, 302, 305, 309, 424, 432, 434, 438, 440
Lorrain glass, 305
Lotharingia. *See* Lorraine
Loti, Pierre, 31, 44, 51
Loubet, Émile François, 277
Louis IX (king of France), 36
Louis XI (king of France), 76

Louis XII (king of France), 20, 55
Louis XIV (king of France), 15, 16, 37, 154, 156, 413, 424
Louis XV (king of France), 16
Louis XVI (king of France), 15, 48, 49, 65
Louis XVIII (king of France), 16, 385
Louis-Philippe (king of France), 16, 390, 392
Louis the Pious (king of France), 68
Loutherbourg, Philip James de, 309, 312
Louvier Island, 116
Lower Brittany, 399
Luther, Martin, 415
lycées, 210
Lyon, 7, 15

MacMahon, Comte de, 277
Maggiolo, Vicomte A., 1, 2
Magistracy of the Rhine, 420
Maine-et-Loire, 384
Maine river, 384
Maison du Chat qui pelote, La (Balzac), 119
Maistre, Joseph de, 154, 423
Malberg, Raymond Carré de, 415
Malte-Brun, 344
Manet, Édouard, 332
Manifeste des Trois Épis, 431
Man village, 427f
maps, 350–52; Burgundy, 161f; Cassini map, x, 159, 160, 251, 350–51; departmental blueprint, 218f; Depository of Maps and Plans, 33; ecclesiastical map of France, 188f; of the general staff, 369f; geological, 352–55, 380n.16; marine maps, 33–34; naval, of Western Europe, 26f; nomenclature, 357; of provinces, 192f; relief, 357; scale, 351–52, 380n.16
maraichains, 384
maraîchinage, 404
Marais, Jean, 96f
Marches, 398
Marigny, marquis de, 300, 309
Marine Academy, 35, 57
marine dictionaries, 63
Marin-Pêcheur (Sea Fisherman) (Lecat), 44

maritime affairs: system of classes, 59; votive practices, 65
maritime archives, 34–36
maritime commemoration, 62–64
maritime commerce, 44
maritime France, 48, 74–76
Marly, forest at, 137–38
Marquet, Albert, 336
Marseillaise, ix, 422; parade of, 230f
Marseille, 15, 46; annexation of, 11; collection of models of commercial ships, 46; metropolitan area of, 219; Rhodian colony in, 7
Martignac project of 1829, 238–39
Martin, Henri, 332
Martin, Jean-Clément, 263
Martin, L., 44
Martinière canal, 45
Mascareignes, 45
Massif Central, 3, 4, 7, 10, 13
Massilia, 46
Massol, Joseph, 414
Matisse, Henri, 336
Mauges, 384, 385, 398
Maupassant, Guy de, 319
Maupeou, René, 154
Maurras, Charles, 154, 272
mayors, nominated by the central government, 235
Mazarin, Cardinal, 418
Meck, Henri, 429
medical topography, 346
medieval France, two images of landscape, 299–300
Mediterranean, 4
Méduse (ship), 66, 73
Meeting of Heart and Humble Request (Master of the Coeur d'amour épris), 304f
Meinecke, Friedrich, 415
Meitzen, Auguste, 366
Méjean, Annie
Mélusine, 273
Mémoires d'outre-tombe (Vernet), 308
Mémoires d'un touriste (Stendhal), 258
memoirs, 197
Mentelle (geographer), 169
Mer, La: Hommes, richesses, enjeux, 77n.6
merchant marine, 35, 47, 59, 62

Mercœur, duc de, 52

Mérite agricole (award), 276

Merovingian period: cultural originality, 8; villa, 372

metalworking-industry, fuel demands, 110–15

metropolises, 224

Mettrier, Henri, 183, 211, 229n.45

Meurthe-et-Moselle, 112

Michel, Georges, 312–13, 314, 323f

Michelangelo, 302

Michelet, Jules, 69, 71, 238, 318, 344, 345, 359, 361; *Histoire de France,* 239–41; *Tableau de la France* (Picture of France), 239–41, 281, 316–17, 355–56

micro-landowners, 5

Middle Ages: domain villa of, 369; rural landscape of, 372

Midi, 1, 4; blocks of Catholic loyalty, 13; extinction of great princely families, 12; heretical leanings, 8; livestock, 5; municipalism of early Middle Ages, 10; Neolithic agriculture, 7; quiritarian advantages of, 20; resistance to taxes, 13; wealth of aristocracy undermined by division of inheritances, 9

Midoux, Étienne, 267

Millet, Jean-François, 300, 317–18, 326f, 362–63

miniatures, 300–302

mining engineers, 201

Ministry of Agriculture, 276

Minquier Islands, 38

Mirabeau, Comte de, 154, 166, 187

Mistral, Frédéric, 17, 74, 260, 281, 296

Mitterand, Françoise, 17

modern art, 337

Mommsen, Theodor, 414

monarchy: assembly of 1871, 272; and centralization, 15, 154; tolerant of provincial personalities and particularisms, 160; unwillingness of Parisian culture to make a place for regional cultures, 159

Monceau, Duhamel du, 35

Monet, Claude, 310, 333, 335f

Monluc, Seigneur de, 15

Monnier, Désiré, 268

Montagnard dictatorship, 169

Montagnes des Sabines, Les (Flandrin), 310

Montaigne, Michel, 15

Montaigut-le-Blanc (Puy-de-Dôme). Castle of Guillaume Revel, 347f

Montalivet, Comte de, 176, 201

Montbard, department of the Côte-d'Or, 172f

Montbret, Coquebert de, 199

Mont des Alouettes chapel, 386

Montesquieu, Baron de, ix

Mont-Faron, 55

Montfort, Simon de, 15

Montmorency family, 12

Montmorency Forest, 102

Montpellier, University of, 19

Mont-Sainte-Odile, 439, 440f

Mont-Sainte-Victoire Seen from the Stone Quarry of Bibemus (Cézanne), 103f

Mont-Saint-Michel, 2

moral landscapes, 356

moral statistics, 176

Morbihan Islands, 40

Morlaix harbor, 41

Morogues, Bigot de, 35

Morvan, 112

Moselly, Émile, 282

Moulins, master of, 300–301

Mourer, J.-P., 431

Mourillon, 55

Mouvement républicain populaire, 437

muleteers, 107

Mulhouse, 422

Muller, Germain, 436

municipal elections of 1789, 234

Musée breton, Quimper, 259

Musée d'Aquitaine, 260

Musée d'Art et d'Archéologie, 260

Musée des Monuments français, 237

Musée d'ethnographie, *salle de France,* 273

Musée du Dessin industriel (Museum of Industrial Design), 260

Musée lorrain, Nancy, 259

Musée Napoléon, 312

Musée national des Arts et Traditions populaires, 260, 286

Museon Arlaten, Arles, 260

Museum of Alise-Sainte-Reine, 255

Museum of Chalon-sur-Saône, 259
Museum of Napoleon, Auxonne, 255
Museum of Natural History, Paris, 33
museums, 232, 254–58; of archaeology, 259; commemorative collections, 260–61; dedicated to individuals, 261; exiguity and poverty of, 258; increase of in provincial towns, 252, 254; pedagogical task of presenting the progress of the human spirit, 258–59; politically elite donors, 257–58; provincial, 258
Muslims, 8, 17
Musset, Alfred de, 311, 313
Musset, René, ix

Nancy, 112
Nancy Program of 1865, 239
Nantes, 45, 53
Nantes-Mulhouse line, 3
Napoleon I, 16, 55, 420; museums, 261; "organic articles," 412; takeover, 176; tight surveillance of Vendée, 392
Napoleon III, 49, 87, 255; law of 1860, 128f; trips aimed at consolidating his personal power, 277
Napoleonic Code, 196
Napoleonic state, 238
Narbonnais, 10
Nardy, Jean-Paul, 250
National Confederation, Paris, July 14,1790, 230f
National Forest Fund, 145f
National Forestry Foundation, 102
National Front, 17
national geographies, 344
National Guard, 399
nationalism: in other countries in the nineteenth century, 322
national model: disintegration of, 232
naturalism, 359, 360, 375, 376
naturalists, 33, 201
naturalization, 364
natural regions, 353–55
natural sciences, 203
natural space, turned into museums, 362
Naurouze, 6
Naval Academy, 57, 59
navigation journals, 32–34

navy: blue uniform of, 62; ceremony in, 60–62; and society, 65–74; technical modernity of, 60; tradition and modernity, 56–65
Nelli, René, 17
Neo-Hippocratism, 158, 346
Nerval, Gérard de, 312, 315, 419
Neufchâteau, François de, 171, 174, 199
Niausssat, Pierre, 80n.52
Nice, 11, 42
Nicot, Jean, 179n.16
Niépce, Nicéphore, 261
Night of August 4, 162, 186
Nîmes, 15
Nîmois, 10
Nivernais, Duc de, 112
Nividic lighthouse, 71
Nodier, Charles, 244–45, 262, 357
Noirmoutier Island, 37, 40
nomenclature maps, 357
Nord department, regional societies, 248
Nordgau, 421
Nordman, Daniel, 282
Norman Association, Caen, 283
Normandie (ship), 46
Normandy, 4; property crimes, 3; regional societies, 248
northern Europe, contrast with Mediterranean Europe, 6
northern France: lineal reclamation, 21; shaped by egalitarianism, 20; suicide rates, 3; *taille* often assessed capriciously, 21
north-south division, 1–24; and crime, 3; and inheritance, 22–23; opposition over contrast between customs and Roman law, 18; during the 1850s, 3–7; Saint-Malo-Geneva line, 2
Norway (ship), 47
Nostradamus, 15
notarii (notaries), 18
Notes sur la province (Taine), 258
Notre France, 281
Nouveaux contes de fées (Ségur), 98
novels, with a regional theme, 282
Numa Roumestan (Daudet), 22

Oak of Flagey, The or *The Oak of Vercingetorix* (Courbet), 327f

Oberlé, Les (Bazin), 434

Occitania, 8; almost fully constituted at end of fifteenth century, 11–12; and French Revolution, 16; leftism, 17; "privileged Occitania," 6; "southern accent," 12

ocean liners, sanctuary for, 44–47

Oceanographic and Hydrographic Service of the Navy, 34

Oceano nox (Hugo), 28

Odile, 439

Office national des fôrets (O.N.F. [National Office of Forests]), 130–32

Office of Longitudes, 57

Oise forests, 139

Oise region, 169

Oléron, 37

Olivier, Laurence, 302

One Hundred Days, 390

open-air painting, 331, 338

optants, 434

Oradour-sur-Glane massacre, 431

Order of Malta, 57

Ordinance of 1669, 106, 126

Ordonnance de la Marine (Colbert), 63

Orléans, 112, 121

orthogonal sectioning, 184f

Ostrogoth, 8

Ouarville (Eure), commune of, 373f

Oudan, 107

Ouessant Island, 38–39, 39f, 55; aid to shipwrecked, 73; cemetery for sailors, 75f; lighthouses, 71

Ozouf, Mona, 1, 162, 167, 236

Ozouf-Marignier, Marie-Vic, 166, 187, 190

Pagès, Georges, 33, 418

Painter's Studio, The (Courbet), 328f

painting: of ideas, 331; portrait, 308; regional schools of, 270

Pal de Limbourg, 303f

papal Zouaves, 392

paper industry, 132, 139

paquebots (pocket boats), 46

Paris, department of, 198f

Parisian agglomeration, 219

Parisian basin, "personalized" taxes, 12

Parisian forests, 136

parlement de Toulouse, 11, 19

parlements, 251

Parmentier brothers, 43

parti communiste français, 428

particular. *See* local space

particularism, 425–28

"Parvenus' seventh" (arrondissement), 117

Pascal-Paoli de Morosaglia museum, 261

Pas-de-Calais department, regional societies, 248

Pasquini, Pierre, 286

Passy, Antoine, 267–68, 352, 354

Pasteur, Louis, 261, 362, 381n.33

pastoral style, 303–4

Path through the Trees (Denis), 92f

patois, 152, 168, 174

patrimony, 258, 259

Patriote (ship), 46

patronage, 12

Paul, Saint, 94

paydrets, 384

Pays, Le, 183, 219, 229n.45, 237, 364. *See also* regions

paysage, 358

pays de France, 282, 359

peasants, 129; change in the image of, 270; legacy of, 101–2; opposition to the Waters and Forests Administration, 129; Peasants' War, 424; tradition, 296; transformation of image, 362–63; utopia, 363

Peirotes, Jacques, 424–25

Penfield river, 55

pensionnaires, 117

Pergaud, Louis, 282

Pérouse, Jean-Francois de la, 33, 46, 65, 66

Perrault, Charles, 98

Perret, Auguste, 45

Perrot, Jean-Claude, 190, 346

Perthes, Boucher de, 257

petite histoire, 284

Petite Rade, 55

Petit Luc, massacre at, 403

Pflamlin, Pierre, 438

Phalsbourg, 434

pharology, 69

Philip II (king of Spain), 52

Philip the Fair, 154
photoengraving, 357
photogrammetry, 344
photography, 344, 357
physiocrats, 157, 346, 348, 349
Picardy departments, regional societies, 248
Picardy-Wallonia, 22
pieds-noirs, 17
Pierre Corneille du Petit-Couronne museum, 261
Piles, Roger de, 303, 309
Pillement, Jean Baptiste, 312
piloting, 72
Pilot's Manual for Use by Breton Pilots (Brouscon du Conquet), 26f
Pinchon, J. P.: *Burgundy,* 285f; *Les Provinces de France illustrées,* 284f
Pineau, Nicolas, 98
pine trees, 132, 133, 140
Pissarro, Camille, 313, 333, 334f
Pitauts, revolt of, 13
Pius II, Pope, 412
places, diffusion of knowledge about, 282–83
plagues, 11
Plailly woods, 139
Planche, James, 331
Planier (lighthouse), 69
Plantagenets, 10, 55
plants, 374
Pleven, René, 432
Poële, Marcel, 375
Pointe du Stiff lighthouse, 71
Poitou, 5
"policy on language," 235
Political arithmeticians, 157
Ponant (Atlantic fleet), 75
Pond, The (Rousseau), 325f
Pontchartrain, Count de, 34
popular imagery, 325, 327, 330
Po River, 415
Pornic castle, 41
Port-Louis, 44, 52
Port of la Rochelle (Vernet), 314f
portrait painting, 308
portulan chart, 33, 69
Port-Vendres, 42
postage stamps, 63

postal almanacs, 325
postcards, 330
Postimpressionism, 299
Poussin, Nicolas, 297, 302, 304, 305
poverty, triangle of, 6
Prat, Oliver de, 32
Praying on the Beach, 30f
prefects, prefectures, 196, 201
Prélot, Marcel, 415
primogeniture, 19, 20
Printemps à travers les branches (Monet), 320
"privileged Occitania," 6
Proëlla, 40
Professor Knatschke (Hansi), 426
Pro Fonteio (Cicero), 7
progressivism, 364
Protestantism, 14f, 398
Provence, 5; annexation of, 11; independent functioning in eighth century, 8; landscape, 362; "real" taxes, 12; unification with the French kingdom, 53
Provence Canal, 206
Provence-Occidentale, 219
proverbs, 179n.16
provinces: divisions within, 199f; imprecise definition of, 155; lost their juridical and political role, 186; map of, 192f; resistance to plan to create departments, 166; retained as the base for division into departments, 237; vague territorial definition, 162
provincial estates, 154
provincial museums, 258
provincial names: persistence of, 237; resurgence of, 232
provincial nostalgia, 196
psychanalyse de l'Alsace (psychoanalysis of Alsace), 436
psychoanalysis, 377
Puget, Pierre, 56
Pyramid Oak, The (Bessa), 134f
Pyrenees, 10
Pyrotechnics (Biringuccio), 108f

Quai de la Fosse, 45
Quai des Chartrons, 45
Quai des Indes, 53
Quai d'Orsay, 117

Quai Henri-IV, 116
Quatre Nations, 116
Quercy, 10
Qu'est-ce que le Tiers État? (What Is the
    Third Estate?) (Sièyes), x
Quimper-Colmar line, 3
Quimper harbor, 41
quiritarian property, 20
quiritarian spirit, 21

Rabelais, François, 42
Raess, André, 423
Raft of the Méduse, The (Géricault), 31,
    67f
railroads, 102, 202
Rance River, 41
Randier, Commander, 48
Rapport sur les idiomes (Barrère), 168
Rapport sur les musées de province, 258
Rassemblement du peuple français
    (Assembly of the French People), 438
Rayons et les ombres, Les (Hugo), 28
Ré, 37
Realist landscape painters, 331
"Realist" movement, 299, 331
Recher, J., 44
Reclus, Élisée, 176, 213, 344, 357
Recueil des travaux, 267
Red Midi, 17, 18
Redon harbor, 41
Referendum of 1969, 150f, 217
reforestation, 132
regionalism: aroused by partition plan
    of 1789, 165–67; in last third of the
    nineteenth century, 176–77; obliter-
    ation of, 152; recrudescence of, 152;
    spontaneous, 214
regionalist congress, first, 296
regions, 175; banking networks, 214;
    cultural movements, 281; diverse
    terms representing, 155; dress, 286;
    elusive concept, 151; ethnographies,
    270; history projects, 159–60; lan-
    guages, 152; literature, 282–83;
    modern, 213; museums, 260; natural,
    353–55
Régions naturelles et noms de pays (Gallois),
    352
Reichsland, 436

relief maps, 357
religion, and rural identity, 399
Rembrandt van Rijn, 313
remote sensing technology, 379f
Renan, Ernst, 433
René, King, 12, 280
Rennes, speech by the mayor of at the
    unveiling of the monument com-
    memorating the union of Brittany
    with France, 1911, 279f
Renoir, Pierre-Auguste, 312
Répertoire archéologique, 262
Republic: agrarianism, 276; attached
    to an exclusively territorial electoral
    system, 216; landscape painting, 331–
    33. *See also* First Republic; Third
    Republic
Republic of the United Provinces of the
    Midi, 13
rescue boats, 73–74
Resistance, 17
*Resources du travail intellectuel en France,
    Les* (Tassy and Léris), 247f
Restoration, 16; establishment of provin-
    cial museums under, 255; kept cen-
    tralization intact, 238
Retz river, 384
Reuss, Edouard, 423
Rêve, Le (Zola), 119
revitalization projects, 232
Revolt of the Red Hats *(Bonnets rouges),*
    399
Revolution of 1789, 16; affirmed the ab-
    solute priority of national unity, 163;
    changed the conditions of experi-
    ence, 162; combined the will to unify
    with the discovery of regional differ-
    ences, 173; creation of departments
    (see departmental division); defined
    the terms of a regionalist nostalgia,
    177; extreme decentralization early
    on, 234; invented local space, 232;
    linguistic policy, 168; and the local as
    memory, 233–71; and private prop-
    erty of the forest, 131
Revue alsacienne illustrée, 425
Revue catholique d'Alsace, 263–64
Revue celtique, 273
Revue d'Alsace, 263

Revue de géographie, 213

Revue de synthèse, 273–76

Revue de théologie et de philosophie chrétienne, 423

Rheinlied (Becker), 418–19

"Rhein Teutschlands Strom aber nicht Teutschlands Grenze, Der" (The Rhine Germany's River but not Germany's Border), 418

Rhenanus, Beatus, 415

Rhenish Catholicism, 421

Rhine Palace, 420

Rhine River, 415, 417–20

Rhône Valley, 4

Rhône Valley departments, 248

Ribot bill, 212

Richelieu, Cardinal, 37, 41–42, 76, 418

Ricklin, Eugen, 429

Rieder, Frédéric, 436

Ripert, Adeline, 283

Ritter, Carl, 355, 357

rituals, 279f

riverbanks, 36

riverboat guild, 420

Road through the Low Trees (Bruandet), 129f

Robert, Hubert, 308, 316f, 321

Robespierre, Maximilien, 23, 401

Robillard de Beaurepaire, Charles de, 266

Roche, Daniel, 159

Rochefort, 49–52; architectural unity, 51; maritime patrimony, 48, 80n.51; marshes, 52; naval hospital, 51

Rocher de Comillon, 172f

Rock of Dabo, 439–40

Rohan family, 12

Rôles d'Oléron, 63

Rolland, Eugène, 273

Roman *campagna,* 305

Roman *castellum,* 412

Roman des provinces de France, Le, 282

Romanesque art, 10

Romania, 273

Roman law, 9–10; emphasized quiritarian property, 21; in the Midi, 18–23

romantic geography, 356

romantic journey, narrative of, 244

Romantic painters, 311–12

Ronarc'h, Admiral, 31

Roos, Karl, 429

Roosevelt, Franklin Delano, 424

Roscoff harbor, 41

Rosenwiller, Jewish cemetery of, 417f

Rossé, Joseph, 424, 429, 431

Rouen, 45

Rouerque, 10

Rouquette, Yves, 17

Rousseau, Jean-Jacques, 308

Rousseau, Théodore, 65, 100f, 141, 170, 313, 315–16, 318, 325f, 332

"Rousseauist" nature painting, 308

Roussillon, 10

routiers, 34

Royale, La (Randier), 47–48

royal *pré carré,* viii

rural exodus, 98, 145f

rural landscape, 345, 359; "fixed" arguments, 378; Haussmanization, 371; as historical problem, 369–70; and naturalism, 376; north vs. south, 367–68; research on, 366; seen from an airplane, 373f; tension between the fixed theses and the meaning of agrarian changes, 375

rural patrimony, 273

rural society: mobility of, 372, 374; two kinds of, 367–68

rustic novel, 282

Ruysdael, Salomon van, 312, 313

Saarbrucken, 431

sailing ships, 45

sailors, cemeteries for, 29

Saint-Cado, 37

Saint-Eulalie, 10

Saint François, Church of, 45

Saint-Gérand (ship), 28

Saint-Honorat, 37

Saint-Jacques, 43

Saint-Jean-de-Luz, 42

Saint Louis, Church of, 62

Saint-Malo, 37, 40

Saint-Malo-Geneva line, 2

Saint Marguerite and Olibrius (Fouquet), 305f

Saint-Mathieu Abbey, 41

Saint-Mathieu Island, 55

Saint-Nabor, 440f
Saint-Nicolas, 116
Saintonge coast, 37
Saint-Pierre, Bernardin de, 28, 53
Saint-Pierre, Louis de, 53
Saint-Pierre-et-Miquelon, 44
Saint-Remy, 43
Saint-Sauveur, 56
Saint Thomas, Strasbourg, 416f
Saint-Tropez, 42
Saisons, Les (Saint-Lambert), 308
Salorges, 45
saltus, 368, 372
Salve Regina, 388
Sambre-et-Meuse Valley, 115
Sand, George, 270, 296, 313, 315
satellite photos, 377, 379f
Schapiro, Meyer, 333
Scharnhorst (ship), 31
Schengen space, vii, xiii n.1
Schmidlin, Joseph, 429
School of Naval Construction, 57
Schuler, Théophile, 84f
Schuman, Robert, 437–38
Schweitzer, Albert, 425
scientific societies, diffusion of, 203–4
scientific works, 152
Scorff River, 52–53
sea: effect on French landscape, 27;
    "great devourer," 25; law of, 63; sea
    power, 75; security at, 72–73; writers
    and artists of, 28–32
seamen: graffiti, 32; plaques of thanks-
    giving, 32
seascapes, 31
Sébillot, Paul, 98, 273
Second Empire: establishment of provin-
    cial museums under, 255; official pa-
    triotic themes used to support local
    celebrations, 279; urban modernism
    of, 272
Segonzac, Dunoyer de, 334
Ségur, Countess of, 98, 400
Seigneurial domains, 9
Sein Island, 38, 40, 55
Selestat, 415, 421
Sellier, Henri, 219
Seltz, Thomas, 429
Sémillante, La, 28, 73

Senancour, Etienne, 314
Sénart forest, 143
Service des archives et bibliothèques
    (Archive and Library Service), 34
Seurat, Georges, 305, 306
Seven Years' War, 48, 55
Sèvre River, 384
She Waits (Henner), 433, 435f
ships: conservation of memories, 59–60;
    launching of, 62; sailing, 45
Shipwreck of Virginia, The (Rogers), 30f
shipwrecks, 46, 73, 80n.45
Sidonius, 9
Siegfried, André, 393–94
Sieyès, Emmanuel-Joseph, ix–x, 163,
    164
Signac, Paul, 336
silviculture, 102, 126
Simmel, Gregor, 415
sinagots, 44
Sion, Jules, 363, 364
Sisley, Alfred, 327, 333
sites and ports, 36
"Six Swans, The," 88–90
social geography, 365
social structures, in north and south in
    the 1850s, 4–5
Société académique de Laon, 264
Société archéologique de Soissons, 264
Société belfortaine d'emulation (Belfort
    Competitive Society), 250
Société bourguignonne de géographie
    et d'histoire, 264
Société centrale des naufragés, 73
Société dauphinoise d'ethnologie et
    d'anthropologie (Dauphiné Society
    of Ethnology and Anthropology),
    270
Société de l'histoire de France (Society
    for the History of France), 243–44,
    265
Société d'emulation du Doubs (Compet-
    itive Society of the Doubs), 263
Société d'emulation du Jura (Competi-
    tive Society of the Jura), 250, 262,
    264, 265
Société des agriculteurs de France, 364
Société des antiquaires, Normandy, 248
Société des antiquaires de l'Ouest, 248

Société des antiquaires de Picardie, 262, 263

Société des archéologues et bibliophiles Lyonnaise, 265

Société des archives historiques de Guyenne, 265

Société des archives historiques de la Saintonge et de l'Aunis, 265

Société des écrivains de province (Society for Writers of the Province), 282

Société des hospitaliers sauveteurs bretons (Charitable Society of Breton Rescuers), 73

Société des Observateurs de l'Homme, 175

Société des régates de Paimpol, 74

Société des sciences historiques et naturelles de l'Yonne, 264–65

Société des traditions populaires, 273

Société d'ethnographie et d'art populaire du bas Limousin (Society of Ethnography and Popular Art of the Lower Limousin), 270

Société d'ethnographie nationale et d'art populaire, 273

Société de Vieux Fécamp, 264

Société du Vieil Arles, 264

Société du Vieux Chinon, 264

Société du Vieux Montmartre, 264

Société française d'archéologie, 248, 262

Société historique du Calaisis, 261

Société historique et archéologique des Vans (Ardèche), 248

Société historique of Gascony, 260

Société humaine des naufragés, 73

Société libre d'agriculture, sciences, arts et belles-lettres of the Eure, 267–68

Société nationale de sauvetage en mer (National Society for Rescue at Sea, 73

Société nivernaise (Nevers) des sciences, lettres et arts, 263

Société philomatique de Perpignan, 263

Société polymathique du Morbihan, 267

Société royale de médecine, 158, 346

Société statistique de Marseille, 203

societies. See learned societies

sociologism, 375

socioprofessionals, 216

Solidor Tower, 41

"Song of the Army of the Rhine," 422

southern France: adoption of Protestantism, 13; economic health in 1950s, 6; fedualism and serfdom less developed, 9; "French" incorporation of, 10; military insubordination and resistance to taxes, 2–3; murder rates, 3; regional semirepresentative system, 12; strong local organizations, 11

southern Gaul: preeminence of, 8; vernacular speech, 9

Souvenir de Mortefontaine (Corot), 307

souvenir français, 426

souvenir Vendéen, 387f, 406n.8

Souvestre, Émile, 269

space, French: diversity of, 153; forest as cultivated, 83; intensity of connection with, vii–viii; leisure, 362; natural, turned into museums, 362; referring to the idea of nature, vii; referring to the notion of territory, vii; representations of, 233; Schengen, vii, xiii n.1; themes of unity and fragmentation, viii; transformed by departments, 167, 177. See also local space; regionalism; regions

Spinner, Auguste, 426

spontaneous generation, 362

Spring through the Branches (Monet), 335f

stained-glass window, Beaune, Maine-et-Loire, 391f

stamps, 286

statistics, 346, 348–50

Statistique des Bouches-du-Rhône, 351

Statistique et atlas des forêts, 126

Statistique générale de la France (General Statistics Office of France), 176, 199, 211, 243, 348–49

statuary, aimed at promoting local patrimonies, 280

staves, 124

Stendhal, 258, 357

stereotypes, 285–86

Stoeber, August, 420

Stofflet, Jean Nicolas, 390

Strabo, viii, 418

Strasbourg, 412–15; annexed to France by Louis XIV, 413; cathedral, 412–

Strasbourg (*continued*)
  14; evolving importance in com-
    merce on the Rhine, 420–21; libera-
    tion of, 438f; Lycée Fustel-de-
    Coulanges, 414; Nazi annexation,
    413; Place de la République, 414;
    Rohan Palace, 414; view of, 410f–
    411f
Strombau, 421
Sturm, Johannes, 436
Sturmel, Marcel, 431
Sturm und Drang, 314
subjective landscape, 377
subprefects, 196
subprefectures, 201
subsistence crops, alliance with forest,
  102
Sue, Eugène, 31
Sundgau, 421
superstitions, 179n.16
suroît, 74
Surrealism, 337
surveillance maritime (Sur Mar), 72

Tableau de la France (Picture of France)
  (Michelet), 29, 239–41, 281, 316–
  17, 355–56
Tableau géographie de la France (Geograph-
  ical Chart of France) (Vidal de La
  Blache), viii–ix, x, 27, 271
taille (taxes), 20
Taine, Hippolyte-Adolphe, 258
Tanguy Tower, 56
Tauler, Johannes, 423
Taureau castle, Morlaix, 41
taxes, 204, 205, 363
Taylor, Baron, 311, 357
*Témoignage Chrétien, Alsace et Lorraine
  terres françaises* (Christian Witness,
  Alsace and Lorraine French Lands),
  430–32
Tenant farming, 4–5
territoire, 183
territorial reorganization, plans for, 176
Ter River, 52
testamentary freedom, favored by the
  south, 23
thanksgiving plaques, 32
theater, 12

Thermidorians, 401
Thibaudet, Albert, 333
Thierry, Augustin, 355
Thierry brothers, 316
Thiers, Jean-Baptiste, 179n.16
Thiesse, Anne-Marie, 282
Third Republic, ix, x, 17; associated
  landscape painting with liberty, 331–
  33; increasingly based institutions
  and functions on local space, 271,
  276–81
Thirty Years' War, 418, 421, 424
Thomas, Philadephe, 257
Thoré, Théophile, 313, 331
Thouret, 164
Thouret, Jacques-Guillaume, 186
Thumb, Tom, 90
Tierny, Gonzague, 270
Tocqueville, 152
Toits rouges (Pissarro), 320
topography, 197, 349
toponymy, 353
Torfou, 385
Toufaire, Pierre, 51
Toulon: college of surgery, 52; harbor of,
  54f; maritime patrimony, 48; as mili-
  tary port, 53–56
Toulousain, 10
Toulouse: counts of, 10; University of,
  19
Tour de France, x
*Tour de France par Camille et Paul, deux
  enfants d'augjourd'hui, Le* (Camille and
  Paul Tour France: Two Children of
  Today) (Pons), 31
Tour de la Découverte, 53
*Tour de la France par deux enfants,
  Le* (Two Children Tour France)
  (Fouillée), 29, 177, 434
Tour d'Ordre, 42, 68
Touring Club of France, 282
tourism, 232; growth of, and quest for
  the past, 311; guides, 362; local of-
  fices, 283; products for, 282–83; role
  in diffusion of stereotypes, 286
Tournelle, 116
Tourville, Comte de, 66
towns, 175, 210; warehouse, 193
Tracy, comte de, 155

Trafalgar, 66, 76

Traité des bois servant à tous usages
   (Caron), 114f

travel narratives, 235, 236, 345–46, 362

Traversins, 124

Treaty of Frankfurt, 424, 425, 434

Treaty of Vienna, 420

trees: attitude toward cutting, 83; fir,
   132, 133, 140; memories of, 143, 145;
   and sex, 143

Trésor du Félibrige, Le, 281

Trésor gastronomique de la France, 285

Très riches heures du duc de Berry, 301, 303f

Trèves, 8

triennial rotation, 369

Tronçais forest, 126

troubadours, 12

Trouvé, 202

Troyon, Constant, 318, 319

Truce of God, 9

Turcos, 415

Über die deutsche baukunst (On German
   Architecture), 413

ultramontane doctrine, 238, 430

Unabhängige Landespartei (Independent
   State Party), 429, 431

Union populaire républicaine (UPR),
   424, 429–30, 437

unity and diversity, interaction between,
   149, 152–53, 231

Universal Exposition of 1937, 277, 286

universal geographies, 344

universal suffrage, 214, 215, 216

urban crisis, 377

urban departments, 193

urban history, 375

urbanization, 224

urban landscape, 361, 375

Urfé, Honoré d', 307

Urville, Dumont d', 33

Utrillo, Maurice, 335

vagabonds, 106

Valenciennes, 310

Valéry, Paul, 29

Valing (ship), 57

Valois, 55

van der Meulen, Adam Franz, 304

Van Eyck, Jan, 300

Van Gogh, Vincent, 300, 323

Varzy (Nièvre), 106

Vauban, Sébastien, 56, 69, 71, 162, 418,
   419f

Veillat, Just, 257

Vendée, xii, 2; alcoholism in, 404; attachment to the Catholic religion,
   394; beatification of martyrs of, 404;
   borders of, 384; "brigands of the
   Vendée," 384–85; common term for
   counterrevolution and the ancien
   régime after March 19, 1793, 392–
   96; desire for enclosure, 392–96; dialectic of memory, 398–401; double
   heart logo, 385; internal threat to the
   Revolution, 383, 400–401; opposition to progress and rejection of any
   outside influence, 394–95; as region
   of memory, 383–84, 388–92, 403–
   4; reminders of the wars of 1793,
   385–88; repression anchored in local
   memory from one generation to the
   next, 401; rural vs. urban, 398–400;
   street names, 388; wars of 1793 to
   1796, 383, 384

Vendée Militaire, 406n.8

Vendéen, The (Maxime Real del Sarte),
   402f

Vengeur (ship), 66

Vercingetorix, 280

Verne, Jules, 66, 68, 243

Vernet, Joseph, 31, 51, 52, 64f, 66, 308,
   309

Verrazano, Giovanni da, 43, 66

Vichy régime, 17, 176, 286–87

Victoria, Queen, 73

Vidal de La Blache, Paul, viii, 27, 149,
   212, 213, 238, 343–44, 355, 370,
   374, 376, 377, 381n.33; *Principes de
   géographie humaine,* 358; *Tableau de la
   géographie de la France,* 358, 359–61;
   Vidalian synthesis, 271–73; Vidal
   school of geography, 345, 357–66,
   378

Vienne, Admiral Jean de, 40, 66

*View from Marly near Saint-Germain-en-
   Laye* (Robert), 316f

View of Auvers-sur-Oise (Cézanne), 336f

View of the Port of la Rochelle from the Petit Riv (Vernet), 64f
village community, 372
village land, 369
Villefranche, 42
Villèle Comte de, 16
Villemarqué, Hersart de La, 269
Villemot, Bernard, poster for Philippe Pétain, 1940, 298f
Villeneuve, Pierre de, 349
Villeneuve-Bargemon, Vicomte de, 202
Villers-Cotterêts, 154
vineyards, 7–8
Visiteurs du soir, Les, 302
Visscherbende, 281
vitalism, 362
Vivenel, Antoine, 257
Vlaminck, Maurice de, 334, 335
Voix intérieures, Les (Hugo), 28
Volksverein (People's Association), 425, 429
Voltaire, 65
von Steinbach, Erwin, 440n.1
Vosges Jura, 140
Vosges Mountains, 420
voting, according to arrondissement, 276
Vovelle, Michel, 170
Voyage pittoresques de la France, ouvrage national dédié au roi, 308
Voyages dans les départements de la France (Lavellée and Brion), 169, 177
Voyages pittoresques et romantiques dans l'ancienne France (1829) (Nodier, Taylor, and Cailleux), 242f, 244–45, 262, 311–12, 356–57

Walter, Michel, 429
Waltz, Jean-Jacques (Hansi), 426

warehouse town, 193
Wars of Religion, 37, 52, 76, 398, 399, 403, 421
Waterloo (Erckmann-Chatrian), 434
Watteau, Antoine, 309
wealth, 4, 9, 119, 210
Weber, Eugen, viii
Weill, Georges, 424, 425
western Europe, naval map of, 26f
Westmark Gau, 431
Wetterlé, Abbé, 425
"What Do You Think of the Universal Soul, My Lord the Oak?" (Schuler), 84f
wheat production, 104
White Terror, 16, 18
Wilhelm II, 414
Wimpheling, Jacob, 415
Wissembourg, 415, 422
Wittich, Werner, 424
wood: as fuel, 112; harvest, 113; markets, 116–17; module, 122–24; panel, 122, 124; as source of energy in the city, 115–18; warehouses, 116
woodcutters: and great strikes of 1891–92, 87; as a symbol of protest, 101
wooden houses, 119–22, 120f
woods. *See* forest; forest myths
Worms, Jean-Pierre, 208
written law. *See* Roman law
Wüstungen (deserted villages), 374

Yeu Island, 40
Young, Arthur, 348
Yvette (de Maupassant), 143

Zola, Émile, 270
zone of silence, 138